The American Bird Conservancy Guide to the 500 Most Important Bird Areas in the United States

MAPS AND
PRODUCTION SUPPORT BY
GAVIN SHIRE

ILLUSTRATIONS BY
MARCIA POLING

The American Bird Conservancy Guide to the 500 Most Important Bird Areas in the United States

KEY SITES FOR BIRDS AND BIRDING IN ALL 50 STATES

Robert M. Chipley, George H. Fenwick,
Michael J. Parr, and David N. Pashley

RANDOM HOUSE TRADE PAPERBACKS | NEW YORK

RANDOM HOUSE and colophon are registered trademarks
of Random House, Inc.

Library of Congress Cataloging-in-Publication Data
The American Bird Conservancy guide to the 500 most important bird areas
in the United States : Key sites for birds and birding in all 50 states /
by American Bird Conservancy in association with the Nature
Conservancy.—1st ed.
p.   cm.
Includes bibliographical references and index.
ISBN 0-8129-7036-5
1. Birding sites—United States.   2. Birds, Protection of—United States.
3. Endangered species—United States.   I. American Bird Conservancy.
II. Nature Conservancy (U.S.)
QL682.A54 2003
598'.07'23473—dc21   2003043229

Random House website address: www.atrandom.com
Printed in the United States of America on acid-free paper
9 8 7 6 5 4 3 2 1
First Edition

FOREWORD

SAVE THE BIRDS, SAVE OURSELVES

Paul R. Ehrlich

Why should we care about the conservation of birds? Ornithologists and ecologists can readily rattle off reasons why we should care ranging from the importance of birds in supplying ecosystem services—controlling insects and rodents, dispersing seed, and pollinating plants—to their value as indicators of environmental health.

Less frequently cited is the role birds have played in affecting human culture: birds live in every ecosystem on Earth, have been present at the rise and the fall of every human civilization, large and small, and have had profound effects on our species throughout our history. Neolithic people scratched migrating geese on cave walls, and Egyptians carved falcons on kings' thrones. Quetzals adorn Mayan temples, and pictures of birds can be found in most American homes today. The reason for this extraordinary use of bird images cannot be traced to their ecological roles but most likely originated in their effects on the human spirit.

Cranes, parrots, corvids, and even sparrows permeate human history, cultures, and religions. Eagles and falcons have long been used to symbolize national power, and doves represent peace. In times of trouble, bird songs soothe our spirits. Storks deliver us at birth, and owls mourn our deaths. The migration of birds—once thought a mysterious annual disappearance, perhaps into the depths of the sea—has exemplified human wonderment and the quest for knowledge. And many of us revel in the vivid colors and fascinating behavior of birds and, in the process, imagine ourselves close to nature.

But in truth we are growing apart from nature. Our own species now dominates the biosphere and is increasingly destroying it. Growing human populations, increasing per-capita consumption (especially among the rich), and the selection of environmentally unfriendly technologies and institutions are sawing off the limb on which humanity is perched. Most people seem to be unaware of the seriousness of the destruction and unable to perceive the message of danger being sent by our avifauna. But we should not be: while only a few North American *species* have disappeared, many bird *populations* have undoubtedly gone extinct, often unheralded. The Whooping Crane, Eskimo Curlew, Spotted Owl, both Prairie-Chickens, Yellow-billed Cuckoo in California, Red-cockaded Woodpecker, Kirtland's Warbler, and Seaside Sparrow are among the better-publicized examples of extensive population loss. Fully 70 percent of eastern neotropical migrants have dwindled in numbers in the past 20 years.

Seven of 12 species endemic to the Great Plains grasslands have declined in the past 25 years. In the West, the Marbled Murrelet and California Gnatcatcher have created concern as species threatened by habitat loss leading to population extinctions. Even though we should be very concerned about species loss, it is populations that supply ecosystem services—including the esthetic and life-enriching services birders value so much.

Outside our borders things are often worse. Almost 300 species are threatened with extinction in the American tropics, and untold populations throughout the developing world are being extirpated as forests and swamps are cleared for grazing, agriculture, silviculture, and aquaculture.

These losses are damaging not just in terms of the environmental services birds provide—though these are substantial—but because of what they say about our cultures and our values today. Birds and their habitats are in decline almost everywhere, and, increasingly, people choose just to look the other way. The generosity of our spirit has diminished to the point where we seem no longer willing to find room for these beautiful and interesting representatives of Earth's disappearing biota. We are heedlessly wiping out a substantial portion of our only known living companions in the universe.

We stand today at a crossroads: Never has the rate of loss of biodiversity been greater during the six million years of human history—and the engine of destruction is *Homo sapiens*. Never has our species been more disconnected from the natural world; but, ironically, never have so many Americans been interested in the welfare of birds. Yet never has a nation had greater financial capacity to provide for nature, and never before has humanity had so much scientific capacity both to understand and protect birds.

Those who care about conservation recognize that the future of our species depends on the future of the other life on our planet—for ecological, economic, and spiritual reasons. There is also a growing awareness that our ability to turn our own species onto a course that allows for the continued sustenance of all life will require reengaging people with nature and a reacquisition of humanity's appreciation for the life around it. Birds—omnipresent, beautiful, and mysterious—can be nature's best ambassadors.

Birds, like all other organisms, face two basic kinds of threats: those that reduce reproduction and those that increase mortality. Factors affecting mortality are legion, ranging from bycatch of seabirds in the world's commercial fisheries and the widespread use of pesticides and other toxic chemicals to the introduction of alien predators and the construction of lighted towers and buildings that attract migrants to their deaths. Reproduction is also affected by many things, but none more significant than the galloping loss of high-quality habitat. Not only is habitat absolutely lost via permanent alteration of the landscape to suburban development, row crop agriculture, and so forth, but more is lost to fragmentation and degradation, invasions of exotic plant species, and land management not conducive to wildlife. Global climate change is likely to exacerbate habitat loss, since natural processes of adjustment could be overwhelmed by unprecedented rates of change, and organisms will certainly face human-created barriers to movement.

Many people believe habitat loss to be the greatest threat to all wildlife, and myriad efforts are underway to stem the tide of these losses—to some effect. Led by broad coalitions such as Partners in Flight (more than 300 groups cooperating for the conservation of bird habitat) and the North American Bird Conservation Initiative (collaborative planning and conservation among the major bird initiatives for waterfowl, shorebirds, raptors, and songbirds), ornithologists have become highly organized in the past decade in targeting conservation of prime breeding, wintering, and migratory areas.

American Bird Conservancy's (ABC) highly collaborative Important Bird Areas (IBA) program is one excellent strategy for bird conservation. By identifying the 500 or so most significant places for birds, ABC accomplishes several things. First, it focuses conservation efforts where they will matter most for North American birds. As a directory of priorities, this book will guide conservation actions for years to come. Second, the IBA program provides a rallying point for hundreds of local groups and thousands of citizens who want to be directly involved in conservation. And, perhaps most importantly, by publishing this book, ABC draws the attention of the American public to the need to identify and protect the most important places for birds. In addition, the conservation briefs scattered throughout the book should aid in educating readers about the world of conservation issues and solutions. It is my strong hope that this book will increase awareness of the plight of birds and arouse citizens of the United States to more determined action in the cause of conservation.

PAUL R. EHRLICH is Bing Professor of Population Studies at Stanford University and President of Stanford's Center for Conservation Biology. He is the coauthor of *The Birder's Handbook* and *Birds in Jeopardy*.

ACKNOWLEDGMENTS

In identifying these sites we have relied greatly on experts within each state, particularly the Partners in Flight coordinators and other experts they have recommended to us. We have also found helpful the many fine state birding guides now available, such as those sponsored by the American Birding Association. Some have gone through several editions and for years have reliably guided travelers to the birds they most want to see. American Birding Association's two publications, *Birding*, and *Winging It* have also proved particularly good sources of site information. National Audubon Society also provided much information of value in preparing these accounts: Fred Baumgarten, Bob Barnes, Doug Faulkner, Noreen Damude, Walker Golder, Bill Pranty, and Dan Niven have been particularly helpful. Books have already appeared on the IBAs of New York State, Pennsylvania, and Washington, and these have been very helpful as well, as have IBA websites for Florida and California. Particular thanks are due to the Audubon Naturalist Society, which supplied extensive information about the Chesapeake Bay and elsewhere in Maryland and Virginia. Thanks are due to our many cooperators who filled out forms to nominate IBAs. Particular thanks is due to the many biologists and land managers at the sites themselves; their review of the site accounts and their helpful suggestions have proved essential. Thanks particularly to our ABC colleagues Gavin Shire, who prepared the maps, and Jane Fitzgerald and Jeff Price, who contributed sidebars. Thanks also to the National Geographic Society for their assistance in preparing the national IBA map on p. xxii. A list of those who contributed information or made useful suggestions is found below. American Bird Conservancy would like to especially acknowledge the important support of BirdLife International, the Council for Environmental Cooperation, LaSalle Adams Fund, and the Laurel, Leo Model, C. S. Mott, National Fish & Wildlife, David and Lucille Packard, Prospect Hill, Felix and Elizabeth Rohatyn, Turner, Underhill, and Weeden Foundations, for their contributions to the Important Bird Areas program that made this book possible. A very special debt of gratitude is also owed American Bird Conservancy's Board of Directors, particularly Howard Brokaw and Alan Weeden, and members (especially the Falcon Club) for their unflagging, steady support. Our thanks, too, to the Disney Corporation, which funded our project to send plaques designating the Globally Important Bird Areas to each of the site managers for display to the public. Finally, much of the funding provided for this book has been supplied by The Nature Conservancy, through its Wings of the Americas Program, funded by a grant from the Canon Corporation. Without this generous support, this project would not have been possible. For anyone we have failed to thank, please accept our apologies!

Christine Abraham
Ray Adams
Sarah Aicher
David H. Allen

Stephanie Allison
Bob Altman
Don Anderson
Ed Anderson

John Richard Anderson
Margaret M. Anderson
Ralph G. Anderson
Brad Andres

Linda Andrews
Robert F. Andrle
Larry L. Apple
Bill Armstrong
Henry T. Armistead
Lyne Askins
Dennis Aslett
Jonathan Atwood
Keith Axelson
Amber Bach
Karen Bachman
Paul J. Baicich
Suzanne Baird
Mark Ball
Scott Ballard
Cindy Barkhurst
Bob Barnes
Ed Barren
Michael Barron
Wylie Barrow
Jack R. Bartholmai
Robert Bastarache
Fred Baumgarten
Andrew Beckington
Laura Beckley
Mike Behrens
Carol Beidleman
Theodore H. Below
Joseph Benson
Jim Bergan
Steve Best
Timothy R. Bigler
Lisa Bigley
Keith L. Bildstein
Laurence C. Binford
Bill Bird
Todd Bittner
Jennifer Bjork
Jon Blanchard
Frank C. Blomquist
Connie Boardman
Martha C. Bogle
Diane Borden-Billiot
Stephen H. Bouffard
Peter V. Bradley
Brian Braudis
Dan Brauning
Daniel Breaux
Richard Brewer
David F. Brinker

Kenneth J. Brock
Ben Brown
Clait Brown
Kelly Bryan
Joe Buchanan
Margaret Buckwalter
David Buehler
Bill Busby
Greg Butcher
Tim W. Byer
Kris A. Cafaro
Carolyn Caldwell
Ellen Campbell
Rick Cantu
Lawrence D. Carlile
Dawn Carrie
Kris K. Carter
Mike Carter
Robin Carter
Dan Casey
John Castrale
John Cely
Andrea Cerovski
Angy Chambers
John Chatt
Graham Chisholm
Jeff Chynoweth
Jeff Clark
Jim Clark
Richard Clayton
Ken Cole
Brian Collins
Marti Collins
Mark Colwell
Scott Comings
Sheila Conant
Jeff Connor
Sarah Connors
Dwight Cooley
Jeff Cooper
Kevin C. Cooper
Jeff Cordes
Dean Corgiat
Troy E. Corman
John Cornelius
Jim Corven
Ralph Costa
Yvonne Cougoulat
Tom Counts
Alan Craig

Nancy Jo Craig
Julie Craves
Gary J. Crossley
Paula Crumpton
Paula Cruz
Lloyd A. Culp Jr.
Natalene Cummings
Noel Cutright
Lisa Cutting
Bill Cutts
Gretchen Cutts
Denise Dachner
Jon Dale
Carol Damberg
Doug Damberg
Noreen Damude
Ken Dancak
Donald Dann
David T. Dauphin
Lynn Davidson
Jerry W. Davis
Tylan Dean
Jeff DeBlieu
James Decker
John Decker
Gina Dello Russo
Pam Denmon
Anthony W. Detoy
Pete DeSimone
Bruce Deuel
Ed DeVries
David Dickey
Jeff Dimaggio
James J. Dinsmore
Stephen J. Dinsmore
Bill Dobbins
John Doremus
Dan Dourson
Jan Dubuisson
Gregory J. DuCote
Katy Duffy
Mark Dumesnil
Charles Duncan
Chris Eberly
Darrell Echols
Tom Edgerton
Bill Eddleman
Jaime Edwards
Jack Clinton Eitniear
Lee Elliott

Dean Elson
Steven R. Emmons
Dave Engebretson
Rex Ennis
A. Sidney England
Eric Epstein
Mark Epstein
Mick Erickson
Terry Esker
Troy Ettel
Cory Evans
Dave Ewert
Norm Famous
Jay Fatooh
Doug Faulkner
David Feliz
Catie Fenn
Marie Fernandez
John Fitch
Jane Fitzgerald
Robert Flores
Todd Forbes
Steve Foree
Doug Forsell
Eric Forsman
Dennis Franklin
Dave Frederick
Andrew C. French
Rand French
Ed Friedman
Carl Frounfelker
Jim Fryer
John T. Fulton
Bill Gaines
John B. Gallegos
Bill Gates
Daphne Gemmill
Mike Getman
T.J. Gostomski
David Govatski
Kenneth M. Giesen
Kathy Gilbert
Douglas Gill
Robert Gill
Bill Glass
Walker Golder
Ken Gordon
Lamar B. Gore
Theodore J. Gostomski
Gordon Gould

Dave Govatski
Gary Graves
Ken Gray
Jim Greaves
Janet C. Green
Jay Greenberg
John J. Grensten
Skip Griep
Jane Griess
Christine Griffiths
Paul Grindrod
Sterling Grogan
Karl Grover
Richard J. Guadagno
Mark Guetersloh
Bruce Hagedorn
Bill Haglan
Freeman F. Hall Jr.
Mic Hamas
Paul Hamel
Bob Hamilton
Jeanne Hammond
Helen Hands
Patty Happe
Paul C. Hardy
Greg Harper
Jim Harper
Dean Harrigal
Bettie Harriman
Stan Harris
Bea Harrison
Craig Harrison
Steve Harrison
Joe Hartman
Thomas E. Harvey
Michael M. Hawkes
Anne Hecht
Scott Hecker
Christopher Heckscher
Cloyce Hedge
Roger Hedge
Jill Hedgecock
Roy E. Heideman
Gary Helbing
Sheri Helon
Brian J. Helsaple
Scott G. Hereford
James Herkert
Tom Henson
Carrie Herziger

Jenna Hestir
Kevin K. Higgins
Dave Hilley
Rebecca E. Hinkle
Toni Hodgkins
Tom Hodgman
Bob Hodorff
Jim Hoefler
Craig Hohlenberger
Deborah Holle
Jean Hookwater
Jeff Hoover
Jeff Horton
Gary Houf
Susan Hootman
Robert L. Howard
Robert W. Howe
Mark Howery
M. Howsh
Craig N. Huegel
Ron Huffman
Tim Hughes
John Hunter
Mike Hupp
Mike Hurst
Gary Hushle
Daria Hyde
Larry Igl
Dianne Ingram
Gary Ivey
Brad Jacobs
Ken Jacobsen
Deborah Jansen
Jack Jeffrey
Jessie Jewell
Mark E. Johns
Aaron Johnson
Kris Johnson
Andrea Jones
Conrad Jones
Drew Jones
R. Joseph
Robert L. Joyner
Richard P. Kane
Marty Kaehny
John Karges
Marsha Kearney
Greg Kearns
Jeff Keating
Ralph Keel

Joseph B. Kelly
Don Kemner
John Kemper
Randall Kennedy
David Kisner
Diane Kitchen
Paul D. Kittle
David R. Kitts
Vernon Kleen
Larry Klimek
Dean Knauer
Mike J. Knezek
Fritz Knopf
Gregg Knutsen
Melinda Knutson
Robin Kobaly
Tom Koerner
Margaret T. Kolar
Barbara Kott
Joe Kraayenbrink
David Krueper
Cyndi Kuehler
Jack Kumer
Robert LaFleur
Bill LaHaye
Christi Lambert
Ron Lambeth
Mike Lang
Tom Langschied
Arthur Langton
Jack Lapinski
Chris Lapp
Stephen A. Laymon
Wendy Ledbetter
David S. Lee
Harry LeGrand
Robin Leong
John Lerg
Fred Lesher
Gary Lester
Steve Lewis
Alan Lieberman
Steven L. Lima
Jim Lind
Ed Lindquist
Bob Lindsay
Dawn Lipton
Ken Litzenberger
Mark Lockwood
Derek Lohuis
Socheata Lor

Joe Lundh
Merrill Lynch
Marcia Lyons
Lynda MacWhinney
Elizabeth Madden
D. Mairs
Paul D. Makela
Anne Mankowski
David Maple
Charles E. Marshall
Jennifer Martin
Larry Martin
Ron Martin
Steve Martin
Larry Master
Randy Matchett
Jeffrey K. Mauck
Jim Mawk
Brian J. McCaffery
Bill McDaniel
Nikki McDaniel
Dianna McDonell
Terry McEneaney
Kevin McIntyre
Don McIvor
Bradley W. McKinney
Will Meeks
Dave Mehlman
Scott M. Melvin
David W. Menke
Paul Meyers
Gary Milano
Glen R. Miller
Carl D. Mitchell
Laura Mitchell
Ronald F. Mize
Pat Momich
Delfinia Monaño
Kenneth Moore
Narca Moore-Craig
Glenn Moravic
Griff Morgan
Marie P. Morin
Elaine Morrall
Daniel Moss
Dave Muench
Bob Murphy
Dan Murphy
Paula Nasiatka
Allan Naydol
Larry Neel

W. Nelson
Chuck Nicholson
Gerry Niemi
Dick Nikolai
Dan Niven
Joan Nitschke
Kit Novick
Paul O'Brien
Jack Oelfke
Mike Oldham
Rebecca Olsen
Bridget Olson
Mike Olson
Len Pardue
Robert Parker
Steve Parris
Joe Patt
Don Paul
John Payne
Lance Peacock
Denise Pengeroth
Rob Penner
John Perkins
William M. Perry
Delia Person
David J. Peters
Gary Peters
Joel Peterson
Wayne Peterson
Carl Petrick
Scott Petrie
Mike Petruchka
Howard Phillips
Nell Phillips
Mark Phipps
Linden Piest
James Ponshair
Linda Poole
John Porter
Tim Post
Bill Pranty
Michael Prather
Thane Pratt
Wayne R. Pray
Dennis E. Prichard
Jeff Price
Leighlan Prout
Lori Pruitt
John Pumilio
Mike Quinlan
Mary Rabe

Roger Radd
Jim Ramakka
Kerry Reese
Bruce Reid
Joe Reinman
Melissa Renfro
Jimmie J. Reynolds
Robert W. Reynolds
Timothy D. Reynolds
Sue A. Ricciardi
Adam Rich
David Richardson
Kory Richardson
Jean Richter
Chris Rimmer
Gerald R. Rising
Donald L. Rivenes
Justin Roach
Joe Robb
Renee L. Robichaud
John Robinson
Jon Rodiek
Bill Rowe
Art Rohrbacher
Carlyle Rogillio
Jim Roscoe
Ken Rosenberg
Eric Rosenquist
Bill Roshak
Terry Rossignol
Richard Roy
Eric Rozowski
Linda Rubenstein
Jeff Rupert
Wayne P. Russ
Bob Russell
Ann Rydgren
Danny Salas
M.J. St. Louis
Douglas A. Samson
Jennifer Sanchez
Kevin Sands
Conrad Sankpill
Eugene J. Scarpulla
Mary Schaefer
Alan Schultz
Thomas Schultz
William A. Schultze
Chris Schumacher
Stan Senner
Bruce Seppi

Nanette W. H. Seto
Darrell Seven
Charles W. Sexton
N. Sferra
Cliff Shackelford
Margaret Shea
Ron Shepperd
Julie Shieldcastle
Mark Shieldcastle
Susanne Shipper
Gavin Shire
Karen C. Short
Bob Siegfried
Mark Silberstein
Michelle Simone
Bobbi Simpson
D. Simpson
Scott Simpson
Eric Sipco
Carey Smith
Eric Smith
Henry T. Smith
John Smith
Karen Smith
Kathleen Lesh Smith
Reed V. Smith
Shannon Smith
Dan Snodgrass
Laura Sommers
Mike Spanel
Paul Springer
Donna Stanley
John D. Stanton
Wendy D. Stanton
George Steger
Dick Steinbach
Charles Stenvall
Terry Stevens
Dennis L. Stewart
Earl Stewart
Kyle Stockwell
Kelli Stone
Brian Stotts
Eileen Dowd Stukel
Ken Sturm
Meyrl Sundove
Lee Sutton
Dan Svingen
Chris Swarth
Ramona Swenson
Bryan Swift

Randy Swilling
Wayne Syron
Brian Taber
Eddie Taylor
Tim Tear
Diane Tecic
Donald E. Temple
Ralph Terry
Daryl Tesson
Bill Thomas Jr.
Nate Thomas
Craig Thompson
Steve Thompson
Dagmar Thurmond
Tim Tibbitts
Donald Tiller
Jeanne R. Tinsman
Todd Tisler
Michael J. Tollefson
Genelle Treaster
Beatrix Treiterer
Charles Trost
Floyd A. Truetken
Barry R. Truitt
Vinnie Turner
Dianne Tyrne
Gregory Ugiansky
Russell Utych
Philip Unitt
Robert Valen
Rosalie Valvo
Brian van Eerden
Julie F. Van Stappen
Bill Vermillion
Alan Versaw
Louise Vicencio
Linda Vidal
William K. Volkert
George E. Wallace
Jeff Walters
Nancy Walters
Patrick Walther
Jo Wargo
Gordon Warrick
Richard Wass
Kerstin Wasson
Keith Watson
Keith M. Weaver
Kenneth Weaver
Ron Weeks
Sarah Welker

William E. Wellman

Jeff Wells

Karen West

Karen Westphall

Robert Wheat

William E. Wheeler

Mark Whisler

Dorn Whitmore

David Wilcove

John Wilker

Brian D. C. Williams

Eric Willman

Brent Wilson

Jim Wilson

John C. Wilson

Ken Wilson

Gerald Winegrad

Brad Winn

Donna Work

John Wright

Dave Wrobleski

D. Yokel

Hana Young

Jessica Young

Rebecca Young

Roy Zipp

Dawn M. Zirrillo

CONTENTS

LIST OF SIDE BARS

INTRODUCTION

This book is the first to identify and describe the globally most significant Important Bird Areas (IBA) in the United States. Though there are books treating some of these areas and which species a birder can find there, no single work has ever put sites into the context of their global meaning to bird conservation.

The Important Bird Area concept originated in Europe and was developed by BirdLife International in the 1980s, and through the years has become a worldwide effort. Conservationists in the United States have taken up the idea with enthusiasm. ABC's contribution began in 1995, with a focus on sites of global, continental, and national significance. Working with partner conservation groups and managers and owners of the sites themselves, we intend the IBA program to be as powerful a force for bird conservation in the United States as it has been abroad. This book is an important step toward this goal. In it we are not just trying to raise or sharpen the awareness of the public and of the managers and owners of these areas as to their critical importance, but to provide information to birders and other conservationists who wish to get directly involved and see the sites for themselves. If one knows what role a site plays in the overall conservation of birds, one sees it through new eyes.

In the last 100 years, the bird landscape in the United States has changed dramatically. Ranges of many species have shrunk (such as Loggerhead Shrike and Lesser Prairie-Chicken), while others have grown (such as Fish Crow, Blue Jay, and Clay-colored Sparrow). Many non-native birds have been introduced into the United States, including several species of parrots and doves, now found widely in the Sun Belt. One that got here on its own—the Cattle Egret—has spread through much of the country and has been sighted in nearly all of the lower 48 states. Two species decimated during the nineteenth century finally died out completely in the early twentieth—the Passenger Pigeon and the Carolina Parakeet—victims of overhunting and persecution by humans. Two denizens of old-growth bottomland forests in the Southeast—the Ivory-billed Woodpecker and Bachman's Warbler—slipped into oblivion as their habitat became scarce. Several species of Hawaiian forest birds fell victim to habitat loss and introduced avian diseases, and became extinct. Yet while the last hundred years have been very bad for some bird species, for others—those that benefit from human activities—they have been very good. Herring and Ring-billed gulls are flourishing, as are Brown-headed Cowbirds and Canada Geese. Helped by feeders, backyard birds such as cardinals, Tufted Titmice, and mockingbirds have expanded their ranges and no doubt their numbers.

Just as bird distributions and abundances have changed, problems facing bird conservation have changed as well. Old problems—such as wholesale slaughter of shorebirds by market hunters and the killing of egrets for feathers for women's hats—have disappeared. Others—such as habitat destruction—are still with us, but in a different form: the clearing of the forests and the breaking of the prairies have given way to suburban sprawl and the vast monocultures of commercial agriculture. And new problems have arisen. Pollution from pesticides and excessive use of fertilizers first arose as a serious issue in the twentieth century. In the last few years, communication towers have sprung up as hazards to migrant birds. And the last few decades have greatly hastened the introduction and spread of non-native plants and animals—often crowding out native species and degrading millions of acres of land. Global warming—though only its earliest effects have been felt so far—may affect the distributions of most species greatly over the next few human generations. Unlike earthbound creatures, birds can pick up and look for places where conditions are better, but there is no guarantee in a very changed world that they will find them.

Despite these problems, the picture for bird conservation has many bright spots. More and more land—including land in and adjacent to Important Bird Areas—is being protected every year. The federal government continues to add lands to refuges and national forests and to designate wilderness areas. Many states are protecting additional lands as well; for example, Florida has an ambitious program to acquire natural areas, spending $300 million a year. Using not only direct purchase but tools such as conservation easements, groups such as The Nature Conservancy, The Conservation Fund, and local land trusts have protected millions of acres of land. Biologists have learned what measures it takes to protect some of our rarest species, and they are carrying them out. In the case of the Red-cockaded Woodpecker and Florida Scrub-Jay, this means direct habitat manipulation through controlled burning or mechanical clearing of brush; for the Kirtland's Warbler and the Black-capped Vireo, it means trapping of cowbirds that parasitize nests; for the Piping Plover it means protecting nests from marauding predators such as gulls, raccoons, and domestic cats and dogs.

Most encouraging is the public support these programs have gained. A powerful constituency has arisen, and it is still growing. Birding is now one of the most popular hobbies in the United States. In the last ten years, the number of birders has more than doubled, from 21 million to 54 million—some estimates are as high as 71 million. Birders tend to be well informed, bright, and curious about their environment. They have gone beyond asking the casual question, "What bird is that," to trying to find out. For many, one thing leads to another, and soon they are buying books, spending money on binoculars and telescopes, and taking trips to add to their life lists. Once hooked, they find birding is a passion that will last them a lifetime. In the process they become an eloquent and powerful constituency for bird and habitat conservation.

Birders are the natural allies of the land managers and research scientists at the sites themselves, not just on federal lands but on state lands and private preserves as well. These dedicated professionals, often working with limited budgets and limited recognition, are not only the ones most knowledgeable about the resource they manage, but also are typically very well informed as to what is happening in bird research and protection elsewhere. To get the resources to make their programs a success, these managers need all the support they can get from birders and other conservationists. If we can direct attention toward these globally important sites and strengthen the bond between those who visit and those who manage them, we will have accomplished much of what we set out to do.

USING THIS BOOK

This book describes 508 IBAs in the form of "site accounts." These accounts provide information on location, size, ownership, official designations (where they exist), habitats, land use, and a general site description, as well as information on the birds found there and concerns regarding their conservation. The *Highlight* section provides an at-a-glance indication of why the site is globally significant to birds. In many cases the account describes a single IBA or pair of closely related IBAs, and this is reflected in the account title. In other cases a single account relates to a cluster of IBAs that occur in close proximity, and/or have common habitats and avifauna. Such clusters are represented by an overarching, descriptive account title, with the names of the individual IBAs shown in sequence immediately below. In some cases, the volume of information or differences between IBAs within these clusters merit each being given individual attention under its own (indented) account. The book also cites many other places that, while not IBAs themselves, may be internal divisions of an IBA (e.g., islands within a chain, or units of a national wildlife refuge or national forest), larger management units responsible for administration of an IBA, or simply nearby places worthy of note.

Numbers in parentheses after the IBA names correspond to the numbers on the maps at the start of each chapter. These maps vary in scale and are provided to indicate the approximate geographical location of IBAs relative to each other and major rivers, cities, and state boundaries. Where the information is available and where the size of the IBA warrants it, sites are represented by polygons. All other sites are marked with dots. Some IBAs are so close together that representation on the maps became too crowded. In such cases the dots were spaced farther apart to aid legibility. The map legends give page references where the account for each IBA can be found. The checklist on page 453 provides the opportunity to record your visits to individual IBAs. This checklist is arranged by state, and contains page numbers referencing all the IBA accounts. In this way it can also be used as an index of IBAs by state, supplemental to the main alphabetical index at the back of the book.

All bird names are taken from the American Ornithologists' Union (AOU) *Check-list of the Birds of North America, Seventh Edition.* Where a subspecies, race, or population segment is mentioned, it is either indicated in the text, or the subspecies portion of the common name is placed in quotes, e.g., the "Yuma" Clapper Rail, and the "Southwestern" Willow Flycatcher. Scientific names are not used, but can easily be found in the comprehensive list maintained by the AOU on their website: www.aou.org.

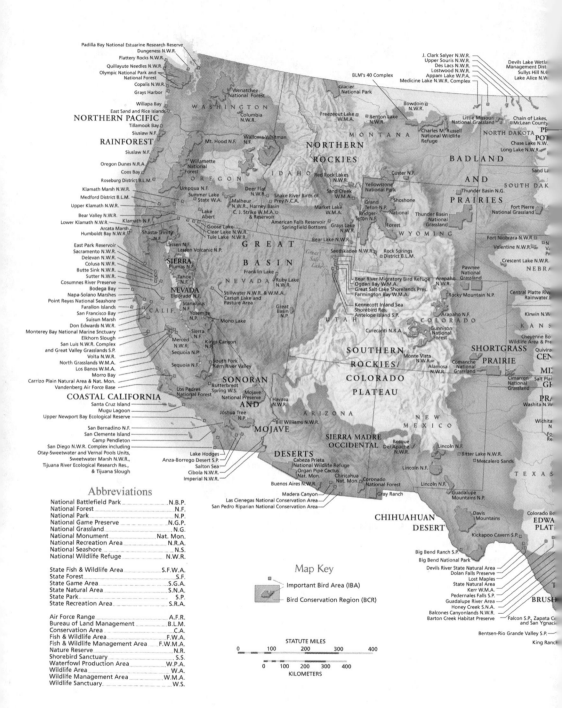

GLOBALLY IMPORTANT BIRD AREAS
IN THE CONTIGUOUS UNITED STATES

ATLANTIC
NORTHERN
FOREST

LOWER
GREAT LAKES/
ST. LAWRENCE
PLAIN

MAINE

Upper St. John
River Project

Baxter
S.P.

Northeastern
Coastal Maine

Waters around
Machias Seal
Island

Mount
Mansfield

VT.

White
Mountain

Merrymeeting Bay

Acadia N.P.

N.H.

Parker River N.W.R.
Crane Beach
Cape Cod N.S.

MASS.

Monomoy N.W.R.
South Chatham Beach
Nantucket Sound
Nantucket
Martha's Vineyard

CONN.
R.I.

Bird Island
Block Island N.W.R.
Stewart B. McKinney N.W.R.
Great Gull Island
Long I. Piping Plover Nesting Beaches

NEW ENGLAND/
MID-ATLANTIC COAST

Agassiz N.W.R.
s Slough
R.

Chippewa
National
Forest

Hawk
Ridge N.R.C.

Isle Royale N.P.

Superior
National Forest

Apostle
Islands

Lake Superior S.F.

Whitefish Point

Hiawatha

Lake Superior S.F.

Rice Lake N.W.R.
McGregor
Marsh
Scientific &
Natural Area

BOREAL HARDWOOD
TRANSITION

Hiawatha
N.F.

Seney
N.W.R.

Hiawatha
N.F.

MINNESOTA

WISCONSIN

Lake Huron

Crex Meadows
Wildlife Area

Nicolet
National
Forest

PRAIRIE
OTHOLES

PRAIRIE HARDWOOD
TRANSITION

Trempealeau N.W.R.

MICHIGAN

Kirtland's Warbler
Management Area

Hamlin Beach S.P.

Derby Hill

Northern Montezuma
Wetlands

NEW YORK

Adirondack
Park

Green
Mtn.

Lake Ontario

L. Erie

Allegheny
N.F.

PENN.

Hawk Mt.
Sanctuary

N.J.

Edwin B. Forsythe N.W.R.
Fortescue W.M.A. & Egg Island
Cape May N.W.R.
Woodland Beach
Cape May Migratory Bird Refuge
Cape Henlopen
Prime Hook N.W.R.
Blackwater N.W.R.

Upper Mississippi River
National Wildlife Refuge &
U.S. Army Corps of Engineers lands

Horicon Marsh
Lake
Michigan

Allegan S.G.A.
& Kalamazoo River

Saginaw Bay

Niagara River
Corridor

Lake St. Clair
Lake Erie Where the Detroit
River Enters it
Maumee Bay

Lakeshore
Metropark

Mt. Zion-
Hiney Run

Bombay
Hook N.W.R.
Little Creek W.M.A.
Ted Harvey W.M.A.
Eastern Neck N.W.R.

IOWA

Upper Mississippi River N.W.R. &
U.S. Army Corps of Engineers Lands

Goose L. Prairie
P.N.A.

Metzger Marsh W.A.
Cedar Point N.W.R.
Ottawa N.W.R.

Sandusky
Bay

Magee Marsh
W.A.

DEL.

MD.

Assateague Island National Seashore
Chincoteague N.W.R.
Smith Island Archipelago
Virginia Coast Reserve
Kiptopeke S.P.
Eastern Shore of Virginia N.W.R.
Fisherman Island N.W.R.
Fishing Bay W.M.A.   Elliott I.
Great Dismal Swamp N.W.R.
Pocosin Lakes & Pungo N.W.R.
Alligator River N.W.R.
Nags Head Woods
Pea Island N.W.R.
Cape Hatteras National Seashore
Mattamuskeet N.W.R.
Cape Lookout National Seashore
Swanquarter N.W.R.
Croatan N.F.

Squaw Creek N.W.R.

Port Louisa N.W.R.

EASTERN TALLGRASS PRAIRIE

LaSalle Lake
S.N.A.

Jasper-
Pulaski
F.W.A.

INDIANA

Morgan Monroe S.F.

OHIO

Wayne
N.F.

Shenandoah
N.P. & The Blue
Washington Ridge Pkwy

VIRGINIA

Piney Grove
Preserve

Banner Marsh & Rice Lake S.F.W.A.
Great River N.W.R.

Swan Lake
N.W.R.

Chautauqua N.W.R.

Lake Shelbyville

ILLINOIS

Reclaimed
Coal Mine
Grasslands

Brown County S.P.
Big Oaks N.W.R.

Clarence Cannon N.W.R.
Mark Twain N.W.R.
Mississippi River S.F.W.A.

Carlyle Lake
W.M.A.

Two Rivers
N.W.R.

Hoosier
N.F.

George
Washington

Roanoke River
Floodplain
& Wetlands

Roanoke River
N.W.R.

MISSOURI

Mark Twain N.F.

Rend Lake
S.F.W.A.

Jefferson
N.F.

Daniel
Boone
N.F.

Cherokee
N.F.

NORTH
CAROLINA

Fort
Bragg

Mark Twain N.F.

Trail of Tears
S.F.

Crab Orchard N.W.R.
Shawnee N.F.

Lower Cache River Complex
Frozen-Head S.P./S.N.A.
& Royal Blue W.M.A.

KENTUCKY

CENTRAL
HARDWOODS

Ozark
N.F.

Mingo
N.W.R.

Fort Campbell

Reelfoot
Lake

Great Smoky Mts.
National Park

Pisgah
N.F.

Coastal Waterbird Colonies
Carolina Sandhills N.W.R.
Congaree Swamp N.M.
Francis Beidler Forest
Tom Yawkey Wildlife Center
Santee Coastal Reserve
Cape Romain N.W.R.
Francis Marion N.F.
ACE Basin

iquaw Creek N.W.R.
rvation

Konza Prairie
Research
Natural Area

John Redmond
Reservoir

CENTRAL
HARDWOODS

Flint Hills
Tallgrass
Prairie
Preserve

Tennessee
N.W.R.

Nantahala
N.F.

Fort
Stewart

Big Lake
N.W.R.

TENNESSEE

Cherokee
N.F.

Sumter N.F.

Chattahoochee N.F.

Kennesaw Mt.
N.B.P.

SOUTH
CAROLINA

grass
rie National
serve

OKLAHOMA

Ozark N.F.

ARKANSAS

Wheeler N.W.R.

William B.
Bankhead
N.F.

GEORGIA

Ouachita
N.F.

White River
N.W.R.

ALABAMA

Hitchiti
Experimental
Forest

McCurtain County
Wilderness Area

WEST GULF
COASTAL PLAIN

MISSISSIPPI

Noxubee
N.W.R.

Talladega
N.F.

Fort
Benning

Piedmont N.W.R.

Fort Stewart
Altamaha River Delta

OAKS
AND
PRAIRIES

Caddo Lake

Ouachita N.F.

Overflow
N.W.R.

Felsenthal
N.W.R.

Yazoo N.W.R.
Complex

Bienville
N.F.

Delta N.F.

Okefenokee
N.W.R.

Cumberland Island National Seashore
Pinhook Swamp

Angelina
N.F.

Kisatchie
N.F.

Catahoula
N.F.

Buckhorn
W.M.A.

Tensas
River N.W.R.

SOUTHEASTERN COASTAL PLAIN

Osceola National Forest

Davy Crockett
N.F.

Fort
Polk

LOUISIANA

Blackwater River N.F.

Elgin Air Force Base

Apalachicola
N.F.

Ochlockonee
River N.W.R.

St. Marks N.W.R.

Fort Hood

Sam Houston
N.F.

Big Thicket
National
Preserve

Sabine
Woods

Lake
Pontchartrain
Causeway

Gulf
Islands
N.S.

Dog I.

Ocala N.F.

Canaveral National Seashore
Merritt Island N.W.R.
Cape Canaveral Air Force Station
Three Lakes W.M.A.
St. Sebastian River State Buffer Preserve

cken N.W.R.

W. G.
Jones S.F.

Lacassine
N.W.R.

Atchafalaya
Basin

Lower Suwannee N.W.R.
Cedar Key Scrub State Reserve
Cedar Keys N.W.R.
Lake Apopka Restoration Area
Honeymoon Island S.R.A.
Cross Bar Ranch Wellfield &
Al-Bar Ranch

FLORIDA

Avon
Park
A.F.R.

PENINSULAR FLORIDA

Katy Prairie

Roy E. Larsen Sandyland Sanct.
McFaddin & Texas Pt. N.W.R.s

Delta
N.W.R.

Jonathan Dickinson S.P.
Belle Glade Area
Arthur R. Marshall
Loxahatchee N.W.R.

water Prairie

Sea Rim S.P.

Anahuac N.W.R.

Coastal Louisiana Is.

Archbold Biological Station &
Lake Placid Scrub Preserve

Lake
Okeechobee

exas City Prairie Preserve

High Is.

Smith Point.

Breton N.W.R.

Chandeleur Islands

Big Cypress
National Preserve

GULF
COASTAL
PRAIRIE

Bolivar Flats S.S.
Brazoria N.W.R.

Gulf Islands
National Seashore

Gulf Coast Least
Tern Colony

Corkscrew Swamp
Florida Panther N.W.R.

Key Largo Hammocks State Botanical Site
Crocodile Lake N.W.R.
John Pennekamp Coral Reef S.P.

PAN

San Bernard N.W.R.
Columbia Bottomlands

Mississippi Sandhill
Crane N.W.R.

Everglades National Park
Great White Heron N.W.R.

Big Boggy N.W.R.

Lower Pascagoula R. W.M.A.
Dauphin Island
Ft. Morgan Historical Park
Bon Secour N.W.R.

National Key Deer Refuge
Torchwood Hammock Preserve

Mad Island Marsh Complex
Matagorda Island
Aransas N.W.R.
Hazel Bazemore County Park

Dry Tortugas N.P.

Key West
N.W.R.

Padre Island National Seashore &
South Padre Island Preserve
Kenedy Ranch
Laguna Atascosa N.W.R.
Sabal Palm Grove Audubon Center
Lennox Foundation Southmost Preserve
Santa Ana and Lower Rio Grande
Valley National Wildlife Refuges

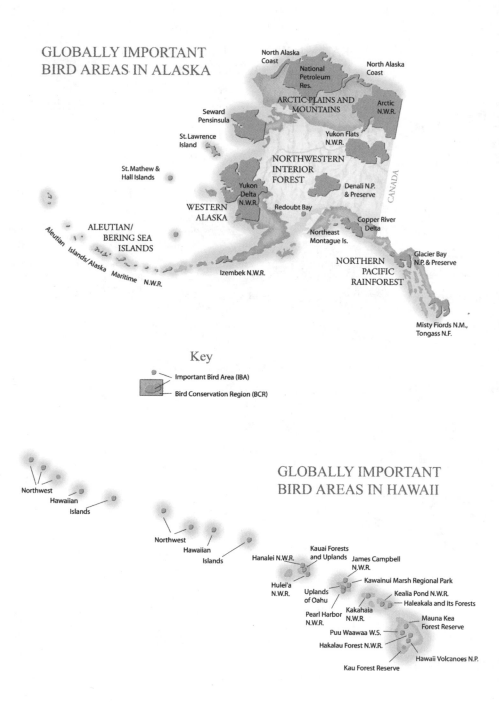

GLOBALLY IMPORTANT BIRD AREAS IN ALASKA

North Alaska Coast

National Petroleum Res.

North Alaska Coast

ARCTIC PLAINS AND MOUNTAINS

Arctic N.W.R.

Seward Pensinsula

Yukon Flats N.W.R.

St. Lawrence Island

St. Mathew & Hall Islands

NORTHWESTERN INTERIOR FOREST

Denali N.P. & Preserve

CANADA

Yukon Delta N.W.R.

Redoubt Bay

WESTERN ALASKA

Copper River Delta

Northeast Montague Is.

ALEUTIAN/ BERING SEA ISLANDS

Glacier Bay N.P. & Preserve

Aleutian Islands/Alaska Maritime N.W.R.

Izembek N.W.R.

NORTHERN PACIFIC RAINFOREST

Misty Fiords N.M., Tongass N.F.

Key

Important Bird Area (IBA)

Bird Conservation Region (BCR)

Northwest Hawaiian Islands

GLOBALLY IMPORTANT BIRD AREAS IN HAWAII

Northwest Hawaiian Islands

Kauai Forests and Uplands

James Campbell N.W.R.

Hanalei N.W.R.

Kawainui Marsh Regional Park

Hulei'a N.W.R.

Uplands of Oahu

Kealia Pond N.W.R.

Haleakala and its Forests

Pearl Harbor N.W.R.

Kakahaia N.W.R.

Mauna Kea Forest Reserve

Puu Waawaa W.S.

Hakalau Forest N.W.R.

Hawaii Volcanoes N.P.

Kau Forest Reserve

Criteria for Site Selection

W hy did we pick the sites we did? For some sites, the reasons are apparent; Aransas National Wildlife Refuge in Texas is internationally known as the winter home to nearly the entire wild population of the Whooping Crane, while Delaware Bay is famous as the place where hundreds of thousands of shorebirds stop each spring to feast on horseshoe crab eggs. But how many people know that Apalachicola National Forest in Florida has the greatest population in the world of the endangered Red-cockaded Woodpecker, or that Fort Hood, Texas, is the world's leading site for two endangered species—the Black-capped Vireo and the Golden-cheeked Warbler? Or that one of the best breeding areas for the green-listed Henslow's Sparrow is reclaimed strip-mined lands in southwestern Indiana? There are plenty of foregone conclusions among the sites listed in this book, but there are plenty of surprises, too.

For a site to be chosen, it must be of significant importance, during at least some part of the year, by containing habitat that supports:

Category 1: a species on the ABC Green List, the criteria for which are set forth below. Note that for species on this list, we do not in general attempt to describe each and every important site, but rather, the few best and most critical of the sites known, while listing or mentioning a few of particular note. Note also that certain subspecies are mentioned in the accounts throughout the text, because of their special conservation concern.

Category 2: a significantly large concentration of breeding, migrating, or wintering birds, including waterfowl, seabirds, wading birds, raptors, or landbirds. For the species in this category, we do not include super-abundant flocking species such as some of the blackbirds or those which are increasing their populations to the point where they, themselves, are presenting management problems, such as Snow and Canada Geese and Herring and Ring-billed gulls. Below are our criteria for including sites with significant congregations:

a. for waterfowl, we count as a globally significant IBA sites with more than 100,000 ducks and geese;

b. for seabirds, we limit this to colonies of 50,000 individuals or more, omitting concentrations of Herring and Ring-billed gulls;

c. for shorebirds, we include sites at the international and hemispheric level in the Western Hemisphere Shorebird Reserve Network (WHSRN) and sites with 50,000 individuals or more at some time of year. Many shorebird species are on the Green List; we include sites that reliably host important contingents of these species.

d. Congregations of raptors, with 25,000 or more individuals regularly counted during a season. It is important to note that these sites are generally "overflight" sites, not used by migrant raptors for resting and feeding, and thus not important to them in the same way many stopover sites are to migrating passerines and other landbirds. There are probably many other places in the United States that would qualify on the basis of 25,000 hawks passing over, but we include only those where long-term counts are available.

e. for wading birds, we limit our sites to those representing the largest colonies or other places regularly used, not merely those with more than 10,000 individuals.

f. for migrating landbirds other than raptors, including passerines, cuckoos, and hummingbirds, the sites we include are stopover sites, though there is a general lack of census data on numbers using such sites, and use can vary greatly from year to year, depending on weather conditions. Among the examples in this category are well-known migrant traps such as Dauphin Island, Alabama, and High Island, Texas.

Many of the sites qualify in both categories. We hope that the "Highlight" given for each site should make it apparent why it was chosen, without the need for the reader to page back to this section. Note that since the appearance of the Important Bird Areas map produced in cooperation with National Geographic, the list has undergone a revision; for example, all those species of very limited total distribution (e.g., Tricolored Blackbird, Yellow-billed Magpie) have now been incorporated into the ABC Green List.

ABC Green List

The ABC Green List reflects the most advanced and consistent reasoning yet attempted concerning the assessment of the status of birds in the United States. In order to focus on the most important conservation objectives, Partners in Flight (PIF) developed a species assessment process. From the beginning, the criteria used included range size, population size, population trend, and threats. Initiatives dealing with shorebirds, waterbirds, and waterfowl all created variations of these criteria, as did increasing involvement by Canadian and Mexican conservationists, and the criteria continue to evolve as new ideas develop.

A list such as this is an interpretation of assessment that includes all of those species that exceed a selected level of cumulative concern on a national or continental scale. PIF has produced a number of Watch Lists over the years, most recently in "Conservation of the Land Birds of the United States" in 2000. Previous lists were inconsistent, in part because divergent interpretations of the various initiatives (shorebirds, waterbirds, etc.) were respected, meaning that different groups of birds were evaluated differently and independently of each other.

Since the 2000 publication, PIF in the three North American countries has made great advances in the science and application of species assessment. ABC has applied this latest thinking to all birds, including shorebirds, waterbirds, waterfowl, and other gamebirds such as grouse and quail. The result is the following ABC Green List. There are three groups of species on the list. The first includes those species of highest continental concern: those showing some alarming combination of population declines, small population size, small ranges, and high threats. The second list includes species that are moderately abundant with population declines or high threats, and the third list includes those with restricted distributions and low population size.

Listing status under the United States Endangered Species Act is indicated (as Endangered or Threatened). Note that the ABC Green List only deals with full species, not considering subspecies that may be of high concern. A separate list of Hawaiian birds on the ABC Green List follows.

Highest Continental Concern

Short-tailed Albatross (Endangered)
Bermuda Petrel (Endangered)
Black-capped Petrel
Pink-footed Shearwater
Ashy Storm-Petrel
California Condor (Endangered)
Steller's Eider (Threatened)
Spectacled Eider (Threatened)
Gunnison Sage-Grouse
Lesser Prairie-Chicken
Yellow Rail
Black Rail
King Rail
Whooping Crane (Endangered)
Snowy Plover (Western ssp. threatened)
Piping Plover (Threatened; Great
  Lakes/Midwest pop. endangered)
Mountain Plover
Eskimo Curlew (Endangered)
Long-billed Curlew
Marbled Murrelet (WA, OR, and CA
  pops. threatened)
Xantus's Murrelet
Craveri's Murrelet
Thick-billed Parrot

Red-cockaded Woodpecker
  (Endangered)
Ivory-billed Woodpecker (Endangered)
Black-capped Vireo (Endangered)
Florida Scrub-Jay (Threatened)
Island Scrub-Jay
Bicknell's Thrush
Bachman's Warbler (Endangered)
Golden-winged Warbler
Colima Warbler
Golden-cheeked Warbler (Endangered)
Kirtland's Warbler (Endangered)
Bachman's Sparrow
Henslow's Sparrow
Saltmarsh Sharp-tailed Sparrow
Tricolored Blackbird

Moderately Abundant Species with Declines or High Threats

Horned Grebe
Greater Shearwater
Audubon's Shearwater
Band-rumped Storm-Petrel
Brandt's Cormorant

Pelagic Cormorant
Little Blue Heron
Brant
American Black Duck
Black Scoter
Swallow-tailed Kite
Swainson's Hawk
Greater Sage-Grouse
Blue Grouse
Greater Prairie-Chicken (Attwater's ssp. endangered)
Scaled Quail
American Golden-Plover
American Avocet
Lesser Yellowlegs
Solitary Sandpiper
Upland Sandpiper
Whimbrel
Marbled Godwit
Sanderling
Semipalmated Sandpiper
Western Sandpiper
Dunlin
Stilt Sandpiper
Short-billed Dowitcher
Wilson's Snipe
American Woodcock
Wilson's Phalarope
Red Phalarope
Gull-billed Tern
Roseate Tern (North Atlantic Coast pop. endangered; Western Hemisphere pop. threatened)
Least Tern (Interior ssp. Endangered)
Black Skimmer
Razorbill
Pigeon Guillemot
White-crowned Pigeon
Band-tailed Pigeon
Mangrove Cuckoo
Short-eared Owl
White-throated Swift
Rufous Hummingbird
Elegant Trogon
Red-headed Woodpecker
Olive-sided Flycatcher
Willow Flycatcher (Southwestern ssp. endangered)
Bell's Vireo (Least ssp. endangered)

Pinyon Jay
Oak Titmouse
Brown-headed Nuthatch
Wood Thrush
Sprague's Pipit
Grace's Warbler
Prairie Warbler
Bay-breasted Warbler
Cerulean Warbler
Prothonotary Warbler
Worm-eating Warbler
Kentucky Warbler
Canada Warbler
Brewer's Sparrow
Baird's Sparrow
Harris's Sparrow
Varied Bunting
Painted Bunting
Dickcissel
Rusty Blackbird

Species with Restricted Distributions and Low Population Size

Yellow-billed Loon
Clark's Grebe
Laysan Albatross
Black-footed Albatross
Cory's Shearwater
Flesh-footed Shearwater
Buller's Shearwater
Manx Shearwater
Black-vented Shearwater
Black Storm-Petrel
Least Storm-Petrel
Red-faced Cormorant
Magnificent Frigatebird
Reddish Egret
Emperor Goose
Mottled Duck
Harlequin Duck
Snail Kite (Endangered)
Mountain Quail
Montezuma Quail
Pacific Golden-Plover
Wilson's Plover
American Oystercatcher
Black Oystercatcher
Bristle-thighed Curlew

Hudsonian Godwit
Bar-tailed Godwit
Black Turnstone
Surfbird
Red Knot
Buff-breasted Sandpiper
Heermann's Gull
Yellow-footed Gull
Red-legged Kittiwake
Elegant Tern
Aleutian Tern
Bridled Tern
Kittlitz's Murrelet
Ancient Murrelet
Whiskered Auklet
Flammulated Owl
Elf Owl
Spotted Owl (Northern and Mexican
    ssp. threatened)
Antillean Nighthawk
Black Swift
Costa's Hummingbird
Calliope Hummingbird
Allen's Hummingbird
Lewis's Woodpecker
Nuttall's Woodpecker
Arizona Woodpecker
White-headed Woodpecker
Thick-billed Kingbird
Gray Vireo
Yellow-billed Magpie
California Gnatcatcher (Endangered)
Black-capped Gnatcatcher
Wrentit
Bendire's Thrasher
California Thrasher
Le Conte's Thrasher
Blue-winged Warbler
Virginia's Warbler
Lucy's Warbler
Hermit Warbler
Swainson's Warbler
Red-faced Warbler
Abert's Towhee
Rufous-winged Sparrow
Five-striped Sparrow
Black-chinned Sparrow
Nelson's Sharp-tailed Sparrow

Seaside Sparrow (Cape Sable ssp.
    endangered)
McCown's Longspur
McKay's Bunting
Audubon's Oriole
Black Rosy-Finch
Brown-capped Rosy-Finch
Lawrence's Goldfinch

Hawaiian Birds

Hawaiian Petrel (Endangered)
Townsend's Shearwater (Newell's
    subspecies threatened)
Hawaiian Goose (Endangered)
Hawaiian Duck (Endangered)
Laysan Duck (Endangered)
Hawaiian Hawk (Endangered)
Hawaiian Coot (Endangered)
Millerbird (Endangered)
*Kamao (Endangered)
*Olomao (Endangered)
Omao
Puaiohi (Endangered)
Laysan Finch (Endangered)
Nihoa Finch (Endangered)
*Ou (Endangered)
Palila (Endangered)
Maui Parrotbill (Endangered)
Oahu Amakihi
Kauai Amakihi
Anianiau
*Nukupuu (Endangered)
Akiapolaau (Endangered)
Akikiki
Hawaii Creeper (Endangered)
Maui Alauahio
*Oahu Alauahio (Endangered)
Akekee
Akepa (Endangered)
Akohekohe (Endangered)
Poo-uli (Endangered)
Iiwi
Elepaio (Oahu subspecies endangered)
Hawaiian Crow (Endangered)

*Denotes species that are possibly extinct.

Extinction and Extinct Species

Extinction is the absolute measure of conservation failure because its approach is clear and undeniable, and because it is unrecoverable. It is the quintessential indicator of society's willingness to sacrifice future options for short-term gain. Thus, the prevention of extinction should be a hallmark of any society that plans for secure future generations.

Extinction is a naturally occurring phenomenon of evolution. Species cease to exist for reasons ranging from natural competition with other species to gradual (e.g., climate change) or catastrophic (caused by events ranging from a cave collapse to an asteroid's impact on Earth) habitat change. However, it is the greatly increasing rate of extinction due to the exploding dominance of man across the planet that gives cause for alarm today.

By far the greatest man-caused threat to birds and all species is habitat loss, fragmentation, and degradation in which extinction is an unintended, often unconsidered consequence. The last Ivory-billed Woodpecker succumbed to logging of the last large tracts of bottomland primary forest in the southeastern United States. Bachman's Warbler fell to conversion of canebrake habitat to agriculture. Sometimes, habitat loss simply stacks the odds too steeply against species survival. When the grasslands and blueberry barrens of Martha's Vineyard, Massachusetts, were reduced to fragments, overhunting, fire, cat and other predation, and disease combined to drive the Heath Hen to extinction.

Perhaps the worst case of man-caused mass extinction on Earth has occurred in Hawaii, resulting first from colonization by the Polynesians, and then by Western cultures during the last 200 years. Polynesians arrived around A.D. 400, bringing a variety of mammalian predators. They introduced weed species, converted much of the dry forest, and were responsible for the extinction of at least 50 percent of Hawaii's bird species. Westerners arrived late in the eighteenth century, bringing grazing mammals, rats, cats, mongooses, insects (including mosquitoes), hundreds of new plant species, and bird diseases. At least 23 bird species have been lost since that time, and many others teeter on the brink of extinction.

Which species will be the next to disappear in the United States? The ABC Green List provides some clues. Most species' declines are due to habitat loss. Those bird species breeding or wintering in restricted or unique habitats, those dependent upon degrading or disappearing "bottlenecks" during annual migrations, and those least adaptable to changing conditions are the leading candidates for the extinct species list. Examples of restricted or unique habitats include breeding islands for seabirds and island endemics, and species whose mainland habitat types have been fragmented into "habitat islands" such as old-growth conifers ("Northern" Spotted Owls and Marbled Murrelets in the West, and Red-cockaded Woodpeckers and Bachman's Sparrows in the East), freshwater wetlands (rails), or native grasslands (shorebirds and sparrows). Species threatened by migratory bottlenecks include shorebirds such as the Red Knot that depend on the eggs of horseshoe crabs in Delaware Bay during spring migration and songbirds needing undeveloped coastal habitats after crossing the Gulf of Mexico.

Adaptation is increasingly an important factor in the survival of bird species. When submerged aquatic vegetation—the primary food for many waterfowl species—suffered widespread decline in eastern estuaries in the 1970s, those species that could adapt to upland field feeding (Tundra Swan, geese, and some ducks) maintained populations. Others, such as diving ducks, adapted to aquatic invertebrate foods (Bufflehead) or declined (Canvasback, Redhead). When habitat change in the Ohio Valley proved unfavorable, Cerulean Warbler populations were able to find suitable habitat in southern Ontario in the 1980s and 1990s. Most obviously, species having adapted to the man-altered suburban landscape, such as the American Robin, Northern Mockingbird, and Northern Cardinal, have flourished.

There are limits to adaptability. Wood Thrushes breeding in suburban forest patches are unlikely to adapt to cat predation, and Dickcissels and other birds of agricultural areas cannot adapt to pesticide poisoning. Albatrosses are unlikely to adapt to longline vessels dragging baits that hook and drown them. And when the beaches are all devoted to human recreation, Piping Plovers are unlikely to adapt to breeding in the uplands. The bottom line is that, for each species, reproduction and survivorship must match or exceed mortality for that species to survive. The growing list of threats to most habitats, the non-habitat-related threats to survivorship, and a look at the extinct species list—a duck, shorebird, alcid, pigeon, parakeet, woodpecker, warbler, grouse, wren, and two sparrows—illustrates that no taxonomic group or species is necessarily secure.

Continental U.S. Species Extinct Since European Colonization

Labrador Duck
Great Auk
Eskimo Curlew
Passenger Pigeon
Carolina Parakeet
Ivory-billed Woodpecker
Bachman's Warbler

Continental U.S. Subspecies Extinct Since European Colonization

Heath Hen
"San Clemente" Bewick's Wren
"Texas" Henslow's Sparrow
"Dusky" Seaside Sparrow

Site Listings by Bird Conservation Region

Many types of Important Bird Areas (IBAs) are represented in the following site accounts. Some are important primarily within a context of a whole suite of sites; they are links or endpoints in a chain along a migratory pathway. In the fall, for example, shorebirds coming down from the Arctic and stopping at the Platte River in Nebraska appear next at Cheyenne Bottoms, Kansas, and then at refuges on the Texas coast. A few are important quite independent of any other: Ocala National Forest is one of the few remaining strongholds for the sedentary Florida Scrub-Jay. Some sites—notably those in Hawaii such as the Alakai Swamp on Kauai, and the complex of sites including Haleakala National Park on Maui—support species found nowhere else on Earth. Nearly all have felt the hand of man to one degree or another, and some—such as the Salton Sea in California and Brazoria Flats Shorebird Sanctuary in Texas—exist as the direct result of human activities. Yet, in the absence of pristine habitats, they have become important for birds.

The sites in this book are arranged within North American Bird Conservation Regions (BCR). Developed by the North American Bird Conservation Initiative (NABCI), the BCR system reflects an emerging consensus among ornithologists as to how to divide up North America to advance bird conservation. Lines defining BCRs were chosen to reflect factors including distribution of birds, patterns of vegetation relevant to birds, prevalent land use practices, and important conservation issues. Those lines are loosely based on a single "spatial language" devised by James Omernik and associates at the Environmental Protection Agency, a method that the three countries involved in NABCI (the United States, Mexico, and Canada) and by various bird initiatives within the United States agreed upon. Lines within this system were chosen by a team of bird conservation experts from a broad spectrum of backgrounds to demarcate the boundaries of BCRs based on factors relevant to birds. Proposed

BCR boundaries were widely reviewed throughout the country, modified as a result, and approved by the United States NABCI Committee in November 1999 with the intent to accept additional suggestions for change at the end of three years.

Unlike most state boundaries, these lines are ecologically meaningful. Just as sites in the mountains of North Carolina are very like those in the adjoining mountains of Tennessee but very unlike those on North Carolina's coast, so do sites on the coast of Oregon have much in common with those on the coasts of Washington and northern California, but very little with sites in the Great Basin in eastern Oregon. It makes sense to treat similar sites together, regardless of the state they are in, since they are often alike in their avifauna and in the management problems they face. Though this organizational scheme may seem somewhat awkward at first, it sorts sites by ecological similarity, and in so doing, adds to the reader's understanding of birds, habitats, and ecological systems.

Already in use in planning for shorebirds and waterbirds, BCRs are increasingly becoming the primary planning units for all bird conservation. A description of each BCR in terms of its characteristic avifauna and habitats precedes the discussion of the sites found within it. Note that several BCRs span the border with Canada and others cross over into Mexico. Because this book deals only with U.S. IBAs, only the portion of BCRs falling within the United States are represented on the maps. There are also three BCRs (*6: Boreal Taiga Plains, 7: Taiga Shield and Hudson Plains,* and *8: Boreal Softwood Shield*) that are exclusively in Canada, and several others only in Mexico. Although no Canadian IBAs are discussed in this book, some brief information on Canada's BCRs is provided. The chapter numbers in this book correspond with the numbers assigned to each BCR by NABCI.

Since we think of the geography of the United States in terms of state boundaries, however, we also present a checklist of the sites by state (p. 453).

Finally, is every globally significant Important Bird Area in the United States in this book? Would that they were, but they are undoubtedly not. Note, for example, that of the 508 sites mentioned in this book, some 60.4 percent are in federal ownership, 27.7 percent are owned by state governments, 6.2 percent are owned and managed by The Nature Conservancy, 3.1 percent by other conservation groups, one percent by municipalities, and only 1.6 percent are on private lands. Does this really reflect the true situation in the United States—that for IBAs, public and conservation lands have everything and private lands next to nothing? Not at all. Then why aren't they better represented? The main reason is that, in general, far less information on birds—both species and numbers—is available for private than for public lands. Many, if not most private lands are not open to researchers, let alone the public, and often the level of their significance is not widely known. Rights of property owners is a sensitive issue in conservation, and many landowners might regard the naming of their holdings as IBAs with suspicion. We would hope that in the future, more private lands might be identified as IBAs, and that landowners might come to regard this recognition with pride.

As with any set of data about birds, the IBA program will benefit from continuous updating and input from the birding community. Birds change, times change, and the importance of areas change—and new information, affecting IBAs both positively and negatively, is always coming to light. If you have new information or information that corrects what appears in our site accounts—or if you know of an area you believe ought to be included among the top IBAs, please contact us through our website, www.abcbirds.org, or call us at 540-253-5780.

1. Aleutian/Bering Sea Islands

Included in this region are the Aleutian Islands, extending westward from the Alaskan mainland for 1,100 miles, and the Bering Sea Islands, including the Pribilofs, St. Matthew, Hall, St. Lawrence, and Little Diomede. The Aleutian chain is volcanic in origin with a maritime climate in which wind is ever present. Vegetation at higher elevations consists of dwarf shrub communities mainly of willow and crowberry. Meadows and marshes of herbs, sedges, and grasses are plentiful, and some islands have ericaceous bogs. Sea ice does not extend to the Aleutians, and permafrost is generally absent; however, sea ice is an important feature of the Bering Sea. Seabirds are a dominant component of this region's avifauna and several species, the Red-legged Kittiwake, Least Auklet, and Whiskered Auklet, breed only in this region. Southern Hemisphere procellariiforms occur regularly in the offshore waters of the southern Bering Sea and northern Gulf of Alaska during Alaskan summers. The breeding diversity of passerines (mainly the Lapland Longspur, Snow Bunting, and Gray-crowned Rosy-Finch), and shorebirds (including the Black Oystercatcher, Dunlin, Ruddy Turnstone, and Rock Sandpiper) is low. However, the McKay's Bunting, the only endemic Alaskan passerine, is restricted to this area.

Bering Sea Islands IBAs, Alaska

St. Lawrence Island (1), St. Matthew and Hall Islands (2), Pribilof Islands (3)

▶ Highlight: Remote windswept islands designated for the breeding McKay's Bunting (St. Matthew and Hall, possibly also St. Lawrence and Pribilofs), and for the Red-legged Kittiwake (75 percent of world population breeds in the Pribilof Islands).
▶ Designation: The Alaska Maritime National Wildlife Refuge, which administers much of the islands, is a National Natural Landmark.
▶ Location: Includes St. Matthew and Hall Islands (60° N, 172° W), the Pribilof Islands (57° N, 170° W), and St. Lawrence Island (63° N, 170° W).
▶ Size: The Bering Sea Unit of the Alaska Maritime Wildlife Refuge is 170,000 acres. The Bering Sea Wilderness Area is 81,340 acres.
▶ Ownership: Private and federal: Alaska Maritime National Wildlife Refuge, Bering Sea Wilderness Area.
▶ Habitats: Windswept tundra, precipitous cliffs, some lower-lying coastal lagoons, and beaches.

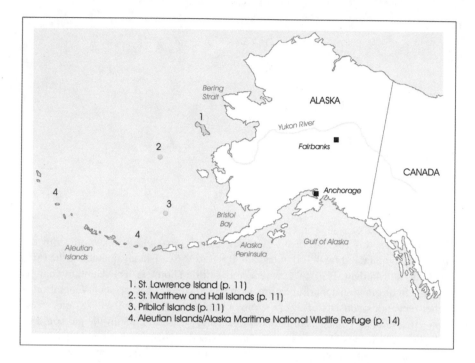

1. St. Lawrence Island (p. 11)
2. St. Matthew and Hall Islands (p. 11)
3. Pribilof Islands (p. 11)
4. Aleutian Islands/Alaska Maritime National Wildlife Refuge (p. 14)

▶ Land Use: Wilderness. Some subsistence hunting and offshore commercial fishing.
▶ Site Description: Two groups of remote, windswept islands separated by 200 miles of ocean, and one larger (100-mile-long) island that lies around 150 miles farther to the north. The islands are treeless and covered in low spongy tundra with grasses reaching a foot high in places. Some dwarf willows are also present. The northerly St. Lawrence and St. Matthew and Hall Islands (81,340 acres, of which 77,000 is St. Matthew) are surrounded by pack ice nine months of the year. The bleak climate is characterized by high winds and frequent fog. St. Matthew rises to 1,500 feet in altitude, and the steep sea cliffs of nearby Pinnacle Island reach 1,200 feet. The tiny, northerly Hall Island has a hauling-out site for Pacific walrus. St. Matthew has a lake with endemic landlocked chinook salmon, and singing voles and Arctic foxes are the common terrestrial mammals. Of the five islets that make up the more southerly Pribilof Islands, St. Paul is the most frequently visited by birders, although 90 percent of the breeding seabirds occur on nearby St. George. The low tundra of the islands is punctuated by rocky outcrops, and the volcanic soil is a reddish color. During the summer the landscape is brightened by a flush of colorful wildflowers, and there are two lakes on St. Paul where waterfowl and shorebirds gather. There is a colony of approximately one million northern fur seals, of which the majority are found on St. Paul, a herd of wild reindeer, and naturally occurring Arctic foxes. The Pribilofs are also home to a large Aleut-Russian community, many of whom are Russian Orthodox.
▶ Birds: The islands are best known for their seabird colonies with two million birds, principally Least Auklets, murres, and fulmars, in the northerly group, and three million in the Pribilofs where a similar mix of species occurs, with the notable addition of

McKay's Bunting

75 percent of the world's Red-legged Kitti-wakes. Other seabirds include the Black-legged Kittiwake, Crested and Parakeet Auklets, and Horned and Tufted Puffins. The majority of the Red-legged Kittiwake population breeds on St. George Island, but the population has declined 50 percent from around 220,000 birds in the mid-1970s. The reason for this decline is not known but appears to be linked to food shortages at sea. The Red-legged Kittiwake has a larger eye than the Black-legged, and this may be an adaptation for specialized night feeding (although both species are known to feed at night). The Pribilofs are also known to birders as a location for Asian vagrants, although the islands are of little, if any, conservation significance for these species. McKay's Bunting has a tiny isolated breeding population on St. Matthew and Hall Islands, where it nests in rocky areas and along shingle beaches (probably also occasionally breeding on St. Lawrence Island). It is also found in the Pribilofs and may have bred there, and migrates to the western Alaska coast in October, returning to breed in May. The population is probably between 3,000 and 6,000 individuals. Other species of interest include the Red-faced Cormorant, Rock Sandpiper, and Gray-crowned Rosy-Finch. St. Lawrence has more than 3.5 million breeding seabirds, including large numbers of Least Auklets (1.3 million at Singikpo Cape alone), as well as Crested Auklets, and Thick-billed and Common Murres. There are also large numbers of nesting Dunlin, and the Pribilofs have an endemic breeding race of the Rock Sandpiper. Recently discovered winter single-species concentrations of Spectacled Eiders in ice-free areas of the Bering Sea may include upward of 300,000 individuals.

▶ Conservation Issues: Seabird nesting success has been variable in recent years, probably in response to natural fluctuations in food availability, but the possibility that the decline of the Red-legged Kittiwake may be linked to overfishing requires research. In 1982, kittiwake nesting cliffs on St. George were purchased by the government and included in the Alaska Maritime National Wildlife Refuge. Introduced Norway rats or mustelids could wreak havoc on seabirds and on the McKay's Bunting, and must not be allowed to establish a foothold. The McKay's Bunting must be considered vulnerable due to its tiny population and limited range. Any major environmental disaster (especially predator introduction) affecting St. Matthew Island could threaten the species' existence. The Fish and Wildlife Service has already developed a rat response plan for the islands, but the development of rat-proof nest boxes may be a useful precaution.

▶ Visitor Information: St. Paul is the most common destination for birders and along with the seabirds, and occasional McKay's Buntings there, Asian vagrants are a major attraction. Visit during the summer as seabirds are present only between May and August. Tours to the Pribilofs can be arranged by contacting Peninsula Airways at 800-448-4226 and the Tanadgusix Native Corporation at 907-278-2312 (three- to eight-day tours of St. Paul). The King Eider Hotel can be reached at 907-546-2477. The hotel on St. George can be reached at 907-859-9222.

Aleutian Islands/Alaska Maritime National Wildlife Refuge (4), Alaska

▸ Highlight: World alcid capital. Includes most of the world breeding population of the rare, endemic Whiskered Auklet and several huge "bird cities" with more than 200,000 breeding seabirds of more than a dozen species. Breeding Red-legged Kittiwakes on one island; significant wintering population of Emperor Geese. Some Steller's Eiders winter in the east. Bristle-thighed Curlews during migration. Classic birding for Asian vagrants on eastern islands.

▸ Designation: Alaska Maritime National Wildlife Refuge is a National Natural Landmark.

▸ Location: A chain of more than 2,400 islands stretching 1,000 miles from 163° W to 172° E, and lying between 52° and 54° N. Of the more than 2,400 islands, the following are the most significant for breeding seabirds: Buldir, Chagulak, Kaligagan, Kiska, Segula, and Gareloi.

▸ Size: Two million acres: Aleutian Islands Unit of the Alaska Maritime National Wildlife Refuge.

▸ Ownership: Mostly federal: Alaska Maritime National Wildlife Refuge is owned by the Fish and Wildlife Service. Adak is a Navy base, and Shemya is an Air Force base. Attu has a small Coast Guard base. Some land is privately owned by native corporations.

▸ Habitats: Low-lying, naturally treeless maritime tundra, snow-covered volcanoes, steep sea cliffs up to 200 feet.

▸ Land Use: Mostly wilderness. Some subsistence hunting. Commercial fisheries based out of Dutch Harbor, Unalaska. Some military installations.

▸ Site Description: The Aleutian Islands extend from the tip of the Alaska Peninsula in the east to remote Attu Island in the west. They comprise around twenty large islands, and more than 2,400 smaller islands, lying at the junction of the northern Pacific Ocean and the Bering Sea, where two crustal plates collide, generating substantial seismic and volcanic activity. The islands are formed from the peaks of an arc of submerged mountains, including 57 volcanoes (13 above 5,000 feet) more than 40 of which have been active during the last 250 years. The archipelago is surrounded by some of the most productive seas in the world, and birds provide a vital link in the ecological chain by contributing large amounts of nitrogen and phosphate through their droppings. The islands include the most southerly land area in Alaska, and are characterized by treeless maritime tundra, snow-capped peaks, boulder beaches, spits, tall sea cliffs, and large kelp beds close to shore. Summer brings colorful wildflowers, and the islands are brought alive by millions of birds, ten million of which are nesting seabirds. The climate is cold (winter average 30°F, summer average 50°F), wet, and inclement, with high winds, fog, and snow. The Aleutians lay to the south of the ancient land bridge known as Beringia, which allowed the free flow of wildlife (and people) between Asia and North America during ice incursions up to 11,000 years ago. During this period, the islands themselves were largely glaciated. Since then they have acted as a partial bridge for the movement of island-hopping colonists, and the prohibitive distance between islands has marooned some immigrant populations that have formed isolated subspecies. For example, the "Evermann's" Rock Ptarmigan (Attu), the "Yunaska" Rock Ptarmigan (Yunaska), and the Amak race of Song Sparrow, which are all of conservation concern. Five endemic plants have also been identified, including the federally endangered Aleutian shield fern.

Whiskered Auklet

▶ Birds: The easternmost island, Attu, is famous for Asian vagrants that are at the edge of, or outside, their normal ranges when they occur there. The Aleutian Islands support huge numbers of nesting seabirds (75 percent of Alaska's marine birds), and the surrounding seas are also important for seabirds, including the endangered Short-tailed Albatross outside the breeding season. Nesting alcids include Horned and Tufted Puffins; Parakeet, Whiskered, Least, Cassin's, and Crested Auklets; Marbled and Ancient Murrelets; Pigeon Guillemots; and Common and Thick-billed Murres. The Red-legged Kittiwake breeds on Buldir Island in the western Aleutians. More than one million Northern Fulmars and 100,000 Cassin's Auklets nest on Chagulak, and Kaligagan holds 100,000 Tufted Puffins. Kiska has more than 1.1 million Least Auklets, and more than 300,000 Crested Auklets. Other large colonies of the Least Auklet can be found on Segula (475,000) and Gareloi (402,000). In total, the Rat Islands (Buldir, Kiska, and Segula) have more than 5.5 million nesting seabirds. Fork-tailed and Leach's Storm-Petrels, Aleutian Tern, Rock Sandpiper, Black Turnstone, Rock Ptarmigan, Tundra Swan, and Red-faced Cormorant also nest.

▶ Conservation Issues: After 1741, the spread of European influence over the indigenous Aleut people, the exploitation of sea otters for fur, and the consumption of other wildlife began the process of permanently changing the natural ecosystems of the Aleutian Islands. The introduction of red and (primarily) Arctic foxes, initially by Russian, and then by American fur trappers, resulted in the near extinction of the "Aleutian" Canada Goose after more than 450 islands had been stocked with foxes. Subsequent removal of foxes has restored goose populations (which had survived on just one island), and improved nesting success for seabirds, waterfowl, shorebirds, and ptarmigan. Today, introduced foxes exist only on 46 islands. Other introduced mammals such as caribou on Adak Island, and Arctic ground squirrel on Unalaska and Kavalga, may present a threat to local ecosystems, but are likely to have little, if any, direct impact on birds. Marine contamination, overfishing, changes in marine ecosystems caused by climate change, floating plastics, fishing nets, and long-lining all present threats to seabirds. Human disturbance could also impact nesting species in some cases. There has been recent documentation of Norway rats killing thousands of nesting auklets on Kiska Island; biologists estimate that the colonies there could be destroyed within 20 years. One researcher has stated, "The number of seabirds that are being killed by rats each year (on Kiska) exceed those killed by the Exxon Valdez oil spill." The Fish and Wildlife Service is developing a plan to eliminate the rats through the use of poison bait dropped from aircraft.

▶ Visitor Information: Commercial flights from Anchorage reach Dutch Harbor, Unalaska, where the only commercial lodgings in the Aleutians can be found. Flights also go to Adak and Shemya, but these islands are controlled by the military, and visitors can travel there only with military clearance (Navy and Air Force respectively). Some areas are owned by native corporations and should be treated as private property. The Coast Guard operates a small base on Attu, but birders can no longer visit the island. For general visitor information, contact: Refuge Manager, Aleutian Islands Unit, Alaska Maritime National Wildlife Refuge, Box 5251, NAS Adak, AK, FPO Seattle, WA 98791, 907-592-2406/2407, e-mail: r7aiuwr@mail.fws.gov.

This region consists of the subarctic Coastal Plain of western Alaska and the Alaska Peninsula mountains. Wet and mesic graminoid herbaceous communities dominate the lowlands and numerous ponds, lakes, and rivers dot the landscape. Tall shrub communities are found along rivers and streams, and low shrub communities occupy uplands. Forests of spruce and hardwoods penetrate the region on its eastern edge. Permafrost is continuous except in southern parts of the region. High densities of breeding waterfowl and shorebirds are found on the coastal plain of the Yukon and Kuskokwim Rivers. Intertidal areas there, and lagoons on the north side of the Alaska Peninsula, support millions of shorebirds during migration, including the Dunlin, Western Sandpiper, Red Knot, and Bar-tailed Godwit. The coast of the Alaska Peninsula supports high concentrations of wintering sea ducks, including the Steller's Eider, Harlequin Duck, Long-tailed Duck, Surf Scoter, and Black Scoter. Passerine diversity is greatest in tall, riparian shrub habitats, where the Arctic Warbler, Gray-cheeked Thrush, and Blackpoll Warbler nest. The Gyrfalcon and Rough-legged Hawk nest along the riverine cliffs. Mainland sea cliffs are occupied by nesting colonies of the Black-legged Kittiwake, Common Murre, and Pelagic Cormorant.

Seward Peninsula (1), Alaska

▸ Highlight: A remote wilderness that provides the bulk of the world breeding habitat for Bristle-thighed Curlews. Wintering McKay's Buntings.
▸ Location: The 20,000-square-mile peninsula lies at approximately 65° N, and between 162° and 168° W, and is surrounded to the north by the Chukchi Sea and to the south by the Bering Sea. The extreme northern tip of the peninsula (Cape Espenberg) lies inside the Arctic Circle.
▸ Ownership: Private and federal, including the 2.7-million-acre Bering Land Bridge National Preserve.
▸ Habitats: Coastal and alpine tundra, extensive lava flows, volcanic crater lakes (known as maars), coastal barrier islands, dunes.
▸ Land Use: Wilderness, subsistence hunting, reindeer herding.
▸ Principal Threats: The remoteness of the area provides natural protection. The Bering Land Bridge National Preserve is one of the most isolated parks in the United States. Few threats are evident.

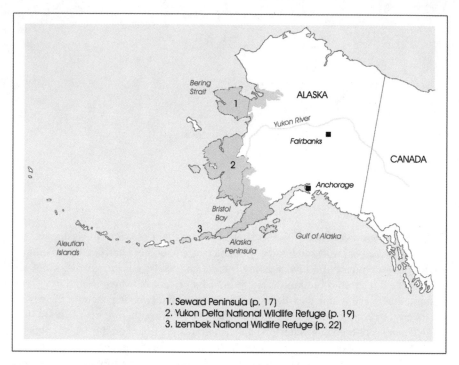

1. Seward Peninsula (p. 17)
2. Yukon Delta National Wildlife Refuge (p. 19)
3. Izembek National Wildlife Refuge (p. 22)

► Site Description: The Seward Peninsula is characterized by open maritime tundra with more alpine tundra inland. The surrounding seas are covered with ice for eight months each year. There is a brief summer growing season during the period of extended daylight when the daily maximum temperature can reach above 70°F. Most of the peninsula is remote and roadless, with the Bering Land Bridge National Preserve reachable only by air taxi, charter plane, or across the snow in winter. There are mountainous areas with rugged glaciated peaks reaching to 4,700 feet and deep valleys. The bedrock is chiefly metamorphic, but includes both volcanic and limestone rocks, each with its own distinctive flora. Shrubs including the dwarf birch, willow, and alder can be found in the southern hills, and tussock cotton grass is the dominant plant across the bulk of the landscape. The south of the peninsula also contains some Boreal Forest. Permafrost reaches close to the surface and occasionally hot volcanic springs can be found. The topography is shaped by ice action, and small hills, or pingos, and thermokarst lakes are both formed as buried ice cores expand and decay. The northern Coastal Plain consists of wet meadows, and the coast is protected by a chain of low-lying barrier islands. More than 400 plant species have been identified, and mammals include the moose, wolf, and brown bear. Local Eskimo communities practice subsistence hunting and reindeer herding. Some domesticated reindeer (domesticated caribou) have been lost after joining migrating caribou herds.

► Birds: The bird conservation highlight of the Seward Peninsula is the breeding population of the Bristle-thighed Curlew, but the McKay's Bunting also winters along the coast. The Hoary Redpoll, Gray-cheeked Thrush, Gyrfalcon, and Arctic Loon breed, as does the Black Turnstone. Both the Steller's and Spectacled Eider occur, the latter breeding in small numbers. The Emperor Goose also occurs during migration. Aside from these species of conservation concern, the peninsula offers outstanding birding, especially around Nome and Wales. Nick Lethaby's book, *A Bird Finding Guide to Alaska* contains an excellent and detailed section on birding these areas. Some of the possible highlight species include the Arctic Warbler, Bluethroat, Northern Wheatear, Yellow and White Wagtails, Wandering Tattler, Red-throated Pipit, and occasional Dotterel and Yellow-billed Loon. The Bar-tailed Godwit nests. The Long-tailed Jaeger and Rock Ptarmigan can be found on the alpine tundra. The Tundra Swan and Sandhill Crane are also present. The Varied Thrush nests in taller willow scrub, and colonies of Aleutian and Arctic Terns can be found along the coast. Passage of seabirds and wildfowl past Wales can be spectacular, with thousands of loons and Parakeet and Least Auklets. Asian vagrants include regular records of the Red-necked Stint.

▸ Conservation Issues: The area's remoteness provides a high degree of natural protection. Birders looking for the Bristle-thighed Curlew should be careful not to disturb the birds (see below). Wolf control has been discontinued, and they are slowly recovering.

▸ Visitor Information: The Bristle-thighed Curlew is the main prize for birders visiting the peninsula, and the species can be found by driving north from Nome on the Kougarok (Taylor) Highway to the Kougarok River. Each year, the Fish and Wildlife Service tries to stake out one pair for birders to see so that other nesting pairs can remain undisturbed. For information on the location of curlews, call Robert Gill at the Fish and Wildlife Service, 907-786-3514. The best time to visit is mid-June, and if you are unable to get information on where to see the birds, you may find them in the vicinity of the bridge over the Kougarok River where it is sometimes possible to see curlews from the road. Wherever you go, please do not walk through curlew territories, keep your distance, and leave as soon as you can. The Bering Land Bridge National Preserve can be reached by air taxi or by charter flight from Nome. For information, contact the refuge at 907-443-2522. The preserve is open year-round for hiking, fishing, camping, hunting, and for skiing in winter. There are a small number of cabins for visitors.

Yukon Delta National Wildlife Refuge (2), Alaska

▸ Highlight: Most important IBA for nesting geese (750,000 nesting swans and geese). Two million nesting ducks. Perhaps up to 20 million breeding and staging shorebirds. The Bristle-thighed Curlew and threatened Spectacled Eider breed, as do small numbers of the Alaska-breeding population of the Steller's Eider, federally listed as threatened. Critical site for the Emperor Goose.

▸ Designation: Wetland of Regional Importance in the Western Hemisphere Shorebird Reserve Network.

▸ Location: The refuge lies on the Bering Sea coast of central western Alaska, extending from the south of Norton Sound in the north, to Kuskokwim Bay in the south. Nelson and Nunivak Islands are included within the refuge.

▸ Size: The refuge's borders encompass more than 26 million acres, of which 19.5 million acres are federally owned, with about seven million acres privately owned by a variety of native corporations.

▸ Ownership: Fish and Wildlife Service, private.

▶ Habitats: The low-lying tundra of the Yukon-Kuskokwim Delta proper includes both wet and moist tundra (with wetter habitats generally found toward the coast), and the uplands north of the Yukon and east of the Kuskokwim include both moist and alpine tundra. Although some of the mountains north of the Yukon are forested, some are not. There are also forested slopes in the mountains east of the Kuskokwim. The most productive and biologically diverse forests within the refuge's borders are found not in the mountains, but in the corridors of the Yukon and Kuskokwim rivers. The forest and shrub habitats of the refuge, most of which are riparian, total nearly 2.5 million acres.

▶ Land Use: The area is sparsely populated but supports the majority of the Yup'ik Eskimo people, who continue an extensive subsistence harvest of fish, wildlife, and plants (including berries). Historically, commercial fishing has been the most important resource-based component of the cash economy. Forty-three villages and thousands of seasonal fish camps are scattered throughout the area, particularly along the coast and major rivers. The largest town, Bethel, has over 5,000 inhabitants.

▶ Site Description: The land within the borders of the refuge comprises the Yukon-Kuskokwim Delta. This remote and wild region on the coast of the Bering Sea is principally low-lying maritime tundra peppered with hundreds of thousands of small pools, and crisscrossed by countless slow-moving creeks and rivulets. It is formed by the deltas of the Yukon and Kuskokwin Rivers. The Yukon is the fifth-largest river in the United States and one of the least affected by human development. With a daily tidal range of more than six feet, maritime influence can extend up to 34 miles upriver, and seasonal storm surges can cause flooding well inland. The area is in the southernmost permafrost and is dominated by sedge-graminoid and dwarf shrub meadows. Riparian shrub corridors provide nesting habitat for passerine birds. The southern Nulato Hills extend into the northern portion of the refuge; the Andreafsky Wilderness encompasses most of this region. Both forks of the Andreafsky River have been designated "Wild and Scenic." The vegetation along the river consists of spruce, poplar, tall shrubs, and low wet bogs. Willows, alders, dwarf shrubs, mosses, lichens, and a rich diversity of flowering forbs cloak the surrounding hills. Across the delta, rivers become ice free in June, and water levels are lowest in July, picking up again through August during summer rains. As well as being important for birds, the delta supports the moose, bear (brown and black), wolf, and caribou. The 1.1-million-acre Nunivak Island holds important herds of introduced musk oxen and caribou.

▶ Birds: This is one of the most important nesting areas for geese in the United States, with large numbers of the Brant, Emperor, Greater White-fronted, and "Cackling" Canada Goose. White-fronted and Canada Goose populations have grown dramatically over the last decade, as a result of cooperative management (through the Yukon-Kuskokwim Delta Goose Management Plan) while those of the Brant and Emperor have remained stable. Large num-

Yellow Wagtail

bers of Tundra Swans and Sandhill Cranes also nest, and the threatened Spectacled Eider is among the nesting ducks (twentyfold decrease from 1971–1992, but with a slow but fairly steady increase since then). The world population of the Bristle-thighed Curlew is approximately 3,500 pairs: half nest on the refuge in the Nulato Hills, and the other half nest on the Seward Peninsula to the north; virtually the entire Alaskan population stages on the delta before autumn migration to the archipelagoes of the central Pacific, where the birds are vulnerable to introduced predators. Other breeding species of interest include the "Harlan's" Red-tailed Hawk, Gyrfalcon, Pacific Golden-Plover, Hudsonian Godwit, Black Turnstone, Surfbird, Rock Sandpiper, Short-billed Dowitcher, Long-tailed Jaeger, Sabine's Gull, Great Gray Owl, Bluethroat, Northern Wheatear, and Yellow Wagtail. Millions of migratory shorebirds stage during the fall, including the Western Sandpiper, Bar-tailed Godwit, and Dunlin. Juvenile Sharp-tailed Sandpipers raised in Siberia migrate east each fall to stage on the delta before migrating to Australasia for the winter. Riparian shrubs and woodlands provide nesting habitat for a number of long-distance neotropical migrants, including the Alder Flycatcher, Gray-cheeked Thrush, Northern Waterthrush, Yellow Warbler, and Blackpoll Warbler. The refuge supports at least 15 species of breeding raptors; in fact, the Kisaralik River watershed has the highest combined diversity and density of nesting raptors in Alaska. The Yukon-Koskokwim Delta is also a primary wintering area for the McKay's Bunting, the only species strictly endemic to Alaska.

Seabird numbers on the refuge are also considerable. Nunivak Island alone hosts between 500,000 and one million nesting seabirds, the most abundant of which are the Common Murre, Black-legged Kittiwake, and Red-faced Cormorant. Arctic and Aleutian Terns, Parakeet and Crested Auklets, and Horned and Tufted Puffins also occur. The refuge also has the only breeding Slaty-backed Gulls in North America, as well as the northwesternmost Caspian Tern colony on the continent, hundreds of miles from the nearest colonies.

▶ Conservation Issues: The refuge is one of the main Alaskan nurseries for geese. Its isolation and inaccessibility provide good protection from most human-induced impacts. Sea level rise in response to global warming is perhaps the most serious potential threat. A very small rise in the level would simultaneously inundate many of the villages as well as the coastal mudflats and meadows, which are probably the most productive bird habitats on the refuge. Of course, once migratory birds leave the refuge, they are vulnerable to other threats. The Fish and Wildlife Service in Alaska has worked with partners in the Alaska native community and hunters in the lower 48 to restore the population of "Cackling" Canada Geese on the refuge. Farther south on the West Coast, the Fish and Wildlife Service has worked with farmers to eliminate these birds as agricultural pests on turf farms during the winter. Likewise, shorebirds leaving the refuge in the fall are subject to wetland habitat loss at staging areas to the south, which may limit their numbers.

▶ Visitor Information: The area is generally inaccessible and difficult to bird. Visitors should consult refuge headquarters in advance. It is necessary to charter boats, guides, and/or floatplanes to reach the best areas, and visiting is more economical for a party of four or more. All the birds that occur in the area can also be seen elsewhere in Alaska. Early summer is the best time if the male Spectacled Eider in breeding plumage is the

Spectacled Eider

objective. During the winter the McKay's Bunting is regular in Bethel (an easy flight from Anchorage), arriving between Thanksgiving and Christmas and departing in early April. More than one quarter of the land within the refuge's borders, particularly along the rivers, is private property, owned by a variety of native village corporations. Visitors must know which lands are public and which private, as permission is required from the respective owners to gain access to private lands.

For information, contact: Refuge Manager, Yukon Delta National Wildlife Refuge, P.O. Box 346, Bethel, AK 99559, 907-543-3151, (fax) 907-543-4413, e-mail: r7ydnwr@fws.gov. Please type "Attention Refuge Manager" on the subject line. People wishing to visit the Andreafsky Wilderness should contact: City of St. Mary's, P.O. Box 163, St. Mary's, AK 99658, 907-438-2247, and/or, Hagland Aviation, P.O. Box 195, St. Mary's, AK 99658, 907-438-2247 or 800-478-2246.

Izembek National Wildlife Refuge (3), Alaska

▶ Highlight: A vital staging area for shorebirds and waterfowl with almost the entire world population of the Emperor Goose passing through each fall, and several thousand wintering. Important staging area for the "Black" Brant; a molting area for the Steller's Eider. Annual shorebird passage up to 285,000 birds each fall, and 100,000 each spring.
▶ Designation: Ramsar Site.
▶ Location: Izembek National Wildlife Refuge is located at the western tip of the Alaska Peninsula at approximately 55° N, 163° W. Izembek and Moffet Lagoons are outstanding representatives of the shorebird staging sites along the northern coast of the Alaska Peninsula, which include Nushagak Bay, Kvichak Bay, Egegik Bay, Ugashik Bay, Cinder-Hook Lagoon, Port Heiden, Seal Islands, and Nelson Lagoon–Mud Bay. In total, hundreds of thousands of shorebirds use these sites, including the entire northern Alaska Peninsula breeding population of the Marbled Godwit, and 30 percent of the world population of the "Pacific" Bar-tailed Godwit.
▶ Size: 417,000 acres.
▶ Ownership: Fish and Wildlife Service.
▶ Habitats: The 417,000-acre refuge contains one of the largest eelgrass beds in the world, contained within a shallow bay surrounded by rocky and muddy shores and low-lying barrier islands. Tussock tundra lies around the lagoons, and the entire area is crisscrossed by narrow rivulets and channels.
▶ Land Use: Wildlife refuge, hunting, recreation.
▶ Site Description: A network of coastal flats and lagoons, separated from the Bering Sea by spits and low-lying barrier islands, which are fringed by sandy beaches and covered in beach rye. The surrounding coast is composed of both rocky and muddy shores, some pebble beaches, and low bluffs. On the inland side of the refuge, one

larger river and several smaller streams cross the tussock tundra. The refuge includes two large lagoons: Izembek and Moffet, and one smaller lagoon: Kinzarof. The lagoons are covered by extensive eelgrass beds (the largest in North America), and there are also unvegetated tidal flats drained by numerous channels. The area is surrounded by rugged, spectacular scenery. In addition to its importance for birds, the refuge is home to the caribou, wolf, wolverine, brown bear, and lemming.

▶ Birds: Most of the world population of the "Black" Brant (up to 200,000) use the refuge as a staging area, and each spring and fall, virtually the entire world population of the Emperor Goose also passes through (several thousand also winter). Thousands of Canada Geese and other waterfowl also occur at Izembek, principally from late August through early November. The Steller's Eider uses the refuge for molting, and is also the commonest wintering duck (the species is present from late July through April). Huge annual shorebird passage with Rock and Western Sandpipers, and Dunlin being the most numerous species. This IBA is representative of the bird populations passing through many of the coastal flats and estuaries along the Alaska Peninsula, but tends to host more Rock Sandpipers and Ruddy Turnstones, and fewer godwits and dowitchers than other areas. Other birds of interest include the Kittlitz's Murrelet, which can sometimes be seen from the ferry. The Gyrfalcon breeds, and the McKay's Bunting has been recorded.

▶ Conservation Issues: The first United States Ramsar Site (listed in 1986). The refuge was established in 1960 to protect this vital shorebird and waterfowl staging area, and, in fact, it is considered one of the better protected shorebird staging areas in the Pacific Flyway. One recent potential problem has been the plan to construct a 30-mile highway that would pass through part of the refuge. If implemented it could also set a dangerous precedent for construction projects at other refuges.

▶ Visitor Information: The refuge provides outstanding opportunities for birdwatching, and is especially good for viewing brown bear. It can be accessed by air (Anchorage to Cold Bay) and by ferry (Homer to Dutch Harbor), and 40 miles of gravel roads provide limited access to the refuge from Cold Bay. For more information, contact: Refuge Manager, Izembek National Wildlife Refuge, 907-532-2445, e-mail: r7izemwr@fws.gov. Accommodation in Cold Bay is available at the Weathered Inn, 907-532-2456, and vehicles can be rented from Cold Bay Truck Rental, 907-532-2404.

3. Arctic Plains and Mountains

This region includes low-lying, coastal tundra and drier uplands of the Arctic mountains across the entire northern edge of North America. Because of thick and continuous permafrost, surface water dominates the landscape (20 to 50 percent of the Coastal Plain). Freezing and thawing form a patterned mosaic of polygonal ridges and ponds and many rivers bisect the plain and flow into the Arctic Ocean. The ocean surface is generally frozen from nine to ten months of the year, and the ice pack is never far from shore. Because of the wetness, waterfowl and shorebirds dominate the avian community, and passerines are scarce. The most abundant breeding birds on the Coastal Plain include the Northern Pintail, King Eider, Long-tailed Duck, American Golden-Plover, Semipalmated Sandpiper, Pectoral Sandpiper, Red-necked Phalarope, and Lapland Longspur. Several Old World species, including the Arctic Warbler and the Bluethroat, penetrate the region from the west. Taiga passerines such as the Gray-cheeked Thrush and the Yellow Warbler reach the region along drainage systems, and raptors, including the Gyrfalcon and the Rough-legged Hawk commonly nest along major rivers. Few bird species winter in the region.

North Alaska Coast IBAs, Alaska

North Alaska Coast (1), National Petroleum Reserve (2), Arctic National Wildlife Refuge (3)

▶ Highlight: The North Alaska Coast represents the only U.S. bird population of the true Arctic tundra. The threatened Steller's Eider breeds in small numbers. This is the only significant breeding area for the Yellow-billed Loon, King Eider, and Brant, and the only breeding population of the Snow Goose in the United States. The Trumpeter Swan also nests. Approximately 20 percent of domestically consumed petroleum is produced in this and nearby areas.

▶ Location: Alaska's north coast is best considered a large IBA complex which extends along the northern (Beaufort Sea/Arctic Ocean) coast of Alaska from Wainright in the west through Barrow and Prudhoe Bay to the Canadian border in the east, and includes: Barrow and its environs; Teshekpuk Lake; the Colville River Delta; inland raptor nesting cliffs and riparian passerine habitat along the Colville River; and the

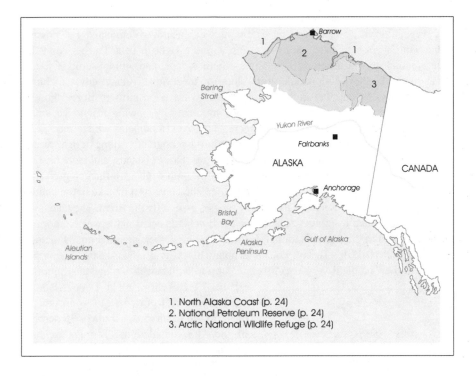

1. North Alaska Coast (p. 24)
2. National Petroleum Reserve (p. 24)
3. Arctic National Wildlife Refuge (p. 24)

Arctic National Wildlife Refuge, which extends inland to include the Brooks Range. The IBA lies at approximately 70° N.

▶ Size: More than 43 million acres (National Petroleum Reserve is 23.5 million acres; Arctic National Wildlife Refuge is 20 million acres).

▶ Ownership: Federal: National Petroleum Reserve—Alaska, State of Alaska, Bureau of Land Management, Fish and Wildlife Service, Arctic Slope Regional Corporation.

▶ Habitats: Principally Arctic tundra, with scattered lakes and braided rivers. The Colville River (largest in the region) has some low riparian scrub, and inland, steep bluffs that reach 500 feet in height. The north slopes of the Brooks Range in the Arctic National Wildlife Refuge include alpine meadow and montane habitats, and the south slope includes dwarf spruce taiga and some Boreal Forest.

▶ Land Use: One large national wildlife refuge; remaining areas are wilderness with few indigenous settlements (with some subsistence hunting); largest being Barrow with 4,000 residents. The Arctic National Wildlife Refuge includes the only true Arctic tundra in the United States with protection. Some hunting and backpacking by visitors. The National Petroleum Reserve occupies a large part of the area, and 4.6 million acres of this are currently slated for new oil development.

▶ Site Description: The coastal Arctic tundra belt lies to the north of the Brooks Range and is characterized by a polygonal-patterned landscape formed by seasonal frost action. Pack ice can be seen from shore even during the summer, and it can snow at any time of the year. The tundra is above the latitudinal tree line, and there is continuous permafrost just below the surface (about 18 inches deep) with a six-week growing season. Vegetation is characterized by extensive wet meadows dominated by mosses, sedge, cotton grass, and tundra grass sitting above a layer of peat. Farther from the coast, tussock tundra becomes the dominant habitat type, and willow scrub is found along rivers. Farther south on the north slope of the Brooks Range, cover includes poplar and willow, and the southern slope includes tracts of northern Boreal Forest. There are thousands of pothole lakes, depressions caused by thawing ground ice, small hills (pingos) formed by underground ice cores, and river floodplains with terraces. Exposed sands and gravel also punctuate the tundra topography along longer water courses. The coastline is mostly low-lying with spits, barrier islands, and lagoons. Occasional storm surges can carry saline water a few miles inland influencing coastal ecosystems. Teshekpuk Lake (at 315 square miles, the largest Arctic lake in the United States) provides stopover habitat for molting geese, especially the Brant. The lake is 20 miles in length but only 20 feet deep. Large caribou herds occur in the western portion of the area and in the Arctic National Wildlife Refuge. Other large mammals include moose; musk ox; Dall's sheep; wolf; and polar, black, and brown bears. The upper reaches of the Colville River have cliffs that support high densities of nesting raptors.

Gyrfalcon

▶ Birds: The Yellow-billed Loon nests in small numbers from close to Wainright to the Colville Delta (5,000 birds or 85 percent of the U.S. population). The Pacific and Red-throated Loon also breed. Breeding waterfowl numbers are generally lower than in the maritime tundra of western Alaska. The Greater White-fronted is the commonest breeding goose (20 percent of the U.S. population), and there are scattered colonies of breeding Brant, especially in the Colville Delta. The Canada Goose also breeds. More than 20 percent of the Pacific Brant population visits Teshekpuk Lake to molt. The largest Snow Goose breeding colony in the United States is on Howe Island in Prudhoe Bay (400 pairs), and up to 325,000 Snow Geese stage in the Arctic National Wildlife Refuge. The Trumpeter and Tundra Swan breed; the latter is increasing. The Spectacled Eider breeds (80 percent of the U.S. population), as does the Steller's Eider (4,000 birds or 95 percent of the U.S. population). The Northern Pintail (10 percent of the U.S. breeding population) and the Long-tailed Duck are the commonest nesting ducks, and pintail numbers are swelled by non-breeding birds in years when drought hits nesting areas in the center of the continent. The King Eider is a fairly common breeder. High concentrations of the Rough-legged Hawk, "Arctic" Peregrine Falcon, and Gyrfalcon nest on bluffs along the Colville River. Willow and Rock Ptarmigans move north from the Brooks Range to nest on the tundra in spring. Snowy Owls are most numerous in lemming years. Colville Delta hosts around 50,000 staging shorebirds, and there are significant numbers of breeding shorebirds including Stilt, Pectoral, Semipalmated, Baird's, and Buff-breasted Sandpipers, American Golden- and Black-bellied Plovers, Red and Red-necked Phalaropes, Long-billed Dowitcher, and Bar-tailed Godwit on the north slope. Shorebird breeding success responds to predator relationships and annual climate. Passerines include the Bluethroat, Snow Bunting, Arctic Warbler, Yellow Wagtail, Northern Wheatear, Northern Shrike, Lapland Longspur, and Smith's Longspur. The Arctic National Wildlife Refuge has recorded a total of 180 species, including 30 species of waterfowl and 30 species of shorebirds.

▶ Conservation Issues: Although the Arctic National Wildlife Refuge protects representative tundra habitats and bird populations, many species such as the Yellow-billed Loon and Spectacled Eider are rare in the refuge and depend on other sites, especially the Colville Delta. Teshekpuk Lake is in an area slated for oil development, and although the lake was given "Maximum Protection" in 1976 under the Naval Petroleum Reserve Protection Act, 1.7 million acres were declared a Special Management Area in 1977. The Bureau of Land Management conducted an Environmental Impact Assessment in 1998 concerning the proposed development of 4.6 million acres of the National Petroleum Reserve—Alaska (which includes the lake). The preferred recommendation was that there should be "strict restrictions" on oil and gas development around the lake though the bureau is currently considering some relaxation of these restrictions. Environmental groups believe that the lake should be declared a National Wildlife Refuge. Along with its importance for bird conservation, the lake's caribou herd is used by the indigenous Inupiat people for subsistence hunting. The 1.5-million-acre Coastal Plain of the Arctic National Wildlife Refuge is the only permanently protected part of the Arctic tundra in the United States (comprising approximately 125 miles, or 10 percent of the coastal belt) although the oil industry and their allies in Congress and the executive branch are still calling for the opening of the refuge to drilling, though they have as yet been unable to pass the legislation that would allow them to do this. The refuge's large caribou herd is used for subsistence hunting by the indigenous Gwich'in people. The refuge contains an eight-million-acre wilderness area, the largest in the National Wildlife Refuge system. In 1977, 2.3 million acres of the Colville River and its tributaries were declared a Special Management Area, and although some landowners opposed the river being afforded protection as a Wild and Scenic River, some groups suggest that it, too, should be declared a National Wildlife Refuge.

▶ Visitor Information: As with many parts of Alaska, much of the area is accessible to the general visitor only by aircraft. The Steller's Eider can be seen in the vicinity of Barrow, and the Spectacled Eider can be seen by visitors to Prudhoe Bay (especially in June). Some roads linked to oil production, for example the roads within the north slope oil fields (at the end of the Dalton Highway), are closed to public traffic. Visitors may wish to call the Alaska Department of Transportation at 907-451-2210 to check on road access. Teshekpuk Lake can be reached only by plane. For information on the Arctic National Wildlife Refuge, contact: Refuge Manager, Arctic National Wildlife Refuge, 101 12th Avenue, Box 20, Fairbanks, AK 99701, 907-456-0250, e-mail: arctic_refuge@fws.gov.

4. Northwestern Interior Forest

The interplay of elevation, permafrost, surface water, fire, and aspect creates an extensive patchwork of ecological types. Forest habitat in the region is dominated by white spruce, black spruce, poplars, and paper birch. Tall shrub communities occur along rivers and near the tree line. Bogs, consisting of low shrubs and shrub-graminoid communities, are common in the lowlands. Alpine dwarf scrub communities are common throughout mountainous regions, and the highest elevations are generally devoid of vegetation. Lowlands, bottomlands, and flats harbor many species of migrating and breeding waterfowl (e.g., the Northern Pintail, Northern Shoveler, and Green-winged Teal) and swans. These, and the forested lowlands and uplands, support breeding shorebirds such as Greater and Lesser Yellowlegs, Solitary and Spotted Sandpipers, and Wilson's Snipe. The American Golden-Plover and Surfbird are found in alpine habitats in mountainous regions. The Western Sandpiper, Long-billed and Short-billed Dowitchers, Hudsonian Godwit, and Dunlin use stopover sites along the coast that are also primary wintering habitat for the Rock Sandpiper. The suite of passerines inhabiting upland communities in the region includes the Boreal Chickadee, Swainson's and Gray-cheeked Thrushes, White-crowned, American Tree, and Fox Sparrows, and Common Redpoll. At high elevations, the Horned Lark and Lapland Longspur are common breeders.

Yukon Flats National Wildlife Refuge (1), Alaska

▶ Highlight: One of the most important nurseries for migratory shorebirds and waterfowl, including the Trumpeter Swan. Contains significant amounts of interior Boreal Forest, which provides habitat for declining species such as the Olive-sided Flycatcher, Gray-cheeked Thrush, and Blackpoll Warbler. The Smith's Longspur is also found.
▶ Location: Eastern interior Alaska is characterized by boreal and riparian forest, marshy floodplains, and the foothills and alpine meadows of the southern Brooks Range. Within the region, the 8.6-million-acre Yukon Flats National Wildlife Refuge lying at 66° N, 146° W (approximately 100 miles north of Fairbanks) is both outstanding and representative of the region's key ecosystems.
▶ Size: 12 million acres.
▶ Ownership: Fish and Wildlife Service, National Park Service, Bureau of Land Management.

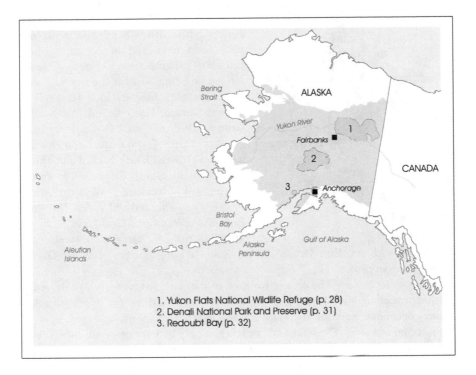

1. Yukon Flats National Wildlife Refuge (p. 28)
2. Denali National Park and Preserve (p. 31)
3. Redoubt Bay (p. 32)

▶ Habitats: Northern Boreal Forest, 40,000 lakes and ponds, bogs, marshes, Yukon River floodplain.

▶ Land Use: Wilderness, recreation. Athabascan and Koyukon Indians use the refuge for a variety of subsistence uses.

▶ Site Description: The refuge centers around the complex of 40,000 small lakes and marshes located at the most northerly reach of the Yukon River. The river's vast floodplain provides an oasis for nesting waterfowl and is surrounded by windswept mountains on all sides. The refuge includes large tracts of northern Boreal Forest and subalpine habitat on the lower slopes of the surrounding ranges. The northern Boreal Forest is largely made up of white and black spruce, with deciduous forest of quaking aspen, balsam poplar, and Alaska paper birch. Natural wildfires occur approximately every 110 years, and stands over 170 years old are rare. Mature trees can reach 100 feet in height. Low scrub vegetation is dominated by open shrub willows and low shrubs such as Labrador tea and low bush cranberry. Bogs with scattered black spruce, mosses, and sedges are known as muskeg and are found in wetter areas. The refuge is important for spawning salmon, and mammals including the moose, caribou, Dall's sheep, black and brown bears, wolves, lynx, snowshoe hare, and beaver.

▶ Birds: Approximately 1.6 million ducks, 10,000 geese (27 species of waterfowl breed, including the Trumpeter Swan), 11,000 Sandhill Cranes, 18,000 loons, at least 100,000 grebes (Red-necked and Horned), and hundreds of thousands of passerines nest on the refuge. At least 12 species of nesting shorebirds, including

Gray-cheeked Thrush

the Upland Sandpiper, Surfbird, and Wandering Tattler. Birds banded in the refuge have been recovered in 26 states, three Canadian provinces, and Mexico. Characteristic breeding birds of the Boreal Forest and associated habitats include the Gyrfalcon; Spruce, Ruffed, and Sharp-tailed Grouse; Willow and Rock Ptarmigan; Northern Hawk, Great Gray, Great Horned, and Boreal Owls; Black-backed and Three-toed Woodpeckers; Boreal Chickadee; Olive-sided Flycatcher; Western Wood-Pewee; Gray-cheeked and Varied Thrushes; Bohemian Waxwing; Gray Jay; Northern Shrike; Yellow, Orange-crowned, and Blackpoll Warblers; Pine Grosbeak; and Smith's Longspur (in open habitats on surrounding slopes).

► Conservation Issues: The present isolation of the refuge provides a high degree of natural protection, but oil and gas exploration are possible threats to its integrity. Any future contamination of the Yukon River could also threaten the area.

► Visitor Information: The refuge can be reached only by river or by air; there are no roads. Access by motorboat, canoe, kayak, or raft is possible during the summer, and Beaver Creek, a nationally designated Wild and Scenic River, can be used to reach the area as it flows into the refuge from the south. For information, contact: Refuge Manager, Yukon Flats National Wildlife Refuge, 101 12th Avenue, Room 264, Fairbanks, AK 99701, 907-456-0440, (fax) 907-456-0447, e-mail: YukonFlats_Refuge@fws.gov.

ENDANGERED SPECIES ACT

In 1973, Congress passed the Endangered Species Act, and President Richard Nixon signed it into law. The act not only authorizes the determination and listing of species as endangered and threatened, but prohibits their unauthorized taking, possession, sale, and transport, while providing authority to acquire land for their conservation. Section seven of the act requires federal agencies to ensure that any action they authorize, fund, or carry out is not likely to jeopardize the existence of listed species or modify their Critical Habitat.

The act has been a potent force in bird conservation, with far-reaching effects. It mandates that listed species be considered in management plans, and many of the natural resource activities on federal lands today can be traced to the act. Some bird species have benefited greatly—the Red-cockaded Woodpecker, Black-capped Vireo, and Golden-cheeked Warbler for example. Much practical knowledge has come from the work that federal agency staff biologists have done to manage and protect endangered and threatened species, and this knowledge can also be applied by biologists working for state governments and private conservation groups.

The Endangered Species Act is a lightning rod for environmental conflict. Because of its potential to limit an owner's use of land—including public use of public lands—it has even helped create an anti-environmental backlash, the so-called "wise use movement." The Act's greatest notoriety derives from the controversy over cutting of old-growth forest, home to the endangered Northern Spotted Owl, in the Pacific Northwest. The Endangered Species Act is a valuable tool in protecting the habitats of our rarest species, and cases of demonstrable economic loss from the act are few.

Denali National Park and Preserve (2), Alaska

▸ Highlight: Most representative large protected area for central Alaskan alpine and montane ecosystems. Birds include the three ptarmigan species, Gyrfalcon, and shorebirds.
▸ Location: A large (6,028,091 acres) national park located in central Alaska at 63° N, 51° W.
▸ Size: 6,028,091 acres.
▸ Ownership: National Park Service.
▸ Habitats: Rich matrix of montane and boreal habitats, some riparian forest, bogs, marshes.
▸ Land Use: Wilderness, recreation.
▸ Site Description: Denali is Alaska's most popular national park and is home to Mount McKinley, which, at 20,320 feet, is North America's highest peak. The park can be accessed by the 85-mile park road, and a bus system (expect a wait, perhaps as long as two days, to be allocated a seat) allows visitors to gain access without disturbing the park's natural beauty and tranquillity. Tourist vehicles are restricted to the first 13 miles of the road. Limited camping facilities within the park provide accommodation for visitors. The central Alaskan wilderness has cold winters (0°F to −30°F), and warm summers (63°F to 72°F). The park has a rich mosaic of habitats, including significant areas of dwarf taiga forest, riparian scrub, alpine meadow, Boreal Forest of black and white spruce, bogs consisting of shrub-graminoid communities, marshes, treeless montane wilderness, rocky ridges, glaciers, and snow-capped peaks. The alpine tundra is generally found above 2,450 feet. The transitional zone from the lower altitude boreal spruce comprises alder, willow, and birch. The scenery is impressive, and large mammals such as the brown bear, wolf, moose, caribou, Dall's sheep, marmot, and ground squirrel can be seen relatively easily.
▸ Birds: The Gyrfalcon (between Polychrome Pass and the Eilson Center); Long-tailed Jaeger (Stony Dome between Highway and Thorofare Passes); Northern Wheatear; Arctic Warbler; Willow, Rock, and White-

Townsend's Solitaire

tailed Ptarmigans (Willow on lower slopes, Rock in alpine tundra, White-tailed on highest ridges) all occur. The Golden Eagle is the commonest raptor. The Surfbird and American Golden-Plover are found in the alpine tundra; the Wandering Tattler is found on gravel streams such as Igloo Creek. The Upland Sandpiper also breeds, as does the Northern Hawk Owl, White-winged Crossbill, Arctic Warbler, Northern Wheatear, Lapland Longspur, Northern Shrike, Say's Pheobe, Townsend's Solitaire, Gray-crowned Rosy-Finch, and Bohemian Waxwing.

▸ Conservation Issues: The significant conservation issue is controlling visitors, although a sophisticated tourism management system is already in place. Hunting is banned within the park.

▸ Visitor Information: The park entrance is easily reached by road from Anchorage, and there are a number of places to stay around the park entrance, including Denali Park Hotel, 907-276-7234; Denali Cabins, 907-683-2773; and River View Inn, 907-683-2663. Healy, which lies eight miles north of the park also has accommodation at Historical Healy Hotel, 907-683-2242; and Dome House Bed & Breakfast, 907-683-1239. Accommodation within the park can be found at North Face Lodge, 907-683-2290; Kantishna Roadhouse, 907-683-2710; and Denali Mountain Lodge, 907-683-2643. Reservations for buses and camping must be made in advance. For information, call the Alaskan Public Lands Information Center at 907-451-7352 or 907-271-2737.

Redoubt Bay (3), Alaska

▸ Highlight: Important stopover for upwards of 500,000 shorebirds annually. Also a major waterfowl stopover site. Nesting White-fronted Geese, tens of thousands of breeding ducks.

▸ Location: The bay is on the western edge of Cook Inlet, about 40 miles southwest of Anchorage.

▸ Size: 171,520 square miles.

▸ Ownership: State of Alaska (managed by the Alaska Department of Fish and Game).

▸ Habitats: Coastal marsh, braided riparian riverine systems, tidal mudflats.

▸ Land Use: Wildlife habitat, hunting, sport and small-scale commercial gillnet fishing.

Spruce Grouse

▸ Site Description: A large coastal wetland complex with huge intertidal flats, lying on the western edge of Cook Inlet and surrounded by high snow-capped peaks. Braided freshwater streambeds and open water comprise the remaining areas.

▸ Birds: Shorebirds, primarily Western Sandpipers, occur in huge numbers during May, with approximately 30,000 birds present per day for most of the month. The White-fronted, Canada, and Snow Goose nest; and the Tundra and Trumpeter Swan also use the area. Tens of thousands of breeding ducks are also found, including the Mallard, Northern Pintail,

Green-winged Teal, American Wigeon, Northern Shoveler, Canvasback, and Common Eider. The Bald Eagle also occurs. The central portion of Redoubt Bay, especially the three to four miles south of the Drift River, is the most important site in Cook Inlet for migrant shorebirds in spring. The high daily count for this area is 162,500 birds, of which some 92 percent are Western Sandpipers, and eight percent are Dunlin.

▶ Conservation Issues: Waterfowl hunting is popular with takes in the thousands. Fishing nets may pose a threat to some diving birds. The entire inlet is vulnerable to oil spills and other marine pollution.

▶ Visitor Information: Access is by plane or boat from Anchorage. Visitors can stay at Redoubt Bay Lodge.

5. Northern Pacific Rain Forest

The coastal rain forest stretches from the western Gulf of Alaska all the way south through British Columbia and the Pacific Northwest to northern California. Its maritime climate is characterized by heavy precipitation and mild temperatures. The region is dominated by forests of western hemlock and Sitka spruce in the far north, with balsam fir, Douglas-fir, and redwood becoming more important farther south. Broadleaf forests are found along large mainland river drainages. High-priority-breeding forest birds include the Spotted Owl, Marbled Murrelet, Northern Goshawk, Chestnut-backed Chickadee, Red-breasted Sapsucker, and Hermit Warbler. The coast of the Northern Pacific Rain Forest is characterized by river deltas and pockets of estuarine and freshwater wetlands set within steep, rocky shorelines. These wetlands provide critical breeding, wintering, and migration habitat for internationally significant populations of waterfowl and other wetland-dependent species. The area includes major stopover sites for migrating shorebirds, especially the Western Sandpiper and Dunlin. The Black Oystercatcher, Rock Sandpiper, Black Turnstone, and Surfbird are common wintering species. Nearshore marine areas support many breeding and wintering sea ducks. Many seabirds breed on offshore islands, including important populations of the Ancient Murrelet, Rhinoceros Auklet, Tufted Puffin, Common Murre, Western and Glaucous-winged Gulls, and Leach's Storm-Petrel. Pelagic waters provide habitat for large numbers of shearwaters, storm-petrels, alcids, and the Black-footed Albatross.

Copper River Delta (2) and Northeast Montague Island (1), Alaska

▸ Highlight: Largest wetland on the Pacific Coast of North America and the largest spring concentration of shorebirds in the Western Hemisphere. Spring stopover site for up to five million shorebirds, including 60–80 percent of the Western Sandpiper population and most of the Pacific Coast Dunlin population. Also an important breeding area for many species of waterfowl, including the Trumpeter Swan and "Dusky" Canada Goose.

▸ Designation: Wetland of Hemispheric Importance in the Western Hemisphere Shorebird Reserve Network. State of Alaska Critical Habitat Area.

▸ Location: 61° N, 144° W, lying immediately east of Cordova on the northeastern

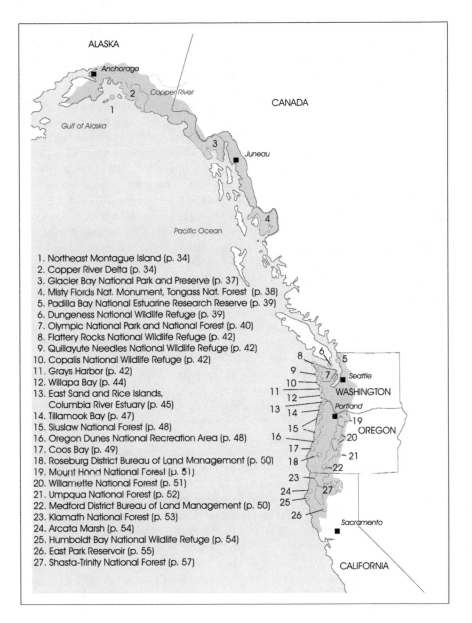

ALASKA

Anchorage

Copper River

2

1

Gulf of Alaska

CANADA

3

Juneau

Pacific Ocean

4

1. Northeast Montague Island (p. 34)
2. Copper River Delta (p. 34)
3. Glacier Bay National Park and Preserve (p. 37)
4. Misty Fiords Nat. Monument, Tongass Nat. Forest (p. 38)
5. Padilla Bay National Estuarine Research Reserve (p. 39)
6. Dungeness National Wildlife Refuge (p. 39)
7. Olympic National Park and National Forest (p. 40)
8. Flattery Rocks National Wildlife Refuge (p. 42)
9. Quillayute Needles National Wildlife Refuge (p. 42)
10. Copalis National Wildlife Refuge (p. 42)
11. Grays Harbor (p. 42)
12. Willapa Bay (p. 44)
13. East Sand and Rice Islands,
    Columbia River Estuary (p. 45)
14. Tillamook Bay (p. 47)
15. Siuslaw National Forest (p. 48)
16. Oregon Dunes National Recreation Area (p. 48)
17. Coos Bay (p. 49)
18. Roseburg District Bureau of Land Management (p. 50)
19. Mount Hood National Forest (p. 51)
20. Willamette National Forest (p. 51)
21. Umpqua National Forest (p. 52)
22. Medford District Bureau of Land Management (p. 50)
23. Klamath National Forest (p. 53)
24. Arcata Marsh (p. 54)
25. Humboldt Bay National Wildlife Refuge (p. 54)
26. East Park Reservoir (p. 55)
27. Shasta-Trinity National Forest (p. 57)

8
9
10
11
12
13
14
15
16
17
18
23
24
25
26
27

5
6
7
Seattle
WASHINGTON
Portland
19
20
OREGON
21
22

Sacramento

CALIFORNIA

coast of the Gulf of Alaska. The Copper River Delta includes the wetlands, mudflats, and barrier islands of the Copper and Bering River Deltas.

▶ Size: Approximately 700,000 acres.

▶ Ownership: Forest Service (Chugach National Forest), Eyak Corporation, Chugach Alaska Corporation.

▶ Habitats: A network of sloughs, shallow ponds, tidal mudflats, and braided glacial streams, interspersed with sedge marshes, alder and willow thickets, and small stands of spruce and cottonwood.

▸ Land Use: Commercial, subsistence, and sport fishing; recreation; hunting; and wilderness. Proposed development for logging, oil drilling, and coal extraction on privately owned parcels.

▸ Site Description: This sizable wetland lies at the base of the Copper and Bering River watersheds, which drain the Alaska, Wrangell, and Chugach Mountains. The delta occupies a relatively narrow strip of low-lying land between the Gulf of Alaska and the nearby mountain ranges. The delta is bordered to the east by the St. Elias Mountains, which, at more than 18,000 feet, are the tallest coastal mountains in the world and contain some of the largest glaciers outside the polar regions. The delta is the largest wetland complex on the Pacific Coast of North America. In addition to its importance for birds, the delta supports populations of brown and black bears, moose, wolf, mountain goat, coyote, otter, and harbor seal. One of the highest densities of beaver in North America also thrives here. The nearby town of Cordova, population 2,500, is separated from the delta by the Heney Range, and is home to the native Eyak community. Some 60 miles to the southeast of Cordova is another site of hemispheric importance for shorebirds, Northeast Montague Island.

▸ Birds: The delta is of outstanding international importance as a shorebird stopover site. As many as five million migrating shorebirds use the area each spring. The majority of shorebirds are Western Sandpipers and Dunlin, but many other species are common as well: the Red Knot, Sanderling, Black-bellied Plover, Pacific and American Golden-Plover, Short- and Long-billed Dowitchers, Marbled Godwit, and Pectoral Sandpiper. Spring migration peaks in early May. In addition to shorebirds, the delta is home to about eight percent of the world's Trumpeter Swan population, as well as nearly the entire population of the "Dusky" race of Canada Goose. The Red-throated Loon, Red-necked Phalarope, Arctic Tern, Aleutian Tern, Mew Gull, Wilson's Snipe, Mallard, and Greater Scaup are also common nesters. Northeast Montague Island has an annual count of shorebirds in excess of 500,000.

▸ Conservation Issues: Most of the delta is part of the Chugach National Forest, with several private parcels, mainly owned by native corporations. The Alaska National Interest Land Conservation Act mandated that the public portion of the delta be managed for the conservation of fish, wildlife, and their habitats. This mandate has helped to keep the federal lands relatively pristine. These regulations, however, do not extend to private inholdings. In addition, this same congressional act guaranteed easements through the national forest to private inholdings, and development on these easements could lead to road building through the area. Chugach Alaska Corporation owns land with timber, coal, and oil deposits, and has proposed extracting these resources. To date, overuse of the area by recreational users has not been a major issue. However, if the delta is connected to the road system, as has been proposed, overuse may be a concern. The re-

Olive-sided Flycatcher

cent "roadless areas rule" promoted by the Clinton administration may help to ensure this does not happen, however.

▸ Visitor Information: Cordova is unreachable by road. Access is via commercial flights from Anchorage (45 minutes) and by ferry from Valdez (five hours). The annual Copper River Delta Shorebird Festival is held in early May and organized by the Cordova Chamber of Commerce, P.O. Box 99, Cordova, AK 99574. Contact: Forest Service, Chugach National Forest, 3301 "C" Street, Suite 300, Anchorage, AK 99503, 907-586-8806. Information on access to Chugach National Forest can be obtained from the Forest Service at 907-586-8806. Cabin rental information can be obtained by calling 877-444-6777.

Glacier Bay National Park and Preserve (3), Alaska

▸ Highlight: An important breeding area for the Kittlitz's Murrelet and Black Oystercatcher.

▸ Designation: A World Heritage site.

▸ Location: The park lies at 59° N, 137° W in southeast Alaska at the northern end of the Alexander Archipelago.

▸ Size: 3,280,198 acres.

▸ Ownership: National Park Service.

▸ Habitats: Coastal, glaciated mountains and fjords, coniferous rain forest, alpine habitats.

▸ Land Use: Wilderness, recreation.

▸ Site Description: The glacial cap has retreated some 65 miles in the last 200 years, providing an unparalleled opportunity to study how life recolonizes the landscape following glacial retreat. The park presents a mosaic of habitats, from spruce-hemlock rain forest and alder thickets to thinly vegetated scree and alpine habitats surrounding glaciated valleys. The park has 16 tidewater glaciers, the ice being generated by the snow-capped Fairweather Range, where Mount Fairweather, at 15,320 feet, is the highest peak. The glaciers dump large icebergs into the sea, and these may remain floating for a week or more before melting into the surrounding waters. The range also separates Glacier Bay from the Gulf of Alaska. The bay has two main arms, and there are numerous small islands and inlets.

Marbled Murrelet

▸ Birds: The park has an important breeding population of the Kittlitz's Murrelet. The species nests on rocky alpine slopes in the coastal mountains. The Marbled Murrelet and Horned and Tufted Puffins also nest. There are large numbers of breeding Black Oystercatchers. The Fork-tailed Storm Petrel occurs, as well as the most southerly breeding populations of the Aleutian Tern and Black-legged Kittiwake. Large rafts of Surf and White-winged Scoters occur, and there are large numbers of Red-necked Phalaropes and loon species during migration.

▶ Conservation Issues: The park is well protected. The possibility of pollution and contaminants from cruise ships entering the bay is a concern, however. Changing quota systems in the halibut fishery could lead to increased conflict between recreational users and commercial fisheries. Although these conflicts are likely to have little impact on birds, seabird bycatch mitigation measures should be employed by all commercial fisheries.

▶ Visitor Information: Access to the park is by boat and plane. The flight from Juneau to Gustavus enables visitors to catch a bus to the Glacier Bay Lodge and Bartlett Cove Campground. It is also possible to reach Gustavus on the Auk Nu Ferry from Juneau. From Glacier Bay Lodge, campers can take a boat that will drop them off at three different sites from which they can hike or kayak back to the lodge, or wait for the boat to return. Cruise boats regularly visit the bay as they travel up the Alaskan coast. There are a number of trails in the vicinity of the lodge. Contact: Glacier Bay National Park and Preserve, P.O. Box 140, Gustavus, AK 99826-0140, 907-697-2230.

Misty Fiords National Monument, Tongass National Forest (4), Alaska

▶ Highlight: Representative of the Alaskan coastal rain forest and riverine forest ecosystems, it supports several bird species of conservation concern, including the federally threatened Marbled Murrelet.

▶ Location: This comprises the most southerly part of mainland Alaska, lying at 56° N, 131° W, abutting the Canadian border, and includes the Stikine River Delta.

▶ Size: 2,294,343 acres.

▶ Ownership: Forest Service.

▶ Habitats: Glaciated mountains, temperate rain forest, riverine systems, lava flows, steep sea cliffs.

▶ Land Use: Wilderness, recreation, one mining concession.

▶ Site Description: The site is a large, remote, and almost pristine wilderness area of spruce-hemlock rain forest, glaciated mountains, fjords, lava flows, and riverine ecosystems. The principal tree species are western hemlock and Sitka spruce, with some red and Alaskan cedar. The forest contains scattered bogs or "muskegs" characterized by sphagnum mosses, sedges, and rushes. Above the tree line, which lies at approximately 3,000 feet, there is an alpine zone with grasses and some dwarf trees. The coast has many small bays and shoals. The mountains rise from approximately 2,000 feet in the southern part of the monument to approximately 7,000 feet close to the Canadian border. Close to the coast they are dissected by steep-sided fjords. The Stikine River flows through the area and its delta has extensive flats used by upward of 100,000 shorebirds during migration. Yearly precipitation averages 160 inches, and it can rain at any time of the year. Mammals include black and brown bears, wolf, and mountain goat.

▶ Birds: Species characteristic of southeastern Alaskan temperate rain forests occur, including the Marbled Murrelet, Blue Grouse, Vaux's and Black Swifts, Rufous Hummingbird, Red-breasted Sapsucker, Western Wood-Pewee, and Hammond's and Pacific Slope Flycatchers. Several of these are at the northern limits of their range here. More than 100,000 shorebirds use the Stikine River Delta as a staging site during migration.

▶ Conservation Issues: In 1980, Congress passed the Alaska National Interest Lands Conservation Act, which designated all but 151,832 acres of the monument as wilderness, where nature is allowed to take its course and evidence of human use is minimized. The non-wilderness portion includes the Quartz Hill molybdenum deposit, which will be mined in a controlled, low-impact fashion.

▶ Visitor Information: The monument can be reached by floatplane or boat, and regular air service is available from Ketchikan. Charters are also available from Wrangell and Petersburg. There are no roads within the monument. There are a number of cabins and campsites that can be reserved in advance. Contact: Ketchikan-Misty Ranger District, 3031 Tongass Ave., Ketchikan AK 99901, 907-225-2148. For cabin reservations call 877-444-6777, or access the web at www.reserveusa.com.

Padilla Bay National Estuarine Research Reserve (5), Washington

▶ Highlight: Up to 200,000 waterfowl overwinter in the bay; important wintering and migratory stopover for "Black" Brant.

▶ Designation: National Estuarine Research Reserve.

▶ Location: On North Puget Sound near Anacortes, Skagit County.

▶ Size: 11,000 acres.

▶ Ownership: Washington State Department of Ecology.

▶ Habitats: Seagrass meadows, tidal mudflats, salt grass marshes, upland forests.

▶ Land Use: Research, wildlife conservation.

▶ Site Description: The bottom of the bay is shallow, flat, and muddy; at low tide the entire bay empties out, exposing a very large area of mudflats, allowing the growth of extensive eelgrass meadows that cover nearly 8,000 acres. These serve as a nursery for fish and crabs and also provide habitat for worms, clams, shrimp, and other invertebrates that provide a rich food source for migrating and overwintering birds.

▶ Birds: As many as 200,000 waterfowl overwinter; important overwintering and migratory stopover for "Black" Brant.

▶ Conservation Issues: As one of 26 National Estuarine Reserves, the site is managed cooperatively by the Washington State Department of Ecology and the National Oceanic and Atmospheric Association. There is an active control program for invasive cordgrass, through the use of mowing, digging the plants up, and some chemical application. From a peak of 17 acres, the infested area has now been reduced to approximately one acre. Extensive research and environmental education programs are in place at the reserve.

▶ Visitor Information: There is a visitor's center with exhibits. Contact: Padilla Bay National Estuarine Research Reserve at 10441 Bayview-Edison Road, Mount Vernon, WA 98273, 360-428-1558.

Dungeness National Wildlife Refuge (6), Washington

▶ Highlight: Important tidal flats for migrants and wintering waterfowl. Up to 15,000 "Black" Brant winter. Up to 26,000 migratory waterfowl and 15,000 shorebirds are found during migration and winter.

▸ Location: The refuge is located in the northeast part of the Olympic Peninsula on the shore of the Strait of Juan De Fuca, Clallam County.

▸ Size: 631 acres.

▸ Ownership: Fish and Wildlife Service.

▸ Habitats: Marine, bays, tidal flats, salt marsh, grassy meadow, shrub, and forest.

▸ Land Use: Wildlife conservation, recreation.

▸ Site Description: The tidal flats on the refuge are protected from the sea by a 5.5-mile-long sand spit, the longest natural sand spit in the United States; at its outer end is a new lighthouse. There are extensive salt marsh areas with eelgrass beds, tidal mud-flats, and drier grassy meadows with some shrubby areas and conifers. The spit may be reduced to a width of just 50 feet during high tides and is occasionally breached. The refuge also includes parts of Dungeness Bay and Harbor.

▸ Birds: Important wintering and stopover site for waterfowl and shorebirds. Up to 15,000 "Black" Brant stay to feed on the refuge's eelgrass beds during the winter. Up to 26,000 waterfowl in total use the refuge on passage, and many of these also stay to winter. Common species include the Canada Goose (including "Dusky" and "Lesser" races), Mallard, Northern Pintail, Green-winged Teal, American Wigeon, Bufflehead, White-winged and Black Scoters, Greater Scaup, Long-tailed and Harlequin Ducks, and Common and Red-breasted Mergansers. The Trumpeter Swan occurs rarely. Breeding waterfowl include the Northern Pintail, American Wigeon, Green-winged Teal, and Common Merganser. Up to 15,000 shorebirds occur during migration and winter, with a total of 31 species having been recorded; among the most numerous are the Dunlin, of which several thousand may be present, and the Black-bellied Plover, for which Dungeness is one of the three most important sites in the Greater Puget Sound area. The Black Turnstone, Surfbird, and Black Oystercatcher occur in winter, and during migration, while the Rufous Hummingbird, Band-tailed Pigeon, and Short-eared Owl breed.

▸ Conservation Issues: The refuge is vulnerable to oil spills in major shipping channels in the Strait of Juan de Fuca. Off-road vehicle (ORV) traffic is banned.

▸ Visitor Information: Best time to visit is fall and winter. There is a short trail through the refuge to the spit. Admission is $2. Contact the refuge at 33 South Barr Road, Port Angeles, WA 98362-9202, 360-457-8451.

Olympic National Park and National Forest (7), Washington

▸ Highlight: The area provides key habitat for the threatened "Northern" Spotted Owl and the threatened Marbled Murrelet.

▸ Designation: Biosphere Reserve, World Heritage Site.

▸ Location: Dominates the central Olympic Peninsula, the most northwesterly land-mass in the lower 48 states; an additional narrow strip of the park runs along 60 miles of the nearby Pacific Coast.

▸ Size: 922,000 acres (national park) and 632,000 acres (national forest).

▸ Ownership: National Park Service and Forest Service; Olympic National Forest in-cludes inholdings of some native American lands, private land, and Washington De-partment of Natural Resources land.

▸ Habitats: Temperate rain forest, glacier-covered mountains, shoreline, alpine mead-ows, lakes, coniferous upland forest.

▶ Land Use: Wilderness, wildlife conservation, recreation, logging (in the national forest).

▶ Principal Threats: Introduced mountain goats, poaching and timber theft, visitor impacts, logging in unprotected areas.

▶ Site Description: Olympic National Park lies in the center of the Olympic Peninsula, surrounding the 8,000-foot peak of Mount Olympus. It is flanked to the east, south, and northwest by Olympic National Forest. A separate 60-mile strip of temperate coastal rain forest is also included in the park. The main section of the park starts around ten miles inland of the Pacific coastal belt. Thirteen rivers radiate from Mount Olympus, and although the park has over 100 miles of road, none traverse it. Rainfall is highest near the coast where 12 feet or more can fall annually, and heavy fog is common. True temperate rain forest extends up the Hoh, Queets, and Quinault Valleys inland toward Mount Olympus. Typical trees of the rain forest are Sitka spruce, western hemlock, Douglas-fir, western red cedar (up to 25 feet in circumference and 300 feet high), and big-leaf maple. Mosses, ferns, and lichens abound, and trees are typically draped with moss. True old-growth forest such as this is made up of trees up to 1,000 years old. The biomass is extremely high, and the forest floor is covered with dead or "nurse" trees that rot away, leaving giant trees standing on stilt-like root extensions. Inland, where there is less rainfall, western pine, madrone, and vine maple become commoner.

▶ Birds: The area provides peak habitat for the "Northern" Spotted Owl and the Marbled Murrelet. In the most recent census, there were 230 pairs of owls estimated in the park; the murrelet is present in good numbers, with the species detected in most suitable habitat. Other typical species include the Varied Thrush, Gray Jay, Pine Grosbeak, Northern Pygmy-Owl, Gray-crowned Rosy-Finch, Blue Grouse, Hermit Warbler, and Rufous Hummingbird. The Black Swift may also nest. The Black Oystercatcher nests along the Pacific Coast, and the Rock Sandpiper and other shorebirds pass through during migration.

▶ Conservation Issues: A serious problem for the "Northern" Spotted Owl is the invasion of the Barred Owl. The latter, first detected on the Olympic Peninsula in 1985, has now spread to the heart of the park; whenever Barred Owls invade Spotted Owl territories, they invariably displace them. Of the park's 922,000 acres, 95 percent is wilderness. With an estimated four million visitors annually, the park is heavily used. The Olympic National Forest comprises two forest districts. Of the forest's 632,000 acres, 89,900 are designated as wilderness, and 417,500 as late successional reserves, where management activities such as silviculture are practiced. Under the Northwest Forest Plan, 125,000 acres have been designated as an Adaptive Management Area that allows for some timber extraction (currently eight to ten million board feet are extracted from a small portion of this land each year). As well as managing recreation activities, a central objective of Forest's management plan is to protect watersheds and restore fish stocks.

▶ Visitor Information: Best time to visit is spring through fall. There is a visitor center and camping and lodges are available. Entry costs $10 per vehicle and a further $5 is payable for visitors wishing to enter wilderness areas (call 360-452-0300 for reservations). Contact: Olympic National Park, 600 East Park Avenue, Port Angeles, WA 98362, 360-565-3130; Olympic National Forest Headquarters, 1835 Black Lake Blvd. SW, Olympia, WA 98512, 360-956-2402.

Washington Island National Wildlife Refuges IBAs, Washington

Flattery Rocks National Wildlife Refuge (8), Quillayute Needles National Wildlife Refuge (9), Copalis National Wildlife Refuge (10)

▶ Highlight: Fifty thousand breeding seabirds of 14 species. Up to one million seabirds and shorebirds gather on these islands during migration.

▶ Location: Coast of the Olympic Peninsula from Cape Flattery to Copalis Beach.

▶ Size: The area comprises a continuous strip of near-shore rocky islets of varying sizes which extend 100 miles along the Washington coast.

▶ Ownership: Fish and Wildlife Service. Includes Flattery Rocks, Quillayute Needles, and Copalis National Wildlife Refuges.

▶ Habitats: Marine, rocky outcrops, small islets.

▶ Land Use: Wildlife conservation.

▶ Site Description: The refuges form a chain of 870 small rocks, islands, and reefs scattered along the Washington coast in one of the richest marine ecosystems in the world. Some of the rocks are exposed only at low tide, while others are permanent islands and are sparsely vegetated with salal, salmonberry, and dwarf conifers. Sea lions, harbor seals, sea otters, and cetaceans are abundant.

▶ Birds: Fifty thousand seabirds of 14 species nest, including Leach's and Fork-tailed Storm-Petrel, Rhinoceros and Cassin's Auklets, Tufted Puffin, Pigeon Guillemot, Common Murre, Glaucous-winged Gull, and Brandt's and Pelagic Cormorants. The Black Oystercatcher also breeds. Up to one million seabirds and shorebirds use the islands and surrounding seas for roosting and foraging during migration.

▶ Conservation Issues: Naval bombardment was halted by a 1993 order signed by the Secretary of the Interior. No visitors are allowed to land on the islands, and boats must remain at least 200 yards away. The potential for a serious oil spill must be considered a threat to seabirds in the area, especially if it were to occur in late summer—shortly after the breeding season for most pelagic species. There is the possibility of offshore oil drilling. The entire set of refuges, except for Destruction Island, is included in the Washington Islands Wilderness Area.

▶ Visitor Information: Visitors cannot land on the islands. The refuges can be viewed from the shore at a number of locations, including near Lake Ozette, Rialto Beach, Second Beach, Ruby Beach, Kalaloch, and from sections of the coastal part of Olympic National Park. For more information, contact: Copalis National Wildlife Refuge, 33 South Barr Road, Port Angeles, WA 98362, 360-457-8451.

Grays Harbor (11), Washington

▶ Highlight: Perhaps the most important shorebird site on the United States Pacific Coast south of Alaska.

▶ Designation: Hemispheric Reserve in the Western Hemisphere Shorebird Reserve Network.

▶ Location: Near Hoquiam in Grays Harbor County (46° 58" N, 123° 56" W).

▶ Size: Surface area varies from about 94 square miles at high tide to 38 square miles at low tide, with nearly 34,000 acres of intertidal mudflats. The Grays Harbor National Wildlife Refuge is approximately 1,500 acres.

► Ownership: Fish and Wildlife Service, Washington Department of Natural Resources, Washington Department of Fish and Wildlife, Washington State Parks, a private conservation group, and private lands.

► Habitats: The site is an estuary with open water, intertidal mudflats, rocky shore, salt marsh, open beaches, shrub-scrub, and forested wetland-willow areas.

► Land Use: Commercial and municipal use; recreation (hiking, biking, kayaking, and birding).

► Site Description: Grays Harbor is one of the six major estuary systems on the Pacific Coast and the third largest in the Pacific Northwest.

► Birds: Grays Harbor is one of the four most important estuaries in the entire continent as a stopover for migrant shorebirds. The other three are Alaska's Copper River Delta, and the Bay of Fundy and Delaware Bay on the East Coast. These stopover areas are sites where migrating shorebirds feed on amphipods and other invertebrates, and can nearly double their weight before moving on. In fact, at Grays Harbor, certain areas support densities of amphipods of more than 55,000 animals per square yard. More than one million shorebirds are recorded annually, representing 24 species. During an aerial survey of Grays Harbor during spring migration, an estimated 300,000 shorebirds were counted on a single day. The five most abundant species are the Western Sandpiper, Dunlin, Short-billed and Long-billed Dowitchers, and Semipalmated Plover. Approximately 50,000 Dunlin winter at Grays Harbor, with an all-time record Christmas Bird Count of 95,500 individuals. Among the species found in winter are the Black Oystercatcher, Black Turnstone, Surfbird, and Rock Sandpiper. The Marbled Godwit, Red Knot, Buff-breasted Sandpiper, and Hudsonian Godwit stop by during migration, while the Snowy Plover nests.

In the spring, shorebirds leaving Grays Harbor fly 1,500 miles to Alaska's Copper River Delta. Some stop along the coast to rest and feed, while many others fly nonstop. At Grays Harbor, the most critical area is Bowerman Basin, not only because of the high amphipod concentration, but because it is the first area to be exposed and the last to be inundated during the tidal surge. Used by up to 50 percent of the migrating shorebirds stopping in the area, the basin supports some shorebirds all year long, both resident and off-peak migrant birds. During winter, it supports up to 20,000 individuals. The harbor is also heavily used by waterfowl, with the American Wigeon making up nearly 60 percent of the ducks present. There is also a high concentration of Peregrine Falcons at Bowerman Basin preying on shorebirds. Gray's Canyon, about 25 to 30 miles offshore, is important for seabirds. Among the species found there seasonally are the South Polar Skua, Black-footed and Laysan Albatrosses, all three jaegers, Sooty and Buller's Shearwaters, Fork-tailed Storm-Petrel, and several species of alcids and gulls.

► Conservation Issues: The area around the estuary is developed, and the refuge forms only a small part of the system. The refuge itself is surrounded by industrial development. Salt marshes and tidal mudflats around the edge of the harbor have been created by dredging and filling, in connection with the shipping channel. The effects of dredging and industrial and residential development have led to decreased water quality. Threats include continued development in the area and increased recreational use and invasive non-native plant species such as Phragmites and cordgrass which pose a threat to the native vegetation. Refuge personnel use mechanical means and selective application of herbicides to control the spread of these plants. The introduced green crab is also a concern. It may be replacing a native crab species and is a threat to the shellfish industry.

Oil spills from tankers are a particular concern; an oil spill during spring migration could potentially wipe out most of the shorebirds on the West Coast. Pollution from pesticides and from industrial runoff is a potential problem affecting the long-term health of shorebird and waterfowl populations. The refuge itself is next to an area for proposed industrial expansion. Further expansion of the airport could also impact the avifauna of the area.

The primary purpose of the refuge is to conserve fish and wildlife populations and their habitats, with a focus on migratory shorebirds. The refuge provides opportunities for wildlife observation and education; there is a boardwalk trail for visitors. Habitat management issues include control of noxious weed species and restoration of native plant communities.

A coalition of citizens and conservation groups, including Grays Harbor Audubon Society and American Bird Conservancy, is working to establish the North Bay Wetlands Preserve, an area of 681 acres of critical feeding, resting, and breeding habitat for several wetland-dependent birds. The project will result in the protection of about two miles of Grays Harbor's shoreline on both sides of the Humptulips River, together with 689 acres of associated wetlands, uplands, and riverbank. Grays Harbor has been identified as a top conservation priority by Partners in Flight and the Pacific Coast Joint Venture.

▸ Visitor Information: Any time of year is good for a visit, but the biggest concentrations of migrating shorebirds occur from April 15 to May 15, with many wintering as well. Pelagic trips to look for seabirds in Gray's Canyon leave at various seasons from Westport, at the south entrance to Grays Harbor. Contact: Nisqually National Wildlife Refuge, 100 Brown Farm Road, Olympic, WA 98516, 360-753-9467.

Willapa Bay (12), Washington

▸ Highlight: Important wintering area for the "Black" Brant, which has, however, declined there in recent years due to infestation by a non-native cordgrass.
▸ Designation: Wetland of International Importance in the Western Hemisphere Shorebird Reserve Network.
▸ Location: Southeastern coast of Washington State.
▸ Size: Willapa Bay covers approximately 80,000 acres, of which the Willapa National Wildlife Refuge is 11,000 acres in five main sections around the bay.
▸ Ownership: Fish and Wildlife Service, private.
▸ Habitats: Sandy beaches, estuarine marsh, dunes, coniferous forest, eelgrass beds in the bay.
▸ Land Use: Commercial shellfish fishing and aquiculture; recreation and wildlife conservation.
▸ Site Description: Willapa Bay lies between Grays Harbor and the mouth of the Columbia River. The bay is separated from the ocean by a long, narrow peninsula. There are several salt marshes around the bay. Low tide exposes approximately 75 square miles of mudflats. The site includes Long Island, which, at 5,000 acres, is the largest estuarine island on the Pacific Coast.

▶ Birds: Willapa Bay supports large concentrations of shorebirds and waterfowl. Up to 300,000 shorebirds stop during spring migration, and the Snowy Plover nests. The Trumpeter Swan sometimes winters; and the "Dusky" race of the Canada Goose grazes on the grassland meadows. The refuge was established to provide a wintering area for the "Black" Brant, which has been present from October through May in numbers up to 3,669 in recent counts. Use by the Brant declined abruptly after 1992, perhaps due to habitat changes brought about by cordgrass. The Black Turnstone also winters, and Willapa is a key wintering area for the Canvasback. Up to 70,000 Dunlin have been counted there during the winter months, and more than 80,000 Western Sandpipers have been recorded during spring migration. Nearly 24,000 Short-billed Dowitchers have also occurred during spring migration.

▶ Conservation Issues: Cordgrass, a non-native and invasive plant, is the biggest problem natural resource managers face in the coastal areas of the Pacific Northwest. It degrades the habitat, making it unuseable by shorebirds, and also damages the shellfish harvest. The outlook at present is not good. Its invasion of Willapa Bay is the largest in Washington. In 1991, there were about 2,500 acres of cordgrass in Willapa Bay. In 1999, the infestation covered between 15,000 to 18,000 acres of tidelands and is projected to occupy 56,000 out of the 80,000 acres of the bay if left uncontrolled. Managers try to control it mechanically, and with an herbicide from airboats, but can treat only 15 or so acres a year that way. In addition, airboats are very expensive, costing $40,000 each. Though it is worst at Willipa Bay, cordgrass similarly threatens Grays Harbor, and the battle is at present not being won. The complete loss of intertidal mudflats and native salt marsh to cordgrass will be devastating for shorebird use and for foraging habitat for the wintering Brant and the rare "Dusky" Canada Goose. Control efforts in the near future will be expanded to include new techniques (including biological control) and to focus on distinct geographic areas within Willapa Bay. Control efforts are a cooperative effort between federal and state agencies, and are supported not only by the oyster and hard-shell clam aquiculture industry, but by local and national conservation groups. A new concern is the green crab, introduced from Europe; it may be replacing a native crab and is a threat to the shellfish industry. The green crab may be associated with the non-native cordgrass.

▶ Visitor Information: Best time to visit is fall through spring. Access to the refuge is by foot only. Contact: Willapa National Wildlife Refuge, HC01, Box 910, Ilwaco, WA 98624, 360-484-3482.

East Sand and Rice Islands, Columbia River Estuary (13), Oregon and Washington

▶ Highlight: Largest Caspian Tern colony in the world, with approximately 30 percent of the total North American population, 75 percent of the West Coast population, and ten percent of the global population.

▶ Location: In the Columbia River estuary on the border of Oregon and Washington.

▶ Size: 53 acres.

▶ Ownership: Army Corps of Engineers.

▶ Habitats: Sandy dredge spoil islands.

▶ Land Use: Dredge spoil from dredging the estuary.

▶ Site Description: East Sand Island was originally a natural island but through dredge spoil dumping has been expanded to 53 acres. It was last used for this purpose in 1983.

▶ Birds: East Sand Island has the largest nesting colony of Caspian Terns in the world. The colony numbers approximately 9,100 pairs. It also has the largest post-breeding concentration of the endangered West Coast population of the Brown Pelican north of San Francisco. The East Sand Island colony is the only Caspian Tern breeding colony anywhere along the coast of the Pacific Northwest, as previous breeding sites have been deliberately or naturally destroyed. Caspian Terns formerly nested in large colonies on islands in Willapa Bay and Grays Harbor, and along the coast of Puget Sound near Everett and Tacoma, Washington; and on Rice Island, also in the Columbia River estuary. The populations have since been intentionally eliminated. The terns no longer nest in Willapa Bay and Grays Harbor.

▶ Conservation Issues: The National Marine Fisheries Service, Idaho Fish and Game Department, the Army Corps of Engineers, and several Native American tribes hold nesting Caspian Terns responsible for declines in salmon stocks in the Northwest. Noting there was no sound science linking terns to salmon declines or to impeding salmon recovery of listed species, in April 2000 American Bird Conservancy, the National Audubon Society, Defenders of Wildlife, and Seattle Audubon Society filed suit in the U.S. District Court in Seattle, to prevent the Army Corps of Engineers and the Fish and Wildlife Service from destroying the Caspian Tern colony on Rice Island. Despite the opposition of conservationists and even their own fishery scientists, the National Marine Fisheries Service and other agencies pushed the Corps to force all terns to relocate to East Sand Island, which is 16 miles closer to the ocean, where the birds might eat fewer hatchery-raised and wild smolt of federally listed coho and steelhead salmon. The Rice Island colony held about 20,000 nesting terns in 1998. Through seeding of bare sand habitat and fencing with flagging to scare terns, Rice Island was made unsuitable for nesting. At East Sand Island, 4.5 acres of bare sand habitat was scarified, and decoys and sound attractants were employed. In 2001, all Caspian Terns nesting in the Columbia River estuary used 3.9 acres of restored habitat on East Sand Island. The estimated size of the East Sand Island colony (9,100 pairs in 2001) was not significantly different from 2000, suggesting that the tern breeding population is no longer increasing. The total number of Caspian Terns nesting in the Columbia River estuary increased in 1998, 1999, and 2000, while numbers of nesting terns were stable or slightly declined in 2001. The East Sand Island colony is now the world's largest. In 2001, 50 percent fewer salmonid juveniles were consumed. While large numbers of Caspian Terns occur in the Columbia River basin relative to the North American population as a whole, the Caspian Tern is not abundant anywhere in its range. There are only seven sites in North America with breeding colonies of 1,000 pairs or more.

The court had issued a preliminary injunction because the Corps failed to prepare a full Environmental Impact Statement (EIS). American Bird Conservancy and other conservationists filed suit only after repeated pleas to federal and state officials for such an EIS were ignored as the Corps continued to extirpate terns from Rice Island. On August 7, 2001, the federal court entered a final judgment in favor of the plaintiffs. The judge based the decision on the failure of the Corps to comply with National Environmental Policy Act requirements and to complete an EIS before further activities were conducted by federal defendants to alter the Caspian Tern or the cormorant habitat in the Columbia estuary, or before any take or harassment of terns or cormorants occurred. The federal defendants appealed to the 9th Circuit Court of Appeals. Settlement negotiations led to an agreement wherein the case was settled and the injunction dismissed on April 2, 2002. Federal defendants agreed to complete an EIS by March 2005, to scarify and keep at least six acres of open sand habitat on East Sand Island for tern breeding at least until the EIS is completed, to conduct predator control as necessary on East Sand Island, to conduct a tern population assessment, to conduct a tern-salmon predation analysis, and to conduct a site assessment to locate viable additional nesting sites outside the Columbia estuary. The Corps has prepared 6.5 acres of suitable habitat for the 2002 breeding season. Although nesting success increased significantly in 2001, conservationists are concerned about concentrating such a large proportion of the breeding population at a single colony due to the risks from disease, storms, predators, human disturbance, and oil spills.

▸ Visitor Information: There is no public access to the island. For information, contact: Gerald Winegrad, ABC, 202-452-1535, e-mail: gww@abcbirds.org.

Tillamook Bay (14), Oregon

▸ Highlight: One quarter of Oregon's coastal wintering waterfowl occur there, including sizable numbers of the Brant. More than 100,000 shorebirds are found annually as migrants. The Marbled Murrelet feeds close to shore, and there is a high concentration of nesting Snowy Plovers.

▸ Location: 60 miles west of Portland, where the Kilchis, Wilson, Trask, Miami, and Tillamook Rivers run into the ocean.

▸ Size: Approximately 11 square miles.

▸ Ownership: State and private lands. Restoration and acquisition projects are under way with federal funds provided to local public-private partnerships.

▸ Habitats: Open water, intertidal flats, salt marsh, eelgrass beds, rocky shoreline.

▸ Land Use: Commercial and recreational fisheries, wildlife habitat.

▸ Site Description: Tillamook Bay is a shallow (six feet deep) tidal bay protected from the Pacific Ocean by a four-mile-long spit. It is fed by four major rivers. Another river, the Miami, feeds in close to the ocean inlet. Intertidal flats cover approximately 60 percent of the water surface of the bay. Salt marsh and eelgrass beds are also present.

▸ Birds: Among the wintering shorebirds are large numbers of Black Turnstones and Surfbirds as well as smaller numbers of Black Oystercatchers and Rock Sandpipers. The Snowy Plover is also found. Grebes, loons, diving ducks, and Brant occur in the bay. Seabirds, including wintering alcids, migrant shearwaters, and storm-petrels can be seen from the shore. Large numbers of American Wigeon graze in the fields close to Bayocean Spit, and at high tide, the fields there often hold Pacific Golden-Plovers and Buff-breasted Sandpipers during migration. Bald Eagles are frequent. Huge numbers of Western and Least Sandpipers are found in early fall. Rare shorebirds are annual, and Bayocean Spit is a notable site for vagrants from Asia. The nearby Cape Meares State Park has one or two resident pairs of Spotted Owls. Cape Meares itself has nesting alcids, including Tufted Puffins. Within the boundaries of the state park is the 138-acre Cape Meares National Wildlife Park.

▶ Conservation Issues: A large local human population, sewage outflow, and agricultural runoff (principally from dairy farms) have led to a decline in shellfish populations. Sedimentation caused by increased erosion from logged areas has decreased the bay's water volume by 35 percent from historical levels. Approximately 72 percent of the original natural wetland has been converted to agriculture. A number of conservation projects are underway involving public-private partnerships and federal funding.

▶ Visitor Information: Most of the area can be reached easily by car. The walk to the tip of Bayocean Spit is best for Snowy Plovers, which are most common during the winter. The refuge can be contacted at 26208 Finley Refuge Road, Corvallis, OR 97333, 541-757-7236.

Siuslaw National Forest (15) and Oregon Dunes National Recreation Area (16)

▶ Highlight: Important breeding site for both the "Northern" Spotted Owl and the Marbled Murrelet.

▶ Location: Pacific Coast of central Oregon.

▶ Size: 630,395 acres.

▶ Ownership: Forest Service.

▶ Habitats: Coastal sand dunes, freshwater ponds, and rocky coast; old-growth temperate rain forests, salmon streams and lakes, subalpine areas.

▶ Land Use: Wildlife conservation, recreation, timber extraction.

▶ Site Description: A large area of old-growth forest and coastal dunes, some reaching 400 feet, the Siuslaw National Forest is one of only two national forests on the Pacific Coast. The adjacent Oregon Dunes National Recreation Area occupies 14,000 acres. The forest extends from sea level to approximately 4,000 feet in altitude at St. Mary's Peak. From around Tillamook in the north to close to Coos Bay in the south, the forest is approximately 135 miles long and 27 miles wide, with 30 lakes, and 1,200 miles of streams. Characteristic tree species include Douglas-fir, western hemlock, western red cedar, Sitka spruce, red alder, and big-leaf maple.

▶ Birds: Three key species here are the "Northern" Spotted Owl, with a recent count of 100 or so territories, the Marbled Murrelet, for which there are almost 500 occupied sites known, and the "Western" Snowy Plover, with approximately 30 nests. The Mountain Quail also occurs in early seral habitats at all elevations. Migrant shorebirds include the Long-billed Curlew and Surfbird, while the Black Oystercatcher is resident. Also among the species either resident or found seasonally are the Aleutian race of Canada Goose, Brown Pelican, Bald Eagle, Blue Grouse, Rufous Hummingbird, and Gray-crowned Rosy-Finch.

▶ Conservation Issues: Because of the unique coastal environments and surrounding private industrial timber lands, the forest can provide habitat for much of the biodiversity dependent on old-growth forests and structurally diverse streams. A primary focus is to enlist private sector partners in Forest Service restoration efforts in these terrestrial and aquatic habitats. Timber production in the forest is limited to thinning stands planted in the 1940s, with no harvest of natural stands. The initiative to preserve roadless areas in national forests will result in only a few areas being protected due to the forest's heavily roaded landscape. The forest contains three wilderness areas totaling 22,600 acres.

▶ Visitor Information: The forest offers a range of facilities, including campgrounds, off-road vehicle areas; and boating, biking, hiking, and horseback riding opportunities. There are 100 miles of trails. For more information, contact: Siuslaw National Forest, 4077 S.W. Research Way, P.O. Box 1148, Corvallis, OR 97339, 541-750-7000.

Coos Bay (17), Oregon

▶ Highlight: The estuary has the largest concentrations in the northwest of migrating and wintering shorebirds, while adjacent Bureau of Land Management lands hold a significant number of "Northern" Spotted Owls.

▶ Location: Pacific Coast of south-central Oregon, near the town of Coos Bay.

▶ Size: The Coos Bay District of the Bureau of Land Management covers 325,000 acres.

▶ Ownership: Bureau of Land Management, private, Oregon State Parks and Recreation Department.

▶ Habitats: Estuarine mudflats, rocky shoreline, sandy beaches, marsh, coniferous forest.

▶ Land Use: Recreation, forestry, commercial use.

▶ Site Description: Coos Bay is Oregon's largest estuary, protected from the ocean by a long sandy spit. The area includes tidal mudflats, some rocky shoreline along the Pacific Coast to the south of the estuary, freshwater marshes, and grassy meadows, while coniferous forest, including old-growth, is found on the Bureau of Land Management lands in the adjacent coastal range.

▶ Birds: Thousands of waterfowl winter in the enclosed bay, including large numbers of American Wigeon, Northern Pintail, Gadwall, Scaup, Bufflehead, and Ruddy Duck. Thousands of shorebirds also use this area, including the Black-bellied Plover, Long-billed Dowitcher, Dunlin, and Sanderling, with smaller numbers of the Pacific Golden Plover, Whimbrel, Greater Yellowlegs, and Short-billed Dowitcher. Rocky areas along the shore near Shore Acres State Park attract the Black Oystercatcher, Surfbird, and Black Turnstone, and there is a small breeding population of the endangered western race of the Snowy Plover. The Hermit Warbler and Rufous Hummingbird nest in the Coos district of the Bureau of Land Management; in addition, 106 sites for the "Northern" Spotted Owl are known for the district.

▶ Conservation Issues: Coos Bay is one of the largest commercial ports in the northwest. The potential for an accidental oil spill or discharge of chemicals from a ship or harbor facility would cause serious damage to the tidal flats and waterfowl populations. In the Coos district of the Bureau of Land Management, most of the known "Northern" Spotted Owl sites have a minimum of a 100-acre core area protected. Of the 106 sites, 71 sites are further protected because the primary site center falls within a late successional reserve; a large block of land managed for late successional species.

▶ Visitor Information: Best time to visit is during migration and winter. The locations of the "Northern" Spotted Owl and the Marbled Murrelet sites are kept confidential to protect the birds. The Hermit Warbler and other breeding birds can best be found from late May to early July. For more information on the Bureau of Land Management lands, contact: Bureau of Land Management, 1300 Airport Lane, North Bend, OR 97459, 541-756-0100.

Roseburg (18) and Medford (22) Districts of the Bureau of Land Management, Oregon

- ▶ Highlight: Important site for the "Northern" Spotted Owl.
- ▶ Location: Near Roseburg, in Douglas County.
- ▶ Size: 423,928 acres (Roseburg District Bureau of Land Management) and 859,096 acres (Medford District Bureau of Land Management).
- ▶ Ownership: Bureau of Land Management, private lands.
- ▶ Habitats: Coniferous forests of Douglas-fir, hemlock, cedar, and oak woodland.
- ▶ Land Use: Timber production, watershed protection, recreation, wildlife conservation.
- ▶ Site Description: In addition to the coniferous forest, some of which is old-growth, many streams and rivers are found on the district; these provide breeding habitat for anadromous fishes and thus contribute to commercial fishing. The Bureau of Land Management lands in western Oregon are unlike the Bureau of Land Management lands elsewhere in that they are heavily forested.
- ▶ Birds: Good numbers of "Northern" Spotted Owls occur here. The population is the most intensively studied of any on public lands. In 2000, there were 122 pairs censused in the Roseburg District, and 150 pairs in the Medford District. A few Marbled Murrelets (approximately seven occupied sites) have also been found on the Roseburg District, and the Hermit Warbler and Rufous Hummingbird breed.
- ▶ Conservation Issues: The Roseburg District contains 192,990 acres considered suitable habitat for the "Northern" Spotted Owl, while the Medford District contains 363,000 acres. Another 215 to 426 acres are capable of being converted to owl habitat but, primarily due to previous timber harvest, are not at present suitable to support nesting pairs. A total of 110,665 acres are considered Critical Habitat for the owl.

The conservation strategy for the "Northern" Spotted Owl in the district is based on the requirements of the Northwest Forest Plan, which required the establishment of 100-acre retention areas for the best habitat in all Spotted Owl activity centers known as of January 1, 1994. A total of 142 activity centers, covering 134,421 acres, were established in the Roseburg District. Additional owl sites have been located in the district since 1994. Many of these new sites are in protected land use categories. The plan established a network of Late Successional Reserves, and Riparian Reserves across the district. Thirty-two percent of the land in the districts taken together is in Late Successional Reserves, whereas approximately 36 percent is in Riparian Reserves. An additional 26,900 acres on Roseburg and 27,200 on Medford are designated as Connectivity/Diversity Blocks with a 150-year rotation designed to provide corridors for movement of owls between different areas. Only 13 percent of the Roseburg District lands are in the General Forest Management Land Use allocation, while some 54.7 percent of Medford District's land is in "matrix" lands. In the most recent count, the number of known activity centers where pairs of owls were observed was 122 on Roseburg and 150 on Medford.

▶ Visitor Information: Best time for a visit is spring through fall. Owl locations are kept confidential to protect the birds. For further information, contact: Bureau of Land Management Roseburg District Office at 777 NW Garden Valley Boulevard, Roseburg, OR 97470, 541-440-4930, and Medford District Office at 3040 Biddle Road, Medford, OR 97504, 541-618-2200.

Mount Hood National Forest (19), Oregon

▶ Highlight: Good population of "Northern" Spotted Owls, in addition to breeding Green List species.
▶ Location: East of Portland, stretching southward from near the banks of the Columbia River.
▶ Size: 1,063,000 acres.
▶ Ownership: Forest Service.
▶ Habitats: Western hemlock–Douglas-fir forest, high subalpine meadows, ponderosa pine forest.
▶ Site Description: Named for Mount Hood, which is 11,235 feet high, the forest straddles the Cascade Range. The dry eastern section is dominated by ponderosa pine, while the western section is a mixture of moist forest types, including western hemlock and cedar forests.
▶ Land Use: Recreation, some timber extraction, wildlife conservation.
▶ Birds: Among the species resident or breeding on the forest are the Band-tailed Pigeon, Hermit Warbler, Rufous Hummingbird, and Gray-crowned Rosy-Finch. In the last census, there were 303 known activity centers (representing a pair or a single territorial male) of the "Northern" Spotted Owl in the forest.
▶ Conservation Issues: The last survey work for the "Northern" Spotted Owl was done in 1995. In accordance with the Northwest Forest Plan implemented in 1994, Late Successional Reserves have been set up on the forest, designed to protect and promote dispersal of the owl. For each owl activity center known in 1994, a 100-acre core was set up. At present, in advance of any habitat-altering project on the forest, survey work is conducted to determine if an owl activity center is located there. Since the introduction of the Northwest Forest Plan in 1994, timber sales have been reduced.
▶ Visitor Information: May to July is the best time to see breeding birds. Most roads in the forest are open from May to November. For information, contact: Mount Hood National Forest, 16400 Champion Way, Sandy, OR 97055, 503-668-1700.

Willamette National Forest (20), Oregon

▶ Highlight: Perhaps the top global site for the endangered "Northern" Spotted Owl.
▶ Location: Western slope of the central Cascade Mountains.
▶ Size: 1,675,407 acres.
▶ Ownership: Forest Service.
▶ Habitats: Old-growth forest, other coniferous forest, deciduous forest, lakes.
▶ Land Use: Forestry, recreation.
▶ Site Description: The Willamette National Forest stretches for 110 miles along the western slopes of the Cascades. With numerous volcanic peaks, it has an elevational range from 1,000 to 10,495 feet. The predominant vegetation is coniferous forest, in-

cluding old-growth, with Douglas-fir, western hemlock, western red cedar, and Pacific yew at the lower elevations; Pacific silver and noble firs at the mid-elevations; and mountain hemlock, subalpine fir, lodgepole and western white pines, and Engelmann spruce at higher elevations. There are many natural lakes bordered by deciduous and mixed coniferous forest.

▸ Birds: The forest is one of the top sites for the endangered "Northern" Spotted Owl, with as many as 1,000 found in the old-growth habitat there, perhaps the largest number found anywhere. The forest is the only place in the state where the Black Swift breeds. Among the other species found there are the Hermit Warbler and Rufous Hummingbird.

▸ Conservation Issues: Because the owl is sensitive to disturbance, its nesting locations are kept confidential.

▸ Visitor Information: Late May through July is best for songbirds. The supervisor's office is in Eugene, at 541-465-6521.

Umpqua National Forest (21), Oregon

▸ Highlight: Important site for the threatened "Northern" Spotted Owl. The most common nesting warbler is the Hermit Warbler.

▸ Location: West slope of the Cascades in southwest Oregon. Seventy-four percent of the forest lies within Douglas County, with the remaining portions in Lane and Jackson Counties. Roseburg is the nearest large town and is the home of the forest supervisor's office.

▸ Size: Approximately 1,000,000 acres, of which half is old-growth.

▸ Ownership: Forest Service.

▸ Habitats: Late successional and old-growth forest of several types (Douglas-fir, white fir, western hemlock, mountain hemlock, Pacific silver fir, Shasta red fir, and Oregon white oak), riparian hardwoods, and ash wetlands. Also intermixed are high meadows, wetlands, dry meadows, oak savannahs, lakes, ponds, rock outcrops, cliff features, and caves.

▸ Land Use: Forestry, mining, grazing, recreation, wildlife conservation.

▸ Site Description: The Umpqua National Forest is noted for having some of the largest remaining contiguous blocks of late successional forest in the Pacific Northwest. In parts of the forest, past timber harvest has created a mosaic of vegetation patterns and younger-aged timber stands of varying densities. The forest is situated at the convergence of the High Cascades, Western Cascades, and the Klamath geological provinces. This has resulted in a wide variety of habitats and species. The forest is bordered by several other national forests, Crater Lake National Park, and Bureau of Land Management lands.

▸ Birds: The forest harbors species found primarily in the Pacific Northwest, and also species characteristic of the east side of the Cascades and of northern California. Species from the east side of the Cascades include the Prairie Falcon, Canyon Wren, Green-tailed Towhee, and Brewer's Sparrow. California species include the California Towhee and Red-shouldered Hawk. Among the birds of prey nesting on the forest are "Northern" Spotted and Great Gray Owls, Bald and Golden Eagles, Peregrine Falcon, and Northern Goshawk. The Mountain Quail is relatively common, and the Band-tailed Pigeon can also be found. The Hermit Warbler is the most common nesting warbler found in the annual surveys for neotropical migrants conducted in the old-growth habitat. Extrapolating from territory size and the amount of suitable habitat, there could be as many as 250,000 on the forest. Through past survey and monitoring efforts a total of 611 "Northern" Spotted Owls are known to reside in the forest. A few Brewer's Sparrows nest in areas that were clear-cut in the 1970s and 1980s.

▶ Conservation Issues: Land allocations in the Umpqua National Forest Plan protect diverse wildlife and fish habitats while providing opportunities for dispersed and developed recreation, carefully regulated timber harvest, mining, grazing, and other uses. Notable among the various land allocations in the forest are Late Successional Reserves and Riparian Reserves. These reserves were established in the Northwest Forest Plan to protect populations and habitats of late successional and old-growth-forest-dependent species. They are the foundation of forest and riparian ecosystem restoration efforts. The largest Late Successional Reserve (LSR) in the Pacific Northwest reserve network (LSR 222 at 508,000 acres), is centered on the Umpqua and extends into adjacent national forests and Bureau of Land Management lands. There are other Late Successional Reserves, including LSR 223 at 14,373 acres, and numerous smaller reserves protecting "Northern" Spotted Owl core areas and other old-growth-dependent species. The forest has three wilderness areas—Boulder Creek, Rogue-Umpqua Divide, and Mt. Thielsen. Other designated areas are the Oregon Cascades Recreation Area, and the North Umpqua Wild and Scenic River.

The Band-tailed Pigeon is present, but numbers have declined in recent years in part due to an outbreak of an infectious disease, trichomoniasis, and reduction of a favorite food, elderberry. In cooperation with Oregon State University, forest managers are conducting studies of gamebirds, including the Mountain Quail. The forest participates in Region 6 Neotropical Songbird Monitoring, which surveys for migrant songbirds in forested habitat.

▶ Visitor Information: Best time to visit is spring through fall. Contact the forest at 2900 N.W. Stewart Parkway, P.O. Box 1008, Roseburg, OR 97470, 541-672-6601.

Klamath National Forest (23), California

▶ Highlight: More than 280 territories of the threatened "Northern" Spotted Owl are found on the forest.

▶ Location: North-central California.

▶ Size: The forest administers approximately 1,700,000 acres.

▶ Ownership: Forest Service.

▶ Habitats: Douglas-fir, mixed conifer, ponderosa pine, lodgepole pine, and a variety of oak communities; on the east side of the forest are shrub steppes and grasslands.

▶ Land Use: Forestry, recreation, wildlife conservation.

▶ Site Description: The forest encompasses a large portion of the Klamath Mountains, which form the link between the Coast Ranges and the Sierra Nevada. The climate is Mediterranean, with warm, dry summers, and cool to cold wet winters. Summertime lightning storms are common and provide the ignition source for wild fires. Forest stand structure and wildland fire behavior has been altered since the commencement of a campaign of fire suppression beginning in World War II. The forest also administers the Butte Valley National Grassland.

▸ Birds: Species include the threatened "Northern" Spotted Owl, Flammulated Owl, White-headed Woodpecker, Mountain Quail, and Hermit Warbler. The "Northern" Spotted Owl is a fairly common resident of the forest, with more than 280 territories identified (pairs and territorial singles). The Flammulated Owl was virtually unknown from this region until audio surveys were conducted beginning in the mid-1970s. The owl also has been detected during nocturnal surveys for the "Northern" Spotted Owl. It is now considered to be fairly common, especially within the dry forest. The White-headed Woodpecker is a fairly common resident in mid- to upper-elevation coniferous forests. The Mountain Quail is a fairly common resident in montane chaparral, mixed-conifer/hardwood, and open mixed-conifer stands with shrub understorey. The Hermit Warbler is a fairly common breeding species in the forest. In an analysis of census points on the west side of the forest, the Hermit Warbler was the eighth most common bird detected.

▸ Conservation Issues: The threatened "Northern" Spotted Owl became an object of conservation concern in the mid-1970s due to the effects of clear-cut logging practices throughout the Pacific Northwest. Several management strategies for National Forest System and Bureau of Land Management lands have been developed over the past 15 years. Currently, the "Northern" Spotted Owl is managed under the Northwest Forest Plan. As a part of that plan, large management units, termed "Late Successional Reserves," have been designated throughout the Pacific Northwest. Most were designed specifically around known owl activity centers. Extensive field surveys in the Klamath National Forest have been ongoing since the early 1980s. The owl nests and forages in mixed-conifer forests of medium- to large-sized trees with closed canopy.

▸ Visitor Information: Best time to visit is during the breeding season, from late May to early July. Contact: Klamath National Forest, 1312 Fairlane Road, Yreka, CA 96097, 530-842-6131.

Arcata Marsh (24) and Humboldt Bay Natural Wildlife Refuge (25), California

▸ Highlight: Almost the entire global population of 200,000 "Black" Brant stop over during migration. Large numbers of shorebirds are present ten months of the year, and the total number is probably more than one million annually. More than 15 percent of the world population of the Marbled Godwit, as well as large numbers of the Western Sandpiper and Dunlin, winter at the site.

▸ Designation: International importance in the Western Hemisphere Shorebird Reserve Network.

▸ Location: At Eureka in Humboldt County.

▸ Size: More than 40,000 acres; Arcata Marsh is 174 acres and Humboldt Bay National Wildlife Refuge is 3,000 acres.

▸ Ownership: Fish and Wildlife Service, City of Arcata, private.

▸ Habitats: Mudflats; eelgrass beds; diked seasonal wetlands; sand spits; uplands; and salt, brackish, and freshwater marshes.

▸ Land Use: Commercial fishing and shellfishing, recreation, logging, cattle grazing; there is a deepwater port at Eureka.

▶ Site Description: Humboldt Bay is from 0.5 to nearly five miles wide, and 14 miles long, and consists of two shallow tidal basins connected by a relatively narrow shipping channel. Eelgrass beds and extensive mudflats provide habitat for large concentrations of waterbirds and serve as important spawning, nursery, and feeding areas for marine life. Included in this IBA are Humboldt Bay National Wildlife Refuge and Arcata Marsh and Wildlife Sanctuary, the latter a 174-acre restoration project consisting of six freshwater ponds, owned and managed by the city of Arcata.

▶ Birds: Mudflats, salt and freshwater marshes, waterways, and pasturelands provide forage and resting areas for more than 30 species of shorebird. During peaks of spring and fall migration more than 100,000 shorebirds may be present. The "Black" Brant depends on the eelgrass beds in the bay, with up to 30,000 birds occurring at any one time; their numbers are highest during March and April. Thousands of other waterfowl are found during migration and winter. Marbled Godwits and Dunlin are abundant in fall, winter, and spring, and Black Turnstones and Surfbirds are also found on the jetties in those seasons. The Short-billed Dowitcher and Heermann's Gull are common in summer and fall. Among the other species found seasonally are the Band-tailed Pigeon and Allen's Hummingbird, both of which are common spring through fall. The Short-eared Owl is common in winter. An abundant and diverse raptor community (buteos, falcons, harriers, accipiters, and owls) feeds on rodents in pastures and takes avian prey (shorebirds and passerines).

▶ Conservation Issues: In the nineteenth century much of the bay was diked and 93 percent of the original salt marsh was converted to pasture and urban development. There are several serious conservation problems in the bay. One is mariculture of oysters. Dredging for oysters is extremely detrimental to the eelgrass, which gets dredged up as well, affecting the Brant population. Local oyster culturalists, however, are converting from bottom to off-bottom culture. The effects of off-bottom culture on birds are unknown. There is pressure to develop a major harbor, deepening and widening the channel and destroying the mudflats. There is an increased rate of siltation due to over-logging in the watershed, making the bay shallower and potentially allowing non-native plants to get a foothold. A small patch of cordgrass was detected recently and eliminated. Nearly all of the remaining marsh is dominated by another cordgrass species introduced before 1900. A major siltation after heavy rains recently smothered the eelgrass, and the Brant were forced to move out into fields during late winter. The Arcata Marsh Project, surrounding an abandoned landfill site, has been launched by the city of Arcata as part of its wastewater treatment system, wherein the discharge from a local wastewater treatment plant is routed through a series of restored freshwater marshes before being released into the bay. Two oil spills (in 1997 and 1999) highlight the vulnerability of the bay's ecosystem to pollution. Humboldt Bay National Wildlife Refuge has an acquisition boundary of approximately 10,000 acres.

▶ Visitor Information: Best time to visit is during spring and fall migration. Contact the refuge at 1020 Ranch Road, Loleta, CA 95551, 707-733-5406.

East Park Reservoir (26), California

▶ Highlight: Three large breeding colonies of the Tricolored Blackbird, a restricted range species.

► Location: Colusa County, near Stonyford.

► Size: 51,000 acres.

► Ownership: Bureau of Reclamation.

► Habitats: Marshes, riparian woodland, oak woodland.

► Land Use: Water management, recreation.

► Site Description: Representing a severely diminished natural community, the riparian woodland at East Park Reservoir is of considerable importance to several bird species that depend on such habitat. In fact, it is a hot spot for riparian species in the Sacramento Valley. Another important habitat type for many bird species, blue oak woodland, is also found at the site.

► Birds: The Tricolored Blackbird is abundant, with three breeding colonies found around the reservoir. The area around East Park Reservoir is one of the best sites in the state to observe this species. The California endemic Yellow-billed Magpie also breeds, and the Oak Titmouse is quite common in the riparian and blue oak habitats. The Lawrence's Goldfinch has also been recorded as a breeding species, but in low numbers. The Nuttall's Woodpecker is common and conspicuous in the reservoir's riparian habitats. The area is also used as a stopover point by migrating landbirds.

► Conservation Issues: In 1996, Point Reyes Bird Observatory began monitoring bird populations at the site. Among the recommendations resulting from these studies is that active management may be warranted to help maintain and possibly augment the Tricolored Blackbird population. Another recommendation is that an effort should be made to assist regeneration of oaks critical for species endemic to oak woodlands. These include the Yellow-billed Magpie and Nuttall's Woodpecker.

► Visitor Information: Best time to visit is during the breeding season, from April to June. For more information, contact: East Park Reservoir, P.O. Box 988, Willows, CA 95988, 530-934-7069.

FIRE AND ITS DIFFERING EFFECTS ON COASTAL SCRUB AND SAGEBRUSH

When fires blaze in the West, media coverage always underscores the devastation and the number of acres burned. While not minimizing the impacts on humans and their belongings or the heroic efforts of firefighters, there is always a question as to whether the fire is doing ecological damage or actually benefiting and restoring the habitat and its birdlife.

Whereas some shrub systems require fire to maintain their health, others suffer great damage from fire. Understanding the differences between systems and the details involved is critical to successful management and bird conservation, and how best to interpret news stories about fires.

Chaparral and coastal scrub systems, such as those that stretch from southern California into the Baja California peninsula, are among the habitat types in which fire is a naturally recurring and beneficial force. Conditions maintained by fires are optimal for birds such as the California Thrasher, Wrentit, and California Gnatcatcher. Over time after a fire, vegetation builds up and forms fuel for a new fire. The dry woody material of some species is actually pyrogenic—that is, the plants create conditions that encourage fires that kill their above-ground growth. Their roots survive, and they undergo a burst of growth after each fire. This process of dynamic regeneration creates conditions to which the aforementioned birds and other species are adapted. The longer the period between fires, the greater the buildup of fuel, and thus the more intense the inevitable fire. The people who live in these systems tend to suppress fires, guaranteeing that the fire that eventually hits them will be devastating to their homes and belongings.

In dramatic contrast, sagebrush systems in the Great Basin and elsewhere suffer serious damage as a result of fires. This was not such a problem in the past but is now a serious one due to the presence of cheatgrass, an aggressive invasive species native to the Old World. Cheatgrass becomes established in sage systems after a fire, particularly where overgrazing has already weakened an area's health. The sage grows much more slowly than the cheatgrass but would eventually regain dominance save for one important fact—cheatgrass is also pyrogenic. Early in the growing season it builds up biomass that becomes fuel for a new fire in the summer. With each fire cycle, sage is less and less likely to reestablish itself, and a diverse shrub community turns into a monoculture of cheatgrass. Breaking this cycle is extraordinarily difficult, and the pervasiveness of this problem is responsible for declines in populations of such birds as both species of sage-grouse, Sage Sparrow, and Sage Thrasher.

Shasta-Trinity National Forest (27), California

▶ Highlight: Important site for the "Northern" Spotted Owl, with good numbers of several breeding Green List species.
▶ Location: North-central California, near Redding.
▶ Size: 2.1 million acres, one quarter of which is designated as wilderness.
▶ Ownership: Forest Service.
▶ Habitats: Coniferous forest, oak woodland, and chaparral.
▶ Land Use: Recreation, wildlife conservation, limited timber harvest.
▶ Site Description: Much of the forest is mixed conifer, with Douglas-fir, ponderosa pine, white fir, lodgepole pine, sugar pine, and red fir; at lower elevations there are upper Sonoran foothill woodlands and mixed chaparral habitats. The forest includes 53,000 acres of lakes and wetlands, and 5,500 miles of rivers and streams. Its highest peak, Mount Shasta, rises to 14,162 feet.
▶ Birds: There are 230 pairs of "Northern" Spotted Owls known in the forest, making it an important site for the species. The Hermit Warbler occurs in the western part of the forest. The Nuttall's Woodpecker is common at lower elevations in oak woodlands; the White-headed Woodpecker occurs in the higher, drier pine stands in the eastern part of the forest. The Oak Titmouse is common at lower elevations within oak woods, and the California Thrasher is present in chaparral in low numbers. The Mountain Quail is found in good numbers. The Band-tailed Pigeon and Lewis's Woodpecker are also present. Many waterfowl are also found during migration.
▶ Conservation Issues: Approximately 75 percent of the forest is an old-growth reserve; a relatively small amount of logging is corrected in the rest of the forest. Forest biologists continue survey work to document new territories for the owl while protecting known territories. Forest managers are now looking into the use of prescribed burning to reduce fuel load and catastrophic forest fires.

▸ Visitor Information: Best time to visit is spring through fall. In winter, many parts of the forest are inaccessible. There are campgrounds in the forest and motels at several towns in the area (e.g., Lewiston, McCloud, Weaverville, Dunsmuir, and Mount Shasta). For information, contact the supervisor's office, Shasta-Trinity National Forests, 2400 Washington Avenue, Redding, CA 96001, 530-242-2242.

6. Boreal Taiga Plains

The Boreal Taiga Plains is the first of three BCRs that occur only in Canada. We provide a very brief description of each of these three boreal regions. BCR 6 extends south to the Prairies and east to central Manitoba. This area is dominated by the Mackenzie River and its tributaries. Black spruce is a dominant species in the open forests of the north, while warmer, better-drained southern areas support mixed forests, including the Aspen Parklands on the southern fringe. The seasonally waterlogged landscape is breeding habitat for the Whooping Crane and Wilson's Phalarope, while Great Gray Owls haunt the forests.

7. Taiga Shield and Hudson Plains

The Taiga Shield and Hudson Plains is perhaps the largest wetland complex in the world. Dense sedge-moss-lichen groundcover is interspersed with open woodlands of black spruce and tamarack on drier sites. Representative birds are Rock and Willow Ptarmigan, Black Scoter, Northern Shrike, and Blackpoll Warbler.

8. Boreal Softwood Shield

The last strictly Canadian area is the Boreal Softwood Shield, which stretches all the way from Saskatchewan to the Atlantic Ocean. It is covered by a closed stand of coniferous forest that becomes more mixed with broad-leaved species such as white birch and balsam poplar in southern transition zones. Wetland birds here include the Purple Sandpiper and Yellow Rail, while forests provide habitat for the Yellow-bellied Flycatcher, Boreal Owl, and a large suite of breeding warblers.

9. Great Basin

T his large and complex region includes the Northern Basin and Range, the Columbia Plateau, and the eastern slope of the Cascade Mountains. This area is dry due to its position in the rain shadow of the Cascades and Sierra Nevada. Grassland, sagebrush, and other xeric shrubs dominate the flats and lowlands, with piñon-juniper woodlands and open ponderosa pine forests on higher slopes. Lodgepole pine and subalpine fir forests occur at higher elevations on north-facing slopes. Several substantial lowland wetlands are extremely important to shorebirds, including breeding American Avocet, Black-necked Stilt, and Willet, migrating Wilson's Phalarope, and other waterbirds, notably the Eared Grebe. The region is also important for breeding Mountain and Snowy Plovers. Most of the North American breeding populations of the White-faced Ibis and California Gulls nest in marshes and lakes scattered across the region. The Great Salt Lake and adjacent marshes host large numbers of American White Pelicans, Cinnamon Teal, Northern Pintails, Redheads, Tundra Swans, and other waterfowl, and many species of migrant shorebirds. The Greater Sage-Grouse, Sage Sparrow, and Brewer's Sparrow are priority land birds of the lowlands, with the White-headed Woodpecker leading the list of characteristic species of the region's pine forests.

Wenatchee National Forest (1), Washington

- ▸ Highlight: One of the top sites for the threatened "Northern" Spotted Owl.
- ▸ Ownership: Forest Service.
- ▸ Location: Wenatchee portion of the Okanogan and Wenatchee National Forest covers an area approximately 40 miles across and 140 miles long, north and east of the town of Wenatchee.
- ▸ Size: 2.5 million acres (Wenatchee portion only).
- ▸ Habitats: Spruce and hemlock forest, Douglas-fir forest, ponderosa pine forest, alpine and subalpine meadows, shrub steppe, lakes, and rivers.
- ▸ Land Use: Recreation, water provision, wildlife conservation, timber, grazing, mining.
- ▸ Site Description: The Wenatchee National Forest portion of the Okanogan and Wenachee National Forest covers a huge area and is representative of the surrounding northern coniferous forests. It stretches from upper Lake Chelan in the north

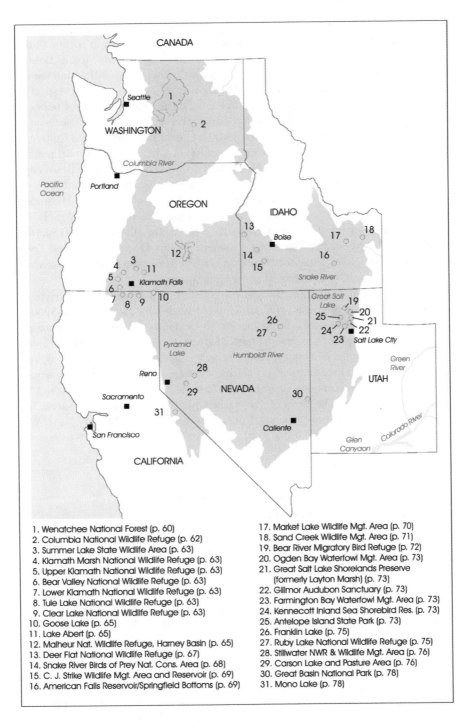

1. Wenatchee National Forest (p. 60)
2. Columbia National Wildlife Refuge (p. 62)
3. Summer Lake State Wildlife Area (p. 63)
4. Klamath Marsh National Wildlife Refuge (p. 63)
5. Upper Klamath National Wildlife Refuge (p. 63)
6. Bear Valley National Wildlife Refuge (p. 63)
7. Lower Klamath National Wildlife Refuge (p. 63)
8. Tule Lake National Wildlife Refuge (p. 63)
9. Clear Lake National Wildlife Refuge (p. 63)
10. Goose Lake (p. 65)
11. Lake Abert (p. 65)
12. Malheur Nat. Wildlife Refuge, Harney Basin (p. 65)
13. Deer Flat National Wildlife Refuge (p. 67)
14. Snake River Birds of Prey Nat. Cons. Area (p. 68)
15. C. J. Strike Wildlife Mgt. Area and Reservoir (p. 69)
16. American Falls Reservoir/Springfield Bottoms (p. 69)

17. Market Lake Wildlife Mgt. Area (p. 70)
18. Sand Creek Wildlife Mgt. Area (p. 71)
19. Bear River Migratory Bird Refuge (p. 72)
20. Ogden Bay Waterfowl Mgt. Area (p. 73)
21. Great Salt Lake Shorelands Preserve
    (formerly Layton Marsh) (p. 73)
22. Gillmor Audubon Sanctuary (p. 73)
23. Farmington Bay Waterfowl Mgt. Area (p. 73)
24. Kennecott Inland Sea Shorebird Res. (p. 73)
25. Antelope Island State Park (p. 73)
26. Franklin Lake (p. 75)
27. Ruby Lake National Wildlife Refuge (p. 75)
28. Stillwater NWR & Wildlife Mgt. Area (p. 76)
29. Carson Lake and Pasture Area (p. 76)
30. Great Basin National Park (p. 78)
31. Mono Lake (p. 78)

to the Yakama Indian Nation in the south, and has five ranger districts. The forest borders North Cascades National Park to the northeast, the Okanogan portion of the Okanogan and Wenatchee National Forest to the north, and Mount Baker–Snoqualmie National Forest to the west. Several wilderness areas fall within the jurisdiction of the forest and are managed jointly with adjacent national forests. The forest contains a great diversity of terrestrial habitats and the large Lake Chelan. It includes several major river systems: the Entiat, Wenatchee, Yakima, Naches, and American. Elevations range from below 1,000 feet near the banks of the Columbia River, to above 10,000 feet on the volcanic summit of Glacier Peak. Annual precipitation, which falls mostly as snow, varies from 10 to 20 inches at the eastern edge of the forest to 60 to 120 inches on the crest of the North Cascades mountains.

▶ Birds: The forest has up to 150 territories of the "Northern" Spotted Owl. Among the other breeding resident species are the White-headed Woodpecker, Rufous Hummingbird, and Black Swift. Other species in the forest include the Northern Goshawk, Blue Grouse, White-tailed Ptarmigan, Northern Pygmy-Owl, Flammulated Owl, Common Poorwill, and Three-toed Woodpecker. The Harlequin Duck and Barrow's Goldeneye have also been confirmed as breeding species.

▶ Conservation Issues: Approximately 40 percent of the forest is designated wilderness and approximately 30 percent is in habitat reserves managed for the "Northern" Spotted Owl and other late-successional forest species. The remainder of the forest is managed for multiple uses, including recreation, timber harvest, grazing, and some mining. Past fire suppression has led to a greater risk of habitat loss due to high intensity wildfires than historically occurred. Present management actions include controlling noxious weeds such as common crupina, dalmatian toadflax, knapweed, and Scotch broom.

▶ Visitor Information: The forest can be reached by paved roads, and there are 2,500 miles of trails and 100 campgrounds. Contact the forest at 215 Melody Lane, Wenatchee, WA 98801, 509-662-4335.

Columbia National Wildlife Refuge (2), Washington

▶ Highlight: More than 100,000 waterfowl winter at the refuge.
▶ Location: Near Othello, in Franklin County.
▶ Size: 23,000 acres.
▶ Ownership: Fish and Wildlife Service.
▶ Habitats: Open water, marshes, sagebrush desert.
▶ Land Use: Hunting, fishing, wildlife observation, and conservation.
▶ Site Description: The refuge forms a biological unit with two Wilderness Recreation Areas, Lava Lake and Goose Lake. All three are important for nesting and wintering waterfowl. This area is part of the Channeled Scablands of the Columbia River Basin, featuring many small- and medium-sized lakes surrounded by sagebrush and grassy uplands and canyons. Irrigated agricultural fields dominate the surrounding landscape.
▶ Birds: This is a very important area for wintering geese and more than 100,000 ducks, mostly Mallards. Several species of ducks nest here also, including the Mallard, Redhead, and Cinnamon Teal. The Long-billed Curlew also nests, and thousands of cranes stop over during migration.

▸ Conservation Issues: The refuge is managed to benefit waterfowl.
▸ Visitor Information: Best time to visit is fall through spring. Contact Columbia National Wildlife Refuge, 735 East Main Street, P.O. Drawer "F," Othello, WA 99344, 509-488-2668.

Summer Lake State Wildlife Area (3), Oregon

▸ Highlight: Thousands of shorebirds stop over during migration.
▸ Designation: Wetland of Regional/International Importance in the Western Hemisphere Shorebird Reserve Network along with Lake Abert and Goose Lake.
▸ Location: Lake County, just south of the town of Summer Lake.
▸ Size: The lake is approximately 12 miles long and three miles wide.
▸ Ownership: Bureau of Land Management, Oregon Department of Fish and Wildlife, private.
▸ Habitats: Open water, alkali flats, marshes, and ponds.
▸ Land Use: Tourism, livestock grazing, hunting.
▸ Site Description: Like Lake Abert, which lies some 20 miles to the southeast, this is a hypersaline-alkaline lake with concentrations of invertebrates such as tabid flies. The lake is broad and shallow and its size varies seasonally. It can almost dry up during droughts.
▸ Birds: Up to 100,000 shorebirds may be present during migration, and counts of 50,000 American Avocets have been recorded in the fall. Tens of thousands of Snow Geese are found during migration, and the Snowy Plover and other shorebirds nest.
▸ Conservation Issues: Water levels in the marshes and ponds are managed principally to benefit waterfowl. There is an extensive series of earthen diversion structures. The Friends of Summer Lake is a local conservation group that believes current water management practices are having a negative effect on the lake and on its critically important brine shrimp population. The lake has been drying up in summer and fall, impacting shorebirds that use it as a stopover during their long migrations.
▸ Visitor Information: Best time in general to visit is during fall migration, in August and September, when most shorebirds are present. Contact: Summer Lake Wildlife Area, 36981 Highway 31, Summer Lake, OR 97640, 541-943-3152.

Klamath Basin National Wildlife Refuge Complex IBAs, Oregon and California

Klamath Marsh National Wildlife Refuge, OR (4), Upper Klamath National Wildlife Refuge, CA (5), Bear Valley National Wildlife Refuge, OR (6), Lower Klamath National Wildlife Refuge, CA (7), Tule Lake National Wildlife Refuge, CA (8), Clear Lake National Wildlife Refuge, CA (9)

▸ Highlight: Important stopover site for most of the waterfowl in the Pacific Flyway.
▸ Location: South-central Oregon and north-central California.
▸ Size: The six refuges in the basin total 192,000 acres.
▸ Ownership: Fish and Wildlife Service, private.
▸ Habitats: Freshwater marshes, lakes, coniferous forest, sagebrush scrub, agricultural lands.

▸ Land Use: Hunting, water management, wildlife conservation, agriculture.

▸ Site Description: The Klamath Basin was once dominated by shallow lakes and freshwater marshes that attracted over six million waterfowl in the fall, and supported abundant populations of other waterbirds during the breeding season. In 1905, the Bureau of Reclamation initiated the Klamath Reclamation Project to convert the lakes and marshes of the Lower Klamath and Tule Lake areas to agricultural lands. As a result, less than 25 percent of the historic wetlands remain. To conserve the basin's remaining wetland habitat, six national wildlife refuges have been established: Lower Klamath (46,900 acres), Tule Lake (39,116 acres), and Clear Lake (46,460 acres) in California; and Bear Valley (4,200 acres), Upper Klamath (15,000 acres), and Klamath Marsh (40,646 acres) in Oregon. The Klamath Basin Refuges consist of a variety of habitats, including freshwater marshes, open water, grassy meadows, coniferous forests, sagebrush and juniper grasslands, agricultural lands, and rocky cliffs and slopes.

▸ Birds: The refuges of the Klamath Basin are a migratory stopover for about three-quarters of the waterfowl using the Pacific Flyway, with concentrations during the peak month of November of over one million birds—among the largest in North America. Up to 45,000 ducks of several species are raised on the refuges each breeding season. Willets breed in the basin, as do Wilson's Phalaropes, Short-eared Owls, and 3,000 pairs of White-faced Ibis. Up to 1,000 Bald Eagles are present in winter, one of the greatest concentrations in the lower 48. Ross's Goose winters, and up to 80 percent of its total world population uses the basin at some time of year. The upland areas at Clear Lake are habitat for the Greater Sage-Grouse, and the Tricolored Blackbird breeds at Lower Klamath and Tule Lake. Klamath Marsh is a consistently used breeding site for the Yellow Rail, with up to 65 individuals detected calling there during the breeding season. It was in this area of south-central Oregon that the Yellow Rail, once thought extirpated as a breeding species from the western United States, was reported by birders in the early 1980s and confirmed by survey work begun in 1988.

▸ Conservation Issues: In an area that receives only ten to 12 inches of rainfall per year, a primary conservation threat is competition for the regional water supply. Agricultural and water programs at the refuges are coordinated under an agreement between the Fish and Wildlife Service and the Bureau of Reclamation. Freshwater marshes, open water, grassy uplands, and croplands are intensively managed to provide feeding, resting, nesting, and brood-rearing habitat for waterfowl and other waterbirds. Approximately 17,000 acres at Tule Lake Refuge are leased by farmers under a program administered by the Bureau of Reclamation, while refuge permit holders farm another 1,900 acres of cereal grain and alfalfa. These crops, together with the waste grain and potatoes from the lease program, are a major food source for migrating and wintering waterfowl. At Bear Valley, past exclusion of fire has led to an excessive buildup of fuel, with a consequent risk of catastrophic fire to Bald Eagle roosting and nesting trees. Selective tree thinning followed by prescribed burning is under way to protect old-growth forest and eagle nesting habitat. The Clear Lake Reservoir is the primary source of water for the agricultural program of the eastern half of the Klamath Basin, with water levels regulated by the Bureau of Reclamation. The Wilderness Society has identified these refuges as being among the 15 most endangered wildlands in the United States and refers to these refuges as "Everglades West."

► Visitor Information: Bear Valley and Clear Lake are closed to the public, except for a limited hunting season. Best times to visit the other refuges are late March through April and late October through November for migrating waterfowl, and late April through June for breeding birds. Peak numbers of the Bald Eagle occur from December through February. For more information, contact: Klamath Basin National Wildlife Refuges Complex, Route 1, Box 74, Tule Lake, CA 96134, 530-667-2231.

Lake Abert (11) and Goose Lake (10), Oregon

► Highlight: Important stopover point for thousands of migrating shorebirds; Lake Abert is probably second only to the Great Salt Lake in importance to migrant Great Basin shorebirds.
► Designation: Wetland of Regional and International Importance in the Western Hemisphere Shorebird Reserve Network along with Summer Lake.
► Location: Lake County, north of Valley Falls.
► Size: Lake Abert is approximaely 15 miles long, and is six miles wide at its widest point.
► Ownership: Most of the land around the shoreline is owned by the Bureau of Land Management, with some private land.
► Habitats: Open water, alkali playa and mudflats, sand and gravel beaches.
► Land Use: Recreation, ranching.
► Site Description: Lake Abert is a relatively deep hypersaline-alkaline lake with large populations of brine shrimp, on which migrant and breeding birds feed.
► Birds: The lake serves as a critical staging and feeding area for large numbers of migratory waterfowl and shorebirds. The alkali flats bordering the lake support one of the state's largest nesting populations of the Snowy Plover. Approximately 100,000 shorebirds use the area during fall migration alone. It is a major stopover point for migrating Wilson's Phalaropes—one of the largest concentrations of this species in the country, and large numbers of American Avocets are seasonally present; these two species make up the greatest proportion of the shorebirds observed here. Goose Lake, which lies mostly in California but extends into Oregon, is an alkaline lake important for breeding Snowy Plovers and migrating shorebirds, though numbers counted there in recent survey work did not match those of either Lake Abert or Summer Lake. The three lakes are within a 55-mile radius, and there is undoubted exchange of birds among the three.
► Conservation Issues: Numbers of birds at this lake and at Summer and Goose Lakes vary from year to year, based on water levels.
► Visitor Information: Best time to visit is during fall migration, during August and September, when most shorebirds are present. Contact: Lakeview District, Bureau of Land Management, 1300 S. G Street, Lakeview, OR 97630, 541-947-2177.

Malheur National Wildlife Refuge, Harney Basin (12), Oregon

► Highlight: As the only significant wetland for miles around, Malheur National Wildlife Refuge attracts not only millions of waterfowl but also serves as an important stopover and breeding area for shorebirds, wading birds, colonial nesting waterbirds, and passerines.

▶ Location: Southwestern Oregon near Burns, in Harney County.

▶ Size: 186,500 acres.

▶ Ownership: Fish and Wildlife Service.

▶ Habitats: Flood-irrigated hay meadows, sloughs, seasonal wetlands, playas, willow-lined rivers, extensive cattail and tule marshes, open water, some grain fields, and shrub steppe.

▶ Land Use: Limited rake-bunch grazing and haying is allowed on the refuge for the purpose of habitat management.

▶ Site Description: Located in the high desert of southeastern Oregon at an elevation of 4,100 feet, Malheur National Wildlife Refuge is a critical link for migratory birds in the Pacific Flyway. In addition to the refuge proper, traditional hay meadow management, and grazing and traditional flood irrigation of meadows on thousands of acres of adjacent private land provides essential habitats for a wide variety of migrating birds. These management practices on private land also provide good breeding habitat for numerous wetland-dependent species.

Malheur National Wildlife Refuge lies within the heart of the Harney Basin. There are 120,000 acres of wetland plus upland and riparian habitats on the refuge. The major features are two large alkali lakes, Malheur and Harney, which at low-water levels are reduced to marshes and shallow channels. Malheur Lake forms the largest freshwater marsh in the lower 48 states. Unfortunately, common carp, an exotic species, has drastically altered the productivity and ecological integrity of wetlands throughout the refuge. For waterfowl, shorebirds, and waterbirds these wetlands are a significant stopover on the route between their wintering grounds to the south and their nesting grounds in eastern Siberia, Alaska, Canada, and the Prairie Potholes.

The marshes and wet meadows found along several river floodplains throughout the Harney Basin attract spectacular numbers of migratory birds of many species. Three major streams flow through the basin and eventually into Malheur and Harney Lakes. The Donner und Blitzen River originates in the Steens Mountains to the southeast, Silver Creek flows from the mountains to the northwest, and the Silvies River flows from the mountains to the north. The significance of the area is hardly limited to the two times per year that migrants stop there. Many species, including waterfowl, wading birds, shorebirds, passerines, hawks, and owls breed throughout the area while other species spend the winter.

▶ Birds: Designated as a bird sanctuary by President Theodore Roosevelt in 1908, Malheur National Wildlife Refuge was originally established to protect a nesting colony of herons, egrets, and ibis from plume hunters. Named by Roger Tory Peterson as one of the top dozen birding hot spots in the United States, this area has many superlatives. The refuge supports up to 20 percent of the world's population of the White-faced Ibis; significant breeding populations of the American White Pelican, Cinnamon Teal, Redhead, and "Greater" Sandhill Crane, Snowy Plover, Long-billed Curlew, Franklin's Gull, and Trumpeter Swan. Up to half of the entire population of the Ross's Goose uses the refuge and surrounding private lands during migration. A significant proportion of the total populations of the Green-winged Teal, American Wigeon, Northern Shoveler, Northern Pintail, Canvasback, and Ruddy Duck use the area as an important migratory stopover. Among the other nesting species are the

Short-eared Owl, Greater Sage-Grouse, and Bobolink. The refuge has one of the highest Breeding Bird Survey counts for the Brewer's Sparrow. Its riparian habitat also supports the highest-known densities of the Willow Flycatcher.

▶ Conservation Issues: On private land the preservation of traditional flood irrigation and management of hay meadows and the increasing possibility of the breakup of traditional family ranches threaten the rural way of life and long-term conservation of wildlife habitat. Without these private lands and current management practices remaining intact, thousands of acres of habitat are at risk.

On the refuge, invasive species (e.g., perennial pepperwood, Canada thistle, common carp) threaten wetland and upland habitats for migratory birds. Wetland habitats on the refuge are managed through a complex and old irrigation system. This system is in need of significant repair and upgrading. Haying and grazing of wet meadows and subsequent flood irrigation on the refuge creates a foraging habitat for many species of migratory birds. Controlled burning on the uplands helps stimulate native grasses, important for many of the grassland/upland nesting species.

Private landowners, the refuge, Ducks Unlimited, Harney Soil and Water Conservation District, Harney Watershed Council, and others are working on the restoration of riparian habitats, wetlands, water quality, fish passage, and screening to benefit migratory birds, native fish species, and other wildlife species.

The role played by private landowners and the refuge in Harney Basin is absolutely critical for the long-term conservation of migratory birds in the Pacific Flyway. The issue is not whether the refuge or private land is more important. Rather, the issue is how can the two work together to protect migratory birds and current lifestyles into the future. For example, refuge data indicate that there are more migratory bird use days on private land than on the refuge during the spring migration. While the white geese, Northern Pintail, and "Lesser" Sandhill Crane may roost on Malheur Lake, they feed in flooded meadows on private land. The highest numbers of nesting Long-billed Curlews in the Harney Basin are on private lands in the Silvies River floodplain. The refuge, however, supports higher numbers of breeding "Greater" Sandhill Cranes and manages more late-season wetland habitat than is typically found on private land.

Refuge staff are actively working with the local community to build bridges and settle a long-standing feud over management of the refuge. The refuge, with several local partners, is proposing to erect permanent interpretive panels along a "private land" tour route for the benefit of visitors to explain the importance of traditional flood irrigation and meadow management to migratory birds. Malheur National Wildlife Refuge provides a good illustration of the constructive relationship that can develop between refuge managers and the surrounding community.

▶ Visitor Information: Spring (late March through late May) and fall (September through October) migrations are good times for a visit. Breeding birds may be seen during June and July, and southward-bound shorebirds turn up in July and August. Be prepared for masses of mosquitoes in the summer. Contact the refuge at 36391 Sodhouse Lane, Princeton, OR 97721, 541-493-2612.

Deer Flat National Wildlife Refuge (13), Idaho

▶ Highlight: A significant waterfowl wintering area in the Pacific Flyway, with winter peaks of 150,000 ducks and 15,000 geese.

▶ Location: Southwest Idaho near Nampa, extending into eastern Oregon.
▶ Size: 11,381 acres.
▶ Ownership: Fish and Wildlife Service, Bureau of Reclamation.
▶ Habitats: Reservoir, riparian woodlands, marsh, mudflats, sagebrush flats.
▶ Land Use: Hunting, fishing, wildlife conservation.
▶ Site Description: The refuge consists of two sections. The larger, the Lake Lowell Sector, at 10,587 acres, is superimposed on a Bureau of Reclamation irrigation project reservoir. Lake Lowell itself is approximately 9,000 acres at maximum water levels and is fed by water out of the Boise River through a canal. Part of the refuge is on the Snake River.
▶ Birds: Lake Lowell is a wintering area for thousands of waterfowl, of which the Mallard is the most abundant species. The Green-winged Teal, Northern Pintail, Common Merganser, and Common Goldeneye also winter in significant numbers. Wintering raptors are attracted by waterfowl concentrations. Many unusual migrants, including species from eastern North America, have been recorded through the years.
▶ Conservation Issues: Annual irrigation drawdown exposes mudflats that attract large numbers of waterfowl and flocks of shorebirds during late summer and early fall. The refuge cooperatively farms 250 acres of cropland for waterfowl. Non-native Russian olive has invaded riparian areas on the refuge.
▶ Visitor Information: Best time to visit is fall through spring. Contact the refuge at 13751 Upper Embankment, Nampa, ID 83686, 208-467-9278.

Snake River Birds of Prey National Conservation Area (14), Idaho

▶ Highlight: One of the densest populations of nesting raptors in North America.
▶ Location: 81 miles of the Snake River in Ada and Owyhee Counties.
▶ Size: 485,832 acres.
▶ Ownership: Bureau of Land Management.
▶ Habitats: Canyon walls ranging up to 600 feet high, shrub-grass steppe, cottonwood gallery forest.
▶ Land Use: Recreation, wildlife conservation.

Prairie Falcon

▶ Site Description: The cliffs along the Snake River provide ledges, cracks, and crevices for nesting raptors while the adjacent shrub-grass steppe north of the river supports dense populations of small mammal prey, in particular the Townsend's ground squirrel and blacktail jackrabbit; as well as the pocket gopher, kangaroo rat, and deer mouse. This unusual combination of ideal nesting habitat close by areas with abundant prey has created a unique situation to benefit raptors.
▶ Birds: Up to 800 pairs of raptors of 15 species nest here, including more than 200 pairs of Prairie Falcons, a significant proportion of the species' entire population.

Among the other raptors common here are Swainson's, Ferruginous (recent counts indicate 55 occupied nests), and Red-tailed Hawks, Golden Eagles, American Kestrels, and several species of owl. In the winter, Rough-legged Hawks are also found here. Sage and Brewer's Sparrows nest in the area. The Snake River is a major migratory route not only for hawks but for waterfowl and landbirds.

▶ Conservation Issues: The ecosystem has been fragmented and degraded by dams, irrigation diversions, levees, riprap, resort development, subdivisions, agricultural development, noxious weed invasion, overgrazing by livestock, and increasing recreational use.

▶ Visitor Information: Best time to visit is March through June, when raptors are nesting. Contact: Bureau of Land Management, Boise Field Office, Lower Snake River District, 3948 Development Avenue, Boise, ID 83705, 208-384-3334.

C. J. Strike Wildlife Management Area and Reservoir (15), Idaho

▶ Highlight: An important wintering site for waterfowl.

▶ Location: Southwest Idaho near Mountain Home.

▶ Size: 20,725 acres, including a 7,500-acre reservoir created by the C.J. Strike Dam.

▶ Ownership: Idaho Power Company, Idaho Department of Fish and Game, the Bureau of Land Management.

▶ Habitats: Reservoir and shoreline.

▶ Land Use: Hunting, fishing.

▶ Site Description: The main feature of significance to birds is the large reservoir and its shoreline. The area is a popular hunting and fishing site.

▶ Birds: An impoundment, it has winter counts of more than 100,000 waterfowl, and, during migration, it hosts many shorebirds and also exceptional numbers of passerines, including counts of 125,000 swallows of four species within a few hours.

▶ Conservation Issues: The area is managed to benefit waterfowl.

▶ Visitor Information: Best time to visit is fall through spring. For more information, contact: Idaho Department of Fish and Game, 600 South Walnut, P.O. Box 25, Boise, ID 83707, 208-334-3700.

American Falls Reservoir/Springfield Bottoms (16), Idaho

▶ Highlight: Staging area for thousands of migrating shorebirds and waterfowl.

▶ Designation: Wetland of Regional Importance in the Western Hemisphere Shorebird Reserve Network.

▶ Location: Bingham County, three miles southeast of Springfield.

▶ Size: 5,000 acres.

▶ Ownership: Bureau of Outdoor Recreation, private.

▶ Habitats: Wetlands, deciduous forest, and mudflats that appear when the reservoir drops in water level.

▶ Land Use: Reservoir, recreation.

▶ Site Description: This area is at the northeastern corner of American Falls Reservoir, a large reservoir of 120 square miles located near the town of American Falls in Power County. The reservoir hosts thousands of ducks and geese during migration and winter and many migrating shorebirds. Springfield Bottoms is particularly important for migrating birds.

▸ Birds: During spring and fall migration, the wetlands are used by large flocks of waterfowl. In March, thousands of ducks (particularly the Northern Pintail) are present, along with Tundra and Trumpeter Swans. The primary interest, however, is the shorebird migration. From July to late fall, during periods when there are extensive mudflats in the area, huge flocks of "peep" sandpipers (mostly Western and Baird's) are often present. Hundreds of Marbled Godwits, Snowy Plovers, Red Knots, and Short-billed Dowitchers are also sometimes recorded.

▸ Conservation Issues: The non-native Russian olive has replaced some of the original vegetation. Outbreaks of botulism occur when water levels in the reservoir remain high. The disease kills large numbers of shorebirds and waterfowl at the reservoir.

▸ Visitor Information: March is the peak of waterfowl migration. April to May and August to October are also good times to see migrating waterfowl and shorebirds. Contact: American Falls Reservoir, Bureau of Reclamation, 214 Broadway Avenue, Boise, ID 83702, 208-678-7206.

Market Lake Wildlife Management Area (17), Idaho

▸ Highlight: A significant stopover site for migrating waterfowl in the spring.
▸ Location: Near Roberts in Jefferson County.
▸ Size: 5,000 acres.
▸ Ownership: Idaho Department of Fish and Game.
▸ Habitats: Approximately 1,700 acres of bulrush and cattail marshes and wetland meadows, surrounded by sagebrush/grassland desert; approximately 0.75 miles of riparian area along the Snake River.
▸ Land Use: Recreation, wildlife management, and conservation.

Sage Sparrow

▸ Site Description: With only 11 inches of annual precipitation, this area has several springs, seeps, and artesian wells supplying water for the wetlands.

▸ Birds: Up to 150,000 ducks of several species and 40,000 Snow Geese use the area during spring migration; it also has significant breeding numbers of White-faced Ibis and Franklin's Gulls plus a few breeding Greater Sage-Grouse, Long-billed Curlews, and Sage Sparrows.

▸ Conservation Issues: There are several invasive non-native weed species infesting the area; these include Canada thistle, musk thistle, Russian knapweed, field bindweed, and whitetop. Biological, mechanical, and chemical methods are used to control and eliminate them. The water output of the springs is only about 25 percent of what it was in the 1970s.

▸ Visitor Information: Best time to visit is March through early July. For more information, contact: Idaho Department of Fish and Game, 600 South Walnut, P.O. Box 25, Boise, ID 83707, 208-334-3700.

Sand Creek Wildlife Management Area (18), Idaho

▸ Highlight: Important area for the Greater Sage-Grouse.

▸ Location: Fremont County in southeastern Idaho, just north of St. Anthony.

▸ Size: 30,000 acres of public land; 25,000 acres of private land are under cooperative management through use-trade agreements.

Lewis's Woodpecker

▸ Ownership: Idaho Department of Fish and Game, private.

▸ Habitats: Sagebrush, grassland.

▸ Land Use: Hunting, fishing, wildlife observation.

▸ Birds: The Greater Sage-Grouse breeds on the site, as does the "Columbian" Sharp tailed Grouse. Sand Creek is the only Wildlife Management Area in Idaho with nesting Trumpeter Swans, though their numbers are low and no more than a few cygnets survive to adulthood each year. Among the other species found are the Lewis's Woodpecker and Brewer's Sparrow.

▸ Conservation Issues: The Greater Sage-Grouse has declined dramatically throughout its range over the past 40 or 50 years, and the populations in Idaho are no exception. In the Sand Creek area, the mean count for males at leks in the 1960s and 1970s was 600, whereas by the 1980s and 1990s, the mean had declined to 200, representing record low numbers. Habitat loss and degradation are the most likely reasons for the decline; much land within the species' winter range has been converted to cropland. Continuing research has provided information and management recommendations that will be implemented to improve habitat in the area. Protecting the birds means protecting not just leks, but nesting and wintering habitat; the birds make annual trips up to 80 miles and use an annual range of nearly 700,000 acres. Prescribed burning to benefit big-game animals is conducted in the area, but research has shown that there is no long-term benefit to the grouse of burning nesting and brood-rearing habitat, and, in fact, burning has negative impacts. The population of the "Columbian" Sharp-tailed Grouse in Sand Creek and the surrounding area had been declining until the initiation of the Conservation Reserve Program in 1985. Since then, the species has expanded into new areas and its numbers are increasing. If the program were to be discontinued, the numbers would likely decline dramatically again. The Wildlife Management Area is managed primarily for big game, including the elk and moose. Management includes not only prescribed burning but the planting of grassland.

▸ Visitor Information: Best time to see the two grouse species is in April and May.

Contact: Sand Creek Wildlife Management Area, Idaho Department of Fish and Game, 758 North 2000 East, St. Anthony, ID 83445, 208-624-7065.

CONSERVING BIRDS OF SAGEBRUSH HABITATS

Sagebrush cover a huge extent of the American Intermountain West, from central Washington, south to northern Arizona, and east to Wyoming, Colorado, and New Mexico. To many urban and suburban dwellers, the perception of sagebrush country is one of a vast wasteland, with little significant life and no real value. This misunderstanding, partially arising from the television westerns of the 1950s and 1960s, is inaccurate from both the standpoint of life and economic value. Approximately 100 bird species and 70 mammal species can be found in sagebrush habitats. Some bird species, such as the Sage Sparrow, Brewer's Sparrow, the Sage Thrasher, and the two species of sage-grouse are "sagebrush obligates," restricted to this habitat during the breeding season or year-round. Sagebrush is a major North American habitat type and, as such, deserving of the attention of conservationists. There is a wide range of sagebrush habitat types, but all good quality stands are characterized by a variety of shrub, grass, and forb species. As with grassland, sagebrush ecology is affected by large and small herbivore grazing, insect infestations, hydrology, climate, non-native plant species such as cheatgrass, and fire.

The chief influence on sagebrush habitat today is cattle grazing. After an extended period of overgrazing—and the resultant decrease in species richness and increase in shrub dominance—ranchers today are increasingly recognizing the importance of proper grazing to maintain system health—for cows and for wildlife.

Bear River Migratory Bird Refuge (19), Utah

▸ Highlight: Thousands of migrating waterbirds.
▸ Location: At the eastern edge of the Great Salt Lake, near Brigham City.
▸ Size: 74,000 acres.
▸ Ownership: Fish and Wildlife Service.
▸ Habitats: Marsh, open water, mudflats.
▸ Land Use: Wildlife conservation.
▸ Site Description: Located at the delta where the freshwater of the Bear River flows into the hypersaline water of the Great Salt Lake, the Bear River Migratory Bird Refuge encompasses a wider continuum of salinity than in a marine estuary.
▸ Birds: The avian highlights are many. Thousands of White-faced Ibis, American Avocets, Black-necked Stilts, Franklin's Gulls, American White Pelicans, and Eared Grebes have been counted on the refuge. The Willet nests here, and hundreds of Marbled Godwits and thousands of other shorebirds pass through during migration. Flocks of migrating swallows of up to 500,000 individuals are observed in the fall, when half a million ducks and geese also concentrate on the refuge's impoundments. As many as 50,000 Tundra Swans can be found in November.
▸ Conservation Issues: The area of the refuge has a varied history. In the early twentieth century, water from the Bear River was diverted for agriculture, drying up the

marshes and leading to outbreaks of avian botulism among the migrating birds, killing millions. Public reaction to these die-offs brought Congress in 1928 to declare the delta a National Wildlife Refuge. In the early 1980s, however, the water level of the Great Salt Lake rose to seven to 11 feet above normal, overtopped dikes, destroying marsh vegetation, and making the refuge inoperable. By 1989, the waters had receded enough so that repair work on the dikes and restoration of the refuge could begin. Salt deposits have now been flushed out enough to reestablish marsh plants. Water levels are now managed to prevent further botulism epidemics at the level of years past, which occur when too many birds are concentrated into too small an area. Nonetheless, outbreaks still continue to kill thousands of birds in late summer and fall, and the refuge is a site for research into how these might be controlled.

Bear River Migratory Bird Refuge is one of the pilot sites in a new conservation partnership developing to connect breeding, migratory stopover, and wintering sites for shorebirds. Called "Linking Communities, Migratory Birds and Wetlands," its goal is to ensure that no stop along the migratory corridor becomes inhospitable to birds. Funded by the North American Free Trade Agreement and sponsored by Wetlands International and the Western Hemisphere Shorebird Reserve Network, the three sites in the pilot project are Chaplin Lakes in Saskatchewan, where many shorebirds breed; Bear River Migratory Bird Refuge; and Marismas Nacionales in Narayit, Mexico, where many shorebirds winter. One strategy behind the project is to show that sustainable ecotourism can act as a powerful incentive to protect a natural resource—in this case the migratory shorebirds and their habitat.

► Visitor Information: The best time to visit is during spring and fall migration. The refuge is open during daylight hours. The 12-mile auto-tour route is open from mid-March to December. Contact the refuge at 58 South 950 West, Brigham City, UT 84302, 435-723-5887.

Great Salt Lake IBAs, Utah

Ogden Bay Waterfowl Management Area (20), Great Salt Lake Shorelands Preserve (formerly Layton Marsh) (21), Gillmor Audubon Sanctuary (22), Farmington Bay Waterfowl Management Area (23), Kennecott Inland Sea Shorebird Reserve (24), Antelope Island State Park (25)

► Highlight: The Great Salt Lake hosts some of the largest flocks of migratory waterbirds and shorebirds in the world.
► Designation: Wetland of Hemispheric Importance in the Western Hemisphere Shorebird Reserve Network.
► Location: North-central Utah, at the easternmost edge of the Great Basin.
► Size: More than 2,000 square miles.
► Ownership: Much of the shoreline is protected by federal and state agencies and The Nature Conservancy.
► Habitats: Open water, shallow marshland.
► Land Use: Recreation, wildlife conservation.
► Principal Threats: Lowering of the water table due to irrigation.
► Site Description: The Great Salt Lake is the outstanding natural feature of the Great Basin and one of the most remarkable natural phenomena in the world. Surrounded by

shallow marshland, it is about the size of the state of Delaware—though its flat basin means that small changes in water level cause large changes in surface area. Having no outlet, and losing water only by evaporation, it has a level of salinity four to eight times that of the ocean. Though too salty to support fish, the lake produces incredible blooms of brine shrimp and brine flies, both rich sources of food for aquatic birds.

Several important sites are associated with Great Salt Lake, including The Nature Conservancy's Great Salt Lake Shorelands Preserve (3,000 acres), the Gillmor Audubon Sanctuary (1,500 acres), Kennecott Utah Copper's Kennecott Inland Sea Shorebird Reserve (2,500 acres), and the state's Farmington Bay Waterfowl Management Area (12,000 acres) and Ogden Bay Waterfowl Management Area (11,000 acres), in addition to five other state Wildlife Management Areas. Another important site is Antelope Island State Park (28,022 acres), which supports species such as Sage and Brewer's Sparrows. Many ducks and shorebirds may be seen from the 7.2-mile causeway leading to the island. One site in particular, Bear River Migratory Bird Refuge, deserves treatment as a site on its own and is described on p. 72.

▸ Birds: As a result of blooms of brine shrimp and brine flies, the lake hosts some of the largest flocks of migratory birds in the world and is critical to several species. Among its many ornithological superlatives are the largest staging concentration area in the world for the Wilson's Phalarope (up to 600,000), the largest assemblage of the Snowy Plover in the world, and the largest breeding population of the White-faced Ibis and California Gull (up to 150,000), plus significant populations of breeding American White Pelicans (up to 20,000) and Eared Grebes. Millions of waterfowl use the lake; it is seasonally important for the Red-necked Phalarope (with an estimated 280,000 in a single day), and heavily used by the American Avocet (250,000), Black-necked Stilt (65,000), Marbled Godwit (30,000), and many other shorebirds.

Fortunately, much of the lake's shoreline habitat used by shorebirds and other waterbirds is protected by state, federal, and nongovernmental refuges. This has proved critical to the Snowy Plover. Since its numbers along the coasts continue to decline from habitat degradation and development, the population on the Great Salt Lake is becoming more and more important to the species' survival. Its breeding population here has been estimated at 10,000. Conditions for the species were ideal in the early 1990s, due to a massive flood event. A creek favored by foraging plovers at Locomotive Springs Waterfowl Management Area had dried up by 1997, apparently due to the lowering of the water table from center-pivot irrigation systems, but many were found on a recently created impoundment on Bureau of Land Management lands. Up to 40,000 American Avocets and 30,000 Black-necked Stilts also breed here.

▸ Conservation Issues: Development of the southern and eastern shores threaten the lake. Plans for a major highway connecting Salt Lake and Davis Counties, called the Legacy Highway, would bisect many of the lake's wetlands and facilitate urban sprawl along its shores. Another threat is the possibility of using the lake as a dumping site for contaminated soil (arsenic and lead) from a SuperFund site. Attempts to stabilize the water level and salinity could severely threaten the lake's ecology. The lake's ecosystem and the effects of alterations is poorly understood, especially as they might affect brine shrimp, brine flies, and, consequently, many shorebirds. The Utah Division of Wildlife Resources is conducting several studies designed to determine the extent of shorebird usage at selected sites around the Great Salt Lake. A study to determine the nesting and foraging habitat requirements of the Snowy Plover around the lake is also being conducted.

▶ Visitor Information: Contact: Antelope Island State Park, 4528 West 1700 South, Syracuse, UT 84075, 801-773-2941.

Franklin Lake (26), Nevada

▶ Highlight: In wet years it is a major stopover site for waterfowl and shorebirds.

▶ Location: Elko County, 65 miles southeast of the city of Elko, adjacent to Ruby Lake National Wildlife Refuge.

▶ Size: 15,400 acres.

▶ Ownership: Nevada Division of Wildlife, The Nature Conservancy, Bureau of Land Management, private.

▶ Habitats: Ephemeral lake and marshes, riparian woodland, alkali playa, shrub steppe, grassland.

▶ Land Use: Wildlife habitat, recreation, hunting, fishing, agriculture.

▶ Site Description: Franklin Lake is a valley playa fed by the Franklin River. It is only five miles from Ruby Lake National Wildlife Refuge. Unlike Ruby Lake, which is spring fed and has several permanent wetlands, Franklin Lake is runoff fed and generally shallow and ephemeral. The size of its marshes varies from year to year, depending on water levels. The state portion is Franklin Lake Wildlife Management Area.

▶ Birds: In wet years Franklin Lake hosts hundreds of thousands of waterfowl. The birds move back and forth from nearby Ruby Lake, and the two sites are really part of the same system. The American Avocet is present during the breeding season and migration, and the "Greater" Sandhill Crane breeds in small numbers and stops by on migration. Forster's, Caspian, and Black Terns use the wetland as foraging and breeding habitat, likely using the relict dace and tadpole shrimp as forage species. The Greater Sage-Grouse can be found on upland portions of the system, and there is a colony of up to 500 Franklin's Gulls. In wet years the American White Pelican has attempted to establish breeding colonies on small islands. Brewer's and Sage Sparrows are common breeding species.

▶ Conservation Issues: Franklin Lake is primarily under private ownership and a small portion is under state ownership. The state of Nevada maintains public access to the southern portion of the area. The Nature Conservancy holds an easement on state property and on a private ranch. Overgrazing has been a problem at the site, and there is some agricultural runoff. The suitability of the lake for waterfowl fluctuates considerably from dry to wet years.

▶ Visitor Information: Public access is limited due to the fact that most of the site is privately owned. Best time to visit is during spring and fall migration. For more information, contact: Nevada Division of Wildlife, 1375 Mountain City Highway, Elko, NV 89801, 715-738-5332.

Ruby Lake National Wildlife Refuge (27), Nevada

▶ Highlight: An important stopover for migrating shorebirds and waterfowl, Ruby Lake also supports the largest nesting population (more than 500 pairs) of the Canvasback west of the Mississippi River outside Alaska, and the highest concentration of that species in North America.

▸ Location: Elko County, approximately 65 miles from the city of Elko.

▸ Size: 37,632 acres.

▸ Ownership: Fish and Wildlife Service.

▸ Land Use: Wildlife conservation, wildlife-oriented activities (including observation, photography, hunting, fishing, and interpretation), research.

▸ Habitats: Freshwater marsh, alkali playa, riparian areas, shrub steppe and grassland, meadow.

▸ Site Description: Located in a high-altitude valley (6,000 feet), this refuge is a vast open-water marsh surrounded by grassland and shrub-steppe communities. It includes 20,000 acres of wetlands with bulrush and grass-covered islands. In an area where average precipitation is only 12 to 13 inches per year, it is a closed water system with more than 160 springs flowing into the wetland. Along with nearby Franklin Lake, this refuge is part of the Ruby Valley Wetlands.

▸ Birds: Large pristine wetlands are extremely rare in the Great Basin, making Ruby Lake National Wildlife Refuge very significant for breeding and migrating birds. There are significant numbers of breeding White-faced Ibis and waterfowl. During migration it is an important stopover for migrating waterfowl and shorebirds. The Long-billed Curlew nests on the refuge, and it has up to 55 wintering individuals and six breeding pairs of Trumpeter Swans. The Brewer's Sparrow is abundant, and the Sage Sparrow is uncommon from spring through fall. Its riparian areas are important to migrating and breeding songbirds. Of special interest are nesting areas for the Canvasback and Redhead in the bulrushes of the South Marsh, a natural depression at the south end of the refuge that has been designated a National Natural Landmark by the National Park Service. This area has the highest Canvasback nesting density anywhere in the world. Among the other waterfowl species nesting in the marsh are the Canada Goose, Gadwall, Lesser Scaup, and Cinnamon and Blue-winged Teal. Shorebirds are abundant during migration only if the shallow playa lakes are flooded. The Greater Sage-Grouse is an uncommon resident.

▸ Conservation Issues: Overgrazing has been a problem in the past. The high density of coyotes on the refuge is impacting both the Sandhill Crane and waterfowl species. Non-native fish species compete with waterfowl for food. Recreational activities have caused disturbance to birds on the refuge in the past, when the lake was heavily used by boaters and water-skiers. As the result of a lawsuit to put wildlife interests above those of motorized recreation, this is now strictly regulated.

▸ Visitor Information: Public access is limited. For further information, contact: Ruby Lake National Wildlife Refuge, HC 60, Box 860, Ruby Valley, NV 89833, 775-779-2237.

Lahontan Valley Wetlands IBAs, Nevada

Stillwater National Wildlife Refuge and Wildlife Management Area (28) and Carson Lake and Pasture Area (29)

▸ Highlight: Major stopover for shorebirds and waterfowl using the Pacific Flyway.

▸ Designation: Wetland of Hemispheric Importance in the Western Hemisphere Shorebird Reserve Network.

▸ Location: Churchill County, near Fallon.

▸ Size: 200,000 acres.

▸ Ownership: Fish and Wildlife Service, Bureau of Reclamation, state lands, private.

▸ Habitats: Salt desert scrub, fresh and alkaline marshes, cottonwood and willow riparian communities.

▸ Land Use: Recreation, wildlife conservation.

▸ Site Description: The Lahontan Valley Wetlands form the most important waterfowl breeding and migratory site in Nevada, and are critical to many species using the Pacific Flyway. At an elevation of close to 4,000 feet, this is a complex of wetlands, the most important of which are Stillwater National Wildlife Refuge and Stillwater Wildlife Management Area (both managed by the Fish and Wildlife Service), and Carson Lake and Pasture Area (managed by the Bureau of Reclamation). Besides their significance to migrating birds, they are an important breeding site for many other species as well. These wetlands sit in a large basin once occupied by Lake Lahontan, sediments from which cover much of the valley floor. The valley's climate is one of the warmest and driest in northern Nevada, with an annual rainfall of only 5.32 inches.

▸ Birds: Depending on water levels, the area is visited by up to 250,000 shorebirds, including the Long-billed Dowitcher, Western and Least Sandpipers, American Avocet, Wilson's Phalarope, and Long-billed Curlew, with peak numbers in the latter part of April, and again in the latter part of August. Nearly 250,000 American Coots have been recorded in the fall from the wetlands. Migration also brings thousands of waterfowl, including the Snow Goose and smaller numbers of Ross's and White-fronted Geese, along with the Gadwall, Northern Pintail, and Green-winged and Cinnamon Teal; the wetlands are particularly critical for the Canvasback, with up to 28,000 individuals recorded, and the Redhead, with up to 29,000 recorded during migration. The area just upstream from the terminus of the Carson River acts as a "migrant trap," particularly during the fall, and large numbers of raptors use the wetlands during the winter.

The wetlands are also important during the breeding season. With up to 10,000 birds, Stillwater National Wildlife Refuge has the world's largest colony of the White-faced Ibis. Up to 5,000 American Avocets remain to breed, as do close to 700 Snowy Plovers.

▸ Conservation Issues: Historically, the Carson River, flowing out of the Sierra Nevada in California, formed on average 150,000 acres of diverse wetlands in the Lahotan Valley. Beginning in the early twentieth century, however, water was diverted from the wetlands for agriculture, so that now the wetlands receive water mainly from irrigation ditches and drains, with increasing agricultural contaminants. Although at present this accounts for about three quarters of the inflow, this percent will gradually be decreased under a program of water rights acquisition, which will allow a blending of fresh water with drain water. The Nevada Division of Wildlife is currently responsible for water management at the Carson Lake wetlands under this program. Though periodic droughts have left less water available for drainage into the wetlands, congressional appropriations and funds from The Nature Conservancy are being used to purchase water rights to alleviate the situation.

▸ Visitor Information: Best time to visit is during spring and fall migration. Contact: Stillwater National Wildlife Refuge, P.O. Box 1236, Fallon, NV 89406-1236, 702-423-5128.

Great Basin National Park (30), Nevada

▶ Highlight: Breeding Black Rosy-Finches and several Green List species.
▶ Location: East-central Nevada, in White Pine County, near Baker.
▶ Size: 77,180 acres.
▶ Ownership: National Park Service.
▶ Habitats: Streams, lakes, sagebrush, piñon-juniper woodland, subalpine forests of limber pine, spruce, and aspen; alpine communities.
▶ Land Use: Hiking, camping, wildlife observation, and conservation.
▶ Site Description: The park includes much of the South Snake Range, with 13 peaks above 11,000 feet, the highest rising to 13,065 feet. Limber and bristlecone pines grow to about 9,500 feet in altitude. The windswept alpine zone includes lichens and dwarf plants, including bristlecone pine, individuals of which can live thousands of years; in fact, one individual was determined to be the world's oldest living thing, at an estimated 4,950 years. The national park is surrounded by other public lands, including Bureau of Land Management lands and the Humboldt National Forest.
▶ Birds: The Black Rosy-Finch, a species found very locally at high elevations within a limited range, can be reliably located within the park. The Greater Sage-Grouse is found in limited numbers in the area, and the Flammulated Owl is a rare resident. The White-throated Swift, Virginia's Warbler, and Brewer's and Sage Sparrows also breed in the park.
▶ Conservation Issues: Cattle grazing on the east side of the park has been phased out, and sheep grazing on the west side may eventually be phased out as well. There is the hope that the Yellow-billed Cuckoo may return as the streamside willows begin to grow back with the removal of cattle. Part of the adjoining land to the park has been set aside in a Bird and Wildlife Sanctuary, under the management of the Nevada Land Conservancy. Work to locate and document sage-grouse leks is underway, and bird inventory studies, building on studies conducted 20 years ago, will be conducted during the coming breeding seasons. The main non-native plant eradication program within the park has focused on spotted knapweed.
▶ Visitor Information: Contact the park at Great Basin National Park, Highway 488, Baker, NV 89311, 775-234-7331.

Mono Lake (31), California

▶ Highlight: The lake is an important stopover for more than two million migrant waterbirds and shorebirds. The lake is critical for large numbers of Eared Grebes, California Gulls, and Wilson's and Red-necked Phalaropes. The lake's tributary streams provide habitat for a variety of nesting birds from the upper canyons down to the lake's shoreline. More than 100 species depend on the lake and its shoreline environs, while more than 325 total species have been recorded within the Mono Basin watershed.
▶ Designation: Site of International Importance in the Western Hemisphere Shorebird Reserve Network, Mono Basin National Forest Scenic Area, Mono Lake Tufa State Reserve, Outstanding National Water Resource.
▶ Location: Near Lee Vining, just east of Yosemite National Park.

► Size: Total acreage for the Mono Basin watershed is 445,000 acres (695 square miles). The lake's surface area is approximately 45,000 acres.

► Ownership: Forest Service, Bureau of Land Management, Los Angeles Department of Water and Power, State Lands Commission (California State Parks), Southern California Edison, Mono County, private.

► Habitats: Lake, stream, marsh, wet meadow, riparian woodland, sagebrush scrub, coniferous forest, piñon-juniper woodland, and alpine habitats.

► Site Description: The Mono Basin is part of the Inyo National Forest. A lake with no outlet, Mono Lake is a hypersaline alkaline lake. Due to its extreme alkalinity and salinity, there are no fish. Nonetheless, the lake is home to a simple and highly productive aquatic ecosystem. Dense populations of brine shrimp and flies draw birds to the lake. The flies and shrimp provide a concentrated and very abundant food supply for six months of the year. There are open marshy areas along the lake's shore. Tufa towers and tufa shoals grace certain shoreline locations. Sagebrush steppe is the dominant vegetation above the lakeshore, while piñon pines dominate the escarpment above Mono's western shore. Along Mono Lake's tributary streams, riparian vegetation composed of pines, willows, cottonwoods, and aspen wind through sagebrush steppe and yield to deltaic lowlands. The Sierra Nevada, young volcanoes, and older volcanic hills surround the lake and define the Mono Basin watershed. Elevations within the basin range from 6,383 feet above sea level to more than 13,000 feet.

► Birds: Mono Lake is an important stopover point for birds on the Pacific Flyway. Among the most numerous migrants are the Eared Grebe and Red-necked and Wilson's Phalaropes; the latter also breeds here in limited numbers. As many as 70,000 Wilson's and 40,000 Red-necked Phalaropes have been estimated on the lake in a single day. For the Wilson's Phalarope, Mono Lake is an essential stopover site where the birds remain for several weeks in the summer, molting and doubling their weight before the 3,000-mile nonstop flight to their South American wintering grounds. Aerial surveys reveal as many as 1.8 million Eared Grebes may be present in the fall, possibly more than half the North American population, doubling or even tripling their weight before departing for wintering grounds at the Salton Sea and Gulf of California.

The lake is important for breeding birds as well. Between 44,000 and 65,000 California Gulls nest on Mono's islands. This California Gull colony is the second largest after the colony at Great Salt Lake. The Snowy Plover nests near Mono Lake, as do the Sage Sparrow, Sage Thrasher, Yellow-headed Blackbird, and American Avocet. Mono Lake's recovering tributary creeks provide riparian habitat for an abundance and diversity of migratory and resident songbirds. The creeks also harbor breeding populations of species that have significantly declined or have been extirpated from other regions of California, including Yellow and Wilson's Warblers, Warbling Vireo, and Willow Flycatcher.

► Conservation Issues: Beginning in 1941, water diversion to Los Angeles withered Mono Lake's tributary streams, and eventually threatened the lake's entire ecosystem and habitat for countless birds. Birds became a rallying point for the lake's protection, and a difficult legal and environmental struggle ensued from 1978 until 1994. In 1994, the California State Water Resources Control Board issued a decision that mandated the lake rise to a specifically managed level between its prediversion level of 1941 and its historic low in 1982. This decision, still in effect, will ensure the health of the lake's ecosystem, improve air quality, maintain minimum stream flows, and allow for continued, managed diversions to Los Angeles. The target average management level of 6,392 feet above sea level is not expected to be reached before 2020. Implementation of the 1994 decision and the water board's 1998 restoration order will help restore waterfowl habitat and Mono Lake's damaged tributary streams. Increased recreation pressure and the potential for increased water diversions remain viable issues.

▶ Visitor Information: Best time to visit for most birds is April through September; October is the time for Eared Grebes, and July and August for phalaropes. August to September is best for the fall shorebird migration. Waterfowl viewing is good from August through October. There are two visitor centers in Lee Vining. Contact: Mono Basin National Forest Scenic Area at 760-647-3044; Mono Lake Committee Information Center and Bookstore at 760-647-6595; and Mono Lake Tufa State Reserve at 760-647-6331.

Included in this area are not only the Northern Rocky Mountains and outlying ranges such as the Blue Mountains of eastern Oregon, but also the intermontane Wyoming Basin. The Rockies are dominated by a variety of coniferous forest habitats. Drier areas are dominated by ponderosa pine, with Douglas-fir and lodgepole pine at higher elevations and Engelmann spruce and subalpine fir even higher. More mesic forests to the north and west are dominated by western larch, grand fir, western red cedar, and western hemlock. High-priority forest birds include the Flammulated Owl, Black-backed Woodpecker, Olive-sided Flycatcher, Black Swift, and Blue Grouse. Barrow's Goldeneyes, Harlequin Ducks, and Trumpeter Swans breed on the slopes and in high elevation lakes and streams. The Wyoming Basin and other lower-lying valleys are characterized by sagebrush shrub land and shrub steppe habitat, much of which has been degraded by conversion to other uses, or by the invasion of non-native plants. High-priority birds include the Greater Sage Grouse, Ferruginous Hawk, Brewer's Sparrow, and Sage Thrasher.

Glacier National Park (1), Montana

▶ Highlight: Several Green List birds breed in the park.
▶ Designation: International Biosphere Reserve, World Heritage Site.

Lazuli Bunting

▶ Location: Northwest Montana adjacent to the Canadian border.
▶ Size: 1,013,572 acres.
▶ Ownership: National Park Service.
▶ Habitats: Alpine tundra, snow-capped peaks, coniferous forest, lakes, streams.
▶ Land Use: Recreation, wildlife conservation.
▶ Site Description: The park includes a range of high-elevation habitats, rising to 10,466 feet at Mount Cleveland. There are 650 lakes, several glaciers, and numerous mountain streams. Although summer temperature in the valleys can reach 90°F, snow

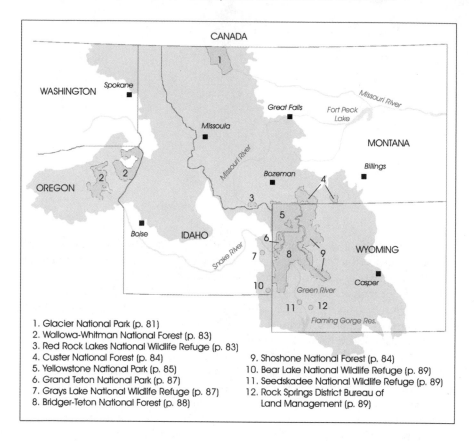

1. Glacier National Park (p. 81)
2. Wallowa-Whitman National Forest (p. 83)
3. Red Rock Lakes National Wildlife Refuge (p. 83)
4. Custer National Forest (p. 84)
5. Yellowstone National Park (p. 85)
6. Grand Teton National Park (p. 87)
7. Grays Lake National Wildlife Refuge (p. 87)
8. Bridger-Teton National Forest (p. 88)

9. Shoshone National Forest (p. 84)
10. Bear Lake National Wildlife Refuge (p. 89)
11. Seedskadee National Wildlife Refuge (p. 89)
12. Rock Springs District Bureau of
    Land Management (p. 89)

can fall at any time of year. Summer rainfall is around two to three inches per month. The largest lake is Lake McDonald, which is ten miles long and 472 feet deep. The forested valleys are covered with coniferous forest dominated by cedar, hemlock, spruce, and lodgepole pine.

▶ Birds: Among the breeding species are the Harlequin Duck, White-tailed Ptarmigan, Short-eared Owl, Gray-crowned Rosy-Finch, Brewer's Sparrow, and Lewis's Woodpecker.

▶ Conservation Issues: In 1932, the park was combined with Alberta's Waterton Lakes National Park to form the Waterton-Glacier International Peace Park. Both parks have been designated as Biosphere Reserves, and together form the Waterton-Glacier World Heritage Site. Strip-mining, logging, and oil and gas development on the Canadian side of the border close to the park's boundaries threaten habitat there. Park officials and conservation groups are working with the Forest Service, the Canadian government, private companies, and the Blackfeet Indian Reservation to protect the park's buffer zone areas. The gray wolf repopulated the park in the 1980s after being extirpated in the 1950s, and the brown bear is also found here. The park is heavily visited, with approximately 1,500,000 visitors per year. There is housing development both inside and around the park

▶ Visitor Information: There is a $10 entry fee. Best time to visit is from spring to fall, as winter snow limits access. There are three visitor centers and 700 miles of trails. For more information on visiting the park, contact Glacier National Park, West Glacier, MT 59936, 406-888-7800.

Wallowa-Whitman National Forest (2), Oregon

▶ Highlight: With among the most diverse avian communities in the Pacific Northwest, this forest include several Green List species.
▶ Location: Northeastern Oregon, near LaGrande.
▶ Size: 2,383,159 acres.
▶ Ownership: Forest Service, private lands.
▶ Habitats: Ponderosa pine forest, riparian deciduous hardwoods, alpine and desert communities.
▶ Land Use: Forestry, grazing, recreation.
▶ Site Description: Consisting of several units in northeastern Oregon, this forest ranges in elevation from 875 feet to 9,845 feet; with a corresponding range in habitats, from desert-like countryside to alpine vegetation. The forest includes a system of high-elevation prairie playas, while the canyons hold excellent examples of dry ponderosa virgin pine forest, although many of the stands have 40- to 60-year-old understoreys of Douglas-fir, as a result of fire control. In the bottoms there are stands of riparian deciduous hardwoods, including quaking aspen, black cottonwood, western water birch, thin-leaf alder, and serviceberry.
▶ Birds: The White-headed Woodpecker and Flammulated Owl are frequently found in the old pine stands. The Northern Goshawk, and Cooper's and Sharp-shinned Hawks nest on the north faces and in the canyons. Prairie and Peregrine Falcons nest on visible rims and cliffs close to the ridgetops. The Swainson's Hawk nests periodically above the playas, and the Ferruginous Hawk has recently nested on the exposed rims. "Columbian" Sharp-tailed Grouse were reintroduced to the forest in 1990, and the Mountain Quail is present and breeding in Devils Gulch, Bear Gulch, and Big Sheep Creek, which frame the playa-topped ridges. In winter, Gray-crowned and Black Rosy-Finches can be found.
▶ Conservation Issues: Management is targeting the restoration of fire to some if not all of the stands of ponderosa pine forest to achieve open parklike, prefire conditions and eliminate the understoreys of Douglas-fir. An increase in off-road vehicles on roads and trails over the last ten years is a problem, leading to wildlife disturbance and mortality, not only direct, but through habitat fragmentation, loss of secure habitat, changes in behavior, and nest failure. Non-approved, user-built trails and cross-country off-road vehicle use can negatively affect soil and water conditions and the quality and condition of the vegetation, while contributing to noxious weed infestations. These types of trails threaten many rare and endangered species in the forest, both plant and animal.
▶ Visitor Information: Best time to visit is during spring and fall. For more information, contact the forest at P.O. Box 907, 1550 Dewey Avenue, Baker City, OR 97814, 541-523-1205.

Red Rock Lakes National Wildlife Refuge (3), Montana

▶ Highlight: Historically one of the most important breeding areas for the Trumpeter Swan in North America.

▸ Location: In the Centennial Valley, approximately 45 miles west of Yellowstone National Park.

▸ Size: 42,000 acres.

▸ Ownership: Fish and Wildlife Service; adjacent lands owned by Bureau of Land Management, Forest Service, and private landowners.

▸ Habitats: High-elevation sagebrush-grasslands, wet meadows and wetlands, cool aspen-conifer forests and coniferous forests in the subalpine zone, harsh alpine habitats on the high peaks.

▸ Land Use: Wildlife conservation, recreation.

▸ Site Description: Called the most valuable bird habitat site in the Greater Yellowstone Ecosystem, of which it is a key component, the refuge lies in a large and remote high-elevation valley. It is an outstanding example of an intact, high-elevation lacustrine wetland ecosystem. In addition to the Trumpeter Swan, the high-quality wetlands support diverse breeding bird communities.

▸ Birds: It was here that the Trumpeter Swan was rescued from extirpation. More than 100 live and breed on the refuge and in the Centennial Valley, making this one of the most important nesting areas for the species in the lower 48 states and a crucial site for the production of this species in the tristate area; up to 600 of the birds may be seasonally present. Fall migration is impressive, when Trumpeter and Tundra Swans and tens of thousands of other waterfowl are found on the refuge, along with the Sandhill Crane and occasional Whooping Crane. The Long-billed Curlew and Brewer's Sparrow breed on the refuge, along with a variety of raptors.

▸ Conservation Issues: Though it is a remote area with a long and harsh winter, there is increasing use by visitors, since it is only an hour's drive from the west entrance to Yellowstone National Park. There is a potential threat from development and resource extraction on adjoining private lands. The Trumpeter Swan is extremely sensitive to human activities and development. Only a limited amount of suitable habitat exists in the region for the species' breeding and wintering activities. If these areas suffer human disturbance such as second-home development, or through logging and road building, the birds will abandon these habitats. Winter habitat is particularly critical. In winter, the swans use lakes and streams that have an adequate food supply, and more important, that never freeze over. Only in these limited areas can the swans survive the severe winters. Disturbance by snowmobiles or other recreational activity may cause the swans to die of starvation. These habitats must be protected during the winter if the Trumpeter Swans are to survive in the region.

▸ Visitor Information: The birding season here is short, since the refuge is generally inaccessible until mid-May. Red Rock Lakes usually freezes over by early November. Area roads are often difficult to travel, and secondary roads are all but impassable when wet. Contact the refuge at 27820 Southside Centennial Road, Lima, MT 59739, 406-276-3536.

Beartooth Plateau IBAs, Montana and Wyoming

Custer National Forest, MT (4) and Shoshone National Forest, WY (9)

▸ Highlight: With the largest area of alpine habitat in the lower 48 states, these sites have good breeding populations of the range-limited Black Rosy-Finch.

▶ Location: Custer and Shoshone National Forests straddle the state line just east of Yellowstone National Park.
▶ Size: High elevation islands of habitat are scattered throughout an area of some 1,500 square miles.
▶ Ownership: Forest Service.
▶ Habitats: Alpine tundra.
▶ Land Use: Recreation, wildlife protection.
▶ Site Description: This area of alpine tundra is comprised of exposed rock, rocky outcrops, cliffs, and, during the breeding season, melting snowbanks.
▶ Birds: Part of the Greater Yellowstone Ecosystem, this is one of the best breeding areas for the range-limited Black Rosy-Finch, a species endemic to the United States, which nests only in alpine tundra at a few scattered localities in the Rocky Mountains of six western states, including the Greater Yellowstone area and northern Utah. With elevations over 9,000 feet, these alpine habitats are islands in a sea of coniferous forests, sagebrush scrub, and grassland.
▶ Conservation Issues: Human disturbance is generally low in alpine tundra areas, but vegetation here is sensitive to disturbance, and the total extent of the habitat is small. A principal threat to alpine tundra is global warming, which might cause this habitat type to disappear altogether.
▶ Visitor Information: Best time to visit is from Memorial Day through late August. Contact: Custer National Forest, 1310 Main Street, Billings, MT 59105, 406-657-6200; or Shoshone National Forest, 808 Meadow Lane, Cody, WY 82414, 307-527-6241.

Yellowstone National Park (5), Wyoming, Montana, and Idaho

▶ Highlight: Largest concentration of the Trumpeter Swan, with up to 700 present in the fall.
▶ Designation: World Heritage site.
▶ Location: The park occupies the northwestern-most corner of Wyoming and small areas of adjacent Montana and Idaho.
▶ Size: 2,219,823 acres.
▶ Ownership: National Park Service.
▶ Habitats: Eighty percent is forested (largely with conifers, most dominant being lodgepole pine); 15 percent is subalpine meadow and montane sagebrush grassland, and about five percent is covered with water. There are more than 10,000 thermal features, including over 200 active geysers.
▶ Land Use: Wildlife observation, conservation, recreation.
▶ Site Description: Yellowstone National Park is at the core of what is termed the Greater Yellowstone Ecosystem, representing the largest remaining area of undeveloped land in the lower 48 states. With elevations ranging from 5,282 to 11,358 feet, the park itself is the largest and topographically most varied national park outside Alaska. Established in 1872, it is also the first and oldest national park in the world. An area of dramatic scenery and intense geothermal activity, it represents probably the most intact natural area in the temperate zone of North America and has the largest concentration of free-roaming wildlife south of Alaska and northern Canada, including the elk, moose, bison, and brown bear.

► Birds: Among its avian superlatives are 30 breeding Trumpeter Swans; as many as 700 may occur during fall migration, the largest concentration for that species. The park has one of the most significant American White Pelican breeding colonies in the Northern Rockies (approximately 500 birds), and the only one in the national park system. There are significant numbers of breeding Bald Eagles and Ospreys, one of the highest concentrations of the Great Gray Owl and Barrow's Goldeneye in North America, and one of the highest concentrations of the Peregrine Falcon in the Northern Rockies. The Harlequin Duck, Short-eared Owl, and Brewer's Sparrow are also found in Yellowstone. Three-toed and Black-backed Woodpeckers frequent the burned woodland, of which there are large expanses after the 1988 fires. The range-limited Black Rosy-Finch breeds above the timberline in the park.

► Conservation Issues: Yellowstone has had active wildlife research programs since the 1920s. It is often used by researchers as a control area, since it has been so little modified by humans. However, the primary threats to the park are overuse from tourism, outdoor recreation, and increased development within and bordering the park. Non-native plant and animal species are also potential threats to the integrity of the ecosystem; these include introduced lake trout, a snail from New Zealand, and various non-native plants. Efforts at controlling or eliminating such species are under way. Use of the park and of other sites in the Greater Yellowstone Ecosystem by noisy and polluting snowmobiles continues to be an issue.

► Visitor Information: Early June to early July are best for breeding birds; mid-August to late October for fall migration. In winter, most roads are closed to vehicular traffic. Contact the park at P.O. Box 168, Yellowstone National Park, WY 82190, 307-344-7381.

FOREST FIRES AND BIRDS

Fire is a natural and necessary force in many forested ecosystems, often creating habitat conditions important or necessary for the health of many bird populations. The frequency, intensity, and resultant conditions of naturally occurring fires varies greatly among systems, but in virtually all cases these natural characteristics have been altered through human-induced changes. Management of these systems must be sensitive to the need to mimic these earlier conditions.

Several systems depend on frequent (every three to seven years) and low-intensity ground fires, including longleaf pine on the Southeastern Coastal Plain and ponderosa pine in the mountainous West.

These fires perpetuate dominance of these trees and maintain open understoreys by eliminating woody growth, particularly other trees more susceptible to fire damage as seedlings. Fire-maintained longleaf creates optimal conditions for the Red-cockaded Woodpecker, Bachman's Sparrow, and Brown-headed Nuthatch, with species such as the Flammulated Owl and White-headed Woodpecker thriving in fire-maintained ponderosa. Extended periods of fire suppression allow species such as loblolly pine and hardwoods to gain dominance in the Southeast and Douglas-fir in the West, all resulting in deterioration of conditions for the above-mentioned high-priority birds.

Other systems and birds rely on less frequent and much more intense fires that often result in complete replacement of aboveground plant matter. Such fires in jack pine systems in Michigan are necessary to create breeding conditions for the Kirtland's Warbler. Aspen groves optimal for the Red-naped Sapsucker in the West also often depend on crown-replacement fires. A few species such as Three-toed and Black-backed Woodpeckers specialize in immediate postfire conditions.

There is clearly some damage done by fires to nesting and adult birds. On an individual basis, many birds will nest again after fires, particularly fires that are of low intensity. In any case, the long-term benefit to the systems greatly exceeds any short-term losses.

Managers must be sensitive to the potential damage to humans and their possessions from smoke and fire, but must work to retain the capacity for careful use of fire as a necessary tool for maintenance of ecosystem health.

Grand Teton National Park (6), Wyoming

▶ Highlight: Greater Sage-Grouse leks are found in the park, and the Black Rosy-Finch breeds in the alpine tundra.
▶ Location: Northwestern Wyoming, just south of Yellowstone National Park.
▶ Size: 309,994 acres.
▶ Ownership: National Park Service.
▶ Habitats: Sagebrush flats, coniferous forests, riparian wetlands, alpine tundra.
▶ Land Use: Tourism, wildlife protection.
▶ Site Description: The most widespread habitat type in the park are sagebrush flats, but other habitats vary from riparian, to lodgepole pine and spruce forests, to subalpine meadows and alpine stone fields. The park is part of the Greater Yellowstone Ecosystem.
▶ Birds: The Greater Sage-Grouse occurs in sage-covered valley bottoms in the park. The Trumpeter Swan, the Brewer's Sparrow, and the range-limited Black Rosy-Finch also occur.
▶ Conservation Issues: Though well-protected, the park receives heavy use by visitors; it is near major ski areas, and there is increasing development outside the park borders.
▶ Visitor Information: A good place to view Greater Sage-Grouse in the spring is north of Jackson in the sage-covered valley bottoms of the park. One of the leks in the park can be visited through a tour run by Grand Teton National Park naturalists. Contact the park at P.O. Drawer 170, Moose, WY 83012, 307-739-3300.

Grays Lake National Wildlife Refuge (7), Idaho

▶ Highlight: This refuge has the largest colony of Franklin's Gulls in the intermountain West, in addition to a large colony of the White-faced Ibis and the world's largest breeding population of the "Greater" Sandhill Crane.
▶ Size: 18,300 acres.
▶ Location: Near Wayan, in Caribou and Bonneville Counties.
▶ Ownership: Fish and Wildlife Service.
▶ Habitats: Bulrush marsh, wet meadow, aspen, willow, and mountain brush.
▶ Land Use: Wildlife observation, conservation.

▸ Site Description: At an elevation of 6,400 feet, Grays Lake is actually a large, shallow marsh with very little open water; it is the largest bulrush marsh in North America.
▸ Birds: With up to 40,000 birds, the refuge supports the largest breeding colony of the Franklin's Gull in the intermountain West, in addition to up to 2,000 pairs of the White-face Ibis and concentrations of other species, including up to 11 pairs of Trumpeter Swans. The Long-billed Curlew and Brewer's Sparrow are common breeding species. The refuge also has the world's largest breeding concentration of "Greater" Sandhill Cranes (150 to 225 pairs). It was the site chosen for the failed experiment to establish a breeding population of the Whooping Crane.
▸ Conservation Issues: Introduced noxious weeds are a problem. There is a complicated pattern of ownership, with many inholdings and hence conflicting interests. Diversion of water for irrigation and renewed interest in mining for gold on nearby national forest lands, with attendant water-quality concerns, are also potential problems.
▸ Visitor Information: There is no access to the refuge from April 1 through early October; there is a loop road from which birds may be seen by using a spotting scope. Contact the refuge at 74 Grays Lake Road, Wayan, ID 83285, 208-574-2755.

Bridger-Teton National Forest (8), Wyoming

▸ Highlight: The Trumpeter Swan is found on the more remote lakes in the forest.
▸ Location: Western Wyoming, adjoining Grand Teton and Yellowstone National Parks.
▸ Size: 3.4 million acres in several units.
▸ Ownership: Forest Service, private.
▸ Habitats: Coniferous forest, saltbrush-sagebrush, riparian forest.
▸ Land Use: Timber harvest, grazing, hunting.
▸ Site Description: Bridger-Teton National Forest in western Wyoming is the second-largest national forest outside Alaska. From within the forest spring the headwaters of the Green, Snake, and Yellowstone Rivers. Some units of the forest are part of the Greater Yellowstone Ecosystem, the largest remaining area of undeveloped lands in the conterminous United States. Another significant part of the forest is in the Wind River Range.
▸ Birds: The Boreal Owl, Great Gray Owl, Northern Goshawk, and Three-toed Woodpecker, all Forest Service Intermountain Region sensitive bird species, are found in forested areas. Trumpeter Swans can be viewed at several of the larger lakes with no recreation developments. Whooping Cranes are recorded occasionally during migration. The Greater Sage-Grouse also occurs as does Brewer's Sparrow. The range-limited Black Rosy-Finch breeds above the timberline in both the Greater Yellowstone and Wind River parts of the forest.
▸ Conservation Issues: The forest has more than 1.2 million acres of dedicated wilderness. Recreational development, now on the increase, can cause sensitive species such as the Trumpeter Swan to abandon an area.
▸ Visitor Information: Best time to visit is late May to early September. Contact the forest at P.O. Box 1888, Jackson, WY 83001, 307-739-5500.

Bear Lake National Wildlife Refuge (10), Idaho

▶ Highlight: Large colonies of the White-faced Ibis and Franklin's Gull.

▶ Location: Near Paris, in Bear Lake County.

▶ Size: 18,000 acres.

▶ Ownership: Fish and Wildlife Service.

▶ Habitats: Marshes, mudflats, grassy meadows, willow thickets, and sagebrush foothills.

▶ Land Use: Recreation, wildlife conservation.

▶ Site Description: At about 6,000 feet, the refuge is largely a bulrush and cattail swamp, with associated sedge, rush, and salt grass meadows. Utah Power and Light owns the right to store water on the refuge, but cooperates with refuge personnel to maximize the benefits of water levels for the birds.

▶ Birds: There is a large colony of the White-faced Ibis (up to 5,000 birds) and one of the Franklin's Gull (up to 13,000 birds) on the refuge. Among the other nesting species are the Redhead, Canvasback, American Avocet and Willet, along with Sage and Brewer's Sparrows.

▶ Conservation Issues: Introduced carp and noxious weeds are management problems; addition of nutrients and sediment from water diversion for agriculture is also a problem.

▶ Visitor Information: Best time to visit is from late April through late June. Contact the refuge at Box 9, 370 Webster Street, Montpelier, ID 83254, 208-847-1757.

Seedskadee National Wildlife Refuge (11) and Rock Springs District Bureau of Land Management, (12) Wyoming

▶ Highlight: The Greater Sage-Grouse is common on Bureau of Land Management lands adjoining the Seedskadee National Wildlife Refuge during breeding. During nonbreeding, the grouse is found commonly on the refuge.

▶ Location: Seedskadee is located on the Green River, near Fontenelle, Sweetwater County.

▶ Size: 26,382 acres for the refuge; Rock Springs District Bureau of Land Management covers some five million acres surrounding the refuge.

▶ Ownership: Fish and Wildlife Service, Bureau of Land Management, private landowners.

▶ Habitats: Riparian vegetation, including narrowleaf cottonwood, coyote willow, Bebb willow, skunkbush sumac, and golden currant. Also wetlands with emergent and submerged aquatic plants, and high desert uplands of sagebrush, greasewood, and wheatgrass. The refuge is completely fenced to exclude livestock grazing, but all lands surrounding the refuge are grazed.

▶ Land Use: Wildlife conservation, hunting, grazing, oil and gas exploration, mining on Bureau of Land Management lands; hunting, fishing, wildlife observation and conservation, environmental interpretation on refuge lands.

▶ Site Description: The refuge is a narrow (1 to 1.5 mile wide) forested riparian corridor on both sides of the Green River for a stretch of 36 miles. The gently sloping floodplain is bounded by rolling shrublands and some cliffs.

▶ Birds: Though there are no leks on the refuge, the Greater Sage-Grouse is common during the nonbreeding season, when they move their broods to the river for food, water, and cover. The leks are on the adjoining Rock Springs District Bureau of Land Management, and on private lands. The refuge is on an important migratory route, and also provides nesting habitat for passerines and waterfowl. The Lewis's Woodpecker and Sage Sparrow occur, and the Mountain Plover is uncommon as a breeding species and during migration. The Gray-crowned Rosy-Finch is found during the winter. The Trumpeter Swan nests and winters on the refuge.

▶ Conservation Issues: Whitetop and other noxious weeds have invaded the riparian habitat. There is little woody-plant regeneration due to changes in river flow as a result of Fontenelle Dam. Beavers and ungulates also browse on regenerating shrubs and trees. The refuge has been fenced to keep out livestock. Some planting of woody vegetation and experimental flooding are planned to help restore riparian communities. Hunting seasons have been established to help control ungulates, and beavers are removed annually. Invasive species are aggressively treated each year.

▶ Visitor Information: The refuge is in a remote area, and the nearest visitor services are a store and service station at Fontenelle, 15 miles away. Some of the gravel roads are seasonally passable. For more information, contact the manager, Seedskadee National Wildlife Refuge, P.O. Box 700, Green River, Wyoming 82935, 307-875-2187. The Rock Springs District of Bureau of Land Management can be contacted at 280 Highway 191, N. Rock Springs, WY 82901, 307-352-0256.

11. Prairie Potholes

The Prairie Pothole Region is a glaciated area of mixed-grass prairie in the west grading toward tallgrass prairie in the east. This is still the most important waterfowl-producing region on the North American continent, despite extensive wetland drainage and tillage of native grasslands. Breeding dabbling duck density may exceed 100 pairs per square mile in some areas during years with favorable wetland conditions. The region comprises the core of the breeding range of most dabbling ducks and several diving duck species, as well as providing critical breeding and migration habitat for more than 200 other birds including priority species such as the Franklin's Gull, Yellow Rail, and Piping Plover. The Baird's Sparrow, Sprague's Pipit, Wilson's Phalarope, Marbled Godwit, and American Avocet are among the many priority non-waterfowl species breeding in this region. Wetland areas also provide key spring migration sites for the Hudsonian Godwit, American Golden-Plover, White-rumped Sandpiper, and Buff-breasted Sandpiper. Continued wetland degradation and fragmentation of remaining grasslands threaten future suitability of the Prairie Pothole region for all of these birds.

Freezeout Lake Wildlife Management Area (1), Montana

▶ Highlight: Important stopover for waterfowl; major breeding colony of the Franklin's Gull.
▶ Location: Just north of Fairfield along U.S. Highway 89.
▶ Size: 12,000 acres.
▶ Ownership: Montana Department of Fish, Wildlife, and Parks.
▶ Habitats: Lake, ponds, surrounding wetlands, shelterbelts, grasslands, agricultural lands.
▶ Land Use: Wildlife observation, hunting, agriculture.
▶ Site Description: Freezeout Lake is a large prairie wetland dominated by a large lake that typically thaws out in March, attracting large numbers of waterfowl. The site is only about 30 miles away from Benton Lake National Wildlife Refuge and has a similar avifauna.
▶ Birds: Up to 18,000 pairs of Franklin's Gulls breed on the refuge. It is a major staging area for the Snow and Ross's Goose, and up to one million waterfowl can be found

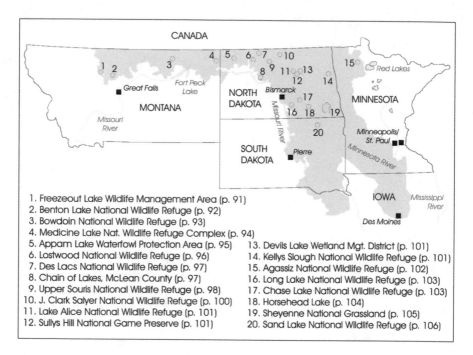

CANADA

Great Falls
Fort Peck Lake
MONTANA
Missouri River

NORTH DAKOTA
Bismarck
Missouri River

SOUTH DAKOTA
Pierre

MINNESOTA
Red Lakes
Minneapolis/ St. Paul
Minnesota River

IOWA
Des Moines
Mississippi River

1. Freezeout Lake Wildlife Management Area (p. 91)
2. Benton Lake National Wildlife Refuge (p. 92)
3. Bowdoin National Wildlife Refuge (p. 93)
4. Medicine Lake Nat. Wildlife Refuge Complex (p. 94)
5. Apparn Lake Waterfowl Protection Area (p. 95)
6. Lostwood National Wildlife Refuge (p. 96)
7. Des Lacs National Wildlife Refuge (p. 97)
8. Chain of Lakes, McLean County (p. 97)
9. Upper Souris National Wildlife Refuge (p. 98)
10. J. Clark Salyer National Wildlife Refuge (p. 100)
11. Lake Alice National Wildlife Refuge (p. 101)
12. Sullys Hill National Game Preserve (p. 101)

13. Devils Lake Wetland Mgt. District (p. 101)
14. Kellys Slough National Wildlife Refuge (p. 101)
15. Agassiz National Wildlife Refuge (p. 102)
16. Long Lake National Wildlife Refuge (p. 103)
17. Chase Lake National Wildlife Refuge (p. 103)
18. Horsehead Lake (p. 104)
19. Sheyenne National Grassland (p. 105)
20. Sand Lake National Wildlife Refuge (p. 106)

during peak migration in spring. Many waterfowl also remain to nest. Thousands of shorebirds stop over during fall migration. Among the nesting species are the American Avocet, Long-billed Curlew, Marbled Godwit, Short-eared Owl, Clay-colored Sparrow, McCown's Longspur, and Lark Bunting.

▶ Conservation Issues: Formerly Freezeout Lake dried up during drought years, becoming an exposed alkali flat. With the development of an irrigation project, there is now water in the lake year-round. Contaminants are associated with this irrigation flow into the lake.

▶ Visitor Information: Best time to visit is spring, particularly mid-March to mid-April, to see concentrations of waterfowl; shorebird viewing in the late summer and fall is excellent. Contact: Freezeout Lake–Great Plains Region, 316 North 26th Street, Billings, MT, 59101, 406-657-6218.

Benton Lake National Wildlife Refuge (2), Montana

▶ Highlight: Important nesting and stopover site for shorebirds and waterfowl; nesting prairie birds.

▶ Designation: Wetland of Regional Importance in the Western Hemisphere Shorebird Reserve Network.

▶ Location: In Cascade and Choteau Counties, north of Great Falls.

▶ Size: 12,383 acres.

▶ Ownership: Fish and Wildlife Service.

▶ Habitats: Marsh, shortgrass prairie.

Chestnut-collared Longspur

▸ Land Use: Wildlife conservation, hunting.
▸ Site Description: A prairie pothole, Benton Lake is actually a 5,800-acre shallow marsh in a closed basin, with surrounding uplands dominated by native shortgrass prairie.
▸ Birds: A colony of up to 25,000 pairs of Franklin's Gulls breed on the refuge, the largest colony of this species in Montana. Thousands of shorebirds occur during migration, including counts of more than 11,500 Long-billed Dowitchers. Up to 100,000 ducks occur during migration, as do several thousand geese, particularly the Snow Goose. The Marbled Godwit and Willet nest on the uplands, as do the Short-eared and Burrowing Owls. The Baird's Sparrow and McCown's Longspur are uncommon breeding species, while the Chestnut-collared Longspur is abundant.
▸ Conservation Issues: Water levels depend on meltwater from the winter snowpack; during most years, additional water from an irrigation project is pumped into the basin. There are contaminants associated with irrigation drainage that end up in the marsh.
▸ Visitor Information: Any time from early spring to late fall is good for a visit. Contact the refuge at 922 Bootlegger Trail, Great Falls, MT 59404, 406-727-7400.

Bowdoin National Wildlife Refuge (3), Montana

▸ Highlight: Important breeding area for grassland birds; important stopover area for waterfowl and shorebirds.
▸ Designation: Wetland of Regional Importance in the Western Hemisphere Shorebird Reserve Network.
▸ Location: Near Malta, Phillips County.
▸ Size: 15,551 acres.
▸ Habitats: Diked impoundments, shortgrass prairie, planted shelterbelts.
▸ Land Use: Wildlife observation, hunting.

Sprague's Pipit

▸ Site Description: Fed by the Milk River, the main feature of the site is Lake Bowdoin, an ancient oxbow and natural basin with several islands supporting colonial nesting birds. Surrounding the lake is shortgrass prairie.
▸ Birds: There are large breeding colonies of the American White Pelican and Franklin's Gull. The Greater Sage-Grouse is an uncommon breeding species. Piping Plovers are some-

times seen during migration and have bred. The American Avocet, Willet, Long-billed Curlew, and Marbled Godwit breed, as do Common and Black Terns; in recent years, Arctic Terns have attempted to breed on the refuge, the only instance in the interior of the lower 48 states in modern times. The Sprague's Pipit and Lark Bunting are common breeding species. The Clay-colored, Brewer's, and Baird's Sparrows, and the McCown's Longspur are uncommon breeding species. Many shorebirds stop over during migration. In September and October, the refuge is a staging area for up to 10,000 Sandhill Cranes. As many as 100,000 waterfowl stop over during fall migration, and thousands of ducks breed on the refuge. A system of dikes and ditches is used to manage water levels.

► Conservation Issues: Historically the basin was filled by spring runoff, which gradually became shallow stagnant water by the end of the summer, leading to outbreaks of botulism and the death of thousands of birds. At present, additional water is diverted from the Milk River, suppressing the conditions that led to these outbreaks.

► Visitor Information: Best times to see migrating waterfowl are late fall and early spring. Contact the refuge at HC65, Box 5700, Malta, MT 59538, 406-654-2863.

Medicine Lake National Wildlife Refuge Complex (4), Montana

► Highlight: Important assemblage of watch-listed grassland and wetland birds, with many species abundant.

► Location: Near the town of Medicine Lake, in the northeastern corner of the state.

► Size: 31,457 acres in two units.

► Ownership: Fish and Wildlife Service.

► Habitats: Grasslands, lake, marshes, shelterbelts, and cropland.

► Site Description: Medicine Lake National Wildlife Refuge Complex lies within the highly productive Prairie Pothole region of the northern Great Plains and has relief typical of the glacial drift prairie: relatively gentle rolling plains with occasional shallow depressions. This is an area of high wetland density, and the resulting prairie-wetland complexes contain a high diversity of wetland types and sizes. The refuge lies in the transition zone between the mixed-grass and shortgrass prairie. The complex includes the three-county Northeast Montana Wetland Management District, with 45 Waterfowl Production Areas encompassing 11,791 acres, and more than 8,500 wetland and 11,000 grassland acres protected under perpetual easements.

Northern Pintail

► Birds: Many grassland species breed on the complex; the four most abundant are the Chestnut-collared Longspur, Grasshopper Sparrow, Savannah Sparrow, and Baird's Sparrow. Among other common breeding species are the Clay-colored Sparrow, Sprague's Pipit, Bobolink, Lark Bunting, Willet, and Marbled Godwit. The Le-Conte's Sparrow and the Nelson's Sharp-tailed Sparrow also breed, as do Short-eared and Burrowing Owls, Yellow Rail, and Lark Sparrow. The refuge is the site of one of the largest American White Pelican rookeries, with approximately 10,000 birds; the colony averages 3,500 nests each year. Other abundant colonial nesting birds on the refuge include the Eared Grebe, Black, Forster's, and Common Terns, Great Blue Herons, and Black-crowned Night Herons. A large colony of Franklin's Gulls nest on nearby Manning Lake (2,000 to 6,000 nests annually), and up to 50,000 of the gulls use the refuge for loafing and foraging during late summer. Up to 250,000 waterfowl may stop over during migration, and many breed, the most abundant of which are the Mallard, Gadwall, Northern Shoveler, Northern Pintail, and Lesser Scaup. Waterfowl breeding success in the complex is among the highest in the Prairie Pothole region. Alkali lakes throughout the complex provide important shorebird migration and breeding habitat. Twelve shorebird species breed, the most commonly the Marbled Godwit, Wilson's Phalarope, Upland Sandpiper, American Avocet, and Willet. A large proportion of the threatened Great Plains population of the Piping Plover breeds on the alkali lakes in the complex. This population was listed as threatened in 1985. As many as 34 pairs have nested on the refuge during low-water years. Plovers nesting in northeast Montana have the highest breeding recruitment of the Great Plains population, largely due to the relatively intact wetland-prairie complexes found there.

▸ Conservation Issues: The biggest threat to conservation in the complex is the conversion of native prairie to agriculture. Coordinated partnerships among federal, state, and local agencies and private organizations (such as The Nature Conservancy and Ducks Unlimited) focus on protection of existing grasslands and wetlands through acquisition of conservation easements. Other private lands extension work include wetland and riparian restoration, grazing systems, and technical assistance to landowners. On refuge grasslands, a combination of prescribed burning, and livestock grazing and rest is used in an effort to mimic the natural disturbance regime that once prevailed. The biggest threat to maintaining quality prairie on the refuge is the invasion by nonnative plants, especially crested wheatgrass, leafy spurge, Canada thistle, and Russian olive. Biological control (e.g., insect predators) is used in the control of some of the non-native plant species. A series of impoundments, water-control structures, and canals are used to optimize habitat for waterbirds. Other management efforts include enhancing nest success by maintaining predator exclosures, and by the planting of tall, dense nesting cover on former croplands.

▸ Visitor Information: Best time to visit is mid-May through early July to see and hear breeding grassland birds. Fall waterbird migration can be spectacular during mid-September through early November. Contact the refuge at 223 North Shore Road, Medicine Lake, MT 59247, 406-789-2305.

Appam Lake Waterfowl Protection Area (5), North Dakota

▸ Highlight: Important breeding site for the Piping Plover.
▸ Location: Near Appam, Williams County, in northwestern North Dakota.
▸ Size: Approximately 600 acres.
▸ Ownership: Fish and Wildlife Service (65 percent), private lands (35 percent).
▸ Habitats: Gravelly beach with adjacent sparsely vegetated uplands.
▸ Land Use: Wildlife conservation.
▸ Site Description: Appam Lake includes several islands and long peninsulas. When

the water level is at its most favorable for the Piping Plover, there are approximately five miles of beach suitable for nesting.

▶ Birds: The breeding population of the Piping Plover fluctuates from approximately ten to 50 pairs, depending on the water level during the nesting season. Appam was among the top five breeding concentrations in the Great Plains during the 1996 international census. Covering less than a square mile, in some years the plover breeding density is unequaled elsewhere. Other common breeding birds on the site include the American Avocet, Willet, Chestnut-collared Longspur, Marbled Godwit, Lark Bunting, Sprague's Pipit, and Baird's Sparrow. Le Conte's and Grasshopper Sparrows are uncommon, and the Nelson's Sharp-tailed Sparrow is occasional.

▶ Conservation Issues: Researchers working at Appam Lake in 1996 and 1997 determined that 21 pairs of Piping Plovers fledged an average of 0.9 young per nest, while eight pairs protected by experimental predator barrier fences fledged an average of 2.3. Coyotes are thought to be the primary predator of plover eggs at Appam; gulls and raptors are generally kept away by the American Avocets that mob them. Though most of Appam Lake is federally owned, owners of adjacent private lands have generously supported the management work.

▶ Visitor Information: Visitors must not disturb nesting plovers. Any open beach is likely to support plover pairs during May through July, and visitors should stay at least 100 yards from these areas. The only reasonable public access is on the southwest part of the Fish and Wildlife Service tract. To reach this, go one mile east of the junction of highways 50 and 85, then turn left (north) on a gravel road and drive 0.4 mile and park. Walk north along the road on the lake edge, or east onto the small grassland area owned by the Fish and Wildlife Service. The hilltop 300 yards east affords a great overlook of the area. Note also that just 1.3 miles north of the junction of highways 50 and 85 there is an access point for birding on Lake Zahl National Wildlife Refuge. For more information on Lake Appam, contact: Crosby Wetland Management District, P.O. Box 148, Crosby, ND, 58730, 701-965-6488.

Lostwood National Wildlife Refuge (6), North Dakota

▶ Highlight: This is the largest contiguous block of Prairie Pothole habitat in federal ownership; it provides excellent habitat for high concentrations of Green List grassland birds.

▶ Location: Northwestern North Dakota, in Burke and Mountrail Counties.

▶ Size: 27,000 acres.

▶ Ownership: Fish and Wildlife Service.

▶ Habitats: Shortgrass and mixed-grass prairie interspersed with pothole wetlands.

▶ Land Use: Wildlife conservation, hunting, grazing.

▶ Site Description: Approximately 70 percent of the refuge is virgin prairie; most wetlands on the refuge were never drained and remain as they were before European settlement.

▶ Birds: Lostwood National Wildlife Refuge is recognized as perhaps the best place in the state to find good numbers of both the Baird's Sparrow and Sprague's Pipit, as well as Clay-colored, Grasshopper, Le Conte's, and Nelson's Sharp-tailed Sparrows, and the Bobolink. Among the other nesting species are the Marbled Godwit, Willet, Upland

Sandpiper, Wilson's Phalarope, Black Tern, and 12 species of ducks, including the Blue-winged Teal, Mallard, Gadwall, Wigeon, and Lesser Scaup, with the Canvasback and Redhead being less abundant. There is a large population of the Sharp-tailed Grouse. Approximately 30 pairs of the threatened Piping Plover breed on the refuge, while the Lark Bunting and Short-eared Owl are of irregular occurrence. During migration the refuge is an important stopover for shorebirds.

▶ Conservation Issues: Drainage for agriculture on private lands has diminished water-dependent wildlife in the area; invasion of woody plants and replacement of native grasses with non-native grasses threatens the prairie. Fire is an important management tool on the refuge to reduce brush and increase grasses and forbs. Cattle grazing is managed to simulate bison grazing. Baird's Sparrows need a combination of fire and grazing to keep down the non-native plants. They need to be able to run around freely under "a forest of grass," which means that too great a buildup of litter prevents the birds from flourishing. A positive link has been demonstrated between the density of the Baird's Sparrow and burning in northwestern North Dakota.

▶ Visitor Information: Best time to see nesting species is mid-May to early July. Contact the refuge at 8315 Highway 8, Kenmare, ND 58746, 701-848-2722.

Des Lacs National Wildlife Refuge (7), North Dakota

▶ Highlight: Important stopover for thousands of waterfowl and Franklin's Gulls.

▶ Location: Along the Des Lacs River in northwestern North Dakota, just south of the Canadian border.

▶ Size: 19,554 acres.

▶ Ownership: Fish and Wildlife Service.

▶ Habitats: Pothole wetlands, mixed-grass prairie, wooded draws.

▶ Land Use: Recreation, wildlife conservation.

▶ Site Description: Des Lacs National Wildlife Refuge is a 28-mile-long riverine refuge with a narrow band of upland covered by mixed-grass prairie and woodland. It has three natural lakes. The flow of water in the river valley is intermittent, with most runoff occurring during the spring snow melt.

▶ Birds: The Le Conte's Sparrow is common in wet years on the refuge. The Baird's Sparrow and Sprague's Pipit occur but are rare. Many ducks, and five species of grebe breed, and the refuge is an important migratory stop for waterfowl, most commonly the Snow Goose, whose numbers may reach half a million in the fall. It is also a late summer staging area for the Franklin's Gull, with more than 100,000 birds in some years.

▶ Conservation Issues: The refuge is managed to benefit waterfowl.

▶ Visitor Information: Best times to visit are May and June and again in late summer through fall. The town of Kenmare hosts a goose festival in October. The refuge can be contacted at P.O. Box 578, Kenmare, ND 58746, 701-385-4046.

Chain of Lakes, McLean County (8), North Dakota

▶ Highlight: Largest breeding concentration of Piping Plover in the United States.

▶ Location: McLean County in west-central North Dakota.

▸ Size: 1,440 acres.
▸ Ownership: The Nature Conservancy, Bureau of Reclamation, private lands.
▸ Habitat: Alkali lakes and mixed-grass prairie.
▸ Land Use: Conservation, recreation, grazing.
▸ Site Description: The most important part of this area, known as The John E. Williams Memorial Preserve, is owned and managed by The Nature Conservancy; it lies in an area of lakes and depressions, typical of the Prairie Pothole region. The alkali chemistry of these lakes limit the growth of most plants along their shores, creating a sparsely vegetated, gravelly beach area ideal for the nesting of the threatened Piping Plover.
▸ Birds: Of the total estimated Great Plains population of the Piping Plover (1,700), approximately 300 to 350 breed in this area, mostly on the Conservancy's preserve. The Baird's Sparrow is found on the site. The American Avocet, Willet, Northern Harrier, and Grasshopper Sparrow also nest on the grasslands.
▸ Conservation Issues: Predation is one of the main threats to the breeding plovers. Among the predators are the Ring-billed Gull, raccoon, skunk, corvids, and possibly the Great Horned Owl. To counteract predators during breeding, The Nature Conservancy has set up electric barrier fences and uses individual nest cages. Seasonal staff are hired to conduct monitoring and management; also, prescribed burning is used to maintain the grassland by preventing the spread of non-native plants, removing dead vegetation, and releasing nutrients into the soil. Prescribed burning is conducted in the spring, before the plovers arrive, or in the fall, after they have left for their wintering grounds on the Gulf of Mexico. Some of the lakes on private lands have also been fenced off to protect nesting plovers. Several years ago, the Bureau of Reclamation flooded two of the lakes, eliminating some of the plover habitat.
▸ Visitor Information: The best time to visit is late May to early July. There is a blind on The Nature Conservancy's preserve for research and monitoring purposes. It is also open to the public, at the discretion of Nature Conservancy staff. There is no public access to the beach areas. For maps and visitor information, contact: The Nature Conservancy, c/o Cross Ranch Nature Preserve, HC 1, Box 112, Hensler, ND 58547, 701-794-8741.

Upper Souris National Wildlife Refuge (9), North Dakota

▸ Highlight: One of a series of critical waterfowl migration sites in the Central Flyway, it hosts up to 350,000 waterfowl during migration.
▸ Location: Northwestern North Dakota, seven miles north of Foxholm.
▸ Size: 32,092 acres.
▸ Ownership: Fish and Wildlife Service.
▸ Habitats: Constructed and natural marshes, native mixed-grass, lowland meadows, constructed lake, wooded river bottomland, brush, and native grass coulees and hills.
▸ Land Use: Wildlife and habitat conservation, fish and wildlife dependent recreation.
▸ Site Description: The refuge, running some 35 miles along the river valley, is one of two national wildlife refuges located on the Souris River, which originates in Saskatchewan, loops into North Dakota, and empties into Manitoba. The refuge in-

cludes the 9,900-acre Lake Darling which was created when the Souris River was dammed in 1935 to provide a year-round source of water for marshes on Upper Souris and on the J. Clark Salyer National Wildlife Refuge located some 110 miles downstream. The lake is designed to hold a two-year supply of water to safeguard marshes downstream against the threat of drought. The dam is also an integral part of the Souris River Flood Control Project which provides 100-year-flood protection for the city of Minot.

▶ Birds: Among the thousands of waterfowl using the refuge seasonally are large numbers of the Lesser Snow Goose, Tundra Swan, Mallard, Northern Pintail, Canvasback, Redhead, Bufflehead, and Ruddy Duck. The American White Pelican occurs commonly but does not breed. Species of conservation concern include the Yellow Rail, Piping Plover, and the Whooping Crane, which stops by occasionally during migration. Grassland species of conservation concern include the Grasshopper Sparrow and Northern Harrier, which are common; the Baird's Sparrow, Sprague's Pipit, LeConte's Sparrow, Nelson's Sharp-tailed Sparrow, Marbled Godwit, and Upland Sandpiper, which are fairly common; and the American Bittern and Chestnut-collared Longspur, which are uncommon. Other species of interest to birders include the breeding Sharp-tailed Grouse and five species of grebes, including the Clark's.

▶ Conservation Issues: Over 100 years of fire suppression, extirpation of the bison, introduction of invasive plants and animals, and wetland drainage have resulted in drastic changes in vegetative succession patterns and water runoff and storage for this region. Dramatic increases in cool-season non-native plants and woody vegetation, and decreases in wetland quantity and quality have altered the prairie landscape forever. These changes have affected birds and other animals dependent on native prairie and wetland habitats. The refuge uses prescribed burning, cattle grazing, haying, biological weed control, invasive woody species removal, and native grass and flower seeding to assist in reversing this habitat deterioration. The Upper Souris Refuge was designated Piping Plover "Critical Habitat" for the northern Great Plains population in 2000. The water levels in approximately 2,000 acres of constructed marshes are managed yearly to provide the nesting, feeding, and resting needs of migratory birds. The water elevation of Lake Darling is managed to provide a minimum of two years of water for marshes in Upper Souris and J. Clark Salyer Refuges. Recent construction of two dams, Rafferty and Alameda, in Saskatchewan is expected to decrease the historical amount of water received and alter water quality and timing of the natural hydrology. Up to 150,000 visitors use the refuge for wildlife observation and photography, walking, environmental education, fishing, and hunting. Lake Darling provides excellent fishing opportunities for more than 100,000 visitors yearly.

▶ Visitor Information: Best time to visit for birding opportunities is April through June and again in September and October. Visitor facilities for birdwatching include the 3.5-mile Prairie Marsh Scenic Drive, four walking trails covering different habitats, two canoe trails on the Souris River, Sharp-tailed Grouse dancing ground blinds in April, a large open-water lake and marsh at the upper end of Lake Darling, educational materials, and some of the most strikingly beautiful scenery of the upper plains region. The Refuge is open from 5 a.m. to 10 p.m. daily. For more information contact: Refuge Manager, Upper Souris National Wildlife Refuge, 17705 212th Avenue NW, Berthold, ND 58718, 701-468-5467, e-mail fw6_rw_upper_souris_nwr@fws.gov.

J. Clark Salyer National Wildlife Refuge (10), North Dakota

▶ Highlight: Hundreds of thousands of breeding and staging waterfowl and shore-birds use this refuge complex, the largest such riparian refuge in the state.

▶ Designation: Wetland of Regional Importance in the Western Hemisphere Shore-bird Reserve Network.

▶ Location: North-central North Dakota, close to the Canadian border.

▶ Size: 58,700 acres.

▶ Ownership: Fish and Wildlife Service, private.

▶ Habitats: Freshwater marshes and ponds, croplands, prairie, grassland, woodland.

▶ Land Use: Refuge and Waterfowl Production Area lands are dedicated to wildlife production and maintenance; other land uses are recreation, agriculture, and oil wells.

▶ Site Description: Running along the Souris River for 50 miles, J. Clark Salyer National Wildlife Refuge is the largest refuge in North Dakota and contains the largest wetland complex of any refuge in the state. The refuge comprises 25,000 acres of wetland, 16,000 acres of prairie, 10,000 acres of grassland, and 1,200 acres of cropland. The refuge complex includes the surrounding privately owned J. Clark Salyer Wetland Management District. The refuge complex also has significant woodlands in the Turtle Mountains portion of the Wetland Management District and in the southern portion of the J. Clark Salyer National Wildlife Refuge. The district contains the largest relatively unfragmented tract (approximately one million acres) of northern mixed-grass prairie in North Dakota. It also contains more than 27,000 acres in 127 publicly owned Waterfowl Production Areas. Easement interests on private land in the district include wetland easements on more than 131,600 wetland acres, grassland easements on more than 11,000 acres, and 8,800 acres in seven "easement refuges."

▶ Birds: This site is representative of the Prairie Pothole habitat, which in total provides habitat for 50 percent of the nesting ducks in the lower 48 states. It is especially important for nesting Gadwall, Mallards, and Blue-winged Teal, in addition to Canada Geese. Waterfowl nest at densities as high as 100 pairs per square mile. The refuge is part of the Central Flyway for staging waterfowl and shorebirds. More than 500,000 waterfowl, including up to 300,000 Snow Geese, can occur there in the fall, and the total use of the complex, including the Wetland Management District, is much higher. As many as 100,000 shorebirds use the area in the course of the year. Other significant species include the Sandhill Crane, Yellow Rail, American White Pelican, and nesting Lark Bunting, Sprague's Pipit, and Le Conte's Sparrow. A colony of 20,000 Franklin's Gulls occurs on the refuge. The woodlands of the Turtle Mountains and the southern portion of J. Clark Salyer National Wildlife Refuge increase overall species diversity. Additional significant species include the Marbled Godwit, Bell's Vireo, Baird's Sparrow, Nelson's Sharp-tailed Sparrow, American Bittern, Willet, Wilson's Phalarope, Black Tern, Black-billed Cuckoo, Red-headed Woodpecker, and Willow Flycatcher.

▶ Conservation Issues: The refuge and management area benefit from the Prairie Pothole Joint Venture under the North American Wetland Management Plan. The joint venture is a public-private partnership designed to improve habitat for birds, primarily nesting waterfowl, while protecting the interests of parties such as private landowners, and state and federal land managers. The joint venture includes Ducks Unlimited, the North Dakota Wetland Trust, the North Dakota Forest Service, the North Dakota Game and Fish Department, county soil conservation districts, and private landowners. As well as developing easements so that land titles can be retained by the original owners while also managing habitat for birds, recent activities include the construction of dikes and water controls to improve habitat in the Benson, Soo Line, and Rubble Masonry sub-impoundments and the Brudvik Waterfowl Production Area by reducing cattails. Approximately 1,150 acres of wetlands have been restored and more than 80 acres have been created, mostly on private land. Several oil wells are in use on the refuge.

▶ Visitor Information: Best times to visit are from April through June and again in September and October. Contact: P.O. Box 66, Upham, ND 58789, 701-768-2548.

Devils Lake Wetland IBAs, North Dakota

Lake Alice National Wildlife Refuge (11), Sullys Hill National Game Preserve (12), Devils Lake Wetland Management District (13), Kellys Slough National Wildlife Refuge (14)

▶ Highlight: Thousands of waterfowl and grassland birds nest there, while thousands of waterfowl pass through during migration.

▶ Location: Parts of eight counties in northeastern North Dakota around the town of Devils Lake.

▶ Size: The complex includes 209 Waterfowl Production Areas totaling 45,000 acres; two National Wildlife Refuges, Lake Alice and Kellys Slough totaling 14,067 acres; Sullys Hill National Game Preserve (1,674 acres); and more than 154,000 acres of easements that protect wetland resources and other wildlife habitat.

▶ Ownership: Fish and Wildlife Service, private.

▶ Habitats: Rolling prairie grasslands and potholes, croplands.

▶ Land Use: Hunting, wildlife observation, and conservation.

▶ Site Description: The area is within the glaciated Prairie Pothole region. Little native prairie remains, most having been farmed at some point. The National Wetlands Inventory has identified 480,165 acres of wetlands within the complex. There is a herd of bison at Sullys Hill National Game Preserve.

▶ Birds: Managed Waterfowl Production Areas provide habitat for ground-nesting waterfowl and passerine species such as Le Conte's, Swamp, Grasshopper, and Clay-colored Sparrows; the Bobolink; and the Western Meadowlark. The Willet, Marbled Godwit, and Upland Sandpiper also nest, while the Black Tern and other marsh birds use managed wetlands extensively. Large concentrations of waterfowl use the area during migration and as an important breeding site; hundreds of thousands of ducks (the Mallard, Gadwall, Blue-winged Teal, Northern Pintail, and Northern Shoveler being the most numerous) use the district. Breeding pairs number in excess of 100 per square mile in portions of the district. Concentrations of the Snow Goose have numbered between 500,000 and one million. White-fronted and Canada Geese, the Sandhill Crane, and the Piping Plover also occur. The world's second largest breeding colony of Franklin's Gull (more than 100,000 pairs) is found on Lake Alice National Wildlife Refuge. Kellys Slough National Wildlife Refuge is regionally known for shorebird concentrations totaling more than 30,000 during migration.

▶ Conservation Issues: Management activities include providing waterfowl and wildlife habitat through prescribed fire; water-level manipulation, restoration, creation; and the enhancement of upland and wetland habitat. Major issues and threats include enforcement of wetland easements to protect the integrity of the prairie wetland community. Hunting is allowed on Waterfowl Production Areas and on some portions of Lake Alice National Wildlife Refuge. The area is benefiting from several North American Wetland Conservation Act grants. Partnering agencies in these grants include Ducks Unlimited, North Dakota Game and Fish Department, and numerous landowners.

▸ Visitor Information: Best time to visit is spring through fall. Devils Lake Wetland Management District may be contacted at P.O. Box 908, Devils Lake, ND 58301, 701-662-8611, e-mail r6rw_dlw@fws.gov.

Agassiz National Wildlife Refuge (15), Minnesota

▸ Highlight: One of the largest colonies of the Franklin's Gull.
▸ Location: Northwestern Minnesota, in Marshall County.
▸ Size: 61,500 acres.
▸ Ownership: Fish and Wildlife Service.
▸ Habitats: Open water and freshwater marshes (40,094 acres), shrubland (10,000 acres), forest (7,000 acres), grassland (4,256 acres), cropland planted for wildlife (150 acres).
▸ Land Use: Wildlife observation, conservation, recreation.
▸ Site Description: Agassiz National Wildlife Refuge is located in the aspen parkland of northwestern Minnesota; this represents the transition between coniferous forest, tallgrass prairie, and the Prairie Pothole region to the west. The moose and gray wolf are found on the refuge and on adjoining state lands.
▸ Birds: The refuge is one of the vital links for migrating waterfowl along the Mississippi Flyway, with up to 40,000 ducks and 14,000 geese during migration, in addition to as many as 1,000 Sandhill Cranes. The main ornithological feature of the refuge, however, is that it consistently hosts one of the world's largest colonies of the Franklin's Gull, with between 25,000 and 50,000 nesting pairs. There are also up to 1,500 Black Terns on the refuge, and between 3,000 and 5,000 nonbreeding American White Pelicans present seasonally. The Le Conte's Sparrow is common, and the Clay-colored Sparrow is abundant during breeding season. Among the other breeding species are the Nelson's Sharp-tailed Sparrow, Bobolink, and Yellow Rail.
▸ Conservation Issues: Water levels are managed with a system of dikes and spillways. There are 19 pools ranging in size from 100 acres to 10,000 acres. In May, the practice has been to draw down some pools to create mudflats for migrating shorebirds. Perhaps the main management problem is that there is pressure from owners of adjoining lands to have the refuge act as a floodwater management impoundment. There are at present no significant problems with non-native invasive plants.
▸ Visitor Information: Best time to visit is during migration in April to May, and September to October. Motel accommodations are available at Grygla and Thief River Falls. Primitive camping sites are available on nearby state wildlife management areas. Camping sites with facilities are available in Middle River, Thief River Falls, Newfolden, and Old Mill State Park. Contact the refuge at 22996 290th Street, NE, Middle River, MN 56737, 218-449-4115.

Long Lake National Wildlife Refuge (16), North Dakota

► Highlight: Important shorebird stopover site during migration, particularly in the fall.

► Designation: Wetland of Regional Importance in the Western Hemisphere Shorebird Reserve Network.

► Location: Burleigh and Kidder Counties, near Moffit.

► Size: 22,300 acres.

► Ownership: Fish and Wildlife Service.

► Habitats: Lake (16,000 acres), rolling prairie, cultivated uplands.

► Land Use: Hunting, fishing, trapping, wildlife observation.

► Site Description: The refuge is part of the Long Lake Wetland Management District, which also includes Florence Lake and Slade National Wildlife Refuges. Long Lake is divided by two dikes allowing manipulation of water levels; fresh ponds and freshwater marshes are found in these areas.

► Birds: The Piping Plover breeds on the refuge, as do the Baird's and Nelson's Sharp-tailed Sparrows, in low numbers. A wide variety of colonial nesting waterbirds nest in isolated areas of emergent vegetation, including the White-faced Ibis, Black-crowned Night-Heron, and Cattle Egret. Up to 35,000 shorebirds use the area annually, including both dowitcher species, the Lesser Yellowlegs, and the American Avocet, which are abundant. Up to 20,000 Sandhill Cranes stop over, and there are occasional Whooping Cranes. An average of 25,000 ducks and 35,000 geese of three species (the Canada, Snow, and White-fronted) are found during fall migration. In late summer there are spectacular congregations of the Franklin's Gull.

► Conservation Issues: Water levels are manipulated to benefit waterfowl; the amount of habitat available to shorebirds depends on water levels, and fluctuates from year to year. Controlled burning is used to enhance marsh and upland vegetation. There have been major outbreaks of avian botulism in the past.

► Visitor Information: Best time to visit is April to May and September to October, for migrating waterfowl and shorebirds. Contact Long Lake National Wildlife Refuge, 12000 353rd Street SE, Moffit, ND 58560, 701-387-4397.

Chase Lake National Wildlife Refuge (17), North Dakota

► Highlight: World's largest breeding colony of American White Pelicans.

► Location: Approximately 15 miles northwest of Medina.

► Size: 4,385 acres of which 4,155 are designated wilderness.

► Ownership: Fish and Wildlife Service.

► Habitats: Lake, grassland, marsh.

► Land Use: Wildlife conservation.

► Site Description: Chase Lake is a highly alkaline lake surrounded by marsh and grassland with prairie potholes. The entire area is surrounded by native prairie grasslands, seeded grasslands, and irrigated cropland.

► Birds: Up to half of all American White Pelicans are hatched at Chase Lake. The pelicans previously nested on two islands, about seven and nine acres in size. However, due to high water levels, the pelicans are now nesting in several new locations on the refuge. Since Chase Lake does not support enough fish or other food sources for the pelicans, the birds feed in surrounding local wetlands. Their primary food is the tiger salamander. In the early 1900s, fewer than 50 birds nested on Chase Lake. In 2000, more than 35,466 breeding pelicans were counted. Much of this increase can be attributed to an abundance of water and an explosion in tiger salamanders, frogs, and fish. The Piping Plover has nested in the past (most recently in 1993), but with higher water levels, there is no suitable habitat for them. The refuge is also an important breeding area for tens of thousands of wetland and grassland birds; among them are the Horned Grebe, Sprague's Pipit, and Clay-colored and Baird's Sparrows.

▸ Conservation Issues: There is a problem with the non-native invasive leafy spurge, the biggest weed problem at many refuges in North Dakota. This European weed, which outcompetes native plants in grassland and is unpalatable to cattle, was first reported in 1909 and now infests nearly one million acres. Programs to combat it include grazing by goats and sheep, chemical control, and a biological control program using species of flea beetles that attack the roots of the plant. There is concern about ground-water levels and about pesticide runoff from irrigated cropland around the refuge. An active banding program is in place, in part to determine wintering patterns of the Chase Lake pelicans. Many American White Pelicans winter in Mississippi and Louisiana.

▸ Visitor Information: The pelicans can be seen from mid-April to late August.

Horsehead Lake (18), North Dakota

▸ Highlight: Important breeding area for many grassland and wetland species, including the Yellow Rail, Baird's Sparrow, and Nelson's Sharp-tailed Sparrow.

▸ Location: Horsehead Lake is in Kidder County, which lies in central North Dakota, about halfway between Bismarck and Jamestown.

▸ Size: The county covers about 1,600 square miles.

▸ Ownership: Predominantly private lands.

▸ Habitats: Grassland, marsh, open water.

▸ Land Use: Predominantly agricultural lands.

▸ Site Description: This extensive area is in the heart of the Prairie Pothole region, consisting of thousands of small wetlands surrounded by grassland. Long Lake National Wildlife Refuge, which also lies partly in Kidder County, is a separate IBA.

▸ Birds: Important staging area for migrating Sandhill Cranes. Important breeding area for many grassland and wetland birds, including the Piping Plover, American Avocet, Wilson's Phalarope, Marbled Godwit, Western and Eared Grebes, Franklin's Gull, Black Tern, Le Conte's, Clay-colored, and Vesper Sparrows, Bobolink, and Lark Bunting. The largest populations of nesting Ferruginous and Swainson's Hawks have been documented in Kidder County. One of the high Breeding Bird Survey counts for the Yellow Rail was also here. In addition to providing the high count of the Marbled Godwit, Baird's Sparrow, and Nelson's Sharp-tailed Sparrow, the area provides the third-highest for the Grasshopper Sparrow and Chestnut-collared Longspur. Kidder County also has large concentrations of nesting ducks, including one million Blue-winged Teal; other breeding ducks include the Canvasback, Redhead, and Lesser Scaup. The Burrowing Owl was once found in the grasslands but has disappeared in the last decade as part of a general range contraction of the species.

▸ Conservation Issues: Changes in agricultural practices, particularly an increase in irrigated potato farms, are detrimental to grassland birds.

▸ Visitor Information: Any time from spring through fall is good for a visit, with June best for seeing the breeding birds.

Sheyenne National Grassland (19), North Dakota

▸ Highlight: As the largest intact tallgrass prairie in the upper Midwest in public ownership, it is an important breeding area for tens of thousands of grassland birds.

▸ Location: Southeastern corner of North Dakota in Richland and Ransom Counties.

▸ Size: 70,000 acres.

▸ Ownership: Forest Service, private.

▸ Habitats: Tallgrass prairie, oak savannah, riparian forest.

▸ Land Use: Grazing, recreation.

▸ Site Description: In a state linked to prairie lands, less than one-tenth of one percent of all tallgrass prairie in North Dakota is still intact, while nationwide, just one percent remains. No other major ecosystem on the North American continent has been so fully altered since European settlement. Today, the Sheyenne National Grassland is a prairie island, a biological oasis in an intensively cultivated region. It offers the last best hope for the restoration of tallgrass prairie in North Dakota. The Sheyenne River is lined by a riparian forest of basswood, American elm, green ash, and bur oak. As elsewhere, American elm has been significantly damaged by Dutch elm disease.

▸ Birds: The state's largest and only viable population of the Greater Prairie-Chicken breeds on the grassland. Numbering fewer than 200 birds, it has declined there in recent years. Its ultimate survival may depend on successful restoration of native vegetation on the grassland. Other species include the Bobolink and the Dickcissel.

▸ Conservation Issues: Once agricultural land abandoned during the Dust Bowl period, the Sheyenne National Grassland now supports a mix of native and non-native grassland species. Besides isolated remnants of native tallgrass, non-native grasses such as brome grass and Kentucky bluegrass thrive. While these species carry some value as forage for cattle—annually stocked at about 10,000 head—they also edge out native plants, and are an impediment to the restoration of tallgrass prairies. Land managers are working to revitalize native grasses by the use of periodic controlled burns. As many as 2,000 acres are burned on the Sheyenne National Grassland each year. Fire not only reinvigorates these grasses but also burns off woody species, such as the non-native Russian olive, which encroaches on tallgrass vegetation in the absence of fire. While it may take generations to restore old-growth forests after timber cutting, restoring prairies can be done much faster. Some prairies can reclaim many of their native qualities in as little as ten years. The effort is hampered, however, by a shortage of funds and personnel to bring restoration about.

One striking feature of the Sheyenne is its undulating sand dune landscape of oak savannah, a rare community type that has now largely vanished from its original range. Within the savannah, leafy spurge is pushing out much of the native vegetation. This European weed was first discovered in North America in Massachusetts in 1827. Unpalatable to cattle, it eventually spread to the Great Plains, where it now infests about 11,000 acres on the Sheyenne National Grassland. An aggressive control program is under way, including the use of herbicides and insects that attack the weed.

▶ Visitor Information: Best time to visit is April through the end of June. The grassland can be contacted at 701 Main Street, P.O. Box 946, Lisbon, ND 58054, 701-683-4342.

Sand Lake National Wildlife Refuge (20), South Dakota

▶ Highlight: World's largest colony of the Franklin's Gull, with close to 50 percent of the global breeding population of the species.

▶ Designation: A Ramsar site.

▶ Location: Brown County, northeastern South Dakota, near Houghton.

▶ Size: 21,498 acres.

▶ Ownership: Fish and Wildlife Service.

▶ Habitats: Open water, marsh, grassland, cropland, riparian woodland.

▶ Land Use: Wildlife observation and conservation, recreation.

▶ Site Description: Located along the James River, the refuge is an isolated riverine landscape in an agricultural setting. It includes 11,000 acres of cattail- and Phragmites-dominated marsh and open water, 7,400 acres of grassland, plus some 200 acres of riparian woodland. There are two major lakes, Sand Lake and Mud Lake.

▶ Birds: The refuge has supported the largest Franklin's Gull nesting colony in the world, with up to 150,000 breeding there; this amounts to approximately 50 percent of the entire population of this species. In addition, many thousands of Franklin's Gulls gather in the fall. Other colonial nesting birds include the White-faced Ibis, and Forster's and Black Terns. There is a large mixed-species heron rookery with up to 6,000 pairs. The Marbled Godwit and Willet nest; as do the Short-eared Owl, Bobolink, and Nelson's Sharp-tailed and Clay-colored Sparrows. Fall migrations of the Snow Goose may reach peaks of 250,000 individuals, whereas the spring migration has been documented at more than 1.2 million. Hundreds of thousands of ducks also stop over on migration. Up to 12,000 American White Pelicans are found on the refuge seasonally. When mudflats are exposed during spring and fall migration, the refuge hosts thousands of shorebirds.

▶ Conservation Issues: The refuge employs water-level manipulation, prescribed burning, reseeding of native grassland, construction of nesting islands, and grazing and haying. Control of Canada thistle is implemented by release of thistle weevils. The most serious potential threat to the refuge is the revival of the Garrison Irrigation Project in North Dakota.

▶ Visitor Information: Best time to visit is spring through fall. Contact the refuge at 39650 Sand Lake Drive, Columbia, SD 57433, 605-885-6320.

12. Boreal Forest Transition

This region is characterized by coniferous and northern hardwood forests, nutrient-poor soils, and numerous clear lakes, bogs, and rivers. All of the world's Kirtland's Warblers breed here, as do the majority of Golden-winged Warblers and Connecticut Warblers. Great Lakes coastal estuaries, rivers, large shallow lakes, and natural wild rice lakes are used by many breeding and migrating waterbirds. The Yellow Rail is among the important wetland species, and islands in the Great Lakes support large colonies of Caspian and Common Terns. Although breeding ducks are sparsely distributed, stable water conditions allow for consistent reproductive success. The Wood Duck, Mallard, American Black Duck, Ring-necked Duck, and Common Goldeneye are common breeding species in this region. Threats to wetland habitat in the Boreal Forest Transition Region include recreational development, cranberry operations, peat harvesting, and drainage.

Chippewa National Forest (1), Minnesota

► Highlight: The forest is an important site for the Golden-winged Warbler, an extremely high priority species, and one that is increasing its numbers here.
► Location: North-central Minnesota, west of Grand Rapids.
► Size: 1.6 million acres are within the forest boundary, of which 666,000 are managed by the Forest Service.
► Ownership: Forest Service, Leech Lake Reservation, state and county, private.
► Habitats: Aspen, birch, pine, balsam fir, with maples on the rolling uplands. There are more than 1,300 lakes, 923 miles of rivers and streams, and 400,000 acres of wetlands.
► Land Use: Timber production, recreation, wildlife conservation.
► Site Description: The forest lies on the southern boreal-northern hardwood border; since the mid-nineteenth century, much of the landscape has been converted from conifers to more deciduous woodland, including aspen and birch. The forest's boundaries overlap with state, county, and private lands as well as with the Leech Lake Reservation.
► Birds: Together with Superior National Forest, the Chippewa provides habitat for a large proportion of the population of neotropical migrants and other forest birds in

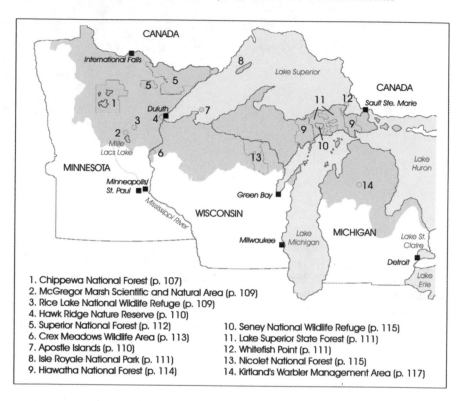

1. Chippewa National Forest (p. 107)
2. McGregor Marsh Scientific and Natural Area (p. 109)
3. Rice Lake National Wildlife Refuge (p. 109)
4. Hawk Ridge Nature Reserve (p. 110)
5. Superior National Forest (p. 112)
6. Crex Meadows Wildlife Area (p. 113)
7. Apostle Islands (p. 110)
8. Isle Royale National Park (p. 111)
9. Hiawatha National Forest (p. 114)
10. Seney National Wildlife Refuge (p. 115)
11. Lake Superior State Forest (p. 111)
12. Whitefish Point (p. 111)
13. Nicolet National Forest (p. 115)
14. Kirtland's Warbler Management Area (p. 117)

Golden-winged Warbler

Minnesota. The Golden-winged Warbler breeds in the Chippewa, where it is relatively common, only slightly less so than on the Nicolet National Forest in Wisconsin. It is now absent from southeastern Minnesota where it formerly bred, and is now most common in the central and north-central regions. It appears to be expanding its range northward. Some Black-throated Blue, Canada, and Connecticut Warblers also breed, as do Nashville and Chestnut-sided Warblers, and Ovenbirds. The Chippewa is also home to the largest breeding population of the Bald Eagle in the lower 48 states. The Yellow Rail and Nelson's Sharp-tailed Sparrow also breed in the wetlands.

▸ Conservation Issues: The forest is a multiple-use area, used for timber extraction. The Golden-winged Warbler benefits from the creation of early successional fields, so it can apparently do well after areas are timbered. Long-term monitoring of bird populations is under way, and 140 40-acre plots have been set up.

▶ Visitor Information: Best time to visit is May to early July, during the breeding season. Contact the forest at 200 Ash Avenue, Cass Lake, MN 56633, 218-335-8600.

McGregor Marsh Scientific and Natural Area (2), Minnesota

▶ Highlight: Important breeding site for the Yellow Rail and other priority species.
▶ Location: Aitkin County, two miles south of McGregor.
▶ Size: 400 acres.
▶ Ownership: Minnesota Department of Natural Resources.
▶ Habitat: Sedge marsh.
▶ Land Use: Conservation, wildlife observation.
▶ Site Description: The marsh is composed of extensive sedge meadows, which lie in the former bed of the glacier-formed Lake Aitkin.
▶ Birds: Though small, this is an important area for the Yellow Rail, with as many as ten pairs nesting. Among the other nesting species are a few Nelson's Sharp-tailed Sparrows and many Le Conte's Sparrows. The Sharp-tailed Grouse is also found.
▶ Conservation Issues: Several small lots were added to the scientific and natural area under the Minnesota Session Laws of 2000. Habitat on the marsh is managed to benefit the Sharp-tailed Grouse.
▶ Visitor Information: Contact the Department of Natural Resources Information Center, 500 Lafayette Road, St. Paul, MN 55155, 651-296-6157.

Rice Lake National Wildlife Refuge (3), Minnesota

▶ Highlight: Major waterfowl stopover during fall migration, particularly for the Ring-necked Duck.
▶ Location: Five miles south of McGregor, in Aitkin County.
▶ Size: 18,000 acres.
▶ Ownership: Fish and Wildlife Service.
▶ Habitats: Deciduous and coniferous forest, open bogs, lakes.
▶ Land Use: Fishing, wildlife observation, hiking.
▶ Site Description: Rice Lake itself is a large, shallow natural lake of 4,500 acres, managed for the production of wild rice and other aquatic vegetation, for the benefit of waterfowl. Native Americans also harvest the wild rice.
▶ Birds: The refuge is an important stopover for waterfowl during fall migration, including flocks of Ring-necked Ducks numbering up to 70,000, with a peak of up to 100,000 representing an important concentration of the species; though average counts of waterfowl are somewhat higher than 100,000, in some years more than a million waterfowl have been counted in the fall. Peaks in the numbers of waterfowl occur in mid-October. The Black Tern and Le Conte's Sparrow breeds, and the Yellow Rail has been heard calling during the breeding season.
▶ Conservation Issues: Water levels are managed to provide optimum conditions for the production of wild rice, an important food source for migrating waterfowl. Peak numbers of waterfowl, particularly dabbling ducks, may result from a poor wild rice crop elsewhere but a good crop at Rice Lake.
▶ Visitor Information: Best times to visit are May and October. For more information, contact the refuge at 36289 State Highway 65, McGregor, MN 55760, 218-768-2402.

NEOTROPICAL MIGRATORY BIRD CONSERVATION ACT

This act was signed into law in 2000, authorizing funds for the protection of migratory birds and their habitats. For 2003, $3 million is available. The act covers North America, Latin America, and the Caribbean, comprising most migratory ranges of U.S. breeding birds. It emphasizes partnerships for on-the-ground projects, with priority given to projects having activities located in important breeding and nonbreeding areas. Approximately 97 percent of the funding must go toward local conservation activities, including community outreach and education, and each federal dollar must be matched by $3 in non-federal contributions. Seventy-five percent of funding is to be spent addressing conservation needs of U.S. birds abroad. The act is administered by the Fish and Wildlife Service. A prime goal is to foster international cooperation for projects to protect neotropical migrant birds, in partnership with conservation groups and academic institutions in Latin America and the Caribbean.

Migrant Concentration IBAs of the Upper Great Lakes, Minnesota, Michigan, and Wisconsin

Hawk Ridge Nature Reserve, MN (4), Apostle Islands, WI (7), Isle Royale National Park, MI (8), Lake Superior State Forest, MI (11), and Whitefish Point, MI (12)

▸ Highlight: Concentration points for migrating songbirds and hawks.
▸ Location: Along the Great Lakes in three states. Individual IBAs are described below.
▸ Ownership: National Park Service, Forest Service, state, and private lands.
▸ Habitats: Northern hardwood and coniferous forest.
▸ Land Use: Recreation, commercial, wildlife observation and conservation.
▸ Site Description: The shorelines of the Great Lakes are important stopover and concentration points for migrant birds. The eastern and western shores of Lake Michigan, for example, are also important migration corridors. Global IBAs in the region are detailed below.
▸ Conservation Issues: Though the Great Lakes themselves suffer from a range of threats including introduced species, shoreline development, pollution, and shipping traffic, the sites covered here are all protected lands. There is logging in Lake Superior State Forest, but it is limited by strict guidelines, and raptor nesting trees are avoided.

Hawk Ridge Nature Reserve (4), Minnesota

This site along Lake Superior in suburban Duluth records thousands of migrant hawks passing over, particularly in the fall, with as many as 60,000 seen in some years. It is owned by the Duluth Audubon Society. There is a festival the second weekend after Labor Day.
▸ Visitor Information: Mid-September is the best time to visit. For more information, see: www.hawkridge.org.

Apostle Islands (7), Wisconsin

Apostle Islands National Lakeshore, at 42,300 acres, incorporates 21 of the 22 islands in this Lake Superior archipelago, along with a 12-mile stretch of mainland shoreline in Bayfield County, Wisconsin. The islands are completely forested with conifer and northern hardwoods. They host thousands of migrating shorebirds and passerines, particularly in the fall, and Black-throated Blue and Canada Warblers breed. The site also recorded the first nesting outside Michigan in many years of a pair of the Great Lakes population of Piping Plovers.

▸ Visitor Information: The headquarters is located one block off Wisconsin Route 13 in Bayfield. For more information, see: www.nps.gov/apis.

Isle Royale National Park (8), Michigan

At 133,782 acres, this island in the northwestern part of Lake Superior is the most isolated national park in the lower 48 states and among the least visited. Travel to the island is possible only from mid-April to October, and it can be reached only by boat or floatplane. Travel on the island itself is limited to the 165 miles of hiking trails. More than 98 percent of the land in Isle Royale is designated wilderness. Isle Royale was designated an International Biosphere Reserve by the United Nations, giving it global scientific and educational significance. Though not well studied, it is known to be important as a stopover for migrant birds, and at least 15 species of warblers nest, including Black-throated Blue and Canada Warblers.

▸ Visitor Information: The National Park Service provides transportation information at: www.nps.gov/isro/getthere.htm

Lake Superior State Forest (11), Michigan

The forest comprises both coniferous trees and northern hardwoods such as oaks and aspens. It provides important habitat for a range of resident and migrant species moving through the Upper Peninsula to and from their breeding grounds to the north in Canada's Boreal Forest

▸ Visitor Information: The Michigan Department of Natural Resources provides information at: http://www.michigan.gov/dnr.

Whitefish Point (12), Michigan

Located on the northeastern-most point of the Upper Peninsula of Michigan and jutting into Lake Superior, this is one of the legendary locations of American migrant-watching. Many raptors, waterfowl, and passerines are recorded during migration. Up to 20,000 raptors and 50,000 waterbirds have been counted, and numbers of the latter in particular are no doubt significantly higher. Migrant bird populations are censused and monitored by the Whitefish Point Bird Observatory located adjacent to the Whitefish Point National Wildlife Refuge. In 2000, The Nature Conservancy and the Observatory, an affiliate of The Michigan Audubon Society, acquired 135 acres with 3,000 feet of shoreline of Lake Superior to be sold to the state's Lake Superior State Forest. The Piping Plover nests in the vicinity, and the acquisition may expand plover habitat. Much of the land on the point is in private ownership.

▸ Visitor Information: The Whitefish Point Bird Observatory provides visitor information at http://www.wpbo.org.

THE GREAT LAKES POPULATION OF PIPING PLOVER

In recent decades, the Piping Plover has declined precipitously. Among its favored breeding habitats are beaches on the Atlantic Coast and the Great Lakes—the very habitat also favored for recreation by an ever-growing human population. And with humans come beachfront development, disturbance, predation by domestic dogs and cats, and even greater numbers of marauding raccoons, foxes, and gulls. All this has taken a toll, and the Piping Plover has ended up on the Endangered Species List. As such, it is an important target of conservation concern.

In this book we name several sites in which it is a component of the avifauna, and in some cases it is the main reason the site is named an IBA at all. Included are some with the greatest breeding populations (Chain of Lakes, North Dakota, Cape Cod and Islands, Massachusetts, barrier islands of Virginia and Maryland) and highest wintering numbers (Padre Island and Bolivar Flats, Texas; and Honeymoon Island State Recreation Area, Florida). Though the sites in this book are perhaps the most critical to the species, that is not to say that other sites—ones with only one or a few breeding pairs—are not important, too.

By way of illustration, of the three populations of the Piping Plover in the United States, we have designated several IBAs for the two most significant of them—the Northern Great Plains and Atlantic Coast populations, both numbering about 1,400 pairs, and both designated as threatened. The population designated officially as endangered is that breeding on the Great Lakes, now reduced to only a small fraction—perhaps five percent—of its presettlement numbers.

Historically, the Great Lakes population of the Piping Plover nested on beaches in all eight Great Lakes states and in Ontario, although the bird probably never numbered more than a few hundred pairs. In recent years the Great Lakes population has consisted only of about 15 to 32 breeding pairs, all in northern Michigan save for one recent nesting in northern Wisconsin. The fact that the species is still around at all is due to state, tribal, federal, and private conservation actions to protect it. This has involved habitat surveys, beach restoration, public education, habitat protection, and protecting nests by using predator exclosure fencing—the same strategies used to protect breeding plovers on the Atlantic Coast. To apply protection to the bird on federal lands, the Fish and Wildlife Service has designated some 35 critical habitat units on the beaches of the Great Lakes.

What is the future of the Great Lakes population of the Piping Plover? The good news is that its numbers have increased somewhat in recent years, much to the credit of the work of conservationists. But its population size is so low and the birds are so scattered that protecting it takes a major commitment, one we would like to recognize in this book, though few Great Lakes Piping Plover sites can be designated "global" IBAs.

Superior National Forest (5), Minnesota

▶ Highlight: With 163 species, Superior National Forest has the greatest number of breeding birds of any national forest; these include 24 species of warbler, including several on the Green List.

▶ Location: Northeastern Minnesota.

▸ Size: 3,866,232 acres of land and water; includes the one-million-acre Boundary Waters Canoe Area, along the Canadian border.

▸ Ownership: Forest Service (64 percent), state and county public lands (23 percent), private (13 percent).

▸ Habitats: Boreal spruce-fir forest, deciduous hardwoods and pines, sphagnum bogs and lakes. Within the jurisdiction boundaries, 90 percent of the land is in native vegetation (forest, shrubland, bog, marsh, fen), one percent is developed, and nine percent is water surface.

▸ Land Use: Timber, grazing, recreation, conservation.

▸ Site Description: An area of dense bogs and forests, the Superior National Forest includes more than 445,000 acres of surface water, with more than 2,200 miles of streams flowing within its borders. Winters are long and cold, with an average of 60 inches of snowfall, and snow covers the ground for approximately 150 days a year. The forest harbors the largest remaining population of the wolf left in the lower 48 states. The Boundary Waters Canoe Area Wilderness is located within the forest.

▸ Birds: This forest and the Chippewa provide habitat for a large proportion of the population of neotropical migrants and other forest birds in Minnesota. Among the breeding species are Golden-winged, Black-throated Blue, and Canada Warblers. Other breeding warblers include the Magnolia, Tennessee, Bay-breasted, Blackburnian, Cape May, Mourning, Connecticut, Nashville, Chestnut-sided, and the Ovenbird; the latter three are among the most abundant species here. Several boreal species are resident, including the Boreal and Great Gray Owls, Spruce Grouse, Black-backed and Three-toed Woodpeckers, Gray Jay, and Boreal Chickadee.

▸ Conservation Issues: Most of the public, non-wilderness land is managed for multiple use, including timber, grazing, and recreation. The southern half of Superior National Forest is crisscrossed by gravel roads used for logging. Storm damage can be severe. On July 4, 1999, a severe windstorm blew down or snapped off trees in an area approximately 30 miles long and three to five miles wide. Long-term monitoring of bird populations is under way, and researchers at the University of Minnesota have set up 168 survey points and have 11 years of data.

▸ Visitor Information: Best times to visit are late May to early July for breeding warblers; November to March for winter finches; early March to mid-April for owls. For more information, contact the forest at 8901 Grand Avenue Place, Duluth, MN 55808, 218-626-4300.

Crex Meadows Wildlife Area (6), Wisconsin

▸ Highlight: Nesting Yellow Rails and other Green List species.

▸ Location: Burnett County in northwestern Wisconsin, half a mile north of Grantsburg.

▸ Size: 30,000 acres.

▸ Ownership: Wisconsin Department of Natural Resources.

▸ Habitats: Brush-prairie-wetland complex, potholes, lakes.

▸ Land Use: Hunting, trapping, wildlife observation and conservation.

▸ Site Description: Once drained for agriculture, restoration of wetlands and brush prairie was begun by the state when it acquired the area in 1946. There are dikes, sedge marshes, potholes, and 100 acres of croplands to provide food for migrating waterfowl. The area contains 32 flowages that flood 6,000 acres. Phantom Lake, with 2,000 acres, is the largest flowage.

▶ Birds: An estimated ten to 12 pairs of Yellow Rails nest, as do Nelson's Sharp-tailed, Clay-colored and Le Conte's Sparrows, Bobolink and Short-eared Owl. The Sedge Wren is an abundant nesting species, and the Black Tern and American Bittern also breed. Several ducks are abundant in the breeding season, including the Mallard, Blue-winged Teal, and Ring-necked Duck. Thousands of ducks stop by during migration. The Trumpeter Swan has been introduced, and is now well established in the area, with most of the larger flowages having breeding pairs. The Upland Sandpiper and Sharp-tailed Grouse breed, as does the Sandhill Crane. The area is also a Sandhill Crane staging site, with more than 8,000 usually present in October. Shorebirds can be abundant during migration, particularly in dry years when mudflats are exposed.

▶ Conservation Issues: Dikes were constructed to restore the drained wetlands and controlled burns have been used to restore and maintain prairie vegetation. Approximately 7,000 acres of brush prairie has been restored to date, and an average of 3,500 acres are burned each year. Potholes that have filled with vegetation and sediment are dug out by bulldozers to maintain nesting habitat for ducks. Platforms have been constructed for Ospreys. Much of the wildlife area is managed for the Sharp-tailed Grouse and other prairie wildlife. Funds for the acquisition and management of the land are provided by fees charged to hunters and trappers.

▶ Visitor Information: Two blinds for observing Sharp-tailed Grouse are available to visitors during the display period from mid-April to mid-May. There is a self-guided auto tour. Biting insects are abundant in summer. The refuge may be reached at Box 367, Grantsburg, WI 54840, 715-463-2896.

Hiawatha National Forest (9), Michigan

▶ Highlight: This forest has among the greatest diversity of nesting warblers in the United States.

▶ Location: Eastern Upper Peninsula of Michigan.

▶ Size: 879,000 acres.

▶ Ownership: Forest Service, with private inholdings.

▶ Habitats: Upland boreal forests, northern hardwoods, rocky shorelines and beaches, grasslands, wetlands.

▶ Land Use: Forestry, recreation, wildlife conservation.

▶ Site Description: About half the Hiawatha is forested, with a mix of northern hardwoods (sugar maple, beech, birch) and boreal conifers (black spruce, tamarack, northern white cedar), while the other half is a mix of marshes, lakes, and patterned fens.

▶ Birds: The Upper Peninsula of Michigan vies with northeastern Minnesota as the richest area in the United States in terms of the number of species of breeding neotropical migrants, including 24 species of warblers. This national forest, which consists of two units, has, along with Superior National Forest, the greatest variety of nesting warblers in the United States. They include the Canada, Black-throated Blue, and Golden-winged. The latter is expanding its range northward and becoming more widespread in the Upper Peninsula, particularly in the western half. Among the other breeding warblers are the Connecticut, Nashville, Magnolia, Black-throated Green, Blackburnian, Tennessee, Bay-breasted, Yellow, Black-and-white, and Chestnut-sided. The Clay-colored Sparrow and Bobolink nest in a grassy plain in the forest, and the Yellow Rail is found in the 10,000-acre Scott's Marsh in the forest. Several species of owl also breed, including the Short-eared. The Trumpeter Swan also breeds, as do a great variety of other waterfowl. Sites in the forest are important stopover points for migrating shorebirds.

▶ Conservation Issues: The forest is a multiple-use area. As in other national forests in the Boreal Forest Transition, nesting Golden-winged Warblers can benefit from timber extraction and reversion to early successional communities.

▶ Visitor Information: Best time to visit is late April through June. Contact: Supervisor's Office, Hiawatha National Forest, 2727 N. Lincoln Road, Escanaba, MI 49829, 906-786-4062.

Seney National Wildlife Refuge (10), Michigan

▶ Highlight: A consistently used breeding site for the Yellow Rail.
▶ Location: Near Germfask, Schoolcraft County, Upper Peninsula.
▶ Size: 95,212 acres.
▶ Ownership: Fish and Wildlife Service.
▶ Habitats: Coniferous and hardwood forests, marshes, bogs, meadows, lakes.
▶ Land Use: Primarily recreation.
▶ Site Description: The refuge encompasses a significant portion of the Great Manistique Marsh. The eastern and central areas are characterized by shrub swamp and impoundments ranging from 27 to 950 acres, drainage ditches, and natural watercourses. The western portion is a relatively undisturbed area of marsh-fen-patterned peatland.
▶ Birds: This refuge is one of the better-known breeding sites for the Yellow Rail, a nocturnal species notoriously difficult to observe, especially on its breeding grounds. Since 1979, it has been the site of a long-term study of the species. Other breeding species include the American Black Duck, American Bittern, Sharp-tailed Grouse, Black Tern, Sedge Wren, Le Conte's Sparrow, and Bobolink. Trumpeter Swans were released at the refuge in the early 1990s, and reproduction has steadily increased since. The population on the refuge is now approximately 100 birds. Several warbler species breed on the refuge, including the Black-throated Blue and Canada.
▶ Conservation Issues: There are 25,150 acres of designated wilderness on the refuge. Small-scale prescribed burning is maintaining small areas of marshland and grassland. Burning is a positive management practice for breeding habitat for the Yellow Rail. Historic ditch-dredging of Great Manistique Swamp has changed the natural hydrology of the area. Non-native purple loosestrife is a potential problem should it become established, and spotted knapweed has already colonized some areas.
▶ Visitor Information: Best time to visit is May to early July. Contact the refuge at HCR #2, Box 1, Seney, MI 49883, 906-586-9851.

Nicolet National Forest (13), Wisconsin

▶ Highlight: The forest supports an estimated 1,300 pairs of Golden-winged Warblers, perhaps the greatest density of this species found in its range.
▶ Location: Covers parts of five counties of northeastern Wisconsin, adjacent to the Ottawa National Forest in the Upper Peninsula of Michigan. The nearest major town is Eagle River.
▶ Size: 661,000 acres.

▸ Ownership: Forest Service, private inholdings.

▸ Habitats: Bog wetlands, sedge meadows, shrub swamps, sugar maple deciduous forest mixed with hemlock, white pine, yellow birch, and other upland tree species, including plantations of red pine.

▸ Land Use: Forestry, recreation.

▸ Site Description: Nicolet National Forest is an extensive area of mostly managed forests with 1,200 lakes, seven rivers, and numerous bogs, sedge meadows, and shrub swamps. It occupies a glacial landscape with a complex topography of ridges and lowlands.

▸ Birds: The forest is near the center of distribution for the Golden-winged Warbler, a species of extremely high conservation priority. In the Nicolet National Forest, Golden-winged Warblers occur in tamarack bogs and shrub swamps, places perhaps less likely to be invaded by Blue-winged Warblers, although Blue-winged Warblers are moving northward toward the area.

In addition to the Golden-winged Warbler, the forest has thriving breeding populations of other neotropical migrants, including the following species (all figures are estimates): the Canada Warbler (700 pairs), Black-and-white Warbler (6,000 pairs), Cape May Warbler (400 pairs), Connecticut Warbler (120 pairs), Yellow-bellied Flycatcher (1,200 pairs), and Olive-sided Flycatcher (475 pairs). Several boreal species are also present in small numbers, including the Gray Jay, Boreal Chickadee, and Spruce Grouse. Singing male Kirtland's Warblers have been observed in recent years, and the Northern Goshawk breeds in the area.

▸ Conservation Issues: For the Golden-winged Warbler, the principal threat is hybridization with and displacement by the closely related Blue-winged Warbler, which is invading its range. Though the overall status of the forest is good from the point of view of bird conservation, there are still several issues facing it. Protection of bogs and other wetlands is a critical concern that needs to be addressed. Browsing by deer has inhibited regeneration of hemlock and cedar and virtually eliminated Canada yew. This reduction in the conifer element of mixed forests is a serious problem. In general, there is little funding available for programs connected with non-commodity resources.

▸ Visitor Information: Best time to visit for breeding birds is late May to early July. Insect repellant is a must. Contact the forest at 68 W. Stevens Street, Rhinelander, WI 54501, 715-362-1300.

BROWN-HEADED COWBIRD

Brown-headed Cowbirds are brood parasites, that is, they deposit their eggs in the nests of other birds and leave the rearing of their young to the foster parents. More than 100 bird species have provided host nests for cowbird eggs. The female cowbird quickly lays a single egg in an unguarded nest, generally after the host bird has laid at least one egg. Young cowbirds don't evict their nest-mates the way European Cuckoos do, but they hatch earlier and typically out-compete the host bird's nestlings.

The strategy evolved when cowbirds occupied the grasslands of precolonial North America, following the bison herds and eating the insects they stirred up. Since bison can move a long way from one week to the next and a nest could be left far behind, the cowbird evolved a strategy of laying its eggs in the nests of other species, freeing it to roam where the buffalo roam. This system worked well, and there is no evidence that the cowbird did its hosts much harm. When Europeans arrived and the herds of bison disappeared, the cowbird did just fine. Clearing the forests and introducing cattle, horses, and sheep allowed it to spread from coast to coast. Getting through the winter is no problem for the species. In the fall the cowbird just switches from insects to the ample waste grain left in agricultural fields.

The problem for other birds nowadays is that the cowbird's range expansion has brought it into contact with host species that had not evolved ways of dealing with brood parasitism, such as building a new nest on top of the old or simply abandoning a nest with cowbird eggs altogether. The populations of most species are not seriously depressed by cowbird parasitism, though it may contribute to the reduced breeding success of some in the fragmented forests of the East. For a few, though, it spells real disaster—unless humans intervene. Two endangered species, the Black-capped Vireo and Kirtland's Warbler, have been particularly hard hit, and the very existence of the latter depends on the annual trapping and killing of cowbirds within its very small breeding range. Trapping only makes a difference for a single season. Come the following year, there are as many cowbirds as ever.

Kirtland's Warbler Management Area (14), Michigan

▶ Highlight: This area of Michigan is the only place in the world where the endangered Kirtland's Warbler is known to breed in any numbers.

▶ Location: North-central part of the Lower Peninsula with some in the Upper Peninsula of Michigan.

▶ Size: Approximately 125,000 acres scattered throughout public lands, with some birds on private lands.

▶ Ownership: Forest Service (Huron National Forest), Michigan state forests, private lands.

▶ Habitat: Stands of jack pine five to 20 feet high.

▶ Land Use: Habitat managed for the Kirtland's Warbler, nature observation, forestry.

▶ Site Description: Early successional forest of jack pines with interspersed openings.

▶ Birds: The Kirtland's Warbler has one of the most limited breeding ranges of any migrant bird in the United States. Wintering in the Bahamas, it breeds almost exclusively within a several-county area in the north-central part of the Lower Peninsula of Michigan. Within this limited area, the birds choose only a very specific and relatively temporary habitat and use it only for a few seasons before moving on. Because of this, no specific set of areas within its small range can be designated as a permanent IBA. And because an active management program is required not only to assure the availability of new suitable habitat, but to protect the bird from Brown-headed Cowbird nest parasitism, this species requires constant vigilance to prevent its extinction.

▶ Conservation Issues: The bird is restricted to areas of jack pines (*Pinus banksiana*) from five to 20 feet tall, with interspersed openings, the best habitat being produced by larger wildfires. The species begins to occupy the habitat six to eight years after the jack pines are established, but abandons it a few years later, as the stand matures. Stands must be at least 75 acres in size, though the bird prefers even larger stands. Since it nests on the ground, there must be enough cover to provide concealment for the nest. Historically, the stands of young jack pine the species prefers were created by natural wildfires that frequently swept through northern Michigan. Modern fire suppression programs altered this natural process, severely reducing habitat for the species.

To reproduce the effects of wildfire, state and federal wildlife biologists and foresters now conduct a combination of clear-cutting, controlled burning, seeding, and replanting within the approximate 125,000-acre area defined as the Kirtland's Warbler Management Area on the Huron National Forest and state forest lands. In 1999, managers planted more than 3,000 acres of jack pines to provide habitat for warblers in six to ten years. In 2000, an additional 1,656 acres were planted. The number of Kirtland's Warblers counted in plantations specifically created to create warbler nesting habitat has continued to increase, accounting for 76 percent of all birds counted in 2000.

Another major threat to the species is nest parasitism by the Brown-headed Cowbird. There is an active cowbird removal program beginning each year before the breeding season. This program is successful in limiting cowbird parasitism in the current year, but apparently has had no effect on the number of cowbirds that turn up the following year. The fledge rate of Kirtland's Warblers with cowbird control is about four times that without control. It is unlikely that the Kirtland's Warbler could continue to exist without cowbird removal.

Though the situation demands constant vigilance, efforts to protect the Kirtland's Warbler have paid off dramatically. This has been shown by the most recent results of the annual population census, conducted every year since 1971. Conducted by biologists, researchers, and volunteers, the yearly census counts singing males during a ten-day period in June. The June 2002 census of the warbler's breeding population found 1,050 singing males, down slightly from the all-time high figure in 2001 (1,085 singing males). Counts are up considerably from the lows recorded as recently as 1987, when only 167 singing males were found. Since the songs can be heard from a quarter of a mile away, the census is conducted with little disturbance to the birds. Females do not sing, so the total minimum breeding population is twice the count of males. Though most of the birds were found in four counties at the center of the species' range (Oscoda, Ogemaw, Crawford, and Alcona), recent counts have found up to 18 singing males in the Upper Peninsula, where females were also observed. Singing males have on rare occasions been seen in Wisconsin and Ontario.

The bird is very poorly known from the Bahamas, its only wintering grounds. However, a team of specialists were recently surprised to find eight of the birds on the islands. This surpasses the total number of sightings in the region in the past 50 years.

► Visitor Information: The best and most reliable way of seeing a Kirtland's Warbler is to take the Fish and Wildlife Service tour departing from the Holiday Inn in Grayling, Michigan (517-351-2555), or the Forest Service tour departing from Mio (517-826-3252) from the latter part of May to early July. On the tour from Grayling, after seeing a short introductory slide show, participants drive in a caravan to a nesting site where one has an excellent chance of seeing at least one singing male and sometimes more than that. Every effort is made to avoid disturbing the birds, and unauthorized entry into the nesting areas is not allowed. In 1999, 917 people went on the Fish and Wildlife Service tour and 485 people went on the Forest Service tour; 91 percent of the people on the Fish and Wildlife Service tour and 95 percent on the Forest Service tour saw a Kirtland's Warbler. There is now an annual Kirtland's Warbler Festival, and information about the event can be found at www.kirtland.cc.mi. us/~warbler. There are motels in Grayling and Mio.

13. Lower Great Lakes/ St. Lawrence Plain

The Lower Great Lakes and St. Lawrence Plain cover the low-lying areas to the south of the Canadian Shield and north of various highland systems in the United States. In addition to important lakeshore habitat and associated wetlands, this region was originally covered by a mixture of oak-hickory, northern hardwood, and mixed-coniferous forests. Due primarily to conversion to agriculture, very little of the forest remains today. The highest-priority bird in remnant forests is the Cerulean Warbler. Because of agriculture, this BCR also now contains the largest and most important area of grassland in the Northeast, providing habitat for such species as the Henslow's Sparrow and Bobolink. Agricultural abandonment may temporarily favor shrub-nesting species, such as the Golden-winged Warbler and American Woodcock, but increasingly, agricultural land is being lost to urbanization. This physiographic area is also extremely important to stopover migrants, attracting some of the largest concentrations of migrant passerines, hawks, shorebirds, and waterbirds in eastern North America. Many of these concentrations are along threatened lakeshore habitats.

Open Waters of the Great Lakes IBAs, Michigan and Ohio

Saginaw Bay, MI (1), Lake St. Clair, MI (2), Lake Erie Where the Detroit River Enters It, MI (3), Maumee Bay, OH (4), Lakeshore Metropark, OH (5)

▸ Highlight: The open waters of the Great Lakes provide vitally important habitat for thousands of wintering and migrant waterfowl and gulls. A few important concentration points are mentioned below, but in winter one can generally observe waterfowl in open water along much of the shoreline of the Great Lakes, including near major cities such as Milwaukee, Chicago, Toledo, and Cleveland.
▸ Location: The shoreline of the Great Lakes is found in four Bird Conservation Regions: 12, 13, 22, and 23.
▸ Ownership: Territorial waters of the United States.
▸ Birds: Large numbers of diving ducks such as the Long-tailed Duck, Bufflehead, Common Goldeneye, Red-breasted Merganser, Common Merganser, Canvasback, Scaup, and many migrating gulls, including thousands of Bonaparte's Gulls. Some sites that attract large numbers of wintering and migrating waterfowl and ducks include the waters off Lakeshore Metropark in Cleveland, with counts of 9,500 Bona-

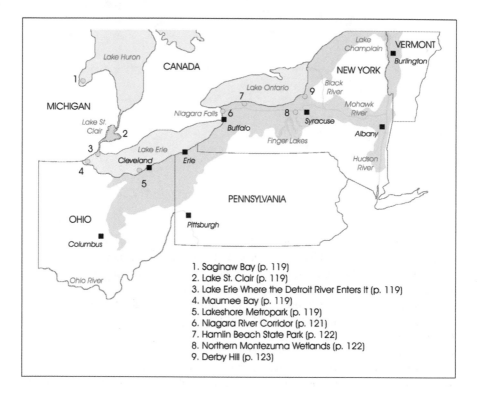

1. Saginaw Bay (p. 119)
2. Lake St. Clair (p. 119)
3. Lake Erie Where the Detroit River Enters It (p. 119)
4. Maumee Bay (p. 119)
5. Lakeshore Metropark (p. 119)
6. Niagara River Corridor (p. 121)
7. Hamlin Beach State Park (p. 122)
8. Northern Montezuma Wetlands (p. 122)
9. Derby Hill (p. 123)

parte's Gulls, 5,000 Common Goldeneye, 4,000 Common Mergansers, and 40,000 Red-breasted Mergansers, and the waters of Maumee Bay, near Toledo, which have about 170,000 waterfowl in winter. Saginaw Bay, on the Michigan shore of Lake Huron, hosts thousands of diving ducks, particularly during migration. Lake St. Clair, the Detroit River, and the waters of Lake Erie where the Detroit River enters it also host thousands of ducks during winter and migration; prominent among these are large numbers of Canvasbacks and Redheads.

▶ Conservation Issues: Oil spills and toxic chemical spills from commercial shipping on the lakes are a threat; discharge of nutrients and other pollutants into the lake from sewage outflow and agricultural runoff are also problems. In 2002, a large die-off of waterfowl in Lake Erie—more than 5,000 birds collected along the shoreline in New York in two weeks in November—was attributed to botulism. The outbreak is thought to have been due to the invasion of exotic species; millions of quagga and zebra mussels, brought from Europe by freighters, have cleaned the waters of the lake considerably, allowing sunlight to penetrate to greater depths and increasing the growth of weeds. Botulism thrives in decaying weeds and is ingested not only by the mussels but by an exotic fish, the round goby. Birds contract the disease and die by eating the infected gobies and mussels. In addition, the filter-feeding mussels accumulate toxins in their tissues and pass these up the food chain. Zebra mussels have become an important food source for diving ducks such as the Greater and Lesser Scaup, American Goldeneye, Bufflehead, and Long-tailed Duck. Since the mussel's arrival in Lake Ontario in 1991, the numbers of diving ducks counted during fall and winter surveys on the Canadian side has increased ninefold. These changes are thought to be the result not only of the new food source but of increased winter temperatures. The number of dabbling ducks has doubled, and that of Canada Geese has increased nearly threefold. The increase in dabblers and geese is probably simply a function of increased continental populations, urban feeding, and warmer temperatures. Recent studies conducted by Bird Studies Canada indicate that the population declines in scaup species may be traced to increased feeding on zebra mussels, leading to increased levels of selenium and other contaminants in their tissues. Another issue in the Lower Great Lakes is the rapidly expanding population of the non-native Mute Swan. Its aggressive disposition and voracious appetite are reducing the carrying capacity of Great Lakes habitats for native waterfowl.

▸ Visitor Information: Best time to observe wintering and migrating waterfowl is October through April.

Niagara River Corridor (6), New York

▸ Highlight: Winter concentrations of waterfowl and gulls, the latter up to 100,000 individuals, and including the largest concentrations of the Bonaparte's Gull in the world.

▸ Location: The Niagara River flows from Lake Erie to Lake Ontario and forms the international border between the United States and Canada.

▸ Size: 32 miles long.

▸ Ownership: New York Department of Environmental Conservation, Niagara Parks Commission, private.

▸ Habitats: Shallow rapids, deeper water, deciduous woodland.

▸ Land Use: Tourism, industrial, commercial, residential, wildlife observation.

▸ Site Description: With parks on both sides and the spectacle of Niagara Falls, the corridor is part of one of the great tourist destinations in North America. Much of the shoreline is developed for industry, including hydroelectric generating stations.

▸ Birds: The roiling waters of the rapids and of the stretches below the falls and the generating plants serve up an abundant supply of fish, attracting as many as 100,000 gulls to the corridor in a single day. The great majority are Herring, Ring-billed, and Bonaparte's, but 16 other gull species have been found through the years. The corridor is also a major wintering area for several species of ducks (such as the Canvasback, Common Goldeneye, Common Merganser, and Greater Scaup) and a major route for migrating songbirds. Several hundred pairs of Common Terns breed in the corridor.

▸ Conservation Issues: Water pollution has been a problem through the years, but an extensive effort at cleanup has brought the levels of most of the injurious chemicals down. Further loss of woodland and shrub habitats along the river will impact the area's importance to migrating songbirds. Protection of the remaining natural vegetation is a priority for conservation.

▸ Visitor Information: Best time to visit for birding is in the winter months.

Hamlin Beach State Park (7), New York

▸ Highlight: This park is a premier location along the shore of Lake Ontario for observing migrating waterfowl in the fall, with numbers peaking at more than 200,000.
▸ Location: Near Hamlin in Monroe County, west of Rochester.
▸ Size: 1,200 acres.
▸ Ownership: New York State Office of Parks, Recreation, and Historic Preservation.
▸ Habitats: Open water, lakeshore, marsh, deciduous woodland, scrub.
▸ Land Use: Recreation.
▸ Site Description: This park is important as a location for monitoring numbers of waterfowl and gulls migrating along the lake. It consists of recreational areas, woods, and beaches protected by stone jetties. The IBA, in this case, really consists more of the waters of Lake Ontario off the park's shore rather than the park itself.
▸ Birds: Among the more than 200,000 waterfowl observed during fall migration are large numbers of loons, Greater Scaup, White-winged Scoters, and Red-breasted Mergansers, plus good numbers of several other species. Thousands of Bonaparte's Gulls pass by, as do many songbirds and raptors.
▸ Conservation Issues: There are no particular threats to the area.
▸ Visitor Information: Best time to visit is during fall migration. Contact the park at 1 Camp Road, Hamlin, NY 14464, 585-964-2462.

Northern Montezuma Wetlands (8), New York

▸ Highlight: One of the largest concentrations of migrating waterfowl in the northeastern United States, including significant concentrations of the green-listed American Black Duck; important breeding population of the Cerulean Warbler.
▸ Location: At the head of Lake Cayuga, near Seneca Falls.
▸ Size: 36,000 acres.
▸ Ownership: Fish and Wildlife Service, New York State Department of Environmental Conservation, private.
▸ Habitats: Wetland, riparian, deciduous woodland, shrubland, pastures, cropland.
▸ Land Use: Agriculture, wildlife conservation, recreation.
▸ Site Description: Much of the area lies within Montezuma National Wildlife Refuge. This glaciated terrain is characterized by wetland basins in the valleys between drumlins. These form a mix of marshes and swamps, upland forests, and agricultural lands, creating a patchwork of diverse habitats important to migratory and resident species. The wetlands are an important stopover for many waterfowl on the Atlantic Flyway.
▸ Birds: More than 100,000 waterfowl use the wetlands during migration, among them up to 25,000 American Black Ducks; the site is also an important stopover site for shorebirds. Breeding birds include a significant population (up to 250 pairs) of the Cerulean Warbler, plus American and Least Bitterns, Bald Eagle, Osprey, and colonies of herons. In the fall, an estimated at 50,000 to 100,000 swallows of several species congregate here.
▸ Conservation Issues: Land acquisition by the Fish and Wildlife Service and New York State Department of Environmental Conservation is continuing, though in-

creased funding is needed to acquire the land from willing sellers. There are some problems with agricultural runoff, and the invading non-native purple loosestrife has been an ongoing problem despite the use of biological controls.

▶ Visitor Information: Best time to visit is during spring and fall migration; Cerulean Warblers can best be found from late May to early July. Contact: Montezuma National Wildlife Refuge at 3395 Route 5 & 20 East Seneca Falls, NY 13148, 315-568-5987.

Derby Hill (9), New York

▶ Highlight: As many as 66,000 hawks have been counted during spring migration.

▶ Location: Near the town of Mexico, Oswego County.

▶ Size: 57 acres.

▶ Ownership: Onondaga Audubon Society, private.

▶ Habitats: Lakeshore, grasslands, residential area, some woodland.

▶ Land Use: Wildlife observation.

▶ Site Description: The observation point is on a bluff overlooking Lake Ontario. Topped with a grassland, it offers a vantage point for seeing hawks during spring migration, as they follow the lake's shoreline and are funneled over the area in great numbers. A nearby woodland harbors many passerines during migration.

▶ Birds: Thousands of raptors pass over Derby Hill during spring migration. At least 20 species have been recorded, the most numerous of which are the Broad-winged Hawk, Red-tailed Hawk, Turkey Vulture, and Sharp-shinned Hawk. Offshore, waterfowl and gulls seasonally number in the thousands.

▶ Conservation Issues: There is erosion of the overlook due to winter storms and spring thaws.

▶ Visitor Information: Best time to visit is during spring migration. The Derby Hill Bird Observatory may be contacted through Onandaga Audubon Society at 313-457-7731. There is a hotline for weather and hawk flight predictions at 315-963-8291.

14. Atlantic Northern Forests

The nutrient-poor soils of northernmost New England and the Adirondack Mountains support spruce-fir forests at more northerly and higher sites, and northern hardwoods elsewhere. Virtually all of the world's Bicknell's Thrushes breed on mountaintops in this region. Other important forest birds include the Canada Warbler and Bay-breasted Warbler. Coastal wetlands are inhabited by the Nelson's Sharp-tailed Sparrow, rocky intertidal areas are important for wintering Purple Sandpipers, and muddy intertidal habitats are critical as Semipalmated Sandpiper staging sites. The Common Eider and Black Guillemot breed in coastal habitats, while the Leach's Storm-Petrel, gulls, terns, and the southernmost populations of many breeding alcids nest on offshore islands. Beaver ponds and shores of undisturbed lakes provide excellent waterfowl breeding habitat, particularly for the American Black Duck, Hooded and Common Mergansers, and Common Goldeneye. The Hudson and Connecticut River valleys are important corridors for the Brant, Green-winged Teal, and other waterfowl migrating from New England and Quebec. Because inland wetlands freeze, coastal wetlands are used extensively by dabbling ducks, sea ducks, and geese during winter and migration.

Adirondack Park (1), New York

▸ Highlight: Nesting habitat for the Bicknell's Thrush and many warblers.

▸ Location: Most of the northeastern part of the state.

▸ Size: Six million acres are included within the boundaries of the park, of which approximately 40 percent is state land while the rest is privately owned.

▸ Ownership: New York State Department of Environmental Conservation, private.

▸ Habitats: Mixed woods, coniferous woods, bogs, lakes, streams.

▸ Land Use: Recreation, tourism, wildlife conservation.

▸ Site Description: The park includes within its boundaries not only much private land but many small towns as well. The woodland is primarily mixed below 3,500 feet and coniferous above 3,500 feet, including subalpine and alpine communities. The Adirondack High Peaks Wilderness Area is 226,435 acres, reaching its maximum elevation of 5,344 feet at Mount Marcy.

▸ Birds: Many forest interior birds nest in the park, including several species of warbler, among them the Canada and Black-throated Blue; for the latter, the high count in

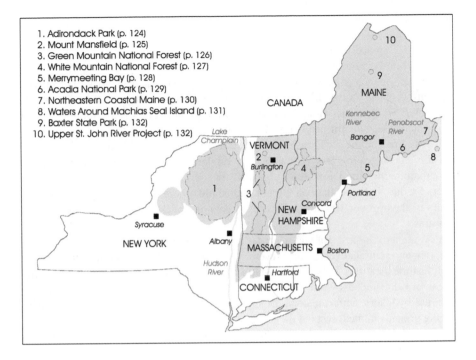

1. Adirondack Park (p. 124)
2. Mount Mansfield (p. 125)
3. Green Mountain National Forest (p. 126)
4. White Mountain National Forest (p. 127)
5. Merrymeeting Bay (p. 128)
6. Acadia National Park (p. 129)
7. Northeastern Coastal Maine (p. 130)
8. Waters Around Machias Seal Island (p. 131)
9. Baxter State Park (p. 132)
10. Upper St. John River Project (p. 132)

the Breeding Bird Survey occurs here. The Wood Thrush also breeds. The higher elevations of the Adirondack High Peaks Wilderness Area are key breeding habitat for the Bicknell's Thrush. Several boreal species breed in the park, among them the Spruce Grouse, Black-backed and Three-toed Woodpeckers, Gray Jay, and Boreal Chickadee.
▶ Conservation Issues: Although the area is managed specifically for wildlife conservation, it is a very popular recreation area, and the number of visitors has increased rapidly over recent years. This can lead to habitat degradation, particularly of fragile alpine habitats. Acid rain deposition continues to have a major effect on lake ecosystems and may affect passerine nesting success at high elevations. The Adirondack Park Agency is charged with developing a Master Plan for the state lands, and a Private Land Use and Development Plan for the private lands. A proposed summit restaurant and lodge at a state-owned ski resort on Little Whiteface Mountain could degrade the high-elevation habitat of the Bicknell's Thrush by removing up to 55,000 trees. The plan is actively opposed by the Adirondack Council and the Audubon Society of New York.
▶ Visitor Information: Best time to visit is late May through early July. For more information, contact: Adirondack Park Agency, P.O. Box 99, Ray Brook, NY 12977, 518-891-4050.

Mount Mansfield (2), Vermont

▶ Highlight: Nesting habitat for the Bicknell's Thrush.
▶ Location: 18 miles northeast of Burlington, near Pleasant Valley.

▶ Size: 1,200 acres.
▶ Ownership: State of Vermont.
▶ Habitats: Spruce-fir forest.
▶ Land Use: Recreation.
▶ Site Description: Mount Mansfield, Vermont's highest peak, rises to 4,393 feet. The habitat occupied by the Bicknell's Thrush is the higher elevations of the mountain, characterized by balsam fir and red spruce forest, in particular the krummholz habitat of stunted spruce and fir just below the tree line.
▶ Birds: The Bicknell's Thrush has a restricted and fragmented distribution within its limited range. In New York and New England, it is found almost exclusively in subalpine forests dominated by balsam fir and red spruce in areas above 3,000 feet. Studies indicate that on Mount Mansfield, there are as many as 50 to 60 pairs of the bird per 100 acres. This represents one of its densest breeding concentrations.
▶ Conservation Issues: Habitat degradation has caused the Bicknell's Thrush breeding range to contract over the past several years, and birds have disappeared from several historic localities. Subalpine habitat has been damaged by acid rain, and breeding areas are threatened by ski development, communication tower construction, and overuse by hikers. Unfortunately, the species also faces severe habitat loss in its wintering grounds in the forests of the Caribbean, especially Hispaniola.
▶ Visitor Information: The thrush is best found on Mount Mansfield from late May to mid-July. There is a toll road to the top of the mountain. Contact: Vermont Department of Forests, Parks, and Recreation, St. Johnsbury District, 1229 Portland Street, Suite 201, St. Johnsbury, VT 05819, 802-751-0100.

Green Mountain National Forest (3), Vermont

▶ Highlight: Nesting habitat for the Bicknell's Thrush.
▶ Location: One unit in southwestern, and another in central Vermont.
▶ Size: 350,000 acres.
▶ Ownership: Forest Service, private.
▶ Habitats: Northern hardwoods, wetlands, spruce-fir forest.
▶ Land Use: Logging, agriculture, hunting, tourism, wildlife conservation.
▶ Site Description: Most of the forest is made up of sugar maple, oak, beech, and birch, with interspersed wetlands and spruce and fir forest. Within the forest boundary is a mosaic of natural lands, rural villages, and farms.
▶ Birds: Species include the Canada Warbler, and Wood and Bicknell's Thrushes. The latter prefers exposed ridges of stunted red spruce and balsam fir at elevations above 3,000 feet. Mount Abraham, near Lincoln, at 4,052 feet, provides nesting habitat for the Bicknell's Thrush.
▶ Conservation Issues: The forest is a multiple-use area; this includes logging. Acid rain deposition is a problem.
▶ Visitor Information: Late spring and early summer are the best times to look for the Bicknell's Thrush. Insect repellant is advisable. Contact the forest at 231 North Main Street, Rutland, VT 05701, 802-747-6700.

DEER AND BIRDS

White-tailed deer have overpopulated much of their range, with profound and negative consequences for both humans and wildlife. At the beginning of the twentieth century, deer populations were in free fall, and deer were in danger of extirpation in some midwestern states. However, by the latter part of the twentieth century, with the disappearance of predators and successful game management, deer populations increased rapidly. Humans altered landscapes and deer successfully adapted to those changed landscapes. As this occurred—in addition to increased crop damage and highway safety issues—heavy deer browsing changed the forest understorey, especially in the eastern United States. The average deer eats 2,000 pounds of vegetation per year.

Researchers who built exclosures in Shenandoah National Park to keep deer out documented higher nesting success for woodland birds inside the exclosures. In many forests, deer have created "browse lines" as high as six feet, below which only woody vegetation can be found. Thus ground- and low-shrub and tree-nesting birds are left with reduced food resources and no visual defenses from predation. A recent study in Pennsylvania showed that deer browsing even caused declines in intermediate canopy nesters. In addition to the immediate loss of plant communities and the wildlife dependent upon them, often no new trees can grow, and the forests are doomed to an unnatural senescence and ultimately death.

One unfortunate consequence of exploding deer populations and the resulting loss of biodiversity is growing polarization between animal welfare and anti-hunting groups on the one hand, and conservation and safety groups (40,000 deer are killed on highways each year in Pennsylvania alone) on the other. All are concerned about compassionate solutions to this issue, but differ on management solutions. Real progress on this issue will require reduced rhetoric, broad participation from differing points of view, clarity between scientific issues and value judgments, and adaptive management across varying landscapes.

White Mountain National Forest (4), New Hampshire and Maine

▶ Highlight: Nesting habitat for the Bicknell's Thrush, Peregrine Falcon, and more than 70 neotropical migratory bird species.
▶ Location: North-central New Hampshire and western Maine.
▶ Size: 780,000 acres.
▶ Ownership: Forest Service.
▶ Habitat: Balsam fir, red spruce, northern hardwood, and paper birch forests.
▶ Land Use: Multiple use forest management.
▶ Site Description: The White Mountain National Forest has spectacular mountain scenery, windswept ridges, clear mountain streams, and beautiful autumn foliage. Much of the forest at lower elevations is lowland balsam fir and red spruce. The middle elevations contain northern hardwood forests consisting of American beech, sugar maple, and yellow birch, along with several other species. Above 3,000 feet the mon-

tane balsam fir and red spruce forest continues until the subalpine krummholz community consisting of balsam fir and black spruce is found. Above this community on the Presidential Range are alpine meadows consisting of sedges and alpine plants.

► Birds: The Bicknell's Thrush is a fairly common breeding species in montane balsam fir and red spruce forest at elevations above 3,000 feet. This is also the habitat for boreal species, including the Spruce Grouse, Black-backed Woodpecker, Gray Jay, Boreal Chickadee, Blackpoll Warbler, and White-winged Crossbill. The American Pipit breeds on the summit of Mount Washington. There is a significant population of the Peregrine Falcon that nests on ledges in the mountains.

► Conservation Issues: The primary conservation issues are similar elsewhere in this BCR and include global warming, acidic precipitation, non-native species, and invasive plants that can alter habitat.

► Visitor Information: The best time to visit is from late May to mid-July, the breeding season for the Bicknell's Thrush and many neotropical migrants. Bicknell's Thrushes are usually found at elevations between 3,000 and 4,500 feet. Access is by numerous hiking trails, and the Jefferson Notch Road and Mount Washington Auto Road, which is a toll road. Contact the forest at 719 Main Street, Laconia, NH 03246, 603-528-8721.

Merrymeeting Bay (5), Maine

► Highlight: The largest freshwater estuary on the Atlantic coast north of Chesapeake Bay, and an important waterfowl staging area.

► Location: Midcoast of Maine, in Sagadahoc County, near Bath.

► Size: Approximately 100 miles of shoreline and 4,500 acres of prime waterfowl habitat.

► Ownership: State of Maine Department of Inland Fisheries and Wildlife, land trusts, conservation organizations, private.

► Habitats: Riverine, bay, tidal flats, marshes, wet meadows, second-growth forest, farmland.

► Land Use: Hunting, farming, wildlife observation.

► Site Description: The estuary is formed by the confluence of two major rivers (the Kennebec and Androscoggin), and several minor rivers. At the mouths of the rivers are extensive freshwater mudflats providing feeding and resting areas for waterfowl and shorebirds. The bay is an inland delta that does not meet the coast. It is affected slightly by the tide, but has a very low salinity. The intertidal zone is 4,300 acres in area, 3,300 of which are tidal flats covered by aquatic vegetation. Common plants include three-square bullrush, bushy pond weed, muskgrass, bladderwort, and sedges. There is also some coniferous, deciduous, and mixed swamp with alder, red maple, and willow. Small stands of spruce and fir are also found.

► Birds: An important waterfowl staging area, with thousands of Canada Geese, some Snow Geese, and large numbers of dabbling and diving ducks, including the American Black Duck, Northern Pintail, Blue-winged Teal, Green-winged Teal, Mallard, Common Goldeneye, and Ring-necked Duck. There is significant potential for use by shorebirds, but this usage has not yet been fully investigated. The site has the largest spring concentrations of migratory geese in Maine.

▶ Conservation Issues: There is the potential of pollution from dioxin release by paper plants upstream. The area is under development pressure, and purple loosestrife is spreading in the wetlands. Upstream dams have reduced the bay's fish stocks. A 275-acre salt marsh on the Back River, a tributary of the Kennebec, was donated to the Maine Chapter of The Nature Conservancy in 1996. Since 1992, the Maine Wetlands Protection Coalition, including the Fish and Wildlife Service, the Maine Department of Inland Fisheries and Wildlife, The Nature Conservancy, and the Maine Coast Heritage Trust, have been working through the Atlantic Coast Joint Venture of the North American Waterfowl Management Plan to protect wetlands in the delta. A number of major grants have enabled the coalition and its members to protect 5,000 acres of wetland and watershed. The Friends of Merrymeeting Bay conduct outreach activities with community members, research water quality, and protect land by establishing easements. The state has set aside a number of parcels as conservation areas including Swan Island, and the Bowdoinham Wildlife Management Area.

▶ Visitor Information: Best time to visit is in late March and April and in September and October; the latter coincides with the hunting season. For more information, contact: Jim Connally, Regional Biologist of the Maine Department of Inland Fisheries and Wildlife, 270 Lyons Road, Sidney, ME 04330. Friends of Merrymeeting Bay can be contacted by e-mail at: fomb@gwi.net.

Acadia National Park (6), Maine

▶ Highlight: 22 species of nesting warblers, and nesting seabirds such as the Leach's Storm-Petrel and Roseate Tern.

▶ Location: Coastal Maine, at Bar Harbor.

▶ Size: 35,000 acres.

▶ Ownership: National Park Service.

▶ Habitats: Marine, marine islands, coniferous forest, birch forest, lakes, rocky coast, mountains to 1,500 feet, fjord, littoral.

▶ Land Use: Recreation, wildlife conservation.

▶ Site Description: The park encompasses parts of two islands—Mount Desert and Isle au Haut—and the whole of the smaller Baker Island. The Schoodic Peninsula, which lies to the northeast, is also included in the park. The coastline is wild and rocky, and the park experiences cold snowy winters, and warm but often misty summers. The range of habitats includes coastal coniferous forest, mixed hardwood, open fields, brushy areas, freshwater marshes and bogs, salt marsh, and mountains scattered with blueberry bushes.

▶ Birds: Breeding species include the Bald Eagle, Common Loon, Leach's Storm-Petrel, Common Eider, American Woodcock, Roseate Tern, Black Guillemot, Northern

American Woodcock

Goshawk, Spruce Grouse, Northern Saw-whet Owl, Black-backed Woodpecker, Gray Jay, White-winged Crossbill, and Evening Grosbeak. The park has more nesting warblers than any other national park except the Great Smoky Mountains National Park and Blue Ridge Parkway. Its 22 nesting warblers include the Canada and Black-throated Blue. In winter, among the sea ducks found there are the King Eider, Barrow's Goldeneye, and Harlequin Duck. Fall shorebird passage includes concentrations of the Red-necked and Red Phalarope, while the Purple Sandpiper winters there. The park is a spring staging area for the Brant.

▸ Conservation Issues: The park is very heavily used by tourists and recreationists. Although it is the fifth-smallest national park, it is also one of the ten most visited, with approximately three million visitors annually. The most serious potential threat is that of an off-shore oil spill.

▸ Visitor Information: The park's visitor center is three miles north of Bar Harbor on Mount Desert Island. The park is open all year, but the visitor center is open only between May 1 and November 1. There are 120 miles of hiking trails, and 45 miles of carriage trails for hiking and biking (these are still closed to cars). There is also a 27-mile Park Loop Road open to vehicles. The vehicle entrance fee is $10 (May to October). There are two campgrounds as well as various hotels and inns. For the boat to Isle au Haut, call 207-367-5193; for the Baker Island boat, call 207-276-3717. For more information on the park, contact: Acadia National Park, P. O. Box 177, Bar Harbor, ME 04609, 207-288-3338.

Northeastern Coastal Maine (7)

▸ Highlight: Thousands of nesting and wintering seabirds are concentrated here, in addition to thousands of shorebirds, particularly during migration.

▸ Location: From Great Wass Island up the coast to Cutler Bay.

▸ Size: Linearly, this section is approximately 20 to 25 miles long, but incorporates several deep inlets.

▸ Habitats: Rocky coast, islands, open water.

▸ Land Use: Wildlife observation, recreation, fishing.

▸ Ownership: A mix of state and private lands, in addition to U.S. territorial waters. Great Wass Island is owned by The Nature Conservancy.

▸ Site Description: This site extends between Cutler Harbor to the east and Great Wass Island to the west, and includes Little Machias Bay, Machias Bay, Englishman's Bay, Little Kennebec Bay, and Eastern Bay. Portions of the towns of Jonesport, Beals, Jonesboro, Machias, Machiasport, Trescott, and Cutler are included. The site includes many seabird nesting islands, extensive mudflats, dense stunted spruce cover (similar to that found below the alpine zone), large areas of alder barrens and bogs, and miles of rocky intertidal habitat. The area is adjacent to Machias Seal Island and its surrounding waters.

The ocean off this section of the coast is very cold throughout the year, and the many upwellings bring nutrients to the surface, which are absorbed by phytoplankton, the base of the food chain. Because of the cold water in the outer portion of the bay, pelagic birds as well as whales are often found nearshore.

▸ Birds: This area supports more than 70 percent of the Maine Razorbill population, the only state in which it breeds. In 1997, Old Mann Island had more than 100 pairs, Pulpit Rock ten to 12 pairs, and Freeman Rock 50 pairs. There are several hundred pairs of Black Guillemots in the area, in addition to more than 1,000 pairs of the Common Eider and perhaps as many as 1,000 Leach's Storm-Petrels. Up to 50,000 Black-legged Kittiwakes winter off the coast. Probably in excess of 30,000 shorebirds use the area at some point during the year. The site is one of the most significant in the United States for fall migrating Whimbrels (400 to 700 birds) and White-rumped Sandpiper. Other shorebirds found in significant numbers include the Semipalmated Sandpiper (12,000–25,000), Semipalmated Plover (1,500–2,500), Black-bellied Plover (800–1,200), Short-billed Dowitcher (1,200–1,500), Greater and Lesser Yellowlegs (700–1,000), and Purple Sandpiper (2,000–3,500). The Short-eared Owl breeds, and the density of nesting Merlins is the highest in the eastern United States. The Bicknell's Thrush may also breed. The headlands along Cutler, east of Little Machias Bay, the Roque Island Archipelago, the Cross Island group, and the Head Harbor Island group support good numbers of the nesting Blackpoll Warbler, a species that typically breeds at high elevations in Maine. In winter, Harlequin Ducks and Barrow's Goldeneyes are present, and national high counts for the American Black Duck and Purple Sandpiper have been recorded in a Christmas Bird Count circle that covers part of the area.

▶ Conservation Issues: Most of these shorebird species have shown sharp declines over the last 15 years. Counts in the 1980s for these species were as follows: Semipalmated Sandpiper, 20,000 to 30,000; Semipalmated Plover, 2,500 to 3,500; Black-bellied Plover, 1,500 to 2,500; and Short-billed Dowitcher, 2,000 to 3,500.

▶ Visitor Information: The area is of interest throughout the year. Fall migration and winter are good times to visit.

Waters Around Machias Seal Island (8), Maine

▶ Highlight: Thousands of seabirds spend the winter in these waters, and terns and other seabird species use the area seasonally.

▶ Location: In the ocean, ten miles southeast of Cutler.

▶ Size: Approximately 50 square miles.

▶ Ownership: U.S. territorial waters.

Atlantic Puffin

▶ Habitats: Open ocean.

▶ Site Description: Machias Seal Island is part of New Brunswick. The Canadian Wildlife Service monitors bird populations and has constructed blinds on the island. It is adjacent to the Northeastern Coastal Maine IBA.

▶ Birds: The waters around Machias Seal Island sometimes support more than 100,000 Wilson's Storm-Petrels, tens of thousands of Greater Shearwaters, and more than 10,000 Sooty Shearwaters. Gannet numbers are in the thousands, and Red and Red-necked Phalaropes number in the tens of thousands.

The Atlantic Puffin is most abundant in Canadian waters, while the Razorbill is common in U.S. waters. Arctic and Common Terns from colonies on Machias Seal Island move to feeding areas in this IBA. This international area is of great significance for wintering seabirds, and also supports 50,000 or more Black-legged Kittiwakes. Other nesting species on the island itself are the Leach's Storm-Petrel, Common Eider, Atlantic Puffin, and Razorbill.

► Conservation Issues: Potential for oil spills and other pollution.

► Visitor Information: Seabirds are in the area throughout the year, but between late May and the end of August there are boat trips to the island, which offer the opportunity to see many seabirds. For commercial trips to Machias Seal Island, visit www.mainebirding.net/puffin/trips/shtml.

Baxter State Park (9), Maine

► Highlight: Important nesting habitat for the Bicknell's Thrush.

► Location: North-central Maine in Piscataquis County.

► Size: 204,000 acres.

► Ownership: Maine Department of Conservation, Bureau of Parks and Lands.

► Habitats: Spruce-fir forest, birch-maple forest.

► Land Use: Wildlife observation, hiking, conservation.

► Site Description: Baxter State Park is in a remote area and includes Mount Katahdin, Maine's highest peak (5,267 feet). This park was given to the state by former governor Percival P. Baxter, who purchased the property between 1931 and 1962, stipulating in his gift that the land remain forever wild. It includes 18 peaks higher than 3,000 feet, many streams and ponds, significant old-growth forests, and the state's most extensive alpine habitat. The park is the northern terminus of the Appalachian Trail.

► Birds: The park is the major area in Maine for the Bicknell's Thrush, which is found among other places on Mount Katahdin above 3,000 feet on sparsely wooded slopes. Twenty warbler species breed, including the Black-throated Blue and Canada Warbler. It is one of the northernmost breeding sites of the Whip-poor-will, and several boreal species are also found, including the Spruce Grouse, Black-backed and Three-toed Woodpeckers, Boreal Chickadee, Gray Jay, and White-winged Crossbill.

► Conservation Issues: The park has a very small staff, and there is no ongoing bird research. The biggest management problem is to keep visitors from trampling the tundra on top of Mount Katahdin.

► Visitor Information: Best time to visit is from June to early July. Insect repellant is a must. Activities within the park are strictly controlled. No oversize vehicles, motorcycles, outboard motors, or pets are allowed, and no audio devices, including cassette players and cell phones, may be operated. Contact the park at 64 Balsam Drive, Millinocket, ME 04462, 207-723-5140.

Upper St. John River Project (10), Maine

► Highlight: This large forested area provides important nesting habitat for many neotropical migrants, including the Black-throated Blue and Canada Warblers.

▸ Location: Extreme northwestern Maine, along the St. John River, near the Quebec border.

▸ Size: The full extent of the Upper St. John River Watershed is approximately 1.8 million acres.

▸ Ownership: The Nature Conservancy.

▸ Habitats: Spruce-fir forest, northern hardwood forest, riparian zones, wetlands.

▸ Land Use: Conservation, timber harvesting.

▸ Site Description: The Upper St. John River is the longest free-flowing river in the eastern United States, and among its wildest and most remote. The watershed of the river contains a matrix of forest communities, including numerous high-quality examples of spruce flats, cedar swamps, and mature hardwood forests. Within it are also several outstanding examples of wetland systems, most notably, some of the state's best ribbed fens. There are essentially no permanent human settlements on the United States' side, and just forest and rural villages in Quebec. The Canadian villages are supported largely by wood product mills and small-scale agriculture. The United States portion of the site is in private corporate ownerships maintained almost exclusively for forest products.

▸ Birds: Large and continuous forested areas in eastern North America are important breeding areas for neotropical migrants, many of which do not do well in fragmented landscapes. This reserve is one of the larger forested areas, and as such has a wide array of breeding flycatchers, thrushes, vireos, and more than 20 species of warblers, including the Black-throated Blue and Canada. Boreal species such as the Spruce Grouse, Three-toed Woodpecker, Gray Jay, Boreal Chickadee, and White-winged Crossbill are among the resident and breeding species.

▸ Conservation Issues: The Nature Conservancy's goal on the St. John River is to preserve one of last remaining free-flowing rivers east of the Mississippi. Of the 180,000 acres it owns in the Upper St. John River watershed, the Conservancy has set aside approximately one quarter as a reserve with no timber harvest. The rest is managed for forestry, with the proceeds used to pay the interest on an internal loan and to support preserve stewardship expenses. The Conservancy is establishing benchmarks for monitoring vegetation change and the health of the ecosystem.

▸ Visitor Information: The area is sparsely settled and relatively inaccessible. Best time to visit is from late May to early July, during the breeding season. Insect repellant is essential. The Conservancy lands are part of a 3.5-million-acre territory that is mostly privately owned and managed for forest products. Public use is overseen by North Maine Woods, Inc. Access for recreation requires registration and a fee. For more information, visit their website at northmainwoods.org.

15. Sierra Nevada

The Sierra Nevada rises sharply from the arid basin and range to the east and slopes gently toward the Central Valley of California to the west. Vegetation at lower elevations is dominated by ponderosa pine on the west and by lodgepole pine on the east, with fir, spruce, and alpine tundra at higher elevations. The area provides habitat for the Hermit Warbler, White-headed Woodpecker, and Mountain Quail at higher elevations; and Nuttall's Woodpecker, Oak Titmouse, and California Thrasher on the western slopes.

National Park and National Forest IBAs of the Sierra Nevada Mountains, California

Lassen National Forrest (1), Lassen Volcanic National Park (2), Plumas National Forest (3), Tahoe National Forest (4), Eldorado National Forest (5), Stanislaus National Forest (6), Yosemite National Park (7), Sierra National Forest (8), Kings Canyon National Park (9), Sequoia National Park (10), Sequoia National Forest (11)

▶ Highlight: The national forests and national parks of California's Sierra Nevada are important for the resident "California" Spotted Owl, several Green List species, and several species that exhibit a strong affinity for riparian or meadow habitats.
▶ Location: The public lands of California's Sierra Nevada stretch some 350 miles from Lassen National Forest in the north to Sequoia National Forest in the south.
▶ Size: Some 8.7 million acres are in federal ownership.
▶ Ownership: Forest Service; National Park Service, private inholdings.
▶ Habitats: Alpine lakes, canyons, reservoirs, streams, coniferous forests.
▶ Land Use: Recreation and tourism, logging, grazing, mineral extraction, watershed protection, water storage, hydroelectric power.
▶ Site Description: These sites are handled collectively because they each have roughly comparable numbers of "California" Spotted Owls, and management for the species, at least on the national forests, is similar. Some of these sites also feature riparian or meadow areas that provide unique habitats for resident and migratory bird species.

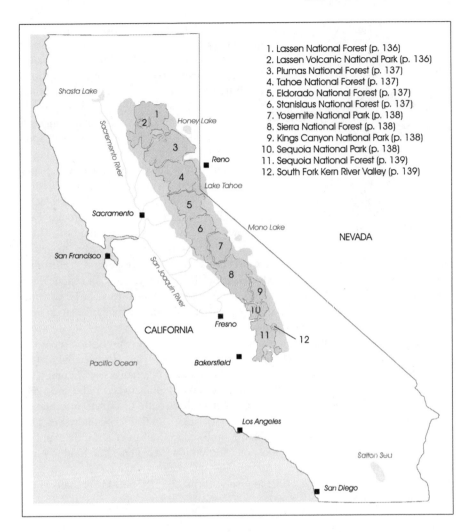

1. Lassen National Forest (p. 136)
2. Lassen Volcanic National Park (p. 136)
3. Plumas National Forest (p. 137)
4. Tahoe National Forest (p. 137)
5. Eldorado National Forest (p. 137)
6. Stanislaus National Forest (p. 137)
7. Yosemite National Park (p. 138)
8. Sierra National Forest (p. 138)
9. Kings Canyon National Park (p. 138)
10. Sequoia National Park (p. 138)
11. Sequoia National Forest (p. 139)
12. South Fork Kern River Valley (p. 139)

▶ Birds: The "California" Spotted Owl is found in isolated populations in the Sierra Nevada and southern coastal mountains of California. In the Sierra Nevada, it is found in five general habitat types, which include mature and old-growth pine or mixed-conifer forests with dense canopies, red fir forests, and riparian hardwood forests or canyons with sycamore and live oak. Habitats used for nesting typically have more than 70 percent total canopy cover. Spotted Owls are found in the Sierra Nevada at elevations ranging from approximately 1,000 feet to approximately 8,000 feet. The total estimated population of this subspecies throughout its range is only 2,000 to 3,000 birds, of which the major proportion are found in the sites mentioned here. The "California" Spotted Owl is distributed relatively evenly throughout suitable habitat in the Sierras; because of factors relating to territory size, there is no one circumscribed area that contains a particularly high density of the species.

Hermit Warbler

Other species for which these public lands are important include the Mountain Quail, Band-tailed Pigeon, White-headed Woodpecker, Hermit Warbler, Yellow-billed Cuckoo, Great Gray Owl, Flammulated Owl, and Willow Flycatcher.

▶ Conservation Issues: There is management action to benefit the "California" Spotted Owl in the national forests; none is specifically in place in the national parks, where extraction of timber or minerals is not allowed. In the forests there is a Protected Activity Center of 300 acres around each owl territory, to which a buffer of 300 to 2,100 acres is added. However, the owl's home ranges may vary from 1,000 acres to more than 7,000 acres. Some "California" Spotted Owl locations are monitored every year. New surveys are also conducted in areas slated for timber harvest. In accordance with the Sierra Nevada Forest Plan Amendment, management is conducted to provide and improve fundamental components of Spotted Owl habitat over time.

The Sierra Nevada Forest Plan Amendment also identifies conservation measures for the Great Gray Owl and Willow Flycatcher, both of which have isolated population distributions in the Sierra Nevada. In the northern parts of its range, the Flammulated Owl is limited to the higher parts of the ponderosa pine belt, between 1,200 and 5,500 feet, though it may be found up to 9,000 feet farther south. Complete information about the distribution of this secretive species is lacking in California, however. Due to the sensitivity of the birds to disturbance, precise locations of "California" Spotted Owl activity centers and nesting locations for Willow Flycatchers and Great Gray Owls are generally not disclosed.

▶ Visitor Information: The best time to visit is spring through fall. Many roads in the Sierras are closed during the winter.

White-headed Woodpecker

Lassen National Forest (1) and Lassen Volcanic National Park (2)

Located at the northern end of the Sierra Nevada, in Lassen and Shasta Counties, the forest occupies 1.2 million acres in three ranger districts, and has three wilderness areas. Lassen Volcanic National Park (106,000 acres) is located in the center of the forest. There are 137 "California" Spotted Owl territories known in the area. The White-headed Woodpecker and Mountain Quail are also readily found.

▶ Visitor Information: Contact: Forest Supervisor's Office, 2550 Riverside Drive, Susanville, CA 96130, 530-257-2151.

Plumas National Forest (3)

Located near the northern end of the Sierras, in Plumas County. The forest occupies one million acres, in three ranger districts. There are 255 "California" Spotted Owl territories. The Flammulated Owl may be found in ponderosa pine forests, especially on the east side of the forest. Diligent searching will be rewarded with sightings of the Mountain Quail.

▶ Visitor Information: Contact: Plumas National Forest, 159 Lawrence Street, P.O. Box 11500, Quincy, CA 95971, 530-283-2050.

Tahoe National Forest (4)

Located next to Plumas and Eldorado National Forests. The forest occupies 841,689 acres in five ranger districts. There are 157 "California" Spotted Owl territories known in the forest. One of the largest-known population centers of the Willow Flycatcher on Forest Service lands in the Sierra Nevada is located here. The forest also supports populations of the Flammulated Owl, Mountain Quail, White-headed Woodpecker, Hermit Warbler, and Band-tailed Pigeon. Great Gray Owls are present, but considered to be quite rare.

▶ Visitor Information: Contact: Tahoe National Forest, 631 Coyote Street, Nevada City, CA 95959, 530-265-4531, or the visitor center at 530-426-3609.

Eldorado National Forest (5)

Located west of Lake Tahoe. The forest occupies 600,000 acres in four ranger districts. There are 200 territories of "California" Spotted Owls known in the forest. The forest also supports populations of the Flammulated Owl, Mountain Quail, White-headed Woodpecker, Hermit Warbler, and Band-tailed Pigeon. Great Gray Owls and Willow Flycatchers are present, but considered to be quite rare.

▶ Visitor Information: Contact the forest at 100 Forni Road, Placerville, CA 95667, 530-622-5061.

Stanislaus National Forest (6)

Adjoins Yosemite National Park to the north and west. The forest occupies 899,000 acres in four ranger districts; the Emigrant Wilderness covers 112,000 acres. There are 195 "California" Spotted Owl territories found in the forest. The Great Gray Owl, whose population center in California is concentrated around Yosemite National Park, is also found in appreciable numbers in the Stanislaus National Forest. The Hermit Warbler may also be found breeding here, and the Flammulated Owl and Band-tailed Pigeon are present. There are recent Willow Flycatcher breeding sites known from the forest.

▸ Visitor Information: Contact: Stanislaus National Forest, 19777 Greenley Road, Sonora, CA 95370, 209-532-3671.

Yosemite National Park (7)

This World Heritage Site is located in east-central California, adjacent to the Sierra, Stanislaus, Inyo, and Toiyabe National Forests. It occupies 748,542 acres and is owned by the National Park Service. There are approximately 30 to 50 activity sites for the "California" Spotted Owl in the park. The Mountain Quail also occurs, and other species include the White-headed Woodpecker, Hermit Warbler, and Willow Flycatcher. The park has four million visitors per year. Fire suppression has led to a high accumulation of fuelwood biomass, which may lead to catastrophic wildfires. The disastrous fires of 1990 destroyed habitat within several "California" Spotted Owl territories. Development and disturbance around known owl territories are limited and controlled. A bird population monitoring program conducted by the Institute for Bird Populations has been in place for the past ten years. Habitat destruction outside the park can affect breeding birds within it; Willow Flycatcher habitat in the park is in good condition, but destruction of its breeding sites outside the park means there is no immigration into the park and the population is not self-sustaining.

▸ Visitor Information: The entrance fee is $20. Many areas are served by a free shuttle bus. There is an extensive system of roads and trails, and numerous campgrounds and hotels. Winter snows can be heavy, and the road through the park is closed part of the year. For more information, contact the park headquarters at P.O. Box 577, Yosemite National Park, CA 95389, 209-372-0200.

Sierra National Forest (8), Kings Canyon National Park (9), and Sequoia National Park (10)

Located in the Sierra Nevada east of Fresno. The national forest is 1.3 million acres; the national parks, managed as one unit, total 863,700 acres. The national forest and the two national parks lie adjacent to one another; the two parks are under a single administration. Habitat ranges from canyons with oak and sycamore, to oak woodlands, coniferous forest, including groves of giant sequoias, and alpine grassland. There are 224 Spotted Owl territories known to occur in the Sierra National Forest. A demographic study of the "California" Spotted Owl was initiated in March of 1990, and this study includes a portion of the Sierra National Forest, and the Sequoia and Kings Canyon National Parks. Seventy-six of the Spotted Owl territories in the Sierra National Forest were included in the demographic study. In 2000, there were a total of 148 California Spotted Owls detected within the demographic study area on both the forest and the parks. In addition, the forest supports populations of the Great Gray Owl, Flammulated Owl, Mountain Quail, White-headed Woodpecker, Hermit Warbler, and Band-tailed Pigeon. Willow Flycatchers are also found in the Sierra National Forest. Nearly 43 percent of the Sierra National Forest is designated wilderness. There is management to benefit the "California" Spotted Owl in the national forest, but none is conducted in the national parks. There is a Protected Activity Center of 300 acres around each territory, to which a buffer of 300 acres is added, to include the best available Spotted Owl habitat in closest proximity to the activity center. Population levels on the forest and the parks fluctuate, but the complex of factors governing this is not well understood. Demographic studies on the owl began in 1990; numbers rose from 1990 to 1994 but have declined from 1995 to 2000.

▶ Visitor Information: Best time to visit is spring through fall. The forest can be contacted at Sierra National Forest, 1600 Tollhouse Road, Clovis, CA 93611, 559-297-0706; the parks can be contacted at Sequoia and Kings Canyon National Parks, 47050 Generals Highway, Three Rivers, CA 93271, 559-565-3341.

Sequoia National Forest (11)

Located at the southernmost end of the Sierra Nevada range within portions of Fresno, Tulare, and Kern Counties. It occupies 1,139,519 acres in five ranger districts. The vegetation in the Sequoia is composed of three major types: chaparral, hardwood, and conifer forests. Giant sequoia groves are located on the western slopes of the Sierra Nevada from 4,000 to 7,000 feet in altitude. There are 38 groves of sequoia in the forest, more than half of all such groves on Earth; these total approximately 10,000 acres. There are 133 "California" Spotted Owl territories found in the forest. The forest also supports populations of the Flammulated Owl, Mountain Quail, White-headed Woodpecker, and Band-tailed Pigeon. The Great Gray Owl and Willow Flycatcher are present, but considered to be quite rare. The largest remaining population of the Yellow-billed Cuckoo in California is found in the Sequoia National Forest at the South Fork Wildlife Area.

▶ Visitor Information: Contact: Sequoia National Forest, 900 West Grand Avenue, Porterville, CA 93257, 559-784-1500. The visitor information center is in Bakersfield. Its phone number is 805-391-6088.

South Fork Kern River Valley (12), California

▶ Highlight: One of the top areas in California for breeding riparian birds, the valley has several Green List species.

▶ Location: Near Kernville in Kern County.

▶ Size: 9,500 acres.

▶ Ownership: Forest Service, Bureau of Land Management, California Department of Fish and Game, National Audubon Society, The Nature Conservancy.

▶ Habitats: Primarily riverine and riparian woodlands, with desert, grasslands, and shrub lands; lakes, streams, valley grassland, chapparal, Joshua tree woodland, piñon-juniper woodland, sagebrush scrub.

▶ Land Use: Agriculture, grazing, conservation.

▶ Site Description: The area has the largest remaining stand of Great Valley cottonwood-willow riparian forest in California. The entire area is a flat alluvial plain. About ten percent of the valley is in agriculture, 50 percent is commercially grazed, and 40 percent is in conservation ownership, including the Kern River Preserve at 1,127 acres.

▶ Birds: Up to 70 endangered "Southwestern" Willow Flycatchers and up to 40 "Western" Yellow-billed Cuckoos breed. An endemic race of the Red-winged Blackbird is found as well. There are five or more colonies of Tricolored Blackbirds, totaling 1,000 to 2,000 pairs, and an estimated 150 to 250 breeding Lawrence's Goldfinches. Also, 145 Nuttall's Woodpeckers and 130 Oak Titmice were counted during a recent Breeding Bird Survey. Other resident species of conservation concern are the Mountain Quail, and Sage and Black-chinned Sparrows. Thousands of hummingbirds move through the area during migration, particularly in the fall, and as many as 27,000 Turkey Vultures also pass over during fall migration,

▶ Conservation Issues: In 1998, The Nature Conservancy transferred ownership of the Kern River Preserve to the National Audubon Society. Brown-headed Cowbird parasitism is a problem for the flycatcher, but there is an active cowbird-control program. Some 300 acres of riparian habitat are being restored. Threats to the area include inundation of some of the riparian forest due to water release from a reservoir, and overgrazing. Overextraction of ground water and urban development are potential future threats to the area.

▶ Visitor Information: Best time to visit is late April through July and during fall migration. The preserve is open dawn to dusk. There is fee parking and a visitor center. For more information, call 760-378-3044.

16. Southern Rockies/ Colorado Plateau

This topographically complex region includes the Wasatch and Uinta Mountains to the west, and the Southern Rocky Mountains to the east, separated by the rugged tableland of the Colorado Plateau. Various coniferous forest types (often lodgepole pine) interspersed with aspen dominate higher elevations. These are replaced by piñon-juniper woodlands on the lower plateaus. Birds also segregate into elevational bands with the Brown-capped Rosy-Finch and White-tailed Ptarmigan in alpine tundra, Williamson's Sapsucker in conifers, Virginia's Warbler and Lewis's Woodpecker in montane shrub, and most of the world's breeding Gray Vireos in piñon-juniper. High arid plains and dry upland shortgrass prairies provide critical breeding areas for the Mountain Plover. San Luis Valley wetlands and surrounding uplands support one of the highest densities of nesting waterfowl in North America, and provide migration habitat for the Sandhill Crane and other wetland species.

Arapaho National Wildlife Refuge (1), Colorado

▶ Highlight: Breeding Greater Sage-Grouse, wintering populations of all three species of rosy-finch.

Williamson's Sapsucker

▶ Location: North-central Colorado, in Jackson County, south of Walden.
▶ Size: 23,267 acres.
▶ Ownership: Fish and Wildlife Service.
▶ Habitats: Wet meadows, streams, sagebrush flats.
▶ Land Use: Recreation, wildlife conservation.
▶ Site Description: The refuge is located in an intermountain glacial basin known as North Park. It is approximately 35 miles wide and 45 miles long, and opens into Wyoming to the north. The basin is crossed by several meandering streams that feed the

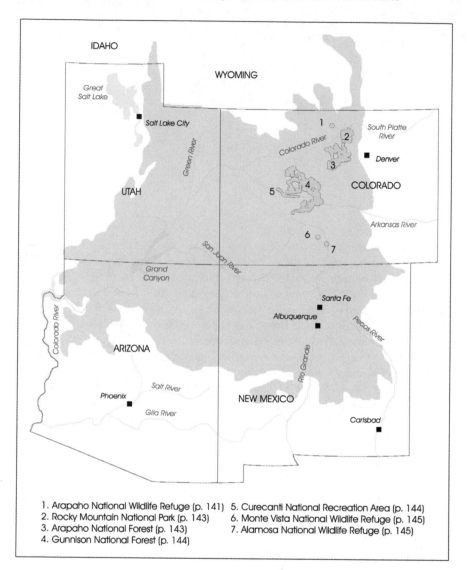

1. Arapaho National Wildlife Refuge (p. 141) 5. Curecanti National Recreation Area (p. 144)
2. Rocky Mountain National Park (p. 143) 6. Monte Vista National Wildlife Refuge (p. 145)
3. Arapaho National Forest (p. 143) 7. Alamosa National Wildlife Refuge (p. 145)
4. Gunnison National Forest (p. 144)

South Platte River. The floodplain along the streams is composed of meadows irrigated by water diverted from the Illinois River. Higher areas are primarily sagebrush flats.
▶ Birds: A population of the Greater Sage-Grouse numbering approximately 200 birds breeds on the refuge. Other breeding species include the Rufous Hummingbird, Brewer's Sparrow, and Lark Bunting. All three species of rosy-finch are common in winter and spring; two of these species have very limited breeding ranges. In late March and mid-April waterfowl begin to gather, with numbers peaking at approximately 5,000 birds in May. Thirteen waterfowl species breed.

▶ Conservation Issues: Management activities include grazing, water-level control, and prescribed burns.

▶ Visitor Information: There are tours to Greater Sage-Grouse leks on weekends in late April and early May led by the North Park Chamber of Commerce and sponsored by the Colorado Department of Wildlife. Contact the refuge manager at P.O. Box 457, Walden, CO 80480, 970-723-8202.

Rocky Mountain National Park (2) and Arapaho National Forest (3), Colorado

▶ Highlight: The Black Swift breeds in the park, as does the range-restricted Brown-capped Rosy-Finch.

▶ Designation: International Biosphere Reserve.

▶ Location: Estes Park on the eastern side, and Grand Lake on the western side of the Continental Divide.

▶ Size: 265,727 acres.

▶ Ownership: National Park Service.

▶ Land Use: Nature study, hiking, camping.

▶ Habitats: Alpine grassland, coniferous forest, open meadows.

▶ Site Description: The Continental Divide passes through the park, dividing it into two distinct parts, with greater rainfall on the west. The park's spectacular scenery is typical of the grandeur of the Rocky Mountains. Some peaks in the park are more than 14,000 feet high. Approximately 60 percent of the vegetation is forest, while 18 percent is bare rock and 13 percent is alpine tundra, with the remaining nine percent a mixture of other habitats. Adjoining the park is Arapaho National Forest, which shares some of the avifauna.

▶ Birds: There are six breeding colonies of the Black Swift in the park. Other birds of particular interest are the White-tailed Ptarmigan, Blue Grouse, Band-tailed Pigeon, Boreal Owl, Flammulated Owl, Calliope Hummingbird, Lewis's Woodpecker, and Virginia's Warbler. The Brown-capped Rosy-Finch is common in the tundra, with numbers estimated between 1,000 to 2,000. It is a range-restricted species breeding only at high elevations in the Rocky Mountains from southeastern Wyoming to northern New Mexico.

▶ Conservation Issues: Approximately 62 percent of the park borders Forest Service lands, of which 70 percent are managed as designated wilderness. The rest of the park is bordered by subdivisions, summer camps, and rapidly growing towns. Visitation is three million visitors annually, approximately the same number as Yellowstone, which is about eight times the size. Approximately 95 percent of the park is roadless and either designated or recommended wilderness, and only one percent is heavily disturbed. There are several non-native invasive plant species that are becoming management problems, found at elevations below 9,000 feet. The water quality in the many lakes in the park has been affected by visitor use and atmospheric depositions. Fire suppression has allowed an excessive buildup of fuel and there is the possibility of a catastrophic fire. There is an active bird monitoring program consisting of 44 transects with 500 point count stations in nine major habitat types.

▶ Visitor Information: From I-25, exit Highway 34 or Highway 36, westbound to Estes Park. Continue on Highway 34 to the north entrance, or Highway 36 to the south entrance, where the park headquarters is located. From I-70, exit on Highway 40 north to Granby, then north on Highway 34 to Grand Lake, and continue on Highway 34 to the west entrance. There is a $10 entrance fee per private vehicle. Contact: Rocky Mountain National Park, 1000 Highway 36, Estes Park, CO 80517, 970-586-1206.

Gunnison National Forest (4) and Curecanti National Recreation Area (5), Colorado

▶ Highlight: The Gunnison Basin contains more than half the entire world range of a newly described species, the Gunnison Sage-Grouse.
▶ Location: Gunnison County.
▶ Size: More than 600,000 acres.
▶ Ownership: Bureau of Land Management; National Forest Service; Park Service; Colorado Division of Wildlife, private.
▶ Habitats: Shrub steppe below 9,200 feet including sagebrush, riparian areas, meadows.
▶ Land Use: Grazing, agriculture, landfill, recreation.
▶ Site Description: The Gunnison Basin watershed is an intermontane basin in west-central Colorado. The site defined here consists of the sagebrush and riparian vegetation types on Bureau of Land Management and Forest Service lands below 9,200 feet. The uplands, dominated by big sagebrush, are moderately to steeply rolling, and dissected by permanent and intermittent stream drainages. Shallow, eroded gulches are common on upland slopes. Steep-sloped mesas with broad, flat tops occur in several areas. Included in the site are private and Bureau of Land Management lands, Curecanti National Recreation Area, state wildlife areas, and Gunnison National Forest. Represented within this large area are isolated populations of the Gunnison Sage-Grouse. This IBA includes a patchwork of habitats, with the grouse using different habitats for leks, nesting, and brood-rearing at various times of the year. Lek habitat is dominated by low, open vegetation within 400 yards of sagebrush areas with a canopy cover of at least 20 percent and a grass cover of at least 25 percent. Nesting takes place within the sagebrush community and is characterized by sagebrush canopy cover of up to 40 percent, grass heights of a minimum of six inches, and grass cover of a minimum of 30 percent mixed with ten percent forbs. Brood-rearing habitat is along the edges and into meadows and riparian areas with a large grass component and a high percentage of forbs. Winter habitat is determined primarily by snow depth. The Gunnison Sage-Grouse eats only sagebrush leaves during the winter, and can often find exposed plants only in drainages where vigorous sagebrush growth occurs during the spring, and on southern or westerly slopes of greater than five percent sagebrush coverage. Other areas used during the winter include windswept mesas and ridge tops.
▶ Birds: The Gunnison Sage-Grouse was recently described as a species separate from the Greater Sage-Grouse. It is characterized by a smaller body size, differing plumage, and low genetic variation; differences in mating displays and vocalizations have also been noted. The total estimated population size is fewer than 4,000 breeding birds, with more than half existing in the Gunnison Basin of Colorado. For the grouse, winter habitat as well as the leks, nesting areas, and brood habitats are equally important. Winter use sites are also critical for the species and may change within and be-

tween years depending on climatic conditions. Lek sites are traditional areas that may have been used for thousands of years. Researchers are discovering new leks, but these were likely always there but overlooked until recently.

▶ Conservation Issues: Concern about the species' conservation status prompted the Colorado Division of Wildlife and the Bureau of Land Management to take the lead in organizing a citizen-based group, the Gunnison Sage-Grouse Working Group, with all stakeholders present to develop a conservation plan for the bird in the Gunnison Basin. The plan was completed in 1997 and is being implemented. As stated in the plan, the overall goal is "to manage the Gunnison Basin watershed in a manner that restores Gunnison Sage-Grouse distribution and numbers as determined by the carrying capacity of the habitat." The plan addresses such threats as decline in habitat quality, habitat loss and fragmentation, and physical disturbance to bird populations. Actions suggested by the plan include lek enhancement, riparian area restoration, nest habitat treatments, improved livestock management, developing best management practices, and nest predator research.

At present, the population of the Gunnison Sage-Grouse is declining in Colorado (it declined 11 percent in 1999 in the Gunnison Basin), and its distribution has been reduced substantially from historical levels. Hunting of the Gunnison Sage-Grouse is currently not allowed anywhere within its distribution. The pressing threat continues to be the loss, degradation, and fragmentation of habitat. Some private landowners on lands where leks are located have put conservation easements on their property. Local, state, and federal agencies are actively trying to work to increase grouse numbers, and those agencies are currently very aware of their importance to sage-grouse conservation. Critical to the population's recovery is keeping specific breeding areas confidential. The use of all terrain vehicles is a threat to the species. Historically in the Gunnison Basin and at other breeding sites, birders have sometimes disrupted the birds and caused leks to decline or be abandoned. One site, however, is available to public viewing.

▶ Visitor Information: There is a designated Colorado Division of Watchable Wildlife site in the Gunnison Basin, the Waunita Lek, which the Gunnison Sage-Grouse Working Group hopes will draw visitors away from areas more easily impacted by viewing. The Bureau of Land Management manages the land surrounding the Waunita lek, which is on private property. The private landowners have entered into a conservation agreement and donated a portion of their land to the Colorado Division of Wildlife for a parking lot for the Watchable Wildlife site. Best time to see the grouse is late March to early May. Directions to the Watchable Wildlife site can be obtained at http://siskadee.org or by calling 970-641-7063 or 303-291-6181. It is important that visitors not disturb this very rare species by looking for it elsewhere within the basin.

Monte Vista National Wildlife Refuge (6) and Alamosa National Wildlife Refuge (7), Colorado

▶ Highlight: Some 20,000 "Greater" Sandhill Cranes stop by during spring and fall migration.

▶ Location: Near the towns of Alamosa and Monte Vista in south-central Colorado.

▸ Size: Alamosa National Wildlife Refuge is 11,168 acres; Monte Vista National Wildlife Refuge is 14,189 acres.

▸ Ownership: Fish and Wildlife Service; the Colorado Division of Wildlife owns San Luis Lakes and other areas in the San Luis Valley.

▸ Habitats: Habitats at Alamosa National Wildlife Refuge include semi-permanent wetlands, wet meadows, river oxbows, short grass, a riparian corridor in the Rio Grande floodplain, and upland shrublands with greasewood, rabbitbrush, and four-wing saltbrush. Monte Vista National Wildlife Refuge includes semipermanent wetlands, wet meadows (primarily baltic rush), salt grass flats, greasewood flats, and approximately 500 acres of farmland.

▸ Land Use: Habitat management and conservation to provide for migratory birds and other wildlife. Wildlife observation and interpretation, waterfowl and small-game hunting.

▸ Site Description: Alamosa and Monte Vista National Wildlife Refuges are separated by 25 miles, but are under joint management. They are located in south-central Colorado, in the San Luis Valley through which the Rio Grande flows. Though in the rain shadow of the San Juan Mountains with an annual rainfall of only seven inches, the valley receives stream flow from surrounding mountains. This is used to grow vast acreages of barley, wheat, potatoes, and alfalfa; and to irrigate native plant meadows for hay and pasture for large numbers of cattle, horses, and sheep. The Fish and Wildlife Service owns water rights and uses this same water to manage a variety of wetland types to provide good wetland habitat for waterfowl, wading birds, shorebirds, cranes, and numerous other species. There are wetland areas scattered throughout the San Luis Valley. Another significant place is the San Luis Lakes, to the north of the refuges, including many wetlands used by nesting and migrating birds. Blanca Wetlands of the Bureau of Land Management also has nesting waterbirds.

The Alamosa National Wildlife Refuge is composed of natural riverbottom wetland and is bordered on the west by the Rio Grande. The refuge is dissected by numerous sloughs and oxbows of the river. Monte Vista National Wildlife Refuge is a more managed landscape but with wetland impoundments; it still has native wet meadows and greasewood flats.

▸ Birds: The combination of wetland habitat and grain availability make the San Luis Valley Colorado's best Waterfowl Production Area and the major stopover for the Rocky Mountain population of the "Greater" Sandhill Crane, moving between its breeding grounds and its wintering grounds at Bosque del Apache National Wildlife Refuge in New Mexico and points farther south. Up to 95 percent of the population (which numbers between 15,000 to 20,000) roosts in shallow water wetlands on the Monte Vista National Wildlife Refuge and feeds on waste grain in farmlands on the refuge in the spring, and on privately owned fields near the refuge in the fall. On average, cranes begin arriving in early September, usually peak in mid-October, and leave by early November. Northbound cranes arrive in late February, peak the second week in March, and are gone by the first of April. Between 3,000 and 5,000 each of the "Lesser" Sandhill Crane and the "Canadian" Sandhill Crane also stop in the San Luis Valley. Both refuges, but especially the Monte Vista National Wildlife Refuge, have dense, short, emergent vegetation (wet meadows), which provide nesting habitat primarily for dabbling ducks such as the Mallard, Blue-winged and Cinnamon Teal, Gadwall, and Northern Pintail. This vegetation also provides nesting cover for the Wilson's Snipe, Wilson's Phalarope, Northern Harrier, Short-eared Owl, Vesper Sparrow, and other species. Deeper water wetlands on the refuges have nesting Ruddy Ducks, Redheads, American Coots, and Canvasbacks. Cottonwood and willow riparian habitat along the Rio Grande on the Alamosa National Wildlife Refuge also provide songbird habitat. Three large colonies of White-faced Ibis, Black-crowned Night-Herons, and Snowy and Cattle Egrets are found in the valley, including the largest ibis colony in the state. A colony of these colonial nesters on Monte Vista National Wildlife Refuge numbers 800 to 1,000 pairs. Early successional stages of wet meadow habitat (i.e., spike rush) supports breeding Wilson's Phalaropes and Soras; on a recent count in one part of Monte Vista National Wildlife Refuge, 1,500 pairs of phalaropes were estimated. Many Bald Eagles and other raptors are found during winter and early spring. During September and October and again in February and March, more than 35,000 ducks are present on the Monte Vista National Wildlife Refuge alone, but because there is adequate wintering habitat for waterfowl to the south, and because winter temperatures in the valley can fall to −30°F, managers no longer manipulate water levels at the refuge to encourage waterfowl to remain during the winter months.

▶ Conservation Issues: Alamosa National Wildlife Refuge has a wilder character than Monte Vista National Wildlife Refuge. To preserve this wildness, the refuge is less intensively managed. However, water is still manipulated and other management tools such as burning, mowing, and grazing are used. Water from the Rio Grande is supplemented by artesian wells and pumped water from the Closed Basin Project. At Monte Vista National Wildlife Refuge, water is managed to provide appropriate water levels for wildlife and to manage vegetation. This in combination with other management practices such as mowing, grazing, prescribed burning, and farming provide food, cover, and nesting habitat for a large array of waterbird species. The Nature Conservancy recently acquired the Baca Land Grant in the San Luis Valley, adding to the protected lands there. Tall whitetop, a Eurasian weed, has invaded a variety of habitats. Currently researchers from the University of Missouri are studying the plant with the goal of finding methods to control and prevent further infestations.

▶ Visitor Information: Spring and fall migrations are the best times for a visit. Contact: Alamosa–Monte Vista National Wildlife Refuge, 9383 El Rancho Lane, Alamosa, CO 81101, 719-589-4021. There are auto-tour routes and short walking trails on each refuge. The town of Monte Vista holds an annual Crane Festival in early March, with guided bus tours, a craft fair, and other scheduled events. The festival draws thousands of visitors. For information, see http://www.cranefest.com/schedule.html.

17. Badlands and Prairies

This is a semiarid rolling plain dominated by a mixed-grass prairie that lies west and south of the glaciated Prairie Potholes region, east of the Rocky Mountains, and north of the true shortgrass prairie. Due in large part to the continued dominance of ranching, many contiguous grassland tracts of significant size persist in this area. As a result, the area provides habitat for some of the healthiest populations of high-priority dry grassland birds on the continent, including the Mountain Plover, McCown's Longspur, and Long-billed Curlew. The relatively small number of wetlands in the region, including small impoundments created to serve as livestock water sources, receive extensive use by upland nesting waterfowl and their broods.

RANGELAND AND GRASSLAND BIRD CONSERVATION

The needs for grassland bird conservation are as different as the various grassland habitats. The extent and type of conservation needed differs greatly from northeastern sandplain vestiges to Kansas tallgrass, southeastern wiregrass to Colorado shortgrass, or desert grassland to western riparian. For these and most other grassland habitats, the knowledge about appropriate management—prescribed burning, grazing regimes, ecology of native mammals, hydrology, invasive weeds, and so on—has grown tremendously in the past 20 years. Thus, the primary limitation to successful grassland bird conservation today is not limits to our understanding of grasslands, but limits to human will in making grassland conservation a priority.

It is important to understand that the future of many grassland birds, especially in the vast western Great Plains, is closely linked to the ranching economy. Though cattle ranch management is rarely ideal for the management of bird populations, it is often sufficient, and always vastly superior to alternatives, such as conversion to row crops. Thus, conservationists must relate to ranchers as partners with the common goal of maintaining grasslands over the long term, and work with them for habitat improvements such as increasing plant heterogeneity, encouraging habitat variation in different grazing units, allowing prairie dogs, and controlling exotic plants.

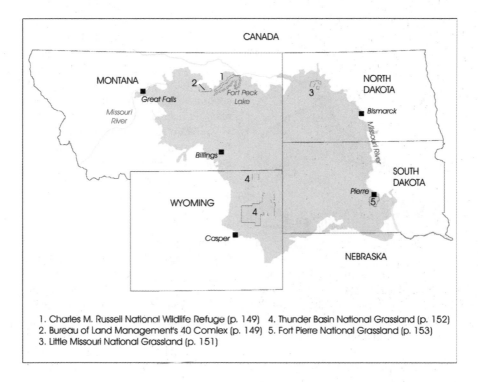

1. Charles M. Russell National Wildlife Refuge (p. 149)   4. Thunder Basin National Grassland (p. 152)
2. Bureau of Land Management's 40 Comlex (p. 149)   5. Fort Pierre National Grassland (p. 153)
3. Little Missouri National Grassland (p. 151)

Charles M. Russell National Wildlife Refuge (1) and Bureau of Land Management's 40 Complex (2), Montana

▶ Highlight: The Bureau of Land Management's 40 Complex and associated private lands contain a significant proportion of the remaining breeding habitat for the Mountain Plover. The adjoining Charles M. Russell National Wildlife Refuge, with its extensive riparian forest, forms an important corridor for migrating land birds, and several listed species breed there.

▶ Location: Along the Missouri River in eastern Montana.

▶ Size: 1.1 million acres.

▶ Ownership: Bureau of Land Management, private, Fish and Wildlife Service.

▶ Habitats: Mixed-grass prairie, sagebrush grassland, cottonwood riparian forest, ponderosa pine-juniper.

▶ Land Use: Hunting, fishing, wildlife observation.

▶ Site Description: The Bureau of Land Management and private lands include extensive prairies, with sagebrush grasslands dominating on rolling slopes with shale soils. There are large colonies of black-tailed prairie dogs. Scattered potholes and reservoirs offer habitat to migratory and nesting waterfowl. Stretching 134 miles along the Missouri River, the adjoining Charles M. Russell National Wildlife Refuge is the second-largest refuge in the lower 48 states. It includes the one place on the Missouri River that is closest to a natural hydrology, including approximately 20 to 25 miles of plains cottonwood riparian habitat in a narrow corridor along the river. It is the only remaining section of this size on the river in a seven-state area that is not grazed, hayed, or farmed. It borders three sides of the UL Bend National Wildlife Refuge, part of the complex of refuges managed by Charles M. Russell National Wildlife Refuge.

Long-billed Curlew

▸ Birds: Bureau of Land Management's 40 Complex and associated private lands contain a significant proportion of the remaining habitat for the Mountain Plover, a candidate for the Endangered Species List, throughout its range. Its total population is estimated at no more than 5,000, of which perhaps half are in Montana. The vast majority nest within prairie dog towns on these lands, where Ferruginous and Swainson's Hawks also occur, as do Burrowing Owls, Prairie Falcons, and Golden Eagles. With the recent releases of America's rarest mammal, the black-footed ferret, on the 40 Complex, the Bureau of Land Management is working to restore a missing component of this ecosystem. There are good populations of Greater Sage-Grouse, and Marbled Godwits, Upland Sandpipers, McCown's and Chestnut-collared Longspurs, Lark Buntings, Grasshopper Sparrows, and Sprague's Pipits are also found on these lands. Least, Common, and Caspian Terns nest in the Charles M. Russell National Wildlife Refuge, as do the California Gull and a small number of Marbled Godwits and Long-billed Curlews. A population of the Greater Sage-Grouse occurs, making more use of this refuge and UL Bend in the winter. Its riparian habitat forms an important corridor for migrating land birds. Another key species, the threatened Piping Plover, breeds along the beaches on Fort Peck Reservoir near Fort Peck except in years when high water inundates the gravel-beach sites the birds need in order to nest.

▸ Conservation Issues: Much of the decline of the Mountain Plover is related to the fact that no more than two percent of presettlement prairie dog complexes remain within its historic range. Recent survey work in the area found 153 nests, of which all but one were on Bureau of Land Management or private lands. Periodic eruptions of sylvatic plague not only decimate local populations of prairie dogs but also cause declines in the preferred nesting habitat of plovers in Montana. Efforts are underway to understand and eventually manage or mitigate plague outbreaks and thereby secure sustainable habitat for the suite of species dependent on prairie dog colonies. Conservation of sagebrush habitat for grouse and other species is also a priority. Principal threats to the diversity of the general area are conversion to cropland, invasion by noxious weeds, and disrupted regimes of fire, grazing, and hydrology. Collaborative efforts by the Bureau of Land Management, ranchers, and others are geared to maintaining the diversity of this landscape in perpetuity. Issues on the refuge include the rapid increase in recreational use, including boating, fishing, and camping.

▸ Visitor Information: The Bureau of Land Management can be contacted at the Bureau of Land Management Malta Field Office, HC 65, Box 5000, Malta, MT 59538, 406–654–5100. The Charles M. Russell National Wildlife Refuge may be entered on the east at Fort Peck and on the west from Highway 191. There is an information kiosk a mile or so north of the bridge over the Missouri River on Highway 191. The refuge can be contacted at P.O. Box 110, Lewistown, MT 59457, 406–538–8706.

Little Missouri National Grassland (3), North Dakota

▶ Highlight: This large block of public land is important for grassland birds, particularly the Sprague's Pipit and Baird's Sparrow.
▶ Location: Western North Dakota close to Theodore Roosevelt National Park.
▶ Size: 1,027,852 acres.
▶ Ownership: Forest Service, interspersed with private inholdings and state school lands.
▶ Habitats: Riparian cottonwood forest, juniper groves on hillsides, mixed-grass prairie on plateaus, ash woodland in canyons.
▶ Land Use: Recreation, oil production, grazing.
▶ Site Description: The Little Missouri National Grassland includes the largest remaining expanse of prairie, estimated at 218,000 acres, in the state. It is also North Dakota's largest block of public land. Western North Dakota is in the Central Mixed-Grass Prairie region, characterized by wheatgrass and needlegrass. The site has open grassland, rolling hills, and more than 200 miles of riparian forest along the Little Missouri River. There are numerous canyons with groves of ash, and the hillsides are dotted with copses of juniper. Grazing cattle and oil wells are also found throughout.
▶ Birds: The site supports tens of thousands of grassland birds. Species occurring there in good numbers include the Sprague's Pipit, Baird's Sparrow, Franklin's Gull, Long-billed Curlew, Dickcissel, Lark Bunting, and Bobolink. A few Greater Sage-Grouse also occur; at last count there were six leks. The Ferruginous Hawk, Upland Sandpiper, and McCown's Longspur also occur; and the Golden Eagle is common.
▶ Conservation Issues: Little Missouri National Grassland composes half the publicly owned land in the state of North Dakota. Since the 1970s, the acreage of roadless areas has halved as a result of oil development. There are now 1,500 wells (many of which are abandoned), and 73 percent of the area's public land is leased to oil companies. Most of the remaining land is still available for leasing. Despite still having two large roadless areas, the Long X Divide and the Bennett Cottonwood, no wilderness has yet been declared, and the grassland is one of only two Forest Service properties with no wilderness. Though the Forest Service is identifying land suitable for wilderness, the members of the state's congressional delegation have stated that they would not propose any wilderness in Congress. Off-road vehicles are damaging some prairie areas, and overgrazing is also a problem, especially for riparian vegetation. Facilities for cattle such as fences and water tanks also impact the ecosystem. The Wilderness Support Center (907-247-8788) and Badlands Conservation Alliance are working to enhance conservation of the area.
▶ Visitor Information: Best time to visit is in the breeding season, in May and June. The Medora Range District has developed a scenic tour of the North Dakota "badlands" in conjunction with the North Dakota Game and Fish Department and Theodore Roosevelt National Park. Hiking and camping opportunities are also available. Contact Little Missouri National Grasslands/Medora Ranger District, 161 West 21st St., Route 3, Box 131B, Dickinson, ND 58601, 701-225-5151, or 701-842-2393.

Thunder Basin National Grassland (4), Wyoming

▸ Highlight: Breeding Mountain Plovers and several other important grassland species.

▸ Location: East-central Wyoming, spanning Campbell, Converse, and Weston Counties.

▸ Size: 571,901 acres, with approximately 1.5 million acres of private lands within the boundaries.

▸ Ownership: Forest Service, private.

▸ Habitats: Ponderosa pine woodland, scoria outcrops, sagebrush steppe, grassland, riparian areas, small wetlands.

▸ Land Use: Grazing, agriculture, coal mining, recreation.

▸ Conservation Issues: Threats posed by mining, grazing, potential for future coal bed methane extraction.

▸ Site Description: A huge area of open prairie mixed with some pine forest, riparian woodland, and small wetlands, Thunder Basin is the second-largest national grassland in the United States. It also contains a variety of irrigated and non-irrigated agricultural land, reclaimed coal mines, and numerous prairie dog towns.

▸ Birds: Designated largely because of its population of the Mountain Plover, the basin also has several important breeding, wintering, and passage species, including the Swainson's Hawk, Long-billed Curlew, Marbled Godwit, Franklin's Gull, Sprague's Pipit, Red-headed Woodpecker, Baird's Sparrow, Harris's Sparrow, Sage Sparrow, Clay-colored Sparrow, Brewer's Sparrow, and McCown's Longspur. Other species of interest include the Ferruginous Hawk, Burrowing Owl, Greater Sage-Grouse, Sharp-tailed Grouse, and Prairie Falcon. The basin also supports a very high density of Golden Eagles.

▸ Conservation Issues: This grassland is one of the three or four most important areas for the Mountain Plover. There are approximately 11,000 acres of habitat occupied by the species. The grassland sends approximately 150 plovers south in the fall. The plover's prime habitat, black-tailed prairie dog towns, has expanded to 19,000 acres, and the plover may expand into this additional area as well.

This is one of the most intact prairie systems in the northern Great Plains but also contains several coal mines, including the largest coal mine in the Northern Hemisphere. There has been controversy about management plans for the grassland, with opponents claiming that the environmental revisions were either too strong or not strong enough. The Forest Service's preferred option is to stay close to current management practices but with the designation of one Wilderness Area, four Research Natural Areas, and four Special Interest Areas. The Bureau of Land Management continues to sell oil and gas leases for the basin, but the leases have some environmental restrictions. Coal bed methane wells are currently prohibited. Overgrazing is damaging some of the basin's riparian woodland. A petition to list the black-tailed prairie dog as endangered failed in February 2000. The basin is the highest-priority reintroduction site for the endangered black-footed ferret.

▸ Visitor Information: Best time to visit is during the breeding season, in May and June. Contact the Forest Service for more information: 125 North Main Street, Chadron, NE 69337, 307-432-0300.

Fort Pierre National Grassland (5), South Dakota

▸ Highlight: Many nesting important grassland birds, including the Greater Prairie-Chicken.

▸ Location: Just south of Pierre.

▸ Size: 116,000 acres.

▸ Ownership: Forest Service.

▸ Habitat: Shortgrass, mixed-grass, and tallgrass prairie; woody draws and riparian areas of cottonwood, green ash, box elder, elm, and juniper; shrub communities; shelterbelts; cropland.

▸ Land Use: Cropland, grazing, hunting, tourism, wildlife conservation.

▸ Site Description: In addition to the prairie communities, the Fort Pierre National Grassland is intermingled with private rangeland and cropland of wheat, sorghum, and sunflower.

▸ Birds: The Greater Prairie-Chicken was common in the mixed prairie region of South Dakota in the late nineteenth century, when millions were killed by market hunters. With the advent of intensive cattle grazing and the conversion of grassland to cropland, the species declined and disappeared from many areas of the state where it had once been common. On Fort Pierre, there are 200 display grounds for both prairie grouse species (Greater Prairie-Chicken and Sharp-tailed Grouse) in the spring, of which approximately 75 percent are the former species. The Upland Sandpiper, Ferruginous Hawk, Marbled Godwit, Lark Bunting, Dickcissel, and Bobolink also nest on the grassland.

▸ Conservation Issues: Much land is in the Conservation Reserve Program, a federal program to restore prairie habitat on private lands in return for subsidies, and this has helped the Greater Prairie-Chicken. Studies suggest that prairie-chickens need at least four square miles of quality grassland habitat to supply roosting cover and protection from predation, intermixed with unharvested food plots providing corn, sunflower, and sorghum. Successful reproduction requires adequate rainfall in spring and summer to provide habitat for nesting and brood cover. On Fort Pierre, there is a hunting season for the two grouse species. The grassland is a multiple-use area, with livestock grazing permitted; at present, approximately 10,000 head are on the grassland from spring to fall. Biologists conduct extensive monitoring of grass height and density after the grazing season.

▸ Visitor Information: In the spring, the Forest Service sets up two blinds from which visitors can observe displaying prairie-chickens. Accommodations are available in Pierre. Phone: 605-224-5517. Website: www.fs.fed.us/r2/nebraska/ftpierre.html.

18. Shortgrass Prairie

The Shortgrass Prairie lies in the rain shadow of the Rocky Mountains, where arid conditions greatly limit the stature and diversity of vegetation. Some of the continent's highest-priority birds breed in this area, including the Mountain Plover, McCown's Longspur, Long-billed Curlew, Ferruginous Hawk, Burrowing Owl, and Lesser Prairie-Chicken. Reasons for the precarious status of these birds are poorly understood but could involve a reduction in the diversity of grazing pressure as bison and prairie dogs have largely been replaced by cattle. For migrants, it is possible that conditions on wintering grounds could also be having a negative impact. Numerous rivers, such as the Platte, drain out of the Rockies through this region toward the Mississippi Valley. These braided and treeless wetlands are heavily used by migrating waterfowl, shorebirds, and cranes. Hydrological simplification has resulted in invasion of trees and shrubs that support breeding eastern riparian birds, but otherwise greatly reduce the value of the areas as wetlands. The Playa Lakes area in the southern portion of this region consists of numerous shallow wetlands that support many wintering ducks, migrant shorebirds, and some important breeding species such as the Snowy Plover.

Pawnee National Grassland (1), Colorado

- ▶ Highlight: Important site for breeding Mountain Plovers and McCown's Longspurs.
- ▶ Location: Weld County in northeastern Colorado.
- ▶ Size: 1,152,000 acres with a checkered ownership pattern; 193,060 acres are national grassland, and the rest is private, state, and Central Plains Experiment Range.
- ▶ Ownership: Forest Service, private.
- ▶ Habitats: Shortgrass prairie surrounded by croplands and grazing lands.
- ▶ Land Use: Nature and wildlife conservation, hunting, other recreational use, agriculture, grazing.
- ▶ Site Description: The Pawnee National Grassland, a mosaic of Forest Service, state, and private lands, is in the heart of the shortgrass prairie, an ecosystem that

McCown's Longspur

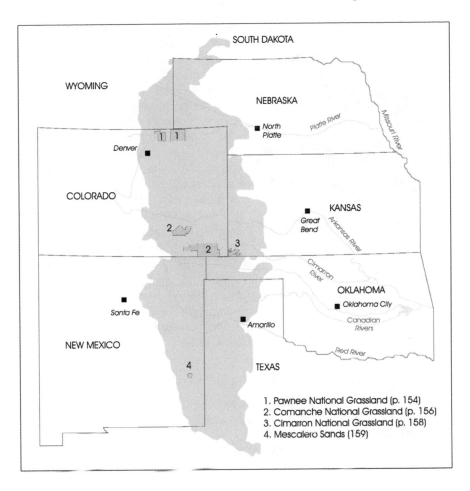

1. Pawnee National Grassland (p. 154)
2. Comanche National Grassland (p. 156)
3. Cimarron National Grassland (p. 158)
4. Mescalero Sands (159)

evolved in a climate with low annual precipitation, most of it coming as spring rains. In this area, characterized by low humidity, high winds, and periodic severe drought, the vegetation is dominated by two short grasses, blue grama and buffalo grass, both adapted to grazing by bison. The area has been the subject of intensive research by the University of Northern Colorado, Colorado State University, Fish and Wildlife Service, and Forest Service.

▶ Birds: This is the habitat favored by two species that are now rare, the Mountain Plover (currently a candidate for threatened species designation) and the McCown's Longspur, a species of extremely high conservation priority. The Mountain Plover prefers areas with patches of bare dirt, such as prairie dog towns or areas resembling prairie dog towns—where there has been overgrazing and burning, for example. Though Pawnee is the hub of the population of the Mountain Plover, with up to 6,000 birds present, numbers have declined greatly since 1995, by as much as 90 percent, due to several years of increased precipitation. This has resulted in vegetation so high that grazing by cattle failed to reduce it to the level that the birds require. Most recently, the weather has been more favorable for the species, and the hope is that the

Mountain Plover

population will recover. The land managers are putting cattle into selected areas, since livestock grazing creates conditions similar to that previously created by the bison.

The McCown's Longspur also prefers the shortgrass habitat, as does the Lark Bunting. Recent reports indicate that both are doing well on the Pawnee, with up to 3,000 McCown's Longspurs and 5,000 Lark Buntings present during the breeding season. The Chestnut-collared Longspur is found in the taller grass, and the Brewer's Sparrow favors the saltbush areas, while the Cassin's Sparrow uses the taller grass along the fence lines, as does the Grasshopper Sparrow.

During migration, many waterfowl and shorebirds make use of the reservoirs and the intermittent ponds on the grassland.

▸ Conservation Issues: Some private lands are being converted from prairie to agriculture; there is increased recreational use of the area.

▸ Visitor Information: Best time to visit is April through June. Contact the grassland at 660 "O" Street, Greeley, CO 80631, 970-353-5004.

Comanche National Grassland (2), Colorado

▸ Highlight: An important site for the United States' endemic Lesser Prairie-Chicken, with more than five percent of its total population; important site for breeding and migrating Mountain Plovers.

▸ Location: Southeastern Colorado in Baca, Otero, and Las Animas Counties.

▸ Size: 435,707 acres; the portion of the grassland with the Lesser Prairie-Chicken is in Baca County.

▸ Ownership: Forest Service.

▸ Habitats: Mixed-grass and shortgrass prairies, and canyonlands.

▸ Land Use: Multiple use, including livestock grazing, wildlife habitat, recreation, mineral production.

▸ Site Description: The Comanche National Grassland had its start in 1938 when the federal government purchased thousands of acres severely damaged during the "Dust Bowl" period and retired it from cultivation. The grassland is in the high plains, with an average elevation of 5,000 feet. Scattered throughout the prairies are canyonlands, with vertical rock walls and woody vegetation including cottonwood, juniper, and piñon pine. The Comanche National Grassland exists within a matrix of public and private lands.

▸ Birds: The Lesser Prairie-Chicken is found in Colorado presently only in the southeastern corner of the state, in Baca and Prowers Counties. A century ago, the species was found more widely in eastern Colorado, but since then its population has dropped dramatically; it is now a threatened species in Colorado. Its present range also includes small parts of four other states: southwestern Kansas, eastern New Mexico, and parts of the panhandles of Oklahoma and Texas. Destruction of the prairie is the main reason for its decline, though excessive market hunting and overgrazing by cattle also played roles.

With ten leks, and an estimated 500 birds, the Comanche National Grassland has played a key role in stabilizing the remaining population. Each spring the males gather at leks to perform their courtship dances to attract mates. The same sites are used year after year. The peak display period is from mid-March to mid-May. A lek may have as many as 40 males. During courtship, the male inflates the reddish-purple sacs on its neck and emits a booming sound that can be heard up to a mile away.

The Mountain Plover also breeds on the grassland. The average number is probably approximately 25 pairs, with up to 49 pairs in years when the habitat has been burned, and probably fewer than ten in years when it has not. Studies indicate that prescribed burning is an important tool in managing habitat for the species. The Mountain Plover also breeds on adjoining agricultural land, but unsuccessfully if wheat is harvested before nesting is completed. The species seems to favor fallow land during migration, and flocks of up to 300 birds have been observed in the area. Other species on the grassland include the Scaled Quail, Long-billed Curlew, Juniper Titmouse, Curve-billed Thrasher, Lark Bunting, and Cassin's Sparrow. It is also a major stopover area for birds during migration.

▶ Conservation Issues: Drought, soil erosion, and habitat degradation due to overgrazing by livestock are among the primary threats. There are 17 producing oil and gas wells on the grassland. The Forest Service cooperates with the Colorado Division of Wildlife and the National Resources Conservation Service to enhance the grasslands through prescribed burns and managed grazing. Prescribed burns of shortgrass prairie are required if the Mountain Plover is to breed successfully.

▶ Visitor Information: The Lesser Prairie-Chicken leks are in the mixed-grass prairie near Campo. For information and reservations to use the blind at the lek, visit the Comanche National Grassland office one mile south of Springfield, or call 719-523-6591.

PLAYA LAKES REGION

Playa lakes are ephemeral wetlands in the Southern Great Plains of Colorado, Kansas, Oklahoma, New Mexico, and Texas. They originate in round depressions where water collects during rainfall. Covering approximately 250,000 acres in 111 counties, the major portion of the lakes occur in the Texas High Plains but reach from the northern Panhandle to southwest Nebraska. The Playa Lakes Joint Venture of the North American Waterfowl Management Plan has identified approximately 25,500 lakes in the five states, of which some 75 percent are in the high plains of Texas. Though they range in size from less than an acre to over 800 acres, most are smaller than 25 acres and usually less than three feet deep. Vegetation associated with the lakes is dominated by annual plants that provide abundant food stocks for migrating birds. Depending on rainfall, playas normally contain water from late spring through fall, with a peak in June. This is an area with as little as 20 inches of annual rainfall and few permanent rivers or streams.

In wet years, the playa lakes region can support two to three million overwintering waterfowl and 400,000 "Greater" Sandhill Cranes; in addition, large numbers of shorebirds use the lakes during migration. When dry, the lakes can attract significant numbers of Mountain Plovers—up to 200 birds—during migration. They also attract large numbers of longspurs and sparrows during migration and winter. Some of the lakes are managed by adding water during the winter, to increase their value to wintering waterfowl.

The area was once dominated by shortgrass prairie but the major land use now is intensively irrigated agriculture. Most of these lakes have become part of irrigation programs and the larger ones are used for grazing. Because the playa lakes are basins, they are greatly affected by surrounding land use, particularly the extensive use of pesticides and fertilizers.

Cimarron National Grassland (3), Kansas

▶ Highlight: Best site to see the Lesser Prairie-Chicken, a species endemic to the United States.
▶ Location: Southwest corner of Kansas, in Morton County.
▶ Size: 108,175 acres.
▶ Ownership: Forest Service.
▶ Habitat: Shortgrass prairie, sagebrush-yucca prairie, riparian woodland.
▶ Land Use: Recreation, conservation.
▶ Site Description: In a semiarid part of the state and bisected by the Cimarron River with its riparian woodland, this national grassland has a topography of rolling hills and rocky cliffs within the shortgrass and sand-sage prairies. Severely impacted by the "Dust Bowl" in the 1930s, the area has been rejuvenated by land-restoration projects over the last several decades.
▶ Birds: Cimarron National Grassland is probably the best place in the world to see the Lesser Prairie-Chicken; it harbors up to 300 and has the highest density per acre of the species on any federal lands. Less widespread and less common than the closely related Greater Prairie-Chicken, this bird is found only in the United States. It has declined dramatically because of plowing and overgrazing of the prairie. Its numbers are still diminishing, and it now inhabits less than ten percent of its historic range. In 1995, 14 leks were known on the Cimarron National Grassland. An assemblage of other grassland birds is also found on the site at various times of the year; these include breeding Long-billed Curlews; Vesper, Cassin's, and Lark Sparrows; Lark Buntings, wintering Harris's Sparrows; and Lapland, Chestnut-collared, and McCown's Longspurs. Mountain Plovers are present and breed in small numbers, probably fewer than 12 birds annually. The Scaled Quail is resident year-round.
▶ Conservation Issues: The Lesser Prairie-Chicken requires a mosaic of bunchgrass and open ground. In the winter, the bunchgrass dies, creating a canopy for hens to nest. Once the chicks have hatched, they need both bunchgrass and open ground where they can forage for insects. The population is limited by the fact that there is not enough residual cover for nesting hens; reduced cover can result from grazing and from oil and gas development, both among the multiple uses on the grassland. Weather is an important factor in the breeding success of the birds; a lack of rain at the right times of year can severely impact the amount of suitable habitat. There is a hunting season for the Lesser Prairie-Chicken, though hunting pressure is not intense. Biologists on the

grassland have established an active management program for the species, and its numbers have increased in the last few years. Prescribed burns are conducted to improve habitat for the nesting Mountain Plover.

▶ Visitor Information: Best time to visit is April and early May. The Forest Service operates two blinds from which visitors can observe displaying birds. Visitors should get to the blinds before dawn. Outside the spring mating season, the birds are very difficult to find. Contact the grassland at 242 E. Highway 56, P.O. Box 300, Elkhart, KS 67950, 620-697-4621.

Mescalero Sands (4), New Mexico

▶ Highlight: Significant population of the Lesser Prairie-Chicken.

▶ Location: Near Caprock, about 40 miles east of Roswell.

▶ Size: Approximately 650,000 acres.

▶ Ownership: Bureau of Land Management, state and private lands.

▶ Habitats: Sand dunes, shinnery oak, shortgrass prairie.

▶ Land Use: Recreation, wildlife observation, grazing, oil exploration.

▶ Site Description: An area of sand dunes that range from small hummocks to 100 feet in elevation; the dunes are stabilized by vegetation, consisting mostly of various grasses and shinnery oak.

Cassin's Sparrow

▶ Birds: The Lesser Prairie-Chicken is resident in the area; the population is estimated at 300 to 400 birds. Among the other breeding species are the Scaled Quail and Cassin's Sparrow. Flocks of Long-billed Curlews migrate through the area.

▶ Conservation Issues: The Caprock Wildlife Habitat Area, designated in 1980, encompasses approximately 645,800 acres, 260,500 of which are public lands. Of these lands, some 328,000 acres are in shinnery oak and suitable for prairie-chickens; of this acreage, 170,000 acres are currently in good condition to support the species. The Bureau of Land Management is not leasing land in the core area for oil and gas exploration, and grazing in that area has been reduced. Near the Wildlife Habitat Area is a 610-acre off-road vehicle recreation area. The Mescalero Sands Outstanding Natural Area, eight miles south of U.S. 380, is designated and protected for its ecological and scenic quality. It is not readily accessible to the public.

▶ Visitor Information: Best time of year to visit is early April when the Lesser Prairie-Chickens are displaying. Summer visits are not recommended, because of extreme temperatures. For more information about Mescalero Sands concerning access, amenities, and observing prairie-chickens, contact the Roswell Resource Area of the Bureau of Land Management, 505-627-0272.

19. Central Mixed-Grass Prairie

T he Central Mixed-Grass Prairie extends from the edge of shortgrass prairie on the west to the beginning of tallgrass prairie and savanna-like habitat to the east. There are vast areas in this region converted extensively to agriculture as well as extensive areas of remaining high quality grassland in the Nebraska Sandhills and other sectors. The BCR includes some of the better remaining areas for Greater Prairie-Chicken and Dickcissel. Sandbars along the larger rivers host a large percentage of the continent's breeding Interior Least Terns. The region is an important spring migration area for American Avocet, Semipalmated Sandpiper, and Buff-breasted Sandpiper. Wetlands concentrated in the Rainwater Basin and other areas, such as Cheyenne Bottoms and Quivira, annually provide habitat for nearly 2 million ducks and 1 million geese. The mid-continent population of Northern Pintail and White-fronted Goose are particularly dependent on these wetland resources. However, wetland drainage and modification and sediment accumulation have jeopardized the integrity of these important landscape features.

Nebraska Sandhills IBAs, Nebraska

Fort Niobrara National Wildlife Refuge (1), Valentine National Wildlife Refuge (2), Niobrara Valley Preserve (3), Crescent Lake National Wildlife Refuge (4)

- ▸ Highlight: Best grassland bird site in the United States.
- ▸ Location: North-central Nebraska, extending a short distance into South Dakota.
- ▸ Size: A total of 19,600 square miles, with dimensions of 256 miles east to west and 125 miles north to south.
- ▸ Ownership: Mostly private, with some federal land, and land owned by The Nature Conservancy.
- ▸ Habitats: Grassland interspersed with wetlands, with isolated deciduous and coniferous forests.
- ▸ Land Use: Grazing, agriculture, hunting, wildlife conservation.
- ▸ Site Description: The Sandhills Region is the largest sand-dune area in the Western Hemisphere and one of the largest grass-stabilized dune regions of the world. The un-

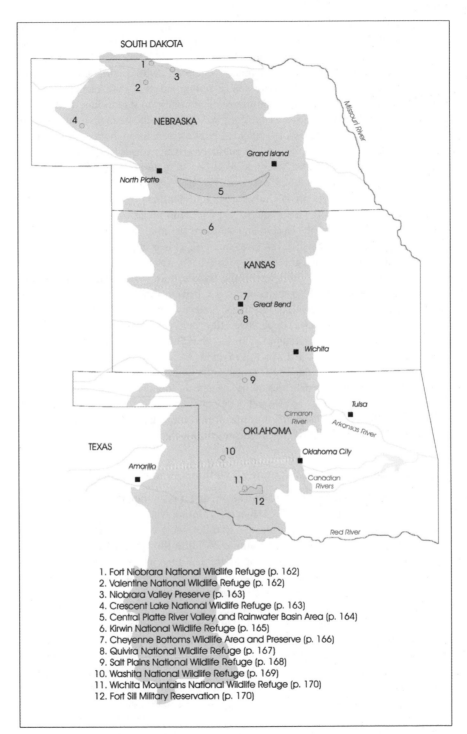

1. Fort Niobrara National Wildlife Refuge (p. 162)
2. Valentine National Wildlife Refuge (p. 162)
3. Niobrara Valley Preserve (p. 163)
4. Crescent Lake National Wildlife Refuge (p. 163)
5. Central Platte River Valley and Rainwater Basin Area (p. 164)
6. Kirwin National Wildlife Refuge (p. 165)
7. Cheyenne Bottoms Wildlife Area and Preserve (p. 166)
8. Quivira National Wildlife Refuge (p. 167)
9. Salt Plains National Wildlife Refuge (p. 168)
10. Washita National Wildlife Refuge (p. 169)
11. Wichita Mountains National Wildlife Refuge (p. 170)
12. Fort Sill Military Reservation (p. 170)

dulating dunes created by the prevailing winds are as high as 403 feet and as long as 25 miles, with slopes up to a gradient of 25 percent. The size of the dunes varies from high, steep hills in the west to small mounds in the east. Principal grass species include sand bluestem, little bluestem, and prairie sandreed, with prairie cordgrass, big bluestem, and switchgrass in the bottomlands; among the shrubs are lead plant and inland ceanothus. The Sandhills remain in excellent condition due to long-term use of virtually 100 percent of the private lands for grazing livestock, the main industry in the area. Some 1.3 million acres of wetlands are scattered throughout. Several areas within the Sandhills representing sites in public or private conservation ownership are designated as individual IBAs: Valentine, Fort Niobrara and Crescent Lake National Wildlife Refuges and The Nature Conservancy's Niobrara Valley Preserve.

► Birds: Sandhill and Whooping Cranes and large numbers of shorebirds are found during migration on or near the Platte River. The main range of the Greater Prairie-Chicken in Nebraska is in the eastern and southern periphery of the Sandhills, where abundance was estimated at 131,484 birds in 1996. This is an area where grain crops have infiltrated the extensive grasslands.

► Conservation Issues: The challenge in the Sandhills is to maintain the grassland-wetland ecosystem while also maintaining the private ranching economy that has helped preserve the biodiversity of the area. The level and quality of groundwater is a prime concern. This requires a cooperative effort between landowners and public entities to protect the Sandhills' natural values. A Sandhills Task Force, representing all interest groups, has been formed with this in mind. As for the Greater Prairie-Chicken, the bird needs a mix of grassland and cropland, the latter as a winter food source. Studies suggest that the greatest densities of the species are found where 30 percent is cropland and 70 percent is native grassland. The development of center-pivot irrigation, especially in the eastern Sandhills, has meant that more land has been converted to cropland, with adverse effects on prairie-chicken populations.

Fort Niobrara (1) and Valentine (2) National Wildlife Refuges, Nebraska

The Greater Prairie-Chicken breeds here, and it is an important stopover site for migrating waterfowl. The 71,516-acre Valentine National Wildlife Refuge is a National Natural Landmark located 20 miles south of the town of Valentine, in Cherry County. Fort Niobrara National Wildlife Refuge is 19,131 acres in size and located four miles east of the town. The Fish and Wildlife Service owns both refuges, which are made up of tallgrass, mixed-grass, and shortgrass prairie, lakes, marshes, and deciduous and coniferous forest. Used primarily for recreation and wildlife conservation, the two refuges are typical of the Nebraska Sandhills, with rolling dunes covered by prairie and wetlands used by migrating waterfowl. Fort Niobrara lies on the Niobrara River and includes both coniferous and eastern deciduous forest. Both refuges have resident populations of the Greater Prairie-Chicken; at Valentine the species is common, and at Fort Niobrara uncommon. Valentine has nesting Long-billed Curlews; it is also an important stopover for waterfowl, with up to 150,000 ducks found there during migration. Many ducks nest at Valentine, including the Blue-winged Teal, Mallard, Northern Pintail, Gadwall, Redhead, Ruddy Duck, and Northern

Shoveler. Many migrant songbirds pass through both refuges. At Valentine, grazing by cattle and prescribed burning are used to mimic the conditions under which the prairie evolved. This not only helps in cycling nutrients but controls non-native grasses which are less favorable for nesting cover for the prairie-chickens and other grassland birds. New ponds have been created on the refuge, and water levels are regulated on some to benefit wildlife. Fort Niobrara is managed primarily for bison, elk, and Texas longhorn cattle.

▶ Visitor Information: Best time to visit is during spring and fall migration. In April through early May, observation blinds are provided at Valentine for viewing the prairie-chickens and Sharp-tailed Grouse courtship displays. For more information, contact the Refuge Manager, Fort Niobrara–Valentine National Wildlife Refuge Complex, HC 14, Box 67, Valentine, NE 69201, 402-376-3789.

Niobrara Valley Preserve (3), Nebraska

Several Green List grassland birds breed here in this 55,000-acre preserve owned by The Nature Conservacy. Located along 25 miles of the Niobrara River in the Sandhills of north-central Nebraska, the preserve in many ways typifies the Nebraska Sandhills. It is shortgrass, mixed-grass, and tallgrass prairie, marsh, shrubland, open water, deciduous forest, ponderosa pine forest. As a large protected area, it is extremely significant as a key area for the conservation of grassland birds. The Greater Prairie-Chicken is found on the preserve, with four or five active leks. Among the breeding birds are the Lark Bunting, Bobolink, and Bell's Vireo. Cranes stop by in greater numbers during the fall, and for the past several seasons, Whooping Cranes have been recorded here. Invasive eastern red-cedar is a problem both in the prairie and deciduous woodland areas. Management includes prescribed burning in the prairies and harvest of the trees where burning is not practicable; some are sold as logs and fence posts, with proceeds used to offset management costs.

▶ Visitor Information: Best time to visit is April through early July, and again during fall migration in September and October. There are trails on the preserve. The office is on site north of Johnstown, in Brown County at 402-722-4440. For further information, contact: Nebraska Field Office, The Nature Conservancy, 1722 St. Mary's Avenue, Suite 403, Omaha, NE 68102, 402-342-0282.

Crescent Lake National Wildlife Refuge (4), Nebraska

Located north of Oshkosh, in Garden County, at the western edge of the Sandhills, this isolated 45,818-acre refuge consists of 18 ponds and lakes within a matrix of sandhills and grassland. Since the sandy soils hold rainfall, the larger lakes have water even in drought years. Grassland birds such as the Sharp-tailed Grouse, Upland Sandpiper, Long-billed Curlew, Lark Sparrow, and Grasshopper Sparrow are common breeding species on the refuge, while the Lark Bunting and Bobolink are uncommon or rare. Up to 45,000 Wilson's Phalaropes can be found on the lakes and ponds in May. Many waterfowl nest on the refuge, and thousands of waterfowl and many passerines stop by during migration.

Portions of the refuge are leased to local ranchers to graze cattle. Grazing and haying are controlled to benefit wildlife. Groves of trees planted on the refuge attract passerines during migration.

▸ Visitor Information: The refuge, owned by the Fish and Wildlife Service, is best reached by dirt road leading north from Oshkosh; few roads in the area are surfaced. Best time to visit is during migration; in April and early May there are blinds for observers to watch displaying Sharp-tailed Grouse. For further information, contact the Refuge Manager, Crescent Lake National Wildlife Refuge, HC 68, Box 21, Ellsworth, NE 69340, 308-762-4893.

Central Platte River Valley and Rainwater Basin Area (5), Nebraska

▸ Highlight: The Platte River and Rainwater Basin form a staging area during spring migration for millions of waterfowl and hundreds of thousands of cranes and shorebirds.

▸ Location: The Rainwater Basin lies south of the Platte River in 17 counties of south-central Nebraska. The northern boundary of the Rainwater Basin Region parallels the central Platte River.

▸ Size: 2,690,000 acres.

▸ Ownership: Private, Fish and Wildlife Service, Nebraska Game and Parks Commission.

▸ Habitats: Scattered wetlands, grain fields.

▸ Land Use: Agriculture, hunting, wildlife observation.

▸ Site Description: Extensive destruction of wetlands in south-central Nebraska began in the early twentieth century, transforming its landscape and diminishing its value to wildlife. After the introduction of center-pivot irrigation, the area became one of the most intensely irrigated regions on Earth. Once there were nearly 4,000 major wetlands totaling nearly 100,000 acres, but of these, only a fraction remain. Still, the Platte River and the Rainwater Basin marshes form a wetland complex of inestimable value to waterfowl. No other stopover area between wintering grounds and nesting grounds can replace the combination of wetlands and grain fields found in close proximity in south-central Nebraska. Most of the remaining wetlands range in size from less than one acre up to 40 acres, with only a few larger than 1,000 acres. They are generally shallow and hold water principally during seasons when precipitation is high. The Fish and Wildlife Service owns and manages some 55 areas ranging in size from 38 to 1,989 acres and totaling 21,742 acres of Rainwater Basin wetlands and adjoining uplands. The Nebraska Game and Parks Commission owns and manages 29 areas, which cover 3,900 acres of wetlands and 3,000 acres of associated uplands.

▸ Birds: More than ten million waterfowl, 500,000 cranes, and 200,000 to 300,000 shorebirds of 30 species use the Platte River and Rainwater Basin during spring migration. The Least Tern and Piping Plover breed, and the Greater Prairie-Chicken is relatively common in the area. Among the other breeding species are the Red-headed Woodpecker, Bell's Vireo, Dickcissel, and Bobolink, while the Short-eared Owl and Harris's Sparrow are found in the winter.

Most of the midcontinent population of approximately 300,000 White-fronted Geese pause in south-central Nebraska each spring, as do 500,000 Canada Geese. In recent years, with the westward expansion of Snow Goose breeding grounds in the Arctic, its numbers in the Rainwater Basin wetlands during spring migration have increased dramatically, rising from approximately 15,000 in 1974 to 353,000 in 1985, and to more than two million in recent years. About half the midcontinental Mallard population and a third of the continental population of the Northern Pintail use the Rainwater Basin–Platte River complex each spring.

In addition, an estimated 200,000 to 300,000 shorebirds of 30 species use the wetlands during spring migration. Wetlands in the central United States are especially important to the White-rumped, Baird's, Buff-breasted, and Pectoral Sandpipers.

▶ Conservation Issues: The importance of the Rainwater Basin–Platte River complex for waterfowl cannot be overstated. Fat reserves acquired during their stay here mean the difference between nest success and failure, influencing both the size and viability of the clutches and broods produced. Recognizing its importance, the North American Waterfowl Management Plan has designated the Rainwater Basin as critical migration habitat for waterfowl, one of only 15 such areas on the continent. Specific goals of the Rainwater Basin Joint Venture call for the protection, restoration, and creation of 50,000 additional acres of wetland and upland. Landowners are provided the technical assistance and incentives for managing and restoring wetlands in the basin.

There is a problem with avian cholera in the basin. Over the past decade, the greatly increased midcontinent population of the Snow Goose has shifted its principal spring migration corridor from eastern to central Nebraska. This means that large numbers of Snow Geese now concentrate on a shrinking wetland base, resulting in greater competition for food with other waterfowl and Sandhill Cranes, and increasing the risk of avian cholera. From 1975 through the 1994 spring migration season, an estimated 200,000 to 237,000 ducks and geese died from avian cholera in the Rainwater Basin.

▶ Visitor Information: Best time for a visit is late February to late April. Contact: Nebraska Game and Park Commission, 2200 N. 33rd Street, Lincoln, NE 68503, 402-471-0641.

Kirwin National Wildlife Refuge (6), Kansas

▶ Highlight: Important site for migrating and wintering waterfowl.
▶ Location: In Phillips County, near Kirwin.
▶ Size: 10,400 acres.
▶ Ownership: Fish and Wildlife Service.
▶ Habitats: Reservoir, river, grassland, riparian woods, cropland.
▶ Land Use: Irrigation and flood control, hunting, fishing, waterfowl conservation.
▶ Site Description: The site includes Kirwin Reservoir, established for irrigation and flood control. Around the reservoir are grass-covered hilltops and croplands, with wooded creek bottoms.
▶ Birds: This refuge is in some ways typical of reservoirs, which have become important to migrating waterfowl. Its prime significance is short-term use by waterfowl. The main function of the reservoir is irrigation. Up to 100,000 geese and 220,000 ducks use the refuge annually, including significant numbers of the Greater White-fronted Goose, with counts up to 39,000. As many as 120 Bald Eagles winter at the site, and the "Interior" Least Tern has bred.

▶ Conservation Issues: Numbers of waterfowl have decreased since peaks in the mid-1970s, due to decreased water levels.

▶ Visitor Information: Best times to visit for migrating waterfowl are April and October. Contact the refuge at Kirwin National Wildlife Refuge, Route 1, P.O. Box 103, Kirwin, KS 67644, 913-543-6673.

Cheyenne Bottoms Wildlife Area and Preserve (7), Kansas

▶ Highlight: The largest marsh in the interior of the United States, Cheyenne Bottoms is one of the most important shorebird migration points in the Western Hemisphere.

▶ Designation: Wetland of Hemispheric Importance in the Western Hemisphere Shorebird Reserve Network, Wetland of International Importance by Ramsar Convention.

▶ Location: Near Great Bend in Barton County.

▶ Size: 41,000 acres.

▶ Ownership: Kansas Department of Wildlife and Parks, The Nature Conservancy, private.

▶ Habitats: Wetlands, upland, native prairie, cropland.

▶ Land Use: Wildlife observation, conservation, recreation, grazing.

▶ Site Description: Considered the most important ecosystem in Kansas, Cheyenne Bottoms is a natural land sink in the center of the state; it represents the state's largest system of wetlands. Of the total acreage, the Cheyenne Bottoms Wildlife Area covers 19,857 acres and is managed by the Kansas Department of Wildlife and Parks, while The Nature Conservancy's Cheyenne Bottoms Preserve covers 7,269 acres; the rest is private land, consisting largely of native-grass prairie and cropland. Approximately 12,000 acres of the wildlife area is generally covered with shallow water, while the rest is wetland habitat with some upland areas. The Nature Conservancy's holdings are higher in elevation than those of Kansas Department of Wildlife and Parks; the Conservancy's land is primarily wet meadow with approximately one dozen semipermanent basins.

Upland Sandpiper

▶ Birds: It has been estimated that 45 percent of the North American shorebird population stops at Cheyenne Bottoms during spring migration, including up to 90 percent of the individuals of several species. Among the most numerous are the Long-billed Dowitcher, Wilson's Phalarope, and Stilt, White-rumped, Semipalmated, and Baird's Sandpipers. More than half of all Pectoral Sandpipers and Marbled and Hudsonian Godwits also stop here during migration. Critical as a stopover for migrating Whooping Cranes and Piping Plovers, it also provides breeding habitat for the Snowy Plover, American Avocet, Wilson's Phalarope, and Upland Sandpiper. As many as 500,000 shorebirds use the site annually. The Harris's Sparrow is common in winter, and the Dickcissel is among the breeding species.

▶ Conservation Issues: The water level at Cheyenne Bottoms fluctuates dramatically, depending on rainfall. It varies from bone dry to five feet deep, and after a heavy rainstorm, the water level can rise as much as ten inches. These fluctuations can help control the growth of cattails, trees, and various herbaceous plants that diminish the value of the habitat to shorebirds. A primary threat to Cheyenne Bottoms is the proliferation of mudflat-invading cattails. The fight to preserve the mudflats has been greatly aided by the acquisition of large tractors. A court decision in 1992 cutting back irrigation at Great Bend has allowed more water to reach the area.

On its preserve, The Nature Conservancy has put a great deal of effort into removing trees around wetland basins, and cattle are used to manipulate the grassland to benefit shorebirds. Prescribed fire management will be used in the future to manipulate the habitat to benefit waterfowl and shorebird use. Plugging of old drainage ditches and the recreation of shallow basins in old crop fields is an ongoing project.

▶ Visitor Information: The best time to visit is during the shorebird spring migration, which peaks in late April and early May; the smaller fall migration peaks in August and September. The birds can be observed from a car, and a scope is a virtual necessity. For more information, contact: Cheyenne Bottoms Wildlife Area, P.O. Box 274, Great Bend, KS 67530, 877-427-9299. Birders will also want to visit Quivira National Wildlife Refuge, only 30 miles to the southeast.

Quivira National Wildlife Refuge (8), Kansas

▶ Highlight: One of the most important stopover points for shorebirds in North America.

▶ Designation: A Ramsar site; Wetland of Hemispheric Importance in the Western Hemisphere Shorebird Reserve Network.

▶ Location: Stafford County, southeast of Great Bend, some 30 miles from Cheyenne Bottoms.

▶ Size: 22,135 acres.

▶ Ownership: Fish and Wildlife Service.

▶ Habitats: Grasslands, wetlands, salt flats.

▶ Land Use: Management for waterfowl and shorebirds.

▶ Site Description: The natural wetlands on the refuge have been modified by dikes and canals. When water levels are high, there are approximately 7,500 acres of surface area in the managed wetland units. The salt flats provide approximately 1,000 acres of high-quality shorebird habitat.

▶ Birds: Quivira National Wildlife Refuge is an absolutely essential stopover point for the thousands of waterfowl and shorebirds using the Central Flyway. It would be hard to exaggerate its importance. During spring migration, half the shorebirds in North America are thought to use this refuge and nearby Cheyenne Bottoms. Up to 500,000 waterfowl pass through seasonally, as well as up to 180,000 Sandhill Cranes and 5,000 American White Pelicans. Occasionally, small groups of Whooping Cranes stop over during migration from mid-March to mid-April, and from October to November. The threatened Piping Plover regularly stops here during migration.

As a wet place in essentially dry surroundings, Quivira is important not only during migration but during the breeding season too. Among the summer residents are the Swainson's Hawk and Mississippi Kite, Wilson's Phalarope, American Avocet, Black-necked Stilt, Snowy Plover, and the largest breeding colony of the endangered "Interior" Least Tern. It is also a good mixed-grass prairie grassland bird area, with nesting Upland Sandpipers, Greater Prairie-Chickens, Bobolink, and Dickcissel. The Bell's Vireo also breeds; and the Harris's Sparrow is present in winter.

▶ Conservation Issues: Management is designed to provide good-quality habitat for both waterfowl and shorebirds. Lowering and raising water levels on units of the refuge are timed to provide shorebirds with habitat at critical times of the year, particularly in the spring. Much of the grassland is managed by prescribed burning and selective grazing. Approximately 1,200 acres of the refuge are planted with winter wheat and milo, part of which is harvested and part of which is left in the fields for migrating cranes and geese. Increased irrigation in the upstream watershed has led to declining water inflow to the refuge. Oil and gas development in the vicinity is a major concern; there are active oil wells in the area, and minor oil spills have occurred.

▶ Visitor Information: Mid-April to early June, and August to early October are the best times to see migrating shorebirds. Waterfowl and Sandhill Crane numbers are greatest from mid-October to late November. Contact the refuge at Rural Route #3, Box 48 A, Stafford, KS 67578, 316-486-2393.

Salt Plains National Wildlife Refuge (9), Oklahoma

▶ Highlight: Largest salt flat in mid-America. It is a major stopover for hundreds of thousands of shorebirds.

▶ Designation: Wetland of Regional Importance in the Western Hemisphere Shorebird Reserve Network.

▶ Size: 32,000 acres.

▶ Location: Approximately 40 miles northwest of Enid, in Alfalfa County.

▶ Ownership: The Fish and Wildlife Service has primary control of approximately two-thirds of the refuge and the Army Corps of Engineers has primary control of one-third of the refuge. The Corps has control of the area that includes the dam and the area of water inflow into the lake from the north. Approximately 400 acres below the dam is the Great Salt Plains State Park, on Corps owned land.

▶ Habitat: Salt barrens, and lake.

▶ Land Use: Wildlife conservation and observation.

▶ Site Description: Located in north-central Oklahoma, Salt Plains National Wildlife Refuge is the state's premier place to observe migrating and breeding shorebirds. Its 32,000 acres are nearly evenly divided between open water, vegetated land, and the feature that gives it its name—some 11,000 acres of almost perfectly flat salt barrens, covered by a thin salt crust formed by seawater flooding millions of years ago. Though devoid of vegetation, these barrens are a major migration stopover area for hundreds of thousands of shorebirds of which "peep" sandpipers are the most abundant; the birds feed on the salt brine larvae, nymphs, numerous other insects, and small crustaceans.

▶ Birds: The refuge is a major stopover site for thousands of waterfowl, cormorants, Sandhill Cranes, and American White Pelicans; many waterfowl also stay for the winter. In terms of numbers, as many as 15,000 "peep" sandpipers have been counted on a single day, with highest counts for the Baird's and Semipalmated; likewise, up to 54,000 American White Pelicans, 50,000 Franklin's Gulls, and 30,000 Sandhill Cranes have been counted in the fall. In the fall, Whooping Cranes also stop over at this refuge more than at any other during their 2,600-mile migration, with up to 18 individually recorded. They stop much less often in spring, though in 1996 up to 12 were observed on a single day. Approximately 200 endangered "Interior" Least Terns and 500 threatened Snowy Plovers breed on the refuge. The Chuck-will's-widow and Red-headed Woodpecker breed on the refuge, as do many songbirds, including the Bell's Vireo, Dickcissel, and Painted Bunting. The Harris's Sparrow is common in winter.

▶ Conservation Issues: Water levels are managed to benefit waterfowl. Salt cedar is invading the grasslands; refuge managers are trying to keep it under control by mechanical means and by annual burns.

▶ Visitor Information: Best times to visit are during spring and fall migration, or in the early breeding season in late May to mid-June to see Snowy Plovers and Least Terns. Summers on the refuge are very hot. Contact the refuge at Tr. 1, Box 76, Jet, OK 73749, 580-626-4794.

Washita National Wildlife Refuge (10), Oklahoma

▶ Highlight: The refuge is a major concentration point for migrant and wintering waterfowl and cranes.

▶ Location: Western Oklahoma, in Custer County in the northwest section of the Foss Reservoir, between the towns of Butler and Hammon.

▶ Size: 8,200 acres.

▶ Ownership: Bureau of Reclamation, managed by the Fish and Wildlife Service.

▶ Habitats: Rolling hills, wetlands, creeks, mixed-grass prairie, bottomland forest.

▶ Land Use: Recreation, wildlife conservation, hunting.

▶ Site Description: The refuge includes 2,000 acres of open water (reservoir and river), 3,000 acres of prairie, 1,200 acres of wetland and forest, and 2,100 acres of planted crops. It lies in the transition zone between tallgrass and shortgrass prairies, and its grasslands include both native and introduced species.

▶ Birds: Waterfowl counts reach 120,000 ducks and geese in winter and migration, with a large portion of the Central Flyway Canada Goose population using the refuge during fall and winter. Other common waterfowl include Snow and Ross's Geese, Mallard, Green and Blue-winged Teal, Gadwall, Ring-necked Ducks, American Wigeon, and Northern Shovelers. The Greater White-fronted Goose is present in smaller numbers, as are the Northern Pintail, Lesser Scaup, Common Goldeneye, and Bufflehead. The American White Pelican is seasonally common, and a few "Interior" Least Terns are seen during migration. Up to 4,000 Sandhill Cranes winter on and near the refuge, and small groups of migrating Whooping Cranes have been seen the last few seasons. Other species include the Red-headed Woodpecker and Bell's Vireo; the Dickcissel is also abundant during the breeding season.

▶ Conservation Issues: The refuge is managed under a cooperative agreement with the Bureau of Reclamation. It lies adjacent to the Foss Lake State Park. Crops are planted to provide winter food for waterfowl. Prescribed burning is used to renew the grasslands, prevent fuel buildup, and control encroachment of woody vegetation.

▶ Visitor Information: The refuge office is located 5.5 miles west and one mile north of Butler. Between October 15 and March 15, the lake is closed to boating to prevent disturbance to waterfowl. Contact the refuge at Route 1, Box 68, Butler, OK 73625, 580-664-2205.

Wichita Mountains National Wildlife Refuge (11) and Fort Sill Military Reservation (12), Oklahoma

Black-capped Vireo

▸ Highlight: Large breeding population of the Black-capped Vireo.

▸ Location: Southwestern Oklahoma, just northwest of Lawton, and adjacent to Fort Sill Military Reservation.

▸ Size: 59,020 acres.

▸ Ownership: Fish and Wildlife Service.

▸ Habitats: Mixed-grass prairie, oak woodlands, intermittent streams, riparian areas, rocky outcrops and canyons, impoundments.

▸ Land Use: Hunting, conservation, tourism.

▸ Site Description: Arising sharply from the surrounding plains, the Wichita Mountains include several peaks higher than 2,000 feet. In the valleys between them are mixed-grass prairies, oak woodlands, and riparian areas. Several impoundments were created in the 1930s, and there are a few natural streams and springs in the area. Immediately adjacent to the refuge is Fort Sill Military Reservation.

▸ Birds: The refuge is the site of the largest breeding population of the endangered Black-capped Vireo in Oklahoma. Approximately 200 pairs of vireos occur here, making it one of the larger breeding populations of the species anywhere. In addition, there are approximately 27 pairs at Fort Sill. The avifauna of the refuge and the adjacent fort is more characteristic of eastern than western North America, but several western birds (the Rock Wren, Canyon Wren, and Rufous-crowned Sparrow) are found here towards the eastern limits of their ranges. The Chuck-will's-widow and Painted Bunting are common breeding species.

▸ Conservation Issues: The refuge is managed primarily for the bison, elk, and Texas longhorn cattle. Bison were reintroduced using animals from the New York Zoological Garden. Texas longhorn cattle were introduced to preserve a diminishing yet historically significant breed. Management of the rangelands includes burning to eliminate eastern red cedar, an invasive species. Management for the endangered vireo includes population monitoring, trapping of Brown-headed Cowbirds, and prescribed burning to enhance or create oak shrub of a suitable height for the species' nests. As a result of management, vireo numbers are increasing. There has also been some cowbird trapping at Fort Sill. On the refuge, the use of tapes to attract the vireo is forbidden, and visitors are steered away from the critical breeding areas.

▸ Visitor Information: Best times to visit are during spring and fall migration; to see the vireo, the best time to visit is late April through mid-June. Contact the refuge at Route 1, Box 448, Indiahoma, OK 73552, 580-429-3222.

20. Edwards Plateau

This dissected hill country of central Texas is clearly demarcated on the east and south by a fault line and grades into the Chihuahuan Desert and Great Plains to the west and north. The native vegetation is a mesquite, juniper, and oak savannah that is the core of the breeding range of two endangered species, the Black-capped Vireo and the Golden-cheeked Warbler. Other priority breeding birds include the Scissor-tailed Flycatcher and the Bell's Vireo. Intensive grazing by goats has caused vegetation to shift from grass to thicket dominance. Suburban expansion is a more recent threat to bird habitat in the Edwards Plateau.

Fort Hood Military Installation (1), Texas

▸ Highlight: Fort Hood has the largest known populations of two endangered species, the Black-capped Vireo and the Golden-cheeked Warbler, under a single management authority.
▸ Location: Near Killeen in central Texas.
▸ Ownership: Department of Defense: Army.
▸ Size: 218,000 acres.
▸ Habitats: 65 percent perennial grassland and 31 percent oak-juniper woodland.
▸ Land Use: Military exercises and training.
▸ Site Description: Fort Hood, an army installation in the hill country of Texas, is the largest armor training center in the United States, housing more than 46,000 active-duty military personnel, 5,000 civilians, and more than 70,000 dependents. The installation is situated in the Lampasas Cut Plains at the edge of the Edwards Plateau. This region is typified by shallow soils, limestone substrates, and isolated, flat-topped mesas covered with dense, mixed oak-juniper woodlands. Streams are clear and rocky, and river bottoms characteristically are grasslands with scattered narrow riparian zones of hardwood. Some portions of the installation have flint outcroppings and post oak-dominated woodlands. Prescribed burning and wildfires caused by military training generate early-successional hardwood scrubland suitable for the Black-capped Vireo. Old-growth oak-juniper woodlands along canyon slopes and remote sections of the post provide habitat for the Golden-cheeked Warbler.
▸ Birds: In addition to its military function, Fort Hood plays an important role in bird

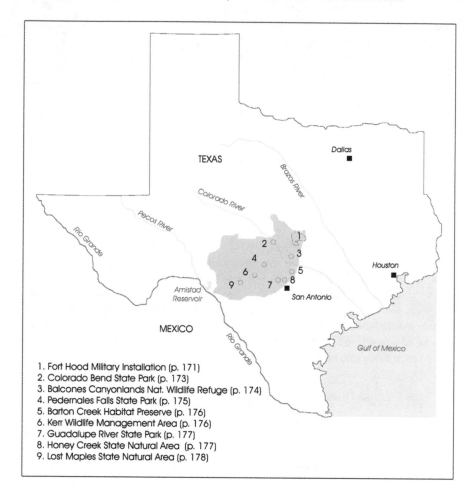

TEXAS

Dallas ■

Brazos River

Colorado River

Pecos River

Rio Grande

1
2 ○
4   ○ 3
6 ○   ○ 5
9 ○ ○ 7 ○○ 8 ■

Houston ■

Amistad
Reservoir

San Antonio

MEXICO

Rio Grande

Gulf of Mexico

1. Fort Hood Military Installation (p. 171)
2. Colorado Bend State Park (p. 173)
3. Balcones Canyonlands Nat. Wildlife Refuge (p. 174)
4. Pedernales Falls State Park (p. 175)
5. Barton Creek Habitat Preserve (p. 176)
6. Kerr Wildlife Management Area (p. 176)
7. Guadalupe River State Park (p. 177)
8. Honey Creek State Natural Area (p. 177)
9. Lost Maples State Natural Area (p. 178)

conservation. It supports the largest breeding populations of the endangered Golden-cheeked Warbler and the endangered Black-capped Vireo under a single management authority. The warbler breeds only in Texas, in and near the Edwards Plateau, while the vireo has a limited and very local breeding range in Oklahoma, Texas, and northern Mexico, though it formerly also bred in southwestern Kansas.

Oak-juniper woodland is a disappearing habitat in Texas, except on public lands. Though the wood is good for fence posts, the woodland itself is regarded by landowners as an invader of pastureland. The result is that it gets cleared, except in less-accessible areas such as ravines. At Fort Hood, however, the woodland is allowed to persist. Both endangered species use oak-juniper woodland, but at different stages of succession. Warblers use the climax stage, but the vireos like the early successional stages; they move in two or three years after a fire and use the habitat for perhaps an additional 15 years. Since they are disturbance-dependent, the habitat for them is patchy. In 1996, there was a large fire on the installation, brought about by drought, and several thousand acres were burned. This resulted in the destruction of warbler habitat and the creation of vireo habitat. At present, there are some 53,000 acres of warbler habitat and 13,000 of vireo habitat at the fort. Though there is no complete census done for the two species, biologists there conduct counts on intensive study areas and then extrapolate. This leads to conservative estimates of 2,000 to 2,500 pairs of warblers (and possibly many more), and in excess of 500 pairs of vireos.

Fort Hood is also important to other neotropical migrants such as the Painted Bunting, Dickcissel, and Bell's Vireo, are common breeders on the installation, probably due to the effective control of cowbird parasitism.

► Conservation Issues: Though cowbird parasitism is a threat to both the warbler and the vireo, the threat to the vireo seems to be particularly critical; if it is to survive, cowbird control is a permanent requirement. At Fort Hood, there is an ongoing program to reduce cowbird numbers; nearly 17,000 cowbirds were trapped and killed in 1998. This has had positive results for the vireo; in 1988, close to 90 percent of the nests were parasitized, but, by 1998, this had dropped to just 6.2 percent. As a consequence, the vireo population has grown considerably. The number of vireos observed in 1998 was nearly double that in 1997, though this may be partly the result of increased experience and/or efficiency in recording observations.

Fire ants are also a serious problem for the birds. Monitoring of vireo nests by cameras to record predation revealed that, of 54 nests filmed, nine failed due to predation, of which six were caused by fire ants. It appears that fire ant control would benefit both vireo and warbler production, since nestlings of the latter are also known to fall victim to the ants.

The warbler and vireo are subject to continued research on the base. In fact, much of the basic research into the biology of these two endangered species has been conducted by the scientists on this base; their program is, according to the Fish and Wildlife Service, one of the most outstanding in the entire country. A cooperative agreement between Fort Hood and The Nature Conservancy involves inventory and monitoring of vireo and warbler populations, as well as characterization of habitat. Studies to evaluate the relationship between cattle grazing and the behavior and movement of cowbirds combined with a cowbird control program, and assessment of the effects of wildfire on the habitats and populations of these endangered species is also underway. Biologists for the fort are also working to generate interest in conserving the warblers on their wintering grounds in the mountains of Chiapas, Mexico, and in Guatemala and Honduras.

► Visitor Information: Fort Hood is an open installation, and the public can use the paved roads. Those wishing to hike or birdwatch should contact the Area Access Office at 254-287-8398. The Nature Conservancy maintains a Fort Hood Field Office with a year-round full-time staff of biologists, a botanist, and Geographic Information System specialist. Organized tours for groups may be arranged by calling 254-287-2885.

Colorado Bend State Park (2), Texas

► Highlight: Breeding Golden-cheeked Warblers and Black-capped Vireos.
► Location: On Colorado River in San Saba County.
► Size: 5,328 acres.

▸ Ownership: Texas Department of Parks and Wildlife.
▸ Habitats: Juniper-oak upland woodland, oak savannah, riparian forest.
▸ Land Use: Wildlife conservation, recreation.
▸ Site Description: The park fronts six miles of the Colorado River. It is in a transitional zone between the prairie to the northeast and the Edwards Plateau to the southwest.
▸ Birds: There are 35 pairs of Golden-cheeked Warblers and 24 pairs of Black-capped Vireos, but the latter is declining here. The Chuck-will's-widow and Painting Bunting also breed in the park.
▸ Conservation Issues: Breeding areas for the endangered birds are closed to the public. Park managers are thinning some vegetation to benefit the vireo, and there is some prescribed burning to improve habitat. Cowbirds are not common in the area and, to date, have not been a problem.
▸ Visitor Information: The best time to visit is March through June. For more information, contact the park at P.O. Box 118, Bend, TX 76824, 915-628-3240.

Balcones Canyonlands National Wildlife Refuge (3), Texas

▸ Highlight: One of the two best sites for the Black-capped Vireo and the Golden-cheeked Warbler.
▸ Location: Close to Austin.
▸ Size: 16,000 acres are at present part of the refuge, with an eventual goal of 46,000 acres.
▸ Ownership: Fish and Wildlife Service, private.
▸ Habitats: Live oak-ashe juniper woodland, post oak-juniper woodland, oak savannah, grassland, riparian corridors, deciduous woodland.
▸ Land Use: Wildlife conservation, recreation.
▸ Site Description: This refuge is made up of several tracts of land in the hills northwest of Austin. It contains a complex of habitats typical of the Texas hill country. Much of the refuge consists of deeply dissected and heavily wooded limestone hills, with an elevational difference of up to 500 feet.

Black-throated Sparrow

▸ Birds: There are approximately 100 territories of the vireo and 800 of the warbler in the area. The warbler is a strict habitat specialist during its breeding season and always uses strips of juniper bark in constructing its nests. It is on its nesting grounds from mid-March to the end of July, while the vireo arrives in late March and leaves in September, but is difficult to find in the late summer.
▸ Conservation Issues: The refuge was established in 1992 to protect the two endangered species. The populations of both are monitored annually. Various management activities are underway to restore additional habitat, particularly for the vireo. These in-

clude cowbird trapping, cutting some encroaching trees, and prescribed burning. Fire is also being used to restore native prairie and savannah in parts of the refuge. A cowbird trapping program was initiated in 1992 at the refuge and elsewhere at vireo colonies in Travis County. Thousands of cowbirds have been removed from the area during the breeding season. This has apparently helped the vireo, and its populations have been expanding at Balcones Canyonlands. Naturally, the cowbird-control program benefits a wider array of nesting songbirds. In the shinoak brush at the refuge, the cowbird traps also protect the nesting efforts of an array of residents and neotropical migrants such as the Scissor-tailed and Vermilion Flycatchers, Yellow-breasted Chat, Bell's and White-eyed Vireos, Painted Bunting, and Field, Rufous-crowned, and Black-throated Sparrows. Cowbird trapping is labor intensive, but it appears to provide an efficient and effective way of regaining some measure of balance in important habitats. Residential development and ranching have been leading factors in the decline of the Golden-cheeked Warbler and Black-capped Vireo. The Austin area is one of the fastest growing in the United States, and residential development continues at a rapid pace, even within the proposed boundaries of the refuge. This will severely diminish the area's biological value. Unfortunately the Fish and Wildlife Service has not received anywhere near adequate acquisition funds to prevent development of prime warbler and vireo habitat. At present, only 16,000 of the proposed 46,000 acres have been protected, and there is a danger that the refuge will not be viable to sustain populations of the two species.

▶ Visitor Information: Guided tours to see the endangered birds are conducted by refuge staff. The refuge can be reached at 512-339-9432.

Pedernales Falls State Park (4), Texas

▶ Highlight: Large breeding population of the Golden-cheeked Warbler.
▶ Location: Blanco County, northeast of Johnson City.
▶ Size: 5,200 acres.
▶ Ownership: Texas Department of Parks and Wildlife.
▶ Habitats: Grasslands, cedar brakes, oak-mesquite woodlands, riverine forest.
▶ Land Use: Recreation, conservation of endangered species.
▶ Site Description: The park lies on both sides of the Pedernales River, with six miles of river frontage. The falls lie in a limestone gorge. The habitats are typical of the Edwards Plateau, with rolling grasslands, rugged cedar brakes, oak-mesquite woodlands, and riverine forest, which includes bald cypress.
▶ Birds: The site holds approximately 70 pairs of the Golden-cheeked Warbler during the breeding season. The Painted Bunting is also found there.
▶ Conservation Issues: In the past, there was some clearing of cedars to improve habitat, but in recent years, in consultation with the Fish and Wildlife Service, this has been discontinued. At present, there is little or no regeneration of hardwoods in the warbler habitat because of heavy deer browsing. Annual deer hunts are conducted, but the deer population continues to have a major impact on the park's vegetation.
▶ Visitor Information: Best time to see the warbler is between mid-March and mid-June. For information, contact: Pedernales Falls State Park, Route 1, Box 450, Johnson City, TX 78636, 830-868-7304.

Barton Creek Habitat Preserve (5), Texas

▶ Highlight: Approximately 60 to 65 pairs of Golden-cheeked Warblers nest on the preserve.

▶ Location: Near Bee Cave, in suburban Austin.

▶ Size: 4,084 acres.

▶ Ownership: The Nature Conservancy of Texas.

▶ Habitats: Live oak-ashe juniper woodland, post oak-juniper woodland, oak savannah, grassland, riparian corridors, bottomland hardwoods.

▶ Land Use: Habitat for endangered species and other wildlife.

▶ Site Description: This preserve is on the outskirts of Austin, one of the fastest-developing areas of the United States. It has a lot of good interior habitat, though isolation and fragmentation of adjoining habitat by residential and commercial development is turning it into an urban retreat. Its habitats are typical of the Texas hill country.

▶ Birds: There are approximately 60 to 65 pairs of Golden-cheeked Warblers breeding on the preserve. The Black-capped Vireo formerly bred, but has not been seen since 1996.

▶ Conservation Issues: The Nature Conservancy acquired this preserve in 1994. At present, it is working to restore bottomland hardwood near Barton Creek, where it had been cleared by previous landowners. Numbers of the warbler are censused each year. Starting in 1999, the Conservancy began working to restore habitat for the vireo in parts of the preserve where it once existed. Restoration is done by mechanical removal of some woody vegetation, followed by prescribed burning and revegetation.

▶ Visitor Information: The preserve is not open to the public. Access is through volunteer workdays and through periodic tours arranged for Conservancy members. For further information, contact: The Nature Conservancy of Texas, Barton Creek Habitat Preserve, 11617 FM 2244, Austin, TX 78733, 512-263-8878 or 512-263-9201.

Kerr Wildlife Management Area (6), Texas

▶ Highlight: One of the largest populations of the endangered Black-capped Vireo. The management program to increase vireo numbers, and those of the endangered Golden-cheeked Warbler, has been particularly successful.

▶ Location: Kerr County, 12 miles northwest of Hunt.

▶ Size: 6,439 acres.

▶ Ownership: Texas Department of Parks and Wildlife.

▶ Habitats: Ashe juniper, live oak-shin oak thickets, springs.

▶ Land Use: Wildlife viewing, hunting, research, conservation of endangered species.

▶ Site Description: The topography of the area is gently rolling and hilly, with occasional draws and small canyons. Dominant trees include several oaks and ashe juniper. The primary goals of the area are directed toward management, research, and demonstration.

▶ Birds: The Black-capped Vireo and Golden-cheeked Warbler are present from March through July. Other breeding species include the Chuck-will's-widow, Bell's Vireo, Painted Bunting, and Cassin's Sparrow; while the Clay-colored Sparrow and Lark Bunting are found in winter.

▶ Conservation Issues: The cowbird-trapping program is a key element in managing the survival of the endangered vireo. Trapping was instituted in 1985. In 1998, 1,658 cowbirds were trapped. Cattle have been concentrated and rotated into areas with cowbird traps, causing trapping success to increase. Without trapping, up to 90 percent of vireo nests were parasitized by cowbirds, whereas with trapping, the level has been kept below 20 percent. The effects of prescribed burns on populations of Black-capped Vireo are also being monitored. Sheep and goats have been removed from the area. Short-duration grazing by cattle is used as a management tool. Cowbird trapping and habitat management in the area has greatly benefited not only the vireo, but also the warbler. In 1986, there were only 27 vireos and 16 warblers, but by 1999 this had grown to 338 vireos and 55 warblers. Much of the research into the vireo and the warbler has been conducted by master's degree students from Southwest Texas University. This has been a successful partnership between a state agency and a university, not only to conduct the research but to implement the resultant recommendations to protect these endangered species.

▶ Visitor Information: Currently birders from all over the world (approximately 600 a season) come to the area to see these birds. Visitors wishing to see either of these endangered species should check in first at the Wildlife Management Area office (830-238-4483). To see the vireo and warbler, the best time to visit is April through June.

Guadalupe River State Park (7) and Honey Creek State Natural Area (8), Texas

▶ Highlight: Nesting Golden-cheeked Warbler.
▶ Location: On the Guadalupe River, on the boundary of Comal and Kendall Counties, north of San Antonio.
▶ Size: 1,900 acres (Guadalupe River State Park) and 1,825 acres (Honey Creek State Natural Area).
▶ Ownership: Texas Department of Parks and Wildlife.
▶ Habitats: Ashe juniper–Texas oak woodland, riparian woodland, live oak-grassland.
▶ Land Use: Wildlife conservation, recreation.
▶ Site Description: Habitats on these adjacent public lands are typical of the Texas hill country, with riverine forest along the Guadalupe River and Honey Creek. Honey Creek State Natural Area was originally acquired by The Nature Conservancy and later transferred to the state.
▶ Birds: The areas combined have approximately 30 pairs of the warbler; Guadalupe has eight to ten pairs, and Honey Creek a few additional pairs. The Painted Bunting and Chuck-will's-widow are among the breeding species.
▶ Conservation Issues: Prescribed burning has been conducted in the past but has been suspended during recent drought years.
▶ Visitor Information: The warbler nests in remote parts of Guadalupe River State Park, and visitors are not very likely to find it here. Honey Creek State Natural Area is closed to visitors except for a guided tour offered on Saturdays at 9 a.m. For information on both areas, contact: Guadalupe River State Park, 3350 Park Road 31, Spring Branch, TX 78070, 830-438-2656.

Lost Maples State Natural Area (9), Texas

▸ Highlight: One of the largest populations of the endangered Golden-cheeked Warbler on publicly accessible land; also the endangered Black-capped Vireo breeds there.
▸ Designation: National Natural Landmark.
▸ Location: Five miles north of Vanderpool, Bandera County.
▸ Size: 2,208 acres.
▸ Ownership: Texas Department of Parks and Wildlife.
▸ Habitats: Oak-juniper woodland, canyons with big-tooth maple.
▸ Land Use: Recreation; primary land use in surrounding areas is livestock grazing.
▸ Site Description: The area is named for relict stands of big-tooth maple that are found in the canyons; these offer a spectacular display of fall foliage. Canyon bottoms support not only maple but sycamore, pecan, walnut, and oaks. On the upper slopes are woodlands of ashe juniper and oaks, while the upland plateaus are mostly grasslands with scattered groves of live oak and madrone.

Zone-tailed Hawk

▸ Birds: In addition to the endangered warbler (95 territories) and vireo (23 territories), the Green Kingfisher and Zone-tailed Hawk occur during the breeding season. The Chuck-will's-widow and Painted Bunting also breed.
▸ Conservation Issues: Habitat for the endangered birds is managed by prescribed burns; cowbird trapping has not been carried out here.
▸ Visitor Information: Best time to visit is April through June; the first warblers arrive in early to mid-March, and vireos in April. This is a good site to see both these endangered species. Park rangers can tell visitors where best to observe them. Use of playback tapes of bird songs is not allowed in the natural area. Contact the Natural Area at 37211 FM 187, Vanderpool, TX 78885, 830-966-3413.

21. Oaks and Prairies

This transition zone between the Great Plains and the forests of the eastern United States is a complex mix of prairie, savannah, cross timbers, and shrubland. Among the priority landbirds that use this mix of woodland and open country are the Scissor-tailed Flycatcher, Painted Bunting, and Mississippi Kite, with a small population of the Black-capped Vireo in areas of denser shrub. Agriculture and urbanization have made tremendous impacts on this region, leaving very little natural habitat available for healthy priority-bird populations.

Attwater Prairie Chicken National Wildlife Refuge (1), Texas

▶ Highlight: Last stronghold for the "Attwater's" Greater Prairie-Chicken, a highly endangered race of the Greater Prairie-Chicken.
▶ Designation: National Natural Landmark.
▶ Location: Approximately 50 miles west of Houston, near Eagle Lake.
▶ Size: 10,200 acres.
▶ Ownership: Fish and Wildlife Service.
▶ Habitat: Coastal tallgrass prairie, marshes, ponds, woodlots, riparian areas, croplands.
▶ Land Use: Wildlife conservation; surrounding lands are developed for agriculture, mostly rice farming.
▶ Site Description: The refuge represents a fragment of coastal tallgrass prairie within an agricultural landscape.
▶ Birds: The refuge is home to one of the only two remaining populations of the "Attwater's" Greater Prairie-Chicken. This highly endangered race of the Greater Prairie-Chicken is close to following the path of another such race, the Heath Hen, which became extinct in the 1920s. It is estimated that more than a century ago, there were one million "Attwater's" Greater Prairie-Chickens on the coastal prairies of Texas and Louisiana; the species had disappeared from the latter state by 1919. Its numbers in Texas dropped from approximately 8,700 in 1937, to 900 in 1986, 456 in 1993, and to approximately 50 in 2000. There are only 20 on the refuge, and, off the refuge, there is only one other site for the species, a Nature Conservancy preserve—the Texas City Prairie Preserve—which has the remaining 30 birds. Its 2,200 acres are landlocked by

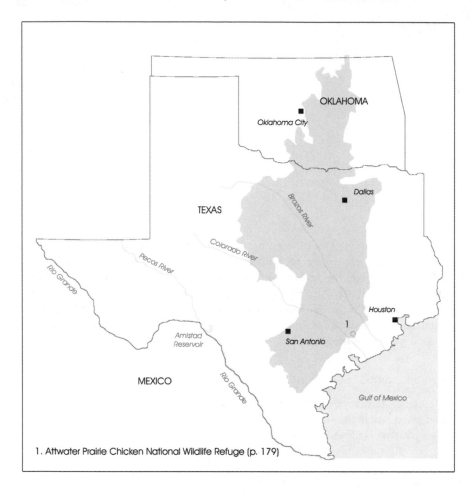

1. Attwater Prairie Chicken National Wildlife Refuge (p. 179)

development, including roads and refineries. Like other prairie-chickens, males perform at leks each morning from February through the middle of May.

The Dickcissel and Painted Bunting commonly nest; the Buff-breasted Sandpiper can be found during spring migration; and in winter, the Sprague's Pipit and several species of sparrows (such as Grasshopper, Le Conte's, and Harris's) are also common in winter and during migration. Three species of interest breeding on the refuge are the White-tailed Hawk, Crested Caracara, and Barn Owl. The Roseate Spoonbill is found in the marshes during the summer months, and many species of waterfowl winter here, as does the Sandhill Crane. Three breeding duck species are the Fulvous and Black-bellied Whistling-Ducks, and the Mottled Duck. Many neotropical migrants pass through in spring and fall.

▶ Conservation Issues: There were once approximately six million acres of coastal prairie, all but a tiny fraction of which has been destroyed by human settlement and agriculture, while suppressing fires has allowed brush species to invade and further reduce the habitat. Among the factors contributing to the prairie-chicken's decline have been urban and commercial development, conversion to cropland, overgrazing, Chinese tallow, and predation. Many of the remaining prairie fragments are now too small to support the species. Research indicates that while the species' life span may range to eight years, half the adults typically die each year from predation or other natural causes. In addition, approximately 70 percent of the nests fall victim to predation, including by introduced fire ants, and fewer than half the remaining chicks survive to adulthood. Periods of harsh weather in the 1990s also led to reduced breeding success.

Management of the refuge includes controlled grazing by cattle and bison, prescribed burning, mowing, replanting of native grasses, cultivation of strip-row crops to supply food for the birds, and control of predation and non-native invasive plants. One such invasive species is the McCartney rose, a woody plant that can destroy a prairie if left unchecked. Control measures include use of herbicides and prescribed burning. The plant offers good cover to skunks and raccoons; skunks are the number one predator of prairie-chicken nests and young during the breeding season. There is a captive breeding program, and 50 birds per year are released onto the refuge. This just keeps the population steady; refuge managers want to be able to release 100 birds per year. Whether or not these measures can prevent the "Attwater's" Greater Prairie-Chicken from becoming extinct after such a precipitous and rapid decline remains to be seen.

▸ Visitor Information: Because of the perilous status of the species, there are no longer any regular tours provided to the booming grounds. An Attwater's Prairie-Chicken Festival is held the second weekend in April; it features guided tours of the refuge, and there is a slight possibility of seeing the species on early morning tours. There is an auto tour from which waterfowl may be seen during the winter months. To reach the refuge from Eagle Lake, travel north on FM 3013 approximately 6.5 miles to the entrance sign on the left. Contact the refuge at P.O. Box 519, Eagle Lake, TX 77434, 979-234-3021.

22. Eastern Tallgrass Prairie

This region includes what was formerly the tallest and most lush grassland in the Great Plains. Beech-maple forest dominated in the eastern sections, and the prairie and woodland ecotone between the two was marked by a broad and dynamic oak-dominated savannah. The modern landscape of the Eastern Tallgrass Prairie is dominated by agriculture. Threats to the upland and wetland habitats of this region include urbanization, recreational development, and agricultural expansion. High-priority grassland birds that persist in some areas include the Greater Prairie-Chicken and Henslow's Sparrow. Worm-eating Warblers are in some wooded areas, and the Red-headed Woodpecker leads the list of savannah specialists.

DeSoto National Wildlife Refuge (1), Iowa and Nebraska

▸ Highlight: Hundreds of thousands of waterfowl stop over during migration.
▸ Location: On the Missouri River in Harrison County, Iowa; and Washington County, Nebraska, east of Blair; and west of Missouri Valley, Iowa.
▸ Size: 7,823 acres (3,499 in Iowa; 4,324 in Nebraska).
▸ Ownership: Fish and Wildlife Service.
▸ Habitats: Open water, marshes, woodland, grassland, croplands.
▸ Land Use: Recreation, wildlife conservation.
▸ Site Description: This refuge on the Iowa-Nebraska state line includes a stretch of the Missouri River, a 750-acre oxbow lake created when the U.S. Army Corps of Engineers channelized the river, ponds, and cattail marshes in addition to cultivated fields, grasslands, and mature woodlands.
▸ Birds: Hundreds of thousands of migratory waterfowl and many Bald Eagles stop over during migration or remain during the winter. In October and November, huge flocks of Snow Geese stop to rest and feed during their southward migration. Peak numbers of 600,000 or more of this "overabundant" species have been observed from the refuge's visitor center. The Red-headed Woodpecker, Dickcissel, and Grasshopper Sparrow are common during breeding season.
▸ Conservation Issues: The refuge is managed to benefit both migratory waterfowl and grassland bird species.
▸ Visitor Information: Best time to visit is when the geese are migrating, in mid-

November and late March. For more information, contact: DeSoto National Wildlife Refuge, 1434 316th Lane, Missouri Valley, IA 51555, 712-642-4121.

HABITAT LOSS

Habitat loss is widely regarded as the leading cause of the decline of birds and biodiversity, but quantifying that loss and documenting its effect on species populations is difficult. Thus, society accepts the loss of habitat for declining—and even rare species—for lack of inarguable evidence of its effects on birds and other wildlife.

Sometimes—especially in unique habitats having small, discrete distributions—the evidence of habitat loss and resulting loss of birds is clear. The Heath Hen succumbed to habitat loss on Martha's Vineyard in Massachusetts, and the magnificent Ivory-billed Woodpecker disappeared with the clearing of the last large stands of bottomland, primary forest in the Southeast. These losses continue today as witnessed by the loss of California chaparral (and California Gnatcatchers) and Florida scrub-oak habitat (responsible for Florida Scrub-jay declines). In the future, we may be faced with even larger-scale problems such as the loss of East Coast barrier islands to sea level rise. With extensive mainland waterfront development, many barrier island and bay breeders will simply have no place else to go.

In a few cases—such as with the loss of more than 90 percent of Mississippi River bottomland forest, or more than 98 percent of tallgrass prairie—scientists have some idea of the extent of loss of particular habitat types. But even for these habitats, it is often difficult to know the effects of those losses. On the one hand, birds can sometimes adapt by concentrating their populations, moving to similar habitats, or otherwise adapting to habitat changes. On the other hand, bird declines can be proportionally greater than habitat losses where numbers of birds sink below minimum viable population thresholds. Habitat loss is not always obvious or absolute. In addition to losing habitat to asphalt or the plow, it can be degraded in ways such that though it might appear to be intact, its usefulness to birds has been compromised. For example, a few acre woodlot might be adequate in extent for a breeding pair of Wood Thrushes, but if deer have browsed all of the undergrowth or neighborhood cats regularly hunt the area, then that woodlot will be essentially sterile in terms of ground or low shrub nesting species.

Thus, habitat quality is as important as quantity in assessing its value to wildlife, and though land acquisition, easements, and other legal protections are critical tools in conservation, they are not sufficient alone. Conservationists and land managers must be prepared to address the full spectrum of land and water quantity, quality, and configuration issues.

Increasingly, land managers and biologists recognize lands need to be managed in ways that promote success for the different stages of the life cycles of target species. Therefore, livestock must be excluded from western riparian habitats if we want breeding Yellow-billed Cuckoos, grasslands must be periodically burned to maintain optimal habitat for some grassland species, and loblolly pines of at least 60 years of age must be maintained for the Red-cockaded Woodpecker.

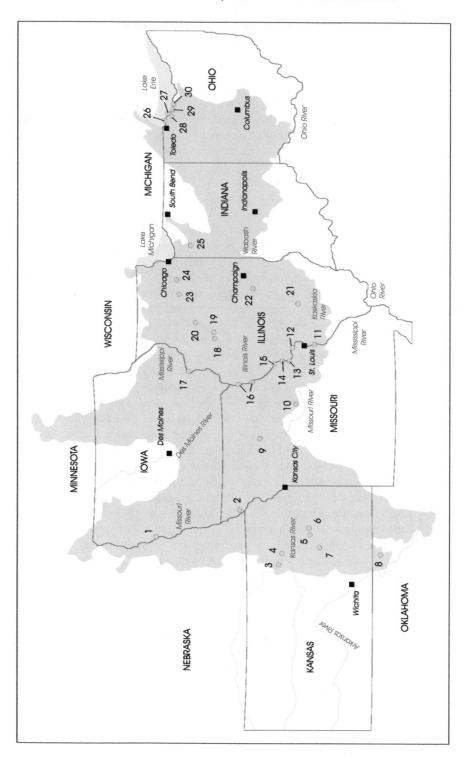

Management prescriptions are becoming increasingly complex as our understanding of birds grows. Some species such as the Greater Prairie-Chicken require large-landscape scale approaches, where others such as the Red Knot require management of smaller migration stopover areas such as the Delaware Bay. Increasingly, we are confronted with land use decisions in which actions to benefit one target species may have deleterious effects on others. For example, allowing the deciduous forests of the Southern Appalachians to mature may be excellent for Cerulean Warblers, but may result in dramatic losses of Golden-winged Warblers, a species dependent on early successional growth.

Finally, what needs to be done for widely distributed, common, but declining species such as the Rufous-sided Towhee? How do we know when to be concerned, when to take action, and where?

These and many more considerations make clear the need for coordinated planning of the entire distributions of habitat types and rangewide planning for declining species. The larger initiatives now underway and cooperating under the umbrella of the North American Bird Conservation Initiative are accomplishing these tasks and hold the best promise for successful, long-term conservation.

Squaw Creek National Wildlife Refuge (2), Missouri

▸ Highlight: Major stopover and wintering area for waterfowl.
▸ Location: The refuge lies in the Missouri River Basin in northwest Missouri, five miles south of Mound City.
▸ Size: 7,178 acres.
▸ Ownership: Fish and Wildlife Service.
▸ Habitats: Man-made marsh and managed impoundments, forest, remnants of upland prairie, cropland.
▸ Land Use: Hunting, wildlife observation.
▸ Site Description: The refuge, which lies along the floodplain of the Missouri River, contains a mixture of habitats including 2,000 acres of grassland, 1,600 acres of forest, 600 acres of cropland, and a complex of wetlands and marshes divided into managed impoundments and dotted with clumps of willow and cottonwood. The eastern edge of the refuge is overlooked by bluffs made from wind deposited soil loess from the last Ice Age, and these are topped by the last remnants of an ancient prairie. There is also some bottomland forest. The Squaw Creek watershed covers approximately 45,000 acres.
▸ Birds: As many as 300,000 geese (mostly Snow Geese) and 200,000 ducks have been counted during late fall; many spending the winter. The refuge is also an important wintering area for the Bald Eagle, with counts of up to 200; during migration it is also heavily used by shorebirds. The Franklin's Gull and American White Pelican are common during migration. Among the common breeding birds are the Bell's Vireo and Dickcissel.
▸ Conservation Issues: The area was once a marsh with meandering creeks that were straightened for agricultural drainage. Water levels and croplands are managed to benefit migrating and wintering waterfowl. The drainage in the Squaw Creek watershed is mostly agricultural, with accompanying sedimentation and runoff of herbicides, pesticides, and fertilizers. The impoundments on the refuge are filling in due to siltation. Some of the highest soil losses in the United States occur in the deep loess deposits along the Missouri River. Among the aggressive non-native plants are garlic mustard, reed canary grass, johnsongrass, and musk thistle.
▸ Visitor Information: To see waterfowl concentrations, the best time to visit is fall through spring. There is a ten-mile loop road, trails, and viewing towers. For information, contact: Squaw Creek National Wildlife Refuge, P.O. Box 158, Mound City, MO 64470, 816-442-3187.

Flint Hills IBAs, Kansas and Oklahoma

Fort Riley Military Reservation, KS (3), Konza Prairie Research Natural Area, KS (4), Flint Hills National Wildlife Refuge, KS (5), John Redmond Reservoir, KS (6), Flint Hills Tallgrass Prairie Preserve, KS (7), Tallgrass Prairie National Preserve, OK (8)

▸ Highlight: One of the great remnant source areas for grassland birds on the continent.
▸ Location: Eastern Kansas, running north-south from near the Nebraska state line into eastern Oklahoma.

▸ Size: Approximately 8,000,000 acres.

▸ Ownership: Mostly private, with some federal and private conservation group lands.

▸ Habitats: Grasslands including native and introduced grasses.

▸ Land Use: Grazing.

▸ Site Description: The Flint Hills contain the largest blocks of tallgrass prairie left in the United States and the only remaining tallgrass area of significant size. This is one of the great remnant source areas for grassland birds on the continent, since it has been dominated by livestock rather than row crops and remains largely in grassland. The vast majority of lands within the region are in private ownership. Lands managed for conservation within it are Konza Prairie Research Natural Area, Flint Hills Tallgrass Prairie Preserve, and Flint Hills National Wildlife Refuge; an important military installation, Fort Riley, is found here as well. Each of these sites receives an individual account. In addition, the Tallgrass Prairie National Preserve, owned by the National Park Trust but managed by the National Park Service, is an important prairie site within the Flint Hills, at present run as a working ranch, but providing habitat for many of the grassland birds.

▸ Birds: A large population of the Greater Prairie-Chicken is found in the Flint Hills, as are good populations of several other important grassland species, including the Upland Sandpiper, Dickcissel, and Henslow's and Grasshopper Sparrows.

▸ Conservation Issues: The Greater Prairie-Chicken is hunted in Kansas. Studies show that the trend in its numbers based on booming ground surveys has been downward in the state, including in the Flint Hills, which represents its prime range. At present, with no significant areas under management for the bird, the outlook for Kansas is uncertain at best. Probably the best populations of the Henslow's Sparrow exists in the Flint Hills. In terms of grassland birds in general, light livestock grazing is largely compatible with their success and should be encouraged as a means of accomplishing bird conservation objectives. One problem for the prairie-chicken is that annual burning on privately owned grassland has become a feature of cattle ranching in the Flint Hills, since it allows ranchers to double the size of their herds. But it is having devastating effects on the prairie-chicken, since the practice removes the vegetative cover and destroys insects, reptiles, and small mammals in addition to forcing female prairie-chickens off the nest. Though periodic fire is a natural and necessary component of grassland ecosystems, if it occurs on an annual basis, it is very damaging to grassland fauna and could lead to the elimination of the prairie-chicken from an important part of its range. One measure of the decline of the prairie-chicken is that the number of birds killed during the hunting season has fallen precipitously, from approximately 109,000 in 1982 to 19,300 in 2000. Researchers attribute the decline in Kansas and Oklahoma to the practice of annual spring burning and the increased size of cattle herds. They recommend rotational burning, whereby patches are burned no more than once every three or four years; this regime is used in Nebraska and South Dakota, where prairie-chicken populations are holding their own. A new alliance of ranchers, conservationists, and state wildlife biologists, the Tallgrass Legacy Alliance, is working on ways to preserve the prairie and its biota, but also making it possible as well for ranchers to raise cattle profitably.

Fort Riley Military Reservation (3), Kansas

One of the top sites for the Henslow's Sparrow; several other grassland birds breed here. The reservation is located in Geary, Riley, and Clay Counties, adjacent to the cities of Junction City and Manhattan. It occupies 100,671 acres, is owned by the Army, and is used for military training, agriculture, and wildlife conservation. Fort Riley is the largest expanse of public land in the Flint Hills. More than half the base

is native or replanted tallgrass prairie. With maximum counts of 2,000, Fort Riley is the best site for the Henslow's Sparrow in Kansas, and one of the very best sites for the bird throughout its range. The fort also contains a representative association of tallgrass prairie species, including the Greater Prairie-Chicken, Upland Sandpiper, Grasshopper Sparrow, and Dickcissel. Unlike private land in the Flint Hills, cattle grazing is excluded from the installation. An extensive agricultural hay lease program is managed here, and the fort has a prescribed burn program that strives to average one burn every three years. In some years, this creates thousands of acres of prime habitat for the Henslow's Sparrow.

Henslow's Sparrow

▶ Visitor Information: Access by the public to Fort Riley is restricted on a daily basis. Call 785-239-6211 for access information. Best time to visit is during the breeding season, from mid-May to early July.

Konza Prairie Research Natural Area (4), Kansas

Located in Geary and Riley Counties, approximately eight miles south of Manhattan, the area occupies 8,616 acres, is owned by The Nature Conservancy, and is used for conservation and research. Because of its relatively steep topography and rocky soils, this grassland has never been plowed. Attracted by its natural qualities, The Nature Conservancy began its work to preserve Konza Prairie in the early 1970s, with the cooperation of Kansas State University. The site is comprised primarily of tallgrass prairie and is an important breeding site for the Henslow's Sparrow, with probably in excess of 100 individuals; the Greater Prairie-Chicken is also a common resident. Among the other breeding species are the Upland Sandpiper, Red-headed Woodpecker, Dickcissel, and Grasshopper Sparrow. The Harris's Sparrow is common during migration and winter. Though it is owned by The Nature Conservancy, the preserve is managed by Kansas State University, with ongoing research projects on the flora, fauna, and ecosystem function. Management includes experimental manipulation of burning frequency and grazing intensity in order to understand patterns

Red-headed Woodpecker

and processes in the tallgrass prairie ecosystem. Forty-eight faculty members and 60 graduate students from 14 departments and five colleges at Kansas State University participate in this research. At present there are almost 20 years of accumulated data on a wide range of population, community, and ecosystem processes in the bluestem prairie ecosystem. Students and scientists from Kansas State University, as well as from other institutions, are actively encouraged to design or participate in research projects on Konza Prairie.

▸ Visitor Information: For information, contact the Biology Division at Kansas State University, Manhattan, KS 66506, 913-532-6620. Best time to visit is in March and April to see prairie-chickens on their leks, and from mid-May to early July to see breeding grassland birds.

Flint Hills National Wildlife Refuge (5) and the John Redmond Reservoir (6), Kansas

Located in Coffey County, near Hartford, the refuge occupies 18,463 acres, is owned by the Fish and Wildlife Service, and is used for fishing, recreation, and wildlife conservation. The refuge is at the upstream end of the John Redmond Reservoir, an Army Corps of Engineers project on the Neosho River. It comprises grasslands, hardwood river bottoms, marshes, sloughs, and agricultural lands. The Greater Prairie-Chicken is resident, and the Upland Sandpiper, Red-headed Woodpecker, Bell's Vireo, and Dickcissel breed on the refuge. The Harris's Sparrow is abundant during migration. The reservoir hosts up to 100,000 waterfowl and up to 500,000 Franklin's Gulls during migration. The refuge is managed to benefit migratory waterfowl.

▸ Visitor Information: Best times to visit are during migration; peak numbers of waterfowl occur in November. Prairie-chickens display in April; in some years there is a blind set up so that visitors can observe the birds without disturbing them. Contact: Flint Hills National Wildlife Refuge, P.O. Box 128, Hartford, KS 66854, 316-392-5553.

Flint Hills Tallgrass Prairie Preserve (7), Kansas

Located in south-central Kansas in Butler and Greenwood Counties, six miles east of Cassoday, the reserve occupies 2,188 acres, is owned by The Nature Conservancy, and is used for conservation and research. The topography includes rolling hills covered with tallgrass prairie of big bluestem, indiangrass, switchgrass, and numerous wildflowers. The hills also contain rocky outcrops, numerous ponds, and woodlands in the riparian corridor along the south fork of the Cottonwood River. Resident or breeding species include the Greater Prairie-Chicken, Chuck-will's-widow, Red-headed Woodpecker, Bell's Vireo, Dickcissel, and Henslow's Sparrow, while the Short-eared Owl is found in winter. The habitat is managed for the prairie-chicken and Henslow's Sparrow. The prairie-chicken requires both open, exposed areas with sparse vegetation for its leks, where the males gather to display to attract mates, and grass-covered areas for roosting and spring nesting cover. Burning and grazing rotation is used to produce this mosaic of habitats. Henslow's Sparrows do best in pastures that have remained unburned for three or more years.

▸ Visitor Information: Access to the preserve is by permission only. For more information, contact The Nature Conservancy, Kansas Chapter, 700 SW Jackson, Suite 804, Topeka, KS 66603, 785-233-4400. Best time to visit is in March and April to see prairie-chickens on their leks, and from mid-May to early July to see breeding grassland birds.

Tallgrass Prairie National Preserve (8), Oklahoma

This is an important protected area for breeding grassland birds. Located in north-central Osage County, the preserve occupies 38,700 acres, is owned by The Nature Conservancy, and is used for conservation of flora and fauna. The Tallgrass Prairie Preserve is located at the southern end of the Flint Hills, the largest intact tallgrass prairie landscape in North America. Approximately 80 percent of the preserve is tallgrass prairie, with the remainder being upland cross timber woodlands (post oak and blackjack oak) and bottomland riparian forests. Breeding grassland birds include the Greater Prairie-Chicken, Dickcissel, Grasshopper and Henslow's Sparrows, and Eastern Meadowlark. The prairie is managed as a functioning tallgrass prairie ecosystem that provides a broad array of habitat patches. The preserve is managed by grazing a reintroduced herd of bison and by prescribed burning that results in a shifting habitat patch mosaic. An extensive research program is focused upon basic ecological studies, remediation of oil field impacted sites, and the development of range management techniques that enhance biodiversity. There is an ongoing radio-collar study of the Greater Prairie-Chicken conducted by the George Miksch Sutton Avian Research Center of Bartlesville, Oklahoma.

▸ Visitor Information: The preserve is open to the public year-round. The best time to visit is from April through early July. The gift shop and interpretive center is run by more than 100 volunteers. Up to 30,000 people visit each year. Contact: Tallgrass Prairie Preserve, P.O. Box 458, Pawhuska, OK 74056, 918-287-4803.

Swan Lake National Wildlife Refuge (9), Missouri

▸ Highlight: A major stopover for migrating and wintering waterfowl and migrating shorebirds.

▸ Designation: Wetland of Regional Importance in the Western Hemisphere Shorebird Reserve Network.

▶ Location: Chariton County, near Sumner.

▶ Size: 10,795 acres.

▶ Habitats: Lakes, marsh, wooded creeks, ponds, hardwood forest, tallgrass prairie, croplands.

▶ Land Use: Hunting, wildlife observation.

▶ Site Description: The refuge is in the floodplain of the Grand River near its confluence with the Missouri River. Among the main features of the refuge are two large lakes, Swan Lake and Silver Lake. Much of the current refuge land was once cleared but frequent flooding made the area poor for agriculture. The Yellow Creek Research Natural Area is one of the few remaining old-growth bottomland hardwood habitats in the state.

▶ Birds: The Bell's Vireo and Prothonotary Warbler breed, and the Red-headed Woodpecker is an abundant resident. When lower water levels leave exposed mudflats, shorebirds can be abundant during migration, with annual use by more than 20,000 birds; most abundant are the Short-billed Dowitcher and Semipalmated Sandpiper. During fall migration up to 100,000 ducks and 100,000 geese (most of them Snow Geese) are found on the refuge, and more than 100 Bald Eagles have been counted during winter. The Dickcissel breeds.

▶ Conservation Issues: Among the management tools used to benefit waterfowl are wetland restoration, cooperative farming, water-level management, and grassland management.

▶ Visitor Information: Best time to visit is August through October to see migrating shorebirds and waterfowl. Contact the refuge at Route #1, Box 29A, Sumner, MO 64681, 660-856-3323.

Mark Twain National Forest (10), Missouri

▶ Highlight: Important source area for the Cerulean Warbler and other breeding neotropical migrants.

▶ Location: Lying mostly in the Ozark Plateau, its several units are scattered throughout the southern part of the state, in 29 counties.

▶ Size: 1.5 million acres.

▶ Ownership: Forest Service, National Park Service, private.

▶ Habitats: Central hardwoods and pine, northern hardwoods, southern coastal species, tallgrass prairie, springs, streams.

▶ Land Use: Forestry, tourism, recreation, wildlife conservation.

▶ Site Description: In an area that was formerly logged and farmed, the forest is the major federal landholding in the Missouri section of the Ozark Mountains. It represents 3.3 percent of the state's land area and ten percent of the state's forests. The landscape varies from gently rolling plains to heavily dissected areas with deep valleys; hills and knobs are scattered throughout. The forest lies within a vegetative transition zone with a wide variety of habitats. The Ozark National Scenic Riverways, managed by the National Park Service, flow through the forest.

▶ Birds: The forest and the scenic riverways are major source areas for the Cerulean Warbler, since the blocks of hardwood forest there are huge, and the habitat structure is favorable for the species.

▶ Conservation Issues: Logging is a major industry in the forest; in a recent year, the

Mark Twain produced approximately 47 million board feet of timber, ten percent of the total for the state. About half of the nation's annual lead ore production comes from federally owned minerals from the forest. There are more than 63,000 acres of wilderness in seven designated areas. The forest also maintains several natural areas, totaling approximately 26,000 acres, managed for scientific studies and for the protection of rare and endangered species.

▶ Visitor Information: Best time to visit is from April to early July, for migrants and breeding birds, and again in September and October, for migrants. Forest headquarters may be reached at 401 Fairgrounds Road, Rolla, MO 65401, 573-364-4621.

Mark Twain National Wildlife Refuge Complex IBAs, Illinois, Iowa, and Missouri

*Middle Mississippi River National Wildlife Refuge, IL, MO (11),
Two Rivers National Wildlife Refuge, IL, MO (12), Mark Twain National
Wildlife Refuge, IL, MO (14), Clarence Cannon National Wildlife
Refuge, IL, MO (15), Great River National Wildlife Refuge, IL, MO (16),
Port Louisa National Wildlife Refuge, IL, IA (17)*

▶ Highlight: Important areas along the Mississippi River for migrant waterfowl, shorebirds, and landbirds.

▶ Location: In addition to the refuges listed above, the IBA includes additional lands from the Rock Island and St. Louis Corps of Engineers Districts managed by the three states, scattered along 340 miles of the Mississippi River from Muscatine, Iowa, to Gorham, Illinois.

▶ Size: Approximately 111,000 acres are in federal ownership.

▶ Ownership: Army Corps of Engineers, Fish and Wildlife Service.

▶ Habitats: River backwaters and side channels, floodplain forest, marshes, wetland impoundments, grassland, cropland.

▶ Land Use: Hunting, fishing, wildlife observation, photography, interpretation, wildlife education.

▶ Site Description: Much of the habitat in the river corridor consists of bottomland forest and wetland. Some of the management units on the refuges have low-level levee systems to control artificial river spiking from the lock and dam system and to maintain wetland water levels. In addition to the floodplain acreage managed by these refuges, the complex also oversees agreements for lands managed cooperatively with the states of Iowa, Illinois, and Missouri. The Corps of Engineers is responsible for forest resource management on Corps-owned lands in the corridor.

▶ Birds: Along with the Upper Mississippi National Fish and Wildlife Refuge area to the north, this corridor area is important to thousands of migrant and wintering waterfowl using the Mississippi Flyway. Thousands of migrant shorebirds and breeding and migrating passerines also utilize the river's habitats. The Red-headed Woodpecker is a common resident, and the Prothonotary Warbler is a common breeder in some sections.

▶ Conservation Issues: The refuge units are managed primarily to benefit migratory birds. Impoundments are drained in the summer to allow plant growth and then flooded in the fall to attract the waterfowl that feed there. Floodplain habitat restoration is a high priority throughout the project area.

▶ Visitor Information: Several of the units are closed during migration to protect waterfowl. For information, contact: Refuge Complex Office at 1704 North 24th Street, Quincy, IL 62301, 217-224-8580, website: http://midwest.fws.gov/marktwain/.

Mississippi River State Fish and Wildlife Area (13), Illinois

▶ Highlight: Thousands of migrant and wintering waterfowl and thousands of migrant passerines and shorebirds in spring and fall.
▶ Location: In Calhoun and Jersey Counties, near Alton.
▶ Size: 33,000 acres.
▶ Ownership: Illinois Department of Natural Resources and U.S. Army Corps of Engineers.
▶ Habitats: Floodplain and riparian forests, riverine wetlands, cropland.
▶ Land Use: Waterfowl habitat, recreation.
▶ Site Description: The site includes 15 management areas stretching along 75 miles of the Mississippi and Illinois Rivers; the areas are backwater lakes and sloughs and bottomland forest. Other public lands occur in this area, including Pere Marquette State Park and a unit of the Mark Twain National Wildlife Refuge.
▶ Birds: Up to 150,000 geese and 80,000 ducks are found in the units during migration and winter, plus hundreds of wintering Bald Eagles. Many breeding and migrant passerines also use the area, as do thousands of migrating shorebirds. Among the breeding birds is the Worm-eating Warbler.
▶ Conservation Issues: The area is managed for waterfowl. Among the potential threats are adjacent development and recreational overuse, with disturbance to the birds.
▶ Visitor Information: Best times to visit are during spring and fall migration. Contact: Superintendent, Rural Route #1, Box 182, Grafton, IL 62037, 618-376-3303.

Banner Marsh and Rice Lake State Fish and Wildlife Areas (18), Illinois

▶ Highlight: Important site for concentrations of migrating waterfowl and shorebirds, and breeding and postbreeding herons.
▶ Location: Fulton County, three miles south of Banner.
▶ Size: 5,660 acres.
▶ Ownership: Illinois Department of Natural Resources.
▶ Habitats: Backwater lakes, floodplain forests, mudflats, croplands.
▶ Land Use: Hunting, fishing, wildlife observation; and conservation.
▶ Site Description: The site consists of large backwater lakes of the Illinois River and adjacent wet floodplain forests and fields farmed for waterfowl. The forests are dominated by silver maple and cottonwood. The agricultural fields are planted with crops to benefit migrating and wintering waterfowl.
▶ Birds: Counts of more than 100,000 waterfowl have been made during migration and winter; in addition, the mudflats host thousands of migrating shorebirds, including an occasional Piping Plover, and thousands of breeding and postbreeding herons are also found. The Prothonotary Warbler breeds in the floodplain forest surrounding the lake.

▶ Conservation Issues: In the past, much of the riparian forest was converted to agriculture. At present, the site is well protected, although it is heavily hunted, and both commercial and sport fishing, and other recreational activities, are popular.

▶ Visitor Information: Best time to visit is during migration, from late March to mid-May, and again in mid-August through October. Contact: Banner Marsh and Rice Lake State Wildlife Areas, Rural Route #3, Box 91, Canton, IL 61520, 309-647-9184.

Chautauqua National Wildlife Refuge (19), Illinois

▶ Highlight: Important stopover for migrating waterfowl and shorebirds. Nighttime observations indicate that more than 1,000 rails use the refuge during fall migration.

▶ Designation: Wetland of Regional Importance in the Western Hemisphere Shorebird Reserve Network.

▶ Location: Near Havana, Illinois.

▶ Size: 4,488 acres.

▶ Ownership: Fish and Wildlife Service.

▶ Habitats: Lake, marshes, woodland, and grassy uplands.

▶ Land Use: Hunting, fishing, boating.

▶ Site Description: Providing an oasis for migrating shorebirds and waterfowl in a landscape otherwise dominated by agriculture, Chautauqua National Wildlife Refuge is one of the most significant stopover points along the Mississippi Flyway. Located in west-central Illinois, the refuge is centered around Lake Chautauqua, historically a backwater lake located on the Illinois River. At present, the refuge is divided into two pools totaling 4,000 acres; one is currently being converted by the Army Corps of Engineers into a stable deep-water lake managed for diving ducks and fisheries, while the other is managed for moist soil plant species and the wildlife associated with that habitat.

▶ Birds: Including seasonal wetlands and bottomland forest, the refuge supports up to 500,000 waterfowl of 24 species, and 150,000 shorebirds in fall migration and lesser usage in the spring. During the fall shorebird migration, key species by order of decreasing abundance are the Lesser Yellowlegs, Stilt and Pectoral Sandpipers, and American Golden-Plover. The endangered Piping Plover has been observed during spring migration. The American Avocet and Buff-breasted Sandpiper may also be observed during migration, and up to 500 American White Pelicans may be present. Among the significant nesting species are the American Black Duck, Black Rail, Black Tern, and American Bittern. Up to 75 Bald Eagles have been counted at the refuge in the winter.

▶ Conservation Issues: Water managers on the refuge strive to mimic the historic flood cycle along the Illinois River. As proof of the success of these management practices, aerial surveys over the past several years have documented the fact that there has been a dramatic increase in waterfowl using the refuge. Since it is located along the Illinois River, water levels can fluctuate dramatically, due to navigation control, agricultural practices, and diversion of Lake Michigan water. Summer floods carrying huge amounts of silt can have a devastating impact on the natural vegetation. The refuge is one of the four units making up the Illinois River Fish and Wildlife Refuges, which together total 10,000 acres along 125 miles of the river. Plans are to acquire lands to total 32,000 acres along the river.

▶ Visitor Information: The nearest town is Havana, in west-central Illinois southwest of Peoria. There is a half-mile nature trail on the refuge and a four-mile auto-tour route. The best time to visit is from late July (when the shorebird migration begins) to October. Contact the refuge at 19031 ECR211ON, Havana, IL 626644, 309-535-2290.

Marshall State Fish and Wildlife Area (20), Illinois

▶ Highlight: Major site for migrating waterfowl, shorebirds, and passerines.
▶ Location: Marshall County, six miles south of Lacon.
▶ Size: 5,658 acres.
▶ Ownership: Illinois Department of Natural Resources.
▶ Habitats: Backwater lakes, floodplain forest, hill prairies, upland hardwoods.
▶ Land Use: Fishing, hunting, boating, wildlife observation.
▶ Site Description: Included in the site are shallow, backwater lakes and floodplain forests along the Illinois River, with adjacent bluffs covered by upland hardwood forests.
▶ Birds: Up to 120,000 waterfowl are found during migration; also thousands of shorebirds and neotropical migrants pass through.
▶ Conservation Issues: There is encroachment by woody vegetation into the hill prairies and prescribed burns are being implemented to address this. Siltation is a problem in the backwater lakes.
▶ Visitor Information: Best time to visit is during spring and fall migration, particularly the latter, from late August through October. Contact: Rural Route #1, Box 238, Lacon, IL 61540, 309-246-8351.

Carlyle Lake Wildlife Management Area (21), Illinois

▶ Highlight: Important migratory stopover for waterfowl, shorebirds, and passerines.
▶ Location: Southwest corner of Fayette County, southwest of Vandalia.
▶ Size: 15,000 acres.
▶ Ownership: Illinois Department of Natural Resources.
▶ Habitat: Open water, bottomland forest.
▶ Land Use: Recreation, waterfowl habitat.
▶ Site Description: The refuge is basically a series of subimpoundments managed for waterfowl found at the north end of Carlyle Lake, constructed by the Army Corps of Engineers in 1967. Nearby is Eldon Hazlet State Park. There are floodplain forests along the Kaskaskia River.
▶ Birds: The site has 175,000 or more migrant and wintering waterfowl, in addition to several thousand migrating shorebirds, including on occasion species such as both godwits, all three phalaropes, the Buff-breasted Sandpiper, and Red Knot. Up to 1,000 American White Pelicans can be found in the spring. The site also has thousands of passerines in transit during migration.
▶ Conservation Issues: Water levels are managed for waterfowl. Holding of water in the lake for flood control has destroyed many acres of bottomland forest along the river.
▶ Visitor Information: Best time to visit is fall through spring. Contact: Rural Route #1, Box 233, Vandalia, IL 62471, 618-425-3533.

Lake Shelbyville Fish and Wildlife Management Area (22), Illinois

▶ Highlight: More than one million waterfowl and thousands of shorebirds occur during migration.
▶ Location: Moultrie County.
▶ Size: 6,400 acres.
▶ Ownership: Illinois Department of Conservation.
▶ Habitats: Man-made lake, subimpoundments, bottomland hardwoods, marsh.
▶ Site Description: The wildlife management area consists of two units. Lake Shelbyville is a man-made reservoir.
▶ Birds: Counts of more than one million ducks have been made in the area during migration, with the Mallard; Green- and Blue-winged Teal; and Wood Duck being the most numerous species. Thousands of shorebirds also occur during migration, particularly the Greater and Lesser Yellowlegs, and Least Sandpiper.
▶ Conservation Issues: Water levels are managed for waterfowl.
▶ Visitor Information: Best time to visit is during spring migration or in late summer, when shorebirds begin to migrate and there is the postbreeding dispersal of herons and egrets. Contact: Shelbyville Fish and Wildlife Management Area, Route 1, Box 42-A, Bethany, IL 61914, 217-665-3112.

LaSalle Lake State Fish and Wildlife Area (23), Illinois

▶ Highlight: Significant stopover for waterfowl and shorebirds.
▶ Location: LaSalle County, near Seneca.
▶ Size: 2,058 acres.
▶ Ownership: Commonwealth Edison.
▶ Habitats: Open water, old fields, planted grassland.
▶ Land Use: Fishing, wildlife conservation, cooling lake.
▶ Site Description: This is one of the more unusual Important Bird Areas; it is a very large man-made cooling lake created by Commonwealth Edison for the nuclear power plant. It remains warm and often unfrozen throughout the winter, providing habitat not otherwise available in the area.
▶ Birds: More than 100,000 waterfowl use the area, and thousands of shorebirds stop on migration; thousands of herons are found there in the postbreeding season.
▶ Conservation Issues: The primary threat is disturbance of waterfowl by recreational use, particularly fishing.
▶ Visitor Information: Best times are during migration, but winter is also of interest. Contact the wildlife area at 2660 E. 2350th Road, Marseilles, IL 61341, 815-357-1608.

Goose Lake Prairie State Natural Area (24), Illinois

▶ Highlight: Large breeding population of the Henslow's Sparrow.
▶ Location: Grundy County, near Morris.
▶ Size: 2,370 acres.
▶ Ownership: Illinois Department of Natural Resources.
▶ Habitat: Grassland.

Sedge Wren

▸ Land Use: Wildlife conservation, recreation.

▸ Site Description: Goose Lake Prairie is the largest native prairie remnant east of the Mississippi River. Adjacent to or near the prairie are three cooling ponds for Commonwealth Edison's Collins Station.

▸ Birds: With as many as 60 breeding pairs of Henslow's Sparrows, this site is one of the few rangewide, with a relatively large and persistent population of the species. Other breeding birds include the King Rail and Sedge Wren.

▸ Conservation Issues: A long-term research project was started in 1987 to monitor the Henslow's Sparrow population.

▸ Visitor Information: Best time to visit is during the breeding season in May and June. For more information, contact: State Natural Area Park Office, 5010 North Jugtown Road, Morris, IL 60450, 815-942-2899.

MIDWESTERN GRASSLAND BIRD CONSERVATION AREAS

Many of the IBAs in this book recognize lands that are important to birds largely because they represent still extant expanses of relatively healthy ecosystems. However, many high priority birds are in peril because the ecosystems they depend upon have been severely disrupted by habitat degradation, fragmentation, and conversion to other land uses. We wish to recognize conservation efforts that seek to "build back" IBAs in regions where high priority birds were once abundant.

In the Eastern Tallgrass Prairie, for example, large expanses of grassland once stretched from eastern Kansas and Nebraska through much of Missouri, Iowa, Illinois, and Indiana, but much of the prairie was plowed and planted with crops or converted to non-native grasses and forage plants as settlement ensued. Birds of the tallgrass were largely able to adapt to life in "surrogate" grasslands such as hay fields and pasture, however, and remained relatively abundant until the majority of those grassland habitats were replaced by more and more row crops and increased urban sprawl. As a result, populations of grassland birds in the Eastern Tallgrass Prairie region have been in severe decline since at least the mid-1900s. A number of large-scale habitat restorations are now underway in an effort to halt further declines.

An outstanding example of habitat restoration work on behalf of grassland birds and other prairie-associated wildlife is occurring in nine landscapes of western and northern Missouri, and another just across the state line in southern Iowa. The ten grassland "focus areas" have embraced the grassland bird habitat recommendations in Partners in Flight bird conservation plans, and have core areas, each well over a thousand acres, centered upon Greater Prairie-Chicken leks. Acquisition and prairie restoration efforts are considered top priority in these zones.

Habitat work that is based primarily on private land incentive programs is targeted in areas encompassing thousands of acres around each focus area core.

Various members of agencies and organizations who are advocates for prairies and grassland wildlife have formed a Grasslands Coalition, with subsets of the coalition's partners contributing to habitat and education efforts in each of the ten grassland focus areas where their interest and jurisdictions overlap. A monitoring and evaluation strategy has also been developed to determine whether the efforts will result in positive population responses by priority bird species such as the Greater Prairie-Chicken, Henslow's Sparrow, Grasshopper Sparrow, and Bobolink. For more information on the grassland focus areas, contact the Natural History Division, Missouri Department of Conservation, P.O. Box 180, Jefferson City, MO 65102.

Jasper-Pulaski Fish and Wildlife Area (25), Indiana

▸ Highlight: Virtually the entire eastern population of the "Greater" Sandhill Crane stops at this site during fall migration.

▸ Location: In Jasper, Pulaski, and Starke Counties, near Medaryville.

▸ Size: 8,000 acres.

▸ Ownership: Indiana Division of Fish and Wildlife.

▸ Habitats: Upland woods, shallow freshwater marshes, open fields surrounded by row-crop fields.

▸ Land Use: Wildlife observation and conservation, hunting, fishing, agriculture.

▸ Site Description: The site is in a flat area with mostly sandy soils. Its upland oak woods, oak savannahs, and pin oak flats are interspersed with seasonal wetlands and freshwater marshes.

▸ Birds: The site is a major staging area for the "Greater" Sandhill Crane in the fall, with annual numbers generally greater than 15,000 and a maximum of 32,000. Up to 7,000 may congregate here in the spring. The Red-headed Woodpecker is a common resident.

▸ Conservation Issues: Surrounding areas are being subdivided for residential development. Because of the large numbers of cranes congregating here in the fall, a disease outbreak could be devastating; additional staging areas for the bird would be desirable. Some land acquisition is taking place in the area through the North American Waterfowl Management Plan.

▸ Visitor Information: Best time to visit is in the fall, from late September to early November. Contact: 5822 North Fish and Wildlife Lane, Medaryville, IN 47957, 219-843-4841

Crane Creek and Lake Erie Marshlands IBAs, Ohio

*Cedar Point National Wildlife Refuge (26), Metzger Marsh Wildlife
Area (27), Ottawa National Wildlife Refuge (28), Magee Marsh
Wildlife Area (29)*

▸ Highlight: Important stopover for thousands of migrating waterfowl, shorebirds, and landbirds.

▶ Designation: Crane Creek and other marshes along Lake Erie are of regional importance in the Western Hemisphere Shorebird Reserve Network.

▶ Location: On Lake Erie in Ottawa and Lucas Counties, just east of Toledo.

▶ Size: Ottawa National Wildlife Refuge is 4,683 acres; Magee Marsh Wildlife Area is 2,000 acres.

▶ Ownership: Fish and Wildlife Service; Ohio Department of Natural Resources, Division of Wildlife.

▶ Habitats: Marshes, open pools, beach, deciduous woodland.

▶ Land Use: Hunting, fishing, wildlife observation, conservation.

▶ Site Description: The two sites lie next to each other where Crane Creek flows into Lake Erie. The area represents Ohio's largest remaining tract of marshlands, more than 90 percent of which were drained for agriculture beginning in the nineteenth century. Another site of interest, the state's 558-acre Metzger Marsh Wildlife Area, lies just to the west, and is similarly important to the Crane Creek refuges as a stopover for migrating waterfowl, shorebirds, and neotropical migrants. An important federal refuge nearby is the 2,500-acre Cedar Point National Wildlife Refuge, administered by Ottawa National Wildlife Refuge, which also hosts many migrating birds. Another refuge administered by Ottawa is West Sister Island Wilderness, an 82-acre island in Lake Erie approximately ten miles offshore from Ottawa, site of the largest and most diverse wading bird colony in the Great Lakes, with 3,500 nests. Five acres are occupied by a Coast Guard station, while the rest is owned by the Fish and Wildlife Service. The nesting herons and egrets fly from the island to the mainland several times a day to find food for their young.

▶ Birds: Crane Creek is a major migration corridor and stopover area for migrant waterfowl and other birds. More than 100,000 waterfowl use the marshes during migration and winter, including up to 70 percent of the Mississippi Flyway population of the American Black Duck, a species that also breeds in the marshes. The refuges are a major stopover for neotropical migrants in the spring, sometimes surpassing Point Pelee across Lake Erie in Ontario. Thousands of shorebirds also stop by during migration; estimates of numbers using the Lake Erie marshes reach nearly 50,000.

▶ Conservation Issues: With the lack of similar appropriate habitat along most of the lakeshore, the Crane Creek refuges play an essential role in sustaining migrating birds during their passage. Water levels at the refuges are managed to benefit waterfowl. Invasive purple loosestrife is a threat in the marshes. Biological control measures using insect predators of the plant are being implemented. The refuges attract millions of visitors each year and are an important source of revenue to the area. The growing number of Double-crested Cormorants at West Sister Island has become a management problem there.

▶ Visitor Information: Best time to visit is during migration; for neotropical migrants, spring is best. The Magee Marsh boardwalk offers a good view of migrating landbirds. For more information on Ottawa National Wildlife Refuge, call 419-898-0014, or on Magee Marsh State Wildlife Area call 419-898-0960.

Sandusky Bay (30), Ohio

▶ Highlight: Perhaps the world's largest staging area for the American Black Duck and Red-breasted Merganser; up to one million waterfowl use the area during fall migration.

▶ Location: A bay of Lake Erie near Sandusky.

▶ Size: Sandusky Bay as a whole contains 36,000 surface acres of water with eight to 10,000 acres of wetlands surrounding it.

▶ Ownership: Mixed, with both state and private, including lands owned by duck hunting clubs. State areas include: Pickerel Creek Wildlife Area, Willow Point Wildlife Area, Pipe Creek Wildlife Area, and Sheldon's Marsh Nature Preserve, owned by the Ohio Department of Natural Resources, Division of Natural Areas and Preserves. Largest private landowners are Winous Point Marsh Conservancy (formerly Winous Point Shooting Club) and Ottawa Shooting Club.

▶ Habitats: Open water, marshes, some woodland.

▶ Land Use: Recreation, wildlife conservation, commercial fishing, sport fishing, hunting.

▶ Site Description: The upper reaches that hold the vast majority of waterfowl during migration include approximately 12,000 acres. This area is held primarily as a wildlife refuge by Winous Point Marsh Conservancy, with main activities of waterfowl hunting and wildlife research.

▶ Birds: This is the largest concentration of waterfowl anywhere in Ohio during migration. The bay area generally makes up two-thirds of all waterfowl counted in the Lake Erie region, which would include Ottawa National Wildlife Refuge and Magee Marsh Wildlife Area. With a fall total of one million waterfowl using the area, the bay hosts a peak of 290,000 at one time, including up to 67,000 American Black Ducks and more than 170,000 Red-breasted Mergansers. Among the other species found here, with maximum counts, are the Canvasback (23,700), Redhead (9,300), Gadwall (13,100) Green-winged Teal (15,525), Northern Pintail (14,800), American Wigeon (8,500), Blue-winged Teal (12,400), Common Goldeneye (3,500), Ruddy Duck (3,300), American Coot (7,000), Mallard (100,200), and scaup species (50,600). Thousands of Canada Geese also occur. As many as 5,000 shorebirds are recorded during peak days during migration, and more than 100 Bald Eagles can occur on a single day during their fall staging in the area. More than 15,000 Double-crested Cormorants have been counted during late summer. Spring passerine migration is extremely heavy, nearly rivaling the concentrations on Ottawa National Wildlife Refuge and Magee Marsh Wildlife Area along the Lake Erie shore.

▶ Conservation Issues: There is a threat of overuse from recreational development. There are also concerns with agriculture runoff and residential development. Most wetlands are protected by the state wildlife agency or the large hunting clubs. Pickerel Creek Wildlife Area wetland restoration is a North American Waterfowl Management Plan flagship project.

▶ Visitor Information: Best time to visit is during fall migration, in October and November for waterfowl and eagles. Passerine migration is best in April and May. Shorebird observation is best during July to September. Contact: Ohio Department of Natural Resources, Division of Wildlife at 614-265-6300, or the Division of Natural Areas and Preserves at 614-265-6453.

P rairies dominate this region in the west and south and beech-maple forest in the north and east, separated by an oak savannah. There are still remnant populations of the Greater Prairie-Chicken in grasslands and the Worm-eating Warbler and other forest breeding migrants to the northeast. Early successional habitat is used by the Golden-winged Warbler, Henslow's Sparrow, and American Woodcock. Glaciation has resulted in numerous pothole-type wetlands and shallow lakes, and the Great Lakes support coastal estuaries and are the destinations of much river water. Additional important lakeshore wetland waterfowl habitats range from emergent marshes and diked impoundments to nearly ice-free deepwater habitats valuable for diving ducks. This region is second only to the Prairie Pothole Region in terms of high densities of breeding waterfowl including the Mallard, Blue-winged Teal, Wood Duck, and Redhead.

Trempealeau National Wildlife Refuge (1), Wisconsin, and Upper Mississippi National Wildlife Refuge and Army Corps of Engineers Lands (2), Minnesota, Wisconsin, Iowa, and Illinois

▸ Highlight: The refuges provide some of the largest areas of wildlife habitat remaining in the central United States and are important for migrant waterfowl, raptors, and passerines; breeding forest interior birds; and wintering waterfowl.
▸ Location: The refuges consist of units along 260 miles of the Mississippi River from Wabasha, Minnesota, to Rock Island, Illinois.
▸ Size: 46,000 acres.
▸ Ownership: Fish and Wildlife Service, Army Corps of Engineers.
▸ Habitats: Wetland-mesic floodplain forest, backwater lake, backwater pond, marsh, urban and developed land, agriculture.
▸ Land Use: Shipping, hunting, fishing, wildlife conservation, agriculture.
▸ Site Description: The refuges hold lands along the Mississippi in four states: Minnesota, Iowa, Wisconsin, and Illinois. The river is an important navigation corridor with an extensive system of locks and dams maintained by the Army Corps of Engineers. The refuge contains among the largest hardwood forests in the upper Midwest, with silver maple, green ash, elm, cottonwood, and swamp white oak, while sand

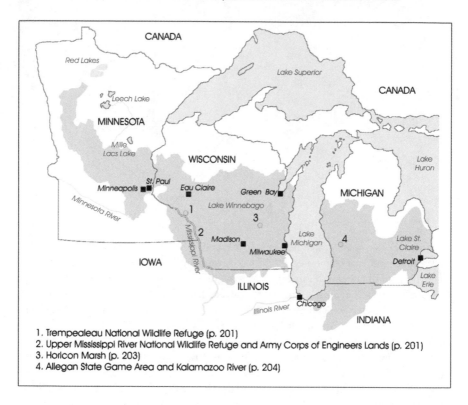

CANADA

Red Lakes

Lake Superior

CANADA

Leech Lake

MINNESOTA

Mille Lacs Lake

WISCONSIN

Lake Huron

St. Paul

Minneapolis   Eau Claire   Green Bay

MICHIGAN

Minnesota River

Lake Winnebago   1

3

2   Madison   Lake Michigan   4   Lake St. Claire

Milwaukee   Detroit

IOWA

Lake Erie

ILLINOIS

Illinois River   Chicago

INDIANA

1. Trempealeau National Wildlife Refuge (p. 201)
2. Upper Mississippi River National Wildlife Refuge and Army Corps of Engineers Lands (p. 201)
3. Horicon Marsh (p. 203)
4. Allegan State Game Area and Kalamazoo River (p. 204)

prairie and hardwoods occur in the uplands. The Corps owns more than half the refuge land, but under a cooperative agreement, the Fish and Wildlife Service manages it as part of the refuge. The Trempealeau National Wildlife Refuge in Wisconsin is part of the refuge system.

▶ Birds: More than 500,000 waterfowl use the refuge during migration, including as much as one fifth of the world's population of the Canvasback (more than 135,000), significant numbers of Lesser Scaup (nearly 100,000), and thousands of other ducks and geese. Thousands of shorebirds and herons use the refuge seasonally, and there are high densities of breeding songbirds in the floodplain forest and many thousands more during migration. Thousands of hawks also use the river as a corridor during fall migration, and feed and rest on the refuge.

▶ Conservation Issues: Introduced zebra mussels threaten native mussels, clams, and snails, while introduced purple loosestrife is responsible for the degradation of many prime wetland habitats; biological control has been instituted to combat it. Upland erosion, channel operation and maintenance, and tow traffic along the river continue to cause degradation and loss of habitat. Sediment deposition and both point and non-point pollution also threaten the biological integrity of habitats along the river. The refuge is heavily used by hunters, fishermen, and other recreationists.

▶ Visitor Information: Best time to visit is during migration from March to late May, and again from August through October. There are many points of access to the refuge along its length. Refuge headquarters are in Winona, MN, 507-454-7351, and there are district offices in each of the four states. Contact the Upper Mississippi National Wildlife Refuge, 51 East 4th Street, Room 101, Winona, MN 55987, 507-452-4232.

Horicon Marsh (3), Wisconsin

▶ Highlight: The largest freshwater cattail marsh in the United States, it is a stopover place for thousands of shorebirds and hundreds of thousands of waterfowl.
▶ Designation: A Wetland of International Importance by the Ramsar Convention.
▶ Location: Dodge and Fon du Lac Counties, near the towns of Horicon, Mayville, and Waupun.
▶ Size: 32,000 acres.
▶ Ownership: The northern two-thirds is a National Wildlife Refuge administered by the Fish and Wildlife Service; the southern one-third is a State Wildlife Area, administered by the Wisconsin Department of Natural Resources.
▶ Habitats: Cattail marsh with stands of bur-reed, Phragmites, reed canary grass, open water, and islands of brush and hardwood forest; the marsh is surrounded by uplands of native grasses and forbs.
▶ Land Use: Fishing, hunting, hiking, canoeing, wildlife observation, agriculture on adjoining lands.
▶ Site Description: Horicon Marsh is a shallow, peat-filled lake bed. In the early part of the twentieth century much of the marsh was ditched and drained, but agriculture proved unsuccessful because fields were too wet during high water years and potatoes grown there tasted like peat. Since the establishment of the refuge in 1941, restoration has involved building a dam at the outlet of the marsh to plug the main ditch, and an extensive system of dikes has been constructed to control and manipulate water levels, including reflooding the drained portions. Horicon is the largest freshwater cattail marsh in the United States.
▶ Birds: Horicon Marsh is known as one of the dozen best birding hot spots east of the Mississippi River. It is the largest nesting grounds for the Redhead east of the Mississippi. It is also the largest stopover site for migrant Canada Geese in the Midwest, about one-half of which use the marsh during migration, with seasonal use by more than one million birds, and peak one-day counts of 300,000 during the fall. Shorebirds are also abundant then. The marsh has the largest heron and egret nesting colony in the state. The Bobolink and Dickcissel breed in the area. Hundreds of American White Pelicans pass through during migration, and the species has recently begun to breed. During the winter, the entire marsh freezes over, restricting its use by birds.
▶ Conservation Issues: The Fish and Wildlife Service and the Wisconsin Department of Natural Resources work together to manage the marsh as one wetland ecosystem. Introduced carp are a problem; they uproot aquatic vegetation and stir up the sediment, suppressing plant growth. Poor farming practices and industrial pollution in the watershed contribute to the sediment in the system, helping to create ideal habitat for the carp. Recently some 1.5 million pounds of carp were removed from the marsh, leading to increased water clarity, regeneration of sago and other pondweeds, and an abundance of aquatic insects. This has benefited the Black Tern, Redhead, and other breeding birds. Non-native purple loosestrife has become estab-

lished; control involves manipulation of water levels, chemical treatment, and introduction of insects that feed on the plant. Nesting platforms have been constructed for the Forster's Tern and Osprey. Rock River Headwaters, Inc., has been created to address problems facing the marsh, particularly those resulting from land use practices on the adjoining private lands. The area receives approximately 400,000 visitors per year, bringing an estimated $3.5 million into the area. Horicon Marsh is open to hunting for deer and small game, but only the state end of the marsh is open to waterfowl hunting.

▸ Visitor Information: Fall migration in September and October is the best time to visit, followed by May through July for migrating and breeding birds. Contact for Horicon National Wildlife Refuge is W4279 Headquarters Road, Mayville, WI 53050, 920-387-2658; contact for Horicon Marsh State Wildlife Area is N7725 Highway 28, Horicon, WI 53032, 920-387-7860.

THE WHOOPING CRANE MIGRATORY REINTRODUCTION PROJECT

Most of the Whooping Cranes in existence breed in Wood Buffalo National Park, in the Northwest Territories of Canada, and winter on the Gulf Coast of Texas, at the Aransas National Wildlife Refuge. But if a group of dedicated biologists and conservationists has its way, there will soon be another migratory population, breeding in Wisconsin and wintering in Florida. The team members of this project are the International Whooping Crane Recovery Team, Fish and Wildlife Service, Operation Migration Canada, International Crane Foundation, National Fish and Wildlife Foundation, Natural Resources Foundation of Wisconsin, the Geological Survey's Patuxent Wildlife Research Center and National Wildlife Health Center, and the Wisconsin Department of Natural Resources.

Starting in summer of 2000, a pilot project testing rearing techniques for Whooping Cranes was conducted at Necedah National Wildlife Refuge in Wisconsin, using Sandhill Crane chicks and involving biologists wearing "crane costumes" so that the chicks would imprint on fellow cranes rather than humans. In 2001, eight Whooping Crane chicks conditioned at Necedah National Wildlife Refuge to follow ultralights began the migration. Seven whoopers made the 1,250-mile trip to Chassohowitzka National Wildlife Refuge, Florida, safely, and five successfully made the unassisted return migration to central Wisconsin the following spring. One bird was lost on migration due to impact with a power line, and two others were lost to bobcat predation during the winter. Both power lines and predation are key threats to all Whooping Cranes. In the fall of 2002, a total of 21 Whooping Cranes successfully completed the southward migration, and the good news is that while 16 of the birds made the long trip to Chassohowitzka following ultralight aircraft, five birds from the previous year made it to Florida on their own. The goal is to establish a new migratory flock by 2020 with at least 25 breeding pairs.

Allegan State Game Area and Kalamazoo River (4), Michigan

▸ Highlights: Important breeding area for the Cerulean Warbler and other Green List species; important migratory corridor for landbirds and waterbirds.

▸ Location: Allegan State Game Area is near Allegan, in Allegan County; the key section of the Kalamazoo River stretches from Galesburg to Saugatuck in Allegan, Kalamazoo, and Calhoun Counties.

▸ Size: Allegan State Game Area is approximately 50,000 acres; river corridor is approximately 40,000 acres and stretches approximately 125 miles.

▸ Ownership: Michigan Department of Natural Resources, private.

▸ Habitats: Oak-pine barrens, lowland hardwood, wetlands, riparian woodland, open water.

▸ Land Use: Hunting, fishing, wildlife conservation, agriculture, residential, commercial, light industrial.

▸ Site Description: These two areas overlap in that a portion of the Kalamazoo River is included within the Allegan State Game Area. The river corridor is lined with deciduous woods and scrub and is surrounded by agriculture, residential, commercial, and light industrial areas. The Allegan State Game Area encompasses a variety of habitats, including oak-pine barrens (savannah) on dry, sandy soils, plus lowland hardwoods, northern hardwoods, wetlands, ponds, and open fields.

▸ Birds: Allegan State Game Area is an important nesting area for neotropical migrants, some of which are near the northern limits of their ranges here. It has the largest populations in the state of the Worm-eating Warbler (approximately 60) and Prothonotary Warbler (75 to 100), as well as the Blue-winged Warbler (more than 250), Wood Thrush (more than 500), and smaller numbers of Red-headed Woodpeckers, Golden-winged Warblers, and Henslow's Sparrows. This stretch of the Kalamazoo River has up to two million landbirds and one million waterfowl during migration.

▸ Conservation Issues: Much of the land along the river above Allegan State Game Area is in private ownership, and there are problems with toxic pollution, especially polychlorinated biphenyls (PCBs) in the Kalamazoo River. There is pressure from increased recreation and residential development.

▸ Visitor Information: Best time for migrating birds is late March to late May, and again from August to October. The breeding neotropical migrants are best seen from mid-May to late June. Contact: Allegan State Game Area, 4590 118th Avenue, Route 3, Allegan, MI 49010, 616-673-2430.

24. Central Hardwoods

The Ozark Mountains on the west and Interior Low Plateaus on the east are geologically similar to each other, but bisected by the floodplain of the Mississippi River and its larger tributaries. The entire area is dominated by an oak-hickory deciduous forest inhabited by interior forest species such as the Cerulean Warbler, Worm-eating Warbler, and Louisiana Waterthrush. The region includes some of the most extensive forests in the middle of the continent, and is probably a source for populations of these birds for many surrounding areas. Among early succession birds, this is the last major stronghold of the "Eastern" Bewick's Wren. Restoration of prairie, glade, and barren habitat is a conservation priority. Although the Wood Duck is the primary breeding waterfowl, the region holds more significance for waterfowl as a migratory staging area. The floodplains of the river systems exhibit a diversity of habitats (i.e., floodplain forests, emergent wetlands, submerged aquatic beds), all of which are utilized by migrating waterfowl. Large concentrations of waterfowl, including the Mallard, Lesser Scaup, and Canvasback, are common during both spring and fall migration. Threats to the habitats of the region include agricultural conversion of floodplain habitats and urbanization.

Ozark Mountains IBAs, Missouri and Arkansas

Mark Twain National Forest (1) and Ozark National Forest (2)

▶ Highlight: The Ozark Mountains are significant for many forest interior species and provide the source populations of several Green List species.
▶ Location: Southern Missouri and northern Arkansas.
▶ Size: Approximately 15,000 square miles.
▶ Ownership: A mix of federal, state, conservation group, and private lands.
▶ Habitats: Central and northern hardwood forest, pine forest, springs, caves, streams.
▶ Site Description: In Missouri, the main public lands or large private holdings in the Ozark Mountains include Mark Twain National Forest, Eleven Point National Scenic River, Pioneer Forest, Sunklands and other Missouri Department of Conservation land, Chilton Creek Preserve (The Nature Conservancy), Ozark Scenic National Riverways (National Park Service), and all interspaced private lands. The

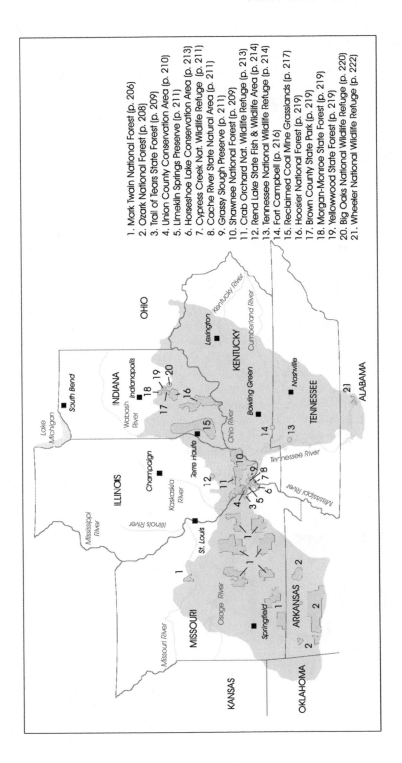

1. Mark Twain National Forest (p. 206)
2. Ozark National Forest (p. 208)
3. Trail of Tears State Forest (p. 209)
4. Union County Conservation Area (p. 210)
5. Limekiln Springs Preserve (p. 211)
6. Horseshoe Lake Conservation Area (p. 213)
7. Cypress Creek Nat. Wildlife Refuge (p. 211)
8. Cache River State Natural Area (p. 211)
9. Grassy Slough Preserve (p. 211)
10. Shawnee National Forest (p. 209)
11. Crab Orchard Nat. Wildlife Refuge (p. 213)
12. Rend Lake State Fish & Wildlife Area (p. 214)
13. Tennessee National Wildlife Refuge (p. 214)
14. Fort Campbell (p. 216)
15. Reclaimed Coal Mine Grasslands (p. 217)
16. Hoosier National Forest (p. 219)
17. Brown County State Park (p. 219)
18. Morgan-Monroe State Forest (p. 219)
19. Yellowwood State Forest (p. 219)
20. Big Oaks National Wildlife Refuge (p. 220)
21. Wheeler National Wildlife Refuge (p. 222)

Mark Twain National Forest is given a separate account on p. 191. The nearby Ozark National Forest in Arkansas, the state's principal area of public lands in the Ozarks, is treated separately below.

▸ Birds: The Ozark Mountains cover much of the southern part of Missouri and the northern part of Arkansas. The core area is of special significance to many forest interior species, with source populations of the Wood Thrush and several species of warbler, including the Swainson's, Kentucky, Cerulean, and Worm-eating. Other neotropical migrants breeding here include the Acadian Flycatcher, Northern Parula; and Hooded, Black-and-White, and Yellow-throated Warblers.

▸ Conservation Issues: The forests in the Ozarks are under various ownerships ranging from commercial (national forest lumber) to conservation (some state lands and The Nature Conservancy).

▸ Visitor Information: Best times to visit are from April through early July and again in September and October. See accounts for Mark Twain National Forest and Ozark National Forest.

Ozark National Forest (2), Arkansas

As the largest remaining unfragmented forest in the south-central United States, this is an important breeding source area for declining neotropical migrants such as the Cerulean Warbler, in addition to large numbers of other breeding warblers, vireos, tanagers, and thrushes. The forest is located in the Ozark Mountains of north-central and northwest Arkansas, the remains of a high plateau eroded by rivers to form a landscape of high bluffs and rolling, forested hills. In the south, the mountains give way to the lower-lying Arkansas River Valley. The forest is bordered to the east by the White River, and in the west reaches close to the state line with Oklahoma. The bedrock is sandstone and limestone. The Ozark National Forest contains some of the best closed-canopy temperate hardwood forest in the United States and is dominated by oak and hickory species. There are also some areas of grassland, brushy thickets, pine, and mixed forest. The understorey is composed of dogwood, maple, redbud, serviceberry, and witch hazel. The highest point is White Rock Mountain at 2,300 feet in

Blue-winged Warbler

altitude. There are several lakes, numerous mountain streams, and five larger rivers. The forest spans 16 counties and six Forest Service ranger districts. There are five Wilderness Areas: Upper Buffalo, Hurricane Creek, Richland Creek, East Fork, and Leatherwood, totaling approximately 66,800 acres. There are six Wildlife Management Areas: Ozark National Forest, Mount Magazine, Piney Creeks, Sycamore, Wedington, and White Rock, which are managed jointly with the Arkansas Game and Fish Commission. Six of the

13 rivers and streams that run through the forest have Wild and Scenic designations. The Buffalo National River, part of the National Park Service, flows not only through the forest but through privately owned lands, and forms important habitat for species such as the Cerulean Warbler. The forest contains some 26 developed recreation areas and approximately 200 miles of trails. In total, the forest covers 1,133,368 acres, and is used for timber production, grazing, gas production, and recreation.

The Ozark National Forest is a major breeding source area for central forest birds. Breeding warblers include the Worm-eating, Kentucky, Cerulean, Swainson's, and Prothonotary. Chestnut-sided and Black-throated Green Warblers were discovered breeding in the forest for the first time in the early 1990s. Other species of conservation concern include the Wood Thrush and a large portion of the remaining population of the eastern subspecies of the Bewick's Wren. Breeding neotropical migrants include the Acadian Flycatcher, Yellow-throated Vireo, Hooded and Blue-winged Warblers, and Scarlet Tanager.

The Land and Resources Management Plan for the Ozark–St. Francis National Forests is due for revision. Some of the current issues for this revision are related to the management of the forest, which includes the use of prescribed burning, herbicides, and timber harvesting (regeneration/thinning). Other concerns include oak regeneration, oak savannah/woodland restoration, pine/bluestem restoration, glade restoration, closed-canopy forest management, old-growth management, all-terrain vehicle use, proposed endangered, threatened, and sensitive species management, indicator species management, converting oak forest to pine, noxious weed eradication and control, road closures and construction, walk-in turkey hunting areas, and medicinal plant use and management.

Best times to visit are during spring and fall. A map of the area can be obtained from the forest headquarters, and visitors who expect to wander off main roads should also take a compass. Care should be exercised on roads, especially during the winter, and everywhere during deer season. There are 21 campgrounds, several scenic byways, and hundreds of miles of hiking trails, including the 169-mile Ozark Highland Trail. For more information, contact the forest supervisor, 605 West Main Street, Russellville, AR 72801, 501-968-2354. Ranger districts can be contacted at the following numbers: Bayou: 501-284-3150, Boston Mountain: 501-667-2191, Buffalo: 870-446-5122, Magazine: 501-963-3076, Pleasant Hill: 501-754-2864, St. Francis: 870-295-5278.

Trail of Tears State Forest (3) and Shawnee National Forest (10), Illinois and Missouri

▶ Highlight: Nesting green-listed neotropical migrants; important site for wintering and migrant waterfowl.
▶ Location: Southernmost part of the state.
▶ Size: Several units totaling 277,500 acres, of which about ten percent is designated wilderness.
▶ Ownership: Forest Service.

▸ Habitats: Mature hardwood and bottomland forest and sloughs, pine forest and pine plantations, old clear-cuts.

▸ Land Use: Hunting, harvesting of mushrooms and ginseng, wildlife observation.

▸ Site Description: Located between the Mississippi and Ohio Rivers in the southern tip of Illinois, the Shawnee National Forest lies in an historically unglaciated area known as the Ozark and Shawnee Hills. Some of the most pristine forest in the state is located in the Pine Hills–La Rue Ecological Area in the forest; it includes the few remaining stands in the state of shortleaf pine; plus large stands of mature oaks, hickories, beech, and tulip trees. Adjoining one of the forest units is the 5,000-acre Trail of Tears State Forest, with much the same habitat and many of the same breeding birds.

▸ Birds: The forest has several important nesting species, most of which are rare elsewhere in the state. These include the Cerulean, Kentucky, Prothonotary, and Worm-

Worm-eating Warbler

eating Warblers, Chuck-will's-widow, and the resident Short-eared Owl and Red-headed Woodpecker. Among the other species are the Whip-poor-will, Mississippi Kite, and Fish Crow. Thousands of ducks, including the Mallard, Gadwall, Wood Duck, and Northern Shoveler, are found during migration and winter, and thousands of migrant passerines and shorebirds also stop over during migration. There is an 830-acre tract of grassland that supports the largest population of the Henslow's Sparrow known from southern Illinois.

▸ Conservation Issues: Land managers flood a portion of the forest to create a wetland where migrating ducks stop and feed. Prescribed burning has been used in the past to manage grassland areas, but in recent years, lawsuits have kept land managers from making use of fire as a primary management tool. This means the formerly burned grassland area where the Henslow's Sparrow occurs will eventually become revegetated to a point where it is no longer useable by the species. It also hinders the conversion of grassland from non-native fescue to native prairie. No logging has been done in the forest for several years. In the past, the Swainson's Warbler was known found, but it is now extirpated from its former locations here.

▸ Visitor Information: Best time to visit is April through October. Contact: 50 Highway 145 South, Harrisburg, IL 62946, 618-253-7114.

Union County Conservation Area (4), Illinois

▸ Highlight: Up to 270,000 waterfowl winter there; thousands of passerines use the area during migration.

▸ Location: Approximately five miles southwest of Jonesboro.

▸ Size: 6,200 acres.

▸ Ownership: Illinois Department of Natural Resources.

▸ Habitats: Floodplain forest, sloughs, mudflats, shallow ponds, lakes, fields, grassland.

▸ Land Use: Wildlife conservation, hunting, fishing.

► Site Description: Much of the site is forested, with 1,100 acres found in shallow sloughs and other open water areas; there are also approximately 2,400 acres under cultivation with crops for wintering waterfowl.

► Birds: Counts up to 200,000 Canada Geese, 20,000 Snow Geese, and 50,000 ducks of several species during winter and migration; up to 1,000 migrating American White Pelicans in spring; also tens of thousands of migrant passerines, including thousands of swallows, stop over in spring and fall, and up to 60 Bald Eagles winter there. Among the breeding species are the Kentucky and Prothonotary Warblers, and Mississippi Kite.

► Conservation Issues: The conservation area is managed to benefit wintering waterfowl; part of the refuge is open to hunting.

► Visitor Information: Best time to visit is winter, when the waterfowl are present. Contact: Refuge Manager, Rural Route #2, Jonesboro, IL 62952, 618-833-5175.

Lower Cache River Complex IBAs, Illinois

Limekiln Springs Preserve (5), Cypress Creek National Wildlife Refuge (7), Cache River State Natural Area (8), Grassy Slough Preserve (9)

► Highlight: Important site for migrating and wintering waterfowl, for migrating landbirds and shorebirds, and for several breeding Green List birds.

► Location: Johnson and Pulaski Counties, near Vienna, in southern Illinois.

► Size: 60,000 acres are included in the Cache River Wetlands Project.

► Ownership: Fish and Wildlife Service, Illinois Department of Natural Resources, The Nature Conservancy, private.

► Designation: A Ramsar site.

► Habitats: Bottomland hardwood forest, upland forest, cropland.

► Land Use: Wildlife conservation, hunting, fishing, agriculture.

► Site Description: The site is located in a floodplain with a mosaic of swamp and bottomland forest of cypress and tupelo, plus upland forest, pasture, and cropland. The Cache River Basin drains the entire southern tip of Illinois. Of the 60,000 acres in the Cache River Wetlands Project, the Illinois Department of Natural Resources owns more than 20,000 acres, including the Cache River State Natural Area and Horseshoe Lake Conservation Area (see separate account for this site on p. 213), and there is a 36,000-acre purchase boundary for the Cypress Creek National Wildlife Refuge, of which 13,000 have currently been acquired. The Nature Conservancy has two preserves here, the Grassy Slough Preserve at 2,000 acres, and the Limekiln Springs Preserve at 1,000 acres. Ducks Unlimited has purchased 1,000 acres, now sold to the Fish and Wildlife Service as the Frank Bellrose Waterfowl Reserve.

► Birds: 250,000 waterfowl winter, approximately 80 percent of which are Canada Geese. Also, thousands of neotropic migrants breed, including the Prothonotary, Yellow-throated, Cerulean, and Kentucky Warblers, and Northern Parula, in addition to Acadian and Great-crested Flycatchers, Red-eyed and Yellow-throated Vireos, and Summer and Scarlet Tanagers. Tens of thousands of other neotropical migrants stop over during migration. The Dickcissel and Henslow's and Grasshopper Sparrows breed commonly in the open areas. Thousands of migrant shorebirds use the area, as do thousands of herons during the breeding and postbreeding seasons. The bottomland forest may be critical winter habitat for the Red-headed Woodpecker; the national high counts for that species are recorded here some years during the Christmas Bird Count. ▸ Conservation Issues: Before European settlement, there were an estimated 250,000 acres of cypress-tupelo forest in the region, but of this, only 5,300 acres remain. The Lower Cache River is the site of studies in habitat restoration, with particular regard to how communities of various animal species, including birds, change in response to increasing tree diversity in the bottomland hardwood forest. The project is designed to give clues as to how restoration of natural communities might best be carried out. The Cache River Wetlands Project was established in 1993 as a joint venture involving the Illinois Department of Natural Resources, the Fish and Wildlife Service, The Nature Conservancy, and Ducks Unlimited. The Nature Conservancy has defined the entire Cache River watershed of 472,800 acres in five counties as a bioreserve project and is pursuing conservation planning and protection work there.

▸ Visitor Information: Any time of year is good for a visit, though summers are hot and there are many biting insects. Contact Illinois Department of Natural Resources, Cache River SNA, 930 Sunflower Lane, Belknap, IL 62908, 618-634-9678, and Cypress Creek National Wildlife Refuge, Rural Route #1, Box 53-D, Ullin, IL 62992, 618-634-2231.

HABITAT CONSERVATION PLANNING

After passage of the Endangered Species Act (ESA), both the federal government and landowners became concerned that property owners' otherwise lawful activities might result in the unintentional harm to ("take") a listed species—even if the landowner were willing to plan and undertake activities to conserve the species. To resolve this problem, Congress amended Section 10 of the ESA in 1982 to authorize "incidental take" through the development of Habitat Conservation Plans or HCPs. This approach was patterned after the San Bruno Mountain HCP, an innovative land use plan in the San Francisco, California, area that began with a conflict between development activities and endangered species protection. This planning effort culminated in the issuance of the first incidental take permit in 1983.

Nonfederal landowners who want to undertake activities on their land that might result in the take of a federally listed species must first obtain an incidental take permit from the Fish and Wildlife Service. To obtain this permit, landowners must develop an HCP designed to offset any harmful effects the proposed activity might have on the species.

HCPs are intended to resolve conflicts regarding development activities in areas harboring endangered species. Because they are developed through negotiation and compromise, HCPs can range from extremely beneficial to the species in question to damaging. Regardless of the outcome, long-term monitoring of HCPs is essential to ensuring implementation of all parts of the plan. HCPs are now the course of choice for many higher profile endangered species conflicts such as with the Red-cockaded Woodpecker, California Gnatcatcher, Least Bell's Vireo, Northern Spotted Owl, Marbled Murrelet, and many others. By February 2001, 341 HCPs had been approved, covering 30 million acres and protecting 200 endangered or threatened species.

Horseshoe Lake Conservation Area (6), Illinois

► Highlight: A major wintering and stopover site for migratory waterfowl; several Green List neotropical migrants breed here.

► Location: Southernmost Illinois, approximately seven miles northwest of Cairo.

► Size: 10,700 acres.

► Ownership: Illinois Department of Natural Resources.

► Habitats: Oxbow lake with cypress swamp, floodplain forest, mudflats, open water, agricultural fields.

► Land Use: Fishing, hunting, wildlife conservation.

► Site Description: A natural oxbow lake with cypress and tupelo, this area resembles the Deep South both in its vegetation and its bird fauna. There are two dedicated nature preserves on the site, one of which is a near-virgin bottomland hardwood forest and designated as a National Natural Landmark. This site is part of the Lower Cache River Complex.

► Birds: Tens of thousands of migrating passerines use the area in transit, as do thousands of shorebirds, including an occasional Piping Plover. More than 300,000 waterfowl—the majority of which are Canada Geese—are found during migration and winter. Thousands of herons are found in the breeding and postbreeding seasons. Among the breeding birds are the Chuck-will's-widow, and Prairie, Cerulean, Prothonotary, Worm-eating and Kentucky Warblers. Other birds at the limits of their ranges are the Mississippi Kite, Fish Crow, Summer Tanager, and Blue Grosbeak.

► Conservation Issues: The area was subjected to severe flooding during the 1993 Mississippi River floods, destroying roads and breaching dikes. One result is that more breeding and foraging areas were created for shorebirds, herons, Least Terns, and other species. The area has a long history of study by the leading ornithologists in the state.

► Visitor Information: Any time of year is good for a visit, with spring and fall migration both excellent, and many waterfowl and passerines are found in the winter. Contact the Conservation Area at P.O. Box 85, Miller City, IL 62962, 618-776-5689.

Crab Orchard National Wildlife Refuge (11), Illinois

► Highlight: Major stopover for migrating and wintering waterfowl; significant numbers of migrating shorebirds and migrating and breeding passerines.

► Location: Southern Illinois, in Williamson County, west of Marion.

► Size: 43,600 acres.

► Habitats: Floodplain forest, upland forest, pine plantations, successional fields.

► Ownership: Fish and Wildlife Service, Bureau of Prisons, private.

► Land Use: Recreation, wildlife management, industry, agriculture, correctional institution.

► Site Description: With three lakes, wetlands, and coniferous and deciduous forests, this is one of the most visited National Wildlife Refuges in the United States. The site is in an area of historically glaciated rolling topography with a few sheer cliffs and overhangs of sandstone up to 40 feet high. Formerly the site of a munitions plant, it still houses 20 industrial plants and a maximum security federal prison within its boundaries.

▸ Birds: Up to 240,000 waterfowl are found on the refuge during migration and winter; shorebirds, waders, gulls, and terns stop over during migration in significant numbers; and thousands of migrant passerines can be seen in the spring and fall. The Prairie, Prothonotary, and Kentucky Warblers breed; the Bell's Vireo is also an uncommon breeding species.

▸ Conservation Issues: Toxic waste, including polychlorinated biphenyls (PCBs), were left by previous industries on the site; cleanup of contaminants has been initiated. The refuge is the site of many studies by students from Southern Illinois University.

▸ Visitor Information: Best time to visit is fall through spring; parts of the refuge are closed to the public. Contact the refuge at 8588 Route 148, Marion, IL 62959, 618-997-3344.

Rend Lake State Fish and Wildlife Area (12), Illinois

▸ Highlight: A major migratory stopover for waterfowl, shorebirds, and passerines, and a major wintering area for waterfowl.

▸ Location: Jefferson and Franklin Counties, near Mount Vernon.

▸ Size: 16,894 acres.

▸ Ownership: Illinois Department of Natural Resources and the Army Corps of Engineers.

▸ Habitats: Man-made lake, old-growth hardwood forest, old fields.

▸ Land Use: Hunting, fishing, and camping.

▸ Site Description: Rend Lake is a relatively shallow impoundment made by the Army Corps of Engineers. It is surrounded by agricultural land, floodplain forests, and wetlands. The state fish and wildlife area is found at the north end of the lake.

▸ Birds: Up to 200,000 waterfowl are found here in the fall and winter; also, thousands of migrant shorebirds use the mudflats around the lake when conditions are right, and many landbirds stop over during migration. The Buff-breasted Sandpiper occurs regularly, and Kentucky and Worm-eating Warblers breed in Ryder's Bottoms, at the north end of the lake.

▸ Conservation Issues: Crops are planted, and water levels are manipulated to attract waterfowl. The area is heavily visited by recreationists, especially for hunting and fishing. There is some pollution from agricultural runoff and mine subsidence.

▸ Visitor Information: Best time to visit is fall through spring. Contact: Route 1, Box 338, Bonnie, IL 62816, 618-629-2320.

Tennessee National Wildlife Refuge (13), Tennessee

▸ Highlight: Major wintering area for waterfowl from the Mississippi Flyway. Important nesting area for forest interior neotropical migratory birds.

▸ Location: Near Paris, on the Tennessee River.

▸ Size: 51,358 acres.

▸ Ownership: Fish and Wildlife Service.

▸ Habitats: Open reservoir waters, bottomland hardwoods, upland oak-hickory forests, freshwater marsh, seasonally flooded herbaceous wetlands, shrub-scrub habitat, agricultural lands.

▸ Land Use: Wildlife observation, hiking, boating, hunting, fishing.

▸ Site Description: Tennessee National Wildlife Refuge is located on Kentucky Lake, an impoundment in west-central Tennessee. It is managed as an important resting, feeding, nesting, and wintering area for migratory birds, along with providing habitat for many resident wildlife species.

Wood Duck

▸ Birds: The refuge is a major wintering area for more than 250,000 ducks and 30,000 geese. Of the 23 species of ducks using the refuge, the Mallard is the most common, followed by the Gadwall, American Wigeon, Northern Pintail, and American Black Duck. The Wood Duck is common and nests on the refuge. The American Black Duck is a species of special concern, with six to 15 percent of the continental population wintering on the refuge during most years. Since the refuge is located within one of the more densely forested regions of the state, it is considered an important area for interior forest nesting birds, including the Wood Thrush, Prothonotary Warbler, Kentucky Warbler, and Worm-eating Warbler. Thousands of migratory shorebirds stop during migration, and large numbers of postbreeding herons and egrets gather in late summer. In excess of 500 Common Loons, and the occasional Pacific and Red-throated Loons, utilize the open waters of the Big Sandy Unit during migration. The refuge usually bands more than 1,000 Wood Ducks each year, more than any other refuge in the nation. The largest population of the "Southern James Bay" Canada Goose, one of the most imperiled populations on the North American continent, also winters here. The refuge is also a major wintering and nesting area for the Bald Eagle, and an important nesting and stopover site for neotropical migratory birds.

▸ Conservation Issues: Water levels on the refuge are managed for wintering migratory waterfowl. A 3,000-acre farming program with milo, corn, soybeans, and winter wheat provides food for the overwintering ducks and geese. Seasonally flooded impoundments are managed using a technique called moist-soil management to produce natural vegetation that provides food and cover for a wide variety of wetland-dependent migratory birds. Problem aquatic weeds such as alligator weed and primrose willow are chemically treated to control their spread. Other invasive vegetation such as black willow is mechanically removed in some areas to improve waterfowl habitat. Controlled fires are also used in certain areas to control woody vegetation. Approximately 20,000 acres of upland oak-hickory forest are actively managed to provide nesting and migration habitats for several species of neotropical migratory birds, many of which are listed as high-priority species of management concern. Breeding Bird Surveys are conducted and point counts established and run during the spring and summer. The surrounding area is being developed as a vacation and retirement area, and the refuge is already heavily visited, with more than 500,000 visitors each year.

▸ Visitor Information: Best time to visit is when the wintering waterfowl are present, from late October to March. Contact: 3006 Dinkins Lane, Paris, TN 38242, 731-642-2091.

MIGRATORY BIRD TREATY ACT OF 1918

The Migratory Bird Treaty Act (MBTA) implemented the 1916 Convention between the United States and Great Britain (for Canada) for the protection of migratory birds. Later amendments implemented treaties between the United States and Mexico (1936), the United States and Japan (1974), and the United States and the Soviet Union (now Russia, 1978). The MBTA makes it illegal, unless permitted by regulations, to "pursue, hunt, take, capture, kill . . . possess, offer for sale, sell, offer to purchase, purchase, deliver . . . , receive for shipment, or export, at any time, or in any manner, any migratory bird . . . or any part, nest, or egg of any such bird." When consistent with respective international conventions, the act provides the Secretary of the Interior authority to determine when ". . . hunting, taking, capture, killing, possession, shipment . . . or export of any . . . bird, or any part, nest or egg . . ." could be undertaken and to adopt regulations for this purpose. Thus, game-bird hunting seasons (not to exceed three and one half months) and some non-game-bird hunting by Native Americans is regulated by federal and state government, but any taking of other birds (". . . except for scientific or propagating purposes under permits") is prohibited.

The MBTA is the broadest legal protection for birds in the United States, but such sweeping legislation can be subject to varying interpretation. For example, timber cutting where there are nesting birds can be interpreted as a "taking" and thus illegal under the MBTA. There are currently cases being heard in different courts to determine whether the MBTA prohibits such activities.

The MBTA is now being considered across a broad front of bird conservation issues ranging from control of Double-crested Cormorants (for purported damage to fish stocks) to tower kills of birds. Is this leading to review and revision of the MBTA just as use of the Endangered Species Act to stop habitat alteration has led to that law's review? Only time will tell.

Fort Campbell (14), Kentucky and Tennessee

▸ Highlight: One of the largest native grassland areas east of the Mississippi River, it is an important site for the Henslow's Sparrow and other grassland birds.
▸ Location: On the Kentucky-Tennessee state line, near Clarksville, Tennessee.
▸ Size: 105,000 acres.
▸ Ownership: Army.
▸ Habitats: Grassland, oak barrens, woodland.
▸ Land Use: Military training and exercises.
▸ Site Description: Fort Campbell is home to the 101st Airborne Division and functions as a training installation for airborne assault troops. With approximately two-thirds of its land area in Tennessee, the fort is at the southern end of a large historic grassland area, the Kentucky Barrens, which once covered some two million acres. At

present, approximately 40,000 acres on the fort are grassland and oak barrens, representing one of the largest existing grasslands east of the Mississippi. A critical link in grassland bird conservation in the East, the vegetation is dominated by native rather than exotic grasses.

▸ Birds: Little bird work was done on the fort until the late 1990s. At present, researchers from the University of Tennessee are sampling birds on 30 to 40 randomly selected plots within the accessible part of the grassland, but much of the area is off-limits as an impact zone for ordnance. In the sampled areas, researchers have found approximately 150 territories of the Henslow's Sparrow, representing probably only a fraction of the bird's numbers there. Also, many Dickcissels and Grasshopper Sparrows nest, and there are a few Bachman's Sparrows.

▸ Conservation Issues: To keep the area open for airborne training, the grasslands are burned on a three-year cycle. There is a program to remove pine plantations and to restore these areas to oak barrens. The area is being considered for reintroduction of the Greater Prairie-Chicken.

▸ Visitor Information: Access to the installation is controlled; biologists there occasionally take birders out to the grassland area. For more information, call 270-798-9855.

Reclaimed Coal Mine Grasslands (15), Indiana

▸ Highlight: Studies in 19 reclaimed coal mines in southwestern Indiana suggest that these large mine grasslands harbor as many as 2,000 pairs of Henslow's Sparrows, amounting to a substantial proportion of the world population of the species.

▸ Location: Southwestern Indiana; the eight top reclaimed coal mine areas for the Henslow's Sparrow among the 19 are (listed in order of importance) Chinook, Lynnville, Squaw Creek, Universal, Dugger, Minnehaha, Ayrshire, Phoenix.

▸ Size: The 19 areas range in size from 240 to 7,500 acres, amounting to some 27,400 acres of suitable habitat for the sparrow (representing 68.7 percent of the grassland in the areas).

▸ Ownership: Of the eight best areas, four are wholly or partially controlled or administered by the Indiana Department of Natural Resources (Chinook, Dugger, Minnehaha, and Ayrshire), and three are owned by Peabody Coal Company (Lynnville, Squaw Creek, and Universal), while others are owned by other coal companies or private owners.

▸ Habitats: Grassland on reclaimed surface mine areas.

▸ Land Use: Wildlife conservation.

▸ Site Description: Large mine grasslands are found mainly in portions of Indiana, Illinois, Kentucky, and Ohio. Under the 1977 Surface Mining Control and Reclamation Act, a mined area is considered reclaimed after the land has been contoured, adequate topsoil put back in place, and vegetation restored. Typically, quick-growing cool-season non-native grasses are planted first, to establish vegetation and prevent soil erosion. Though tree planting and crop production follow, this is often only on a small portion of the reclaimed area, and the majority remains in grassland. Soil conditions and isolation from forest habitat often inhibit invasion by woody plants, and these grasslands can persist for many years with no management. In addition to the advantage of size, these areas are largely unsuitable for other purposes and are often owned by a single entity. Mine grasslands of the Midwest are probably among the largest contiguous grasslands, native or otherwise, east of the Mississippi River. Avian communities of these reclaimed grasslands are similar to those of extant midwestern grasslands and presettlement tallgrass prairies. Such native tallgrass prairie has been almost entirely converted to agriculture, and the remnants are small and dispersed. Grassland created through surface coal mine reclamation has considerable potential for grassland bird conservation. Reclamation produces large grasslands, some larger than 4,500 acres, which exceeds the apparent size thresholds for even the most area-sensitive grassland species.

▶ Birds: The total estimated number of Henslow's Sparrows in this area of south-western Indiana is put at 2,000 pairs. Other grassland birds breeding on these re-claimed mines are the Eastern Meadowlark, Grasshopper Sparrow, Dickcissel, Field Sparrow, Northern Bobwhite, and Horned Lark, all among the more common species found there; small numbers of Upland Sandpipers, Short-eared Owls, Sedge Wrens, and Bobolinks also breed there. Other species occur in wetland areas of these mine grasslands, including the American Bittern, Least Bittern, and King Rail; while in the shrubland and savannah areas the Willow Flycatcher, Bell's Vireo, and Prairie Warbler can be found.

▶ Conservation Issues: The Henslow's Sparrow has declined perhaps the most signifi-cantly of any grassland bird, and more than most forest-dwelling neotropical migrants. It needs large, undisturbed grasslands with relatively little woody vegetation, dense grass-dominated vegetation, and a significant amount of dead litter. Such habitat, native or otherwise, is very scarce in the Midwest, where the Henslow's Sparrow's breeding range is concentrated. Management for this kind of vegetative structure on mine grass-land could greatly increase the species' numbers there. These grasslands could play a significant role in stabilizing not only the populations of the Henslow's Sparrow but of other grassland birds as well. Mine grasslands offer an additional advantage. Studies of nesting success of grassland and savannah birds here indicate a relatively high nesting success; one factor is that the rate of cowbird parasitism is as low as one percent, prob-ably due to the large size of such grasslands and their relative isolation from forested areas.

▶ Visitor Information: Best time to visit the area is May and June. For information about access, contact the Division of Fish and Wildlife, Indiana Department of Natural Resources, 402 West Washington Street, Room W-273, Indianapolis, IN 46204, 317-232-4094.

HUMAN-MADE SITES

The most devout listers in the birding world have all had the experience of going to a totally trashy, ugly, evil-smelling place and finding lots of birds there, some-times even unusual ones. Though hardly any sites in this book fall into that cat-egory, the hand of humankind rests at least lightly on nearly every one of them.

Some sites are out-and-out human creations—dredge spoil islands, sewage plants, reservoirs, airports, reclaimed strip mine lands—that birds have turned to their own uses.

Shorebirds, waterfowl, and grassland birds are among those that benefit most. For the former two categories, it is usually migrants that use such places, since birds on the move demonstrate a plasticity they often do not show once they get to their breeding grounds.

Turf farms and airfields can be important as stopover or wintering sites for shorebirds and longspurs, while during breeding some airfields also support grassland birds such as the Upland Sandpiper and Grasshopper Sparrow. Reclaimed strip mine lands are likewise new sites for grassland birds, among them the Henslow's Sparrow, a species having dense breeding populations on reclaimed coal lands in Indiana and Pennsylvania. Built after World War II for flood control, reservoirs in the Great Plains can host huge concentrations of migrating waterfowl and Franklin's Gulls. Dredge-spoil islands off the coasts of North Carolina and Louisiana host colonies of thousands of terns, skimmers, and pelicans; while the Savannah Spoil Area of South Carolina, a site where thousands of migrating shorebirds stop by each year, is the product of dredging by the Army Corps of Engineers in the Savannah River. It is a great site for shorebirds with 10,000 sometimes present. Many rarities have been recorded from the area. It is recommended by leading birders as one of the top ten sites in the state.

Aesthetically, the least appealing to most human visitors are sewage treatment plants, yet they can draw migrating birds by the thousands. Perhaps the flagship among America's sewage treatment plants is the site known euphemistically as the Memphis Earth Complex. With its shallow water, sparse vegetation, and high levels of nutrients and invertebrates, the Memphis Earth Complex is one of the most significant shorebird stopover sites in the entire Mississippi Valley. In fact, a significant portion of the entire shorebird population migrating along the Mississippi Flyway is thought to stop there. Studies indicate that nine state and federal wildlife management areas in the lower Mississippi Valley recorded from 1,000 to 40,000 shorebird-use days annually, while from 1994 to 1997 the complex never recorded fewer than 50,000 shorebird-use days annually; and in 1997 recorded nearly 150,000 shorebird-use days during fall migration alone. Similarly, Michigan's Muskegon Wastewater System is a premier site to see migrants in the spring and fall, and hosts up to 50,000 waterfowl in the fall.

Though those seeking a pristine natural experience should look elsewhere, these sites play an important role in the conservation of some bird species, and they are instructive as to the adaptability of some birds to a human-dominated landscape.

Brown County Hills IBAs, Indiana

Hoosier National Forest (16), Brown County State Park (17), Morgan-Monroe State Forest (18), Yellowwood State Forest (19)

▶ Highlight: Good populations of breeding Cerulean and Worm-eating Warblers and other neotropical migrants.
▶ Location: Just east of Bloomington, including all of Brown County, and eastern Monroe, northwest Jackson, small portions of northeastern Lawrence, and southern Morgan counties.
▶ Size: 340,000 acres.
▶ Ownership: Forest Service, state lands, private.

► Habitats: Primarily oak-hickory and beech-maple forest; some pasture, hayfields, wetlands, lakes, cropland, developed areas. Steep slopes are common resulting in diverse microhabitats.

► Land Use: Recreation, limited logging, wildlife observation.

► Site Description: This area of south-central Indiana, consisting of the Pleasant Run Unit of the Hoosier National Forest together with a mosaic of private and state lands, forms the largest block of contiguous densely forested land in the state. It consists of all or parts of five counties. Public land ownership is approximately 154,000 acres: Forest Service (67,391); and state lands (86,654), which include Brown County State Park, Yellowwood State Forest, Morgan-Monroe State Forest, and Monroe Reservoir. Oak-hickory forest predominates, with beech-maple, and mixed mesophytic forest types secondary.

► Birds: This contiguous block of forest is probably the single most important area in the state for neotropical forest migrants, and may be one of the few source areas for these species not only in Indiana but in surrounding states. Some 19 species of warbler breed, with good populations in the forest of the Worm-eating, Cerulean, and Kentucky Warblers; the Prothonotary Warbler also breeds; and the Prairie Warbler and Wood Thrush are common. The Red-headed Woodpecker occurs, and the Henslow's Sparrow occurs locally in appropriate habitat.

► Conservation Issues: The Forest Service has established point counts for birds that are conducted every three to five years. Researchers have conducted numerous studies on land use, timber management activities; and bird occurrence, abundance, and productivity for several years. Some Prothonotary Warbler research has also been done in this area. Currently, some Cerulean Warbler research is being conducted by a graduate student at Ball State University. Since much of the land is in public ownership, it is afforded a good degree of protection for birds, particularly compared to other places in the state. The Hoosier National Forest, the state Department of Natural Resources, The Nature Conservancy, and a local land trust (the Sycamore Land Trust) have purchased lands in recent years, and plan to continue to do so. Probably the biggest threat to birds in this area is the development of home sites and the resulting decline in forest quality and increased fragmentation. Timber management is also an issue, with groups disputing how and how much public land should be timbered. At present, not much timber cutting is going on; timber cuts are usually small, so early successional and gap species (e.g., Cerulean Warbler) may be suffering.

► Visitor Information: Best time to see breeding neotropical migrants is from mid-May to early July. During migration in spring and fall is also a good time for a visit. Contact for the Hoosier National Forest is 811 Constitution Avenue, Bedford, IN 47421, 812-275-5987.

Big Oaks National Wildlife Refuge (20), Indiana

► Highlight: Grassland on the site supports one of the largest-known populations of the Henslow's Sparrow, populations of which have declined precipitously throughout much of its range.

► Ownership: Army; most of the area is managed by the Fish and Wildlife Service as an overlay refuge.

▶ Size: The refuge is approximately 50,000 acres; Jefferson Proving Ground was originally 55,264 acres.

▶ Location: Jefferson, Jennings, and Ripley Counties.

▶ Habitats: Mature forest, successional forest, shrubland, grassland, wetlands.

▶ Land Use: Formerly ammunition testing for the military; at present, wildlife conservation.

▶ Site Description: Formerly the Jefferson Proving Ground, historically the majority of the site was forest, but most had been cleared and converted to agriculture prior to 1940, when the Army acquired it as an ammunition testing site. Surrounded by agriculture, the site has largely reverted to forest, in various stages of succession. Periodic burns originally prescribed to reduce the threat of fire connected with munitions testing have also maintained approximately 5,000 acres of grassland. The refuge is very important as the largest tract of public land in the region, with many rare plants and animals found on it, including several maternity colonies of the federally endangered Indiana bat. Big Oaks National Wildlife Refuge is an overlay refuge. The area is managed as a national wildlife refuge by the Fish and Wildlife Service, though it remains in Army ownership because of the liability problems associated with munitions.

▶ Birds: A recent census counted 900 pairs of Henslow's Sparrows, one of the largest-known breeding populations of this species. The site also supports many area-sensitive nesting birds in both the grassland and the forest. The Northern Harrier, Dickcissel, and Prairie Warbler breed, the latter being common. The Worm-eating Warbler breeds in the forests in good numbers, as do the Wood Thrush, Acadian Flycatcher, Ovenbird, Kentucky Warbler, and Hooded Warbler. The Red-headed Woodpecker is also found at the site.

▶ Conservation Issues: Under a recent agreement with the Army and Air Force, the Fish and Wildlife Service will operate Big Oaks National Wildlife Refuge through a 25-year real-estate permit with the Army retaining ownership of the land. The Air Force will retain use of a bombing range (Jefferson Range: 1,033 acres), which is not included in the portion designated as a National Wildlife Refuge, and is located near the center of the former proving ground. Large safety buffer areas separate the Air Force range from public use areas of the refuge. Most of the grasslands located on the former installation's containment area (the area south of the former firing line) have been leased to commercial enterprises and subsequently converted to agriculture. The Fish and Wildlife Service manages the grasslands on the refuge through an annual prescribed-burning program. Since the military mission ceased in 1995, fires associated with munitions testing were discontinued, and the refuge reinstated periodic fire for the welfare of the Henslow's Sparrow. Successional forest areas are being allowed to reconnect larger blocks of mature forest for neotropical migrants. Development potential on much of the refuge is limited because of the presence of unexploded munitions and the prohibitive cost associated with efforts to remove them—some of the bombs are seven feet below the surface of the ground. Much of the munitions are in areas that are burned; since the hazard precludes entry, the fires are managed from the edges and the area cannot be mowed. A complete census of the birds there is not possible, but birds are surveyed through road transects and study plots.

▶ Visitor Information: Due to the presence of unexploded ordnance, visitor access to the refuge is limited. Four thousand acres in the northeastern corner of the refuge are seasonally open for wildlife observation, fishing, photography, interpretation, and environmental education. An additional 15,000 acres are open to seasonal deer and turkey hunting. The refuge can be contacted at 1661 West JPG Niblo Road, Madison, IN 47250, 812-273-0783.

Wheeler National Wildlife Refuge (21), Alabama

▶ Highlight: Up to 100,000 waterfowl use the area during migration and winter, and more than 50,000 shorebirds pass through during migration.
▶ Location: Southeast of Decatur, on the Tennessee River.
▶ Size: 36,000 acres.
▶ Ownership: Fish and Wildlife Service.
▶ Habitats: Bottomland hardwoods, open water, riparian woodlands, backwater embayments, pine uplands, croplands.
▶ Land Use: Fishing, hunting, wildlife observation.
▶ Site Description: Lying on both banks of the Tennessee River for about 20 miles, from Decatur to Huntsville, the refuge is at the upper reaches of the Wheeler Reservoir. Little old-growth forest is found there; the second-growth forests are now about 70 years old.
▶ Birds: Large numbers of migrating and wintering waterfowl use the refuge, with maximum numbers exceeding 100,000 in a season, while more than 50,000 shorebirds pass through during migration; a few remain in the winter. The Prairie, Prothonotary, Kentucky, and Worm-eating Warblers nest on the refuge; as do the Chuck-will's-widow, Red-headed Woodpecker, Wood Thrush, and Dickcissel.
▶ Conservation Issues: The refuge is located in a rapidly urbanizing area, and visitors number approximately 750,000 each year. Water levels and the production of crops are managed to benefit waterfowl.
▶ Visitor Information: Any time from fall through spring is good for a visit. Contact the refuge at 2700 Refuge Headquarters Road, Decatur, AL 35603, 256-350-6639.

P ines dominate this area, largely shortleaf in the north, including the Ouachita
Mountains, and longleaf in the south. This westernmost part of the eastern forest also includes hardwood-dominated bottomlands along the Arkansas River
and other drainages. The Red-cockaded Woodpecker is the highest-priority bird in
pine habitat, which is also inhabited by the Bachman's Sparrow and Brown-headed
Nuthatch. Conversion of the native pine forests to industrial loblolly plantations provides some bird habitat, but is less useful for the highest-priority species. The river and
stream bottoms provide habitat used by the Swainson's Warbler and large numbers of
nesting herons and egrets. Bottomland hardwoods and associated wetlands support
substantial wintering populations of a number of waterfowl species, principally the
Mallard, and breeding and wintering Wood Ducks. They are also a primary migration
corridor for significant numbers of other dabbling ducks. The principal threats to bottomland hardwood wetlands in the region are from reservoirs and timber harvest and
subsequent conversion to pine plantation, pasture, or other land uses.

Ouachita National Forest (1), Arkansas and Oklahoma

▸ Highlight: This site is important to a large suite of forest birds, including the Worm-
eating, Kentucky, and Hooded Warblers, Ovenbird, Louisiana Waterthrush, Wood
Thrush, Summer and Scarlet Tanagers, and Chuck-will's-widow. The Ouachita Mountains and similarly the Ozark Mountains are a stronghold and source of neotropical
migrants for many surrounding sink habitats in the mid-South and Midwest. The endangered Red-cockaded Woodpecker and several Green List birds are among the 300
species that use these habitats.
▸ Location: Spanning two states, the forest is the largest and most contiguous in the
eastern United States, stretching from central Arkansas to east-central and southeastern Oklahoma. Twelve district offices in two states and a supervisor's office and visitor center in Hot Springs, Arkansas, provide a variety of services to the public.
▸ Size: 1,777,000 forest acres.
▸ Ownership: Adjacent to and within the forest boundaries is a mosaic of industrial
timberlands, state, and private inholdings.

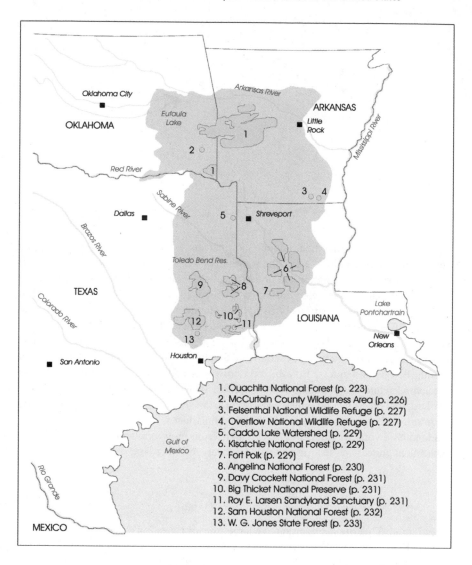

1. Ouachita National Forest (p. 223)
2. McCurtain County Wilderness Area (p. 226)
3. Felsenthal National Wildlife Refuge (p. 227)
4. Overflow National Wildlife Refuge (p. 227)
5. Caddo Lake Watershed (p. 229)
6. Kisatchie National Forest (p. 229)
7. Fort Polk (p. 229)
8. Angelina National Forest (p. 230)
9. Davy Crockett National Forest (p. 231)
10. Big Thicket National Preserve (p. 231)
11. Roy E. Larsen Sandyland Sanctuary (p. 231)
12. Sam Houston National Forest (p. 232)
13. W. G. Jones State Forest (p. 233)

▸ Habitats: A variety of 37 forest and woodland types, including: shortleaf and loblolly pines; mixed pine-hardwood; southern scrub oak, oak-hickory; mixed, dry, mesic, and bottomland hardwoods; oak-gum-cypress; and elm-ash-cottonwood add to the diversity.

▸ Land Use: Forest products, recreation, wildlife observation and conservation.

▸ Site Description: In contrast to most other North American mountain ranges, the Ouachita Mountains are ridges running east and west. The Ouachita National Forest, most of which lies in Arkansas, represents one of the best-preserved expanses of woodland in the United States. Though large volumes of timber were removed from the area by the early twentieth century, the rugged topography prevented wholesale conversion to agriculture, and the harvested areas are now reforested with mature trees. More than 800,000 acres are in hardwoods managed for old-growth.

Scissor-tailed Flycatcher

▸ Birds: One of several premiere birding areas within the forest is the Buffalo Road Demonstration Area, south of Waldron, Arkansas. This area contains a small and growing recovery population of the Red-cockaded Woodpecker, along with the Bachman's Sparrow and Brown-headed Nuthatch. The number of active clusters of the woodpecker has risen from 13 in 1990 to 21 in 2000. Forest birds for which the Ouachita Mountains are a stronghold are the Chuck-will's-widow and Worm-eating and Kentucky Warblers. Other species breeding in the forest are the Short-eared Owl, Wood Thrush, and Prothonotary, Cerulean, and Prairie Warblers. The forest also forms the core of the population of the imperiled eastern subspecies of the Bewick's Wren.

Another important place for birds is Red Slough in southeastern Oklahoma. Red Slough is used by at least 269 species of birds at recent count. This wetland and hardwood mix is used by the migrating, endangered Piping Plover and the Least Tern, and it is the most outstanding shorebird and wading-bird area in the state. At the peak of the season up to 35,000 birds pass through, including many shorebird species and several species of herons and egrets. The White-faced Ibis, Wood Stork (up to 73 in a recent survey), Mottled Duck; Roseate Spoonbill (up to seven were detected in a recent survey), and Yellow Rail (during migration) also occur. Elsewhere in the forest, one can see the Western Kingbird, Scissor-tailed Flycatcher, and Greater Roadrunner, at the easternmost edge of their distribution. Red Slough is popular among birders and its avifauna is very well documented.

▸ Conservation Issues: Forest managers are using prescribed fire to restore the short-leaf pine–bluestem grass ecosystem. This ecosystem provides habitat for many species, including the Red-cockaded Woodpecker, Bachman's Sparrow, Brown-headed Nuthatch, and Prairie Warbler. In 2000, more than 100,000 acres were burned on the forest. In December 2000, a severe ice storm hit Arkansas, but the area where the woodpecker is found was not significantly affected. The large amount of downed timber scattered over 340,000 acres of the forest can mean a heightened wildfire danger, but also, new areas of early successional habitat used by a cadre of bird species. An active bird-monitoring program is in place, including 309 landbird monitoring points, Arkansas and Oklahoma Breeding Bird Atlas plots, and five Breeding Bird Survey routes run by professional biologists. Knowledgeable amateur birders make an important contribution to the knowledge and the databases of birds in the forest.

▸ Visitor Information: There is an auto tour to the Buffalo Road Demonstration Area, featuring a program on managing the Red-cockaded Woodpecker, and a site map is available for Red Slough. The best times for a visit are April to May and September to October. Contact: Ouachita National Forest Supervisor's Office at P.O. Box 1270, Hot

Springs, AR 71902, 501-321-5202. Additional information can be found on the forest's website: http://www.fs.fed.us/oonf/ouachita.htm.

BIRDING THROUGH THE YEARS

The last century has brought big changes in our awareness of birds. One hundred years ago, few people took an interest in birds other than as game. Market hunters were still blasting away at waterfowl and shorebirds to provide food for the city, and shooting egrets to provide feathers for ladies' hats. The change from birds as commodities to birds as recreation came slowly. Not until Frank M. Chapman's book, *Handbook of the Birds of Eastern North America* came out in 1912 was there even a handy, one-volume reference to bird identification in the eastern United States. And it was really the appearance of Roger Tory Peterson's *Field Guide to the Birds* in 1934 that launched modern interest in birds and birding. From an activity limited in the public eye to a few eccentrics, birding has become, for many, close to a competitive sport, with its own rules, code of ethics, stars, and publications. In response to demand, modern binoculars and telescopes have developed far beyond the opera glasses used by the birders who flipped through Chapman's books, looking at the colorized line drawings. While most people once waited for the birds to come to them, they now go to the birds in increasing numbers. Commercial tours are a lucrative business, catering to nearly every pocketbook and taking birders to every continent, even Antarctica. Whereas a hundred years ago people put up gourds for Purple Martins and House Wrens, now there are successful franchises, such as the Wild Bird Centers, with an extensive line of feeders, birdhouses, and bird food, in addition to books, videos, and recordings of birdsongs. New guides appear regularly and sell well; the Sibley guide, covered in the pages of *Time* and *Newsweek,* is a best seller. There's even a *Birdwatching for Dummies* book. Birding has become big business.

McCurtain County Wilderness Area (2), Oklahoma

▸ Highlight: Oklahoma's only population of the Red-cockaded Woodpecker.
▸ Designation: National Natural Landmark.
▸ Location: McCurtain County in southeastern Oklahoma, 15 miles north of Broken Bow and eight miles south of Smithville.
▸ Size: 14,000 acres.
▸ Ownership: Oklahoma Department of Wildlife Conservation.
▸ Habitats: Old-growth oak-shortleaf pine forest, oak-hickory forest.
▸ Land Use: Recreation, wildlife conservation.
▸ Site Description: Located at the north end of the Broken Bow Reservoir, the area is dissected by the Mountain Fork River and several creeks. It contains the largest tract of unlogged, old-growth oak-shortleaf-pine habitat in the United States. The topography consists of narrow dissected ridges with an elevational range of some 600 feet.
▸ Birds: This site represents the only occurrence of the Red-cockaded Woodpecker in Oklahoma; the nearest population is 42 miles away, to the east, in the Ouachita Na-

tional Forest, Arkansas. The Brown-headed Nuthatch and Chuck-will's-widow; and Hooded, Kentucky, and Worm-eating Warblers also breed.

► Conservation Issues: The Department of Wildlife Conservation has developed an ecosystem-based management plan for the wilderness. The primary goal of the plan is to restore the open pine-grassland or open hardwood-woodland that existed before the advent of fire suppression in the mid-1920s. This will increase understorey forage and improve habitat quality for many species of wildlife, including the Red-cockaded Woodpecker. The principal tools for restoring open forest conditions are prescribed burning and limited mid-storey removal. Other management for the woodpecker includes creating corridors linking clusters and prospective recolonization sites, and installation of cavity and predator guards. Translocation of birds from Sam Houston National Forest has also been tried, but so far without much success. From the 1940s to the 1980s the number of colonies of the woodpecker declined from 49 clusters to the present 11, but that number was stabilized in the 1990s.

► Visitor Information: Best time to visit is during migration and the early breeding season, from late April to mid-June, although the woodpeckers and nuthatches can be found at any time of year. Contact: McCurtain County Wilderness Area at HC75, Box 308-12, Broken Bow, OK 74728, 580-241-7875.

Felsenthal National Wildlife Refuge (3) and Overflow National Wildlife Refuge (4), Arkansas

► Highlight: Important wintering area for thousands of waterfowl; small population of the Red-cockaded Woodpecker.

► Location: The refuge is in Ashley, Bradley, and Union Counties, five miles west of Crossett.

► Size: 65,000 acres.

► Ownership: Fish and Wildlife Service.

► Habitats: Lakes and sloughs, bottomland hardwoods, pine forests.

► Land Use: Hunting, fishing, wildlife observation.

► Site Description: Located where the Ouachita and Saline Rivers flow together, much of the refuge is covered by swampy bottomland forest, with pine forests on the uplands. Up to 21,000 acres of the forest are seasonally flooded. The refuge was first established in mitigation for the locks and dams constructed by the Army Corps of Engineers on the Ouachita River.

► Birds: The Red-cockaded Woodpecker population on the refuge is part of the best population in the coastal plain of Arkansas, much of it on lands of timber companies, extending into north Louisiana. On the refuge, there are Brown-headed Nuthatches and Bachman's Sparrows, and breeding Chuck-will's-widows, Red-headed Woodpeckers; and Prothonotary, Hooded, Worm-eating, Cerulean, and Kentucky Warblers. Up to 300,000 waterfowl are found in winter. The refuge also administers the 18,000-acre Overflow National Wildlife Refuge, some 25 miles to the east, which supports up to 200,000 waterfowl in winter, and many shorebirds during migration.

► Conservation Issues: Habitat is managed for the Red-cockaded Woodpecker; among the management tools is prescribed burning. Pileated and Red-bellied Woodpeckers sometimes take over Red-cockaded nest cavities and drive the latter out. Biologists have put metal plates restricting the size of the entrance hole to the dimensions preferred by the Red-cockaded Woodpecker on some of the trees; nest and roost trees have been marked with white bands. There is some problem with predation on the nests by flying squirrels. Despite management, the number of colonies on the refuge itself has declined from 20 in 1992 to 15 in 2000. Water levels are managed on part of the refuge for waterfowl, Wood Storks, and for wading bird rookeries.

▸ Visitor Information: Best time to visit is fall through spring. Contact the refuge at 5531 Highway 82 West, Crossett, AR 71635, 870-364-3167.

HUNTING

No word could be more value-laden or emotion-inciting among many bird lovers than *hunting*. Historically, intensive hunting (or collecting or control) has contributed to the extinction of several New World species, including the Passenger Pigeon and Great Auk. The numbers of many shorebirds—notably the Eskimo Curlew—were decimated by hunting at the turn of the century. Even songbirds were extensively hunted until laws prohibiting this were enacted early in the last century. And today, birds in decline, including the Lesser Prairie-Chicken, Greater Sage-Grouse, and Steller's Eider, are still hunted in some states.

Is this the picture nonhunting citizens should have of hunting today? The answer in North America is clearly no. Regardless of one's ethical and moral view of hunting, it can't be denied that hunters today do far more to help birds than harm them. In fact, collectively, the hunting community may be the strongest contributor of all to land conservation. Conservation organizations such as Ducks Unlimited and the Wild Turkey Federation are leaders in acquiring, restoring, and managing land and water for wildlife, and their work benefits not just hunted species but all birds. In fact, the strong rebound of once declining and locally extirpated species including turkeys and many ducks and geese is attributable to the efforts of the hunting community. And, for the most part, the laws regulating hunting result in healthy and predictable populations, year after year. The birding community could learn a lot from the successful conservation work of hunters' groups in terms of organizing, fund-raising, and advocacy.

Does hunting have a damaging effect in areas important for bird conservation such as IBAs? The answer is, as with most places, well-managed hunting has few adverse effects on bird populations or habitats. Then what, if anything, should concern bird lovers about hunting? One is the practice of introducing large nonnative mammals for hunting or for food. In case after case—especially on islands or in discrete continental habitats, introduced deer, hogs, goats, sheep, pigs, and other mammals have wreaked havoc on native plant communities, denuding habitat, destroying food sources, and causing serious declines in native wildlife populations. The sheep in Hawaii have devoured vegetation important for native birds, and openings created by pigs in mountain forests are responsible for the spread of mosquitoes carrying avian diseases.

Subsistence hunting by Native Americans is not regulated in the same way as other hunting, and given the availability and use of modern weapons and means of transportation, the future of some species is now threatened in part by overhunting.

Today, rather than being divided by the issue of hunting, both hunters and nonhunters are increasingly coming together to address habitat loss and other common concerns. We should encourage this trend.

Caddo Lake Watershed (5), Texas

▶ Highlight: With some of the best cypress swamp in Texas, this site has good numbers of nesting neotropical migrants, including Prothonotary, Kentucky, and Swainson's Warblers.

▶ Designation: Ramsar site (Wetland of International Importance).

▶ Location: Near Kernack, Marion County, close to the Louisiana state line.

▶ Size: 32,000 acres.

▶ Ownership: Texas Department of Parks and Wildlife, Army, private.

▶ Habitats: Lake, bottomland hardwood forest, cypress swamp, marsh, pine forest.

▶ Land Use: Hunting, fishing, boating, wildlife observation.

▶ Site Description: The site includes Caddo Lake, Caddo Lake Wildlife Management Area, and Caddo Lake State Park. The site contains some of the best cypress swamp in the state, with trees up to 400 years old. The lake includes not only cypress swamp and open water but bayous, sloughs, and channels through hardwood and pine forest. Adjacent is the 8,400-acre Longhorn Army Ammunition Plant, also part of the Caddo Lake ecosystem. On the facility is the 1,200-acre Harrison Bayou, about half of which is virgin forest. Caddo Lake is a popular destination for sportsmen, and there are several family-owned fishing outfits and duck-hunting lease properties in the area.

▶ Birds: Many neotropical migrants breed in the area, including large numbers of Prothonotary and Yellow-throated Warblers, and Northern Parulas. Other species include the Chuck-will's-widow; Kentucky, Swainson's, and Prairie Warblers; Dickcissel, and Painted Bunting, in addition to resident Brown-headed Nuthatches. In winter, a few Le Conte's Sparrows are found, as are good numbers of waterfowl.

▶ Conservation Issues: Altered hydrology in the area resulting in a permanently flooded substrate inhibits or prevents regeneration of cypress, though mature trees are surviving. Introduced nutria and populations of beavers are potential risks to forest regeneration. Several non-native plants, including water hyacinth, are problems, as are elevated levels of heavy metals and increasing nutrient input in the lake. The Caddo Lake Institute, a private foundation, played a key role in the designation of the wetland as a Ramsar site. It sponsors local wetland research and conservation education and provides wetland science training to local colleges and schools.

▶ Visitor Information: Any time of year is good for a visit, though summers are hot and there are biting insects. The best way to see the area is by canoe or boat, which can be rented at several locations around the lake during the warmer months. For information, contact: Caddo Lake State Park and Wildlife Management Area, 3103 Rouncival Drive, Longview, TX 75605, 903-757-9572.

Kisatchie National Forest (6) and Fort Polk (7), Louisiana

▶ Highlight: Significant numbers of the Red-cockaded Woodpecker and Bachman's Sparrow.

▶ Location: Vernon Parrish.

▶ Size: There are about 85,000 acres of habitat for the Red-cockaded Woodpecker on the Vernon Unit of Kisatchie National Forest and approximately 90,000 acres on adjacent Fort Polk.

► Ownership: Forest Service, Army.

► Habitats: Pine forests, mixed woodlands, some grassland.

► Land Use: Forestry, recreation, military training exercises.

► Site Description: The site represents one of the best examples of the longleaf pine–bluestem community. There is also some bottomland hardwood forest and a few pitcher plant bogs. Louisiana's only national forest, the Kisatchie consists of six widely separated districts, but the habitat for the woodpecker is on the Vernon Unit of the Calcasieu District.

► Birds: The area supports approximately 250 active clusters of the Red-cockaded Woodpecker (estimated to be up to 700 birds); this represents a significant percentage of the entire world's population. Of these, some 200 clusters are on the Vernon Unit, which abuts Fort Polk, where there are approximately 50 clusters. The area has a good population of the Bachman's Sparrow and provides wintering habitat for the Henslow's Sparrow.

► Conservation Issues: The area has a burn history going back to the 1930s and closely resembles the original habitat. Land managers manage woodpecker habitat to protect the species.

► Visitor Information: Best time to visit the national forest is in April and May and the winter months. Contact the refuge at 2500 Shreveport Highway, Pineville, LA 71360, 318-473-7160. For information about Fort Polk, call 318-531-6088.

Angelina National Forest (8), Texas

► Highlight: There is a large population of the resident Bachman's Sparrow on the forest, in addition to several clusters of the Red-cockaded Woodpecker.

► Location: East Texas just east of Lufkin, in Angelina, Nacogdoches, San Augustine, and Jasper Counties.

► Size: 154,245 acres.

► Ownership: Forest Service.

► Habitats: Bottomland hardwood forest, longleaf pine savannah, pitcher-plant bogs, riparian.

► Land Use: Forestry, recreation, oil and gas wells.

► Site Description: The forest is in the Neches River Basin and on the north and south shores of Sam Rayburn Reservoir, a 114,500-acre impoundment on the Angelina River. The terrain is gently rolling. Longleaf pine is dominant in the southern part of the forest whereas shortleaf and loblolly are dominant in the north.

► Birds: The forest has a large resident population of the Bachman's Sparrow. There are 19 clusters of the Red-cockaded Woodpecker in the longleaf pine savannah, and nine in the shortleaf-loblolly pine community; this land is now managed for the woodpecker. Among the other breeding species are the Swainson's, Kentucky, and Prothonotary Warblers, the resident Brown-headed Nuthatches, and the wintering Henslow's and Le Conte's Sparrows.

► Conservation Issues: There is damage to sensitive soils in longleaf pine savannahs, riparian zones, and pitcher plant bogs, and possible impact on the Red-cockaded Woodpeckers from off-road vehicle use in the forest. A trail system is being established to address this issue. Prescribed burns are used to maintain habitat for the woodpecker and to maintain the seepage bogs, where many rare plants grow. Various preservation and conservation groups oppose burning, and the forest is under federal court injunction restricting burning in Red-cockaded Woodpecker habitat, longleaf pine savannahs, and bogs at this time. As a multiple-use area, much of the forest is managed for sustained timber production. There are oil and gas wells on the forest; mineral rights were retained by many of the landowners who sold their lands to the Forest Service.

▶ Visitor Information: Best time to visit is late April to early June, and during the winter months. Contact the forest at Walnut Ridge Road, Zavalla, TX 75980, 936-897-1068.

Davy Crockett National Forest (9), Texas

▶ Highlight: Good population of the Red-cockaded Woodpecker and several green-listed species.
▶ Location: Just west of Lufkin in Houston and Trinity Counties, east Texas.
▶ Size: 161,497 acres.
▶ Ownership: Forest Service, private.
▶ Habitats: Shortleaf and loblolly pine-hardwood woodland, bottomland hardwood forest.
▶ Land Use: Recreation, logging, wildlife protection.
▶ Site Description: The forest lies in the Trinity and Neches River Basins and includes cypress swamps and hardwood bottoms in addition to pine woodland with a component of sweetgum and various species of hickories and oaks.
▶ Birds: There are 53 active clusters of the Red-cockaded Woodpecker in the forest, and several inactive clusters. The Brown-headed Nuthatch is found here, but the Bachman's Sparrow, a species that needs more frequent fires than now occur, is absent. Prothonotary, Kentucky, and Swainson's Warblers are found in the bottomland forests, and the Red-headed Woodpecker and Painted Bunting also breed.
▶ Conservation Issues: Management for the woodpecker includes prescribed burning, artificial cavities, and timber sales to thin the mid-storey. Since management began in 1990, the species has responded very well, and the populations have increased about five percent per year. The forest is also thinned to prevent infestation by southern bark beetle. Historically the woodland burned every five years or so, but because of the urban interface with nearby towns and cities, this is not practicable on the Davy Crockett today.
▶ Visitor Information: Best time to visit is during spring and fall migration and in the early breeding season, to late June. The forest can be contacted at Route 1, Box 55 FS, Kennard, TX 75847, 936-655-2299.

Big Thicket National Preserve (10) and the Roy E. Larsen Sandyland Sanctuary (11), Texas

▶ Highlight: Many Green List birds breed or winter on the preserve.
▶ Designation: International Biosphere Reserve.

► Location: Southeastern Texas, north of Beaumont.

► Size: 96,757 acres.

► Ownership: National Park Service.

► Habitats: Pine, pine-oak savannah, prairie, marsh, riparian, bottomland forest.

► Land Use: Recreation, wildlife conservation.

► Site Description: The Big Thicket National Preserve consists of 12 units scattered over an area 45 miles long and 50 miles wide. Some of these sites lie along the Neches River corridor. The original Big Thicket covered 3.5 million acres, of which only 300,000 acres remain, with only 96,757 acres protected in the national preserve; but other areas are protected under state or private conservation ownership, most notably The Nature Conservancy's 5,654-acre Roy E. Larsen Sandyland Sanctuary and the Texas Parks and Wildlife Department's 1,003-acre Village Creek State Park and 705-acre Martin Dies, Jr. State Park. On the Sandyland Sanctuary, there are many large trees, including 15 that are the largest of their kind in the nation. The state parks lie in the Neches River floodplain and are heavily forested with bottomland hardwoods. They are particularly significant in representing public lands in a state where relatively few exist.

► Birds: The Swallow-tailed Kite is often observed during the breeding season and presumably nests. The Chuck-will's-widow and Red-headed Woodpecker also breed; as do the Brown-headed Nuthatch, Bachman's Sparrow, Prairie, Worm-eating, Prothonotary, Kentucky, and Swainson's Warblers, and Painted Bunting. In winter, the Harris's Sparrow occurs commonly, and the Henslow's and Le Conte's Sparrows are also present. There was until recently a remnant population of the Red-cockaded Woodpecker, but this became extirpated in the early 1990s.

► Conservation Issues: The National Park Service and The Nature Conservancy conduct prescribed burning on their lands to maintain longleaf pine savannah, home to some of the rarer birds. The Park Service plans to reintroduce Red-cockaded Woodpeckers to the preserve. The closest population at present is just to the north of one of the units, on the Alabama-Coushatta Indian Reservation. The Park Service, The Nature Conservancy, and Texas Parks and Wildlife act together as partners to protect habitat in the Big Thicket complex. The water problems of the rapidly expanding urban sprawl around Houston threaten the area. A proposed larger dam at B.A. Steinhagen Reservoir, if constructed, would inundate part of Martin Dies, Jr. State Park, destroying valuable bird habitat.

► Visitor Information: April and May are the best months to see migrants and nesting birds. Many birds winter in the area. Contact: Big Thicket National Preserve at 3785 Milam, Beaumont, TX 77701, 409-246-2337, and Roy E. Larsen Sandyland Preserve at P.O. Box 909, Silsbee, TX 77656, 409-385-0445. Village Creek State Park can be reached at P.O. Box 8565, Lumberton, TX 77657, 409-755-7322 or 800-792-1112, and Martin Dies, Jr. State Park at Rural Route #4, Box 274, Jasper, TX 75951, 409-384-5231.

Sam Houston National Forest (12), Texas

► Highlight: The largest concentration of Red-cockaded Woodpeckers in Texas, plus good numbers of breeding Swainson's Warblers.

► Location: North of Houston, near Cleveland, Conroe, and Huntsville.

▸ Size: 162,984 acres.

▸ Ownership: Forest Service.

▸ Habitats: Pine forest, bottomland hardwoods, palmetto flats, native prairies.

▸ Land Use: Wildlife protection, recreation, logging.

▸ Site Description: Several types of forest exist at the site, with loblolly and shortleaf pines in the uplands, and magnolias and tupelo on lower sites. Bottomland hardwoods include beech, river birch, swamp chestnut oak, and various other oaks.

▸ Birds: With 169 clusters, Sam Houston National Forest has the largest number of Red-cockaded Woodpeckers in Texas. Among the other typical piney woods birds are the Brown-headed Nuthatch and Bachman's Sparrow. The Swainson's Warbler breeds in good numbers; other breeding warblers include Worm-eating and Kentucky. Henslow's and Le Conte's Sparrows are found in the winter (November to February). The Broad-winged Hawk nests and migrates over the area in huge numbers in April and again in September. Several pairs of Bald Eagles nest from November to May.

▸ Conservation Issues: Habitat for the Red-cockaded Woodpecker is managed to benefit that species as well as other species dependent upon fire-maintained communities. Native prairies are being restored to benefit the Henslow's Sparrow and other grassland species.

▸ Visitor Information: Best time to visit is late April through late June, and again in winter. Contact the forest at 394 FM 1375 West, New Waverly, TX 77358, 936-344-6205 or 888-361-6908.

W. G. Jones State Forest (13), Texas

▸ Highlight: Population of the Red-cockaded Woodpecker in a forest surrounded by urban development.

▸ Location: Near Conroe, north of Houston.

▸ Size: 1,725 acres.

▸ Ownership: Texas State Forests.

▸ Habitats: Pinewoods.

▸ Land Use: Research, conservation, wildlife observation.

▸ Site Description: Primarily loblolly pine with some trees up to 100 years old. The forest is in a rapidly urbanizing setting, surrounded on three sides by a planned community of 80,000 people; on the fourth side is undeveloped, private forest. Busy public roads run along two sides; one is a four-lane parkway. The site is well known as an easy place to see the Red-cockaded Woodpecker, and attracts visitors from all over the world, since it is easily accessible from the Houston International Airport.

▸ Birds: There are 14 active clusters of the Red-cockaded Woodpecker on the forest. The Red-headed Woodpecker and Brown-headed Nuthatch are common residents, while the Chuck-will's-widow, Worm-eating, Kentucky, and Swainson's Warblers, and Painted Bunting are among the species that have bred there, though none are common.

▸ Conservation Issues: W. G. Jones State Forest is designated as a Demonstration Forest, and applied research into forest management techniques, forest genetics, and forest-product utilization have always been a focus there. Several demonstration areas for the protection of water quality from nonpoint source pollution have been established. There are occasional epidemics of southern pine bark beetle, with subsequent replanting or reseeding of affected areas. Habitat in the forest is managed to benefit the woodpecker. The understorey is kept in check by mechanical means and by the use of herbicides and prescribed burning; the latter is used sparingly because of the forest's urban setting. Banding and recovery of the woodpeckers show that there is interchange between the population here and on Sam Houston National Forest, 20 miles away; there are also a few birds on intervening private lands. Landscape architecture students from Texas A&M have written a master plan for the forest and there are plans to turn the site into a conservation education center.

▶ Visitor Information: Any time of year is good for a visit, with late April through early July good for seeing breeding birds. For more information, contact: W. G. Jones State Forest, Texas Forest Service, Route 7, Box 151, Conroe, TX 77384, 979-458-6600.

26. Mississippi Alluvial Valley

T he Lower Mississippi Alluvial Valley consists of approximately 24 million acres of alluvial floodplain south of the river's confluence with the Ohio River. Prior to European settlement, this was the greatest bottomland hardwood forest on Earth and was subject to massive annual flood events of the Mississippi River and its tributaries. These forested wetlands were the main wintering area for the midcontinent Mallard, Wood Duck, and other waterfowl species. Flood control and deforestation for agriculture began more than 100 years ago. Today less than 25 percent of the region remains forested, and flooding has been reduced by approximately 90 percent. Despite these changes, the region still supports large numbers of wintering waterfowl, estimated at nine percent of the continental duck population. With the large reduction in native habitat and natural flooding, the major waterfowl-management issue today is providing enough foraging habitat on managed private and public lands to reliably meet the needs of wintering ducks and geese. Many shorebird species also use managed wetlands as migration stopover sites. Remnant forests harbor populations of the Swainson's Warbler, Prothonotary Warbler, and Swallow-tailed Kite. The region provides excellent colonial waterbird habitat, particularly to the south, where large numbers of White Ibis, Yellow-crowned Night-Herons, and other herons and egrets nest.

Mingo National Wildlife Refuge (1), Missouri

▶ Highlight: More than 200,000 waterfowl winter at the refuge, and several Green List species breed, while many shorebirds stop over during migration.
▶ Location: In the "boot-heel" of southeastern Missouri, 40 miles west of the Mississippi River.
▶ Size: 21,676 acres.
▶ Ownership: Fish and Wildlife Service.
▶ Habitats: Variety of successional habitats from farmland to forest, seasonally flooded basins, limestone bluffs.
▶ Land Use: Wildlife preservation, farming, hunting, recreation.
▶ Site Description: The refuge lies in an ancient channel of the Mississippi River. Approximately 16,000 acres are bottomlands, contained within a perimeter of limestone

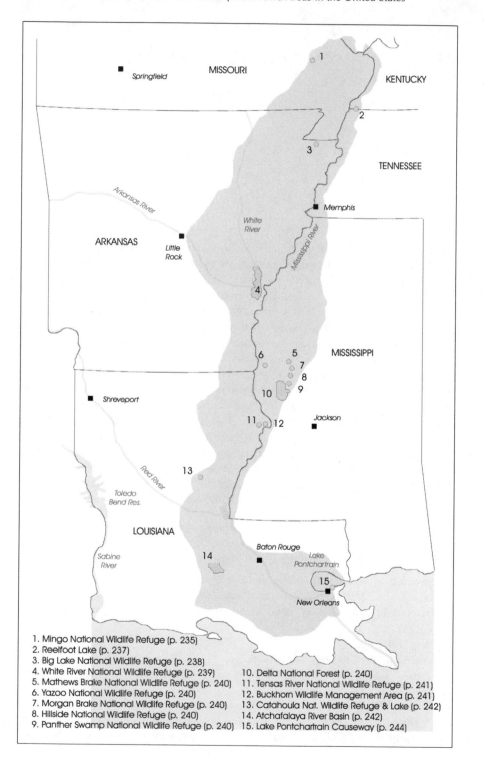

1. Mingo National Wildlife Refuge (p. 235)
2. Reelfoot Lake (p. 237)
3. Big Lake National Wildlife Refuge (p. 238)
4. White River National Wildlife Refuge (p. 239)
5. Mathews Brake National Wildlife Refuge (p. 240)
6. Yazoo National Wildlife Refuge (p. 240)
7. Morgan Brake National Wildlife Refuge (p. 240)
8. Hillside National Wildlife Refuge (p. 240)
9. Panther Swamp National Wildlife Refuge (p. 240)
10. Delta National Forest (p. 240)
11. Tensas River National Wildlife Refuge (p. 241)
12. Buckhorn Wildlife Management Area (p. 241)
13. Catahoula Nat. Wildlife Refuge & Lake (p. 242)
14. Atchafalaya River Basin (p. 242)
15. Lake Pontchartrain Causeway (p. 244)

bluffs and steep hills of the Ozark Uplift, which lie to the east and west. Much of the refuge is forested, with oaks being dominant. The refuge contains the only remaining large tract of bottomland cypress-tupelo forest in the "boot-heel" of Missouri.

Mississippi Kite

▶ Birds: Twenty-one species of waterfowl winter on the refuge, with up to 125,000 Mallards, 75,000 Canada Geese, thousands of Gadwall, Northern Pintails, American Wigeon, and Ring-necked Ducks. Trumpeter Swans are occasional. Raptors include nesting Bald Eagles and Mississippi Kites. Breeding species include the Chuck-will's-widow, Red-headed Woodpecker, Wood Thrush, and Prothonotary and Kentucky Warblers. More than 25,000 annual shorebird-use days have been recorded at the refuge.

▶ Conservation Issues: The refuge is an important link in the chain of sites along the Mississippi Flyway. Forest clearance and drainage in the past was only partially successful, allowing Mingo to retain its potential as a wildlife haven. Management activities instituted since the refuge was established have restored its bird populations. Water levels are manipulated using a system of dikes and ditches, and 700

Hooded Merganser

acres are planted with crops to help provide supplemental food for wintering wildfowl. Nest boxes have been put up for Wood Ducks and Hooded Mergansers. Hunting on the refuge is limited and strictly controlled. Other management activities include prescribed burns, and timber and grassland management. The refuge has approximately 150,000 visitors annually. In 1976, 7,730 acres of the refuge were designated as wilderness. In 1993, a large storm destroyed many of the larger trees. The 6,190-acre State Duck Creek Wildlife Management Area lies adjacent to the reserve along its northeast boundary.

▶ Visitor Information: The refuge has visitor trails and boardwalks. Best time to visit is fall through spring, but visitors should stop at the refuge center before venturing onto the refuge during hunting season, between October 1 and March 14. Contact the Refuge Manager, Mingo National Wildlife Refuge, Route 1, Box 103, Puxico, MO 63960, 314-222-3589.

Reelfoot Lake (2), Tennessee

▶ Highlight: Major stopover and wintering area for migratory birds using the Mississippi Flyway.

▶ Location: Obion County, Tennessee, and Fulton County, Kentucky; headquarters is 15 miles southwest of Union City, Tennessee.

▶ Size: The National Wildlife Refuge is 10,428 acres.

▶ Ownership: Fish and Wildlife Service, Tennessee Department of Conservation, Tennessee State Parks, private.

▶ Habitats: Bottomland forest (1,850 acres), open water (25,000 acres, all of which is managed by the refuge), mixed cropland.

▶ Land Use: Hunting, fishing.

▶ Site Description: Reelfoot Lake was created by a series of violent earthquakes (the New Madrid Earthquakes) from December 1811 to February 1812. These earthquakes changed the course of the nearby Mississippi River and caused a great depression to form in northwestern Tennessee. This depression, which quickly filled with water, became Reelfoot Lake. Public lands included in Reelfoot Lake and its surrounding wetlands are Reelfoot Lake National Wildlife Refuge, Black Bayou and Reelfoot Wildlife Management Areas, and Reelfoot Lake State Park.

Swainson's Warbler

▶ Birds: As many as 400,000 ducks and 150,000 Canada Geese inhabit Reelfoot Lake during the winter. Included are several thousand Ruddy Ducks, and American Black Ducks, and what has in some years been the highest Christmas Bird Count in the United States for Ring-necked Ducks. The refuge has one of the largest concentrations of wintering Bald Eagles in the lower 48 states, with counts sometimes exceeding 200 birds. The refuge also supports considerable numbers of migratory shorebirds and wading birds, while many migrating and breeding neotropical migrants are found in the bottomland hardwoods. The Chuck-will's-widow is common during breeding season, as are the Prothonotary Warbler and Wood Thrush. While the Kentucky and Swainson's Warblers breed occasionally, the Red-headed Woodpecker is a common resident.

▶ Conservation Issues: Management tools include mechanical and chemical control of non-native invasive plant species. Other management activities include forest management, protection and enhancement of wetland habitats, production of waterfowl foods through managed croplands, manipulation of native wetland vegetation, and management of water levels in Reelfoot Lake.

▶ Visitor Information: Refuge lands are open to the public from March 15 to November 15; the auto-tour route is open year-round. For more information, contact the refuge headquarters at 4343 Highway 157, Union City, TN 38261, 901-538-2481.

Big Lake National Wildlife Refuge (3), Arkansas

▶ Highlight: A major site for wintering waterfowl, with up to 500,000 ducks present.

▶ Location: Near Manila, in Mississippi County, northeastern Arkansas.

▸ Size: 11,038 acres.

▸ Ownership: Fish and Wildlife Service.

▸ Habitats: Bottomland hardwood forest, cypress-tupelo-willow swamp, shallow open water, farmlands, levees.

▸ Land Use: Hunting, fishing, hiking, wildlife observation.

▸ Site Description: Located in the Mississippi River Delta, Big Lake was, like Tennessee's Reelfoot Lake, created by the New Madrid Earthquakes of 1811–1812. It represents a small remnant of the vast area of cypress swamp and seasonally flooded bottomland hardwood forest that once covered much of northeastern Arkansas.

▸ Birds: Up to 500,000 ducks are found on Big Lake itself during the winter. Though as many as 90 percent may be Mallards, many other duck species are included. Up to one million ducks and geese are present in the Big Lake area, many feeding on nearby rice fields. Hundreds of young Wood Ducks are produced every year during the breeding season, and many Hooded Mergansers breed as well. The Red-headed Woodpecker is a common resident, and the Chuck-will's-widow, Wood Thrush, and Prothonotary and Kentucky Warblers nest.

▸ Conservation Issues: The refuge receives large amounts of runoff from agricultural lands, creating problems with siltation and water quality. Siltation has favored growth of black willow and American lotus, which are targets of chemical control.

▸ Visitor Information: There are hiking trails, but the refuge is best explored by boat, since as much as 99 percent of it is flooded during the spring. Call for local conditions. The refuge is two miles east of Manila off Highway 18. Phone number is 870-564-2429.

White River National Wildlife Refuge (4), Arkansas

▸ Highlight: With one million or more wintering ducks and geese, this is one of the major waterfowl wintering sites in the United States.

▸ Designation: Together with Cache River National Wildlife Refuge and several nearby Game and Fish Commission areas, it has been named as a Ramsar site (a Wetland of International Importance).

▸ Location: Along the White River east of De Witt, in Arkansas County.

▸ Size: 160,000 acres.

▸ Ownership: Fish and Wildlife Service.

▸ Habitats: Bottomland hardwood forest, sloughs, lakes, streams, bayous.

▸ Land Use: Hunting, fishing, wildlife conservation.

▸ Site Description: With 154,000 forested acres, the refuge is the largest contiguous block of bottomland hardwood forest in one ownership in the United States. Located in the floodplain of the lower White River, just a few miles above its confluence with the Mississippi River, the refuge is from three to ten miles wide and extends along the White River for approximately 90 miles. Much of the refuge is under water during the winter and spring.

▸ Birds: The area calls itself the "mallard capital of the world," with up to ten percent of the entire Mississippi Flyway population wintering there. A good population of Swainson's Warblers breed, as do the Prothonotary, Cerulean, and Kentucky Warblers, and Wood Thrush. The Red-headed Woodpecker is a resident.

Prothonotary Warbler

▶ Conservation Issues: The refuge is managed to benefit waterfowl. There is an ongoing study on the Prothonotary Warbler being conducted on the refuge by researchers from the University of Georgia.

▶ Visitor Information: During winter and spring, much of the refuge is flooded. The roads are closed from November to February and can be muddy in the early spring. Some roads on the refuge can be closed due to high water into May and June. Mosquitoes are a problem during the warmer parts of the year. Visitors should stop at refuge headquarters and ask about road conditions. Mosquito repellent is needed during the warmer weather. Contact the refuge at 321 West 7th Street/P.O. Box 308, DeWitt, AR 72042, 870-946-1468.

Yazoo National Wildlife Refuge Complex and Delta National Forest IBAs, Mississippi

Mathews Brake National Wildlife Refuge (5), Yazoo National Wildlife Refuge (6), Morgan Brake National Wildlife Refuge (7), Hillside National Wildlife Refuge (8), Panther Swamp National Wildlife Refuge (9), Delta National Forest (10)

▶ Highlight: Thousands of wintering waterfowl use this five-refuge complex, as well as the forested wetlands of Delta National Forest.

▶ Location: The Yazoo Basin of the Mississippi River; the area lies north of Vicksburg and west of Yazoo City.

▶ Size: The five refuges total 73,320 acres; Delta National Forest is 60,115 acres.

▶ Ownership: Fish and Wildlife Service, Forest Service.

▶ Habitats: Seasonally flooded bottomland hardwoods, cypress-tupelo sloughs, marshes, and some agricultural areas managed for waterfowl.

▶ Land Use: Hunting, fishing, camping, wildlife observation, hiking and all-terrain vehicle trails; wildlife openings are managed for turkey, deer, and quail.

▶ Site Description: The refuge complex includes Yazoo National Wildlife Refuge and four satellite refuges: Panther Swamp, Morgan Brake, Hillside, and Mathews Brake National Wildlife Refuges. Surrounding the refuges are agricultural fields and commercial catfish ponds. Delta National Forest lies just west of Panther Swamp National Wildlife Refuge. It is a large, contiguous block of bottomland hardwood forest, seasonally flooded timber, and small sloughs draining into the Big and Little Sunflower Rivers. It is the only national forest in the entire system with bottomland hardwoods.

▶ Birds: Up to 250,000 ducks are found on the refuges and the forest during fall and winter. A mixed heron and egret colony of up to 25,000 birds nests on Yazoo National Wildlife Refuge. All forested wetlands in the Yazoo Basin provide nesting, brood-rearing, and wintering habitat for the Wood Duck. Breeding species on the refuges and the forest include the Red-headed Woodpecker, Wood Thrush, Prothonotary Warbler, Painted Bunting, and Dickcissel.

► Conservation Issues: Federal lands in this area of the delta conserve the few remaining forested wetlands where most of the landscape has been converted to agricultural use. Some reforestation by private landowners is in progress through incentive programs such as the Wetlands Reserve Program.

► Visitor Information: Contact: Yazoo National Wildlife Refuge Complex, Route 1, Box 286, Hollandale, MS 38748, 662-839-2638, and Delta National Forest, 402 Highway 61 North, Rolling Fork, MS 39159, 662-873-6256. Refuges are closed in January and February.

Tensas River National Wildlife Refuge (11) and Buckhorn Wildlife Management Area (12), Louisiana

► Highlight: Large concentrations of wintering waterfowl; nesting Green List species, including the Swainson's Warbler.

► Location: Tensas River Basin, northeastern Louisiana, in Madison, Tensas, and Franklin Parishes, south of Waverly.

► Size: Tensas National Wildlife Refuge (64,012 acres); Buckhorn Wildlife Management Area (8,955 acres).

► Ownership: Fish and Wildlife Service, Louisiana Department of Wildlife and Fisheries.

► Habitats: Forest, bayous, lakes, open areas with some croplands.

► Land Use: Hunting, fishing, wildlife observation.

► Site Description: This complex of federal and state lands forms one of the largest remnants of Mississippi alluvial floodplain bottomland forest, a habitat that has been reduced to just 20 percent of its original extent. The understorey is dense over much of the area.

► Birds: The last documented sighting of the Ivory-billed Woodpecker occurred in the 1940s on what is now national wildlife refuge property; the Bachman's Warbler also once occurred here. The area has what may be the highest concentration of Barred Owls in the United States. The Prothonotary Warbler is an abundant breeding species, and Swainson's and Kentucky Warblers are common. Other breeding birds include the Little Blue Heron, Chuck-will's-widow and Painted Bunting. Up to 100,000 waterfowl are found in winter.

► Conservation Issues: Management activities include tree planting and selective thinning, control of water levels, and cooperative agreements with adjacent farms to leave part of their crop as feed for wintering waterfowl. Some cropping also takes place on refuge lands. Water levels are managed for waterfowl, wading birds, and shorebirds.

► Visitor Information: Best time to visit is fall through spring. Contact Tensas National Wildlife Refuge, Route 2, Box 295, Tallulah, LA 71282, 318-574-2664. Information on the Buckhorn Wildlife Management Area can be obtained from the Louisiana Department of Wildlife and Fisheries, P.O. Box 1640, Ferriday, LA 71334, 318-757-4571.

Catahoula National Wildlife Refuge and Catahoula Lake (13), Louisiana

▸ Highlight: Major concentration of wintering waterfowl.
▸ Designation: The lake is a Wetland of International Importance, designated under the Ramsar Convention.
▸ Location: LaSalle and Catahoula Parishes, in east-central Louisiana, 12 miles southeast of Jena.
▸ Size: The refuge is 25,001 acres and the lake 26,000 acres.
▸ Ownership: Fish and Wildlife Service (14,744 acres), American Electric Power (10,257 acres).
▸ Habitats: Open water, bottomland hardwood forest, bayous.
▸ Land Use: Hunting, fishing, wildlife observation.
▸ Site Description: The Catahoula Unit of the refuge borders nine miles of the northeast boundary of Catahoula Lake. It is composed primarily of seasonally flooded bottomland hardwoods, with some wooded swamps and sloughs. A 1,200-acre impoundment has been created for water management and additional waterfowl habitat. Adjacent to the refuge is the state-owned Dewey Wills Wildlife Management Area. The Bushley Bayou Unit is approximately two miles north of the Catahoula Unit. It is comprised of fallow fields with scattered cypress brakes, shallow lakes, and meandering bayous.
▸ Birds: In winter, more than 500,000 ducks have been counted on the lake and refuge; among the most common are the Canvasback (98,000), Northern Pintail (77,000), and Ring-necked Duck (50,000), with Gadwall, Mallard, and Green-winged Teal also numbering in the thousands. Thousands of shorebirds stop by during migration, and thousands of herons are found seasonally. Breeding species include Kentucky and Prothonotary Warblers, and Painted Bunting.
▸ Conservation Issues: In 2001, the 18,372-acre Bushley Bayou Unit was acquired in partnership with the Fish and Wildlife Service, American Electric Power Company, and the Conservation Fund. Approximately 12,000 acres of former farmland within the refuge is being reforested. Levels in freshwater impoundments are also managed for waterfowl. Annual flooding of bottomlands within the refuge from the lake can be severe. Currently there are four oil companies operating facilities on the refuge, and there is a potential threat from oil and saltwater spills.
▸ Visitor Information: Best time to visit is in October and November; access to the interior of the refuge may be restricted between February and June because of high water. The refuge can be contacted at P.O. Drawer Z, Rhinehart, LA 71363. Phone: 318-992-5261, e-mail: FW4_RW_Catahoula@fws.gov.

Atchafalaya River Basin (14), Louisiana

▸ Highlight: The river basin seasonally supports up to nine percent of the duck population in the North American continent, plus large numbers of green-listed neotropical migrants during the breeding season.
▸ Location: South-central Louisiana at the southern end of the Lower Mississippi River Valley.
▸ Size: 595,000 acres.

▸ Ownership: Fish and Wildlife Service, Army Corps of Engineers, Louisiana Department of Wildlife and Fisheries, private.

▸ Habitats: Swamps, lakes, bayous.

▸ Land Use: Hunting, fishing, boating, agriculture, oil and gas extraction, wildlife conservation.

▸ Site Description: The Atchafalaya River Basin is the largest complex of forested wetlands in the nation, comprising approximately 1.2 million acres of seasonally flooded hardwood swamps, lakes, and bayous. A resource as important as the Everglades, only a small proportion is protected as wildlife refuges or parks. Public lands there include the Atchafalaya National Wildlife Refuge (15,220 acres) and the Sherburne Wildlife Management Area (11,780 acres); in addition, the Army Corps of Engineers owns 16,600 acres at the Bayou Des Ourses Area. These public lands are managed jointly by the Corps, the Fish and Wildlife Service, and the Louisiana Department of Wildlife and Fisheries. The Corps owns another 28,480 acres in the Indian Bayou area and 2,230 acres within the Shatters Bayou Area.

The Atchafalaya River is one of five major distributaries of the Mississippi River, which discharges 30 percent of its flow into the Atchafalaya. Ecologically, the basin has four sections. To the north are woodlands and farmlands. The middle section contains North America's largest river basin swamp. Farther south is marshland. Finally, where the Atchafalaya River empties into Atchafalaya Bay, a new delta is being formed. The basin provides one the largest fish harvests in the United States and yields 23 million pounds of crawfish annually.

▸ Birds: Thousands of migratory waterfowl winter in the overflow swamps and lakes of the basin; it is a particularly important wintering area for the Canvasback, but also supports the nation's largest concentration of the American Woodcock. The Swallow-tailed Kite and many wading birds (herons, egrets, and ibis) breed on the Atchafalaya. Many species of neotropical songbirds use the wetlands for resting and feeding during migration. There is also a healthy breeding population of the Mottled Duck, good shorebird habitat, and wading-bird nesting colonies, including some of the Roseate Spoonbill. The area also includes the highest Breeding Bird Survey counts for the Prothonotary, Swainson's, and Kentucky Warblers.

▸ Conservation Issues: Most of the Atchafalaya Basin is in private hands. By the late 1920s, landowners had logged out the old cypress trees and soon after began to lease mineral rights to oil and gas companies. Much of the northwest part of the basin has already been turned into soybean and corn fields, but farther south, vast stretches of the swamp remain, and it is here where the battles over water levels, land use, and resource management have occurred. Beginning in the late 1920s, the Corps turned the Atchafalaya River into a floodway between levees that diverts water from Baton Rouge and New Orleans. In 1985, Congress approved a compromise flood control plan agreed on by the Corps, state agencies, landowners, timber interests, fishers, and conservation groups. This plan authorizes the Corps to purchase 50,000 acres and obtain easements on another 338,000 acres, to restrict damaging aspects of logging and prevent expansion of soybeans and corn fields into the swamp. Without protected status, the Atchafalaya faces logging of its remaining cypress and bottomland hardwoods.

Among the other problems in the basin are dredging, causing siltation that has resulted both in filling in of some of the wetlands, and in creating oxygen-deprived dead zones where no aquatic life can survive; pollution, including contamination with mercury, which has resulted in a fish advisory being issued for one lake; levees, which have cut off freshwater flows, harming fishing and creating saltwater intrusion; and increased development south of Interstate 10. In response to these concerns, two master plans have been developed for the Achafalaya Basin, one by the Louisiana Department of Natural Resources and one by the Corps of Engineers. These master plans complement each other in an effort to address various issues within the basin.

▶ Visitor Information: Best time to visit is fall through spring; summers are hot and humid. Contact for the refuge is Fish and Wildlife Service, Southeast Louisiana Refuges, 1010 Gause Boulevard, Slidell, LA 70458, 504-646-7555. Contact for Sherburne is Area Supervisor, Sherburne Wildlife Management Area, 5652 Highway 182, Opelousas, LA 70570, 337-566-2251. Contact for Corps of Engineers areas is Park Manager, 112 Speck Lane, Port Barre, LA 70577, 337-585-0853.

Lake Pontchartrain Causeway (15), Louisiana

▶ Highlight: From June through August, more than 200,000 Purple Martins roost in the understructure on the southern end of the Lake Pontchartrain Causeway.

▶ Location: Near Metairie.

▶ Ownership: State of Louisiana.

▶ Site Description: This causeway is well known for its roosting Purple Martins, but other bridges and causeways along the Gulf Coast also host evening roosts of martins. These include one in Biloxi, Mississippi; one at Dauphin Island, Alabama; and one at Galveston Island, Texas; there is also a roost at Lake Murray, South Carolina.

▶ Birds: The martins at Lake Pontchartrain congregate at dusk to roost under the causeway.

▶ Conservation Issues: During the summer, as many as 3,000 spectators gather each evening along the lake's shoreline near the causeway. This has created demand for crowd control, safety measures, more adequate viewing space, and facilities for an interpretive center to protect and explain the phenomenon of the birds. Project Swallow has initiated the Save the Swallows program, which enlisted the help of the causeway management to put up 6,700 feet of fencing to eliminate collisions between cars and birds at both ends of the causeway. It was estimated that, prior to putting up fencing, as many as 12,000 birds per year were being killed by automobiles. There is a proposal to create a sanctuary at the end of the bridge where the martins roost.

▶ Visitor Information: Best time to visit is late spring through early fall.

27. Southeastern Coastal Plain

T his region includes extensive riverine swamps and marsh complexes along the Atlantic Coast. Interior forest vegetation is dominated by longleaf, slash, and loblolly pine forests. Priority landbirds include the Red-cockaded Woodpecker, Painted Bunting, Bachman's Sparrow, Swainson's Warbler, and Swallow-tailed Kite. Coastal intertidal habitats provide critical wintering areas for the American Oyster-catcher, important wintering and spring migration areas for the Short-billed Dowitcher and Dunlin, and important fall staging areas for the Red Knot. Sizable numbers of Brown Pelicans and various tern species breed on offshore islands. Coastal areas provide important nesting and foraging habitats for large numbers of herons, egrets, ibis, terns, and other species. Coastal areas hold large numbers of wintering Canvasbacks, Mallards, American Wigeon, Redheads, and the majority of the continent's population of the Tundra Swan. Managed impoundments in coastal areas are important to migrating and wintering dabbling ducks, including the American Black Duck.

Noxubee National Wildlife Refuge (1), Misslssippi

▶ Highlight: Small population of the Red-cockaded Woodpecker; several nesting Green List species.
▶ Location: In Noxubee, Winston, and Oktibbeha Counties, south of Starkville.
▶ Size: 48,000 acres.
▶ Ownership: Fish and Wildlife Service.
▶ Habitats: Old-growth pine forest, bottomland hardwood forest, lakes.
▶ Land Use: Wildlife conservation and management, environmental education, outdoor recreation.
▶ Site Description: Most of the refuge is woodland, some of it old-growth. Several thousand acres of bottomland forest are managed as wilderness.
▶ Birds: There are 45 clusters of the federally listed endangered Red-cockaded Woodpecker on the refuge; the Brown-headed Nuthatch is also resident. Among the nesting species are the Chuck-will's-widow; and Prothonotary, Kentucky, and occasionally Swainson's Warblers. Waterfowl number 10,000 to 20,000 during the winter.
▶ Conservation Issues: The old-growth pine on the refuge is managed for the Red-cockaded Woodpecker, which is also the subject of long-term studies here; the species

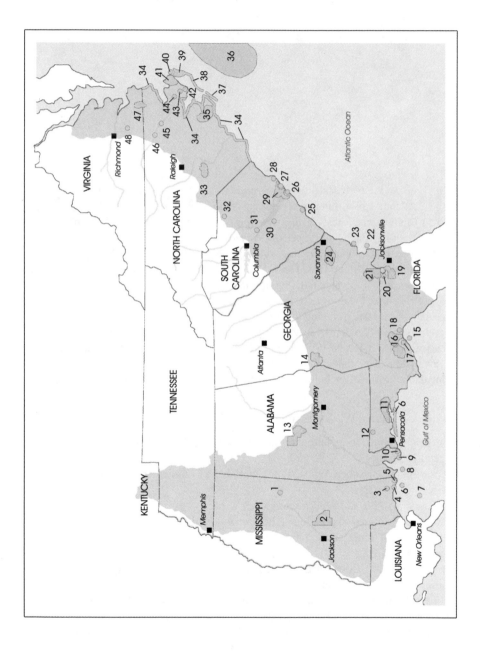

has increased on the refuge in recent years. The adjacent unit of the Tombigbee National Forest has a multiple resource use purpose including timber harvesting and outdoor recreation.

▶ Visitor Information: Red-cockaded Woodpeckers are easy to observe along a trail built through a grove of old-growth pines. Late fall through spring is the best time to visit. Contact is Noxubee National Wildlife Refuge, 224 Office Road, Brooksville, MS 39739, 662-323-5548, website: http//noxubee.fws.gov.

Bienville National Forest (2), Mississippi

▶ Highlight: Largest population of the Red-cockaded Woodpecker in Mississippi.
▶ Location: Near Forest, east of Jackson.
▶ Size: 178,400 acres.
▶ Ownership: Forest Service.
▶ Habitats: Shortleaf and loblolly pine hardwood forest.
▶ Land Use: Recreation, logging, wildlife protection.
▶ Site Description: The great majority of the forest is pine hardwood, and there are no significant wetland habitats. Most of the forest consists of land purchased directly from four large lumber companies.
▶ Birds: The forest has the state's largest number of Red-cockaded Woodpeckers, in addition to Brown-headed Nuthatches, Prairie Warblers, and a few Bachman's Sparrows.
▶ Conservation Issues: Approximately 125,000 acres of the forest are in the habitat management area for the Red-cockaded Woodpecker. Management includes prescribed burning, mid-storey removal, and artificial nest cavities. This active management program has shown success; there are currently 104 active clusters of woodpeckers on the forest, up from 86 clusters in 1990. Wildlife resources on the Bienville are managed cooperatively by the Forest Service and the Mississippi Department of Wildlife, Fisheries, and Parks. Three designated wildlife management areas have been established cooperatively in the forest.
▶ Visitor Information: Best time to visit is fall through spring. The forest can be contacted at 3473 Highway 35 South, Forest, MS 39074, 601-469-3811.

Mississippi Sandhill Crane National Wildlife Refuge (3), Mississippi

▶ Highlight: Only site for an endangered subspecies, the "Mississippi" Sandhill Crane.
▶ Location: Near Gautier, in Jackson County.
▶ Size: 19,000 acres in four units.
▶ Ownership: Fish and Wildlife Service.
▶ Habitats: Wet pine savannah communities.
▶ Land Use: Wildlife conservation; adjacent areas are all being developed for residences; the refuge is bisected by an interstate highway.
▶ Site Description: Historically the area was nearly all wet pine savannah, an endangered community of which only about five percent of the original acreage remains. On the present refuge there are scattered remaining pine plantations, and cypress-tupelo swamp and bayheads. The topography is flat; the refuge is only ten miles from the Gulf of Mexico.

▸ Birds: The wet pine savannahs on the refuge are habitat for the only remaining "Mississippi" Sandhill Cranes, a nonmigratory subspecies of which approximately just 100 individuals remain, including approximately 20 breeding pairs. The Yellow Rail winters and the Brown-headed Nuthatch and Bachman's Sparrow are found in the pines. During the winter the refuge hosts hundreds of Henslow's Sparrows, in addition to Le Conte's and Grasshopper Sparrows. The Red-headed Woodpecker is resident. Among the species found there in the breeding season are the Swallow-tailed Kite, Chuck-will's-widow, and Prairie Warbler.

▸ Conservation Issues: Adjacent development has made this refuge an island of habitat surrounded by areas unsuitable for most wildlife. Much of the original wet pine savannah has been destroyed by conversion to pine plantations and by fire suppression. Refuge managers are now working to restore the savannah by removing trees through bulldozing and cutting to create more habitat for the cranes. The habitat will then be maintained by prescribed burning. Since cranes breed so slowly, there is a captive breeding program for the birds. Cranes were once harassed and shot and may suffer from environmental pollutants. The refuge is bisected by highway I-10. Cordgrass is threatening to replace native vegetation. Coyotes and other predators are a serious threat to crane nests, chicks, and reintroduced adults.

▸ Visitor Information: Tours are offered by the refuge in January and February. Much of the refuge is closed to protect the cranes. Contact the refuge at 7200 Crane Lane, Gutier, MS 39553, 228-497-6322.

Gulf Coast Least Tern Colony (4), Mississippi

▸ Highlight: Perhaps the world's largest Least Tern colony.
▸ Location: Main colony now in Biloxi, Harrison County, with seed colonies scattered along the coast.
▸ Size: Suitable habitat is within a 26-mile stretch of man-made beach.
▸ Ownership: State; maintained by the county.
▸ Habitat: Sandy beach.
▸ Land Use: Tourism.
▸ Site Description: The site consists of a man-made beach developed for tourism. The beach is white sand, brought in from the bottom of Mississippi Sound. The beach has to be churned by heavy equipment to keep grass from growing. A four-lane highway, I-90, runs along the shore immediately in from the beach.
▸ Birds: As many as 6,000 pairs of Least Terns have nested in the colony in the past, but numbers have declined and then risen again somewhat in recent years. In 2000, there were approximately 2,000 pairs in the combined colonies. The area may be seen from I-90, which passes right by it. The birds started nesting on this beach within a few years of its creation, which began in the 1950s. Black Skimmers are also found here.
▸ Conservation Issues: Local birders have worked with officials of Harrison County to protect the colonies, which consist of one large main colony and a number of seed colonies. County beach maintenance crews work closely with the Mississippi Coast Audubon Society to identify where colonies are located each year. The area is fenced and posted during nesting. In summer, the Harrison County Sheriff's Department has a Beach Patrol but it is not there specifically to protect the birds. Intense volunteer efforts protect the colonies during the holidays of Memorial Day and July 4.

▶ Visitor Information: The colony can be seen from the highway from late April to mid-July.

Lower Pascagoula River (5), Mississippi

▶ Highlight: The largest undammed river in the lower 48 states, the Pascagoula River and its associated habitats support several key species, including the Swallow-tailed Kite, Prothonotary and Swainson's Warblers.
▶ Location: Southeastern Mississippi, in George and Jackson Counties.
▶ Size: 63,000 acres.
▶ Ownership: Mississippi Department of Wildlife, Fisheries, and Parks, Mississippi Department of Marine Resources.
▶ Habitats: Bottomland hardwood forest, sandbars, oxbow lakes, coastal marsh.
▶ Land Use: Recreation, wildlife conservation.
▶ Site Description: Several important managed areas make up much of the land along the Lower Pascagoula. The Pascagoula River Wildlife Management Area, at 37,124 acres, consists of three units and includes more than 50 miles of mostly contiguous bottomland hardwood forest along the Pascagoula. Other habitats in the area include sandbars, low ridges, high and low flats, pine forest, and more than 50 oxbow lakes. Another site, the Pascagoula River Coastal Preserve, is just downriver from the wildlife management area and consists at present of 11,685 acres, with 14,500 acres within the planned acquisition boundaries. Some private lands exist between these two managed areas, which the state is currently working to protect. A third important managed area on the Lower Pascagoula is Ward Bayou Wildlife Management Area, at 13,234 acres.
▶ Birds: Recent studies indicated that at least several pairs of Swallow-tailed Kites breed along the Pascagoula, with a maximum count of 167 birds made from an aerial survey of the river. Other breeding birds include Prothonotary, Swainson's, and Kentucky Warblers. In the coastal marshes, Yellow and Black Rails, and Seaside and Nelson's Sharp-tailed Sparrows occur seasonally, along with the Reddish Egret and Snowy and Piping Plovers.
▶ Conservation Issues: Water withdrawal by existing industry and alteration of water-flow by a proposed dam and dredging threaten the hydrology of the system. Sedimentation from road construction, gravel mining, and development threatens the marshes and associated wildlife, as do heavy metals from paint from shipbuilding, discharge from paper mills, and potential pipeline spills in the lower river. A dam and reservoir are proposed on the Bouie River, a tributary of the Pascagoula. Land protection work continues in the area. The Nature Conservancy was involved with the original state acquisitions in the early 1970s, and recently added a 3,300-acre preserve in the area, the Charles M. Deaton Nature Preserve. It is currently fund-raising for an additional 1,700-acre tract.
▶ Visitor Information: Best time to visit is fall through spring. For information, write the Pascagoula River Wildlife Management Area at 816 Wade/Van Cleave Road, Moss Point, MS 39562, 228-588-3878; or the Coastal Preserve at 1141 Bayview Avenue, Suite 101, Biloxi, MS 39530, 228-374-5000. Ward Bayou Wildlife Management Area can be reached at 228-826-1012.

Gulf Islands National Seashore (6), Florida and Mississippi

▸ Highlight: Some of the sections making up this national seashore are important stopover sites for migrating landbirds and migrating and wintering shorebirds.

▸ Location: The National Seashore, comprising 11 sections, is dotted along 150 miles of the Gulf of Mexico coastline from Fort Walton Beach in the Florida Panhandle to Gulfport, Mississippi.

▸ Size: 12,276 acres.

▸ Ownership: National Park Service.

▸ Habitats: Dunes, lagoons, salt marsh, pine forest.

▸ Land Use: Recreation, wildlife conservation.

▸ Site Description: Six sections of the national seashore are in Florida: Okaloosa (19 acres on Choctawhatchee Bay), Santa Rosa (1,598 acres), Fort Pickens (1,742 acres), Naval Live Oaks (1,378 acres), Fort Barrancas and Advanced Redoubt (64 acres), and Perdido Key (1,041 acres). Five sections are in Mississippi: Davis Bayou (401 acres), Horn Island (3,650 acres), Petit Bois Island (1,466 acres), East Ship Island (362 acres), and West Ship Island (555 acres). The coastal barrier islands that make up Gulf Islands National Seashore consist of sand eroded and washed down rivers from the Appalachian Mountains. Sea oats and other salt-tolerant plants make up the vegetation. The largest single site within the national seashore is Horn Island, a designated wilderness accessible only by private boat.

▸ Birds: Several sections, including Fort Pickens Park, host thousands of birds during migration, particularly in the spring. The sections are also important for wintering shorebirds and passerines; the high winter counts for the Sharp-tailed Sparrow (representing two species) and Seaside Sparrow are in the Gulf Islands National Seashore near Biloxi, Mississippi.

▸ Conservation Issues: Among the threats to the seashore are the potential for oil spills, marine debris along the shore, hurricane damage, and recreational overuse.

▸ Visitor Information: Best time to visit is fall through spring, with mid- to late April best for migrating passerines. Contact: Superintendent, Gulf Islands National Seashore, 1801 Gulf Breeze Parkway, Gulf Breeze, FL 32561, 850-934-2600.

Breton National Wildlife Refuge (including the Chandeleur Islands) (7), Louisiana

▸ Highlight: The refuge includes the largest tern colony in North America.

▸ Size: 6,923 acres.

▸ Ownership: Fish and Wildlife Service.

▸ Location: In the Gulf of Mexico, southeasternmost Louisiana, St. Bernard Parish.

▸ Land Use: Commercial fishing, shrimping, crabbing, wildlife conservation and observation, primitive camping.

▸ Habitats: Coastal dune grassland, black mangrove thickets, tidal marshes, and submerged beds of manatee grass, shoal grass, turtle grass, and widgeon grass. Only turtle grass beds remaining in Louisiana.

▸ Site Description: Established in 1904, Breton National Wildlife Refuge is the second-oldest refuge in the national wildlife refuge system. It includes Breton Island

and all the Chandeleur Islands. The barrier islands that make up Breton National Wildlife Refuge are dynamic—their sizes and shapes constantly altered by tropical storms and other wind and tidal action. The area above mean high tide is approximately 7,000 acres. Elevations range from sea level to 19 feet above mean sea level. There was once a settlement on Breton Island, but the inhabitants were evacuated before a hurricane, which destroyed the dwellings. The island was never resettled.

▶ Birds: The refuge has the largest tern colony in North America, which once had 60,000 birds but has declined at present to 15,000 to 20,000 birds; most numerous are Sandwich and Royal Terns. More than 10,000 Brown Pelican nests are found in the island chain, along with the Reddish Egret, other waders; the American Oystercatcher, Snowy Plover, and many other shorebirds. There are also colonies of Laughing Gulls and Caspian Terns. The islands are also an important loafing and roosting area for the Magnificent Frigatebird. The Chandeleur Islands are important for wintering Piping Plovers. Thousands of songbirds also stop over during migration, especially in the spring, and thousands of migratory waterfowl winter in the surrounding waters. Most numerous are the Redhead and Lesser Scaup.

▶ Conservation Issues: These barrier islands have been heavily impacted by hurricanes in recent years and are fast disappearing. This accounts for the decrease in the size of the tern colony. All of the federally owned lands in the refuge, except for North Breton Island, are part of the National Wilderness Preservation System. North Breton was excluded because an oil facility, owned by Kerr-McGee, Inc., is located there. The only visible improvement is the Chandeleur lighthouse on the north end of the islands, constructed before the turn of the century. To avoid visitor disturbance to nesting birds, each colony is posted as a closed area during the nesting season; approximately five percent of the islands are used by nesting birds. Visitor use is confined mainly to the spring, summer, and early fall months, with approximately 2,500 visits per year.

▶ Visitor Information: The refuge is accessible only by boat or floatplane. For more information, contact: Southeast Louisiana Refuges, 1010 Gause Boulevard, Slidell, LA 70458, 985-646-7555.

Dauphin Island (8) and Fort Morgan Historical Park (9), Alabama

▶ Highlight: These two adjacent sites are among the best known "migrant traps" for birds crossing the Gulf of Mexico.

▶ Location: The mouth of Mobile Bay.

▶ Habitats: Woods, marshes, beaches, grassy fields.

▶ Land Use: Residential, recreation, wildlife observation.

▶ Size: Approximately 4,500 acres.

▶ Ownership: Dauphin Island Park and Beach Board, Alabama Department of Conservation, Alabama Historical Commission, private.

▶ Site Description: Migrant traps along the Gulf Coast share one feature—islands or peninsulas separated by water from the mainland. Their location on a major flight path for migrating birds means they are the last place southbound migrants touch down before setting out over the gulf going south and the first place they land after crossing it going north. They function as traps because unfavorable weather conditions can hold birds in the area for several days. The more distant the migrant trap is from the mainland, the more birds are likely to land there.

▶ Birds: Both Dauphin Island and Fort Morgan play critical roles in the survival of trans-gulf migrants. Since it is seven miles from the mainland, Dauphin Island is a classic migrant trap and perhaps the best known of all. A 14-mile barrier island at the mouth of Mobile Bay, it is linked to the mainland by a causeway; much of it is developed. The eastern part of the island is largely residential while the western end is a long, narrow barrier island consisting mostly of sand dunes. The best spot to see migrants is Shell Mound Park, operated by the Alabama Department of Conservation. It is managed primarily to benefit migrant birds and is interlaced with trails that birders can use. Another prime area on the island is the 164-acre Audubon Sanctuary, with beaches and maritime forests of pine, live oak, and magnolia. The Park and Beach Board has entered into a formal agreement with the National Audubon Society, so that it is officially included as part of the national system of Audubon wildlife sanctuaries. In addition to the myriad neotropical passerine migrants that stop here, especially during a "fallout" which occurs during spring migration as a result of storms or strong low pressure centers, the island has attracted a number of vagrant species through the years.

Visible from Dauphin Island across Mobile Bay and reachable by ferry is another famous migrant trap—Fort Morgan. Fort Morgan, operated by the Alabama Historical Commission, is at the end of a peninsula that acts as a funnel; it can be an excellent place to see migrants both in the spring and fall, when the funnel effect can create major hawk flights overland and major passerine concentrations at ground level. Various shorebirds, gulls, terns, herons, and rails can also be found seasonally at Fort Morgan. Its list of vagrant or rare birds is even more impressive than that of Dauphin Island.

▶ Conservation Issues: The area is subject to intense development pressure. Hurricanes and tropical storms striking the Alabama coast can cause considerable damage to the area.

▶ Visitor Information: The best time to visit is late March through mid-May, and secondarily, September through November. Reservations at local accommodations are a must on weekends during spring migration. For more information, contact Dauphin Island Bird Sanctuaries, P.O. Box 1295, Dauphin Island, AL 36528, 251-861-2120, e-mail: dibirder@earthlink.com; or Fort Morgan Historical Park, 51 Alabama 180 West, Gulf Shores, AL 36542, 251-948-7275.

BIRD CONSERVATION IN LATIN AMERICA AND THE CARIBBEAN

Every year many of us look forward to the return of migrant thrushes, tanagers, vireos, and warblers, but we tend not to think of them when they're not around. In some ways the birds we think of as "our birds" are really "their birds," since they spend longer on their wintering grounds than on their breeding grounds or during passage in the United States. What is happening to them when they're not here is a subject of real concern.

When they head out over the water, most of these songbirds breeding in eastern North America go only as far as they must to reach land. Unlike some shorebirds and terns, few of them ever get as far as northern Argentina; half or so winter in the Greater Antilles and Mexico. Just like the United States, these places have changed considerably. The Greater Antilles, in particular, are among the most densely populated areas in the Western Hemisphere; the forests there may exist in the collective memories of the birds looking for them, but, save a few parks and other protected areas, they are not there in reality. The same is true of much of Mexico and Central America; the forests have been cut down to become pastureland. For some species—such as the Indigo Bunting, Yellowthroat, and Palm Warbler—deforestation is no big problem; they can get by in disturbed and scrubby habitats. But many of those species breeding in forests in North America also head for forests during nonbreeding, and with progressive deforestation, they have fewer and fewer places to go. Among them are several watchlisted species, such as the Chuck-will's-widow, Wood Thrush, and Prothonotary, Swainson's, Worm-eating, Black-throated Blue, Cerulean, Kentucky, and Canada Warblers. Unless enough habitat for these birds exists to keep them alive during the nonbreeding season, our efforts to protect them in the United States during breeding will be useless.

What is to be done? First, we must recognize that conservation beyond our borders is of vital concern to bird conservationists in this country and, second, that the issues of deforestation and habitat degradation have to be addressed in a local context, by local organizations. These countries have fine and dedicated conservation groups, and they deserve all the support and cooperation we can give them. After all, their efforts may be even more important than our own. Contact ABC for information on how to help at: 590-253-5780.

Bon Secour National Wildlife Refuge (10), Alabama

▶ Highlight: An important stopping place for thousands of trans-gulf migrants.
▶ Location: Fort Morgan Peninsula at the lower end of Mobile Bay.
▶ Size: 6,700 acres.
▶ Ownership: Fish and Wildlife Service.
▶ Habitats: Beach and dune systems, scrub-oak, pine-oak woodland.
▶ Land Use: Recreation, wildlife management; second-home development in surrounding area.
▶ Site Description: There are several units of the refuge around Mobile Bay; among the most significant lands owned or managed by the refuge are five miles of gulf beach on the Fort Morgan Peninsula, a short ferry ride from Dauphin Island. Home to the endangered Alabama beach mouse, this area also contains nesting beaches for the threatened loggerhead sea turtle. The refuge also has habitat for the gopher tortoise. It is also a stopping place for migrating monarch butterflies.
▶ Birds: Similar to nearby Dauphin Island, Bon Secour is also a noted migrant stopover site, especially during times of "fallout" in the spring, when a southward-moving cold front with rain and northerly winds can cause thousands of migrants to land there and linger until conditions improve. It is the first or last landfall for many landbirds crossing the Gulf of Mexico in transit between their breeding and wintering grounds. Hundreds of hawks pass over, particularly during fall migration. The threatened Piping Plover winters on the beaches.
▶ Conservation Issues: The site is subject to severe hurricane damage, such as oc-

curred in 1979 when Hurricane Frederick struck the Alabama Gulf Coast, flattening the pine forest and destroying many summer homes. Much of the Fort Morgan Peninsula is being subjected to intense development. Invasive non-native plants such as Chinese tallow and cogon grass are problems.

▶ Visitor Information: Mid-April is the best time to visit to see the peak of spring migration. Contact the refuge at 12295 State Highway 180, Gulf Shores, AL 35603, 251-540-7720.

Eglin Air Force Base (11) and Blackwater River State Forest (12), Florida

▶ Highlight: Site of intensive and successful management to increase the population of the Red-cockaded Woodpecker.

▶ Location: Panhandle, just east of Pensacola.

▶ Size: 464,000 acres, of which more than half are accessible to the public.

▶ Ownership: Air Force.

▶ Habitats: Longleaf pine savannah, rivers and streams, lakes, estuarine shoreline, shoreline on the Gulf of Mexico.

▶ Land Use: Military base.

▶ Site Description: Much of the base consists of sandhills and longleaf pine savannah; other habitats include approximately 810 miles of rivers and streams, 32 lakes, 26,000 acres of other wetlands, and 20 miles of frontage on the Gulf of Mexico.

▶ Birds: Eglin Air Force Base is an excellent place to see the birds of the longleaf pine savannah community. The base is at present the fourth best site for numbers of Red-cockaded Woodpeckers, and the numbers are growing. As of August 2000, there were 301 active clusters on the installation, up more than four percent per year since 1994. Management for the woodpecker has also resulted in a great increase in the number of Bachman's Sparrows. Near Eglin is Blackwater River State Forest (189,374 acres), which has 20 clusters of the Red-cockaded Woodpecker, along with Brown-headed Nuthatches, Bachman's Sparrows, and breeding Prothonotary, Hooded, and Swainson's Warblers.

▶ Conservation Issues: Eglin's Natural Resources Branch and Virginia Tech University have recently completed a five-year experimental assessment of Red-cockaded Woodpecker management to determine the most cost-effective way to manage this endangered species across the entire 464,000-acre military reservation. Researchers conducted a landscape-level ecological experiment using a standard scientific design, with four treatment groups and replicates of each. In this case the treatments involved different management strategies, and the replicates were different blocks of land on the base in which these strategies were followed. The simplest and cheapest strategy was ecosystem management: the biologists applied management to promote the longleaf pine ecosystem in which the bird lives, but employed no single-species management techniques for the woodpecker. The most complicated and expensive strategy involved ecosystem management plus virtually every single-species management tool known to benefit the woodpecker. The other two strategies included only a subset of these single-species tools. Among the management tools are prescribed burning (land managers burn up to 50,000 acres each year), establishing artificial cavities, translocating young birds, and control of hardwood mid-storey through removal by mechanical means.

Researchers found that management strategies are able to produce high rates of growth in the woodpecker population on Eglin, and that the different management strategies resulted in appreciably different rates of population growth. Over five years, the most expensive management treatment resulted in a 73 percent increase in the number of active cavity tree territories (clusters of cavity trees currently occupied), the next most expensive 53 percent, the next most expensive 32 percent, and the least expensive 11 percent. All but the least expensive significantly exceed the base goal of four percent growth per year.

Now that experiment is complete, the researchers and land managers are weighing the trade-offs between costs and conservation, but at the least there is solid scientific information to use in making these hard decisions. This information can be used to set reachable conservation goals for both ecosystem and single-species management and to make accurate projections as to the cost.

An important partner in natural resources management at Eglin is The Nature Conservancy, involved since 1990 in conservation planning and research at the base on managing and protecting habitat for the woodpecker and other rare species of the longleaf pine community.

▶ Visitor Information: Visitors must have a permit for which there is a nominal charge; permits are available at the Natural Resources Division, Eglin AFB, 107 Highway 85 North, Niceville, FL 32578, 850-882-4164.

Talladega National Forest (Oakmulgee Division) (13), Alabama

▶ Highlight: Largest population of the Red-cockaded Woodpecker in Alabama.
▶ Location: Central Alabama, in Bibb, Chilton, Perry, Hale, Dallas, and Tuscaloosa Counties.
▶ Size: 156,804 acres.
▶ Ownership: Forest Service with some private inholdings.
▶ Habitats: Pine and pine-hardwood forests, including fire-maintained longleaf pine forests. The longleaf pine forest is the South's most imperiled ecosystem. Both the Talladega Division (made up of the Talladega and Shoal Creek Ranger Districts) and the Oakmulgee Division are excellent places to see this special forest type and the Red-cockaded Woodpecker that inhabits it. Longleaf pines regenerate slowly from a seedling that has a "grass stage." Their seedlings need fire to reduce competition from other tree species. Mature longleaf can be over 300 years old. The long life expectancy of longleaf pine makes it a favored tree species for Red-cockaded Woodpeckers, which, unlike most other woodpeckers, excavate their roost cavities in living pine trees.
▶ Land Use: Timber harvest, wildlife conservation, recreation.
▶ Site Description: The Oakmulgee Ranger District has large expanses of longleaf pine forest, which once covered over 20 million acres of the South. In areas managed for the longleaf pine ecosystem, visitors can expect to be able to see for long distances. Views are of mature forests with a canopy dominated by large longleaf pines and scattered individual oaks, on undulating hills covered by diverse grasses and herbaceous plants.
▶ Birds: Mature longleaf pine ecosystems provide essential habitat, not only for the Red-cockaded Woodpecker, but also the Northern Bobwhite, Bachman's Sparrow, Sum-

Northern Bobwhite

mer Tanager, Black-throated Green Warbler, and many other species that prefer open, park-like forests with large, mature trees and a grassy groundcover. More than 350 Red-cockaded Woodpecker colony sites in the Oakmulgee Division. Approximately 130 colony sites are presently active. This population is large enough to be a donor site for birds being moved to other national forests in the South.

▶ Conservation Issues: Across much of the southern landscape, loblolly pines were planted following the widespread land abandonment caused by the "Dust Bowl" period. Longleaf pines proved impossible to regenerate once fire prevention campaigns excluded fire from the landscape, and domestic animals were allowed free range. Areas replanted with loblolly pines were often managed on short rotations, meaning that they were harvested at younger ages than the longleaf pines they replaced. This style of forest management left few suitable habitats for the Red-cockaded Woodpecker. The Forest Service has managed Talladega to protect the woodpecker, but prescribed burning, which is necessary to halt the encroachment of hardwoods, has become difficult in a landscape that is becoming more suburban. Timber harvest, which is necessary to remove trees that have encroached into the former longleaf forest, has also become controversial. Well-intentioned environmentalists, who often mistakenly oppose all timber harvests, have delayed necessary habitat improvements for the Red-cockaded Woodpecker. At present, the main difficulties facing the birds are a lack of suitable cavity trees and the encroachment of hardwoods that make habitat unattractive to the birds and instead favor nest predators and cavity competitors. Managers plan to use timber harvests, artificial nests, and prescribed burning to restore Red-cockaded Woodpecker habitat.

▶ Visitor Information: The woodpecker can be seen at any time of the year, but summers are often oppressively hot. Look for the waxy, whitish, buildup of pinesap, 30 to 60 feet up on mature pine trees. These "candled" trees are often being used as roost trees by individual Red-cockaded Woodpeckers. For more information, contact the forest supervisor, 2946 Chestnut Street, Montgomery, AL 36107, 334-832-4470.

Fort Benning (14), Georgia

▶ Highlight: One of the most important sites for the Red-cockaded Woodpecker.
▶ Location: Just east of Columbus.
▶ Ownership: Army.
▶ Size: 180,000 acres.
▶ Habitats: Mixed pine forest, old-growth upland forest.
▶ Land Use: Military training, wildlife conservation.
▶ Site Description: This Army installation lies near the fall line dividing the Piedmont and the Coastal Plain. Most is covered by mixed pine forest, in which the dominant

tree is loblolly pine (approximately 70 percent), with lesser numbers of longleaf and shortleaf pine, and an understorey of sweetgum, dogwood, broomsedge, holly, and wax myrtle. Originally longleaf pine dominated the forest, but after timbering, the fort was replanted with loblolly.

▶ Birds: There are 197 active colonies of the Red-cockaded Woodpecker on the installation. Other pinewood species such as the Brown-headed Nuthatch are also common. The Bachman's Sparrow also breeds.

▶ Conservation Issues: Approximately 94,000 acres are suitable Red-cockaded Woodpecker habitat and are managed for the species; approximately 25,000 to 30,000 acres are burned annually. Artifical nest cavities are in use, and the population is carefully monitored. The number of woodpeckers has been steadily increasing, and has grown from about 170 clusters in the last five years. The population has been named one of the 15 recovery populations in the recovery plan for the species. The Nature Conservancy was involved in the initial phases of the management program, and is at present doing a vegetation map of the facility, as well as working on an integrated natural resources plan.

▶ Visitor Information: Best time to visit is fall through spring. The post is open to visitors, though some areas are restricted, due to military activities. For information, call 706-544-7080.

Dog Island (15), Florida

▶ Highlight: Important wintering area for the endangered Piping Plover.
▶ Location: Located in the Gulf of Mexico, off Carrabelle in the Panhandle.
▶ Size: 1,700 acres.
▶ Ownership: The Nature Conservancy, private.
▶ Habitats: Beach, dunes.
▶ Land Use: Wildlife conservation, recreation.
▶ Site Description: Dog Island lies approximately three miles off the coast; some 75 percent of the island is a nature preserve owned by The Nature Conservancy, with the rest privately owned. There are approximately 100 houses on the island, but only a few permanent residents.
▶ Birds: Up to 90 Piping Plovers winter on the island, making it one of the most significant wintering sites for this species in the eastern United States. Snowy and Wilson's Plovers, American Oystercatcher, and Least Tern breed on the island. It is also heavily used by migrant passerines during spring and fall migration.
▶ Conservation Issues: During the nesting season, breeding areas within the preserve are posted. There is also a banding station on the island.
▶ Visitor Information: There are no public recreation facilities on the island and the preserve is not open to visitors. The island is accessible only by boat. For more information, call the Florida office of The Nature Conservancy at 407-682-3664.

Apalachicola National Forest (16), Florida

▶ Highlight: World's largest population of the Red-cockaded Woodpecker; the Apalachicola Ranger District contains the world's only population of this endangered species to be declared "recovered" by the Fish and Wildlife Service.
▶ Location: Florida Panhandle, southwest of Tallahassee.

▸ Size: 569,600 acres.

▸ Ownership: Forest Service.

▸ Habitats: Flatwoods and sandhills of longleaf, slash, loblolly pine forests, and pine savannah.

▸ Land Use: Forestry, recreation.

▸ Site Description: Apalachicola National Forest is characterized by extensive flatwoods and sandhills of longleaf, slash, and loblolly pine forests. These fire-dependent ecosystems are maintained by the largest prescribed burning program of any national forest in the nation. To stand in one of these woodlands is to experience what much of the Coastal Plain of the Southeast was once like. Within this landscape there are bay, cypress and titi swamps, seepage bogs, and open savannahs, home to several species of endemic plants; in fact, the forest has more rare and endemic plant species than any other in the United States. The adjacent Tates Hell Forest of the Florida Division of Forestry, with 159,000 acres currently acquired, is part of the Apalachicola system and shares much of the same plant and animal diversity.

▸ Birds: With its great variety of plant communities and many rare and endangered plant species, the Apalachicola National Forest is not only botanically the most important national forest in the Southeast, but also one of the most important for birds. Its extensive stands of longleaf pine savannah have become the leading site for the Red-cockaded Woodpecker. The Bachman's Sparrow and Brown-headed Nuthatch, like the woodpecker, are also limited to fire-adapted southern pine woods, and also found here in good numbers. The Swallow-tailed Kite; Chuck-will's-widow; and Swainson's, Kentucky, and Prothonotary Warblers also breed. Henslow's Sparrows occur as migrant and winter residents, and among the other wintering species are the Yellow Rail, and Grasshopper and Le Conte's Sparrows.

▸ Conservation Issues: To maintain longleaf pine savannah in the forest in its presettlement state, the Forest Service conducts controlled burns of 30,000 to 50,000 acres each year. The two ranger districts, the Apalachicola and the Wakulla, support approximately 630 active breeding groups of the woodpecker, the majority of which are on the former. Together, the districts support approximately 13 percent of the entire known population of this endangered species; in fact, the species is considered to be recovered at this site. Recent studies indicate, however, that while woodpecker numbers in the Apalachicola District are stable, those at the Wakulla are declining. Biologists in the Apalachicola District have been translocating woodpeckers to locations throughout the Southeast to help recover the species elsewhere. The adjacent Tates Hell Forest has some 27 clusters of Red-cockaded Woodpeckers. This forest was purchased by the state within the last decade, having been extensively altered by the timber industry.

▸ Visitor Information: Spring and fall are best for a visit; summers are very hot. There are accommodations in Tallahassee and nearby towns, and at Wakulla Springs State Park, which is also worth a visit. For more information, contact: National Forests in Florida, Woodcrest Office Park, 325 John Knox Road, Suite F-100, Tallahassee, FL 32303, 904-942-9300.

MANAGING FORESTS FOR THE RED-COCKADED WOODPECKER

Endemic to the southeastern and south-central United States, the Red-cockaded Woodpecker excavates its nest cavities only in pines at least 70 years old and affected with red heart disease. Since the rotation time for the commercial harvest of pines falls far short of that, the distribution of this woodpecker has become more and more limited to lands specifically managed for its survival. Its favored habitat, longleaf pine savannah, now covers only about three percent of its original extent. Where savannah once grew, the lands have been planted with loblolly and slash pine, commercially more profitable but much less suitable for the birds. Of its estimated current population of 5,000 birds, some 40 percent are on national forests, 20 percent on Department of Defense lands, 20 percent on private lands, five percent on national wildlife refuges, and the rest on other federal agency lands including those of the National Park Service and the Department of Energy.

With its listing as endangered under the Endangered Species Act and the subsequent development of a recovery plan, land managers have taken aggressive measures to stabilize and increase populations of the woodpecker on public lands. Working with biologists from the Fish & Wildlife Service, biologists on Forest Service and Department of Defense lands have become experts in the business of managing habitat to benefit the woodpecker. Timber companies have also set aside some private lands for the species.

The prime management tool is fire. Longleaf pine savannah cannot exist unless it burns from time to time. Fire keeps the habitat open by eliminating invading hardwoods and is, in fact, needed in order for longleaf pine cones to germinate. Periodic fires once occurred through natural causes, but are now applied by land managers to mimic this natural process. Programs at the most successful sites for the bird burn thousands of acres each year, generally on about a three-year cycle, under carefully controlled conditions. Where fuel buildup has become too great and fire brings unacceptable risks, land managers use mechanical means to thin mid-storey plants. Biologists augment woodpecker nesting success by installing artificial nest cavities; they also translocate birds from areas with high production to areas with good habitat but no birds, to establish new colonies. Management has generally been quite successful, and the number of woodpeckers at many sites has increased.

St. Marks National Wildlife Refuge (18) and Ochlockonee River State Park (17), Florida

▶ Highlight: Major stopover and wintering area for waterfowl, wading birds, shorebirds, rails, hawks, and passerines; resident Red-cockaded Woodpeckers.
▶ Location: Wakulla, Jefferson, and Taylor Counties along the Gulf Coast south of Tallahassee.
▶ Size: 68,000 acres; the refuge also protects 31,500 acres of open water in the adjacent gulf.
▶ Ownership: Fish and Wildlife Service.
▶ Habitats: Impoundments, ponds, lakes, marshes, pine flatwoods, hardwoods.
▶ Land Use: Recreation, wildlife conservation.
▶ Site Description: Divided into three units, the refuge was originally established to provide habitat for wintering birds. The wetlands include needlerush salt marsh,

wooded swamp, freshwater marsh, and open water. The uplands are dominated by longleaf pine, and longleaf pine-scrub-oak communities, plus slash pine, loblolly, and hardwoods.

▸ Birds: During winter, many waterfowl, shorebirds, and rails use the refuge, and, during spring, it is the first landfall for many northbound neotropical migrants. Among the resident species are the Bald Eagle, Swallow-tailed Kite, Black Rail, Wood Stork, Least Tern, Chuck-will's-widow, Red-cockaded Woodpecker, Brown-headed Nuthatch, Prairie and Prothonotary Warblers, and Seaside Sparrow.

▸ Conservation Issues: Heavy and indiscriminate logging in the nineteenth and early twentieth centuries removed most of the old-growth longleaf pine and bottomland hardwoods. Thinning and prescribed burning are used to manage the pine forests to simulate natural conditions and to maintain habitat for the Red-cockaded Woodpecker. In 2000, there were seven active clusters of woodpeckers on the refuge, representing 19 adults and 14 young; this represented the highest count in 20 years. Birds are color-banded for monitoring. There is an active installation program of artificial cavities and translocation of birds from other areas, including, in the past, adjacent paper company lands. One additional colony of three adults and two young is found on the adjacent Ochlockonee River State Park. A nesting platform has been erected for the Least Tern. The refuge includes 17,500 acres of wilderness and nine Research Natural Areas. It receives approximately 300,000 visitors per year. The refuge has continued to acquire adjacent lands; the last 500 acres was added in 1999; the goal is to increase the refuge size to 74,500 acres.

▸ Visitor Information: Best time to visit is fall through spring. Contact the refuge at P.O. Box 68, St. Marks, FL 32355, 850-925-6121.

Osceola National Forest (19), Pinhook Swamp (20), and Okefenokee National Wildlife Refuge (21), Georgia and Florida

▸ Highlight: One of the largest wetland areas in the Southeast, the Okefenokee is an important breeding area for many wading birds while also supporting bird communities of the longleaf pine savannah. The refuge, together with Osceola National Forest and Pinhook Swamp, forms one of the largest blocks of wildlife habitat east of the Mississippi River.

▸ Designation: Ramsar site and wilderness.

▸ Location: Charlton, Ware, and Clinch Counties, Georgia, and Baker County, Florida.

▸ Size: Okefenokee National Wildlife Refuge is 395,085 acres; Osceola National Forest is 179,732; Pinhook Swamp is 57,379 acres.

▸ Ownership: Fish and Wildlife Service, Forest Service, Florida Department of Environmental Protection, and the St. Johns River Water Management District.

▸ Habitats: Upland pine forest, mixed pine-hardwoods, hardwood hammocks, cypress-tupelo swamp, shrubland, freshwater marsh.

▸ Land Use: Fishing, hunting, canoeing, wildlife observation.

▸ Site Description: The Okefenokee National Wildlife Refuge represents the most significant remnant of the swamps that once covered much of this area. It forms the headwaters of both the St. Marys River and the Suwannee River. In the late 1800s there was an attempt to drain the swamp, and the area was logged extensively in the early 1900s. The refuge, along with Florida's Osceola National Forest and Pinhook Swamp, the latter currently being acquired by the state, together form a contiguous block of public land of more than 1,000 square miles.

► Birds: Many wading birds nest on the Okefenokee, and there is a resident population of the Sandhill Crane. The refuge also supports good numbers of wintering migrant cranes, with crane counts in February 2001 reaching more than 1,500. There are 35 active clusters of Red-cockaded Woodpeckers at the Okefenokee National Wildlife Refuge and 52 active clusters in Osceola National Forest. Other species resident or breeding on these lands include the Swallow-tailed Kite, Chuck-will's-widow, Red-headed Woodpecker, Bachman's Sparrow, Brown-headed Nuthatch, and Prothonotary Warbler.

► Conservation Issues: More than 350,000 acres, or 88 percent of the land area of the Okefenokee, is designated wilderness. Management on both the refuge and the national forest includes prescribed burning to maintain habitat for the Red-cockaded Woodpecker and other native species. Negotiated by The Nature Conservancy, the Florida Department of Environmental Protection and the St. Johns River Water Management District have reached an agreement to purchase the Baker County Forest (Pinhook Swamp) from Rayonier, an international forest products company. The 57,379-acre tract is being purchased with funds from the Conservation and Recreation Lands Program. The size of this block of combined public lands alone makes it one of the great conservation resources of the southeastern United States.

► Visitor Information: Any time of year is good for a visit, but October through April are the cooler months. Best way to see the Okefenokee is to explore it by canoe; there are shelters, but reservations are required two months in advance. For more information on the refuge, contact: Okefenokee National Wildlife Refuge, Route 2, Box 3330, Folkston, GA 31537, 912-496-7836; the Osceola National Forest can be reached at Osceola Ranger District, P.O. Box 70, Olustee, FL 32072, 386-752-2577.

Cumberland Island National Seashore (22), Georgia

► Highlight: Many shorebirds, including the Piping Plover, winter on the island's beaches.

► Location: Coastal island in southeastern-most Georgia.

► Size: 36,000 acres.

► Ownership: National Park Service, private.

► Habitats: Beach and dunes, maritime forest with live oaks behind the dunes, pines and mixed hardwood forest in the central and northern parts of the island, tidal salt marsh on the western side of the island, tidal flats.

► Land Use: Recreation, wildlife conservation.

► Site Description: A relatively undisturbed barrier island, 18 miles long and up to three miles wide, Cumberland Island is the largest and southernmost of Georgia's barrier islands. The ocean shore is dominated by beaches and dunes with some freshwater ponds, while the inland shore is largely saltmarsh; at the center of the island is a rich maritime forest. As the Atlantic Coast in the Southeast becomes more and more developed, Cumberland Island takes on even greater significance.

► Birds: Cumberland Island is an important site for migrating shorebirds, raptors, and passerines. In winter, it is particularly good for shorebirds and waterbirds; a recent one-day survey in January resulted in 14,764 individuals of 47 species, including 26 Piping Plovers, 128 Red Knots, 911 Sanderlings, 3,012 Semipalmated Sandpipers, and 3,022 Dunlin. The American White Pelican winters here. There is a rookery of Wood Storks on the island, and the Painted Bunting is common during breeding season. Saltmarsh Sharp-tailed and Seaside Sparrows are resident.

► Conservation Issues: There is a considerable amount of damage to the vegetation caused by feral horses and hogs.

► Visitor Information: Best times to visit are during the cooler months, from September and October through March and April. From St. Marys it is a 45-minute ride by private passenger ferry to the island. Reservations are recommended (912-882-4335). Take insect repellant. There are marked trails on the island, and there is a reservations-only campground, but no supplies, though drinking water is available. Contact the park at Cumberland Island National Seashore, P.O. Box 806, St. Marys, GA 31558, 888-817-3421 or 912-882-4335.

Altamaha River Delta (23), Georgia

► Highlight: Georgia's most important wintering area for the Piping Plover; important migratory stopover and wintering site for thousands of shorebirds; significant breeding area for shorebirds, terns, and the Brown Pelican.

► Designation: Wetland of Regional Importance in the Western Hemisphere Shorebird Reserve Network.

► Location: Glynn and McIntosh Counties.

► Size: 83,000 acres.

► Ownership: Fish and Wildlife Service, Georgia Department of Natural Resources, private.

► Habitats: Sandy beach, intertidal flats, dune grassland, saltmarsh, bottomland hardwood forest.

► Land Use: Wildlife conservation, recreation.

► Site Description: The Altamaha River Delta, a remote area of the Georgia coast, comprises three land management entities: Little Egg Island Bar is a state protected area, and Little St. Simons Island is privately owned, catering to nature-based tourism. Wolf Island National Wildlife Refuge is a federal refuge.

► Birds: The delta is an important wintering and migration stopover for shorebirds. Up to 80 Piping Plovers spend the winter here, representing half of the state's entire wintering population of this threatened species. As many as 12,000 Red Knots are present at any one time during migration. Other species commonly present during migration and/or winter are the Dunlin (3,000), Black-bellied Plover (1,000), Sanderling (3,000), Semipalmated/Western Sandpiper (2,000), Whimbrel (500), and Marbled Godwit (200). Several species of terns breed in the delta, including up to 9,000 pairs of Royal, 130 pairs of Gull-billed, and 300 pairs of Sandwich Terns; as well as 300 pairs of the Black Skimmer. The Wilson's Plover, American Oystercatcher, and Willet also breed, and there is a breeding colony of about 3,000 pairs of Brown Pelicans. The delta is an important staging area for Whimbrels in the spring.

▶ Conservation Issues: Recreational boating, beachgoing, and low-flying aircraft (private and military) cause disturbance to the birds. Beach erosion, increasing human population in the area, marine pollution, and the potential for oil and chemical spills are also problems. The Nature Conservany has identified the Altamaha Delta as a bioreserve and has established a staffed program to concentrate on its protection. It was instrumental in protecting Wolf Island National Wildlife Refuge and Little Egg Island. The Conservancy, the Georgia Department of Natural Resources, and the Fish and Wildlife Service are operating under a partnership to address the conservation of the Altamaha Delta.

▶ Visitor Information: Wolf Island National Wildlife Refuge is closed to the public; the only access to the area is through the Lodge on Little St. Simons Island, which is open to lodge guests only, and use is limited to nature-based recreation. Contact the Lodge on Little St. Simons Island, P.O. Box 21078, Little St. Simons Island, GA 31522-0578, 888-733-5774, or 912-638-7472, website: www.LittleStSimonsIsland.com.

Fort Stewart (24), Georgia

▶ Highlight: One of the largest populations of the Red-cockaded Woodpecker.
▶ Location: Just west of Savannah.
▶ Size: 280,000 acres.
▶ Ownership: Army.
▶ Habitats: Longleaf pine and wiregrass sandhills, longleaf pine and slash pine flatwoods, cypress ponds, gum ponds, riverine bottomland hardwoods, military and game management clearings.
▶ Land Use: Military training, hunting, fishing, wildlife observation.
▶ Site Description: Uplands were historically dominated by longleaf pine and wiregrass-saw-palmetto flatwoods, much of which still remain. Prior to acquisition by the Army, land use was dominated by cattle grazing, naval stores production, timber production, and small family farms. Wetlands compose approximately 100,000 acres.
▶ Birds: There were 215 active Red-cockaded Woodpecker clusters during the 2000 breeding season. Common breeding birds include the Brown-headed Nuthatch, Wood Thrush, Loggerhead Shrike, Yellow-throated Vireo, Prothonotary Warbler, Parula Warbler, and Bachman's Sparrow. Less common but important breeders include the Bald Eagle, Swallow-tailed Kite, Common Ground-Dove, Swainson's Warbler, and Kentucky Warbler. The Henslow's Sparrow winters on the installation in small numbers.
▶ Conservation Issues: Approximately 130,000 acres of the installation are suitable, or potentially suitable for the woodpecker. The goal is to burn one third of the installation per year with most burns conducted in the growing season, but this goal has not been met in recent years because of severe drought, which makes such burning hazardous. There is extensive use of artificial cavities for the Red-cockaded Woodpecker; 757 have been installed since 1994; 389 were active at last count. Red-cockaded Woodpeckers are recruited into unoccupied stands using artificial cavities, which are generally placed within half a mile of an existing active cluster. In 1994, there were 100 Red-cockaded Woodpecker nests on the installation, and by 2000, there were 170. Much of the success in increasing the population size has been due to these artificial

cavities, combined with prescribed burning, timber thinning, and augmentation of adult bachelor males with hatch-year females.

▸ Visitor Information: Best time to visit is fall through spring. Fort Stewart is an open installation but an access pass is required. There is also a fee. Areas may be closed for military training exercises. Call the Pass and Permit Office at 912-767-5032 for access information.

ACE Basin (25), South Carolina

▸ Highlight: Large numbers of waterfowl, shorebirds, colonial waterbirds, and neotropical migrants, including several green list species.

▸ Designation: National Estuarine Research Reserve.

▸ Location: Southern coastal South Carolina; in Beaufort, Charleston, Colleton, and Hampton Counties; about 45 miles south of Charleston.

▸ Size: 350,000 acres.

▸ Ownership: Fish and Wildlife Service, South Carolina Department of Natural Resources, Westvaco, Nemours Wildlife Foundation, Low Country Open Lands Trust, The Nature Conservancy, Ducks Unlimited, private.

▸ Habitats: Inland maritime forest, longleaf pine flatwoods, bottomland hardwood forest, cypress-gum swamp, salt and brackish marsh, freshwater tidal marsh, tidal flats, barrier islands, beaches, isolated freshwater wetlands, managed waterfowl impoundments, agricultural lands.

▸ Land Use: Recreation, agriculture, timber, commercial fishing, recreational hunting, sport fishing.

▸ Site Description: The ACE Basin is formed where three major rivers, the Ashepoo, Combahee, and the South Edisto meet the coast. An area with a great variety of habitats, it is important not only for its bird populations but also for the threatened loggerhead turtle and endangered shortnose sturgeon.

▸ Birds: The ACE Basin has large numbers of wintering and staging waterfowl and shorebirds, in addition to many neotropical migrants on passage and during the breeding season. Large colonies of herons, egrets, and the endangered Wood Stork also breed while the endangered Piping Plover winters. Among the nesting species are the Swallow-tailed Kite; Black Rail; Swainson's, Prothonotary, Prairie, and Kentucky Warblers; Bachman's Sparrow, Painted Bunting, and Seaside Sparrow. Henslow's and Saltmarsh Sharp-tailed Sparrows also winter.

▸ Conservation Issues: The basin is the watershed drained by the three rivers. Pollution and upstream development of any or all of these could cause serious problems for the area's wildlife. There is rapid development and growth from Charleston and Beaufort. Of the basin's 350,000 acres, more than 137,000 are currently protected either as public lands, private reserves, or under easements or other management agreements with private owners. The ACE Basin National Wildlife Refuge, created in 1990, is 11,062 acres. Other public lands include Bear Island and Donnelley Wildlife Management Areas (20,000 acres), Edisto Beach and Hunting Island State Parks, and the ACE Basin National Estuarine Research Reserve. The ACE Basin Task Force, formed in 1988, works to preserve the area through purchase or conservation easements on private lands; the task force includes The Nature Conservancy, Ducks Unlimited, South

Carolina Department of Natural Resources, Westvaco, Nemours Wildlife Foundation, Low Country Open Lands Trust, Fish and Wildlife Service, private landowners, and dozens of other stakeholders. The Estuarine Research Reserve is managed jointly by the South Carolina Department of Natural Resources and the National Oceanic and Atmospheric Administration. The continued cooperation of private landowners will be critical for the future conservation of the area, as will the protection of the three major watersheds, and the prevention of upstream pollution. The basin also has a steering committee and a friends group, and is considered a high-priority site under the North American Waterfowl Management Plan. For contact details for the various management authorities, see below.

▶ Visitor Information: Not all of the basin is open to visitors, and those planning a trip should check with the various management units listed for access information. Bear Island and Donnelley Wildlife Management Areas, South Carolina Department of Natural Resources, 585 Donnelley Drive, Green Pond, SC 29445, 843-844-8957. National Estuarine Research Reserve (access by boat), 843-844-8822, or 803-762-5000. ACE Basin National Wildlife Refuge, P.O. Box 848 Hollywood, SC 29449, 843-889-3084. Edisto Beach State Park, 843-869-2756. Hunting Island State Park, 843-838-2011. South Carolina Department of Natural Resources website: http://www.dnr.state.sc.us/.

Cape Romain National Wildlife Refuge (26), South Carolina

▶ Highlight: A leading area on the Atlantic Coast for migrating and wintering shorebirds and colonial breeding species.
▶ Designation: Wetland of International Importance in the Western Hemisphere Shorebird Reserve Network.
▶ Location: Northeastern Charleston County, adjacent to Francis Marion National Forest.
▶ Size: 64,000 acres.
▶ Ownership: Fish and Wildlife Service.
▶ Habitats: Saltmarsh, fresh and brackish marshes, salt creeks, forested uplands, open salt water.
▶ Land Use: Hunting, fishing, wildlife conservation.
▶ Site Description: The refuge stretches for 22 miles along the South Carolina coast and includes several islands, including the 5,000-acre Bulls Island, covered with a forest of live oaks, magnolias, pines, and palmettos. It is one of the most important wildlife refuges for nesting and migrant shorebirds and for colonial nesting species along the Atlantic Coast.
▶ Birds: Most Atlantic shorebird species utilize the refuge at some point during the year. Approximately 5,000 Brown Pelicans nest on the refuge; more than 20,000 other colonial nesting birds, including Royal, Least, Sandwich, and Gull-billed Terns also breed. The refuge has the largest population of wintering American Oystercatchers and significant numbers of wintering Piping Plovers. Many waterfowl winter, and the Painted Bunting is among the nesting species.
▶ Conservation Issues: Cattails are removed from artificial ponds to keep them from becoming unusable by wintering waterfowl. There is a threat of oil spills or other contamination from the nearby Charleston Harbor. This coastal area is subject to hurri-

canes; on the night of September 21, 1989, Hurricane Hugo swept through the area, destroying nearly all old-growth timber and most recreational facilities on the refuge. Most of the maritime forest on Bulls Island was blown down or killed by salt water. It is estimated that the refuge will show the effects of that storm for at least a century.

▶ Visitor Information: Fall through spring are good for a visit to see migrants and wintering birds. Bulls Island can be reached by scheduled ferry from Moores Landing. For information, contact: Refuge Manager, Cape Romain National Wildlife Refuge, 5801 Highway 17N, Awendaw, SC 29429, 803-928-3368.

Santee Coastal Reserve and Washo Reserve (27), South Carolina

▶ Highlight: The oldest continuously used wading bird rookery known in the United States, with hundreds of herons, ibis, and egrets.
▶ Location: In Charleston County, near McClellanville.
▶ Size: 23,000 acres.
▶ Ownership: South Carolina Department of Natural Resources, The Nature Conservancy.
▶ Habitats: Barrier islands, waterfowl impoundments, extensive salt marsh, cypress-tupelo swamps, old-growth longleaf pine forest.
▶ Land Use: Wildlife conservation.
▶ Site Description: Considered the most significant conservation donation on the East Coast when donated to The Nature Conservancy in 1975, the Santee Coastal Reserve protects an outstanding suite of lower Coastal Plain and coastal habitats. Within the boundaries of the reserve, The Nature Conservancy retains ownership of the 1,000-acre Washo Reserve, which is managed under lease by the South Carolina Department of Natural Resources.
▶ Birds: In addition to nine clusters of the Red-cockaded Woodpecker, both the Bachman's Sparrow and Brown-headed Nuthatch are found in the pine forest. There is a Wood Stork rookery, and the Bald Eagle and Swallow-tailed Kite also nest. Thousands of shorebirds and passerines stop during migration, and up to 50,000 waterfowl spend the winter on the reserve.
▶ Conservation Issues: Prescribed burning is used to maintain habitat for the woodpecker; water levels on the preserve are manipulated to benefit wintering waterfowl.
▶ Visitor Information: Best time to visit is during spring and fall migration. The Washo Reserve and the marshland nature trail are open from February 1 to October 31, Monday through Saturday, from 8 a.m. to 5 p.m., and on Sunday afternoons. The area is often infested with mosquitoes and biting flies. For information, contact: South Carolina Department of Natural Resources, P.O. Box 167, Columbia, SC 29202, 803-546-8665 or 803-734-3888.

Tom Yawkey Wildlife Center (28), South Carolina

▶ Highlight: Major stopover for migrating shorebirds, important wintering area for American Avocet; small population of the Red-cockaded Woodpecker.
▶ Designation: Biosphere Reserve.

▸ Size: 21,000 acres.
▸ Ownership: South Carolina Department of Natural Resources.
▸ Location: Winyah Bay, near Georgetown.
▸ Habitats: Barrier islands, impoundments, longleaf pine forests.
▸ Land Use: Wildlife conservation.
▸ Site Description: The preserve consists of North and South Island and most of Cat Island, three coastal islands at the mouth of Winyah Bay.
▸ Birds: The preserve has probably the largest wintering concentration of the Avocet on the East Coast, with some 6–800 present from October to June, the peak count being 1,400. The site is a major stopover for shorebirds, with up to 100,000 in the spring but fewer in the fall, when water levels managed for waterfowl are higher. Thousands of waterfowl winter there. There are eight clusters of the Red-cockaded Woodpecker on Cat Island. The Brown-headed Nuthatch, Prothonotary Warbler, and Bachman's Sparrow also breed on the preserve.
▸ Conservation Issues: Willed to the state by Tom Yawkey, who owned the Boston Red Sox, the preserve is dedicated to the management of waterfowl habitat. The number of wintering waterfowl has declined considerably from the 1950s, when there were up to 150,000; in 2000, there were only 15,000. The cause for this decline is unknown. There are 3,500 acres of predominantly longleaf pine on Cat Island, and half is burned each year, in a checkerboard pattern, to maintain habitat for the Red-cockaded Woodpecker. The goal of this management is to build up the numbers of the woodpecker to 20 clusters. The Nature Conservancy has assisted in adding additional tracts to the preserve.
▸ Visitor Information: The preserve is accessible only by boat. Visitor use is restricted; there is one organized field trip per week, and it is booked up for several months in advance. For more information, call 843-546-6814.

Francis Marion National Forest (29), South Carolina

▸ Highlight: Important site for the Red-cockaded Woodpecker, although the population was severely impacted by Hurricane Hugo in 1989.
▸ Location: Berkeley County, near the coast, between Charleston and Georgetown.
▸ Size: 253,062 acres in two ranger districts.
▸ Ownership: Forest Service.
▸ Habitat: Longleaf pine savannah, swamp forest.
▸ Land Use: Forestry, recreation, wildlife conservation.
▸ Site Description: Much of the forest is covered with longleaf pine savannah. Among the other habitats are bottomland hardwood forest, maritime forest, salt marsh, and some managed impoundments. The forest lies along the Intracoastal Waterway and is adjacent to Cape Romain National Wildlife Refuge.
▸ Birds: Though it is still an important site for the endangered Red-cockaded Woodpecker, the species' population was greatly reduced by Hurricane Hugo in September 1989. The Brown-capped Nuthatch and Bachman's Sparrow are found in the pine forests; and Swainson's, Prothonotary, and Prairie Warblers nest. The forest includes the I'on Swamp, among the last places the presumably extinct Bachman's Warbler was known to exist.

► Conservation Issues: The case of the Red-cockaded Woodpecker at Francis Marion National Forest illustrates how a catastrophic natural event can have not only immediate but longer-lasting effects on a population of an endangered species. In September 1989, Hurricane Hugo struck the coast of South Carolina and had a devastating effect on the Francis Marion National Forest and its population of the Red-cockaded Woodpecker. The hurricane destroyed 87 percent of the bird's cavity trees, 63 percent of the woodpeckers, and 59 percent of the foraging habitat. Before Hugo, the population exceeded 475 groups and was expanding. It has been estimated that Hugo would have reduced the population to the level of 100 to 125 groups had restoration activities not occurred, including the installation of more than 900 artifical cavities and the stabilization of damaged nest trees, many of which have since died off. By 1995, the population was at 361 groups, but by 1999, a decline had set in, reducing the population to 314 groups, brought about primarily because of limited prescribed burning, lack of mid-storey control, and aging artificial cavities. At that point, the Forest Service, National Fish and Wildlife Foundation, South Carolina Department of Natural Resources, and a coalition of sportsmen and a public utility supplied funds for woodpecker management, including prescribed burning, mid-storey removal, and the installation of 600 new artificial cavities. The population decline has since been reversed, and in 2000 the number of woodpecker groups rose to 336. The goal is to achieve 450 groups: close to the population level prior to the hurricane.

► Visitor Information: Best time for a visit is fall through spring, though the woodpeckers can be seen at any time of year. Contact the forest at 4931 Broad River Road, Columbia, SC 29212, 803-561-4000.

Francis Beidler Forest (Four Hole Swamp) (30), South Carolina

► Highlight: Largest tract of blackwater, bald cypress-tupelo gum swamp in the United States, with large numbers of breeding neotropical migratory birds, many of which also occur on passage; some cypress trees are more than 1,000 years old.

► Location: Near Harleyville in Berkeley, Dorcester, and Orangeburg counties.

► Ownership: National Audubon Society, The Nature Conservancy.

► Size: 11,700 acres.

► Habitat: Bald cypress-tupelo gum and bottomland hardwood forest, pools, blackwater streams, bordering gentle to steep slopes supporting various upland forest types.

► Land Use: Wildlife conservation and observation, environmental eduction.

► Site Description: With 1,800 acres of old-growth forest, the Audubon Center and Sanctuary at Francis Beidler Forest represents what much of the bottomland forest in the Southeastern Coastal Plain once looked like.

► Birds: Among the many breeding species at the site are the Northern Parula; Yellow-throated, Hooded, Prothonotary, and Swainson's Warblers; and Red-headed Woodpeckers.

► Conservation Issues: Changes in contiguous and nearby land uses, from farming and forestry to rural homesteads, small subdivisions, and other less compatible uses, reduce net habitat and fragment large areas of forest.

► Visitor Information: There is a 1.75-mile boardwalk; the best time to visit is late

April to early June. Contact: Francis Beidler Forest, 336 Sanctuary Road, Harleyville, SC 29448, 843-462-2150.

Congaree Swamp National Monument (31), South Carolina

▶ Highlight: Congaree Swamp is the largest tract of old-growth bottomland hardwood in the United States, and features high densities of neotropical migrants and important permanent resident species.

▶ Designations: International Biosphere Reserve, Ramsar site, National Natural Landmark.

▶ Location: Lower Richland County, about 18 miles southeast of Columbia.

▶ Size: 22,200 acres.

▶ Ownership: National Park Service.

▶ Habitats: Bottomland hardwood forest, about 12,000 acres of which is old-growth.

▶ Land Use: Wildlife conservation.

▶ Site Description: The site has a very diverse bottomland hardwood forest, with 87 species of trees, including seven that are the largest examples in the United States, and more than 150 individual trees with a circumference of more than 12 feet. Much of the forest there has experienced little or no logging. Congaree represents one of the very few intact examples of the great freshwater swamps that were once found along much of the southern coastline from Texas to North Carolina. Much of the forest is flooded during parts of the year, particularly in late winter and early spring.

▶ Birds: The Congaree has high densities of migrating and wintering landbirds and high densities of typical bottomland hardwood residents such as the Pileated Woodpecker and Barred Owl. Many Red-headed Woodpeckers make use of the standing dead trees. The site also supports a few Red-cockaded Woodpeckers on an upland pine bluff adjacent to the floodplain. Among the breeding birds are the Chuck-will's-widow, Brown-headed Nuthatch, Prothonotary, Kentucky, Hooded, and Swainson's Warblers, and Bachman's Sparrow.

▶ Conservation Issues: Ninety-eight percent of the monument is congressionally-designated wilderness. There are pollutants due to upstream urban and agricultural development. The site is only 20 miles from Columbia and receives 90,000 visitors per year. Along with Francis Marion National Forest and Cape Romain National Wildlife Refuge, it was damaged by Hurricane Hugo in September 1989.

▶ Visitor Information: Best time to visit is during spring migration; the best time to see the Red-cockaded Woodpecker is during the nesting season, in May and June. Contact: Congaree Swamp National Monument, 100 National Park Road, Hopkins, SC 29061-9118, 803-776-4396.

Carolina Sandhills National Wildlife Refuge (32), South Carolina

▶ Highlight: Largest number of Red-cockaded Woodpeckers on any National Wildlife Refuge.

▶ Location: Chesterfield County, near McBee.

▶ Size: 43,000 acres.

▶ Ownership: Fish and Wildlife Service.

► Habitats: Longleaf pine–wiregrass savannah, wet hillside seeps.

► Land Use: Recreation, wildlife conservation.

► Site Description: Located near the fall line dividing the Coastal Plain from the Piedmont, the refuge is in a rolling landscape of sandhills.

Whip-poor-will

► Birds: With approximately 140 clusters of Red-cockaded Woodpeckers, this refuge is the most important in the system for conservation of this endangered species. Other species include the Chuck-will's-widow, Whip-poorwill, Red-headed Woodpecker, Brown-headed Nuthatch, Prairie and Prothonotary Warblers, and Bachman's Sparrow. Many migrant passerines spend the winter.

► Conservation Issues: Habitat is managed for the woodpecker, including prescribed burning, mechanical removal of hardwoods, and the use of artificial nest cavities. There is a long-term project to convert 2,000 acres of slash pine into longleaf pine, the habitat type used by the woodpecker.

► Visitor Information: Best time to visit is between December and early June. Contact: Route 2, Box 330, McBee, SC 29101, 843-335-8401.

HABITAT FRAGMENTATION

Habitat fragmentation is frequently cited as one cause for declines in populations of some bird species. There is reason to believe that there is truth to this claim, but imprecise use of terms and a lack of clarity regarding causation have resulted in its frequent overuse.

To make sense as a cause for population declines, fragmentation must refer to newly created conditions. Many habitat types naturally and historically occur as small fragments, such as Western riparian habitat, as well as forest types in elevational bands around small mountain ranges. Fragmentation that causes concern results when large contiguous blocks of habitat are broken into smaller pieces.

The most immediate and important result of such a change is that habitat has been lost, and less habitat supports fewer birds. Fragmentation is only an issue if the area in the remnant fragments supports fewer birds, or different bird species, than the same area would support if it were part of a large contiguous block.

One possible result is edge effect. The ratio of edge to interior area increases as patches become smaller (or more irregularly shaped). Edges can be bad for birds if they result in increases in nest predation or brood parasitism by cowbirds. Edges between forest and pasture may result in increased densities of predators such as crows and jays, or raccoons or feral cats, as well as cowbirds. Edges between grassland and encroaching woodland can expose grassland birds to heavier rates of predation from raptors or mammals. On the other hand, edges between mature forest and early successional habitat caused by logging may have no impact on these types of predators and parasites. So, the intensity of edge effects depends upon the habitat matrix within which fragments are embedded.

A lack of connectivity is another result of fragmentation that can affect some organisms. If a population is extirpated from a fragment, the future of that species in that fragment depends on recolonization. Birds with high dispersal ability may not be affected by this, but some sedentary resident species (as well as other vertebrates and many plants) may be less likely to persist in isolated fragments than in fragments close to, or connected with, potential sources for colonization.

The birds themselves may limit their own success in fragments. If the number of individuals in a fragment is low, factors such as unbalanced sex ratios may reduce the use of habitat by breeding pairs. There may even be deliberate avoidance of small patches by one or both sexes of some species.

Fort Bragg (33), North Carolina

▶ Highlight: One of the top four sites for the endangered Red-cockaded Woodpecker.
▶ Location: Just west of Fayetteville.
▶ Size: 160,000 acres.
▶ Ownership: Army.
▶ Habitat: Longleaf pine savannah.
▶ Land Use: Military installation.
▶ Site Description: This military installation, home to the 82nd Airborne Division, is used for training and for military exercises. Much of the facility is covered with longleaf pine savannah.
▶ Birds: Fort Bragg has one of the largest-known populations of the Red-cockaded Woodpecker—some 280 groups are found on the installation, and the numbers are relatively stable; the woodpecker is also found on some of the adjoining private lands. The Brown-headed Nuthatch and Bachman's Sparrow are also found in the pine savannah.
▶ Conservation Issues: Training involving use of tanks and other armored vehicles can cause soil erosion. The woodpecker colonies are mapped, and military maneuvers are conducted to minimize impact on the colonies. Approximately 30,000 acres are burned per year during the growing season to maintain the open pine savannah that the bird requires. The fort has the largest natural resources program of any military installation in the country, with a staff of 70 people, including 12 biologists. Management has also brought an increase in the population of the Bachman's Sparrow, and there are even a few Lark Sparrows on the grassy areas kept open for paratrooper landing zones.
▶ Visitor Information: Though the fort is open to traffic on paved roads, all off-road areas are closed to the public.

Colonial Waterbird Colonies (34), North Carolina

▶ Highlight: Important area for colonial waterbird nesting.
▶ Location: Islands in sounds near the coast.

▸ Size: The islands range in size from ten acres to 100 acres.

▸ Ownership: State, National Audubon Society, Fish and Wildlife Service.

▸ Habitats: Beach, dredge islands.

▸ Land Use: Dredging operations, wildlife observation and conservation.

▸ Site Description: Included in this IBA are a number of islands in sounds near the North Carolina coast, many of them dredge spoil banks, where terns, pelicans, and other colonial species nest. Some of these sites are highly unstable, and the size of the colonies can vary greatly from year to year. A few islands with larger numbers of birds are:

Battery Island, Brunswick County: Partly formed of dredged sand and occupying 100 acres. A recent survey found 18,000 White Ibis plus a mixed heron and egret colony of more than 1,500 birds. The most numerous species were Great and Snowy Egrets, and Little Blue and Tricolored Herons.

White Ibis

Beacon Island, Pamlico Sound, Hyde County: Colony of 1,360 Brown Pelicans and 6,000 Laughing Gulls.

Big Foot Island, Hyde County: This dredge spoil island of eight acres has supported a colony of Royal Terns with a censused figure in 1993 of 4,752 birds. Least and other tern species have also nested.

Clam Shoal, Dare County: This is a natural shoal of just half an acre. A 1993 colonial waterbird survey censused 1,214 Royal Terns nesting. Least and other tern species have also nested.

Ferry Slip Island, New Hanover County: This is a dredge spoil island of seven acres. It had 6,336 Royal Tern and 2,680 Sandwich Tern nests in 1997.

Monkey Island in Currituck Sound, Currituck County: This five-acre island has a mixed heron and egret colony of approximately 500 birds. Monkey Island is part of the Currituck National Wildlife Refuge and the island is closed to public access, though visitors may boat around its perimeter.

Old House Channel Island, Dare County: This dredge spoil island of 45 acres had 1,339 Royal Terns and 90 Sandwich Tern nests, and 1,402 Brown Pelican nests in a recent survey. Other tern species have nested there in other years.

Sand Bag Island, Carteret County: This ten-acre dredge spoil island had 2,050 Royal Tern and 504 Sandwich Tern nests in 1997.

South Pelican Island, Brunswick County: This ten-acre dredge spoil island had 1,708 Brown Pelicans in a recent survey.

Wainwright Island, Carteret County: This 12-acre island had 1,475 Brown Pelicans and 1,140 Royal Terns in a recent survey.

Wells Island in Dare County: This ten-acre dredge spoil island had 2,509 Royal Tern and 837 Sandwich Tern nests in 1995.

▶ Conservation Issues: Most of these islands are posted, and visitors are prohibited from March 1 to September 1. Several of these state-owned islands are leased to the National Audubon Society for management, with the exception of Beacon Island, which National Audubon owns.

▶ Visitor Information: Best time to visit is during the breeding season from early May to early July. The islands can be observed from a boat.

Croatan National Forest (35), North Carolina

▶ Highlight: Significant area of old-growth longleaf pine flats with Red-cockaded Woodpeckers and Bachman's Sparrows.

▶ Location: Atlantic coast of southern North Carolina between Morehead City, Cedar Point, and New Bern.

▶ Size: 159,000 acres.

▶ Ownership: Forest Service.

▶ Habitats: Pine flats, flooded forest, pocosin.

▶ Land Use: Hunting, fishing, wildlife conservation, timber extraction.

▶ Site Description: Croatan National Forest is a complex of pine flatwoods, flooded coastal forest, saltwater estuary, and raised bogs known as pocosin. It is crisscrossed by creeks and dotted with lakes. More than half of the forest is made up of pocosin, although there are some significant tracts of old-growth longleaf pine, as well as cypress swamp and some saltmarsh. Notable nonavian wildlife includes a few alligators and black bears.

▶ Birds: There are 62 active clusters of the Red-cockaded Woodpecker in the forest; when monitoring began in 1989, there were 47. The Brown-headed Nuthatch and Bach-

man's Sparrow also occur, as do the Chuck-will's-widow, Red-headed Woodpecker; and Swainson's, Prothonotary, Worm-eating, and Prairie Warblers; and wintering Henslow's Sparrow. The South Atlantic Coastal subspecies of the Black-throated Green Warbler (Wayne's) also nests. The Swallow-tailed Kite and Painted Bunting are found during the breeding season in small numbers.

▶ Conservation Issues: Croatan is one of the few places in the mid-Atlantic Coastal Plain where small patches of old-growth longleaf pines can still be found. Some artificial nesting cavities are being provided for the Red-cockaded Woodpecker. There is the potential for damage from hurricanes; woodpecker nesting cavities can weaken trunks significantly, and in coastal South Carolina, nesting trees have been broken off at the level of the woodpecker nest entrance by hurricane-force winds. Periodic prescribed burning and mechanical removal of mid-storey hardwoods in the forest benefit both the woodpecker and Bachman's Sparrow. The sparrow tends to move into areas the season following a fire when there is plenty of grass seed available.

Bachman's Sparrow

▶ Visitor Information: Best time to visit is fall through spring. The Mills Road savannah in the north section of the forest is best for the Red-cockaded Woodpecker and Bachman's Sparrow. Some woodpecker nest trees are marked with blue paint. Contact: Croatan National Forest, 141 East Fisher Avenue, New Bern, NC 28560, 252-638-5628.

Gulf Stream/Continental Shelf Edge Marine Zone (36), North Carolina

▶ Highlight: High diversity of pelagic birds.
▶ Location: Approximately 45 miles west-northwest of the point at Cape Hatteras, at the western boundary of the Gulf Stream.
▶ Size: Approximately 10 by 20 miles.
▶ Ownership: U.S. territorial waters.
▶ Habitat: Open water, with sargassum along frontal boundaries.
▶ Site Description: The Outer Continental Shelf off North Carolina has the largest documented species diversity of pelagic seabirds and marine mammals in the western North Atlantic. The area provides relatively rich foraging grounds with highly variable local marine microenvironments, and within this small geographic area, seabirds are often represented simultaneously by temperate, Arctic, and subtropical species. Two major ocean currents meet here, the cold Labrador current and the warm Gulf Stream. For the past two decades the area has been the subject of intensive study by the North Carolina State Museum, and much of the information in this account is taken from that work.
▶ Birds: In addition to the species commonly found there (Northern Fulmar, Cory's and Greater Shearwaters, Wilson's Storm-Petrel), the area regularly has records of the highly endangered Black-capped Petrel, a species known to nest only in the mountains of Hispaniola, where it faces a number of serious conservation problems. Another endangered species for which there is a confirmed observation in the area is the Bermuda Petrel. Many other tropical species—such as Sooty and Bridled Terns, and White-tailed and Red-billed Tropicbirds—have also been recorded in the area. Many rarities have also appeared; among the more recent are the Swinhoe's Storm-Petrel from the western Pacific and northern Indian Oceans, and Bulwer's Petrel from temperate and tropical waters in the Pacific, Indian, and eastern Atlantic Oceans. The area is also of great importance to endangered whales and sea turtles.
▶ Conservation Issues: Off-shore oil exploration is a potential threat, as are overfishing in the area and excessive sargassum harvest. It is also a popular commercial and sport fishing area.
▶ Visitor Information: Organized bird tours depart from Cape Hatteras periodically throughout the year. Contact: Brian Patteson, Inc., P.O. Box 772, Hatteras, NC 27943, 252-986-1363.

Outer Banks IBAs of North Carolina

Cape Lookout National Seashore (37), Cape Hatteras National Seashore (38), Pea Island National Wildlife Refuge (39), Nags Head Woods Preserve (40)

▶ Highlight: The Outer Banks are a major stopover, wintering, and breeding area for waterfowl, shorebirds and wading birds.

▶ Location: The Outer Banks are a series of barrier islands in the Atlantic off the east coast of North Carolina, stretching from the Virginia line some 140 miles south to just east of Morehead City.

▶ Size: More than 100,000 acres.

▶ Ownership: National Park Service, Fish and Wildlife Service, The Nature Conservancy, private.

▶ Habitats: Dune systems, marshes, beach, maritime forest, coastal scrub.

▶ Land Use: Tourism and recreation, second-home development, wildlife observation and conservation.

▶ Site Description: The islands are barrier islands where the predominant habitats are beach and dunes toward the Atlantic side and marshes toward the sound side; there is one area of extensive maritime forest. Key sites are Cape Hatteras National Seashore, Pea Island National Wildlife Refuge, Cape Lookout National Seashore, and The Nature Conservancy's Nags Head Woods Preserve. The individual sites are described below.

▶ Birds: A significant breeding population of the Piping Plover is found on the Outer Banks, which are also important for the plover during the winter. Thousands of shorebirds and waterfowl use the Outer Banks seasonally.

▶ Conservation Issues: The Outer Banks are one of the most popular vacation destinations on the East Coast, drawing more than two million visitors per year; use of the beaches is particularly heavy in summer and early fall. Off-road vehicle access to the beaches is permitted in several areas and has had a negative impact on colonial nesting birds and Piping Plovers for many years. Predation by raccoons and feral cats on the ground-nesting plovers and colonial birds is also a significant conservation problem. Dune building, channelization, and ditching have diminished the extent and quality of seashore habitat and vegetation. The area is subject to hurricanes and lesser, but still damaging storms. Programs to monitor the status and evaluate the threats to the breeding species are underway.

▶ Visitor Information: Best time to visit is fall through spring; the major tourist season is from Memorial Day to Labor Day, during which time there are thousands of visitors on the beaches.

Cape Lookout National Seashore (37)

This site, marking the southern extent of the Outer Banks, consists of three islands in Carteret County with significant populations of breeding Piping Plovers and Least Terns. The National Seashore occupies 28,000 acres, is owned by the National Park Service, and is used for recreation and wildlife conservation. The park consists of three barrier islands separated from one another by inlets. The islands (North Core Banks, South Core Banks, and Shackleford Banks) vary in length from 9 to 25 miles. While the first two are made up of low dunes, a shrub zone, and saltmarsh, the last has a higher dune system, some freshwater marshes, and approximately 90 acres of maritime forest. There are many small scattered islands on the sound side and nearshore waters around the barrier islands. Approximately two thirds of the state's population of the endangered Piping Plover nests in the park (up to 39 pairs); up to 583 pairs of Least

Terns also nest there and there are significant numbers of nesting Wilson's Plovers, Whimbrels, and American Oystercatchers. Portsmouth Flats, a 3-mile-by-1.5-mile expanse of sand and mudflats provides a migratory stopover spot for thousands of shorebirds, including the Red Knot, Short-billed Dowitcher, and Marbled Godwit. The loggerhead turtle also nests on the beaches of the barrier islands. The park receives more than 300,000 visitors each year; off-road vehicle use on North and South Core Banks alters habitat, disturbs birds, and destroys nests. Feral cats on North and South Core Banks threaten nesting birds, and introduced nutria and horses on Shackleford Banks alter habitats there.

▶ Visitor Information: Transportation to the islands is by private boat or commercial ferry, from Harkers Island, Morehead City, and Beaufort. For more information, contact: Cape Lookout National Seashore, 131 Charles Street, Harkers Island, NC 28531, 252-728-2250.

Cape Hatteras National Seashore (38)

This is an important shorebird stopover and wintering site that extends 70 miles from Nags Head to Ocracoke Island, covering major parts of Bodie, Hatteras, and Ocracoke Islands. It occupies 31,000 acres, is owned by the National Park Service, and is used for recreation and wildlife conservation. The site consists of a low-lying barrier island system with a width varying from 200 feet to three miles, and an average elevation of six feet, with a maximum of 61 feet. Consisting of beach and dune habitats, the major vegetation types include coastal scrub and shrub, sound-side marsh, and maritime forest. The area is subject to severe tropical and northeast storm systems. It is an important area for breeding, migrating and wintering shorebirds and waterbirds. Pea Island National Wildlife Refuge adjoins the national seashore. A few pairs of Piping Plovers breed, but the species is also present during migration, and in significant numbers in winter. There are also significant numbers of breeding Common Terns (500 to 700 pairs) and Least Terns (200 to 250 pairs). Many pairs of the American Oystercatchers also breed on the beaches each summer. Sanderlings are found from fall through spring, and as many as 4,700 Red Knots have been counted during spring migration. Large numbers of other shorebirds use the site seasonally. Feral cats are threatening species such as the Piping Plover; Black Skimmer; American Oystercatcher; and Least, Common, and Roseate Terns while they are attempting to nest. Humane trapping of these predators is being implemented by land managers working to protect these species.

▶ Visitor Information: Any time from fall through spring is worth a visit. Contact the seashore at 1401 National Park Drive, Manteo, NC 27954, 252-473-2111.

Pea Island National Wildlife Refuge (39)

This is a major stopover, wintering, and breeding site for migratory waterbirds, located on the north end of Hatteras Island, approximately ten miles south of Nags Head. It occupies 5,915 acres of land and includes 25,700 acres of Pamlico Sound. It is owned by the Fish and Wildlife Service and used for recreation and wildlife conservation. Pea Island is a typical barrier island comprising ocean beach, barrier dunes, saltmarshes and salt flats, fresh water and brackish ponds and impoundments, tidal creeks, and bays. Its climate is moderated by the ocean and the Gulf Stream. The refuge adjoins Cape Hatteras National Seashore. The refuge hosts thousands of migrating and wintering waterfowl and hundreds of thousands of shorebirds. The Piping Plover is recorded during migration and winter and a few pairs breed. Approximately 150 pairs of Least Terns and 50 pairs of Gull-billed Terns also breed on the refuge. A maximum of 30,000 Sanderlings, 60,000 Least Sandpipers, 40,000 Dunlin, and 15,000 Short-billed Dowitchers have been recorded on a single day during migration. The Saltmarsh Sharp-tailed Sparrow is found in winter, and the Seaside Sparrow is a resident breeding species. Thousands of migrating landbirds can be present during fall migration under certain weather conditions. Up to 5,200 Redheads and 1,200 American Black Ducks have been recorded in winter. The impoundments are managed for migratory birds, and two of the three are closed to public entry to prevent disturbance, as are the areas where gulls, terns, and shorebirds nest. The area of Pamlico Sound adjacent to the refuge is closed to waterfowl hunting. Prescribed burning is used to perpetuate early successional habitat. Beach erosion on the island is due to the dredging of Oregon Inlet. Feral cats are a problem at nesting colonies; the non-native Phragmites is a major management concern. The refuge is administered by Alligator National Wildlife Refuge.

▸ Visitor Information: The best time to visit is from fall to spring. Contact the refuge at P.O. Box 1969, Manteo, NC 27954, 252-473-1131.

Nags Head Woods Preserve (40)

One of the largest maritime forests along the North Carolina coast, it is an important stopover for neotropical migrants, and is located in the municipalities of Nags Head and Kill Devil Hills. The preserve occupies more than 1,200 acres, and is owned by The Nature Conservancy, the Town of Nags Head, and the Town of Kill Devil Hills. It is used for conservation with scattered private inholdings that have been developed as individual homesites. The site is one of three sizable maritime forests on the North Carolina Outer Banks and is considered one of the region's most important natural areas. Nags Head Woods is composed of a complex of densely wooded relict dunes, freshwater ponds, hardwood swamps, and brackish and freshwater marshes. The forest formed in the wind shadow of an extensive dune system, with some dunes being 70 to 80 feet in elevation. This provides significant topographic variation and a mix of extremely diverse habitats within a relatively small area. Although there are not large numbers of breeding birds in the forest, there is high diversity. More than 50 breeding species have been documented, including the Pileated Woodpecker, Yellow-billed Cuckoo, Acadian Flycatcher, Great Crested Flycatcher, Summer Tanager, White-eyed and Red-eyed Vireos, Prothonotary Warbler and Northern Parula. Like other coastal forests, it is perhaps most important as a stopover for long-distance migrant songbirds. Fall migrants include most warblers breeding in eastern North America, including the green list species. As with any natural area on the islands, Nags Head Woods is under considerable pressure from human use. Water is withdrawn from the aquifer to supplement the public water system during the summer, and may be disruptive to the normal rise and fall of the water table. The forest is narrow and fragmented by the development of inholdings, a transmission line right-of-way, and a public road. Feral cats and cowbirds are threats to the forest birds.

▸ Visitor Information: Best time to visit is during fall migration, in September and October. Contact: Nags Head Woods, The Nature Conservancy, 701 West Ocean Acres Drive, Kill Devil Hills, NC 27948, 252-441-2525.

Alligator River National Wildlife Refuge (41), North Carolina

▸ Highlight: The extensive pocosin habitat on the refuge provides nesting habitat for significant numbers of neotropical migrants.

▸ Location: Mainland of Dare County, bordered by Alligator River, Croatan/Pamlico Sound, and Albemarle Sound.

▸ Size: 152,195 acres.

▸ Ownership: Fish and Wildlife Service.

▸ Habitats: Pocosin, bogs, fresh and brackish marshes, hardwood swamps, Atlantic white-cedar swamps, natural lakes and waterways, farmland.

▸ Land Use: Hunting, fishing, canoeing, wildlife observation.

▸ Site Description: The refuge has extensive pocosin habitat; these are wetlands with deep organic soils resulting in peat deposits. Under dry conditions they are susceptible to wildfire and long-lasting subsurface fires. Plant species in the bogs and pocosins include carnivorous species such as pitcher plants and sun dews, while swamps include Atlantic white-cedar, pond pine, black gum, and red maple. Mineral soils on the refuge support a non-alluvial wet hardwood habitat. The refuge is the first reintroduction site for the red wolf. The refuge encloses the Dare County Air Force Range, jointly used by the Air Force and the Navy.

▸ Birds: Concentrations of several thousand ducks and swans occur during the winter. Many wading birds, shorebirds, and neotropical migrants are found during migration and breeding. Breeding Bird Survey routes run between 1993 and 1996 counted 75 Prothonotary, 90 Prairie, 27 Worm-eating, and two Swainson's Warblers; the surveys were done from roads, and the total numbers of birds in the area are likely to be considerably higher. There are three known clusters of Red-cockaded Woodpeckers on the refuge, with the possibility that as many as ten may exist there. The Red-cockaded Woodpecker clusters are in remote and hard-to-reach parts of the refuge. Red-cockaded Woodpeckers are also found on the Dare County Air Force Range.

▸ Conservation Issues: Much of the pocosin habitat in the Carolinas has been destroyed by logging for old-growth bald cypress and Atlantic white-cedar, and by draining for agriculture. Alligator River National Wildlife Refuge was established through a donation of 118,000 acres by the Prudential Life Insurance Company and the cooperative effort of The Nature Conservancy and federal and state agencies. A major objective has been to restore the former hydrologic regimes, through plugging up drainage ditches and installing water-level-management structures. This will reduce adverse impacts from catastrophic fires, to which drained and dried-out pocosin is susceptible. Some farmland is managed for waterfowl through water level manipulation, encouraging production of moist soil plant species and cooperative farming to provide a winter food source. During fall flooding and drawdown in late winter/early spring, these areas are also used by shorebirds. A survey to determine the current condition of regenerating Atlantic white-cedar has been completed and the need for release work is being assessed. Efforts are also underway to reestablish quality hardwoods on non-alluvial wet mineral soils. Hurricane damage, insect and disease outbreaks, and wildfire are among the principal threats for most habitat types on the refuge.

▶ Visitor Information: Many miles of logging roads in the refuge are open to vehicles and hikers; the best time to visit is fall through spring. Be prepared for wet, muddy roads. Contact: Alligator River National Wildlife Refuge, P.O. Box 1969, Manteo, NC 27954, 252-473-1131.

Mattamuskeet National Wildlife Refuge (43) and Swanquarter National Wildlife Refuge (42), North Carolina

▶ Highlight: Leading refuges for wintering waterfowl, they harbor as much as 35 percent of the Atlantic population of the Tundra Swan during the nonbreeding season.

▶ Location: Hyde County, nine miles northeast of Swan Quarter.

▶ Size: 50,180 acres.

▶ Ownership: Fish and Wildlife Service.

▶ Habitats: Lake, freshwater marsh, forest, cropland.

▶ Land Use: Forestry, agriculture, wildlife conservation.

▶ Site Description: The largest feature of the area is Lake Mattamuskeet, the largest natural lake in North Carolina. With an average depth of only 2 feet, it is 16 miles long by five to six miles wide and covers approximately 40,000 acres. Wetland forests on the refuge consist of sweetgum, bald cypress, red maple, and loblolly pine. Swanquarter National Wildlife Refuge (16,411 acres) on Pamlico Sound, has similar habitats of open water, brackish marsh, and wetland forest habitats.

▶ Birds: Mattamuskeet is one of the most important refuges on the Atlantic Coast for wintering waterfowl, with total counts averaging approximately 120,000. As many as 35,000 Tundra Swans have been recorded at the refuge during Christmas Bird Counts, though a range of 15,000 to 30,000 is more typical. Large numbers of ducks also winter, including many Northern Pintail, American Wigeon, American Black Ducks, and Green-winged Teal. Shorebirds also use the area during migration. Swanquarter also hosts thousands of waterfowl during migration; the birds move back and forth between the two refuges. It also has many shorebirds during migration.

▶ Conservation Issues: Repeated attempts to drain the lake in the early twentieth century were unsuccessful, but much of the surrounding land once covered by pocosins and forested wetlands has been converted to agriculture. Housing development along the north shore of the lake has the potential to disturb waterfowl and to impact the water quality. Hurricanes and flooding also diminish water quality by leading to increased runoff from agriculture and other development.

▶ Visitor Information: The refuge has most to offer during the winter months. There is a local birding festival, Swan Days, in December, celebrating the return of migratory Tundra Swans. Contact the refuge at 38 Mattamuskeet Road, Swan Quarter, NC 27885, 252-926-4021.

Pocosin Lakes and Pungo National Wildlife Refuge (44), North Carolina

▶ Highlight: Important site for wintering waterfowl and breeding green list species.

▶ Location: Eastern North Carolina, in Tyrrell, Hyde, and Washington Counties.

▶ Size: 113,000 acres.

▶ Ownership: Fish and Wildlife Service.

▶ Habitats: Lakes, rivers, pocosins, bottomland hardwood forest, some farmland.

▶ Land Use: Hunting, wildlife observation, and conservation.

▶ Site Description: Pocosin is a characteristic plant community on the refuge. Vegetation on the site is dominated by dense broadleaf evergreen shrubs and scattered pond pines. There is some open water, including the 1,000-acre Pungo Lake, the 4,000-acre New Lake, and the adjacent 16,000-acre Lake Phelps. The Alligator and Scuppernong Rivers pass through the refuge, and there are tracts of bottomland hardwood forest dominated by blackgum and Carolina ash, with some red maple, water tupelo, loblolly pine, and bald cypress. There is at least one Atlantic white-cedar stand. Large pitcher plants are visible in some areas. This IBA includes Pungo National Wildlife Refuge, now a unit of Pocosin Lakes National Wildlife Refuge.

▶ Birds: Flocks of wintering waterfowl occur on Lake Pungo and Lake Phelps, including up to 30,000 Tundra Swans, 40,000 Snow Geese, 2,230 American Black Ducks, and thousands of Canada Geese, Mallards, Northern Pintail, Green-winged Teal, and American Wigeon; peak numbers reach 100,000 birds during winter. Breeding species at the refuge include the Chuck-will's-widow, Red-headed Woodpecker, Wood Thrush, and Prothonotary, Swainson's, and Prairie Warblers. The Short-eared Owl and the Henslow's Sparrow occur seasonally.

▶ Conservation Issues: Pocosin Lakes National Wildlife Refuge comprises 93,000 acres of land donated to the Fish and Wildlife Service in 1990 by the Conservation Fund with support from the Richard King Mellon Foundation. Most pocosin has been subjected to some degree of drainage, and managing water levels is a key factor in preserving the ecosystem. Other key issues include waterfowl management, swamp restoration, and fire management. There is a high risk of wildfire in the area, and the site is also in the hurricane belt. More than 10,000 hunters utilize the refuge during the waterfowl season. The refuge is crossed by 100 miles of roads and 175 miles of major drainage canals.

▶ Visitor Information: Best time to visit is from fall through spring; summers are hot and there are many biting insects. For further information, contact the refuge at P.O. Box 329, 205 South Ludington Drive, Columbia, NC 27925, 252-796-3004.

Roanoke River Wetlands IBAs, North Carolina

Roanoke River National Wildlife Refuge (45) and Roanoke River Floodplain and Wetlands (46)

▶ Highlight: With breeding Cerulean and Swainson's Warblers, the extensive floodplain in the lower reaches of the Roanoke River is considered the largest intact, least disturbed bottomland forest ecosystem remaining in the mid-Atlantic region.

► Location: Near Williamston, Martin County.
► Size: 150,000 acres.
► Ownership: Fish and Wildlife Service, North Carolina Wildlife Resources Commission, The Nature Conservancy, private.
► Habitats: Bottomland cypress-tupelo forest with an intermittent ridge and swale topography consisting of levee forests, hardwood flats, and cypress-tupelo swamps.
► Land Use: Fishing, hunting, boating, wildlife observation, timber production.
► Site Description: The floodplain of the Roanoke River contains the largest intact, least disturbed bottomland hardwood and cypress-tupelo forests on the Atlantic Coast. The protected areas in the floodplain consist of several tracts along the river, some of which are part of the Roanoke River National Wildlife Refuge, which totals some 18,000 acres. Approximately 17,500 acres in the floodplain comprise the Roanoke River Floodplain and Wetlands, which are owned by the North Carolina Wildlife Resources Commission. As part of its Roanoke River Project, The Nature Conservancy owns some 1,500 acres, but also holds easements and management agreements on an additional 21,000 with a timber company, and one conservation easement on 1,800 acres with Weyerhaeuser.
► Birds: There is a disjunct population of the Worm-eating Warbler in the old-growth, mature floodplain forest. The Swainson's Warbler also breeds here, as do Prothonotary and Kentucky Warblers and a good number of other neotropical migrants. Included in the floodplain is the largest inland heron rookery in the state, with approximately 2,600 herons and Anhingas. The Wood Thrush also breeds, and many waterfowl use the area during the winter.
► Conservation Issues: Upstream reservoirs regulate the flow of water in the lower Roanoke River. Regulated flows and their effect on vegetation and wildlife is a subject of ongoing research by The Nature Conservancy. Findings indicate that in areas flooded during the growing season (April to June), there is little regeneration of cypress and other canopy species, resulting in a lack of understorey and mid-storey vegetation. In areas once periodically inundated but now permanently dry, American beech is invading and becoming dominant in the canopy. By pointing out how the changed hydrology of the Roanoke is affecting important ecosystems, the Conservancy plans to work with managers upstream to bring water release policies more in line with the natural processes that created these ecosystems in the first place. Road construction in the national wildlife refuge along the tops of levees through canebrakes is reducing the amount of suitable habitat for the Swainson's Warbler, a high-priority species.
► Visitor Information: Best time to visit is fall through spring. For more information, contact: Roanoke River National Wildlife Refuge, P.O. Box 430, Windsor, NC 27983, 252-794-3808.

Great Dismal Swamp National Wildlife Refuge (47), Virginia and North Carolina

► Highlight: The Swainson's Warbler is a common breeding species.
► Location: South of Norfolk, on the state line dividing Virginia and North Carolina.
► Size: 107,000 acres.
► Ownership: Fish and Wildlife Service.

▶ Habitats: Successional black gum and red maple forest; bald-cypress and Atlantic white-cedar forest.

▶ Land Use: Recreation, wildlife observation and conservation.

▶ Site Description: The refuge is on the border of Virginia and North Carolina, with the greater part located in Virginia. The 3,000-acre Lake Drummond is a prominent feature of the swamp. Some 85,000 acres of the refuge are wooded wetlands. The principal vegetation type is black gum and red maple, but with stands of Atlantic white-cedar, bald-cypress, and evergreen shrubbogs.

▶ Birds: The Prothonotary Warbler is an abundant breeding species on the refuge, and the elusive and often hard-to-observe Swainson's Warbler is more common here than almost anywhere else on the Atlantic Coast. This is, in fact, its northernmost viable population. A recent study conducted at the site indicates that habitat favored by territorial males is significantly drier and floristically more diverse than unoccupied habitat, with extensive understorey thickets, greenbrier tangles, deep shade at ground level, and abundant leaf litter. When such territories are flooded during the breeding season, the birds abandon them. Among the other breeding species are the Chuck-will's-widow, Wood Thrush, "Wayne's" Black-throated Green Warbler, and Kentucky, Prairie, and Worm-eating Warblers. The Brown-headed Nuthatch is also found locally. The swamp also hosts an immense winter mixed roost of blackbird species—once estimated at over 30 million individuals.

▶ Conservation Issues: The hydrology of the swamp has been greatly altered by drainage and by repeated logging, beginning with George Washington; one of the main ditches bears his name. This has meant that most of the once dominant bald-cypress and Atlantic white-cedar stands have been replaced by other forest types, notably red maple. Agriculture, and commercial and residential development, have destroyed much of the swamp, so that less than half its original extent remains. The present management goal is to work to restore the ecosystem diversity that existed before humans began to alter it. This has meant efforts to re-create original hydrological conditions, and to use fire as a management tool. A long-term Swainson's Warbler project, involving a habitat and population monitoring study, also includes experimental habitat manipulation. In areas managed primarily for the warbler, it is recommended that the water table be maintained at subsurface levels from late March through September.

▶ Visitor Information: Best time to visit is during spring migration and the early breeding season, from April to June. The refuge is off-limits to cars, and the trail to Lake Drummond, reachable from U.S. 17 south of Norfork, is five miles each way. Biting insects and limited visibility due to foliage make summer birding difficult. Contact: Great Dismal Swamp National Wildlife Refuge, 3100 Desert Road (office), P.O. Box 349 (mail address), Suffolk, VA 23439, 757-986-3705.

Piney Grove Preserve (48), Virginia

▶ Highlight: The northernmost colony of the Red-cockaded Woodpecker, and the only one remaining in Virginia.

▶ Location: Sussex County, near Wakefield.

▶ Size: 2,600 acres.

▶ Ownership: The Nature Conservancy.

▶ Habitats: Pine woods, mixed pine-hardwoods.

▶ Land Use: Conservation.

▶ Site Description: Pine forest on the preserve is of mixed age classes, with a core of approximately 1,000 acres of old-growth pine, dominated by loblolly with a component of shortleaf and pond pine.

▶ Birds: There are three clusters of woodpeckers on the preserve, with a total of approximately 15 to 20 birds. The woodpecker is restricted largely to the 1,000 acres of old-growth pine forest on the preserve. The Brown-headed Nuthatch is also found, and the Bachman's Sparrow has recently been reported nearby.

▶ Conservation Issues: This Nature Conservancy preserve is at the center of the northernmost population of the Red-cockaded Woodpecker. The nearest population is some 75 miles to the south, at a site in North Carolina. The woodpecker has persisted at Piney Grove because the timber company that owned it for many years practiced selective cutting rather than short rotation, and fires occasionally swept the area. The Conservancy has encouraged neighboring landowners to carry out habitat improvements to benefit the species. The Virginia Safe Harbor Program for the woodpecker was approved by the Fish and Wildlife Service in July 2000, and resembles similar programs for the woodpecker in several other states, except that instead of being administered by a state or federal agency, it is overseen by The Nature Conservancy. Among the activities to improve habitat for the bird are prescribed burning, installation of artificial nest cavities, and selective thinning to allow the open canopy structure that the species requires.

▶ Visitor Information: Due to the small number of woodpeckers present and the need to minimize stress on the bird, the preserve is closed to visitors.

Other Red-cockaded Woodpecker Sites in the Southeastern Coastal Plain

▶ Highlight: There are a number of sites—in the order of 150 or so—in the southeastern United States that support smaller numbers of Red-cockaded Woodpeckers. Though not in the league of large population centers that qualify as global IBAs, such as Apalachicola National Forest, Fort Stewart, or Fort Bragg, they still merit protection, and are of interest to conservationists. The list below mentions only a few of them.

▶ Location: Though sites in the southeastern Coastal Plain predominate here, sites in other parts of the bird's range are also included; its present distribution is south from Virginia to Florida, and west to Texas and Oklahoma.

▶ Ownership: Forest Service, Department of Defense, state lands, private lands.

▶ Habitats: Pine savannah with old-growth longleaf, shortleaf, and loblolly pine.

▶ Land Use: Timber production, recreation, wildlife conservation.

▶ Site Description: Sites supporting the Red-cockaded Woodpecker are typically pine savannah with old-growth pines at least 75 years old, which the species uses to excavate its nesting cavities.

▶ Birds: Typically, sites supporting the Red-cockaded Woodpecker also support the Brown-headed Nuthatch, and often the Bachman's Sparrow. At the sites listed below, the number of clusters of the woodpecker range from just a few to 50 or so; where available, these figures have been included.

▶ Conservation Issues: The woodpecker needs sites where periodic fires prevent the succession of open pine forest to hardwoods. Sites where fire is suppressed and where trees are harvested on a short rotation are not suitable habitat. The woodpecker is the object of management concern, and typically land managers use some combination of prescribed burning, mechanical removal of hardwood mid-storey, and the placement of artificial nests to stabilize or increase the species' population. In some cases, as in DeSoto National Forest, Mississippi, managers are restoring longleaf pine forest by selectively cutting loblolly and slash pine that had been planted there, and even translocating birds from other locations to establish new clusters.

▶ Visitor Information: The woodpecker is non-migratory. Since these sites have hot and humid summers, the best time to visit is fall through spring.

SITES:

Camp Lejeune Marine Base, North Carolina: 54 clusters. With active management, the site has had a ten percent increase in each of the past several years.

Homochitto National Forest, Mississippi: 51 clusters, up from 22 clusters in 1992.

Savannah River (DOE), South Carolina: 28 clusters.

Goethe State Forest, Florida: 28 clusters.

Camp Blanding, Florida: 25 clusters.

Holly Shelter Game Land, North Carolina: 25 clusters.

Shaw Air Force Base, South Carolina: 20 clusters.

Conecuh National Forest, Alabama: 19 clusters.

Oconee National Forest, Georgia: 18 clusters.

Big Branch Marsh National Wildlife Refuge, Louisiana: 13 clusters.

DeSoto National Forest, Mississippi: Six clusters.

Sabine National Forest, Texas: Five clusters.

D'Arbonne National Wildlife Refuge, Louisiana: Five clusters.

Other public or conservation lands: Several other sites in public ownership have a few clusters; these include Gulf State Park and Lake Purdy in Alabama; Big Branch Marsh National Wildlife Refuge in Louisiana; The Nature Conservancy's Green Swamp Ecological Preserve in North Carolina; and Cheraw State Park and Fish Hatchery, Oketee Plantation, and James K. Webb Wildlife Center in South Carolina. The Venus Flatwoods Preserve of The Nature Conservancy in peninsular Florida also has a few birds.

Private lands: Several hundred woodpecker clusters are located on private lands, particularly on the large holdings of paper companies. There are partnerships between conservationists and these companies to manage lands for the bird, and much land has been set aside.

28. Appalachian Mountains

Included in this area are the Blue Ridge, the Ridge and Valley Region, the Cumberland Plateau, the Ohio Hills, and the Allegheny Plateau. The rugged terrain is generally dominated by oak, hickory, and other deciduous forest types at lower elevations, and various combinations of pine, hemlock, spruce, and fir in higher areas. While flatter portions are in agricultural use, the majority of this region is forested. Priority forest birds include the Worm-eating Warbler at low elevations, and the Black-throated Blue Warbler higher up. Golden-winged Warblers are in early successional habitats, and Henslow's Sparrows in grasslands. While not as important for waterfowl as coastal regions, the Appalachian Region contains the headwaters of several major eastern river systems that are used by various waterfowl species during migration. In addition, large wetland complexes such as Canaan Valley in West Virginia and isolated wetlands created by beavers provide Wood Duck breeding habitat.

DECLINE OF EASTERN FOREST INTERIOR SPECIES

Older birders sometimes reminisce about the great spring flights of warblers in days gone by. Are they turning their youth into a golden age, or was it really better back then?

It appears it *was* better back then. Since the end of World War II, the numbers of many species have gone down precipitously. Particularly hard hit are those breeding in northeastern forests and wintering in Latin America and the Caribbean. In one state alone—Illinois—Breeding Bird Survey data show that between 1966 and 1991, more than two-thirds of the state's Ovenbirds and Acadian Flycatchers disappeared, along with more than a third of the Eastern Wood Pewees, Great Crested Flycatchers, and Red-eyed Vireos. Breeding Bird Survey data from elsewhere show much the same trend. In Rock Creek Park, Washington, D.C., with one of the longest histories anywhere of breeding bird records, Red-eyed Vireos decreased by 79 percent over the last few decades and Ovenbirds by 94 percent, while Black-and-white Warblers and Hooded Warblers have vanished altogether.

What is going on? Forest-interior birds need forest interior, and there is just not as much of that as there used to be. More and more roads have been built

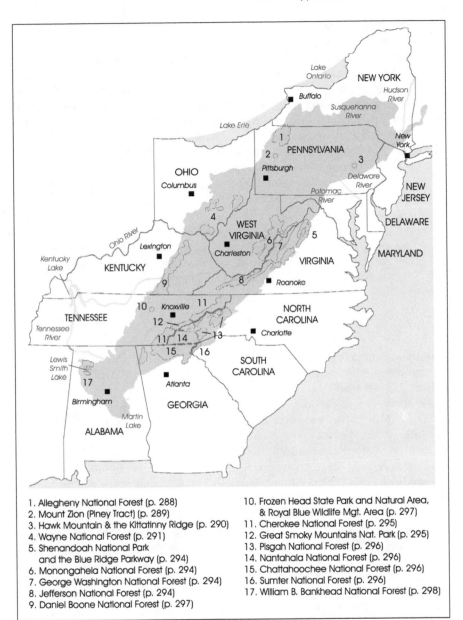

1. Allegheny National Forest (p. 288)
2. Mount Zion (Piney Tract) (p. 289)
3. Hawk Mountain & the Kittatinny Ridge (p. 290)
4. Wayne National Forest (p. 291)
5. Shenandoah National Park
   and the Blue Ridge Parkway (p. 294)
6. Monongahela National Forest (p. 294)
7. George Washington National Forest (p. 294)
8. Jefferson National Forest (p. 294)
9. Daniel Boone National Forest (p. 297)

10. Frozen Head State Park and Natural Area,
    & Royal Blue Wildlife Mgt. Area (p. 297)
11. Cherokee National Forest (p. 295)
12. Great Smoky Mountains Nat. Park (p. 295)
13. Pisgah National Forest (p. 296)
14. Nantahala National Forest (p. 296)
15. Chattahoochee National Forest (p. 296)
16. Sumter National Forest (p. 296)
17. William B. Bankhead National Forest (p. 298)

through existing forests, cutting them up into smaller and smaller parcels—a process known as forest fragmentation—and that means less interior and more edge. Woodland edge is a habitat more favored by nest-parasitizing cowbirds and nest-robbing birds like jays, crows, and grackles, not to mention raccoons, possums, red foxes, and domestic cats. One estimate is that as much as 7,000 acres of relatively unbroken forest may be needed for a full complement of forest interior breeding birds, and in much of the northeastern United States, places like that are getting harder and harder to find.

Furthermore, suburbs have spread farther into the countryside, eating up more and more farmland and forests. This has been hard on many neotropical migrants looking for a secure place to build their nests. Residential areas bring with them an abundance not just of nest-robbing birds but of squirrels, raccoons, possums, and feral cats. City parks such as Rock Creek have become more and more isolated from other wooded areas as development has grown up around them, and as populations of certain species decline everywhere else, there just are not enough of them left to breed in the marginal habitats where they were once found.

To make matters worse, the problem seems to be not only what is happening here, but what is happening in the birds' wintering grounds. Deforestation in Latin America and the Caribbean means there is less habitat, and less habitat means that fewer migrants make it through the winter. There just are not as many migrant songbirds as there used to be, and for many of them, the numbers are still decreasing. The result is that species that used to be abundant are now on the Green List, and spring migration is a trickle instead of a flood.

Allegheny National Forest (1), Pennsylvania

▸ Highlight: High concentrations of breeding neotropical migrants, including a dense population of the Blackburnian Warbler.

▸ Location: Northwestern Pennsylvania, with headquarters in Warren.

▸ Size: 513,000 acres.

▸ Ownership: Forest Service.

▸ Habitat: Mostly hardwood forest; contains some of the oldest tracts of beech-hemlock–white pine forest in the eastern United States.

▸ Land Use: Forestry, recreation.

▸ Site Description: The forest occupies a rolling plateau cut by many creeks and streams, with a relief of 1,300 feet. A location of particular interest within the forest is the Tionesta Scenic and Research Natural Area. At 4,131 acres, it contains the largest old-growth forest between the Adirondacks and the Great Smoky Mountains. Another

Black-throated Blue Warbler

large block of undisturbed forest within Allegheny's boundaries is the Hickory Creek Wilderness Area/Hearts Content Natural Area: 8,763 acres of mature mixed hardwoods and forested stream bottoms. Both these areas support large concentrations of breeding neotropical migrants of several species. Just south of the forest is Cook Forest State Park, at 7,182 acres. This includes several tracts of virgin forest and it also has good numbers of breeding neotropical migrants. Its stand of old-growth white pine and hemlock, called the Forest Cathedral, is a National Natural Landmark.

▶ Birds: Forest-interior breeding birds abound in various habitats in the forest, including many warblers, among them Canada, Nashville, Golden-winged, Blue-winged, Yellow-throated, Yellow-rumped, Black-and-white, Cerulean, Worm-eating, and Mourning; plus Ovenbirds, and Northern and Louisiana Waterthrushes. There are particularly high concentrations of breeding Blackburnian, Black-throated Green, Magnolia, and Black-throated Blue Warblers. In fact, it is estimated that Blackburnian Warblers occur here in densities approximately 40 times that in second-growth forests. The Wood Thrush, Swainson's Thrush, and Yellow-bellied Flycatcher also nest, as do several pairs of the Northern Goshawk.

▶ Conservation Issues: Threats to the forest include disease, insect pests such as the gypsy moth, and a lack of forest regeneration due to overbrowsing by deer. A tornado damaged approximately 1,000 acres of the Tionesta area in 1985.

▶ Visitor Information: Best time to visit is late May to early June, for nesting forest interior birds. For more information, contact the forest at P.O. Box 847, 222 Liberty Street, Warren, PA 16365, 814-723-5150.

Mount Zion (Piney Tract) (2), Pennsylvania

▶ Highlight: Important breeding site for the Henslow's Sparrow and other grassland birds.

▶ Location: Southwestern Clarion County, near Knox, in northwestern Pennsylvania.

▶ Size: 2,300 acres.

▶ Ownership: Private.

▶ Land Use: Restoration of strip-mined lands.

▶ Site Description: Similar in its history and avifauna to the Reclaimed Coal Mine Grasslands in Indiana, Mount Zion was strip-mined and afterward revegetated, principally with grasses but also with some tree species. In the process, much of the site has become good habitat for grassland birds. At present, pines are invading some of the grassland there.

▶ Habitats: Grassland, ponds, brushy and wooded streams.

▶ Birds: The area now hosts a good diversity and large population sizes of several grassland birds, including the Henslow's Sparrow, with the largest breeding colony in the state, numbering hundreds of pairs; the species also occurs on other reclaimed strip-mined grasslands in southern Clarion County. Good numbers of Grasshopper and Savannah Sparrows are found, as are a few Upland Sandpipers and Northern Harriers. The first state breeding record of the Dickcissel was recently made in the area, and the Clay-colored Sparrow has recently bred as well. It is the only reliable area in the state for breeding Short-eared Owls, which are also found sparingly in winter.

▶ Conservation Issues: In many ways the argument can be made that keeping the site in grassland is the optimal use of reclaimed strip-mined lands. Periodic burning will be necessary to control encroaching woody vegetation, which is not suitable for these grassland birds. The site is owned by a coal company, with which agreement must be reached before such management can take place. Pollution from acid mine drainage is a problem in some parts of the site. Several conservation and sportsmen's groups are cooperating to conserve the area, with the involvement of the Pennsylvania Game Commission.

▶ Visitor Information: The area is accessible to visitors. Best time to see the breeding birds is in late May to early July. For current status, call Audubon Pennsylvania at 717-213-6880.

Hawk Mountain and the Kittatinny Ridge (3), Pennsylvania

▶ Highlight: Hawk Mountain is on the Kittatinny Ridge, the most heavily used raptor migration corridor in the northeastern United States.
▶ Designation: Hawk Mountain is a National Natural Landmark.
▶ Location: Near Eckville, Schuylkill County.
▶ Size: The Kittatinny Ridge is about 280 square miles; the sanctuary is 2,400 acres.
▶ Ownership: Hawk Mountain is owned by the Hawk Mountain Sanctuary Association; most of the ridge is in private ownership.
▶ Habitat: Deciduous forest with rocky outcrops.
▶ Land Use: Conservation, research.
▶ Principal Threat: Proposed construction of communication towers.
▶ Site Description: Pennsylvania's Kittatinny Ridge forms a corridor where great numbers of migrating hawks can be seen during fall migration. The ridge is an important migration route for other landbirds as well. The area of the ridge extends from the Susquehanna River to the Pennsylvania–New Jersey state line. The valleys on either side of the ridge have mixed farmland and small towns. Though there are many sites along the ridge from which to observe hawk migration, two are particularly well known. One is Waggoner's Gap, a site with a history of long-term research and monitoring of hawk migration; the other, more prominent site is Hawk Mountain, one of the best-known hawk-watching sites in the world. Called "one of the greatest monuments of the American conservation movement," Hawk Mountain Sanctuary was established in 1934 as the world's first refuge for birds of prey at a site where hunters once stood and killed migrating hawks by the thousands. As the oldest continuously operating hawk watch in the world, it engages in long-term monitoring studies of migrating hawks, applied conservation research, and public education. It was with the help of monitoring studies at Hawk Mountain that ornithologists were able to document the recovery in numbers of several raptor species affected by DDT.
▶ Birds: Approximately 23,000 hawks pass over each fall. In addition to the 16 species of raptor that regularly use the corridor, some 140 other species of birds are recorded regularly, as are migrating monarch butterflies and bats.
▶ Conservation Issues: Development along the ridge is a potential threat, particularly the construction of communications towers (see p. 431). Surrounding lands are crucial for feeding and resting for migrant hawks and other birds. Visitors to the Hawk Mountain Sanctuary are largely restricted to four miles of trails.
▶ Visitor Information: The hawk migration season begins in mid-August when Ospreys, Bald Eagles, and Kestrels pass through. In mid-September thousands of Broad-winged Hawks fly over, followed by thousands of Sharp-shinned and Red-tailed Hawks in October. In November the species to look for are the Northern Goshawk and Golden Eagle. The best days are those with northwest winds, after the passage of a cold front. Contact Hawk Mountain Sanctuary, 1700 Hawk Mountain Road, Kempton, PA 19529, 610-756-6000 or 610-756-6961.

Wayne National Forest (4), Ohio

▸ Highlight: Good breeding populations of the Cerulean and Worm-eating Warblers.

▸ Location: The forest consists of three units in two districts in southeastern and south-central Ohio.

▸ Size: 232,926 acres.

▸ Ownership: Forest Service, private inholdings.

▸ Habitats: Upland forest of hardwoods and pine, rivers, streams.

▸ Land Use: Timber production, hunting, wildlife observation, oil and gas wells, off-road vehicle use on designated trails.

▸ Site Description: Located in the foothills of the Appalachian Mountains, the Wayne National Forest came into existence during the Great Depression, when many farmers abandoned their eroded farms, and the lands were taken for taxes. Within its boundaries there is still much private land. Its hills are covered with diverse stands of hardwoods and pine, and there are lakes, rivers, and streams in the area. Besides upland oak-hickory and beech-maple forests, there is a small area of native white pine, along with scattered areas of native shortleaf and Virginia pines. Much of the Wayne National Forest was mined for coal, iron, clay, and limestone; strip-mining began in the late 1940s, and some of the land is in various stages of reclamation and revegetation.

Cerulean Warbler

▸ Birds: The Cerulean Warbler is a common breeding species in the forest, with birds detected at most census points on all three units. Another common forest-interior species is the Worm-eating Warbler, while the Prairie Warbler is common on maintained open areas. The Wood Thrush is also common, and there are a few breeding Kentucky Warblers. In the reclaimed strip mines on the forest there are good populations of the Henslow's Sparrow, a species also found in southeast Ohio on other reclaimed strip mines owned by the Ohio Division of Wildlife.

▸ Conservation Issues: The forest is committed to inventory and monitoring of breeding birds and monitoring protocols are being established. A recent three-year project concentrated on censusing forest interior birds. There is an active reforestation project, and also a project to restore water quality in streams affected by acid mine drainage. The forest is managed for multiple use.

▸ Visitor Information: Best time to visit for migrating and breeding forest birds is from late April to early July, and again in August to October, for fall migration. The forest can be reached at 13700 Highway 33, Nelsonville, OH 45764, 740-753-0101.

Southern Appalachian Mountains IBAs

Shenandoah National Park and the Blue Ridge Parkway, VA (5),
Monongahela National Forest, WV (6), George Washington National
Forest, VA (7), Jefferson National Forest, VA (8), Cherokee National Forest,
TN (11), Great Smoky Mountains National Park, NC, TN (12), Pisgah
National Forest, NC (13), Nantahala National Forest, NC (14),
Chattahoochee National Forest, GA (15), Sumter National Forest, SC (16)

▸ Highlight: A key source area for neotropical migrants including the Wood Thrush, Worm-eating, Canada, Black-throated Blue, Golden-winged, and Swainson's Warblers. Several subspecies have breeding ranges confined to the Southern Appalachians, including races of the Ruffed Grouse, Northern Saw-whet Owl, and Black-capped Chickadee.
▸ Location: This IBA complex is spread among six states: West Virginia, Virginia, North Carolina, South Carolina, Georgia, and Tennessee. The area is best viewed as a mosaic of ten separate but interconnected IBAs (detailed below), which share common habitats, birds, and often management issues.
▸ Size: 20,000 square miles.
▸ Ownership: National Park Service, Forest Service, private.
▸ Habitats: A wide range of habitats, including spruce-fir forest at the high elevations, mixed mesophytic forest, rhododendron thickets, grassy balds.
▸ Land Use: Wilderness, timber production (in national forests), recreation.
▸ Site Description: The Southern Appalachian IBAs consist of ten blocks of public land and one narrow, winding habitat corridor along the Blue Ridge Parkway. The public lands include Shenandoah National Park, Monongahela, George Washington, Jefferson, and Cherokee National Forests, Great Smoky Mountains National Park, Pisgah, Nantahala, Chattahoochee, and Sumter National Forests; the Park Service also owns the Blue Ridge Parkway. Unlike the national parks, the national forests typically consist of several units and incorporate a greater number of private inholdings. Although there are important sites in state and private ownership, only the larger blocks under federal ownership are treated in separate accounts below. The area is composed of forest and upland meadows on a series of ridges and valleys running from the southwest in Tennessee to the northeast in Virginia. The predominant base rock consists of varying amounts of metamorphic and igneous rocks. Along with the high-altitude spruce-fir forest above 4,000 feet, the area contains extensive mid-altitude mixed-hardwood forest dominated by oaks, and lower altitude mixed forest with locust, hickory, and birch, often with a thick understorey of rhododendron. Also occurring are hickory, hemlock, sprouts of American chestnut, poplar, spruce, mountain ash, fire cherry, mountain maple, beech, buckeye, serviceberry, Virginia pine, sassafras, and dogwood. At the highest elevations are grass balds, probably originally cleared by Native Americans or early European settlers. Ecosystems typical of more northerly latitudes also occur, such as cranberry bogs. There are also numerous streams, rocky outcrops, and brush. These forests provide a source of breeding neotropical migrants and comprise the largest block of forested public land in the East. The area contains numerous towns and is crossed by many roads. At 6,684 feet, Mount Mitchell is the highest mountain in eastern North America. Most forest is secondary growth; small

patches of unlogged forest can still be found, however, with larger remnants in Great Smoky Mountains National Park. A few isolated patches of old-growth cove forest at mid-elevations that support massive tulip poplars can also be found.

▸ Birds: The Southern Appalachians are an important breeding area for many neotropical migrants, several at the southern limit of their breeding ranges. The cool high-elevation (above 2,000 feet) areas form islands of habitat for species normally confined to more northerly regions such as the Black-capped Chickadee and Northern Saw-whet Owl. Both are represented by particular subspecies in the region, as are the Ruffed Grouse, Yellow-bellied Sapsucker, Brown Creeper, Winter Wren, Blue-headed Vireo, Black-throated Green Warbler, Black-throated Blue Warbler, Red Crossbill, and Dark-eyed Junco. The eastern subspecies of the Bewick's Wren now appears to have been extirpated from this part of its former range. Subspecies of particular conservation concern are those of the Northern Saw-whet Owl, Black-capped Chickadee, Red Crossbill, Yellow-bellied Sapsucker, and Brown Creeper, all of which survive only in small and fragmented populations, principally in higher altitude spruce-fir forests. Prairie and Golden-winged Warblers are found in early successional forests, and Cerulean, Black-throated Blue, Kentucky, Canada, Blackburnian, Worm-eating and Yellow-throated Warblers all breed. Swainson's Warblers also breed in lower-altitude forests with a thick rhododendron understorey.

▸ Conservation Issues: According to which agency owns them, these areas are managed very differently. Forest in the national parks is strictly protected, but the national forests are managed for multiple use, including for timber extraction, with the exception of wilderness areas and some other large areas of forest canopy. Declining budgets are an issue on national forest lands, where funds are needed for monitoring and implementing habitat-improvement projects, and for training and funding personnel. The Forest Service, however, has taken the lead in organizing a bird-population monitoring program that incorporates off-road point counts during the breeding season. There are few effective tools to deal with damage to the forests by deer overpopulation and introduced pest species. The Great Smoky Mountains National Park has an active research program, including important studies on the effect of habitat fragmentation on breeding success of forest interior birds and on the park as a source area for these species. A recent study estimated that a breeding population of approximately 10,000 pairs of Wood Thrushes in the park produce a surplus of approximately 3,000 female young each year, which can potentially return to nest in surrounding fragmented habitats. Second-home development in the Southern Appalachians is resulting in rapid land use changes on both inholdings and lands surrounding the forests. There is more pressure for recreational use—more demand for roads, areas for all-terrain and off-road vehicles, and additional visitor facilities. The impact of the construction of cell towers throughout the Appalachians poses a significant threat to migratory species from all along the Eastern Flyway. Air pollution from coal-fired power plants and other sources is a serious problem, threatening plants and animals as well as visitors and residents. The park has some data on the effects of pollution but needs funding to monitor air and water quality.

▸ Visitor Information: The best time to visit is spring through fall to see both migrating and breeding songbirds. The Southern Appalachians are a popular tourist destination, and in the fall the area is particularly crowded with sightseers there for the brilliant fall colors.

Shenandoah National Park and the Blue Ridge Parkway (5), Virginia

The park occupies 194,630 acres and reaches its highest elevation at 4,051 feet. It extends along the Blue Ridge Mountains for 75 miles from Front Royal in the north to Rockfish Gap in the south. The park is approximately five miles wide with an average elevation of approximately 3,000 feet. Skyline Drive provides access to the entire length of the park. The vegetation is mostly second-growth oak forest, but there are scattered tracts of old-growth hemlock, with cove forest in many of the ravines. Among the many neotropical migrants breeding there are Black-throated Blue, Cerulean, Worm-eating, Canada, Kentucky, and Hooded Warblers, and Wood Thrushes.

The 469-mile Blue Ridge Parkway and its associated narrow winding band of protected habitat connects the Shenandoah and Great Smoky Mountains National Parks. It is important for spring warbler migration and fall hawk migration and has small pockets of habitat for nesting Cerulean Warbler.

▸ Visitor Information: The best time to visit is spring through fall to see both migrating and breeding songbirds. Contact the Shenandoah National Park, Luray, VA 22835, 703-999-2266. Contact the Blue Ridge Parkway at 199 Hemphill Knob Road, Asheville, NC 28803, 828-259-0779.

Monongahela National Forest (6), West Virginia

The forest is 909,174 acres in five ranger districts with five wilderness areas totaling 78,131 acres. A patchwork of federal and private ownership within its boundaries, the forest has important populations of several breeding species, including Cerulean, Black-throated Blue, Prairie, Worm-eating, Golden-winged, Kentucky, and Canada Warblers, and Wood Thrushes. It lies inside West Virginia, meeting the George Washington National Forest at the Virginia state line along its eastern flank; its most northerly extent is also the most northerly reach of this IBA complex.

▸ Visitor Information: The best time to visit is spring through fall to see both migrating and breeding songbirds. Contact the Forest Supervisor, 200 Sycamore Street, Elkins, WV 26241, 304-636-1800.

George Washington (7) and Jefferson (8) National Forests, Virginia and West Virginia

The George Washington is 1,054,922 acres in three sections. The Jefferson is 700,000 acres. These two national forests cover most of Virginia's Blue Ridge Mountains outside of Shenandoah National Park and the Blue Ridge Parkway, with a slight overlap into West Virginia and Kentucky. The George Washington borders the Monongahela, and the Jefferson borders the Cherokee in Tennessee. The Jefferson has the highest point in Virginia and one of the highest summits in the central Appalachians, the 5,728 foot Mount Rogers. Starting in 1993, Forest Service biologists established a bird monitoring program within the almost 1.8 million acres of land encompassed by the two forests. As of 2001, more than 800 point counts were incorporated into this program. The survey stations are located off-road, within mature (greater than 70 years old) deciduous and deciduous-pine forests. Worm-eating and Hooded Warblers, and Wood Thrushes are among the 15 species that accounted for almost 70 percent of detections, with the Worm-eating Warbler occurring on approximately one-third of all survey sites. Among the other breeding birds found in the two national forests are Cerulean, Kentucky, Black-throated Blue, and Blue-winged Warblers. Also of note is the spectacular fall hawk migration. Locations such as Hanging Rock Tower on the New River Valley Ranger District offer some of the best hawk-viewing opportunities in Virginia.

▸ Visitor Information: The best time to visit is spring through fall to see both migrating and breeding songbirds. Contact: George Washington and Jefferson National Forests, 5162 Valleypointe Parkway, Roanoke, VA 24019, 540-265-5100.

Cherokee National Forest (11), Tennessee

The Cherokee National Forest is 632,000 acres. It runs along the east Tennessee border and is separated into two units by the Great Smoky Mountains National Park. It also borders units of the Pisgah and Nantahala National Forests in North Carolina and of the Chattahoochee National Forest in Georgia. Ten percent of the forest is wilderness, divided into 11 areas, and 44 percent is available for timber production. This is the largest tract of public land in Tennessee. Hooded, Canada, Black-throated Blue, Worm-eating, Swainson's, Kentucky, and Prairie Warblers all breed there.

▸ Visitor Information: The best time to visit is spring through fall to see both migrating and breeding songbirds. Contact the Forest Supervisor, Cherokee National Forest, P.O. Box 2010, Cleveland, TN 374320, 423-476-9700.

Great Smoky Mountains National Park (12), North Carolina and Tennessee

The park is 520,976 acres, and is the most-visited national park in the United States with nearly ten million visitors annually. It lies on the North Carolina–Tennessee state line. Its large blocks of intact forest retain reasonably unaltered bird life and provide a valuable source area for breeding neotropical migrants such as the Wood Thrush; as well as Black-throated Blue, Canada, Worm-eating, Kentucky, and other warbler species. Brown-headed Cowbird nest parasitism is at very low levels due to continuous forest cover over 95 percent of the park. Cooperating scientists have completed an extensive inventory of breeding birds.

▸ Visitor Information: The best time to visit is spring through fall to see both migrating and breeding songbirds. Contact: Great Smoky Mountains National Park, Gatlinburg, TN 37738, 865-436-1200. The park is an International Biosphere Reserve and World Heritage Site.

Pisgah (13) and Nantahala (14) National Forests, North Carolina

Pisgah is 505,226 acres in three ranger districts. Nantahala is 530,412 acres in four ranger districts. These two national forests span the rugged mountains of western North Carolina. A variety of ecosystems—from high elevation spruce-fir forests to rich hardwood coves—provide habitat for many bird species. Within Nantahala, an old-growth forest of 400-year-old trees is preserved as

Joyce Kilmer Memorial Forest. The mature forests are breeding habitat for Cerulean, Blackburnian, Black-throated Blue, and Worm-eating Warblers, while the high-peak forests provide habitat for the Northern Saw-whet Owl, Black-capped Chickadee, Red-breasted Nuthatch, Winter Wren, Golden-crowned Kinglet, and Red Crossbill.

▶ Visitor Information: Contact the National Forests in North Carolina, 160A Zillicoa Street, Asheville, NC 28801, 828-257-4200, website: www.cs.unca.edu/nfsnc.

Northern Saw-whet Owl

Chattahoochee National Forest (15), Georgia

The forest is 750,000 acres. Bordering the Cherokee National Forest in Tennessee and Nantahala National Forest in North Carolina, it is divided into three ranger districts, the Brasstown, Cohutta, and Tallulah. The Swainson's Warbler nests on the latter, while other nesting warblers in the forest include the Black-throated Blue, Black-throated Green, Blackburnian, and Canada Warblers and a few Worm-eating Warblers. There is an ongoing effort to create habitat for the Golden-winged Warbler.

▶ Visitor Information: The best time to visit is spring through fall to see both migrating and breeding songbirds. Contact: Brasstown Ranger District, Highway 19/129S, Box 216, Blairsville, GA 30512, 404-745-6928.

Sumter National Forest (16), South Carolina

At 364,908 acres the forest is divided into three separate ranger districts, extending across 11 counties, but only the Andrew Pickens Ranger District in the northwest corner of the state is in the Southern Appalachian IBA complex. Habitats include coniferous and mixed forests ranging from upper piedmont into the foothills, including the 1,546-foot Rich Mountain.

▶ Visitor Information: The best time to visit is spring through fall to see both migrating and breeding songbirds. Contact: Sumter National Forest, 4931 Broad River Road, Columbia, SC 29212, 803-561-4000.

Daniel Boone National Forest (9), Kentucky

▶ Highlight: Good breeding populations of Swainson's, Cerulean, and Worm-eating Warblers.
▶ Location: The six forest districts are located in eastern Kentucky, with headquarters in Winchester.
▶ Size: 680,000 acres.
▶ Ownership: Forest Service, private inholdings.
▶ Habitats: Mixed mesophytic forest, beech-maple-hemlock forest, white pine–hemlock forest in gorges, ridges with Virginia, shortleaf, and pitch pines. Rhododendron is an important understorey component of several forest types.
▶ Land Use: Recreation, conservation.
▶ Site Description: The forest is in the Cumberland Plateau; in terms of its biota and forest types, it has much in common with the Southern Appalachians. Many species of fish and mussels occur in the streams, several of them endangered. There are many limestone and sandstone arches, caves, and many miles of cliff face in the forest.
▶ Birds: Cerulean, Worm-eating, and Kentucky Warblers are common breeding species. A good population of the Swainson's Warbler breeds in rhododendron thickets in the upper reaches of the North Fork of the Red River, an area that is virtually inaccessible except by canoe or kayak. The state's only known breeding and resident population of the Red-breasted Nuthatch occurs in white pine and hemlock in the Rock Bridge area; these were discovered only in the mid-1990s. Saw-whet Owls have been heard calling during the nesting season, though positive evidence of nesting has not yet been found. Red-cockaded Woodpeckers existed in the forest, but when insect pests destroyed the old-growth pines, leaving the birds no habitat, biologists trapped and removed them.
▶ Conservation Issues: Though logging has occurred in the past, there has been no removal of timber in recent years, due to lawsuits. Two wilderness areas are found in the Daniel Boone National Forest: the Clifty Wilderness (13,000 acres) and Beaver Creek Wilderness (4,700 acres). The Red River Gorge has been designated as a National Natural Landmark and a National Geologic Area. With its many cliff faces, the forest is one of the most popular climbing areas in the world. Kayaking and canoeing are also popular activities. The forest has more than one million visitors per year. There has been some thinning for habitat improvement for wildlife, in addition to pond construction. Autumn olive, a non-native, invasive plant, is a problem at the edges of openings; land managers use mechanical means to control it. Other problem non-native plants are pampas grass and Japanese grass, which colonize disturbed areas such as roadsides.
▶ Visitor Information: Best time to visit is late May to early July for breeding warblers. For more information, call the Stanton Ranger District at 606-663-2852. The forest can be contacted at 1700 Bypass Road, Winchester, KY 40391, 859-745-3100.

Frozen Head State Park and Natural Area, and Royal Blue Wildlife Management Area (10), Tennessee

▶ Highlight: Dense breeding population of the Cerulean Warbler; other Green List species breed here also.

► Location: In the Cumberland Mountains near Wartburg.

► Size: 11,876 acres.

► Ownership: Tennessee Department of Environment and Conservation.

► Habitats: Hardwood forest, streams, waterfalls.

► Land Use: Recreation and conservation; adjoining land uses include agriculture, mining, and timber extraction.

► Site Description: The second-growth forest in the park is a diverse assemblage of hardwood trees, some more than 100 feet in height. There is a high, closed canopy, a distinct shrub layer, and lush ground cover with spectacular wildflowers. The park contains high-quality examples of mixed mesophytic forest, with some stands exhibiting old-growth conditions. The mountainous terrain varies from an elevation of 1,340 feet to more than 3,000 feet on 14 different mountain peaks.

► Birds: Frozen Head State Natural Area and its environs, including the entire southern Cumberland Mountains, have dense populations of nesting Cerulean Warblers, perhaps the densest throughout the species' range. There are an estimated 3,000 pairs of the warbler at Frozen Head, with peak densities of 58 per 100 acres. Another large public land area with a high number of Cerulean Warblers, the 45,000-acre Royal Blue Wildlife Management Area, is approximately 15 miles away. Several large timber company land holdings, including tracts immediately bordering Frozen Head, also provide habitat for the species. Canada, Kentucky, and Black-throated Blue Warblers also breed at Frozen Head, as do a few Swainson's. There are good numbers of Wood Thrushes.

► Conservation Issues: There are developed recreational facilities at Frozen Head but no plans at present to expand them. Much of the surrounding land is privately owned, including by coal and timber companies. At present, there is little mining going on but much timber production and clear-cutting of hardwoods. An adjacent state prison farm causes undesirable edge effects. The state is working to add another 2,600 acres to the natural area. Timber companies own land adjacent to Frozen Head and Royal Blue Wildlife Management Areas in extremely large tracts, keeping the area more than 90 percent forested and maintaining fairly contiguous forest tracts.

► Visitor Information: Best time to see the Cerulean Warbler is mid-May to early July. The park can be contacted at 964 Flat Fork Road, Wartburg, TN 37887, 423-346-3318.

William B. Bankhead National Forest (17), Alabama

► Highlight: Prairie and Worm-eating Warblers are common breeding species, along with several other high-priority species.

► Location: Northwestern Alabama, in Winston, Lawrence, and Franklin Counties.

► Size: 350,000 acres are within the forest boundaries, of which 180,000 are owned by the Forest Service.

► Ownership: Forest Service, private inholdings.

► Habitats: Mesic hardwood and mixed pine-hardwood forest, shortleaf pine forest, white pine–hemlock forest, oak-hickory forest, and mountain longleaf pine forest.

► Land Use: Recreation, hunting, timber production.

► Site Description: The forest is an island of mature forest surrounded by intensely managed timber industry lands. There are many limestone bluffs, swift-flowing streams and waterfalls, and Alabama's only nationally designated Wild and Scenic River, the Sipsey.

▸ Birds: Besides Prairie and Worm-eating Warblers, the Swainson's Warbler is known to breed in the forest. Kentucky and Black-throated Green Warblers are found most commonly in hemlock stands near streams and in bottomland hardwoods, while nesting Worm-eating Warblers are found in mesic hardwood stands with trees more than 80 years old in the Sipsey Wilderness portion of the forest. The Wood Thrush breeds commonly, and there are also a few Brown-headed Nuthatches and Chuck-will's-widows on the forest. The Red-cockaded Woodpecker formerly existed here but has not been reliably observed since 1993.

▸ Conservation Issues: The forest's 26,000-acre Sipsey Wilderness is the second-largest wilderness area east of the Mississippi. It represents an important block of habitat for forest interior birds, particularly neotropical migrants. Forest Service biologists have established 122 permanent Breeding Bird Survey points in seven major forests types and five age classes to represent forest composition in the Bankhead. Of the 71 species detected in these surveys, more than half were more abundant in older-aged stands. There is a network of off-road vehicle trails in the forest. In recent years timbering in the forest has been the subject of lawsuits, and there has been a drastic reduction of timber harvest in the last decade. The forest is currently undergoing an unprecedented outbreak of southern pine beetles; this will lead to more early successional habitat within the next few years.

▸ Visitor Information: April through late June is a good time to visit to see migrant birds and breeding birds; September and October are the height of fall migration. For more information contact the Forest Service, P.O. Box 278, Double Springs, AL 35553, 205-489-5111.

The Piedmont is transitional between the mountainous Appalachians and the flat Coastal Plain, and is dominated by pine and mixed southern hardwoods. Priority landbirds include the Red-cockaded Woodpecker, Bachman's Sparrow, and Brown-headed Nuthatch. Interior wetlands, reservoirs, and riverine systems provide migration and wintering habitat for waterfowl and some shorebirds. The fragmented patchwork of pasture, woodlots, and suburban sprawl that now dominates most of this region creates significant bird conservation challenges.

Kennesaw Mountain National Battlefield Park (1), Georgia

▶ Highlight: One of the best inland locations for observing migrant landbirds in the entire Southeast.
▶ Size: 2,884 acres.
▶ Location: Northwestern Atlanta, in Cobb County.
▶ Ownership: National Park Service.
▶ Habitat: Woodland.
▶ Land Use: Historical preservation, wildlife preservation.
▶ Site Description: This battlefield park reaches an elevation of of 1,808 feet. There is a road leading from the visitor center to the summit of the mountain.
▶ Birds: This is one of the best inland locations for observing migrant landbirds in the entire Southeast. One interesting feature is the high counts of Cerulean Warblers, which are commonly seen during spring, but especially during fall migration.
▶ Conservation Issues: The park receives heavy use by visitors throughout the year.
▶ Visitor Information: Best time to visit is during migration—early April through mid-May, and mid-August through mid-October. Contact Superintendent, Kennesaw Mountain National Battlefield Park, 905 Kennesaw Mountain Drive, Kennesaw, GA 30152, 770-427-4686.

Piedmont National Wildlife Refuge (2) and Hitchiti Experimental Forest (3), Georgia

▶ Highlight: The Red-cockaded Woodpecker and several breeding green list species.
▶ Location: Jones County, near East Juliette.

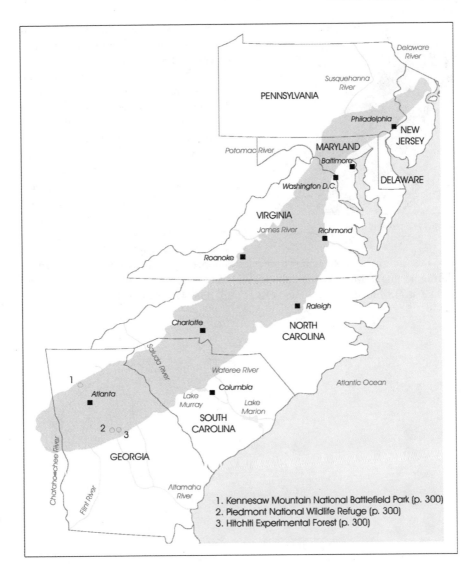

1. Kennesaw Mountain National Battlefield Park (p. 300)
2. Piedmont National Wildlife Refuge (p. 300)
3. Hitchiti Experimental Forest (p. 300)

▶ Size: 35,000 acres.

▶ Ownership: Fish and Wildlife Service.

▶ Habitats: Pine forest, mixed-pine hardwood, floodplain forest.

▶ Land Use: Hunting, fishing, wildlife observation.

▶ Site Description: Much of the site (about 19,000 acres) is loblolly pine forest, managed for the Red-cockaded Woodpecker. In addition to woodland, there are also creeks, streams, and impoundments on the refuge.

▶ Birds: There are 39 active clusters of Red-cockaded Woodpeckers on the refuge, in addition to 12 to 14 clusters in the nearby Hitchiti Experimental Forest, together making this area one of the more significant for the species in the state. Other species

Brown-headed Nuthatch

include the Bachman's Sparrow, Brown-headed Nuthatch; and the Prairie, Hooded, Kentucky, and Swainson's Warblers.

▸ Conservation Issues: The loblolly pine forest on the refuge is managed to benefit the Red-cockaded Woodpecker. Land managers have installed artificial nest cavities in strategic areas where foraging birds are likely to find them. As a result, the number of clusters rose from approximately 25 to the recent count of 39. The woodpecker is easy to see here, and the refuge is one of the only two easily accessible sites for the bird in Georgia, as the others are on military reservations or private land.

▸ Visitor Information: Best time to see the woodpeckers and other pinewoods birds is during nesting in May to early July, but any time of year is worth a visit. Contact the refuge at 718 Juliette Road, Round Oak, GA 31038, 478-986-5441.

30. New England/
Mid-Atlantic Coast

This area has the densest human population of any region in the country. Much of what was formerly cleared for agriculture is now either in forest or residential use. The highest-priority birds are in coastal wetland and beach habitats, including the Saltmarsh Sharp-tailed and Nelson's Sharp-tailed Sparrows, Seaside Sparrow, Piping Plover, American Oystercatcher, American Black Duck, and Black Rail. The region includes critical migration sites for the Red Knot, Ruddy Turnstone, Sanderling, Semipalmated Sandpiper, and Dunlin. Most of the continental population of the endangered Roseate Tern nests on islands off the southern New England states. Other terns and gulls nest in large numbers, and large mixed colonies of herons, egrets, and ibis form on islands in the Delaware and Chesapeake Bay regions. Estuarine complexes and embayments created behind barrier beaches in this region are extremely important to wintering and migrating waterfowl, including approximately 65 percent of the total wintering American Black Duck population, along with large numbers of the Greater Scaup, Tundra Swan, Gadwall, Brant, and Canvasback. Exploitation and pollution of the Chesapeake Bay and other coastal zones, and the accompanying loss of submerged aquatic vegetation have significantly reduced their value to waterfowl.

IBAs of the Delmarva Peninsula Tip, Virginia

Fisherman Island National Wildlife Refuge (1), Eastern Shore of Virginia National Wildlife Refuge (2), Kiptopeke State Park (3)

▶ Highlight: Globally important coastal migration route and stopover site for millions of songbirds, raptors, shorebirds, waterfowl, swallows, herons, and egrets.
▶ Location: The southern 15 miles of the Delmarva Peninsula, on Virginia's Eastern Shore, in Northampton County.
▶ Size: The area is approximately 50 square miles. Contained in the area are Fisherman Island National Wildlife Refuge (approximately 1,800 acres), Kiptopeke State Park (540 acres), and Eastern Shore of Virginia National Wildlife Refuge (780 acres): the southern part of the Virginia Coast Reserve also extends into this area, and The Virginia Department of Game and Inland Fisheries owns a small parcel of land of approximately ten acres.

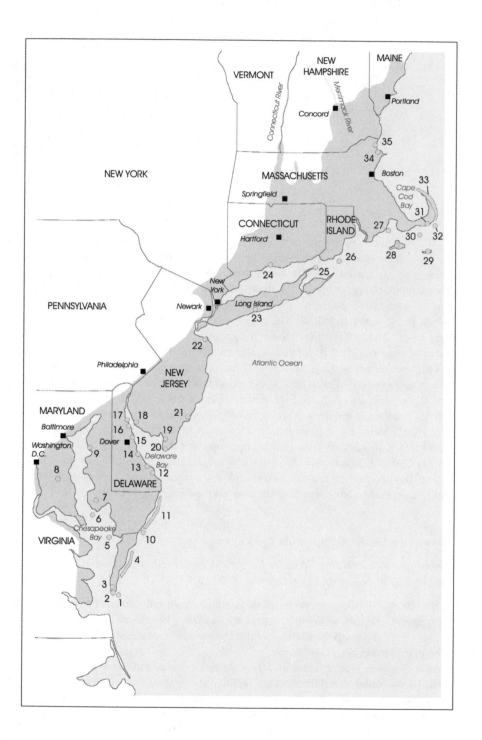

▶ Ownership: Private landowners, Commonwealth of Virginia, Virginia Department of Game and Inland Fisheries, The Nature Conservancy, Fish and Wildlife Service.

▶ Habitats: Mixed deciduous and pine forests, wax myrtle thickets, agricultural and fallow fields, salt marsh, beach, dunes, mudflats, small freshwater impoundments.

▶ Land Use: Intensive wildlife research, conservation, camping, hiking, agriculture.

▶ Site Description: Fragmented forests and agricultural fields are bordered by Chesapeake Bay and Atlantic Ocean shorelines.

▶ Birds: Similar to Cape May, the funneling effect of the narrowing peninsula, together with the hazardous water-crossing at the mouth of Chesapeake Bay, causes a concentration of millions of songbirds at the Delmarva tip during late summer and fall migration. Most are neotropical migrants; others are species that winter in the area. Tens of thousands of raptors and waterfowl also use the corridor at that season. An estimated 90 percent of the birds are only a few months old. Research on songbirds in this area has been annual since 1963, with nearly 300,000 birds banded at Kiptopeke. Research on raptors has been annual since 1977, with more than 500,000 recorded at Kiptopeke, and thousands banded at Kiptopeke and at the Eastern Shore of Virginia National Wildlife Refuge. The research at Kiptopeke was started by volunteers and since 1995, has been conducted by professional biologists hired by Coastal Virginia Wildlife Observatory.

In 1996, the observatory began late winter and spring migration research, including songbird banding, point count censusing, and breeding bird documentation, mainly at the Eastern Shore of Virginia National Wildlife Refuge. Results show that the area is also an essential migration corridor at that season for hundreds of thousands of land-birds and waterbirds.

The Delamarva tip may be the best place in the world to view migrating Merlins and Peregrine Falcons, because of the high annual numbers and close views.

In addition to the birds studied by the observatory and other groups in the area, tens of thousands of shorebirds, waterfowl, swallows, and other species migrate through the area.

▸ Conservation Issues: This small area is vulnerable to the pressures of development. Planned reduction of the fee for crossing the Chesapeake Bay Bridge–Tunnel and the subsequent development will impact the area. Development from the northern part of the peninsula has been steadily increasing as well.

Many species of songbirds have been documented to be in decline over the past several decades, mainly due to habitat loss in North, Central, and South America, making migration corridors and stopover sites like this one crucial to survival. Research to monitor populations, document changes, and encourage conservation must continue in the area.

▸ Visitor Information: Camping is permitted at Kiptopeke State Park; hiking is permitted at Kiptopeke and at the Eastern Shore of Virginia National Wildlife Refuge. Fisherman Island National Wildlife Refuge, administered by the Eastern Shore of Virginia National Wildlife Refuge, is closed to visitors, though there are organized tours to the island between October and March, when no nesting birds are present. Contact Kiptopeke State Park, 3540 Kiptopeke Drive, Cape Charles, VA 23310, 757-331-2267 and Eastern Shore of Virginia National Wildlife Refuge, 5003 Hallett Circle, Cape Charles, VA 23310, 757-331-2760. The Coastal Virginia Wildlife Observatory can be contacted at P.O. Box 111, Franktown, VA 23354.

"IF YOU BUILD IT, THEY WILL COME."

Is it possible to create an IBA intentionally? Yes—wildlife managers have been doing it for years. By building impoundments where water levels can be manipulated, and by planting fields of corn, they have attracted hundreds of thousands of migratory waterfowl to their refuges. But can it be done for other birds as well? Perhaps not so readily for old-growth forest birds—no one alive today would be around to judge the results. But how about grassland birds? Their decline is well documented and a matter of real concern.

In 1998, a conservation-minded landowner and birder, Dr. Henry Sears, approached Dr. Douglas Gill of the University of Maryland with the idea of restoring grassland on a tract of his land on the Eastern Shore. In March 1999, Dr. Gill and his students planted a 230-acre tract with nine species of native grasses, components of the native coastal warm-season grassland that once covered much of the area. The results were remarkable. Within one month of planting,

Grasshopper Sparrows—one of the target birds—arrived, in great numbers; Dr. Gill and his colleagues banded 362 of them at the end of the first season. In the second year, another of the target species—the Dickcissel—arrived and there were eight nesting pairs that year. It is doubtless just a matter of time until more of the target species—such as the Upland Sandpiper, Northern Harrier, Bobolink, and Henslow's Sparrow—turn up as well. Since the community is fire-adapted, the researchers are using fire to maintain it; the first prescribed burn was conducted on part of the site in March 2001. Now refuge managers throughout the Eastern Shore, impressed by the project's success, are beginning to convert some of the cornfields planted for wintering geese to warm-season grasses for grassland birds. The result? Bird diversity on wildlife refuges goes up, and grassland birds gain a new hold in an historic part of their range.

Chesapeake Bay IBAs, Maryland and Virginia

Smith Island Archipelago, MD (5), Fishing Bay Wildlife Management Area (Elliott Island), MD (6), Blackwater National Wildlife Refuge, MD (7), Jug Bay, MD (8), Eastern Neck National Wildlife Refuge, MD (9)

▸ Highlight: Critical migratory and wintering area for waterfowl, with significant percentages of the world's population of several species seasonally present. Prime breeding area for waterbirds such as herons.

▸ Location: A major topographic feature of the Atlantic Coast, enclosed by Maryland and Virginia.

▸ Size: With a surface area of 2,300 square miles and 5,600 miles of tidal shoreline, the bay's watershed drains 64,000 square miles in six states and the District of Columbia.

▸ Ownership: Federal, state, private.

▸ Designations: Chesapeake Bay Estuarine complex is a Ramsar site; Chesapeake Bay Reserve is a National Estuarine Research Reserve.

▸ Habitats: Open water, marshes (freshwater, brackish, and salt), tidal creeks, loblolly pine; mixed and hardwood forest.

▸ Land Use: Commercial and sport fishing, crabbing, hunting, boating, wildlife observation, shipping, urban sprawl, shoreline development.

▸ Site Description: The Chesapeake Bay is the largest estuary in the contiguous 48 states and forms a major feature along the Atlantic Coast of North America. Much of the land along the bay is private, but there are important state and federal holdings in the immediate area of the bay. Those given separate treatment are Blackwater National Wildlife Refuge, Jug Bay, Eastern Neck National Wildlife Refuge, and Fishing Bay Wildlife Management Area (Elliott Island). Many other areas on or near the bay are also important. Sandy Point State Park and Beverly-Triton Beach Park are among the several other significant protected areas, whereas the tidal portion of the Potomac River and the Choptank River are important bodies of water hosting thousands of waterfowl in the winter. Smith Island Archipelago, including the Martin National Wildlife Refuge, is a complex of low salt marsh islands with scattered small hammocks of woody vegetation, located in the bay just west of Crisfield, Maryland; these host a mixed heronry of up to 4,500 birds, plus many waterfowl that winter nearby. Hart-Miller Island has thousands of migrant shorebirds and terns, and thousands of migrant and wintering gulls and waterfowl. The Nature Conservancy's Nanjemoy Creek Great Blue Heron Sanctuary has one of the largest Great Blue Heron colonies north of Florida, plus breeding Prairie and Kentucky Warblers.

Two sites that form part of the Chesapeake are also worth special mention. One is the tidal portion of the Potomac River, a stretch of 92 miles starting just above Washington, D.C. About 60 percent of this section of the river is wooded, 25 percent is agricultural, and 15 percent is urban and/or developed. This is an important migratory pathway for landbirds and waterfowl; during the winter, up to 50,000 waterfowl use the lower Potomac. Another prime wintering and migratory stopover area for waterfowl is the brackish estuary at the mouth of the Choptank River, near Cambridge, Maryland. Among the species numbering in the thousands are the Common Loon, Horned Grebe, Tundra Swan, Canada Goose, Canvasback, Long-tailed Duck, Surf Scoter, Common Goldeneye, and Bufflehead. Many Ospreys and several pairs of Bald Eagles nest near and on the estuary.

Prairie Warbler

▶ Birds: The Chesapeake Bay is a critical migratory stopover and wintering area for waterfowl, with midwinter estimates of up to one million birds. Among its many superlatives, the bay and its surrounding lowlands seasonally support 33 percent of the Atlantic Coast Great Blue Heron population, 23 percent of the world's population of the Red-breasted Merganser, and between 15 and 20 percent of the world's population of the Common Goldeneye, Tundra Swan, and Black and Surf Scoters. In a recent survey, 3,000 Osprey nests were counted, triple the number found in the late 1960s, indicating that the species may have regained its historic numbers on the bay. Among the breeding species on the bay are the Chuck-will's-widow, Brown-headed Nuthatch, and Prothonotary and Prairie Warblers.

▶ Conservation Issues: The bay and its surroundings face a number of tough conservation problems; among them are pollution from pesticides, agricultural fertilizers, and sewage, particularly from poultry farms; urban and recreational development and an increase in recreational boating; overfishing; and oil pollution. At least in the case of pollution, there is a multistate effort to reduce the problem and restore the damaged fisheries in the bay. Shoreline erosion and invasion of marshes by *Phragmites* are also threats. Non-native Mute Swans, the population of which has exploded in the Chesapeake from five in 1962 to 4,500 today, are a concern. They are resident year-round and deplete submerged aquatic vegetation, a valuable food source for the Tundra Swan and the American Black Duck. There is a hunting season on waterfowl. The Chesapeake Bay Foundation is active in conservation in the area. A leading regional conservation group, Audubon Naturalist Society, coordinated and provided information to prepare this account.

Global climate change could have a ruinous effect on the Chesapeake and the Delaware Bays, with untold negative effects on the bird life there. New research by the University of Maryland indicates that almost all coastal marshes along the bays could disappear before 2100, if the sea level continues to rise at present rates, or the higher rates predicted by climate models. The loss of these marshes would be devastating, the researchers say, due to its effect on the food chain, water quality, and the amount of carbon that would be released into the oceans and atmosphere.

▶ Visitor Information: The Chesapeake Bay is worth a visit at any time of year; spring and fall migration are impressive, and winter is particularly rewarding.

IBAs on or near the bay are discussed below.

Fishing Bay Wildlife Management Area (Elliott Island) (6), Maryland

This is an important breeding site for the Black Rail. It is located in Dorchester County, near Vienna, and occupies 20,000 acres. It is owned by the Maryland Department of Natural Resources. Fishing Bay consists of brackish marsh habitat surrounded by estuarine waters and a loblolly pine forest. A few loblolly hammocks also occur in the marsh. Elliott Island has been called the "Everglades of Maryland," with its vast expanse of brackish marsh containing several wetland communities, especially those dominated by salt meadow cordgrass, black needle rush, and cattails. The saltmarsh habitat on Elliott Island has several imported breeding species, including the Black Rail (25 to 100 or more pairs), Seaside Sparrow (no population estimates available, but the species is abundant), and Saltmarsh Sharp-tailed Sparrow (100 plus pairs). The Black Rail, for which Elliott Island is well known, represents a significant proportion of the total population of this elusive and hard-to-observe species, probably between one to five percent, though a recent report documents a sharp drop in the number of Black Rails detected during June at the site. Brown-headed Nuthatches also occur in pinewoods near the marsh. Introduced and invasive species include *Phragmites* and nutria. Raccoons, foxes, and other predators may restrict the Black Rail population. Tapes have been regularly used by birders, and this disruptive practice may account for the fact that the rail is now not found in some habitats near the road where it was previously known. High marsh pools are ditched for mosquito control, and marsh is regularly burned. The Maryland Department of Natural Resources is making attempts to control *Phragmites* and nutria; acquisition of marsh and adjoining upland is active and ongoing.

▶ Visitor Information: For breeding marsh birds, the best time to visit is from late May to early July. Take plenty of insect repellant; wear long pants and a long-sleeved shirt. Visitors should stay on the road and not enter the marsh. Black Rails call generally between 10 p.m. and 2 a.m. Contact: Maryland Department of Natural Resources, Wildlife Division, at 410-260-8540.

Blackwater National Wildlife Refuge (7), Maryland

This is an important site for migrating and wintering waterfowl and for breeding and wintering Bald Eagles. It is located in Dorchester County, south of

Saltmarsh Sharp-tailed Sparrow

Cambridge, and occupies 22,000 acres. The refuge is owned by the Fish and Wildlife Service. The refuge is used for fishing, hunting, crabbing, wildlife observation. The refuge consists of forest (12,000 acres of loblolly pine, pine-oak, pine-hardwood, and mixed hardwood), brackish marsh (6,500 acres), tidal creeks and open water (3,000 acres), with the remaining acreage in agricultural crops left unharvested for wildlife. Up to 60,000 ducks and geese use the refuge during migration and in winter; 50 breeding adult Bald Eagles are found on the refuge, with numbers growing to as many as 200 adults and juveniles during the winter. Among the breeding birds are the Chuck-will's-widow, Prothonotary Warbler, and Saltmarsh Sharp-tailed Sparrow. A few resident Brownheaded Nuthatches also occur in the loblolly pine woods. It is also an important stopover site for migrating shorebirds. With probably the best remaining terrestrial habitat on the bay, it is also vital to migrating landbirds. A combination of sea level rise, land subsidence, saltwater intrusion, and herbivory, particularly by introduced nutria, is leading to accelerating marsh loss with consequent threats to wintering and foraging birds. Management activities include prescribed burns, suppression of wildfire, water management, and control of muskrats and nutria.

▸ Visitor Information: Spring and late fall are the best times to visit, but many species may also be seen during the winter months. Contact the refuge at 2145 Key Wallace Drive, Cambridge, MD 21613, 410-228-2677.

Jug Bay (8), Maryland

This is one of the largest freshwater tidal wetlands on the East Coast. The site is also an important staging area for migrating Soras and Virginia Rails. It is located on the Patuxent River, where Prince George's, Anne Arundel, and Calvert Counties converge, and occupies 3,000 acres. It is owned by Anne Arundel County, the Maryland Department of Natural Resources, the Maryland National Capital Parks Commission, and private owners. Jug Bay is used for recreation, research, wildlife observation, and for commercial and residential developments. Approximately 75 percent of the site as described is in public ownership, including Jug Bay Wetlands Sanctuary, Patuxent River Park, and Merkle Wildlife Sanctuary. The site is a good example of an eastern freshwater marsh system including riparian tidal wetlands, non-tidal wetlands, mixed woods, and shrub lands.

More than 4,000 migrating Soras and Virginia Rails have been known to use the area during fall migration, one of the greatest concentrations of these species anywhere. High counts of the former are in the second half of September. The site also provides habitat for migrating shorebirds and wintering waterfowl, one of the most abundant of which is the American Black Duck, though its numbers have declined here in the last several years. There is encroaching commercial and residential development in the watershed, with resulting sedimentation and runoff. This can result in a decline of wild rice and consequent negative impact on the migrating rails whose numbers have recently decreased. A further cause of decline in wild rice is a flock of 300 to 500 Canada Geese, which have taken up residence in recent years. It is estimated that current stands of wild rice in Jug Bay's marshes represent only ten percent of stands existing 30 to 40 years ago. Land managers at the marsh are working to control goose population size by coating eggs with vegetable oil, which stops embryo development. Tree and shrub planting has been initiated to increase the size of the buffers around the area.

▸ Visitor Information: Contact the sanctuary at 1361 Wrighton Road, Lothian, MD 20711, 410-741-9330.

Eastern Neck National Wildlife Refuge (9), Maryland

This is an important waterfowl concentration point, especially for the Canvasback and American Black Duck. It is located five miles south of Rock Hill, Queen Anne's County, and has 2,200 acres of land and 3,000 subtidal acres. It is owned by the Fish and Wildlife Service. The refuge is used for fishing, boating, crabbing, hunting, and wildlife observation. Eastern Neck National Wildlife Refuge is a relatively flat island with extensive intertidal wetlands. Surrounding the island are shallow coves and inlets that provide foraging and loafing areas for large numbers of waterfowl. The adjacent waters once supported extensive submerged aquatic vegetation beds that are now recovering. Habitats included mixed hardwoods and conifers, and agricultural lands used to provide forage for wintering waterfowl. In addition to more than 20,000 Canada Geese during the winter and migration, there are important populations of Greater and Lesser Scaup (20,000), Canvasback (15,000, representing 2.4 percent of the world's estimated population), American Black Duck (4,000), and sizable numbers of Ruddy Ducks and American Wigeon. Dredging for hydraulic clams in surrounding waters produces excessive turbidity and prevents growth of submerged aquatic vegetation. An increasing population of feral Mute Swans also threatens the recovery of this vegetation. Introduced *Phragmites* is also a problem; control programs are underway for both these non-native species. Erosion has been controlled on the western shore, but may need to be expanded to the northern shore.

▸ Visitor Information: Contact: Eastern Neck National Wildlife Refuge at 1730 Eastern Neck Road, Rock Hall, MD 21661, 410-639-7056.

GLOBAL WARMING AND IBAs

IBAs are already subject to many different threats. How is global warming affecting IBAs and what does the future hold? The average annual temperature in the United States has increased by 1° to 4°F (greater at higher latitudes) over the twentieth century. Precipitation has increased by more than ten percent in many parts of the country, often as heavy precipitation events that lead to flooding. The global mean sea level has already increased by four to eight inches—more in areas undergoing subsidence (e.g., South San Francisco, some Louisiana coastal areas), less in areas where land is rising (e.g., Willapa Bay NWR). Accompanying these changes have been observations of some species arriving earlier (e.g., Black-throated Blue Warblers, Rose-breasted Grosbeaks), breeding earlier (e.g., Tree Swallows, Prothonotary Warblers), and of some northward shifts in species ranges (e.g., Golden-winged Warblers, Orchard Orioles).

For IBA managers, global warming brings both immediate and future challenges. Some coastal IBAs are likely already experiencing increased erosion attributable to the rise in sea level. Even in coastal areas where few direct effects have been noted, there is an increased risk of flooding because of storm surge. Earlier arrival and breeding dates may necessitate shifts in seasonal closures or require modifying monitoring dates. Many invasive species are likely to benefit from global warming (as are many pest species such as bark beetles) necessitating increased monitoring and eradication efforts. Attention needs to be paid not only to invasive species of the IBA, but also to those located south of an IBA (or at lower elevations) that may migrate northward (or upward) with increasing temperatures (e.g., fire ants, avian malaria). Drought will likely become more prevalent in many areas, possibly leading to increased need for water management, especially to avoid disease outbreaks such as avian botulism. Drought will also likely increase the risk of fire in many cases.

Global-warming-associated threats to IBAs will almost certainly increase with time. Mid-range estimates of temperature increases in the United States are 5° to 9°F higher by the year 2100 (up to 15°F in Alaska). Even in areas with increased precipitation there will likely be reduced summer soil moisture in many parts of the country. Accompanying these changes will likely be large shifts in the ranges of many birds and their habitats, often at unequal rate. Also, as sea levels continue to rise over the next 100 years, the impacts to some IBAs will range from increased erosion and saltwater intrusion into freshwater sources to complete loss of critical shorebird migration habitats and coastal saltmarshes. Shifts in critical habitats and species' ranges may necessitate acquiring buffers around IBAs as well as managing for species "migration" to new areas.

While global warming may not be of immediate concern to IBA managers, by factoring it into future management plans the challenges it poses may be easier to tackle as problems arise.

Barrier Island IBAs of Maryland and Virginia

Virginia Coast Reserve, VA (4), Chincoteague Island National Wildlife Refuge, VA (10), Assateague Island National Seashore, MD, VA (11)

▸ Highlight: Important breeding area for Piping Plovers and colonial nesting birds; important migratory stopover for shorebirds.

▸ Designation: Wetland of International Importance in the Western Hemisphere Shorebird Reserve Network. The Virginia Coast Reserve is an International Biosphere Reserve.

▸ Location: Atlantic coast of the Delmarva Peninsula; Maryland and Virginia.

▸ Size: The Nature Conservancy's Virginia Coast Reserve is 47,000 acres, including all, or part, of 13 islands (amounting to 35,000 acres), plus an additional 12,000 acres on the adjacent mainland. The reserve amounts to about 55 miles of Atlantic coastline and includes the majority of the barrier islands off Virginia. Assateague, which is 37 miles long, is nearly 18,000 acres, with Chincoteague National Wildlife Refuge at 9,460 acres, the Assateague Island National Seashore at 7,897 acres, and nearby Assateague State Park at 680 acres. The total size of the refuge is 13,600 acres, including all or part of three other barrier islands and several islands in the Chincoteague Bay.

▸ Ownership: Fish and Wildlife Service, National Park Service, The Nature Conservancy, State of Maryland, Commonwealth of Virginia.

▸ Habitats: Tidal marshes, dunes, beach, deciduous and loblolly pine forests, shrub thickets, mudflats, impoundments.

▸ Land Use: Conservation, camping, hiking, surf-fishing, wildlife observation.

▸ Site Description: The barrier islands extend for 109 miles along the Atlantic Coast of Maryland and Virginia, from the northern end of Assateague Island, just south of Ocean City, to just north of the tip of the Delmarva Peninsula. The entire chain is a series of sandy barrier islands, with dunes and low shrubs. The islands are subject to frequent alteration by storms. Habitats on the larger islands include wide sand beaches bordered by herbaceous plant communities on the dunes, followed by shrub thickets and pine woodlands in the island's midsection, and saltmarsh at the western margin.

Red Knot

▸ Birds: The barrier islands are an important nesting area for the Atlantic Coast population of the Piping Plover. The mean number of nesting Piping Plovers in Virginia is 102 pairs, with 94 percent being found on the northern barrier islands from Assateague to Cedar Island; the largest counts are on Metompkin Island (Virginia Coast Reserve) and Assateague. In 1999, 82 pairs were counted, considerably below the mean; mammalian predators may be deterring plovers from sites on some of the southern islands in the chain. A total of 29 pairs of Wilson's Plovers were also detected. For Maryland, 55 pairs of Piping Plovers were censused in 2001, most or all of which were on the Maryland portion of Assateague Island, while the Virginia portion of the island had 25 pairs. In 2002, for Maryland, the Assateague Island breeding population was an estimated 59 to 63 pairs, which fledged 111 chicks. When monitoring began in 1986, the breeding population in Maryland was 17 pairs. The area is also important for hundreds of pairs of nesting Least Terns. A 1993 survey in Virginia indicated that the seaside barrier island/lagoon system is the state's most important region for breeding colonial waterbirds, with more than 70 percent of all breeding pairs and 23 of 24 of its colonial species.

The area is also key for migrating shorebirds. Spring surveys were conducted in a two-year study on Virginia's portion of the barrier islands, including all the islands from the state line on Assateague south to Fisherman Island. More than 100,000 observations of shorebirds were made, with peak single-day counts of more than 20,000 birds, in mid-May. Peak densities were much higher than on coastal beaches just south of the Chesapeake Bay but much lower than those reported for the Delaware Bay. The Red Knot accounted for 38.4 percent of the observations, "peeps" for 30.1 percent, Dunlin for 15.5 percent, and Sanderling for 13.9 percent. Among the highest known densities of Whimbrels in the Western Hemisphere have been recorded on the barrier islands. Estimates from the Western Hemisphere Shorebird Reserve Network are that up to 500,000 shorebirds may use the area annually, with up to 170,000 shorebirds on Chincoteague alone. In fact, of all the 600 sites surveyed in the International Shorebird Surveys, Chincoteague ranks second in species diversity during both spring and fall migrations, and is among the top ten sites with the greatest maximum counts.

Significant numbers of shorebirds winter as well, as do waterfowl, including thousands of American Black Ducks, and as many as 12,000 Brant—perhaps the highest counts for these two species on the Atlantic Coast south of New Jersey. Thousands of Snow Geese, Mallards, Northern Pintails, and other duck species are found in winter as well.

The barrier islands of Virginia are critical for breeding and wintering American Oystercatchers; 562 birds were detected during a recent breeding season, and 1,869 at roosts during the winter. These figures represent a sizable percentage of the global population of the species, which is estimated at just 7,500. In fact, a winter coastal survey of the American Oystercatcher in 2000 indicated that the system supports more than 25 percent of that species' East Coast population.

Among passerines, a few Brown-headed Nuthatches are resident in the loblolly pinewoods on Assateague. Seaside Sparrows breed on the islands, and Nelson's Sharp-tailed Sparrows winter.

▶ Conservation Issues: Among the conservation issues facing Assateague Island are heavy visitor use to parts of the island, off-road vehicle use on certain stretches of beach, overgrazing by feral ponies on the dune and salt marsh communities, and accelerated erosion along seven miles of shoreline resulting from the maintenance of inlet jetties in nearby Ocean City, Maryland. The National Park Service is working with the Army Corps of Engineers and state agencies to mitigate erosion rates. Feral ponies are being treated with fertility control to lower populations. The Assateague Coastal Trust is a citizen advocacy group, the goal of which is the protection of the island's ecosystems and biota.

As part of a long-term monitoring program for colonial waterbirds, a census is conducted on the barrier islands of the Virginia Coast Reserve every five years. Those in 1993 and 1998 revealed that five species had increased significantly, that 11 had declined, and that the total number of colonies had declined by five percent. The number of Gull-Billed, Common, and Least Tern colonies all declined in number during this period; all three nest on barrier island beaches, and their decline might be related to an increase in mammalian predators on the islands.

Because of nesting Piping Plovers, some beaches are closed to the public during the breeding season. Predator control and predator-proof enclosures around nests are used to protect the birds from foxes and raccoons. Nesting plovers are similarly protected at the Virginia Coast Reserve. Population studies on the Piping Plover and other shorebirds are currently underway involving the Fish and Wildlife Service, The Nature Conservancy, and the College of William and Mary.

The Nature Conservancy continues to work to protect the barrier islands and habitat on the adjacent mainland. It includes the whole shore south of Wallops Island within its protection program.

▸ Visitor Information: Assateague is accessible by car. Fall through spring are good for a visit. The Virginia Coast Reserve is accessible only by boat; some of the islands are closed to the public. No camping or pets are allowed. The islands of the reserve should not be visited during the nesting season (from early April to mid-August). For more information, contact: Assateague Island National Seashore, 7206 National Seashore Lane, Berlin, MD 21811, 410-641-1441; Chincoteague National Wildlife Refuge, P.O. Box 62, Chincoteague Island, VA 23336, 757-336-6122; and Virginia Coast Reserve, The Nature Conservancy, P.O. Box 158, Nassawadox, VA 23413.

HORSESHOE CRAB HARVEST

The horseshoe crab (*Limulus polyphemus*), is one of only four species of an ancient class (Merostomata) that has been in existence for 350 million years. The species occurs from Maine to the Gulf of Mexico and is most abundant in the Delaware Bay. Millions of crabs migrate from offshore to the bay to breed and lay eggs on its beaches every spring. A dozen species of shorebirds have synchronized their annual northward migration to coincide with the crab's egg laying, and to feast on eggs found on these beaches. In all, 1.5 million shorebirds use the Delaware Bay en route to their Arctic breeding grounds.

Unfortunately, the horseshoe crabs are declining due to the combined effects of shoreline development and erosion, water quality degradation, beach use by humans, and greatly increased commercial harvest. The increase in harvest is especially alarming as huge new markets have emerged which cause crabs to be used as bait for conch and eel fisheries. In the five-year period from 1991–1996, researchers estimated the horseshoe crab population in the Delaware Bay declined from one million to 300,000 crabs, and this decline continues.

Delaware Bay's shorebird populations show a corresponding decrease. Between 1986 to 1989 and 1990 to 1996, shorebird populations declined by 45 percent. Among these birds are approximately 80 percent of the hemisphere's Red Knots, as well as five other species for which Delaware Bay and its horseshoe crab eggs are considered critical for their survival in the Western Hemisphere. Significant research on multiple aspects of bay, crab, and shorebird ecology make it clear that crab and shorebird populations are on the verge of collapse.

In reaction to this crisis, most Mid-Atlantic states have taken steps to limit harvest and landings of crabs, to encourage the most efficient use of crabs as bait, and to increase education. In addition, a rectangular area extending 30 nautical miles off the mouth of the Delaware Bay has been made a horseshoe crab sanctuary. While these steps are encouraging, further conservation measures need to be taken along the Atlantic Coast, the sanctuary must be maintained, and formal monitoring must be established for the crabs and their eggs, shorebirds, and the crab harvest. In situations where a resource has become so depleted, the cost may be not just short-term economic and aesthetic loss, but also the cost of permanent vigilance.

Delaware Bay IBAs, Delaware and New Jersey

Cape Henlopen State Park, DE (12), Prime Hook Wildlife Area and National Wildlife Refuge, DE (13), Ted Harvey Wildlife Area, DE (14), Little Creek Wildlife Area, DE (15), Bombay Hook National Wildlife Refuge, DE (16), Woodland Beach, DE (17), Fortescue Wildlife Management Area, NJ (18), Cape May National Wildlife Refuge, NJ (19), Cape May Migratory Bird Refuge, NJ (20)

▸ Highlight: Over one million shorebirds congregate in the spring on the shores of the Delaware Bay, the second-greatest shorebird congregation in North America.

▸ Location: The Delaware Bay is the body of water between southern New Jersey and Delaware.

▸ Size: More than 126,000 acres of Delaware Bay wetlands were dedicated as a Wetland of International Importance in May 1992. This includes 70 sites along the Delaware Bay in New Jersey and Delaware. On the Delaware side of the bay, approximately 50 percent of the coastline, amounting to 51,054 acres of wetlands, is in state and federal ownership and thus protected. In New Jersey, some 51,910 acres of wetlands associated with the bay are in state ownership, mostly as Fish and Wildlife Management Areas.

▸ Ownership: Land ownership is mixed, with a large percentage owned by New Jersey Fish and Game, the Delaware Fish and Wildlife Departments, and the Fish and Wildlife Service. Other land is owned by local agencies, by The Nature Conservancy, and by private landowners. Land within the Shorebird Reserve Network is technically state owned, since it includes only land below the mean high-tide line.

▸ Designations: Ramsar site, Wetland of Hemispheric Importance in the Western Hemisphere Shorebird Reserve Network.

▸ Habitats: There are extensive freshwater and saltwater wetlands throughout the Delaware River and Bay estuary. The shoreline area is primarily made up of narrow, sandy beaches; some mudflats; shorefront and lowtide flats, including dunes, and sandy/muddy mouths of rivers; adjacent tidal salt marshes; and saltwater impoundments.

▸ Land Use: Recreation, wildlife observation, conservation.

▸ Site Description: Four major estuaries in North America are critical shorebird stopover areas, and each supports more than one million shorebirds during migration. These are the Bay of Fundy and the Delaware Bay on the East Coast, and Alaska's Copper River Delta and Washington's Grays Harbor on the West Coast. At these stopover areas shorebirds feed on amphipods, and can nearly double their weight before moving on. Such areas are unique in their mix of resources, and consistently support high percentages of the entire world populations of certain species. They are presumed to have played an essential role in the evolution of the migratory strategies of these birds.

Land included in the Delaware Bay is in a mix of ownerships. Federal areas under protection include Cape May National Wildlife Refuge, New Jersey, and Bombay Hook and Prime Hook National Wildlife Refuges, Delaware. New Jersey Wildlife Management Areas include Mad Horse Creek, Dix, Egg Island, Fortescue, Nantuxent, Heislerville, Dennis Creek, and Higbee Beach. Delaware Wildlife Management Areas include Woodland Beach, Little Creek, Ted Harvey, Prime Hook, and Cape Henlopen and Prime Hook Wildlife Area and National Wildlife Refuge. The Nature Conservancy has established the Cape May Migratory Bird Refuge, and has launched a multimillion-dollar fund-raising campaign for protection projects along the Delaware River Basin. Additional areas are protected by the Natural Lands Trust, New Jersey Natural Lands Trust, and the Cape May County Park Commission. These sites are treated collectively here, but Cape May is given a separate account describing its importance as an observation point for migrating passerines and hawks.

Part of the Delaware Bay is a component of Delaware's Coastal Zone, which also includes the coastal areas of the state south of Delaware Bay to the Maryland state line. This section of the state has populations of the Brown-headed Nuthatch, in addition to migrant shorebirds.

▶ Birds: Up to 200,000 Red Knots (80 percent of the Western Hemisphere population), 10,000 Short-billed Dowitchers, half the Sanderlings along the Atlantic Coast, and half the Ruddy Turnstones in North America visit the Delaware Bay shore to feed on the eggs of horseshoe crabs. The birds increase their body fat by 40 to 50 percent during the process. The Delaware Bay is the site of the largest spawning concentration of horseshoe crabs in the world. Red Knots fly 19,000 miles round-trip between their wintering and breeding grounds, relying on only a couple of "staging areas," where they stop to feed on what has nearly always been an abundant food supply. After leaving its wintering grounds in southern Argentina, the Red Knot makes only one stop on the coast of Brazil, and then flies nonstop to Delaware Bay—a distance of 5,000 miles, the majority of birds arriving at the same time—in late May. Survival depends on having plentiful food at the exact time they arrive. This plentiful food is supplied by the eggs of the spawning horseshoe crabs.

Total birds counted on beaches in aerial surveys over the six-week migration period range from 250,000 to more than 600,000 (May through mid-June). Birds observed in tidal marsh habitats are estimated at 700,000. Red Knots, Sanderlings, Ruddy Turnstones, and Semipalmated Sandpipers make up about 97 percent of the individuals of 30 species of shorebirds stopping over in the Delaware Bay. Many migratory raptors, and waders and waterfowl also use the area, including Brant and up to 200,000 Snow Geese.

▶ Conservation Issues: Harvest of horseshoe crab for eel and conch bait has rocketed in recent years, greatly reducing its populations and hence the availability of its eggs to the migrating shorebirds that depend on this food source during their passage northward in the spring. Recent research indicates that the amount of eggs had been reduced by between 41 percent and 90 percent since 1990, and the number of days eggs were available had gone from 70 in the early 1990s to only 30 by 1998. There is increasing evidence that this has affected shorebird numbers. Red Knots, for example, have declined by more than 50 percent since the 1980s, and an international team of scientists found that many Red Knots were leaving the Delaware Bay for their northern breeding grounds at below the minimum breeding body weight. Since horseshoe crabs do not reach sexual maturity until nine to ten years of age, they are very vulnerable to overexploitation. Researchers predict that if Red Knots, Ruddy Turnstones, and other migrant shorebirds are unable to continue using this resource at Delaware Bay, the entire flyway could collapse.

The Secretary of the Department of Commerce recently announced the establishment of a 1,500 square-mile horseshoe crab sanctuary at the mouth of the Delaware Bay. This area will be closed to all take of horseshoe crabs. The state of Virginia, the prime offender in the overexploitation of the animal, has capped its fishery at the required quota of 152,000 crabs. The states of Delaware, Maryland, and New Jersey have subsequently also capped their fisheries at similar levels. There had been a vigorous effort on the part of environmental organizations, including American Bird Conservancy, National Audubon Society, and 29 other organizations, to bring this about. A recent study showed that the ecotourism industry based around shorebird/horseshoe crab interactions along the New Jersey coast of Delaware Bay alone was worth more to local businesses than the entire East Coast horseshoe crab fishery.

In 2003, the states of Delaware and New Jersey closed all horseshoe crab harvesting in the Delaware Bay between May 1 and June 7. This is the peak time when the crabs come ashore to spawn, and when the shorebirds are present. This is a significant victory for the conservation not only of the horseshoe crab but of shorebird—particularly the Red Knot—as well. Delaware and New Jersey will also require the use of bait-saving devices such as bait bags, already required in Virginia. These bags can reduce crab use for bait by up to 50 percent. Restrictions will also be imposed on access to state and federal beaches during peak spawning time. This will apply to birders, beachgoers, local residents, and researchers alike. American Bird Conservancy, along with National Audubon Society and New Jersey Audubon Society, had urged New Jersey and Delaware to adopt measures to protect the horseshoe crab and the migrant shorebirds.

There are other threats in Delaware Bay. More than 1,000 oil tankers pass through the bay annually. The lower bay is an area where oil from tankers is transferred to barges and pipelines, while the upper bay is the second-largest petrochemical port in the United States. The Delaware Bay and River have the largest oil transfer port of entry on the East Coast. In the river and upper estuary, industrial land use includes chemical industries. Some of the coast of New Jersey and Delaware is heavily developed for second homes and tourism. The populations of many towns on the bay swell in the summer. Damaging disturbance by humans includes the use of all-terrain vehicles on some beaches, and dogs chasing birds.

A draft "Plan to Protect Shorebird Habitat on Delaware Bay" was first prepared at the New Jersey Division of Fish, Game, and Wildlife in 1989. The agency has been working under a management plan since 1994, one developed cooperatively among all interested groups. The plan has resulted in the formation of the Delaware Bay Shorebird Working Group that meets annually to discuss progress.

The New Jersey Division of Fish, Game, and Wildlife has cooperated with local landowners, the Fish and Wildlife Service, the Cape May County Mosquito Control Commission, and the Park Commission in a marsh restoration project to control *Phragmites* and benefit shorebirds and waterfowl. Marsh restoration by the New Jersey Division of Fish, Game, and Wildlife has progressed to include water-level control and the area was flooded in the spring of 1992. Additional marsh area has been restored to tidal flow as of 1996.

▶ Visitor Information: Best time to see the shorebirds is the last week in May. Some of the contact sites are Cape Henlopen State Park, 42 Cape Henlopen Drive, Lewes,

DE 19958, 302-645-8983; Prime Hook National Wildlife Refuge, Road #3, Box 195, Milton, DE 19968, 302-684-8419; Bombay Hook National Wildlife Refuge, 2591 Whitehall Neck Road, Smyrna, DE 19977, 301-653-6872.

Cape May National Wildlife Refuge (19), and Cape May Migratory Bird Refuge (20), New Jersey

One of North America's greatest birding hotspots, Cape May experiences fallouts of migrating birds, with counts of a single species sometimes numbering in the hundreds of thousands. It also is one of the premier hawk-watching sites in the United States. Located at the southernmost point in New Jersey, with the Atlantic Ocean on one side and Delaware Bay on the other, Cape May is 29,225 acres in size, of which 5,935 acres are public. The lands are under the ownership of the New Jersey Division of Environmental Protection, The Nature Conservancy, and private holdings and consist of primarily of tidal flats, wetlands, dunes, and scrub lands. Cape May acts as a funnel in fall migration to collect birds that often linger before setting out over 12 miles of open water of Delaware Bay. It has a history of ornithological study stretching back to John James Audubon and Alexander Wilson. This tradition survives into modern times, such that the primary land use of the area is tourism and wildlife observation. It is now home to the Cape May Bird Observatory, an important research facility for the study of bird migration. In addition to the public lands, 126 property owners are participating in a program to make sure that their backyard habitats are suitable for birds. Fallouts of migrant birds occur several times a year, sometimes including thousands of birds of a single species; 100,000 Yellow-rumped Warblers were once seen on a single fall day, and more than 500,000 American Robins were estimated to pass through in just three hours. Thousands of hawks fly over in the fall—an average of 50,000 are counted from early September to the end of November. Thousands of waterfowl are seen during migration, and in the spring, thousands of shorebirds are found there. At The Nature Conservancy's Cape May Migratory Bird Refuge there are six to eight nesting pairs of the Piping Plover. The Piping Plover nesting beach is intensively managed during the nesting season. People are kept out, dogs are banned, and the nests are enclosed with chicken wire and netting, allowing the nesting pair access while excluding predators. A threat to migrant and breeding birds alike is the number of colonies of stray cats, abandoned by their owners but fed by locals. The cats prey on migrant birds and are a particular threat to rare breeding species such as the Piping Plover and Least Tern.

▶ Visitor Information: Best times to visit are during spring migration in April and May, but particularly during fall migration from August to October, with a peak of warblers and flycatchers occurring in the last week of August and the first week of September. Among the best areas at Cape May to observe migrant birds are Cape May Point State Park, The Nature Conservancy's Cape May Migratory Bird Refuge, 609-884-2736; Higbee Beach Wildlife Management Area 609-628-2103; and Cape May National Wildlife Refuge, 24 Kimbles Beach Road, Cape May Courthouse, NJ 08210, 609-463-0994.

Edwin B. Forsythe National Wildlife Refuge (21), New Jersey

▸ Highlight: Main wintering area for the Atlantic population of the Brant.

▸ Designation: Wetland of Regional Importance in the Western Hemisphere Shorebird Reserve Network, Ramsar site.

▸ Location: Two units on the coast, north of Atlantic City.

▸ Size: 43,000 acres.

▸ Ownership: Fish and Wildlife Service.

▸ Habitats: Tidal salt marsh and meadow, impoundments, eelgrass beds, upland woods.

▸ Land Use: Hunting, fishing, crabbing, wildlife observation and conservation.

▸ Site Description: The refuge consists of two separate units, the Barnagat Division and the Brigantine Division. The latter was originally a separate refuge. Almost 90 percent of the refuge is tidal salt meadow and marsh, interspersed with shallow coves and bays. These provide important resting and feeding habitat for waterbirds. Abundant marsh vegetation provides important food and cover for wildlife. Some 5,000 acres of woodland—dominated by pitch pine, oaks, and white cedar—are also on the refuge.

▸ Birds: The eelgrass beds on the refuge support about 75 percent of the total population of Atlantic Coast Brant during the winter; this represents about 110,000 individuals out of a total estimated population of 157,000. This figure is down by eight percent from 1999, probably due to conditions on the nesting grounds. Brant are so dependent on eelgrass that the species nearly became extinct during an eelgrass blight in the 1930s. Thousands of other waterfowl are found in migration and winter as well, including up to 15 percent of American Black Ducks. Recently there were 31 pairs of Piping Plovers breeding at two sites on the units, plus 35 pairs of Least Terns and 125 pairs of Black Skimmers. In addition, Saltmarsh Sharp-tailed and Seaside Sparrows are common breeding birds. At least 57,000 shorebirds use the refuge annually.

▸ Conservation Issues: Nesting areas for the plovers, terns, and skimmers are closed to visitors during the breeding season. *Phragmites* is a problem on the refuge. Control efforts include burning in the spring and spraying once a year. Water levels in the impoundments are managed to benefit waterfowl. More than 6,000 acres of the refuge are a National Wilderness Area, including two of the few remaining undeveloped barrier beaches in New Jersey. These beaches are closed to visitors during the nesting season.

▸ Visitor Information: Best times for a visit are late March through early June, and late August through mid-December, when migrant shorebirds and waterfowl are present. Insect repellant is advisable from mid-May to mid-October. There is a wildlife drive at the Brigantine Division. Contact: Edwin B. Forsythe National Wildlife Refuge, P.O. Box 72, Great Creek Road, Oceanville, NJ 08231, 609-652-1665.

Sandy Hook Bay Complex (22), New Jersey

▸ Highlight: Largest number of breeding Piping Plovers in New Jersey; thousands of wintering waterfowl and migrating shorebirds.

▸ Location: Sandy Hook and Raritan Bays form the southeastern portion of the New

York–New Jersey Harbor between the southern shoreline of Staten Island, New York, and the northern shoreline of Monmouth County, New Jersey.

▸ Size: The inshore portion of the bays within this habitat complex is approximately 33,500 acres.

▸ Ownership: Sandy Hook is part of the Gateway National Recreation Area administered by the National Park Service. Portions of the New Jersey shoreline are owned by the Department of Defense and the New Jersey Department of Environmental Protection, while portions of the Staten Island shoreline are owned and managed by the New York City Department of Environmental Protection and New York City Parks Department. Other portions of the shoreline are a mix of public and private ownership.

▸ Habitats: Shallow estuarine open waters, sandy beach, maritime forest, salt marsh, mudflats, riparian forest.

▸ Land Use: Recreation, wildlife observation, industry, residences.

▸ Site Description: Raritan and Sandy Hook Bays receive direct inflow from three rivers and numerous smaller tributaries along the shorelines of Staten Island and New Jersey. Along the shoreline is salt marsh with lowland forests of cottonwood and sweet gum. Sandy Hook is a nine-mile sand spit extending north from New Jersey into New York Harbor. The shoreline on the ocean side is reinforced but continues to erode. Sandy beach is accreting at the northern end of the spit, with an extensive foredune vegetated with American beach grass, and extensive areas of backdune habitat toward the northern end. There are two maritime forest areas on Sandy Hook, totaling approximately 285 acres. On the back side of the spit are tidal mud, sand flats, and salt marsh.

▸ Birds: As the only undeveloped barrier beach area in the northern part of the New Jersey, Sandy Hook has the largest number of breeding Piping Plovers in the state, with 43 pairs in a recent census. Productivity of Piping Plovers there is consistently the highest in New Jersey, averaging nearly 1.5 chicks fledged per nesting pair, compared with the statewide average of about 1.0 chick fledged per nesting pair. More than 600 Least Terns have nested on Sandy Hook, as have Common Terns and Black Skimmers. The migratory and midwinter concentrations of waterfowl average more than 60,000 birds, including scaup, Canvasbacks, Brant, and American Black Ducks; the latter also breed there. Approximately 20,000 shorebirds use the area seasonally, of which about 85 percent are Sanderlings, Ruddy Turnstones, and Semipalmated Sandpipers. During migration many passerines stop by in the forest remnants, and seasonal hawk counts average nearly 5,000 birds.

▸ Conservation Issues: Despite its environmental problems, the area remains important for many bird species. Much of the upland and wetland shoreline of Raritan Bay and the watersheds of these bays have been developed for industrial, commercial, and residential uses. Industries have discharged toxins including heavy metals, and sediments in western Raritan Bay were found to be relatively toxic. Oil and chemical spills in the bays and surrounding areas are frequent. Nutrients, organic matter, and suspended solids enter the watershed from sewage treatment plants and other sources. There are proposals to construct more marinas and residential areas in the few remaining areas of undeveloped marsh and coast along the bay's south shore. The Army Corps of Engineers is evaluating the hardening of the Staten Island shoreline for flood protection. This would result in loss or degradation of the shoreline and near shore habitats.

The Hudson-Raritan Estuary was ranked by the National Oceanic and Atmospheric Administration as highest overall among estuaries sampled in contaminant concentration. Floating garbage and debris impact wildlife and the shoreline, and the use of recreational watercraft lead to disturbance and further pollution. Heavy human use of the beaches at Sandy Hook results in disturbance of nesting birds. There is increasing public pressure for more parking lots and open beach areas that would further erode what is left of natural habitats in this area.

New Jersey Audubon Society has conducted a 20-year bird-monitoring program at a network of sites along the south shore. Sandy Hook hosts some of the largest and most successful beach-nesting bird populations in the region, and protection efforts such as fencing for beach-nesting birds should be expanded.

Feral cats are threatening species such as the Piping Plover, Black Skimmer, American Oystercatcher, and Least and Common Terns while they are attempting to nest. Humane trapping of these predators is being implemented by land managers working to protect these species.

▸ Visitor Information: Best time to visit is during spring and fall migration. Contact: Gateway National Recreation Area, Public Affairs Office, 210 New York Avenue, Staten Island, NY 10305, 732-872-5970.

URBAN GREEN AREAS

Urban green areas—such as city parks and cemeteries—are often the only spots for migrant birds to alight for miles around. Surrounded by roads and buildings, they offer at least temporary respite during the long journey north or south, and birds head for them by the thousands. Resident species tend to be few, but at two seasons of the year a sharp observer can find scores of species in a single morning. Every birder has a few favorite spots like this, but some are justifiably famous for the numbers and variety of birds they attract—some far outside their normal ranges. These include Central Park in Manhattan; Prospect Park in Brooklyn; Mt. Auburn Cemetery in Cambridge, Massachusetts; Rock Creek Park in Washington, D.C.; the Magic Hedge on Chicago's Lakefront; the "Migrant Trap" in nearby Hammond, Indiana; and Golden Gate Park in San Francisco.

Just as these sites are important to birds, they fulfill an important recreational function for birders. Since many of the same people turn up in the spring and the fall, just like the birds do, these urban green areas can provide to the new and to the seasoned birder alike, a nucleus of friends and field trip companions. Many of the top birders in each region are among the regulars, and most are willing to share their knowledge and skills with those just getting started. A visit to one of these spots can be as exciting and as memorable as to one hundreds of miles away.

Long Island Piping Plover Nesting Beaches (23), New York

▸ Highlight: Critically important breeding areas for the Piping Plover on the Atlantic Coast.

► Location: Coastline of Long Island, New York.

► Size: 64 sites, each typically no more than a few acres.

► Ownership: A mix of federal, state, municipal, and private lands.

► Habitat: Barrier island beaches, tidal wetlands.

► Land Use: Primarily recreation.

► Site Description: Beaches and dune systems in a heavily settled area. The nesting habitat for the Piping Plover here requires intense management for the birds to breed successfully. The best nesting beaches are on the South Shore, but Piping Plovers also breed on beaches on the North Shore and the east end of Long Island. All the Long Island barrier beaches, tidal wetlands, coastal shoreline, and bays form a single global IBA, having a significant proportion of the Piping Plover population breeding on the East Coast.

► Birds: The New York State Department of Environmental Conservation conducts Piping Plover surveys on Long Island annually. In 1999, a total of 247 pairs were counted at 64 sites. Of these, 69 pairs were on Westhampton Island, and, of these, 39 were on Westhampton Island West. On many of these beaches the Least Tern and Roseate Tern also nest. Beaches on which the plover nests include the following (and each deserves protection as a component of the Global IBA): North Shore: Huntington and Northport Bays, Smithtown Bay/Nissequogue River Watershed, and Crane Neck to Misery Point. East End: Orient Point and Plum Island, Northwest Harbor/Shelter Island Complex, Peconic Bays/Flanders Bay, Ababonack Harbor. South Shore: Jamaica Bay (including Far Rockaway to Rockaway Point), West Hempstead Bay/Jones Beach West, Captree Island Vicinity, Fire Island, Moriches Bay, Shinnecock Bay.

► Conservation Issues: Heavy recreational use (including by ORVs) during the nesting season and increasing development present a problem for the plover. The site including Jones Beach presents interesting and challenging management issues— protecting birds at a beach heavily used by recreationists. Closing sections of beach during peak summer tourist season has caused conflicts with residents and visitors. The Nature Conservancy is managing the nesting sites there, in cooperation with New York State Office of Parks, Recreation, and Historic Preservation, and the town of Babylon. During nesting, sections of the beaches are posted and patrolled to exclude visitors. Protective wire cages, open at the top, are placed around the nests, allowing the parent birds to enter easily but protecting against predators, including dogs and cats, foxes, raccoons, and gulls. Salt marsh habitat in Jamaica Bay, utilized by many nesting and migrating birds, is vanishing at an increasing rate, as a Columbia University study shows. Aerial photographs show that 51 percent of the marshes there have disappeared since 1924, with 38 percent of that loss occurring since 1974. A recent threat to plovers comes from a group of feral cat advocates who have established feral cat colonies on a beach on Long Island's North Shore where the plovers nest. Biologists report that plover nests on that beach are surrounded by cat tracks. In addition to feeding these cats, the advocates are releasing more cats into a pristine marsh in the area and are lobbying the state for laws to protect their colonies.

► Visitor Information: Best time to visit is late May to early July. For more information, call the Long Island Chapter of The Nature Conservancy at 631-367-3225.

Stewart B. McKinney National Wildlife Refuge (24), Falkner Island, Connecticut

▸ Highlight: Important colony of Roseate and Common Terns.
▸ Location: In Long Island Sound, three miles south of Guilford, in New Haven County.
▸ Size: 4.5 acres.
▸ Ownership: Fish and Wildlife Service.
▸ Habitats: Beach, grassy areas.
▸ Land Use: Conservation, research.
▸ Site Description: The island is a unit of the Stewart B. McKinney National Wildlife Refuge. The island's management was transferred from the Coast Guard to the Fish and Wildlife Service in 1985.
▸ Birds: The site has the largest Common Tern and Roseate Tern colonies in Connecticut, and the third-largest Roseate Tern colony in the northeastern United States. Each year, 6,000 to 8,000 pairs of Common Terns, and 260 to 360 pairs of Roseate Terns nest on the island.
▸ Conservation Issues: The island's tern populations are the subject of the Falkner Island Tern Project run by Patuxent Wildlife Research Center of the Fish and Wildlife Service, Connecticut Audubon Society, The Nature Conservancy, the Little Harbor Laboratory, and the Connecticut Department of Environmental Protection. Researchers place nest boxes for Roseate Terns and conduct other nesting-habitat enhancement activities. Coastal development along the eastern seaboard has significantly reduced the amount of nesting habitat for Roseate Terns. Competition with expanding gull populations has also had an impact on nesting success. The island provides one of the last few refuges for the species on the north Atlantic seaboard.
▸ Visitor Information: The island is closed to visitors during the nesting season. For more information, contact the Refuge Manager, Stewart B. McKinney National Wildlife Refuge, P.O. Box 1030, Westbrook, CT 06498, 860-399-2513.

Great Gull Island (25), New York

▸ Highlight: Largest colony of Roseate Terns in North America.
▸ Location: In Long Island Sound, about halfway between Long Island and Block Island.
▸ Size: Seven acres.
▸ Ownership: American Museum of Natural History.
▸ Habitats: Grassland, shrub, scrub.
▸ Land Use: Conservation, research.
▸ Site Description: A small, rocky island with low vegetation.
▸ Birds: One of the most important tern nesting areas in the world, with recent counts of 1,500 pairs of Roseate and 7,700 pairs of Common Terns. Roseate Terns use the more marginal habitat. The island once housed a military facility.
▸ Conservation Issues: The area is the subject of a long-term research project on tern populations, and the site is well managed by the staff of the museum. The principal threat is the potential of oil spills.

▶ Visitor Information: The terns may be seen from a boat; the best time to visit is late May through July. For more information, contact: Great Gull Island Research Station, Helen Hays Department of Ornithology, American Museum of Natural History, Central Park West at 79th Street, New York, NY 10024, 212-769-5794.

OVERABUNDANT SPECIES

Not all species of birds are those for which we want or need to establish IBAs, no matter how numerous they might be at a particular spot. In addition to introduced bird species that compete for food and nesting sites with native birds and can act as reservoirs for disease, there are native species that present ecological problems, mostly due to their ready adaptation to human-altered landscapes and consequent exploding populations. The Brown-headed Cowbird is one of them, and its threat to some species is so dire that it merits its own sidebar. But certain gulls and geese present problems of their own.

Ring-billed and Herring Gulls

Ring-billed and Herring Gulls are scavengers that thrive on the gleanings from civilization such as are readily available at garbage dumps. These food sources have allowed gulls to expand their numbers so much that they are a threat to other colonially nesting birds such as terns and alcids by destroying nests and preying on the young. Their greatly increased numbers means increased predation pressure on the nests and young of several species of shorebirds as well. Anyone who passes by a landfill has seen the swarms of gulls heralding the arrival of the garbage trucks or following the bulldozers as they push trash from one place to another. Purely in terms of concentrations of large numbers of birds, these places might qualify as Important Bird Areas, but to name them as such would do violence to the entire IBA concept.

Snow and Canada Geese

The Snow Goose is a species that has dramatically increased its numbers in recent years. Populations counted along the St. Lawrence have gone from fewer than 3,000 in 1900, when market hunters were putting severe pressure on the species, to over 400,000 by 1990, after years of restricted hunting and the creation of reserves. Meanwhile, the mid-continent population of Snow Goose has gone from one million to 4.2 million in the last 25 years. The problem, in this case, is that too many geese means overgrazing and destruction of the slow-growing vegetation in their Arctic breeding grounds, and this can adversely affect shorebirds, which depend on the same habitat. Approximately 30 percent of the coastal salt marsh around Hudson and James Bay has been destroyed by geese, and another 30 percent has been damaged. The geese have even begun breeding in areas such as those near Churchill, Manitoba, where they had never been seen before. One reason for this goose explosion is that croplands now cover their wintering grounds in the United States, and this means a superabundant food supply from the spilled grain and planting of winter grasses. There is disagreement as to what to do to reduce the populations. Some favor an increased harvest by hunters, while others think that hunting cannot remedy the problem. In the meantime, destruction of sensitive Arctic habitats continues.

The Canada Goose has taken up residence in many urban and suburban areas where a generation or two ago it was unknown. It is particularly partial to golf courses and large lawns in parks, especially near artificial ponds; its copious droppings have become an unwelcome feature of many such landscapes. Ponds with lawns around corporate headquarters are also favorites; they are sometimes known as "corporate goose factories." There is a good business in training border collies to keep the geese in the water and thus make it impossible for them to feed nearby, ultimately driving them away. The Canada Goose can degrade natural areas as well. Rails and other birds feed on wild rice at Jug Bay, Maryland, during their journey south in the fall, but current wild rice stands in the marshes there represent only ten percent of stands existing 30 to 40 years ago. Much of the decline is due to a flock of 300 to 500 Canada Geese that has taken up residency in recent years. The Canada Goose is a species with a growing image problem.

Block Island National Wildlife Refuge (26), Rhode Island

▸ Highlight: Important migrant stopover point, particularly in the fall.
▸ Location: 12 miles off the coast of Rhode Island.
▸ Size: 6,400 acres.
▸ Ownership: Fish and Wildlife Service, Block Island Conservancy, Block Island Land Trust, Rhode Island Department of Environmental Management, The Nature Conservancy.
▸ Habitats: Dunes, beaches, shrublands, clay bluffs, freshwater ponds.
▸ Land Use: Residential, recreational, conservation.
▸ Site Description: Block Island National Wildlife Refuge is 46 acres of sandy beaches and dunes. Much of the adjacent property is managed as a conservation area by the Fish and Wildlife Service, The Nature Conservancy, and the town of New Shoreham (the incorporated name of Block Island). There are 365 freshwater ponds on the island.
▸ Birds: Spectacular flights of migrants occur in the fall, when thousands of birds on their way south alight on the island to rest and feed and, most importantly, rehydrate; the shrub-covered ponds are particularly heavily used at that time. The Piping Plover recently nested successfully on the island for the first time in 20 years. Northern Harriers and Barn Owls nest on the island and nowhere else in the state, and American Oystercatchers also breed there. In the spring and the fall, when the winds are right, many songbirds can be found. Due to Block Island's shrub habitat, the birds are much lower down and easier to see.
▸ Conservation Issues: Much of the natural habitat on Block Island has been maintained due to the protection efforts of The Nature Conservancy, Block Island Conservancy, the Block Island Land Trust, Audubon Society of Rhode Island, and the Committee for the Great Salt Pond. The town of New Shoreham, the state government, the Fish and Wildlife Service, and the Environmental Protection Agency have been

key partners in conservation on Block Island. The residents of the island have supported these efforts to a degree virtually unheard of elsewhere. In the last 20 years, the amount of permanently protected open land has increased from less than five percent to more than 30 percent.

► Visitor Information: Best time to visit is during fall migration. During the summer season the island is crowded with visitors.

There is frequent ferry service from Galilee and regular flights from Westerly, Rhode Island. Contact the refuge at P.O. Box 307, Charlestown, RI 02813, 401-364-9124, and The Nature Conservancy at 159 Waterman Street, Providence, RI 02906, 401-273-4902.

Bird Island (27), Massachusetts

► Highlight: The second-largest Roseate Tern colony in the Northeast.
► Location: Off the town of Marion in Buzzard's Bay, just west of Cape Cod.
► Size: Five acres.
► Ownership: Town of Marion.
► Habitats: Beach, grasses.
► Land Use: Wildlife conservation, historical preservation.
► Site Description: The island has a lighthouse that is no longer in use.
► Birds: More than 1,000 pairs of Roseate Terns breed here, of a world population estimated at approximately 40,000 pairs. Approximately 2,000 pairs of breeding Common Terns also occur.
► Conservation Issues: This island is well protected.
► Visitor Information: The island is best seen from a boat. Landing on the island is prohibited.

Cape Cod and Nearby Islands IBAs, Massachusetts

Martha's Vineyard (28), Nantucket (29), Nantucket Sound (30), South Chatham Beach (31), Monomoy Wildlife Refuge (32), Cape Code National Seashore (33)

► Highlight: A major breeding area for Piping Plovers on the Atlantic Coast. Thousands of shorebirds stop over during migration, and thousands of waterfowl winter in the waters off the cape and its islands.
► Location: Southeastern Massachusetts; Cape Cod is a major topographic feature along the East Coast.
► Size: About 200,000 acres.
► Land Use: Tourism, agriculture, wildlife observation and conservation.
► Ownership: Fish and Wildlife Service, National Park Service, state, county, municipal, private.
► Habitats: Beaches, dunes, salt marsh, tidal flats, pine barrens.
► Site Description: The region of Cape Cod and offshore islands has many saltwater bays, freshwater ponds, thickets, and swampy woods. Its mild winter climate means that waters remain largely open. Sites treated as part of the region are Martha's

Vineyard, Nantucket and Nantucket Sound, Monomoy National Wildlife Refuge, South Chatham Beach, and Cape Cod National Seashore.

▸ Birds: Massachusetts has more than one third of all the Piping Plovers censused on the species' East Coast breeding range, from Atlantic Canada south to North Carolina. The surrounding waters are important for the large numbers of wintering waterfowl, especially sea ducks such as the Common Eider and Long-tailed Duck. The area is also important for breeding and migrating Roseate Terns.

▸ Conservation Issues: The area attracts hundreds of thousands of visitors and summer residents during the peak season. Piping Plover nesting beaches are closed to visitors and protected during the nesting season. Massachusetts Audubon Society has played a major role in protecting and managing these nesting beaches.

Martha's Vineyard (28)

This 125-square-mile island, located in the southwestern part of Cape Code, is home to breeding Piping Plovers, thousands of migrant shorebirds and passerines, and thousands of wintering ducks. Martha's Vineyard is a popular vacation destination with extensive beaches and heathland, plus ponds, marshes, woodland, and headland cliffs. The western tip, Gay Head, rises to 170 feet and is a good place to observe migrating birds. The island is in state and private ownership. Many sea ducks are found offshore during winter. Thousands of migrant songbirds can be seen in the fall from Gay Head, including vagrants from the West, as well as many migrating Merlins and Peregrine Falcons. As elsewhere around the Cape and islands, many Roseate Terns gather offshore in the fall, and thousands of shorebirds stop during migration. Short-eared Owls are found commonly from October to April. Public land on the island includes the 4,500-acre Manuel F. Correllus State Forest, where Prairie Warblers breed. Up to 30 pairs of the watch-listed Barn Owl nest in nest boxes put up at the Felix Neck Wildlife Sanctuary. In 2000, 47 breeding pairs of the Piping Plovers were censused. There is the threat of oil spills from shipping; the island receives very heavy tourist use, especially in the summer.

▸ Visitor Information: Fall through spring is good for a visit. For ferry schedules, contact the Steamship Authority at 508-477-8600 or 508-693-9130.

Nantucket (29) and Nantucket Sound (30)

Many ducks winter in the waters around Nantucket, including up to 250,000 Long-tailed Ducks. The Piping Plover nests there. Nantucket lies approximately 20 miles south of Cape Cod, with Nantucket Sound intervening. The island and sound cover approximately 700 square miles. The island is largely privately owned, with some protected lands. Nantucket is a popular destination for vacationers during the summer, and its many miles of beaches attract thousands of visitors. Much of the interior is grassland and heathland, with few trees, though there is a forest at the easternmost part of the island. There are also several commercial cranberry bogs. Three conservation organizations protect more than 1,600 acres and nearly 18 miles of shoreline. The largest portion of protected lands is Coskata-Coatue Wildlife Refuge, owned by the Trustees of Reservations. It has 1,117 acres of beach, dunes, estuary, and woodlands. Breeding and migrant Roseate, Common, and Least Terns are found on Nantucket, and many migrant landbirds stop over, particularly in fall. Approximately 44 pairs of Piping Plovers bred on Nantucket and adjacent Tuckernuck Island in 2000. Large rafts of all three scoters and Red-breasted Mergansers occur in winter, and the waters around Nantucket are also important to sea ducks, including Common Eiders. From December to March, as many as 250,000 Long-tailed Ducks fly out of Tuckernuck Channel each dawn and return at dusk. The American Black Duck breeds on the island, and thousands of shorebirds occur during migration. The primary potential threat is from oil spills from shipping. There is increasing development for summer and permanent residences on the island. One problem is a rookery of Herring and Great Black-backed Gulls, which has grown considerably in the last few years, drawn by local garbage dumping, since restricted. These gulls occupy much of the potential breeding area for shorebirds and prey on the young of those that do attempt to nest there. A plan to site a wind turbine farm on Nantucket Shoals also has the potential to impact the shorebirds.

▸ Visitor Information: Best time to visit is March through November, though the spectacular morning and evening flights of Long-tailed Ducks occur in midwinter. Nantucket is accessible by ferry from Hyannis. For those wishing to take a car to the island, reservations on the ferry are essential. Round-trip passage for a car is between $200 and $320, depending on the season, but rental cars and bicycles are available on the island.

South Chatham Beach (31)

Located adjacent to Monomoy and part of the same system, South Beach is a new beach, in effect, created by the blizzard of 1978, when North Beach was breached. Like Monomoy, South Beach is an important site for migrating shorebirds and breeding and migrating Roseate Terns. In 2000, there were 34 breeding pairs of Piping Plovers there. Nesting beaches for the plover and tern are managed by Massachusetts Audubon.

Monomoy National Wildlife Refuge (32)

This 2,710-acre Fish and Wildlife Service refuge is a designated Wetland of Regional Importance in the Western Hemisphere Shorebird Reserve Network. It consists of two barrier islands off the southern coast of Cape Cod; the eastern side of the islands faces the Atlantic Ocean while the western side faces Nantucket Sound. Much of the eastern side of the islands is open sandy beach, with salt marsh and tidal flats on the west. As is the case with barrier islands, the system of which Monomoy is a part, is unstable and rapidly changing. When the refuge was established in 1944, the two islands were a continuous barrier spit attached to Morris Island; in 1958, it became separated from Morris Island, and, in 1978, as the consequence of a severe storm, what had been one island became the two that exist today. North Monomoy is about 1.5 miles long, while South Monomoy is about six miles long. It is part of the same system as South Chatham Beach (see separate account on page 329).

The refuge is extremely important as a shorebird stopover site in July to September, when thousands of shorebirds of many species feed at low tide on the tidal flats and then fly to their roosts elsewhere on the island at high tide. Good numbers of Hudsonian Godwits stop regularly at the refuge in the course of their migration between Hudson Bay and Argentina, and the largest concentrations of roosting Whimbrels, up to 600 individuals, occur on North Monomoy. Annual counts of shorebirds reach close to 40,000 birds. Thousands of Roseate Terns gather here in the fall—a major percentage of the entire population of this species.

This is also an important breeding site for several species, though predation pressure on tern colonies limits them to secure offshore islands. Willet and American Oystercatchers breed successfully there, and the numbers of breeding Piping Plovers have increased in recent years, with 31 pairs present in 2000, of which 29 pairs are on South Monomoy. The Saltmarsh Sharp-tailed Sparrow nests in the marshes, and there are colonies of Roseate and Common Terns, in addition to colonies of Black-crowned Night-Herons and Snowy Egrets. The waters around Monomoy host hundreds of thousands of ducks, which feed on blue mussels. This includes up to 500,000 Common Eiders, and significant numbers of Long-tailed Ducks, all three species of scoters, and Red-breasted Mergansers.

Approximately 90 percent of the refuge is a designated Wilderness Area. The Black-crowned Night-Heron is a leading predator on nesting colonies of Common and Roseate Terns, Black Skimmers, and Laughing Gulls. Mammalian predators are absent on the two islands, having been eradicated by the Fish and Wildlife Service, but Great Horned and Short-eared Owls take chicks of the terns and other colonial nesting species. In recent years, the Fish and Wildlife Service has removed Herring and Greater Black-backed Gulls from parts of the refuge to foster nesting success of Common and Roseate Terns. Though this policy stirred much controversy, it has considerably augmented the tern population.

▶ Visitor Information: There are ferries to the islands in the summer, and Massachusetts Audubon Societies, the Cape Cod Museum of Natural History, and Brookline Bird Club offer guided tours. For more information, contact refuge headquarters at Morris Island, Chatham, MA 02633, 508-945-0594.

Cape Cod National Seashore (33)

Located between Provincetown and Chatham on outer Cape Cod, Cape Cod National Seashore is made up of a 40-mile-long stretch of pristine sandy beach, dozens of clear, deep, freshwater kettle ponds, and uplands, totaling 43,557 acres.

The national seashore is an important breeding area for Piping Plovers, with 96 pairs censused in 2000. The area receives extremely heavy use by visitors in the summer. Off-road vehicle use is restricted to limited portions of the outer beach of the national seashore and a seasonal permit is required. Piping Plover nesting sites are protected during the breeding season. There are indications that beach use by pedestrians near plovers, if managed by roping the nest sites, does not seriously disturb the birds and may even reduce the effects of diurnal predation.

▶ Visitor Information: For more information, contact: Cape Cod National Seashore, 99 Marconi Site Road, Wellfleet, MA 02667, 508-349-3785.

Crane Beach (34) and Parker River National Wildlife Refuge (35), Massachusetts

▶ Highlight: Breeding area for the Piping Plover and important stopover site for migrating shorebirds.
▶ Designation: Wetland of Regional Importance in the Western Hemisphere Shorebird Reserve Network.
▶ Location: Northeastern corner of the state, in Essex County.
▶ Size: Parker River National Wildlife Refuge is 4,662 acres, and Crane Beach and nearby properties total 2,000 acres.
▶ Ownership: Fish and Wildlife Service, Trustees of Reservations.
▶ Habitats: Beach and dune systems, shrubland, tidal salt marsh, impoundments.
▶ Land Use: Conservation, recreation.
▶ Site Description: Parker River National Wildlife Refuge and Crane Beach, the latter owned by the Trustees of Reservations, lie on opposite sides of Ipswich Bay and Plum Island Sound. The refuge occupies much of Plum Island; at the southern tip of the island is Plum Island State Park.
▶ Birds: This is an important breeding area for the Piping Plover and Least Tern. In 2000, there were 13 breeding pairs of the plover. Up to 40,000 shorebirds use the area seasonally. Parker River also provides habitat for the American Black Duck. At Crane Beach, numbers of plovers rose from only five pairs in 1986 to 46 in 2000.
▶ Conservation Issues: At Crane Beach, which includes the entire ecosystem of Castle Neck, there is an active program to protect the Piping Plover by exclosures around nests, to prevent predation and disturbance by humans. These measures, together with the banning of off-road vehicle use, have led to a dramatic increase in the number of birds in recent years. At Parker River, visitors are limited to boardwalks in the dune areas, to protect this fragile system. There is also salt marsh restoration there and controlled burning, in addition to plant control. Water levels in the impoundments are manipulated. The refuge is heavily visited by birders.
▶ Visitor Information: Best time to visit is late May through early July and in August and September. Contact: Parker River National Wildlife Refuge, 261 Northern Boulevard, Plum Island, Newburyport, MA 01950-4315, 978-465-5753; for Crane Beach, contact the Trustees of Reservations, Long Hill, 572 Essex Street, Beverly, MA 01915, 978-412-2590.

31. Peninsular Florida

The northern portion of peninsular Florida is a transitional zone where the pine and bottomland hardwood elements of the Coastal Plain begin to merge with the tropical elements of south Florida. Many of the important pine and bottomland birds of the Coastal Plain, including the Red-cockaded Woodpecker and Swallow-tailed Kite, extend into this area. The central scrub oak Lake Wales Ridge is a center of endemism that includes most of the world's Florida Scrub-Jays. Colonies of Wood Storks, Glossy Ibis, and other herons and egrets are found throughout the region, while coastal islands support important continental breeding populations of the Brown Pelican, various terns, and the Black Skimmer. Farther south, in the subtropical zone of the state, normally frost-free climate creates conditions for mangroves, everglades, and tropical hammocks, tying this area more closely to the Bahamas and Caribbean than to the rest of the United States. Snail Kites, Short-tailed Hawks, and Limpkins breed in interior wetlands, with Mangrove Cuckoos and Black-whiskered Vireos in coastal mangroves. One of the greatest wading-bird concentrations in the world is in the Everglades. White-crowned Pigeons inhabit the Florida Keys, and the only Brown Noddy, Sooty Tern, and Magnificent Frigatebird breeding site in the country is on the Dry Tortugas. Wintering waterfowl abound in coastal waters, including large numbers of Lesser Scaup, Ring-necked Ducks, and Green-winged Teal. Three species of waterfowl, the endemic Florida subspecies of the Mottled Duck, Wood Duck, and Fulvous Whistling-Duck, also breed in the area. Most of the remaining nesting Snowy Plovers in the Southeast occur along Florida's Gulf Coast. Extraordinary numbers of wintering and migratory shorebirds also use the region, particularly Short-billed Dowitchers, but also Piping Plovers, Dunlin, and Red Knots.

Lower Suwannee National Wildlife Refuge (1), Florida

- ► Highlight: An important stopover for migrating and wintering waterfowl and shorebirds; roosts of thousands of herons, egrets, and ibis.
- ► Location: Mouth of the Suwannee River, in Dixie and Levy Counties.
- ► Size: 52,935 acres.
- ► Ownership: Fish and Wildlife Service.
- ► Habitats: Salt marsh, tidal flats, streams, cypress swamps, upland pine forest.
- ► Land Use: Wildlife conservation, recreation.

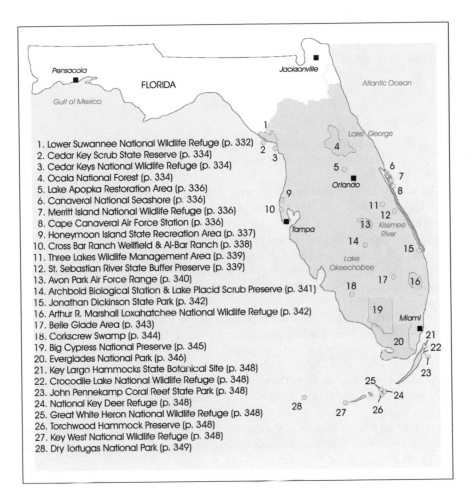

1. Lower Suwannee National Wildlife Refuge (p. 332)
2. Cedar Key Scrub State Reserve (p. 334)
3. Cedar Keys National Wildlife Refuge (p. 334)
4. Ocala National Forest (p. 334)
5. Lake Apopka Restoration Area (p. 336)
6. Canaveral National Seashore (p. 336)
7. Merritt Island National Wildlife Refuge (p. 336)
8. Cape Canaveral Air Force Station (p. 336)
9. Honeymoon Island State Recreation Area (p. 337)
10. Cross Bar Ranch Wellfield & Al-Bar Ranch (p. 338)
11. Three Lakes Wildlife Management Area (p. 339)
12. St. Sebastian River State Buffer Preserve (p. 339)
13. Avon Park Air Force Range (p. 340)
14. Archbold Biological Station & Lake Placid Scrub Preserve (p. 341)
15. Jonathan Dickinson State Park (p. 342)
16. Arthur R. Marshall Loxahatchee National Wildlife Refuge (p. 342)
17. Belle Glade Area (p. 343)
18. Corkscrew Swamp (p. 344)
19. Big Cypress National Preserve (p. 345)
20. Everglades National Park (p. 346)
21. Key Largo Hammocks State Botanical Site (p. 348)
22. Crocodile Lake National Wildlife Refuge (p. 348)
23. John Pennekamp Coral Reef State Park (p. 348)
24. National Key Deer Refuge (p. 348)
25. Great White Heron National Wildlife Refuge (p. 348)
26. Torchwood Hammock Preserve (p. 348)
27. Key West National Wildlife Refuge (p. 348)
28. Dry Tortugas National Park (p. 349)

▶ Site Description: The refuge is part of one of the largest undeveloped river delta-estuarine systems in the United States. It contains the mouth and more than 20 miles of the Suwannee River, which rises in the Okeefenokee Swamp. The refuge also administers nearby Cedar Keys National Wildlife Refuge, which consists of 13 offshore islands, totaling 800 acres.

▶ Birds: Thousands of shorebirds pass through during migration, and thousands of Redheads and other ducks winter here. There is a roost of up to 20,000 herons, egrets, and ibis of several species. The Swallow-tailed Kite and Chuck-will's-widow are common breeding species. There is a remnant population of the Florida Scrub-Jay located on private lands nearby, and sometimes the birds cross onto the refuge. Cedar Keys National Wildlife Refuge has a mixed colony of herons, egrets, and ibis of some 3,650 pairs; the refuge once supported an average of 25,000 pairs. Several thousand shorebirds are found in winter on Cedar Key.

▶ Conservation Issues: Plantations of slash pine are being thinned out or reforested with native longleaf pine.

▶ Visitor Information: Best time to visit is fall through spring. Biting insects can be abundant, especially during the summer. Much of the refuge is inaccessible to cars. Contact the refuge at 16450 N.W. 31st Plaza, Chiefland, FL 32626, 352-493-0238.

Cedar Key Scrub State Reserve (2) and Cedar Keys National Wildlife Refuge (3), Florida

▶ Highlight: Northernmost population of the Florida Scrub-Jay on the Gulf Coast.
▶ Location: Six miles northeast of Cedar Key on State Route 24.
▶ Size: 5,028 acres.
▶ Ownership: State of Florida; the property is managed by the Division of Recreation and Parks, the Fish and Wildlife Conservation Commission, and the Division of Forestry.
▶ Habitats: Salt marsh, pine flatwoods, sand-pine scrub.
▶ Land Use: Hunting, saltwater fishing, wildlife conservation.
▶ Site Description: Most of the reserve is low and flat, but relict dune ridges on the western edge rise to 30 feet above sea level and are covered with sand pine scrub and scrubby flatwoods.
▶ Birds: There is a small, isolated population of the Florida Scrub-Jay in the area, some 50 miles from the nearest populations near Ocala. In 1998, there were 17 family groups (approximately three birds per group) in the area, but only one is on the state reserve proper, the others being on adjacent private lands, including a junkyard and an as-yet-undeveloped scrub area. The population has been reduced to its present numbers by fire exclusion. This population is in imminent danger of extirpation.
▶ Conservation Issues: Prescribed burning has not been possible in recent, very dry years, but will be implemented if weather conditions allow. There has been some mechanical removal of vegetation to create habitat for the jay. The state also plans to add additional acreage to the reserve.
▶ Visitor Information: Fall through spring is best for a visit. Contact: Cedar Key Scrub State Reserve, P.O. Box 187, Cedar Key, FL 32625, 352-543-5567.

Ocala National Forest (4), Florida

▶ Highlight: Site with the greatest numbers of the threatened endemic Florida Scrub-Jay.
▶ Location: North-central Florida, east of Ocala.
▶ Size: 382,664 acres.
▶ Ownership: Forest Service.
▶ Habitats: Xeric oak scrub with scattered slash and sand pines, longleaf pine flatwoods, freshwater springs, pothole marshes, sinkhole lakes.
▶ Land Use: Forestry, recreation.
▶ Site Description: Ocala National Forest contains the largest concentration of sand pine in the world. This sand-pine scrub grows on deep, prehistoric sand dunes, which form an important recharge area for the Florida aquifer. In addition, the forest also has freshwater springs, pothole marshes, and sinkhole lakes. Within the sand pine scrub landscape there are islands of longleaf pine savannah.

▶ Birds: Ocala National Forest has the largest population of the state endemic Florida Scrub-Jay, a threatened species strictly limited to fire-maintained, low-growing oak scrub, with a ground cover of saw and sand palmetto, and scattered slash and sand pines. The scrub habitat is best for the birds from five to 15 years after a fire, but after about 20 years it becomes unsuitable. Because of fire suppression and extensive development, the scrub habitat in Florida has severely declined, resulting in a dramatic decline in the jay population, estimated now at only a few thousand breeding pairs, no more than ten percent of its presettlement numbers. Ocala maintains an active burn program to assure that adequate habitat for the species continues to exist. The number of jays has increased from 697 groups in 1994 to 763 groups in 2000.

In addition to the jay, the count of Red-cockaded Woodpeckers in 2000 was 22 clusters, up from 12 in 1991. There are also several other species in the forest, including the Bachman's Sparrow, Brown-headed Nuthatch, Chuck-will's-widow, Wood Stork, and Short-tailed Hawk.

▶ Conservation Issues: The forest plans at Ocala involve intensive management and monitoring of the jay. The goal for the jay is to maintain a dynamic system of 45,000 to 55,000 acres of suitable habitat, with a ten-year population objective of 742 to 907 groups. The forest plans also involve management by use of prescribed burns to maintain and increase the numbers of the endangered woodpecker, found on the "islands" of longleaf pine savannah within the xeric scrub. At present, managers burn up to 50,000 acres per year, more than on any other national forest. Off-road vehicles are a problem in the forest. In October 2002, the Forest Service closed 7,000 acres of Ocala National Forest to off-road vehicles. This will remain in effect until a decision is reached on the ongoing access designation process, dealing with motorized vehicle access in the national forests. According to Defenders of Wildlife, illegal trails in parts of the forest have increased by 20 percent over a period of 11 months. Illegal mud bogging and off-road vehicle activities have torn up, and, in many cases, destroyed 80 percent of the ecologically important wet prairies and isolated wetlands in surveyed areas of the Ocala. Off-road vehicle users run over and crush birds, salamanders, and plants, and they damage scientific study sites and restoration areas. Off-road vehicle users are also displacing hikers, campers, and other less destructive recreationists, and disturbing wildlife and degrading habitat. Law enforcement has been underfunded and lax in the forest. Unless controlled and eventually eliminated, off-road vehicle use could present a severe threat to the values the forest has to birds.

The reach of this IBA might be expanded to include lands adjacent to the forest, also of conservation value to the scrub-jay and other species. The state has already acquired several thousand acres of scrub and other habitat bordering Ocala and is working to protect more. These lands contain significant numbers of Florida Scrub-Jays, though the numbers there have decreased sharply since fire suppression has resulted in succession to habitat unsuitable for the bird. There is the potential that management will in time create habitat capable of supporting as many as 100 additional scrub-jay groups.

▶ Visitor Information: Since the jay and woodpecker are resident species, they may be seen any time of year, but the summer months are hot, and October through April is more favorable for a visit. Ocala's Hopkins Prairie is one of the best places for observing Florida Scrub-Jays. Contact: National Forests in Florida, Woodcrest Office Park, 325 John Knox Road, Suite F-100, Tallahassee, FL 32303, 904-942-9300.

Lake Apopka Restoration Area (5), Florida

▸ Highlight: Thousands of shorebirds and ducks use the area during migration and winter.

▸ Location: Lake and Orange Counties, near Apopka.

▸ Size: Approximately 18,000 acres.

▸ Ownership: St. Johns River Water Management District.

▸ Habitats: Marshes, lake, pine flatwoods, scrub, former farm fields being restored as shallow marsh.

▸ Land Use: Conservation, water filtration to improve water quality in Lake Apopka.

▸ Site Description: The area is one of former farm fields now being restored as habitat for migrating shorebirds and other birds after purchase by the state. Due to agricultural runoff, Lake Apopka was reportedly Florida's most polluted body of water.

▸ Birds: The area seasonally hosts thousands of shorebirds, waterfowl, wading birds, and migrant passerines, particularly swallows. At least one group of Florida Scrub-Jays remains in scrub near the edge of the property. The state's first breeding record of the Dickcissel occurred in 1999 in fallow fields of the Restoration Area.

▸ Conservation Issues: Pesticide residues in the soil were the probable cause of a recent die-off of American White Pelicans at and near the site. As a result, fields were drained by early 1999 and have remained dry. Following management recommended by Audubon of Florida, in the future land managers plan to create a permanent Shorebird Management Area on the site, consisting of a mosaic of habitats, including shallow-flooded fields, others left fallow, and others kept as bare ground. Human disturbance of the area should be kept at a minimum, meaning a ban on hunting, boating, and dogs. Prescribed burning is recommended to manage scrub for the Florida Scrub-Jay.

▸ Visitor Information: Best time to see the migrating shorebirds is from August to October. Contact: St. Johns River Water Management District, P.O. Box 1429, Palatka, FL 32178, 386-329-4500.

Canaveral Seashore IBAs, Florida

Canaveral National Seashore (6), Merritt Island National Wildlife Refuge (7), and Cape Canaveral Air Force Station (8)

▸ Highlight: One of the larger populations of Florida's only endemic bird species, the Florida Scrub-Jay.

▸ Location: Atlantic Coast near Titusville.

▸ Size: 212,000 acres.

▸ Ownership: NASA (managed by the Fish and Wildlife Service), National Park Service, Air Force.

▸ Habitats: Brackish estuaries and marshes, coastal dunes, coastal strand, oak scrub, pine forests and flatwoods, palm and oak hammocks.

▸ Land Use: Military, NASA facility, wildlife conservation, recreation.

▸ Site Description: Merritt Island National Wildlife Refuge is a 139,000-acre overlay of the John F. Kennedy Space Center; this means that while NASA owns the land, the Fish and Wildlife Service manages much of it. Adjacent to it are the Canaveral National Seashore (57,600 acres) and the Cape Canaveral Air Force Station (15,400 acres). The refuge administers Archie Carr National Wildlife Refuge, Lake Wales Ridge National Wildlife Refuge, Pelican Island National Wildlife Refuge, and St. Johns National Wildlife Refuge as part of the complex. The 24-mile-long national seashore is the longest stretch of undeveloped beach on Florida's Atlantic Coast. The Air Force administers Patrick Air Force Base, Cape Canaveral Air Force Station, Malabar Tracking Annex, Jonathon Dickinson Missile Tracking Annex, Antigua Air Station, and Ascension Island Auxiliary Airfield.

▶ Birds: The Florida Scrub-Jay is resident on this complex of sites; the species is extremely sedentary and birds rarely wander more than a few miles from where they hatched. Wood Storks and Reddish Egrets occur on the refuge; the former, which now winters there, used to breed but has not done so since a freeze in the late 1980s killed much of the mangrove community. Up to 200,000 waterfowl winter in the area. The American Wigeon, Lesser Scaup, and Green-winged Teal are the most abundant species. Other species include the Mottled Duck, Redhead, Willet, Brown Pelican, Least Tern, Black Skimmer, Wilson's Plover, Black Rail, and breeding Chuck-will's-widow. The Bachman's Sparrow is a rare resident also recorded as a breeding species. Up to several thousand wading birds visit seasonally, and the area is important for wintering and migrating shorebirds.

▶ Conservation Issues: About ten years ago there were some 400 groups of scrub-jays found on the refuge with another 100 or so groups on Cape Canaveral Air Force Station, to which public access is limited, and about 20 groups on Canaveral National Seashore. (Cape Canaveral Air Force Station numbers have remained stable over the years, with 111 groups in 2001.) The cause of the decline is probably due primarily to habitat succession because of 40 years of fire suppression, and a suspected viral disease that struck the state in 1994 and impacted the entire scrub-jay population. At present, some new habitat is being created for the species by clearing areas with heavy equipment followed by controlled burning. Water levels within the refuge's 76 impoundments are managed for wading birds, shorebirds, and other native species of plants and wildlife. Non-native invasive plants such as the Brazilian pepper are managed through chemical and mechanical control. The refuge area is subject to intense development pressure, bringing with it pollution and recreational overuse, including disturbance to the birds by watercraft. Management of the national seashore and the air station is similar to that at the refuge (the Air Force spends approximately $500,000 per year for scrub habitat restoration; since 1998, more than 1,100 acres of scrub habitat have been mechanically cut and burned); the scrub-jay population has remained stable over the last several years. Merritt once had one of the only two populations of the now extinct Dusky Seaside Sparrow; mosquito control measures were a factor in its demise.

▶ Visitor Information: Best time to visit is fall through spring. Contact: P.O. Box 6504, Titusville, FL 32782, 321-861-0667.

Honeymoon Island State Recreation Area (9), Florida

▶ Highlight: One of the most important wintering areas in the eastern United States for the endangered Piping Plover.

▶ Location: Near Dunedin, on the Gulf Coast, in Pinellas County.

▸ Size: 408 acres.
▸ Ownership: Florida Department of Environmental Protection.
▸ Habitat: Marshes, beach, sand spits, pinewoods, mangroves.
▸ Land Use: Recreation.
▸ Site Description: Sand spits at this state recreation area provide habitat for many shorebirds at low tide. Marshy areas and stands of pine are among the other habitats on the island, reached by causeway. This site is part of the largest undeveloped dune and beach system left along the peninsular Gulf Coast.
▸ Birds: Snowy and Wilson's Plovers breed on the island beaches, and Saltmarsh Sharp-tailed Sparrows breed in the marshes. The northern end of the sand spit at the northern end of the beach has a great concentration of shorebirds during most of the year, including as many as 110 Piping Plovers in winter, along with significant numbers of wintering Snowy and Wilson's Plovers.
▸ Conservation Issues: The area receives considerable recreational use. Parts of the beach are posted to protect bird nesting and roosting areas.
▸ Visitor Information: Best time to visit is fall through spring. Contact: Honeymoon Island State Recreation Area, c/o Gulf Islands Geopark, 1 Causeway Boulevard, Dunedin, FL 34698, 727-469-5942.

Cross Bar Ranch Wellfield and Al-Bar Ranch (10), Florida

▸ Highlight: Important regional population of the Florida Scrub-Jay.
▸ Location: North-central Pasco County.
▸ Size: 16,115 acres of public land.
▸ Ownership: Pinellas County Utilities, private.
▸ Habitats: Oak hammock, overgrown xeric oak scrub, pine plantations, seasonal wetlands, pastureland, gallberry/fetterbush/saw palmetto community.
▸ Land Use: Wellfield, buffer area, cattle ranching.
▸ Site Description: The site includes not only the 12,023 acres of the wellfield and the 4,100-acre Al-Bar Ranch, both owned by Pinellas County Utilities (the county where Tampa is located), but also four surrounding private cattle ranches.
▸ Birds: A regionally significant and probably isolated population of the Florida Scrub-Jay occurs on the county-owned land and on several adjacent private cattle ranches. A scrub restoration project is underway at Al-Bar Ranch. In a survey conducted by Audubon of Florida in spring 2000, only four or five groups of jays were found on site, with 17 groups found on four adjacent ranches. Since the owners of one ranch refused access to the surveyors, there may be more, particularly since aerial photography indicates that good habitat for the jay exists on much of the southern half of that property. Though the relative numbers of jays here is low, the site has potential under proper management and is important for the conservation of the species. This population also indicates the precarious situation it faces on private lands.
▸ Conservation Issues: Most scrub habitats used by jays are extremely overgrown from decades of fire suppression, and most oak scrub in the area has succeeded to oak hammock, habitat unsuitable for the jay. Currently the jay is found in patches of gallberry/fetterbush/saw palmetto, which is a marginal habitat for the species. This indicates that the adjacent oak habitats are clearly suboptimal. Subpopulations of fewer than ten groups of jays are thought to be doomed to extirpation if isolated from immi-

gration. Pinellas County has designated a management area for the jay of about 1,500 acres on the Al-Bar Ranch, but much of this acreage is unsuitable even as short-term habitat. Habitat restoration has begun in the approximately 400 acres of oak in the management area. Audubon of Florida has set up vegetation transects within the management area. Surrounding habitat will be cut by chain saw and burned to create conditions to allow the bird to survive there.

▶ Visitor Information: The ranches are open to groups by prior appointment only, and then only with a Utilities employee escort. Pinellas County Utilities can be contacted at 727-464-3438.

Three Lakes Wildlife Management Area (11), Florida

▶ Highlight: Breeding Red-cockaded Woodpeckers and Florida Scrub-Jays.
▶ Location: Southern half of Osceola County, west of U.S. 441 and north of S.R. 60, about 25 miles southeast of St. Cloud.
▶ Size: 61,835 acres.
▶ Ownership: Florida Game and Freshwater Fish Commission.
▶ Habitats: Sand pine scrub, scrubby flatwoods, xeric oak scrub, xeric prairie.
▶ Land Use: Hunting, recreation, grazing, timbering, conservation of endangered, threatened, and rare species and communities, natural flood storage area.
▶ Site Description: This site is on the Kissimmee Prairie. Some 95 percent of the vegetation on the site is native. The site includes the Prairie Lakes Unit at 8,859 acres, contiguous to Three Lakes Wildlife Management Area at 52,976 acres; the former is subject to different hunting regulations and is the site of much of the recreation on the area. There are numerous small patches of scrub on the site.
▶ Birds: The site has 52 active clusters of the Red-cockaded Woodpecker, as well as Brown-headed Nuthatch and Bachman's Sparrow. The most recent census of the Grasshopper Sparrow is 280 birds. Two pairs of Florida Scrub Jays were recently discovered on the area. The Crested Caracara is also found there. This and nearby areas are sites of release for captive-raised Whooping Cranes in a program to establish a self-sustaining, non-migratory population of this endangered species.
▶ Conservation Issues: The site was purchased by the state in 1974, under the Environmentally Endangered Lands Program. Management for both the woodpecker and the jay includes prescribed burning; approximately 10,000 to 15,000 acres are burned each year. All the adult woodpeckers are banded, as part of a demographic study. Management to create habitat for the jay also involves mechanical removal of vegetation. The state recently acquired 2,100 acres of inholding, and plans to acquire other land to add to this wildlife management area. Grazing and selective timbering are permitted in some areas, while other areas are closed to such uses.
▶ Visitor Information: Best time to visit is fall through spring. For further information, contact: Florida Game and Freshwater Fish Commission, 1239 Southwest 10th Street, Ocala, FL 34474, 352-732-1225 or 407-436-1818.

St. Sebastian River State Buffer Preserve (12), Florida

▶ Highlight: The site has a significant population of Florida Scrub-Jays, in addition to a few clusters of Red-cockaded Woodpeckers.

▶ Location: In Brevard and Indian River Counties, near Sebastian.

▶ Size: 21,500 acres.

▶ Ownership: St. Johns River Water Management District, Florida Division of Marine Resources.

▶ Habitats: Scrub, longleaf pine flatwoods, hardwood swamp.

▶ Land Use: Conservation, recreation, limited grazing.

▶ Site Description: The preserve has a diversity of ecological communities, including old-growth longleaf pine and Florida scrub, mostly in good to excellent condition. Sebastian River is an important site for the West Indian Manatee.

▶ Birds: In addition to the Florida Scrub-Jay and Red-cockaded Woodpecker, both the Bachman's Sparrow and Brown-headed Nuthatch are found on the preserve.

▶ Conservation Issues: The preserve is managed to protect and enhance habitat for the Florida Scrub-Jay and Red-cockaded Woodpecker. At present there are 51 groups of the jay and ten clusters of the woodpecker. In addition, 88 Bachman's Sparrows have been observed on the Brevard County portion of the preserve. Prescribed burning and mechanical removal of vegetation is used to manage habitat for these species. Cattle grazing is allowed on about 900 acres of the preserve but will be terminated after the pasture has been restored to natural grassland.

▶ Visitor Information: The best time to visit is fall through spring, though the jay and woodpecker can be found at any time of year. Contact: St. Sebastian River State Buffer Preserve, 1000 Buffer Preserve Dr., Fellsmere, FL 32948, 321-953-5004.

Avon Park Air Force Range (13), Florida

▶ Highlight: One of the larger populations of the Florida Scrub-Jay occurs there, along with the endangered "Florida" Grasshopper Sparrow and Red-cockaded Woodpecker.

Swallow-tailed Kite

▶ Size: 106,110 acres.

▶ Ownership: Air Force.

▶ Location: East of the town of Avon Park.

▶ Habitats: Longleaf and slash pine flatwoods, dry prairies, oak and sand pine scrub, riverine and hardwood forests, freshwater marshes.

▶ Land Use: Military training and exercises.

▶ Site Description: This is an active military base where training exercises are conducted. There is gunnery practice and live ordnance remains from bombing exercises during World War II. Adjoining the range is a privately owned site of about 39,000 acres, which the state plans to acquire.

▶ Birds: Avon Park Air Force Range has one of the larger populations of the endangered Florida Scrub-Jay (about 50 groups, but down from 100 a decade ago) and a small population of the Red-cockaded Woodpecker (about 20 clusters). Characteristically found in the same habitat as the woodpeckers, the Brown-headed Nuthatch and Bachman's Sparrow are also found here. The endangered Florida race of the Grasshopper Sparrow also occurs on the native dry prairie. In the breeding season, Swallow-tailed Kites and, rarely, Short-tailed Hawks can be found. The adjoining private land also has several clusters of the Red-cockaded Woodpecker.

► Conservation Issues: Prescribed burning is used to maintain habitat for the rare and endangered species. Dry prairie becomes unsuitable for the "Florida" Grasshopper Sparrow unless it is burned at least every three years. Woodpecker nest and roost trees are marked. Population studies are conducted on the Florida Scrub-Jay, and the birds are color-banded.

► Visitor Information: Public access to the open parts of the facility is limited to Thursday noon to Monday evening, except during the hunting season in late October to December, when access is limited to hunting permit holders. Call 941-452-4119 for information.

Archbold Biological Station and Lake Placid Scrub Preserve (14), Florida

► Highlight: This private research station and the adjacent preserve have together about 150 family groups of Florida Scrub-Jay.

► Location: Near Lake Placid, Highlands County.

► Size: 5,200 acres for Archbold; the scrub preserve has about 3,150 acres.

► Ownership: Archbold Biological Station, state of Florida.

► Habitat: Xeric oak scrub.

► Land Use: Conservation, research.

► Site Description: The privately owned biological station and the preserve are adjacent to each other. The station contains one of the largest stands of xeric oak scrub in the Lake Wales Ridge. This endangered habitat type is the subject of ongoing research projects at the station.

► Birds: Approximately 100 family groups of Florida Scrub-Jays inhabit the station; they total about 300 to 350 birds. The preserve has some 50 groups and about 150 birds. The combined total of jays in the Lake Wales Ridge Ecosystem area is approximately 250 groups. The Bachman's Sparrow also is found on the station.

► Conservation Issues: Much of what is known of the biology of the Florida Scrub-Jay is a result of long-term research conducted at the Archbold Biological Station; this has implications for protecting and managing jay habitat to conserve this rare bird. Limited to the Florida Peninsula, the Florida Scrub-Jay is a very sedentary species that travels no more than a few miles from its birthplace. Known for its cooperative breeding behavior, the offspring from one season typically remain to help the parents raise the offspring from the next. They participate in feeding the young, defending the territory, and watching for predators. The station and the preserve are part of the Lake Wales Ridge ecosystem, an area of some 66,000 acres that includes state land, federal land, a Nature Conservancy preserve, and private land. Although the habitat on the station and the adjacent preserve is protected, more than 85 percent of the endangered scrub habitat in the Lake Wales Ridge has been lost, mostly to citrus orchards. Through its Conservation and Recreation Lands program, the state has acquired some 41,000 acres in Highlands, Lake, Osceola, and Polk Counties and is working to acquire more.

▸ Visitor Information: Hours for visitors are from 8 A.M. to 5 P.M. Monday through Friday but closed on weekends. Due to the nature of the research, much of the station is off-limits to visitors, but there is a self-guided nature trail. Contact the station at P.O. Box 2057, Lake Placid, FL 33862, 863-465-2571.

Jonathan Dickinson State Park (15), Florida

▸ Highlight: The park has one of the larger populations of the Florida Scrub-Jay.
▸ Location: In Martin County, near Hobe Sound, about 12 miles south of Stuart.
▸ Size: 11,383 acres.
▸ Ownership: Florida Department of Environmental Protection.
▸ Habitats: Sand-pine scrub, floodplain forest.
▸ Land Use: Conservation, recreation.
▸ Site Description: The Loxahatchee River, named a National Wild and Scenic River in 1985, runs through the park, bordered by floodplain cypress forest. About 20 percent of the park is covered in coastal sand pine scrub, an endangered community type.
▸ Birds: There are about 25 to 30 groups of jays in the sand-pine scrub at the park, but more precise numbers are difficult to arrive at because of the distribution of the habitat there and the difficulty in sampling it. The Bachman's Sparrow is also found there.
▸ Conservation Issues: Mechanical means and prescribed burning are used to manipulate the sand pine scrub to create good habitat for the jays.
▸ Visitor Information: Best time for a visit is fall through spring. The park may be contacted at 16450 S.E. Federal Highway, Hobe Sound, FL 33455, 561-546-2771.

Arthur R. Marshall Loxahatchee National Wildlife Refuge (16), Florida

▸ Highlight: Important breeding area for the Snail Kite and several breeding or wintering Green List species.
▸ Location: The headquarters are 12 miles west of Boynton Beach, in Palm Beach County.
▸ Size: 147,368 acres.
▸ Ownership: Fish and Wildlife Service.
▸ Habitats: Sawgrass, wet prairies, sloughs, hardwood hammocks.
▸ Land Use: Water management, wildlife conservation, recreation.
▸ Site Description: The refuge is part of the remaining northern Everglades system. Surrounded by levees and canals, it is one of three large freshwater storage areas built by the Army Corps of Engineers and is now under the jurisdiction of the South Florida Water Management District. More than 90 percent of the refuge consists of saw grass marshes, wet prairies, sloughs, and hardwood hammocks.
▸ Birds: Snail Kites are found on the refuge, but largely in its inaccessible interior although they are sometimes observed along one of thc canals. The species is nomadic, feeding only on aquatic snails, including both native and non-native species. It is relatively abundant on the refuge only when water levels are adequate for its prey. Black and Yellow Rails winter there, as do Painted Buntings. Mottled Ducks are resident, and the Chuck-will's-widows and Prairie Warblers are common breeding species.
▸ Conservation Issues: Due to a recent drought, the numbers of Snail Kites are down

on the refuge. Poor water quality on the refuge is altering the vegetation and facilitating the further spread of non-native, invasive species, including several aquatic snails and fish, including the Asian swamp eel. Non-native plants now cover much of the refuge. Melaleuca infests 102,000 acres, Brazilian pepper is abundant along the dikes, and the Old World climbing fern is smothering the vegetation on the hammocks. Seeds of Brazilian pepper are spread by birds such as the American Robin and Cedar Waxwing, which feed on the fruits. Some control of Melaleuca is in place, but such efforts are underfunded; in a recent year there were only enough funds to remove Melaleuca from 133 heavily infested acres. Herbicides and mechanical means are used, but defoliating insects offer some hope if tests can determine they limit their activities to Melaleuca. Insects are kept in quarantine at research facilities for seven or eight years to evaluate their potential impact on agricultural and native plants. The refuge is covered under the Comprehensive Everglades Restoration Plan, which unfortunately does not include sufficient measures to deal with non-native species.

▶ Visitor Information: There is a marsh trail, a boardwalk, and a canoe trail, but parts of the refuge are accessible only by motorboat, and much of the refuge is off-limits to visitors. Contact the refuge at 10216 Lee Road, Boynton Beach, FL 33437, 561-734-8303.

Belle Glade Area (17), Florida

▶ Highlight: Thousands of shorebirds stop over during fall migration.
▶ Designation: Wetland of International Importance in the Western Hemisphere Shorebird Reserve Network.
▶ Location: East side of Lake Okeechobee, near Belle Glade and South Bay in Palm Beach County.
▶ Size: One million acres.
▶ Ownership: Private.
▶ Habitats: Agricultural fields.
▶ Land Use: Agriculture.
▶ Site Description: The site consists of agricultural lands used to grow sugar cane and winter vegetables.
▶ Birds: The area was first documented as important for birds in a 1978 article by P. W. Sykes and G. S. Hunter. They pointed out at that time that intertidal mud and sand flats had already become very limited on the southeast coast of Florida, due to dredge and fill operations to create waterfront property and deep water for recreational and commercial vessels. Shorebirds instead were congregating on agricultural lands of Palm Beach County during periods of flooding, drawdown, and drying. During late spring and summer, when crops are not being grown, some of the fields are flooded to suppress growth of weeds and to kill nematodes; the fields are then drained by late August or early September, providing good feeding and resting areas during the fall migration of many shorebirds, including thousands of "peeps," Greater and Lesser Yellowlegs, and Short-billed Dowitchers. On one September day, a count yielded 57,778 birds of 16 species. In addition, thousands of herons, egrets, and ibis are found in the area at that time of year.
▶ Conservation Issues: The lands are managed for agriculture, and it is only by coin-

cidence that this management is favorable to shorebirds during migration. Only a small percentage of the region is flooded in any given year. A change in the flooding regime could adversely impact the value of this site for shorebird species.

▶ Visitor Information: These private lands are not very accessible to those who wish to observe birds there. Some of the fields can be observed from public roads, but birders should not enter farmlands without permission.

IMPORTANT BIRD EDUCATION AREAS

The three best-known kinds of bird places are good birding spots, places important for conservation, and places important for education, research, or monitoring. For the first, there is a growing plethora of books, magazines, and websites from which to learn. For the second, we hope this book and others similar for different regions of the world provide a good start. But to date there has been no central source for finding information about the third. To overcome this deficiency, Partners in Flight members around the country are beginning Important Bird Education Area (IBEA) programs.

Three southern states lead this effort: Florida, Georgia, and Texas. They have established their own guidelines and printed certificates for varying levels of achievement for landowners in conservation, education and outreach, survey and monitoring, and research. Georgia and Texas refer to their guidelines as Flight S.T.A.R. (Saving Tomorrow's Avian Resources), and Florida's program is named Birds Beyond Borders.

Even if not critical for direct conservation reasons, these sites are important to protect for a host of other reasons. For example, much bird research and monitoring depends on long-term study, and nothing could be as devastating as losing a long-term site for these activities. In addition, sites of historic importance— for bird research, sites where species were first described, sites where extinct species were seen for the last time, and so forth—are in danger of being lost due simply to ignorance of their significance. Perhaps most importantly, without sites for citizens to learn about birds—and to become personally involved—we cannot succeed in building the public constituency needed for comprehensive bird conservation. ABC encourages development of these programs, and hopes to find funding to begin a national recognition program for these sites.

Corkscrew Swamp (18), Florida

▶ Highlight: With the largest stand of old-growth cypress in the country, the refuge has a large colony of Wood Storks and many other colonial wading birds also nest there.

▶ Location: In Collier County, northeast of Naples.

▶ Size: 10,720 acres.

▶ Ownership: National Audubon Society.

▶ Habitats: Pine flats, wet grassland, marsh, cypress forest.

▶ Land Use: Wildlife conservation, tourism.

▸ Site Description: The preserve contains the largest remaining stand of old-growth bald cypress in the country, with trees up to 130 feet tall and as old as 600 years. Other habitats include pine flatwoods; wet grassland dominated by sedges and sand cordgrass; saw grass marsh with pickerelweed, cattail, and bulrush; lettuce lakes and sloughs; pond cypress, and some coastal plain willow.

▸ Birds: The breeding colony of Wood Storks peaked at around 6,000 birds during the 1960s but has decreased in recent years. If water levels are either too high or too low, the birds will not attempt to nest. Since the preserve opened, there have been only two years without a single breeding attempt. Many colonial-nesting herons, egrets, and ibis are found there. Swallow-tailed Kites occur during breeding, and many Painted Buntings winter. Short-tailed Hawks are seen occasionally in spring and summer.

▸ Conservation Issues: The preserve has been well protected since it was established in 1954. When visitation first reached 100,000 per year, there were problems with wastewater, but these have since been solved. Prescribed burns are conducted to limit damage by wildfire. The state of Florida has acquired some adjacent lands in the Corkscrew Swamp Watershed and plans to acquire more. The goal is to connect this sanctuary and other adjacent lands to the Big Cypress National Preserve and other protected lands to the south. Water drawn down from uncontrolled growth around the preserve threatens water availability.

▸ Visitor Information: There is an interpretive center and a 2.25-mile boardwalk. Entry fee is $8. Summers are hot and rainy but winters are dry, with temperatures in the 70s. For information, contact: Corkscrew Swamp Sanctuary, 375 Sanctuary Road West, Naples, FL 34120, 941-348-9151.

Big Cypress National Preserve (19), Florida

▸ Highlight: Significant numbers of Snail Kites, Swallow-tailed Kites, Wood Storks, and Red-cockaded Woodpeckers. Many wading birds forage during the wet and dry season transition (November to March).

▸ Location: South Florida; it is intersected by I-75 (formerly Alligator Alley) and by U.S. Highway 41.

▸ Size: 729,000 acres.

▸ Ownership: National Park Service.

▸ Habitats: Cypress, sawgrass prairie, pinewoods, tropical hardwoods, marshes.

▸ Land Use: Wildlife conservation, recreation, tourism.

▸ Site Description: Big Cypress National Preserve is part of the Big Cypress Swamp ecosystem; it has a subtropical climate and gets 50 to 60 inches of rain a year. It consists of a mosaic of interspersed habitats including cypress strands and domes, wet and dry prairies, marshes, estuarine mangrove forests, slash pine flatwoods, and hardwood hammocks. It is inundated from June through December with the best-quality surface water in South Florida. Other significant adjoining sites include Fakahatchee Strand State Preserve, Water Conservation Area 3A, Florida Panther National Wildlife Refuge, and the Big Cypress Seminole and Miccosukee Indian Reservations. On the coast is Ten Thousand Islands National Wildlife Refuge, with significant mangrove forests and much habitat for shorebirds and wading birds. Near this complex of lands is Marco Island.

▶ Birds: Counts of more than 1,000 nesting Wood Storks, more than 100 Swallow-tailed Kites, and several Short-tailed Hawks have been made in the preserve. There are 45 active groups of Red-cockaded Woodpeckers, numbering about 150 birds, which is the southernmost population of this endangered species. Marco Island supports up to 50 wintering Piping Plovers, a significant number of this species, threatened throughout its wintering range.

▶ Conservation Issues: This was the nation's first national preserve, established by Congress in 1974. Its main objectives were to protect the water supply into Everglades National Park and conserve the South Florida ecosystem while allowing for a variety of human activities, including hunting, fishing, and off-road vehicle use. Problems such as water impoundment, non-native plants, and off-road vehicle damage are being addressed in management plans. Private companies are proposing exploratory drilling for oil, which would involve building new roads.

▶ Visitor Information: Best time to visit is fall through spring. The visitor center is on U.S. Highway 41, halfway between Naples and Miami. Contact the preserve at 33100 Tamiami Trail East, Ochopee, FL 34141, 941-695-4111.

Everglades National Park (20), Florida

▶ Highlight: Populations of wading birds in the Everglades, once close to 250,000 individuals, exist in significant but greatly diminished numbers, now estimated at 20,000 to 30,000.

▶ Designations: A Ramsar site, World Heritage site, and International Biosphere Reserve.

▶ Location: Southern tip of peninsular Florida.

▶ Size: 1.5 million acres covering much of south Florida.

▶ Habitats: Saw grass and cypress prairies, West Indian hardwood hammocks, slash pine rocklands, mangrove forests, coastal shoreline.

▶ Land Use: Wildlife conservation, tourism.

▶ Site Description: The only subtropical park in the continental United States, the Everglades has been severely degraded by water diversion for agriculture such that today only about half the original system survives. The largest continuous stand of sawgrass prairie in North America and the largest mangrove ecosystem in the Western Hemisphere, the Everglades and the adjacent Big Cypress National Preserve together cover 4,500 square miles of wetland, hardwood hammocks, and mangrove swamps in the southern tip of the Florida peninsula. The Everglades ecosystem depends on fresh water from rainfall flowing through it from north to south (over a gradient of only 15 feet in 100 miles, starting at the southern shore of Lake Okeechobee and running to Florida Bay). This "river of grass" has been described variously as a 50-mile-wide shallow, slow-moving river and a vast, shallow expanse of water flowing slowly southward through a sawgrass prairie. Of the present extent of the Everglades, about 40 percent is in the national park, while the other 60 percent is in other protected areas. The park itself is the largest east of the Mississippi River. Adjacent to the park and part of the same system are Water Conservation Areas 2 and 3.

▶ Birds: Though populations were once much higher, the Everglades remains a significant breeding location for many species of wading birds, including not only herons, egrets, and ibis, but also the Wood Stork, Roseate Spoonbill, Reddish Egret, and Great White Heron, a local race of the Great Blue Heron. About half the state's population of the White-crowned Pigeon breeds there, and Short-tailed Hawks occur, especially in the winter, while Mottled Ducks are resident. Snail Kites are seen occasionally on the park but are more common in the adjoining Water Conservation Areas 2 and 3. The "Cape Sable" subspecies of the Seaside Sparrow occurs only within the Everglades National Park and Big Cypress National Preserve. The Everglades also provides critical habitat for migrant shorebirds and landbirds.

▶ Conservation Issues: Unfortunately, the Everglades is also famous for the ecological disasters that have befallen it, and this has, of course, been mirrored in changes in the bird life: populations of wading birds in the Everglades have plummeted from close to 250,000 birds in the past to 20,000 to 30,000 in recent years. Most of the problem lies outside the boundaries of the park. Farmers, developers, and engineers have changed the hydrology drastically. A network of levees, ditches, pumps, and canals have changed the water flow, all designed to drain lands for agriculture and to control floods, such that the Everglades is now described as "a series of pools connected by canals and pumping stations." The fact that much less water now passes through the Everglades has led to droughts, fires, and the spread of non-native plant species such as the Australian tree melaleuca, and the Brazilian pepper tree, which now covers about 100,000 acres in the park. Another introduced plant spreading rapidly and smothering native vegetation is lygodium, an Old World climbing fern and common houseplant, while the Asian swamp eel is now in canals in South Florida and may soon arrive in the Everglades. Reduced water flow has resulted in salt water intruding into mangrove and coastal marsh areas, reducing the food supply available to wading birds. Another problem is agricultural runoff, resulting in a degradation of water quality and consequent algae blooms, fish kills, and changes in the composition of the vegetation. It is estimated that if the current rate in the rise of the sea level continues, much of the Everglades will become a shallow salt- or brackish-water estuary within the next 50 years. Congress has recently passed the "Restoring the Everglades, an American Legacy" bill and has approved the Comprehensive Everglades Restoration Plan. Over the next 30 years the plan will spend about $7.8 billion on more than 60 projects designed to restore the natural hydrology to the Everglades. The plan, however, is controversial. In 2002, *The Washington Post* reported that the $7.8 billion effort to restore the Everglades, which is supposed to help save big cats, wading birds, alligators, and other wildlife, may never benefit the shrinking ecosystem. The paper's investigative series on the Everglades says the plan—the biggest environmental project in American history—may not help the Everglades, but it "delivers swift and sure economic benefits to Florida homeowners, agribusiness and developers."

Interestingly, in 2002, biologists recorded nearly 70,000 nests of wading birds, a dramatic increase over past years, in the Everglades and surrounding areas (some of which are treated under the Big Cypress account, but all are part of the same hydrologic system). The five "indicator species" (White Ibis, Snowy Egret, Wood Stork, Great Egret, and Tricolored Heron) have increased sevenfold in the last five years, with more than 60,000 nests recorded in 2002. One "super colony" of 35,000 nests was found on Water Conservation Area 3, just north of the Everglades and just east of Big Cypress. This included an unprecedented 12,000 pairs of breeding Snowy Egret.

There are many theories for the dramatic increase, including a weather pattern during 2002 that was very favorable for nesting, but more enlightened water management policies may have played a role.

▶ Visitor Information: Best time to visit is October through April. Summers are oppressively hot. Though mosquitoes are present throughout the year, they can be so horrendous during the summer months as to make outdoor activities impossible. Contact the park at 40001 State Road 9336, Homestead, FL 33034-6733, 305-242-7700.

Florida Keys IBAs, Florida

Key Largo Hammocks State Botanical Site (21), Crocodile Lake National Wildlife Refuge (22), John Pennekamp Coral Reef State Park (23), National Key Deer Refuge (24), Great White Heron National Wildlife Refuge (25), Torchwood Hammock Preserve (26), Key West National Wildlife Refuge (27)

▶ Highlight: Several species otherwise breeding in the Bahamas and West Indies are found here, including the White-crowned Pigeon.
▶ Designation: National Marine Sanctuary.
▶ Location: An archipelago of islands stretching from the southern end of the Florida peninsula.
▶ Size: About 23,000 acres of the islands, spread out over 1,400 square miles.
▶ Ownership: Fish and Wildlife Service, Florida Division of Recreation and Parks, Monroe County, The Nature Conservancy, private.
▶ Habitats: Pinelands, West Indian hardwood hammocks, mangrove forests, beaches, mudflats, open water.
▶ Land Use: Tourism, residences, recreation, wildlife conservation.
▶ Site Description: The Florida Keys offer a taste of the Caribbean one can reach by car. Much of the keys have been developed for residences and for recreation, but some natural habitat remains. The largest remaining hardwood hammock forest is found on Key Largo Hammocks State Botanical Site. IBAs include the federally-owned Crocodile Lake National Wildlife Refuge (6,686 acres), John Pennekamp Coral Reef State Park (2,350 acres on land), and National Key Deer Refuge (8,005 acres); the state owns Key Largo Hammocks State Botanical Site (2,100 acres), the largest remaining hardwood hammock forest. The Nature Conservancy owns three tracts there: Torchwood Hammock Preserve (244 acres), and Terrestris Preserve (30 acres). The Braff Tract (230 acres) is another significant site owned by the Conservancy. The rest of the keys are in private ownership. The open water within the boundaries of Key West and Great White Heron National Wildlife Refuges comprises about 358,000 acres.

▶ Birds: Breeding specialties of the Florida Keys (some of which are also found in south Florida but in fewer numbers) are the Man-

Black-whiskered Vireo

grove Cuckoo, Antillean Nighthawk, Black-whiskered Vireo, and White-crowned Pigeon. All four have their main breeding ranges in the Bahamas and the West Indies. The total number of breeding White-crowned Pigeons in Florida (the only state where it occurs) is estimated at 8,000 to 9,000 pairs. Elsewhere in its range its numbers are decreasing due to hunting and the taking of squabs. The species requires two different habitats to reproduce. It nests on undisturbed mangrove-covered islands where raccoons are absent, and it feeds on fruits of the tropical hardwoods found in hardwood hammocks. Least and Roseate Terns and Prairie Warblers breed and the Short-tailed Hawk occurs sparingly in the winter. The Magnificent Frigatebird also occurs. Up to 19 species of West Indian birds have occurred there. At least one, the Key West Quail-Dove, was common on Key West during Audubon's day, in the early nineteenth century, but presumably disappeared due to the destruction of hardwood forests in the keys. Among the many shorebirds wintering in the keys are several threatened or Green List species, including the Piping Plover, Marbled Godwit, and Red Knot. Among the other wintering species are the Prairie and Black-throated Blue Warblers. In addition, many shorebirds and passerines stop over during migration. The keys can also on rare occasions serve as the first landfall for songbirds crossing the gulf, sometimes with disastrous results for most of those landing in settled areas. Due to rain and winds in spring 2001, a massive fallout of migrant warblers descended on the keys. Thousands were killed outright by flying into windows, cars, and other reflective objects, and many of the injured or exhausted birds were killed by stray and feral cats.

▶ Conservation Issues: The explosive development in the keys has destroyed much of the mangrove forests and West Indian hardwood hammocks, making the existing protected areas all the more important. Mangrove forests are now protected, and the state is working to purchase some of the remaining hammocks. Expansion of raccoons onto mangrove islands where White-crowned Pigeons nest would present a danger to the species and destruction of tropical hardwood hammocks limits its available food. The keys are the second priority in Florida Forever, a state program to acquire lands for conservation purposes. The federal agencies continue to pursue additional acquisitions. The Nature Conservancy is playing an important role in helping these public entities to protect land for conservation purposes.

▶ Visitor Information: The White-crowned Pigeon and the other primarily Caribbean birds can be found most easily from May to September; small numbers of the pigeon spend the winter in the Florida breeding range, but most depart for the Bahamas or Cuba. Crocodile Lake National Wildlife Refuge on Key Largo is closed to visitors, to protect its population of endangered American crocodiles. Key Largo Hammocks State Botanical Site offers only limited access. The easiest refuge to visit is the National Key Deer Refuge on Big Pine Key. Key West and Great White Heron National Wildlife Refuges are accessible only by boat. For information on National Key Deer Refuge, contact the refuge at P.O. Box 430510, Big Pine Key, FL 33043, 305-872-2239. For information on Key West National Wildlife Refuge, contact: P.O. Box 430510, Big Pine Key, FL 33043, 305-872-2239.

Dry Tortugas National Park (28), Florida

▶ Highlight: Large colony of terns, two species of which nest at no other U.S. site; stopover for transgulf neotropical migrants.

▶ Location: This isolated national park consists of seven small sand islands 68 miles to the west of Key West.

▶ Size: About 50 acres total; Garden Key is 16 acres, but the total area of the park, most of which is open water, is 47,000 acres.

▶ Ownership: National Park Service.

▶ Habitats: Beach, scrub, groves of non-native Australian pine.

▶ Land Use: Tourism, wildlife conservation.

▶ Principal Threats: The park is subject to hurricane damage, but not at the time of year best for observing birds.

▶ Site Description: The most-visited key, Garden Key, is the site of the remains of Fort Jefferson. There is a large lawn and plantings of West Indian trees and shrubs, attractive to migrants. The largest key, Loggerhead Key, has a dense grove of the non-native invasive Australian pine, which also attracts many birds during migration.

▶ Birds: The Dry Tortugas offer two major avian spectacles. One is that of a stopping point for cross-gulf migrants. Loggerhead Key attracts not only numerous landbirds in spring migration but many hawks that prey on them, while others, in an exhausted state, fall victim to one of the several resident Cattle Egrets. Another is the large breeding colonies of terns on Bush Key, including some 20,000 pairs of the Sooty Tern and 1,000 of the Brown Noddy, the only U.S. breeding sites for these species; the Roseate Tern, Least Tern, Black Noddy, Masked Booby, and Magnificent Frigatebird also breed on the keys in smaller numbers, with the latter three also at their only U.S. breeding site. Many strays and vagrants from the Caribbean have turned up on the keys through the years.

▶ Conservation Issues: Invasive non-native plants are a problem, in particular Australian pine on Loggerhead Key. The Park Service is working to eradicate this species and replace the vegetation with native Caribbean species.

▶ Visitor Information: The Dry Tortugas are reachable by seaplane or boat (the latter offers more opportunities to observe the birds), and there are regular tours leaving from Key West. The park is a favorite destination for tours by commercial bird tour companies in April and May. The best time to visit is from early April to mid-May at the height of spring migration. Bush and Long Keys, which host the nesting colonies, are off-limits during the breeding season, but both keys can be seen from Garden Key, where passengers from both the seaplanes and the boats disembark. Plane passengers are limited to Garden Key, but those arriving by boat also have the opportunity to visit Loggerhead Key. Though camping is available, no water, food, fuel, supplies, or other accommodations are available in the park. Contact: Dry Tortugas NP, 40001 State Road 9336, Homestead, FL 33034, 305-242-7700.

32. Coastal California

A Mediterranean climate of hot, dry summers and cool, moist winters creates conditions for chaparral vegetation in the low mountains along the coast that extend into Baja California, Mexico. Characteristic high-priority chaparral birds include the Nuttall's Woodpecker, Oak Titmouse, California Thrasher, and Lawrence's Goldfinch. The coastline provides habitat for several waterfowl and shore-bird species, and is an important wintering area for the Marbled Godwit, American Avocet, and Surfbird. Most of the world's populations of the Ashy Storm-Petrel and Xantus's Murrelet nest on a small number of offshore islands. A sizable proportion of the Elegant Tern and Heermann's Gull populations spend the nonbreeding season here. Millions of Sooty Shearwaters gather in pelagic waters each fall, joined by num-bers of other shearwaters, storm-petrels, and alcids. The Central Valley of California lies in this region between the Coast Ranges and the Sierra Nevada. Wetlands and as-sociated uplands in the Central Valley provide roosting and foraging habitat for 60 per-cent of the waterfowl that winter in the Pacific Flyway, including a majority of the continental Northern Pintail population. Approximately 95 percent of the Central Val-ley's depressional wetlands and 84 percent of riparian habitat have been lost, primarily to agriculture. A good deal of the remaining wetland habitat is protected within Na-tional Wildlife Refuges; the majority is privately managed for waterfowl hunting. Among landbirds, the Central Valley is the center of the small ranges of the Tricolored Blackbird and Yellow-billed Magpie, and also provides dwindling habitat for a host of riparian birds such as the "Least" Bell's Vireo.

Sacramento National Wildlife Refuge Complex IBAs, California

Sacramento National Wildlife Refuge (1), Delevan National Wildlife Refuge (2), Colusa National Wildlife Refuge (3), Sutter National Wildlife Refuge (4), Butte Sink National Wildlife Refuge (5)

▶ Highlight: The complex forms a critical area for wintering waterfowl in the Pacific Flyway, including most of the world's population of the Ross's Goose.
▶ Location: Tehama, Butte, Glenn, Colusa, and Sutter Counties; nearest larger towns are Chico, Willows, Colusa, Williams, and Yuba City.
▶ Size: 35,000 acres.

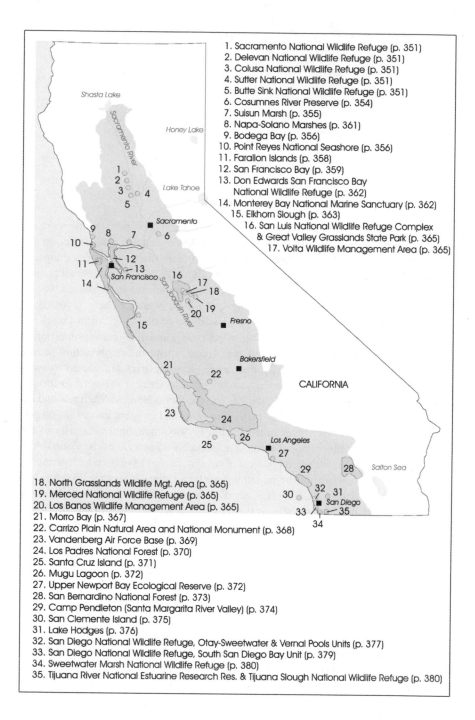

1. Sacramento National Wildlife Refuge (p. 351)
2. Delevan National Wildlife Refuge (p. 351)
3. Colusa National Wildlife Refuge (p. 351)
4. Sutter National Wildlife Refuge (p. 351)
5. Butte Sink National Wildlife Refuge (p. 351)
6. Cosumnes River Preserve (p. 354)
7. Suisun Marsh (p. 355)
8. Napa-Solano Marshes (p. 361)
9. Bodega Bay (p. 356)
10. Point Reyes National Seashore (p. 356)
11. Farallon Islands (p. 358)
12. San Francisco Bay (p. 359)
13. Don Edwards San Francisco Bay National Wildlife Refuge (p. 362)
14. Monterey Bay National Marine Sanctuary (p. 362)
15. Elkhorn Slough (p. 363)
16. San Luis National Wildlife Refuge Complex & Great Valley Grasslands State Park (p. 365)
17. Volta Wildlife Management Area (p. 365)

Shasta Lake

Honey Lake

Lake Tahoe

Sacramento River

Sacramento

San Francisco

San Joaquin River

Fresno

Bakersfield

CALIFORNIA

Los Angeles

Salton Sea

San Diego

18. North Grasslands Wildlife Mgt. Area (p. 365)
19. Merced National Wildlife Refuge (p. 365)
20. Los Banos Wildlife Management Area (p. 365)
21. Morro Bay (p. 367)
22. Carrizo Plain Natural Area and National Monument (p. 368)
23. Vandenberg Air Force Base (p. 369)
24. Los Padres National Forest (p. 370)
25. Santa Cruz Island (p. 371)
26. Mugu Lagoon (p. 372)
27. Upper Newport Bay Ecological Reserve (p. 372)
28. San Bernardino National Forest (p. 373)
29. Camp Pendleton (Santa Margarita River Valley) (p. 374)
30. San Clemente Island (p. 375)
31. Lake Hodges (p. 376)
32. San Diego National Wildlife Refuge, Otay-Sweetwater & Vernal Pools Units (p. 377)
33. San Diego National Wildlife Refuge, South San Diego Bay Unit (p. 379)
34. Sweetwater Marsh National Wildlife Refuge (p. 380)
35. Tijuana River National Estuarine Research Res. & Tijuana Slough National Wildlife Refuge (p. 380)

▸ Ownership: Fish and Wildlife Service.

▸ Habitats: Seasonally flooded freshwater marsh, vernal pools, riparian woodland, valley grassland.

▸ Land Use: Wildlife observation, photography, interpretation, environmental education, hunting, fishing.

▸ Site Description: This complex in the north-central Sacramento Valley is scattered through five counties northwest of Sacramento. It includes six refuges: Sacramento National Wildlife Refuge, Delevan National Wildlife Refuge, Colusa National Wildlife Refuge, Sutter National Wildlife Refuge, Butte Sink National Wildlife Refuge, and Sacramento River National Wildlife Refuge, Llano Seco Unit. Wetland habitats are almost entirely man-made and managed intensively for the benefit of wildlife. They exist as oases for waterfowl and other birds in a sea of agriculture.

Yellow-billed Magpie

▸ Birds: This complex forms one of the most important seasonal waterfowl areas in the Pacific Flyway, with peak populations that can exceed two million ducks during the late fall and winter; most common among these are the Northern Pintail, American Wigeon, and Green-winged Teal. Up to 500,000 geese may also be present; the most common species are the Snow, Ross's, and Greater White-fronted Geese. Shorebirds are particularly abundant during spring migration, including good numbers of Dunlin, Western Sandpipers, and others that use the seasonal wetlands during the drawdown phase. "Greater" Sandhill Cranes, are abundant at the Llano Seco Unit of the Sacramento River National Wildlife Refuge from October through March. Among the other birds present are the Nuttall's Woodpecker, Tricolored Blackbird, and Yellow-billed Magpie. Tricolored Blackbirds nest here in large numbers, but colony locations can vary annually. Gray Lodge Wildlife Area (owned by the California Department of Fish and Game), which is also a major area for wintering waterfowl, is located approximately 20 miles east of Delevan National Wildlife Refuge. It includes freshwater marsh and riparian woodland, with much the same birdlife as the other refuges in this part of California's Central Valley. The commonest wintering duck is the Mallard, but there are 5,000 wintering Ross's Geese present on average, with a peak of 25,000. Avocets, Long-billed Dowitchers, and Long-billed Curlews are common in winter and spring.

▸ Conservation Issues: Among the problems facing the refuges are the presence of non-native or invasive plants. Among the most troublesome are the yellow star thistle, perennial pepperweed, cocklebur, giant reed, Bermuda grass, annual ryegrass, perlagrass, and Johnson grass. These plants compete with, and often exclude, native plants, including rare and endangered vernal pool species. Control methods include mechanical or chemical treatment, management of water levels, prescribed burning, and intensive grazing. Outbreaks of avian cholera and avian botulism occur periodically and can kill thousands of birds in some years. There is also runoff from surrounding agriculture and mosquito-control activities on some units. Periodic large-scale floods can cause damage to levees, water-control structures, and other facilities; deposit trash, and spread weed problems on the refuges.

▸ Visitor Information: October through February is the best time to see wintering and migrating waterfowl, with peak waterfowl numbers in November and December. The Sacramento National Wildlife Refuge has a visitor center and is headquarters for the complex. The two most accessible of the refuges, both of which have auto-tour routes and foot trails, are the Sacramento and the Colusa National Wildlife Refuges. The Sacramento River National Wildlife Refuge, Llano Seco Unit, has only a walking trail. Gas, food, and lodging are available in Chico, Willows, Colusa, Williams, and Yuba City. Contact is Sacramento National Wildlife Refuge Complex, 752 County Road, 99W, Willows, CA 95988. Phone: 530-934-2801.

Cosumnes River Preserve (6), California

▸ Highlight: Important as a breeding site for the Tricolored Blackbird; important wintering area for the Sandhill Crane; several Green List birds are found as residents or migrants.

▸ Location: Central Valley, about midway between Sacramento and Stockton, just east of Interstate 5 at Twin Cities Road.

▸ Size: 40,000 acres.

▸ Ownership: The Nature Conservancy, Bureau of Land Management, Ducks Unlimited, Sacramento County, and California Departments of Fish and Game and Water Resources, State Lands Commission, private.

▸ Habitats: Seasonal, permanent, and intertidal freshwater wetland, valley oak forest, riparian woodland, grassland, vernal pool.

▸ Land Use: Wildlife and habitat conservation, agriculture, and recreation.

▸ Site Description: This preserve contains a mosaic of native habitats, including California's largest stand of valley oak woodland. The Cosumnes is the last free-flowing river from the Sierra Nevada into the Central Valley. As such, its habitats continue to respond to natural cycles of flood and drought. The preserve's prime location on the Pacific Flyway attracts a wide range of migratory birds, from the Least Sandpiper to the "Greater" Sandhill Crane. The owning groups and agencies act as a partnership, and, in addition, many individual landowners adjacent to the project have conservation easements and are also considered partners.

▸ Birds: This is an important wintering site for up to 10,000 Sandhill Cranes (including the "Greater" Sandhill Crane, a state threatened bird) and a breeding area for the Tricolored Blackbird. It is also a stronghold breeding area for the Swainson's Hawk, another state threatened species. The Common Yellowthroat, Blue Grosbeak, and Song Sparrow nest at the preserve (identified as priority species in the Riparian Bird Conservation Plan of the Riparian Habitat Joint Venture in the Central Valley). Also the Nuttall's Woodpeckers, Oak Titmouse, and Yellow-billed Magpie are resident there. White-tailed Kites and a large array of raptors, including all five falcons and two eagle species, inhabit the area as residents or during migration.

▸ Conservation Issues: Though a significant amount of habitat has been protected, priority conservation targets are still threatened. Spurred by close proximity to the booming economy of the greater Sacramento region, urban development pressures and encroachment on habitat and floodplain remain extremely high. These impacts are exacerbated by groundwater overdraft, intensification of agriculture, and existing incompatible flood-management practices. Other threats are posed by non-native invasive plants, such as the star thistle, perennial pepperweed, and annual grasses, and by non-native wildlife, such as introduced fishes, European Starlings, European House Sparrows, and black rats.

▸ Visitor Information: The preserve concentrates its public visitation around the visitor center and on two developed walking trails. The preserve offers monthly guided walks and paddles, led by trained volunteer naturalists. Any time of year is good to visit, with April through July highlighting breeding birds and spring migrants and with November through February showing thousands of wintering birds, including cranes and waterbirds. The visitor center is located at 13501 Franklin Boulevard, Galt, CA 95632, 916-684-2816.

Suisun Marsh (7), California

▸ Highlight: The largest estuarine marsh in the United States, it provides habitat for up to 250,000 wintering waterfowl and the endangered "California" Clapper Rail and Black Rail.

▸ Location: Solano County, about eight miles east of Vallejo.

▸ Size: 84,000 acres.

▸ Ownership: California Department of Fish and Game, private.

▸ Habitats: Salt and freshwater marshes, coastal scrub, bays and lagoons.

▸ Land Use: Hunting, fishing, livestock pasture, wildlife conservation.

▸ Site Description: Suisun Marsh is a brackish-water tidal wetland connected on one side to San Pablo Bay through the Carquinez Straights, and on the other to the Sacramento Delta. Some 12,629 acres are protected in three state-owned areas: Grizzly Island Wildlife Area (10,487 acres), Peytonia Slough Ecological Reserve (281 acres), and Hill Slough Wildlife Area (1,861 acres).

▸ Birds: Up to 250,000 waterfowl winter in the area; the "California" Clapper Rails, Black Rail, and Short-eared Owl are resident, and Tricolored Blackbirds are found there, generally in small numbers, in the winter. The Christmas Count, which includes the marsh, has had the nation's high count of Black Rails, Virginia Rails, Soras, and Cinnamon Teal. The area is an important migratory stopover and wintering site for shorebirds as well, with high counts of up to 10,000. An endemic subspecies of the Song Sparrow, the "Suisun" Song Sparrow, is found in the marsh.

▸ Conservation Issues: Among the chief problems are runoff from agriculture and residential development in the area. Whitetop (*Lepidium latifolium*), an invasive plant in uplands, is a serious problem, since it creates a monoculture and crowds out native vegetation. The state is working to control this plant by spraying, but this will need to be increased if the weed is to be controlled. Water quality and salinity are issues, and there are plans to manipulate the salinity of the marsh. The marsh is protected by law as part of the Suisun Marsh Resource District, but the adjoining area is starting to fill up with homes. This will mean an increase in dogs and feral cats. There have been proposals for wind farms, which may be a threat to some birds.

▶ Visitor Information: The three protected areas are accessible to visitors at certain times of the year; visitors are encouraged to call the number below to find out which areas are open at any given time. Contact: California Department of Fish and Game, 2548 Grizzly Island Road, Suisun City, CA 94585, 707-425-3828.

WIND FARMS AND BIRDS

There are currently 15,000 wind turbines operating in the United States. A study by the National Wind Coordinating Committee estimates that these towers killed 33,000 birds in 2001 alone. Specific reported kills included 448 raptors, the majority of which were killed at Altamont Pass in California, a site with 2,000 turbines that has a known problem with raptor kills due to its location in a raptor flyway. Birds are killed by the moving rotors and may be attracted by lighting that is required on taller towers to avoid plane collisions. Although older design wind towers with larger frames and faster rotors tend to kill more birds, all towers can kill birds. Numerous new wind farm projects are scheduled to be built over the coming years, potentially causing the deaths of thousands more birds. These projects, expected to cost in the region of three billion dollars in total, are made possible partly by a congressional wind energy production tax credit, subsidizing wind energy to make it competitive with other forms of energy production. Industry groups aim to increase production to six percent of national electricity needs by 2020. Research has shown that turbines supported by a single pole with larger, slower moving rotors are less likely to kill birds. The location of wind farms is also of great importance. Farms located in raptor flyways can be especially harmful. While wind power can clearly be a beneficial new technology for the environment, the design and placement of farms and turbines can make the difference between high and low bird impacts. To help prevent these impacts, concerned groups and individuals can monitor proposed new wind farm developments in their states and counties and demand that any new projects conduct a full Environmental Impact Assessment, paying special attention to migrant raptor flyways. Groups can also request that any towers have the minimum lighting required and use white strobe lights rather than red flashing lights (which, studies show, may attract fewer neotropical migrants) until more comprehensive study results are available on lighting regimes.

Point Reyes National Seashore (10) and Bodega Bay (9), California

▶ Highlight: An outstanding and famous locale for observing migrant waterfowl, shorebirds, raptors, and landbirds.
▶ Location: Coast of Marin County, about 20 miles north of San Francisco.
▶ Size: 86,000 acres.
▶ Ownership: National Park Service.
▶ Habitats: Sandy beach, mudflats, dunes, coastal bays and lagoons, rocky headlands, coastal prairie and scrub, salt and freshwater marshes, riparian woodland, coniferous forest.
▶ Site Description: Much of the area is rolling grassland, with clumps of trees that can

act as magnets for vagrant landbirds. The site is home to an internationally known research facility, the Point Reyes Bird Observatory. Not far from the observatory is Bolinas Lagoon, of regional significance in the Western Hemisphere Shorebird Reserve Network and a Ramsar site. Another important site lying just up the coast from the National Seashore is Bodega Bay.

▶ Birds: Among the resident Green List species are the Snowy Plover, Black Oystercatcher, Band-tailed Pigeon, Nuttall's Woodpecker, and Oak Titmouse, while the California Spotted Owl is found in small numbers. Tricolored Blackbirds breed in the region and congregate there during the winter. During the summer, Heermann's Gulls and Allen's Hummingbirds are present, while wintering species include the Long-billed Curlew and Black Turnstone. Migrant species include the Black Brant, Marbled Godwit, and Short-billed Dowitcher. Point Reyes is important as a stopover for migrating shorebirds and a good site for observing migrant raptors. Many vagrant landbirds from eastern North America have been observed here, particularly during fall migration. Bolinas Lagoon alone has a total annual count of 30,000 shorebirds, while Bodega Bay hosts thousands of shorebirds in winter and during migration, in addition to thousands of waterfowl, including significant numbers of Black Brant. Black Oystercatchers and Snowy Plovers are found throughout the year, and Black Rails nest.

▶ Conservation Issues: Much of the shoreline consists of treeless coastal prairie, with dairy cattle operations as private enterprises using National Park Service land. Flocks of Tricolored Blackbirds (up to 14,000 birds) make use of dairies and feed lots during the winter. Continued spread of non-native plants such as pampas grass are threatening native vegetation.

▶ Visitor Information: Any time of year is good for a visit. Contact Point Reyes National Seashore, Point Reyes, CA 94956, 415-464-5100.

SUPPORTING NONPROFIT CONSERVATION ORGANIZATIONS

There are hundreds of nonprofit organizations dedicated to birds in the United States. In fact, more than 900 are listed by the American Birding Association. The vast majority are local groups dedicated to recreational birdwatching but with bird conservation as an area of concern. There are also hundreds of conservation organizations ranging from small, local land trusts to huge organizations with memberships in excess of one million. These groups cover a broad spectrum of interests from conservation land easement purchase to those advocating or opposing innumerable government policies. And there are hundreds more groups specializing in natural history education. The National Association of Interpreters lists more than 400 nature centers alone.

Then there are a few dozen organizations of mostly modest size whose mission is the conservation of birds. These groups often specialize, in the work they do (for example, the Cornell Laboratory of Ornithology specializes in "citizen science," which is education through involvement, and Point Reyes Bird Observatory develops science to inform conservation decision making), in the special role of their locality to birds (most bird observatories are located at migration concentration points), or even in particular groups of birds (for example, the International Crane Foundation and The Peregrine Fund).

Among this confusing array of nonprofits, how does one decide which to join and which to support financially? Virtually all of these organizations are worthwhile, will inform you about their work with literature, and will welcome your participation. With very little effort, your good intentions to support bird conservation can empty your pockets, fill your mailbox, and leave you wondering what good, if any, your efforts and money have done. Here are a few ideas for wending your way through the maze of good conservation organizations.

1. Don't become irritated or impatient at the many conservation-related mailings you receive. These are sent by good people at good groups trying to interest you in their work. They are driven not by profit but by the desire to devote their lives to work beneficial to the environment. Instead of throwing their mail unopened into the trash, think of it as a screening device for deciding which groups are worth your personal support.

2. Investigate local bird and conservation organizations and join the one that you feel is doing the best job to protect habitat, promote good policies, or educate citizens. This can be a bird club, nature center, or land trust.

3. Decide which aspects of conservation are most important to you. Is it setting aside nature preserves? Reporting conservation news? Policy monitoring? Waterfowl? Personal involvement? Citizen education? Shorebirds? You might want to support the best large, national organizations specializing in your area of interest.

4. Please don't stop there. Many people who feel overwhelmed by the multitude of groups limit themselves to the large broad-spectrum, national-level, nonprofits, not taking the time to learn of the excellent work done by smaller bird conservation organizations. However, many of the best new ideas for conservation and the best and most efficient use of your conservation donations will come from the small- and medium-sized groups whose support is limited—the very groups that are fast to respond, more creative, and more willing to take risks. These groups are often the proving grounds for programs later adopted by the larger organizations. So, again, think about your personal areas of interest, educate yourself about the groups, and support the ones that most suit your interest.

5. Get involved. Nonprofit organizations are looking for "wealth, work, and wisdom" from their members. Your financial support is critical for nonprofits, but these groups need you to be fully informed about issues, and then to offer opinions, serve on committees and boards, and help out as a volunteer.

Farallon Islands (11), California

▶ Highlight: The islands contain the largest seabird-breeding colonies on the Pacific Coast south of Alaska, including the world's largest colony of the watch-listed Ashy Storm-Petrel.

▶ Location: The islands are located approximately 30 miles offshore of San Francisco.

▶ Size: 211 acres.

▶ Ownership: Fish and Wildlife Service.

▶ Habitats: Extensive marine terrace, cliffs, sea caves, intertidal zone.

▸ Land Use: Biological research.

▸ Site Description: These rocky islands are significant not only for birds but for marine mammals; Stellers sea lions and northern elephant seals breed and pup on the South Farallon Islands, and California sea lions, harbor seals, and northern fur seals haul out on the islands.

▸ Birds: The Farallon Islands host a large and remarkably diverse assemblage of seabird species, among them the largest breeding colony of the Ashy Storm-Petrel (average number 2,661 individuals) and the largest colonies of the Western Gull (average number 17,305 individuals) and Brandt's Cormorant (average number 5,606 individuals). There are also important colonies of the Leach's Storm-Petrel (1,600 individuals), Cassin's Auklet (15,251 individuals), and Common Murre (61,499 individuals), in addition to breeding Pelagic Cormorants, Rhinoceros Auklets, Tufted Puffins, Pigeon Guillemots, and Black Oystercatchers. Colonies on the Farallons contribute significantly to West Coast seabird populations south of Alaska.

▸ Conservation Issues: Biologists have monitored seabird populations on the Farallon Islands and conducted research on the marine ecosystems associated with the islands for the past 30 years. Data collection is conducted in a way to minimize disturbance. Among the threats to the islands' avifauna are potential toxic chemical spills and oil pollution, the potential for human disturbance at nesting sites, and inshore commercial gill-net commercial fisheries, which cause significant mortality and reduce the quality and quantity of food available to the seabirds. In the past, Ashy Storm-Petrels nesting at the Farallon Islands did so in an area free of nesting gulls, which, since 1976, have nested densely throughout the islands. Introduced house mice eat storm-petrel eggs, as cats (now extirpated) once ate adults.

▸ Visitor Information: The islands are closed to visitors. There are strict regulations against commercial or recreational marine activity on or close to the islands. However, the birds and breeding marine mammals can be observed, studied, and photographed at a distance from boats. Conservation groups sponsor wildlife observation trips to the Farallon Islands. Information regarding these trips can be obtained from the San Francisco Bay National Wildlife Refuge Visitor Center, P.O. Box 524, Newark, CA 94560, 415-792-0222.

San Francisco Bay IBAs, California

Napa-Solano Marshes (8), San Francisco Bay (12), Don Edwards
San Francisco Bay National Wildlife Refuge (13)

▸ Highlight: Millions of birds spend the winter in San Francisco Bay, with rafts of thousands of diving ducks on the open water and thousands of shorebirds per mile along the edges.

▸ Designation: Wetland of Hemispheric Importance in the Western Hemisphere Shorebird Reserve Network.

▸ Location: The bay extends from San Pablo Bay in the north to South San Francisco Bay in the south. It is bordered by nine counties: Santa Clara, Alameda, Contra Costa, Solano, Napa, Sonoma, Marin, San Francisco, and San Mateo.

▸ Size: 55,572 acres of protected lands in an area of close to 1,000 square miles.

▸ Ownership: Fish and Wildlife Service, California Department of Fish and Game, various municipalities.

▸ Habitats: Mudflats, sandy beach, coastal bays and lagoons, salt and freshwater marshes, coastal scrub.

▸ Land Use: Commercial, recreational, wildlife observation and conservation.

▸ Site Description: The San Francisco Bay Estuary system includes the North, Central, and South San Francisco Bays, and San Pablo Bay. Within it are tidal marshes, mudflats, salt ponds, seasonal brackish or freshwater wetlands, tidal pools, islands, rivers, creeks, and bay shoreline. Extensive mudflats are exposed at low tide, and a system of dikes provides prime nesting habitat for shorebirds, especially Black-necked Stilt and American Avocet. Two IBAs within the bay, Don Edwards National Wildlife Refuge and the Napa-Solano Marshes, receive individual treatment below. A third site, Alameda National Wildlife Refuge, is at present on the former Alameda Naval Air Station but is scheduled to be added to the Don Edwards National Wildlife Refuge.

▸ Birds: Millions of birds depend on San Francisco Bay not only during migration but during the winter, when there are rafts of thousands of diving ducks on the open water and thousands of shorebirds per mile along the shore. At least 34 species of shorebirds occur regularly within the San Francisco Bay Estuary, including good numbers of wintering Long-billed Curlews, American Avocets, Willets, both dowitchers, and Marbled Godwits. Counts conducted by the Point Reyes Bird Observatory Pacific Flyway Program in 1989 recorded 930,000 shorebirds in San Francisco Bay during the spring, 340,000 during the fall, and 225,000 birds in the winter. About 90 percent of all shorebirds censused during migration were Western Sandpipers or Dunlin. Tricolored Blackbirds breed and winter there, and Western Snowy Plovers, California Clapper Rails, and Black Rails all breed on the bay.

▸ Conservation Issues: Since the 1950s, approximately 85 percent of tidal wetlands within the bay have been lost to industrial development, salt production, urbanization, and private use. Water quality is degraded by pollution from agricultural, industrial, and urban runoff. Predictions are that the bay will suffer grave effects from global warming, with rising sea levels altering and destroying habitat for shorebirds and other species. Saltwater intrusion is resulting from the draining of tributaries to the bay for agricultural and residential use. Particularly serious is the invasion of non-native plants and animals. Smooth cordgrass has spread throughout the area and colonized mudflats and tidal sloughs used by shorebirds. Non-native invertebrates from ballast water have replaced many of the native species in the bay, affecting food supplies for shorebirds and other birds. Federal, state, and local land managers in the South Bay are cooperating to control the non-native cordgrass and a predator-management program is being implemented to protect endangered species and migratory birds. Several tidal marshes and seasonal wetlands will be restored over the next few years in the San Pablo National Wildlife Refuge, which forms part of the Napa-Solano Marshes. In December 2002, the Department of the Interior, in partnership with the state of California and four private foundations, purchased 16,500 acres of San Francisco Bay salt ponds from Cargill, Inc. These lands will be restored to tidal marshes and other wildlife habitat. Most of the acquired land, which Cargill had used for salt production, will become part of Don Edwards San Francisco Bay National Wildlife Refuge, while some 7,000 acres will be managed by the state as a wildlife reserve. This puts into public hands the largest parcel of privately owned shoreline in San Francisco Bay. Surrounded by a heavily urbanized area, this represents the single-largest wetlands restoration effort on the West Coast. Many species of birds use the salt ponds as habitat, including ducks, cormorants, terns, gulls, and shorebirds. Some areas will remain ponds while others will be restored to tidal marsh. Cargill will take responsibility for dealing with toxic waste, brine, and other contamination.

▶ Visitor Information: Best time to visit is October through March. For information on the National Wildlife Refuges, contact Refuge Manager, San Francisco Bay National Wildlife Refuge Complex, P.O. Box 524, Newark, CA 94560, 510-792-0222.

Napa-Solano Marshes (8)

In addition to a significant population of the endangered "California" Clapper Rail, these marshes support the greatest-known concentration of the endangered "California" Black Rails. The marshes are located in the northern reaches of San Francisco Bay, north of San Pablo Bay and east of Sonoma Creek, in Napa and Solano Counties. They total 16,570 acres in size, and are under Fish and Wildlife Service, California Department of Fish and Game, and private ownership. Part of the site is included in the San Pablo Bay National Wildlife Refuge, established for the conservation of wintering Canvasbacks. These wetlands are among the largest and least disturbed marshes in the entire San Francisco Bay, where more than 90 percent of the wetlands have been destroyed. Included also are Petaluma Marsh Wildlife Area (3,497 acres in eight parcels) and the Napa-Sonoma Marshes (2,010 acres in two parcels), both owned by the California Department of Fish and Game. The land consists of salt evaporation ponds, tidal salt marsh and brackish marsh, and is used for wildlife conservation and hunting. More than 80 percent of the population of "California" Black Rails are confined to the northern reaches of the San Francisco Bay estuary, and the highest abundances are found in these marshes. In addition, up to 40 pairs of "California" Clapper Rails are resident here. Thousands of waterfowl winter in the area, including up to 17,000 Canvasbacks. The salt ponds and mudflats seasonally support tens of thousands of shorebirds. Up to 1,000 nesting pairs of Tricolored Blackbirds have been recorded. Funds are needed to restore and enhance the protected wetlands, the majority of which are former salt evaporation ponds. The higher salinities in some of these ponds do not provide the optimal food sources for birds. There has been an increase in non-native red foxes and feral cats in the area. These need to be controlled before they decimate the rail population. Tidal marshes are being invaded by the non-native pepperweed. Increased residential and industrial development in the area will bring more disturbance, pollutants, and an increase in the number of predatory domestic animals.

▶ Visitor Information: Fall through spring are good for observing shorebirds and waterfowl. Contact: San Pablo National Wildlife Refuge at P.O. Box 2012, Mare Island, CA 94592, 707-562-3000.

Don Edwards San Francisco Bay National Wildlife Refuge (13)

The majority of the remaining numbers of "California" Clapper Rails are resident on this 19,000-acre Fish and Wildlife Service refuge, located in South San Francisco Bay, in Alameda, San Mateo, and Santa Clara Counties. The refuge includes most of the undeveloped land in the area of South San Francisco Bay. Besides wetland habitats of tidal and brackish marshes, salt ponds, mudflats, and open water, there are uplands with shrubs and native and non-native grasses. Land not dedicated to wildlife conservation or recreation is used for salt-evaporation ponds. The refuge has 600 "California" Clapper Rails, approximately 60 percent of the entire population of this endangered subspecies. There are up to 120 breeding "Western" Snowy Plovers. In addition to the thousands of shorebirds stopping at the refuge and elsewhere on the bay, thousands of diving ducks are found on the open water, while others use the adjacent salt ponds, including up to 40,000 Northern Shovelers and 18,000 Ruddy Ducks. Only about half the acreage originally authorized has been acquired to date. There is pressure from animal rights and other groups to allow feral cat colonies in parks and other public lands. This presents a serious threat since cats and non-native red foxes are decimating the population of the endangered "California" Clapper Rail and other birds in the refuge.

▸ Visitor Information: Best time to visit is October through March. Contact the refuge at 510-792-0222.

Monterey Bay National Marine Sanctuary (14), California

▸ Highlight: Several Green List species are found seasonally.
▸ Designation: National Marine Sanctuary.
▸ Location: Coast and offshore waters from Marin to Cambria.
▸ Size: Includes 276 miles of shoreline and 5,322 square miles of ocean up to 30 miles offshore.
▸ Ownership: Federal government.
▸ Habitats: Marine, coastal rocks and beaches, kelp beds. The giant marine canyon reaches a depth of 10,663 feet.
▸ Land Use: Recreational and commercial fishing, coastal developments, wildlife areas.
▸ Site Description: The rocky coastline is interspersed with sandy beaches while a giant marine canyon close to the shore provides an upwelling of nutrients creating a rich marine biodiversity with 26 species of marine mammals and 94 species of seabirds. Large kelp "forests" are found close inshore. The seabed rapidly falls off close to the coast, reaching a depth of more than two miles within sight of land. Big surf and heavy seas are frequent. Large numbers of marine mammals, including migrating gray whales, seals, and sea otters are commonly seen. Wild headlands and bays flank a combination of natural areas, coastal golf courses, suburban and urban areas with small landings and harbors.
▸ Birds: Large numbers of seabirds use the bay for feeding during migration and outside the breeding season. Thirteen Green List species occur regularly within the bay,

and one endangered species, the Short-tailed Albatross, is occasionally seen. Reintroduced California Condors also feed on dead seals on the periphery of the sanctuary along the Big Sur coast. Coastal species of conservation concern include the Black Turnstone, Surfbird, Black Oystercatcher, and Marbled Godwit. Pelagic species include the Black-footed and Laysan Albatrosses, and large numbers of Black and Ashy Storm-Petrels. In warm-water years Least Storm-Petrels and Black-vented Shearwaters are sometimes found. The Craveri's and Xantus's Murrelets are also present in small numbers, October being the best month to find them. The Heermann's Gull is also found in moderate numbers both inshore and following boats. Massive numbers of Surf Scoters and loons migrate close inshore during the spring. Concentrations of breeding Brandt's and Pelagic Cormorants can be found on rocky outcrops.

▶ Conservation Issues: Some recurrent oiling of murres and other seabirds has been traced to a long-sunken vessel that releases oil after being disturbed in storms. Oil drilling and ocean dumping are prohibited. Black-footed and Laysan Albatrosses that occur in the bay are in serious decline due to longline mortality elsewhere in the North Pacific.

▶ Visitor Information: For more general information, contact the National Oceanic and Atmospheric Administration, Monterey Bay National Marine Sanctuary, 831-647-4201. Regular pelagic birding tours are conducted by Shearwater Journeys: www.shearwaterjourneys.com.

Elkhorn Slough (15), California

▶ Highlight: One of the most important staging areas for migrating shorebirds in California, Elkhorn Slough also has a significant breeding population of the "Western" Snowy Plover.

▶ Designation: Wetland of International Importance in the Western Hemisphere Shorebird Reserve Network, National Marine Sanctuary, National Estuarine Research Reserve.

▶ Location: On the central coast between Santa Cruz and Monterey.

▶ Size: The slough winds inland seven miles from its mouth at Moss Landing, encompassing more than 2,500 acres of marsh and tidal flats.

▶ Ownership: California Department of Fish and Game, Elkhorn Slough Foundation, The Nature Conservancy, private.

▶ Habitats: Extensive tidal mudflats and pickleweed-dominated salt marshes, tidal channels and lagoons, sandy beaches, coastal prairie, scrub, oak woodlands.

▶ Land Use: Wildlife conservation and observation, environmental education.

▶ Site Description: Elkhorn Slough is the largest wetland on the central California coast and, after San Francisco Bay, hosts the most extensive salt marshes in the state. The muddy tidal flats and lagoons harbor flourishing populations of invertebrates and fish, which provide a rich diet to migratory and resident shorebirds and waders. Upland of the estuary, farmland is interspersed with protected oak woodlands and grassland, so a diversity of terrestrial birds are found in close proximity to the wetland species. Introduced eucalyptus and Monterey pines are also used by birds. A number of small freshwater ponds in the area host waterfowl and other species. More than 4,000 acres of valuable habitat are now protected in the Elkhorn Slough watershed; large areas are owned by the

Brown Pelican

Elkhorn Slough National Estuarine Research Reserve, the Elkhorn Slough Foundation, The Nature Conservancy, and the Packard family. Adjacent are Moss Landing Wildlife Area and Moss Landing State Beach, which together supply much of the shorebird habitat of the area.

▸ Birds: Elkhorn Slough serves as a major stopover and staging area for shorebirds, many of which winter there. Up to 30,000 shorebirds use the area seasonally. The most abundant species are the Western Sandpiper, Least Sandpiper, Marbled Godwit, both dowitchers, the Willet, American Avocet, Black-bellied Plover, Sanderling, and Long-billed Curlew. The Western Sandpiper accounts for at least 75 percent of the slough's shorebird population. Both American White and Brown Pelicans and Heermann's Gulls are common in the summer and fall. In addition to supporting migratory birds, the slough provides breeding habitat for many species. Up to 70 Western Snowy Plovers breed in the salt ponds, and recent counts indicate that the slough population had the highest fledging rate of any site in the Monterey Bay area. Other nesting shorebirds in the salt ponds include American Avocets and Black-necked Stilts. On the Elkhorn Slough Reserve, Caspian Terns breed on an island in a restored wetland, and Great Blue Herons, Great Egrets, and Double-crested Cormorants nest in a grove of Monterey pines. Tricolored Blackbirds nest in local freshwater marshes, and become common in fall and winter. Many upland birds breed in the grasslands and woodlands surrounding the slough, including Allen's Hummingbird. Important for wetland and upland birds year-round, Elkhorn Slough is consistently among the top ten Christmas Bird Counts in the country in terms of numbers of species recorded.

▸ Conservation Issues: The slough has a long history of human use, and the remaining rich habitats are embedded in a variety of different land use contexts. A number of threats face slough habitats and communities. Tidal erosion due to alteration to slough hydrology by the Army Corps of Engineers results in significant loss of salt marsh habitat each year. High levels of nutrients and pesticides enter the slough with runoff from adjacent agriculture. A main railroad line runs directly through the slough wetlands, with the potential for damaging oil or chemical spills. Non-native, invasive plants abound on the slough's uplands, introduced predators such as red foxes and feral cats threaten nesting shorebirds, and non-native invertebrates dominate some of the wetland habitats. The Moss Landing Power Plant takes a huge volume of water from the Moss Landing Harbor area into its cooling system daily. Recreational visitors, such as the ever-increasing number of kayakers, have the potential to disturb foraging or resting birds and marine mammals.

Local conservation efforts have been very successful and continue to meet challenges to the protection of habitats and wildlife in the area. The Elkhorn Slough National Estuarine Research Reserve, run in partnership between the California Department of Fish and Game and the National Oceanic and Atmospheric Administration, has strong education, community outreach, volunteer, research, restoration, and management programs. The nonprofit Elkhorn Slough Foundation is a land trust, protecting remaining areas with healthy wetland or upland communities, and restoring degraded areas. The Point Reyes Bird Observatory (now known as PRBO Conservation) manipulates water levels and removes introduced predators, greatly enhancing reproductive success of nesting Snowy Plovers at the salt ponds. Partnerships between these and other conservation-oriented organizations and the local community hold great promise for continued protection and enhancement of wetland habitats at the slough. A citizens' group, Friends, Artists, and Neighbors of Elkhorn Slough (www.saveourslough.org), is a grassroots organization formed in response to the high-density development threatening the slough and its watershed. It promotes local efforts to protect the slough.

▸ Visitor Information: The Elkhorn Slough National Estuarine Research Reserve (1700 Elkhorn Road, Watsonville, CA 95076, 831-728-2822), has a delightful visitor center, public trails, and guided tours. The nonprofit Elkhorn Slough Foundation (831-728-5939) also operates out of the same location; for more information on both organizations and the slough, visit their joint website (www.elkhornslough.org). Trails are also available at Kirby Park and the Moss Landing Harbor. A good time to visit is in the fall, when the Monterey Bay Bird Festival is held.

The Grasslands Ecological Area IBAs, California

San Luis National Wildlife Refuge Complex and Great Valley Grasslands State Park (16), Volta Wildlife Management Area (17), North Grasslands Wildlife Management Area (18), Merced National Wildlife Refuge (19), Los Banos Wildlife Management Area (20)

▸ Highlight: Most noted for its wintering waterfowl concentrations, supporting up to one million birds, representing approximately 20 percent of the waterfowl in the entire Pacific Flyway. This includes over three percent of the entire North American populations of Gadwall, Northern Pintails, Green-winged Teal, Northern Shovelers, and Canvasbacks, plus half the world's population of the watch-listed Ross's Goose. There are significant colonies of the range-limited Tricolored Blackbird within the site.

▸ Designation: A Ramsar site, and a Wetland of International Importance in the Western Hemisphere Shorebird Reserve Network.

▸ Location: Merced County between Merced and Gustine, or from Interstate 5 east to Highway 59.

▸ Size: 160,000 acres in a block approximately 30 miles long by 25 miles wide.

▸ Ownership: Fish and Wildlife Service, California Department of Fish and Game, California Department of Parks and Recreation and Grassland Resource Conservation District, conservation groups, private.

▸ Habitats: Seasonally flooded marshlands, semipermanent marsh, riparian cottonwood/willow forest, riparian oak woodlands, wet meadows, streams, lakes, vernal pools, native uplands, pastures, farm fields, native valley grassland.

▸ Land Use: Wildlife conservation, hunting, agriculture.

▸ Site Description: The Grasslands Ecological Area (GEA) is a mosaic of wetlands, uplands, vernal pools, and riparian areas in California's Central Valley. It forms the largest contiguous block of wetlands remaining in California, representing the last five percent of the three to four million acres of wetlands once found in the state. The various habitats for birds within the grasslands are a mosaic of ownerships, including private duck clubs, state parks, state fish and game wildlife areas, federal and state wildlife easement areas, and National Wildlife Refuges. The GEA is a good representative of a vernal pool complex, an ecologically distinctive and increasingly rare habitat type. Ninety percent of California's vernal pools have been destroyed. The vernal pools provide habitat for rare flowers, fairy shrimp, tadpole shrimp, and other protected species of special concern. Individual IBAs are San Luis National Wildlife Refuge Complex, Merced National Wildlife Refuge, North Grasslands Wildlife Management Area, Volta Wildlife Management Area, Los Banos Wildlife Management Area, and Great Valley Grasslands State Park.

▸ Birds: With little wetland and riparian habitat remaining in California, these sites have become increasingly important not only for the one million waterfowl wintering there but for other migratory birds as well, including songbirds, raptors, and shorebirds. Shorebird counts are highest during the fall and spring migrations when hundreds of thousands of birds utilize the GEA as a stopover point, including significant numbers of the Western Sandpiper, Dunlin, Long-billed Dowitcher, Black-necked Stilt, and Long-billed Curlew. In addition, tens of thousands of shorebirds make use of this habitat on a year-round basis, as do several species of waterfowl and raptors. The total number of shorebirds has been estimated at 500,000. Among the limited range species found in the GEA are the Tricolored Blackbird, of which up to 63,000 have been counted in the fall, and the Yellow-billed Magpie, a California endemic.

A breeding colony of the Tricolored Blackbird at San Luis National Wildlife Refuge in the mid-1990s was estimated to reach 105,000 birds.

▸ Conservation Issues: Due to flood-control and irrigation projects, the entire hydrology of the Central Valley has been dramatically altered. The water levels of most of the valley's wetlands are now managed. Of recent concern to the integrity of the wetlands has been the availability of adequate water supplies, both with regard to quantity and quality of water. With inadequate supplies in the 1980s, public and private wetlands were forced to use agricultural drain water, laden with selinium and high concentrations of other toxins. In 1983, substantial bird die-offs and deformities occurred at Kesterson Reservoir, where most of this agricultural drain water ends up. The extent of the problem at the reservoir was alarming, and illustrated dramatically the dangers of using poor quality water for wildlife. With the passage of the Central Valley Improvement Act in 1992, the public and private wetlands of the grasslands were at long last to receive an assured water supply.

The largest threat to remaining wetlands is urban development. The Central Valley is expected to triple its human population by the year 2030, and Merced County specifically is expected to grow rapidly. The Fish and Wildlife Service therefore made this area a priority for easements during the 1980s and 1990s, and progress has been swift in protecting these lands.

Approximately one-third of the area is in public ownership. Recent acquisitions by the Fish and Wildlife Service have included restoration of wetlands on former agricultural land. In addition, approximately 75 percent of the private lands are under perpetual conservation easement. The Fish and Wildlife Service holds the development rights on these lands, ensuring that they remain as native, wetland habitats, and that major topographical alterations do not occur.

Several other properties are currently being appraised for Fish and Wildlife Service conservation easements. In addition to the Fish and Wildlife Service, the Natural Resource Conservation Service, California Department of Fish and Game, and private organizations such as Ducks Unlimited and California Waterfowl Association are extremely active in the area. These organizations and the Fish and Wildlife Service work cooperatively to continually protect, enhance, and restore habitat in the GEA. Each year many such projects are undertaken in the GEA, to the benefit of hundreds or thousands of acres.

► Visitor Information: Best time to visit is during migration (April to May and September to October) and winter (November to March). For more information, contact: Grasslands Wildlife Management Area, c/o San Luis National Wildlife Refuge Complex, P.O. Box 2176, Los Banos, CA 93635, 209-826-3508.

Morro Bay (21), California

► Highlight: Important wintering site for the Brant; important site for migrating and wintering shorebirds.

► Designation: Wetland of Regional Importance in the Western Hemisphere Shorebird Reserve Network.

► Location: Northwest of San Luis Obispo.

► Size: 56,740 acres.

► Ownership: California Department of Parks and Recreation, private.

► Habitats: Tidal and brackish marshes; mudflats; open bay and ocean waters; rocky shoreline and sandy beaches and coastal dunes; willow riparian, mixed and conifer woodlands, eucalyptus forest, coastal scrub, chaparral.

► Land Use: Fishing, recreation, wildlife conservation, agriculture.

► Site Description: This site consists of Montana de Oro State Park (at 8,000 acres, the largest of the public lands at the site), Morro Bay and its tidal estuary, Morro Strand State Beach, and Estero Bay. Elevation ranges from sea level to 1,373 feet at Oates Peak in Montana de Oro State Park. A channel to the ocean is maintained by dredging. The confluence of two streams forms a delta of salt marsh habitat. The bay is an estuary sheltered from the ocean by a four-mile-long sand spit. The area has a Mediterranean climate augmented by cool summer fog. There are many rare and endangered plants and animals; among the latter are the endangered and endemic Morro Bay kangaroo rat and Morro Bay banded dune snail.

► Birds: The area is important for wintering Brant, with counts as high as 5,000; 50 pairs of the Snowy Plover breed there and up to 2,600 Willets, 2,100 Marbled Godwits, and 500 Long-billed Curlews are found in winter, along with several thousand other shorebirds. Tens of thousands of shorebirds also stop over during migration. The "California" Black Rail, Black Oystercatcher, Black Turnstone, Surfbird, and Heermann's Gull also occur. Other species of conservation interest include the Nuttall's Woodpecker, Yellow-billed Magpie, Oak Titmouse, Band-tailed Pigeon, California Thrasher, and "California" Spotted Owl.

► Conservation Issues: Volunteers monitor the Snowy Plover nesting area, which is posted during the breeding season. The introduced red fox is a leading predator of the birds. Soil erosion is a problem, and there is potentially the danger of pollution from off-shore oil drilling. Access to the ocean is maintained by dredging.

▶ Visitor Information: Best time to visit is during migration, in April and May and again from August to October. Contact: Morro Bay State Park, Morro Bay State Park Road, Morro Bay, CA 93442, 805-772-2560.

Carrizo Plain Natural Area and National Monument (22), California

▶ Highlight: An important area for wintering Mountain Plovers.
▶ Location: Eastern San Luis Obispo County.
▶ Size: 246,726 acres.
▶ Ownership: Bureau of Land Management, California Department of Fish and Game, The Nature Conservancy.
▶ Habitats: Iodine bush scrub, saltbush scrub, valley grasslands, juniper woodland.
▶ Land Use: Recreation, wildlife conservation.
▶ Site Description: Carrizo Plain is the largest remaining example of the San Joaquin Valley grasslands as they existed in California 300 years ago. It is an internal drainage basin with surface water draining into 3,000-acre Soda Lake, which, as the water evaporates in the dry season, becomes a salt-encrusted playa. Summer temperatures often exceed 100 degrees. Several endangered animals are found there, including the San Joaquin kit fox, the giant kangaroo rat, and the blunt-nosed leopard lizard. Several endangered plant species are also found there. Carrizo Plain National Monument also includes Elkhorn Plain, lying just to the east.
▶ Birds: This is a significant wintering area for the Mountain Plover, found on bare shortgrass fields. Significant numbers of wintering raptors, Long-billed Curlews, Golden Eagles, Burrowing Owls, Horned Larks, and Western Meadowlarks are found there; the Le Conte's Thrasher is rare and irregular as a breeding species. During winter, hundreds of Sandhill Cranes can be found on Soda Lake. The California Condor, once known from the Carrizo Plain, has been reintroduced nearby and may again become part of the area's avifauna.
▶ Conservation Issues: The Nature Conservancy began acquiring land in Carrizo Plain in 1988, with a purchase of 88,000 acres, later turned over to its partner agencies, which have continued to add land to the national monument. The endangered species there are a primary focus of management by The Nature Conservancy, Bureau of Land Management (BLM), and the California Department of Fish and Game, as is restoration of native ecosystems. Prescribed burning and grazing are used to help give native annual and perennial grasses an advantage over introduced annual grasses. Several research projects are being conducted, including those on restoration of native shrub and grassland.
▶ Visitor Information: Best time to visit is from December to May; daytime hours in the summer are extremely hot, and Carrizo Plain is one of the areas of the state with the most annual sunlight. For more information, contact: Guy L. Goodwin Education Center, Carrizo Plain Visitor Center, P.O. Box 3087, California Valley, CA 93453, 805-475-2131. The Goodwin Education Center is open Thursday through Sunday, 9 a.m. to 5 p.m., December through May. In other months, call the Bureau of Land Management at 661-391-6000 Monday through Friday, 7:30 a.m. to 4:15 p.m.

Vandenberg Air Force Base (23), California

▸ Highlight: Important breeding area for the "Western" Snowy Plover and "California" Least Tern, in addition to several resident and/or breeding Green List birds.

▸ Location: Coast near Lompoc, Santa Barbara County.

▸ Size: 98,600 acres.

▸ Ownership: Air Force.

▸ Habitats: Grassland, fresh and salt marshes, estuary, chaparral, coastal sage scrub and dune scrub, sand beach, rocky shoreline, Bishop pine forest, and oak woodlands.

▸ Land Use: Military base.

▸ Site Description: With a great variety of coastal and upland habitats, Vandenberg represents an important island of natural habitat surrounded by development. Several rare and endangered plant species are found on the base. A site for space and missile launches, its military mission means that much of the base is not open to visitors.

▸ Birds: Up to 250 breeding and nearly 500 wintering "Western" Snowy Plover have been found on the base, as have up to 120 breeding "California" Least Terns. The numbers of Snowy Plovers declined drastically following the 1997–1998 El Niño, but recovery appears to be occurring with over 200 breeding birds observed in 2002. Among the common wintering or migrant shorebirds and waterfowl are Brant, Long-billed Curlews, Black Turnstones, Short-billed Dowitchers, and Heerman's Gulls, while Mountain Plovers and Black Oystercatchers are rare. The Allen's Hummingbird is a common breeding species, while the Black-chinned Sparrow, Lawrence's Goldfinch, and the endangered "Southwestern" Willow Flycatcher are rare breeding species. Common residents include the Nuttall's Woodpecker, California Thrasher, and Oak Titmouse; the Sage Sparrow is resident, with up 325 pairs breeding on the base; up to 100 pairs of Tricolored Blackbirds breed there, with as many as 400 birds wintering.

▸ Conservation Issues: Non-native invasive plants are a problem; ice plant, veldt, and European beach grass are increasing, but pampas grass is under control. A restoration plan is being developed to eradicate ice plant and European beach grass from Snowy Plover nesting areas. Staff biologists cooperate with La Purisima Audubon Society in developing and maintaining a system of ponds designated as the Waterfowl Natural Resource Area. Grazing, formerly allowed on 60,000 acres, has been reduced to 23,000 acres, with cattle excluded from wetlands and oak woodlands.

▸ Visitor Information: Much of the base is closed to visitors, but the Santa Ynez River estuary is open to the public via Ocean Park. Barka Slough, an extensive riparian area, can be seen from San Antonio Road East, and is also open to visitors. For further information, contact: 30 CES/CEVPN, Natural Resources, 806 13th Street, Suite 116, Vandenberg Air Force Base, CA 93437, 805-605-8399. Access to the Waterfowl Natural Resources Area, maintained by La Purisima Audubon Society, is also available on a limited, advance-reservation basis by calling the 30th Security Forces Fish and Wildlife office, 805-606-6804. Beach access is limited during the Snowy Plover nesting season (March 1 through September 30); for current status, call at the number above.

Los Padres National Forest (24), California

▶ Highlight: With several breeding green-listed species, the forest also includes the first reintroduction site for the California Condor.

▶ Location: Divided into two sections, both in central/southern California from just south of Monterey in the north to around Los Angeles in the south.

▶ Size: 1,950,000 acres of which 226,000 are under private ownership.

▶ Ownership: Forest Service, private.

▶ Habitats: Chaparral, grasslands, oak woodland, coniferous forest.

▶ Land Use: Grazing, recreation, mineral extraction, wildlife conservation.

▶ Site Description: The third-largest national forest in California, Los Padres extends approximately 220 miles from mid-Monterey County to west Los Angeles County. From sea level along the wild Monterey coast, it climbs to the 9,000-foot peak of Mount Pinos and includes a wide range of habitats from open chaparral to upland pine forest, oak woodland, grassland, the intertidal ecosystem of the Big Sur coast and the semidesert of the Cuyana Badlands. In total, around 500,000 acres are forested; species include ponderosa pine, piñon, coastal redwood, Douglas-fir, and the rare bristlecone pine. Of the forest's 500 miles of streams, many carry water only in the wet winter season. Rainfall varies widely, from six to 80 inches, according to elevation.

▶ Birds: Los Padres is where the first captive-reared California Condors were reintroduced to the wild. The first release took place in the Sespe Condor Sanctuary, where two California along with two Andean Condors were released on January 14, 1992. Six additional birds were released on December 2 the same year. After three of the birds were killed in collisions with power lines, and one from ingesting antifreeze, the remaining birds were relocated to the more remote Lion Canyon near the San Rafael Wilderness in 1993, where five additional birds were also released during December (the Andean Condors were recaptured and sent back to South America in September 1992). Additional releases at Lion Canyon and in the Ventana Wilderness have taken place on an annual basis since. It is hoped that these releases will re-establish a breeding population of the species in California. At last report, 31 birds are flying free in Los Padres and its environs. In addition to its importance for the California Condor, the forest contains important breeding populations of the White-headed Woodpecker, Mountain Quail, California Thrasher, Oak Titmouse, Lawrence's Goldfinch, and Band-tailed Pigeon. A few pairs of the "California" Spotted Owls are known from the forest, and the endangered "California" Least Tern and Brown Pelican occur along the coast.

▶ Conservation Issues: The various watersheds in the forest supply surrounding communities, industry, and farms. Prescribed burns are carried out to enhance water yield, while protecting water quality and soil productivity. The prevention of flooding, erosion, and mud slides is a management priority. A minimal amount of logging, principally for fuel wood, takes place each year. Approximately 6,000 cattle and horses and 1,000 sheep and goats graze on Forest Service lands, and an equivalent number on private inholdings. The 106 campgrounds and more than 1,000 miles of trails provide recreational facilities for more than three million visitors each year. An average of 20,000 acres per year is burned in wildfires. The small population of condors is subject to a variety of threats, including deliberate attacks, collisions with power lines, and lead poisoning.

▸ Visitor Information: The Los Padres National Forest offers a wide range of facilities for visitors. Contact the forest at 6755 Hollister Avenue, Suite 150, Goleta, CA 93117, 805-968-6640. Information on the California Condor in the Ventana Wilderness can be obtained from the Ventana Wilderness Society, 831-455-9514.

Santa Cruz Island (25), California

▸ Highlight: Only location for the Island Scrub-Jay.
▸ Location: The island is located 20 miles off the coast of California (from Ventura/ Santa Barbara) within the Channel Islands National Park, Santa Barbara County, California.
▸ Size: 60,645 acres.
▸ Ownership: The Nature Conservancy, National Park Service.
▸ Habitats: Rugged rocky mountains, streams, valleys, marshes, sea cliffs and caves, pine-oak woodland.
▸ Land Use: Wildlife conservation.
▸ Site Description: The Nature Conservancy owns 90 percent of the island as its Santa Cruz Island Preserve and the National Park Service the remaining ten percent. Santa Cruz is the largest of California's coastal islands, lying between Santa Rosa and Anacapa. It is made up of igneous, sedimentary, and metamorphic rock, and is surrounded by rugged cliffs. The island reaches an altitude of 2,450 feet at Devil's Peak. The habitat includes rocky outcrops, pine-oak woodland, scrubby chaparral, streams, marshes, and grassland. The surrounding seas are extremely rich in sea life, and large kelp forests lie close to the coast. The island is 24 miles long, six miles across, and has an annual rainfall of approximately 20 inches. The Channel Islands have a large number of endemic species, including a deer mouse and a fox. Santa Cruz itself has nine endemic plants.
▸ Birds: The Island Scrub-Jay is found nowhere else. The Snowy Plover, Black Oystercatcher, and Allen's Hummingbird also occur. The Xantus's Murrelet and Ashy Storm-Petrel nest here and in other parts of the Channel Islands. Several endemic subspecies occur, including races of the Loggerhead Shrike and House Finch.
▸ Conservation Issues: Until it was donated to The Nature Conservancy under an agreement with Dr. Carey Stanton in 1978, most of the island was privately owned. In 1988, after Dr. Stanton died, the entire property passed to the ownership and management of The Nature Conservancy. The Santa Cruz Island Foundation, which was established under Dr. Stanton's will, continues to support research and conservation work throughout the Channel Islands. The Channel Islands National Park was established in 1980, and since then the Park Service has developed a major ecological research and management program throughout the Channel Islands, including Santa Cruz. The service owns land in the eastern portion of the island (ten percent of the total land area), and acquired the last remaining privately owned property in 1997 (6,500 acres). Grazing animals have now been removed so that native vegetation may recover, but the ever-present threat of visitors (some 30,000 annually) introducing non-native plants or animals requires ongoing vigilance by the island's managers. Feral pigs are still present, and introduced fennel and thistle are spreading in parts of the island, the former especially in the east where it is being controlled by the Park Service. The national park includes a large marine reserve, which is one of the best places on Earth to see the endangered blue whale.

▶ Visitor Information: Visitors must have a permit to land on Santa Cruz. For information on Channel Islands National Park, call 805-658-5730. Island Packers, based in Ventura, organize trips to the island, 805-642-1393, as does Channel Island Aviation, 805-987-1301. For information on The Nature Conservancy's preserve, contact: Santa Cruz Island Preserve, 79 Daily Drive #294, Camarillo, CA 93010, 805-488-8840. A strain of the hantavirus has been identified in mouse populations on the island. Visitors should be aware of necessary precautions.

Mugu Lagoon (26), California

▶ Highlight: Up to 60,000 shorebirds have been counted here in a single day, and hundreds of thousands of waterfowl use the area annually.
▶ Location: Near Oxnard, Ventura County.
▶ Ownership: Navy.
▶ Size: 2,000 acres.
▶ Land Use: Military base.
▶ Habitats: Tidal wetland, shrub/scrub, coniferous and mixed woods, riparian, marine.
▶ Site Description: Mugu Lagoon is located within the Naval Air Weapons Station, Point Mugu and is adjacent to a hunting club. The lagoon is fed with fresh water by Calleguas Creek and Revolon Slough. The surrounding wetlands compose the largest coastal wetland between Morro Bay and Bolsa Chica, a linear distance of some 175 miles. The lagoon is surrounded by a major weapons testing facility with hundreds of buildings, airstrips, and more than 50 aircraft.
▶ Birds: The lagoon receives heavy seasonal use by waterfowl (including up to 100,000 Northern Shovelers and 70,000 Northern Pintails) and shorebirds (up to 60,000 in a daily count); the adjacent hunting club reports that 300,000 waterfowl use its lands annually. "Western" Snowy Plovers and "California" Least Terns, "Lightfooted" Clapper Rails and "Belding's" Savannah Sparrows all breed there.
▶ Conservation Issues: High pesticide and nutrient levels have been measured in the water of the lagoon because of agricultural runoff. High concentrations of banned pesticides are found in the sediment and the biota. Further, there is also potential pollution from oil exploration or spills. The Navy has restored 23.5 acres of tidal mudflat, sand flats, channels, ponds, salt marsh, and sand islands in three separate wetland restoration projects. It plans to restore a 37-acre site to salt marsh.
▶ Visitor Information: There is no public access to the site.

Upper Newport Bay Ecological Reserve (27), California

▶ Highlight: As the largest estuary in California, it is an important wintering site for shorebirds and waterfowl.
▶ Designations: Wetland of Regional Importance in the Western Hemisphere Shorebird Reserve Network, a California Ecological Reserve.
▶ Location: Near Irvine, Orange County.
▶ Size: 752 acres.
▶ Ownership: California Department of Fish and Game, private.

▶ Habitats: Tidal marsh, mudflats, open water, offshore sandbars, coastal sage scrub, freshwater pond, adjacent bluffs.

▶ Land Use: Ecological reserve, recreation.

▶ Site Description: This estuary is one of the few remaining in southern California. Bordered by the Pacific Coast Highway, it is close to heavily settled residential areas. Upper Newport Bay Regional Park, comprising 140 acres of bluffs, surrounds the Ecological Reserve.

▶ Birds: Well over half of the endangered "Light-footed" Clapper Rails north of the Mexican border are found in the bay. The "California" Black Rail has also been reported in the past. Shorebirds are present all year long; during migration they number in the thousands, and up to 30,000 can be seen in a day in the winter, including Willets, Long-billed Curlews, Marbled Godwits, and Short-billed Dowitchers. The area is also important for wintering waterfowl. A few pairs of California Gnatcatchers are resident.

▶ Conservation Issues: As one of the top hot spots for birding, the area attracts many visitors, particularly during the shorebird migration. Approximately 80 percent of the area is an ecological reserve managed by the California Fish and Game Department. An artificial channel connects the bay with the ocean. Among the issues are nutrient and sediment control. A partnership managing Upper Newport Bay exists between the California Department of Fish and Game and the County of Orange Department of Harbors, Beaches, and Parks in cooperation with the city of Newport Beach and the Fish and Wildlife Service.

▶ Visitor Information: Any time of year is good for a visit, but fall migration, from late July to the end of October, is particularly good for shorebirds. Contact: Upper Newport Bay, 600 Shellmaker, Newport Beach, CA 92660, 949-640-1751.

San Bernardino National Forest (28), California

▶ Highlight: Important site for the "California" Spotted Owl.

▶ Location: In eastern San Bernardino County, near San Bernardino and Palm Springs.

▶ Size: The entire San Bernardino National Forest contains some 816,000 acres, of which about 450,000 acres are in the San Bernardino Mountains. There are three ranger districts.

▶ Ownership: Forest Service, private inholdings.

▶ Habitats: Desert scrub, chaparral, oak woodlands, pine-oak woodlands, mixed conifer forests, subalpine forests, alpine, piñon woodland, meadows, numerous endemic plants, including some conifers found only in southern California (Coulter pine; big-cone fir, a close relative of Douglas-fir).

▶ Land Use: Recreation (skiing, hiking, mountain biking, birding), mineral extraction. Currently very limited logging and grazing.

▶ Site Description: The San Bernardino Mountains are very rugged, ranging from 2,000 to 11,500 feet in elevation. The vegetation is diverse, including various desert scrub types, chaparral, and forest. Tree line is at about 11,000 feet, where snow is found year-round. South-facing slopes typically contain various forms of chaparral with pockets of trees, and north-facing slopes are usually forested. Precipitation occurs mainly in the winter and ranges from 20 to 50 inches, with snow above and rain below about 6,000 feet. Many areas receive more than 300 days of sunshine, but thunderstorms are possible in July, August, and September. Access is good with several highways and numerous unpaved roads through the national forest.

▶ Birds: There are 70 to 90 pairs of "California" Spotted Owls in the forest. Also occurring there are Mountain Quails, Nuttall's Woodpeckers, White-headed Woodpeckers, California Thrashers, Gray Vireos, Oak Titmice, and Lawrence's Goldfinches.

▶ Conservation Issues: The biggest management issues are urbanization and mining. However, there are a large number of minor issues that collectively may be contributing to conservation problems. These include depletion of water in lower-elevation watercourses to meet domestic water needs, air pollution, particularly on south- and west-facing slopes, development of ski areas at the higher elevations, an altered fire regime wherein fires burn hotter and more often than historically, and invasive non-native plants such as cheatgrass.

▶ Visitor Information: "California" Spotted Owls are found year-round in most of the major forested canyons. Best birding is in the spring and summer while all of the migrants are present. However, there is good access all year for anyone interested in the resident birds. Contact: San Bernardino National Forest Supervisor's Office, 1824 South Commercenter Circle, San Bernardino, CA 92408, 909-383-5588; San Bernardino National Forest Discovery Center, 909-866-3437.

Camp Pendleton (Santa Margarita River Valley) (29), California

▶ Highlight: The scrub lands and oak woodlands of the Santa Margarita River Valley support one of the largest remaining populations of the endangered California Gnatcatcher; Camp Pendleton alone supports over 600 pairs according to its 1998 basewide survey. This Marine Corps base includes the largest undeveloped section of coastline remaining in southern California. The base also has an abundant population of the endangered "Least" Bell's Vireo.

▶ Size: 125,000 acres.

▶ Location: San Diego County, near Fallbrook.

▶ Ownership: Marine Corps (Camp Pendleton), Fallbrook Public Utility District, San Diego State University.

▶ Land Use: Camp Pendleton is a Marine Corps training facility with limited public access.

▶ Site Description: One of the few mostly undammed rivers in southern California, the Santa Margarita flows largely through steep-sided canyons and has a narrow floodplain, except near its mouth. Its nearly continuous riparian corridor adjoins vast scrublands and some oak woodlands and forms the only connection for many animals between the interior and the coast.

▶ Birds: Besides its importance to the endangered California Gnatcatcher, its extensive riparian corridor provides habitat for up to 900 "Least" Bell's Vireos, representing about 50 percent of the entire breeding population of this endangered subspecies. The natural resources program on the base is very active and successful. It has established a program to trap cowbirds, nest parasites of the vireo, and other neotropical migrant birds. The base conserves the estuary through managing military training use that is compatible with species recovery efforts. Due to successful natural resource management by the base, the estuary and surrounding beach area now support 20 percent of the entire "California" Least Tern nesting population. The river valley and estuary also serve as a refuge for the Brown Pelican, "Western" Snowy Plover, and "Southwestern" Willow Flycatcher. Other species occurring include the Nuttall's Woodpecker, Wrentit, Oak Titmouse, and California Thrasher, while the Lawrence's Goldfinch is an uncommon resident.

▶ Conservation Issues: The main threat to the area is potential urban development surrounding the base. Upstream development in the watershed is among the fastest in the country. Other potential threats are large development projects planned for off-base portions of the watershed. These could cause large-scale sedimentation into the river and the estuary.

▶ Visitor Information: Camp Pendleton is an active military base, much of which is used for training exercises. Most public access to the base requires specific written permission from the commanding general. This permission is granted only for scientific and educational purposes consistent with the research mission of the base. However, visitors may take a self-guided tour of the base after receiving a pass at the main gate near Oceanside, California.

San Clemente Island (30), California

▶ Highlight: Two federally listed endemic subspecies are found only on the island. Also nesting Snowy Plovers.

▶ Location: Approximately 70 miles offshore, northwest of San Diego.

▶ Size: 35,800 acres.

▶ Ownership: Navy.

▶ Habitats: Beaches, maritime shrub land.

▶ Land Use: Training facility for the Navy and Marine Corps.

▶ Site Description: This 21-mile-long island and its surrounding waters make up an important military training area. There are buildings and a landing strip associated with military activities. The island rises to an elevation of 730 feet.

▶ Birds: The "San Clemente" Loggerhead Shrike is one of the rarest birds in North America. A subspecies of the more widespread Loggerhead Shrike, it lives only on San Clemente Island. The "San Clemente" Sage Sparrow, a federally listed threatened subspecies, inhabits the shrub habitat along the island's west shore. The Snowy Plover also nests on its beaches.

▶ Conservation Issues: Many groups and agencies, including American Bird Conservancy (ABC), have been active in efforts to prevent the extinction of the "San Clemente" Loggerhead Shrike. The Navy uses the southern end of San Clemente Island as a naval bombardment area to calibrate ships' guns. Unfortunately, this is the main breeding territory of the shrike. Shrike habitat on the island is also used to conduct Marine and Navy Seal training exercises. ABC and several partners on its Policy Council have met with the Navy to promote better conservation measures. ABC encouraged the Navy to reduce military operations such as bombardment and Marine training exercises, especially during shrike nesting. Fires, habitat destruction, and disturbance all have occurred due to these operations. The Navy has intensified recovery efforts and has retained a full-time shrike recovery coordinator. The Navy is now spending approximately $2.5 million annually to restore the shrike population, which at one point had shrunk to just 14 birds.

These efforts seem to be paying off, and prospects for the bird have improved. In January 2002, 71 shrikes were detected on the island, up from 39 in January 2001 and the low point of 14 in the spring of 1999. Much of the increase is due to a successful captive-breeding program conducted by the San Diego Zoo, in addition to improved breeding and fledging success in the wild and to supplemental feeding of released birds over the winter. In all, 53 birds were released from captivity in 2001, and in that year 21 pairs of wild shrikes produced nestlings, contrasting with only four pairs in 2000. Predator control of introduced rats and cats is ongoing, and the island's plant nursery is propagating more than 1,000 native plants for shrike-habitat enhancement. The Navy has also installed artificial perches at sites where captive shrikes are released and is beginning a habitat evaluation system based on characteristics of occupied territories. PRBO Conservation, formerly the Point Reyes Bird Observatory, does the shrike monitoring and the predator-management program to protect nesting shrikes and their offspring. The carrying capacity of the island is estimated at 550 to 700 birds, but to reach even half that number in 20 years will require continued population monitoring, captive propagation and release, predator management, and habitat conservation.

▶ Visitor Information: The island is not open to visitors.

Lake Hodges (31), California

▶ Highlight: The coastal sage scrub habitat here supports a good population of California Gnatcatcher.
▶ Location: Southwest of Escondido, near Rancho Bernardo, in San Diego County.
▶ Size: 4,600 acres.
▶ Ownership: City of San Diego.
▶ Habitats: Coastal sage scrub, chaparral, oak woodland, riparian woodland, freshwater marsh, open water (of the reservoir).
▶ Land Use: Water management, recreation.
▶ Site Description: Lake Hodges, also referred to as San Dieguito River Park, is a man-made reservoir, completed in 1918. At full capacity, the lake is 6.5 miles long and has 19 miles of shoreline. There are three maintained trails in the area. It includes about 2,350 acres of coastal sage scrub, the diminishing habitat type in which the California Gnatcatcher lives.
▶ Birds: There are an estimated 80 pairs of California Gnatcatchers found there. The California Thrasher and Sage Sparrow are also resident.
▶ Conservation Issues: Trail bikes are causing erosion. Joint Powers Authority and Water Utilities of the city have administrative control and attempt to control this and other abuses. Tamarisk and giant reed infest the shoreline and the riparian woodland and are not being adequately controlled. Commercial development in the form of a golf driving range is also a threat to the area. Free-roaming cats from the residential neighborhoods surrounding the area are a threat, and the law requiring dogs to be leashed is widely ignored.
▶ Visitor Information: California Gnatcatchers may be seen here all year long but are easiest to find in April and May, during the breeding season. The similar Blue-gray

Gnatcatcher is present in the area during migration and winter. Contact: San Dieguito River Park, 18372 Sycamore Creek Road, Escondido, CA 92025, 858-674-2270.

San Diego National Wildlife Refuge Complex IBAs, California

San Diego National Wildlife Refuge, Otay-Sweetwater and Vernal Pools Units (32); San Diego National Wildlife Refuge, South San Diego Bay Unit (33); Sweetwater Marsh National Wildlife Refuge (34); Tijuana River National Estuarine Research Reserve and Tijuana Slough National Wildlife Refuge (35).

▶ Highlight: Important breeding populations of several endangered California endemic subspecies; migrant and wintering waterfowl and shorebirds.
▶ Location: These IBAs are located around San Diego Bay in southern California, close to the Mexican border.
▶ Size: 69,612 acres.
▶ Ownership: Fish and Wildlife Service, Navy, City and County of San Diego, San Diego Unified Port District, State Lands Commission, California Department of Parks and Recreation, private landowners.
▶ Habitats: Sage scrub, oak woodland, vernal pools, tidal marsh, tidal mudflats.
▶ Land Use: Wildlife conservation, recreation, watershed protection.
▶ Site Description: The San Diego National Wildlife Refuge Complex includes the Otay-Sweetwater and Vernal Pools Unit, the South San Diego Bay Unit, Tijuana Slough National Wildlife Refuge and Tijuana River National Estuarine Research Reserve, and Sweetwater Marsh National Wildlife Refuge. A refuge in Orange County, Seal Beach National Wildlife Refuge, is also administratively part of the complex. The sites comprise a range of habitats from coastal sage scrub, to riparian woodland, chaparral, wetlands, and saltmarsh. The IBAs are treated individually below.
▶ Birds: The California Gnatcatcher breeds, as do the "Least" Bell's Vireo, "Southwestern" Willow Flycatcher, and several other important populations of California endemic subspecies. Several large tern colonies include significant numbers of the Elegant Tern. Migratory shorebirds include the Long-billed Curlew. In total, more than 500,000 migrant and wintering birds use the area.
▶ Conservation Issues: These IBAs are situated in a region of dense human settlement. Threats include development, invasive species, cat predation, and recreational disturbance.

San Diego National Wildlife Refuge, Otay-Sweetwater and Vernal Pools Units (32)

These units have resident California Gnatcatchers, "Least" Bell's Vireos, and "Southwestern" Willow Flycatchers. They are located in southwestern San Diego County. The approved boundary for the Otay-Sweetwater Unit includes 43,860 acres, of which 4,224 have been acquired. For the Vernal Pools Unit, the approved boundary includes 8,220 acres, of which 53 have been acquired. The units are owned by the Fish and Wildlife Service, with some adjacent land owned by private individuals. They are used for conservation, recreation, and watershed protection. Both the Otay-Sweetwater and Vernal Pools Units support several highly endangered and very localized plants and invertebrates. Habitats include 3,289 acres of coastal sage scrub (of which between 70 and 90 percent has been lost in California), 500 acres of chaparral, and 209 acres of riparian woodland (90 percent of this has been lost in California). A significant part of the area has been declared as Critical Habitat for the endangered "Least" Bell's Vireo. There is also oak woodland, native grassland, and some vernal pools. Recent censuses showed that 120 pairs of California Gnatcatchers, and 47 pairs of "Least" Bell's Vireos are found on the Otay-Sweetwater Unit. The endangered "Southwestern" Willow Flycatcher breeds, and the Sage Sparrow also occurs. Uncontrolled human activity in biologically sensitive areas, both in off-road vehicles and on foot, is a major concern. Control of exotic species and restoration of native habitats are among the goals of this new refuge, which was established in 1998. The refuge staff is working with the surrounding communities, local officials, and other interest groups, to plan recreational activities that are compatible with protection of endangered and threatened species and their habitats.

▶ Visitor Information: Any time of year is good for a visit, but from mid-April to the end of June is best for breeding birds. For more information contact the refuge at: 13910 Lyons Valley Road, Suite R, Jamul, CA 91935, 619–669–7295.

THE DOMESTIC CAT AS BIRD PREDATOR

There are estimated to be more than 70 million pet cats in the United States, at least one in every three American households. Polls show that approximately two-thirds of these cats roam free part or all of the time. In addition, there are estimated to be up to 100 million additional domestic cats that are either stray or feral. All cats kill wildlife. In a recent study in Wichita, Kansas, all of 42 cats observed killed birds, and a declawed cat killed the most! A 1998 study estimated the typical cat allowed to roam outdoors kills 40 animals per year, and other studies suggest some cats kill 80 or more per year. No matter which numbers one uses, at a minimum, hundreds of millions of birds are killed by cats each year. A Wisconsin study published in 1995 estimated that cats kill as many as a million birds per year in that one state!

A well-fed, inoculated and disease-free, well-rested, free-roaming cat is a superpredator, subject to few of the limiting factors of native predators, and able to increase at rates far in excess of natural, wild mammal reproduction. Domestic cats are not a natural part of our ecosystem; they compete with native predators and spread diseases to them. Cats are documented to have killed at least ten endangered species ranging from the Piping Plover to the California Gnatcatcher. Introduced cats have an even greater impact on islands where birds have evolved in isolation from predators. Approximately 40 bird species have become extinct due to cat predation on islands, and on Marion Island in the Indian Ocean, cats killed 450,000 seabirds annually prior to cat eradication efforts. As continental habitats become increasingly fragmented into "habitat islands," the effect of cats is to sterilize these places of ground and low-shrub nesting species.

Cats are genetically programmed for this killing behavior and are not to blame. This slaughter of birds is the result of human ignorance and indifference. Solutions include a nationwide campaign to remove cats from all areas important to or set aside for wildlife and an education campaign to convince pet owners to keep their animals indoors. For more information, see American Bird Conservancy's website, www.abcbirds.org.

San Diego National Wildlife Refuge, South San Diego Bay Unit (33)

This unit hosts important breeding colonies of terns, plus many migrating and wintering waterfowl and shorebirds. It is located in the southern part of San Diego Bay, where five cities come together: San Diego, National City, Chula Vista, Coronado, and Imperial Beach. It is designated as a Wetland of Regional Importance in the Western Hemisphere Shorebird Reserve Network; the unit has 4,772 acres within its acquisition boundary. The land is owned by the Fish and Wildlife Service, San Diego Unified Port District, State Lands Commission, Navy, the City of San Diego, and private landowners. It is principally used for recreation and wildlife conservation. South San Diego Bay's shallow water, eelgrass, tidal mudflats, salt ponds, and saltmarshes are habitats that have virtually been eliminated elsewhere in the bay through dredging and filling for airports, industry, and naval facilities. The south bay unit presently consists of properties for which the Fish and Wildlife Service has already entered into leasehold deals, and other areas within the acquisition boundary of the south bay refuge that have yet to be acquired. The remaining properties are controlled by the San Diego Unified Port District, the State Lands Commission, and the Navy. In 2000 there were approximately 3,000 pairs of Elegant Terns, 300 pairs of Caspian Terns, and 50 pairs of Royal Terns nesting on the refuge. More than 175 pairs of Forster's Terns, 29 pairs of Gull-billed Terns, and 25 pairs of Least Terns also nested, along with approximately 400 pairs of Black Skimmers. "Belding's" Savannah Sparrow also occurs. The salt ponds of the southern bay also provide irreplaceable habitat for many migratory bird species. Each year, these birds use the ponds to nest, feed, and roost. The ponds form one of the few large natural areas remaining along the highly urbanized southern California coast where large bird concentrations can gather. In a recent year, more than 522,000 birds were counted in the salt ponds, including 312,000 shorebirds, 70,000 waterfowl, and 64,000 seabirds. The open water also provides critical wintering habitat for migratory waterfowl. Counts of ducks have reached 79,000, with many Surf Scoters and scaup, in addition to 10,000 gulls and terns, and large numbers of Brown Pelicans and Brant. Intense pressure for real estate development is a primary threat to the refuge. Non-native species, including both plants and invertebrates, degrade habitats in the bay. Perhaps even more serious are native species such as corvids, kestrels, skunks, possums, raccoons, and coyotes, whose populations have grown due to continuing urbanization. They are major predators on endangered bird species, and on other ground-nesting birds in the area. Domestic dogs and feral and domestic cats also prey on these birds. Land protection continues: recently, the Trust for Public Land acquired and transferred 631 acres to the refuge that had been slated for development as a golf course. The salt ponds, purchased from the Western Salt Company by the Port of San Diego, and conveyed to the Fish and Wildlife Service, will continue to be used to produce salt until 2004, and the ponds will be maintained well into the future. The Fish and Wildlife Service is now beginning to develop a Comprehensive Conservation Plan, as well as a restoration plan for the area. Ducks Unlimited will be a cooperator in future habitat restoration projects.

▸ Visitor Information: There are birds of interest at any time of year. Contact the refuge at 1000 Gunpowder Point Drive, Chula Vista, CA 91910, 619-691-1262.

Sweetwater Marsh National Wildlife Refuge (34)

The marsh is located on the east side of San Diego Bay in the cities of Chula Vista and National City. It comprises 316 acres, and is owned by the Fish and Wildlife Service. Ninety-one percent of San Diego Bay's wetlands have been filled in, drained, or diked, and this site includes key natural areas of tidal marsh and adjacent upland habitats. It is used for education and wildlife conservation. The "California" Least Tern nests on the refuge, with as many as 60 pairs in some years. A few endangered "Light-footed" Clapper Rails are found, and approximately 150 pairs of the "Belding's" Savannah Sparrow nest in the upper marsh. A variety of migrating shorebirds and wintering waterfowl also make use of the refuge. Feral cats are a problem, and several Clapper Rails have been brought in with their necks broken by cats. The refuge has an outreach program aimed at local residents, one aspect of which is to ask cat owners to keep their cats indoors. Cats trapped on the refuge are turned over to the pound, and their owners given the opportunity to reclaim them.

▸ Visitor Information: There is an interpretive center reached by shuttle bus from the parking lot at the foot of E Street. Thousands of school children visit the refuge each year. The remainder of the refuge is closed to the public to limit disturbance of these highly sensitive and endangered birds. For more information call: 619-422-2481.

Tijuana River National Estuarine Research Reserve and Tijuana Slough National Wildlife Refuge (35)

One of the only two intact estuaries in southern California, the site has several breeding and migrant green-listed birds. The area has been designated one of the 23 Estuarine Research Reserves in the United States by the National Oceanic and Atmospheric Administration. It is located at Imperial Beach, on the coast just north of the border with Mexico. This IBA occupies 2,800 acres and is owned by the Fish and Wildlife Service, California Department of Parks and Recreation, the Navy, and the City and County of San Diego. Land use includes research, and wildlife conservation and observation. Habitats include dunes, salt pans, salt marsh, mud flats, brackish ponds, riparian habitats, coastal sage scrub, and vernal pools. The IBA includes Tijuana Slough National Wildlife Refuge, Border Field State Park, and lands belonging to the Navy, San Diego County, and the City of San Diego. The estuary is the endpoint of the Tijuana River watershed covering some 1,735 square miles. The reserve is managed cooperatively by the Fish and Wildlife Service and the California Department of Parks and Recreation. There is a biological field station operated by San Diego State University. Breeding birds include the endangered "Light-footed" Clapper Rail, "California" Least Tern, "Least" Bell's Vireo, and "Belding's" Savannah Sparrow. A few "Western" Snowy Plovers also breed, but the bird is common in fall and winter. Marbled Godwits (non-breeding) are common in all seasons. The Long-billed Curlew and Red Knot are common fall migrants. The Heermann's Gull is common from spring through fall, but does not breed. The area is surrounded by urban development. Among the concerns are predation by domestic and feral cats and dogs, the spread of non-native species into native habitats, and sedimentation and contaminants from adjoining areas.

▸ Visitor Information: The area is open throughout the year; there are foot trails and an interpretive center. For more information, contact the visitor center at 619-575-3613 or the National Wildlife Refuge at 619-575-2704.

ENCOURAGING BACKYARD BIRDS

Most of our backyards are not going to be Important Bird Areas (IBAs). However, there are ways to improve conditions for your yard's relatively common birds and enhance your opportunities to appreciate them.

The most important thing you can do to improve backyard bird habitat is to increase the structure, density, and diversity of vegetation. Most birds find little of interest in a mowed lawn. What you grow in your yard depends on where you live, but whether it be deciduous forest, coniferous forest, grassland, or arid shrub land, you'll get the most interesting birds by maintaining or restoring native vegetation.

In most places and times when the weather is warm, birds benefit from a continuous supply of shallow, clean water. They also need food. Putting out seeds, thistle, nectar, or fruit helps you see birds and is beneficial at times. In southern states, plants that produce fleshy fruits during fall migration can be very helpful, and may even attract some rare birds to your yard for brief visits. The real key to providing food for birds, however, is in providing insects. Even seed eaters rely on the protein in insects and other invertebrates to feed growing young. To really encourage birds, you must allow the plants you grow to grow insects. Stop using pesticides and start appreciating the basic elements of biological diversity!

At the very least, even if you can't provide conditions in which birds can thrive, you should avoid creating conditions that cause them to die. Keep your cats indoors. Don't cut down rank vegetation while birds are breeding.

A few "backyards" that are hundreds or thousands of acres in size could be IBAs if managed appropriately. If you have a chance to do this, contact the Partners in Flight or waterbird experts in your state wildlife agency.

33. Sonoran and Mojave Deserts

The Mojave Desert is centered in southeastern California and southern Nevada and grades into the Sonoran Desert of southwestern Arizona, which extends south on both sides of the Gulf of California into the Mexican states of Baja California, Sonora, and Sinaloa. This arid region is dominated by creosote, cacti, and other desert shrubs and is the center of distribution of the Rufous-winged Sparrow, Le Conte's Thrasher, Bendire's Thrasher, Lucy's Warbler, and Abert's Towhee. Riparian wetlands are habitat for the "Yuma" Clapper Rail and "Southwestern" Willow Flycatcher. The Salton Sea hosts large numbers of American White Pelicans, Eared Grebes, and other colonial waterbirds; shorebirds such as Black-necked Stilts and Long-billed Curlews; and waterfowl during both migrations and winter. The Colorado River and adjacent wetlands provide habitat for ducks and other wetland birds, including some of the most important habitat in the arid southwest for Western and Clark's Grebes and American Avocets.

Butterbredt Spring Wildlife Sanctuary (1), California

▶ Highlight: One of the Mojave Desert's best birding localities, this site is an outstanding migrant trap, especially in the spring.

Le Conte's Thrasher

▶ Location: 35 miles southwest of Ridgecrest, Kern County.
▶ Size: The area of the fenced sanctuary is approximately seven acres.
▶ Ownership: The fenced spring is within 720 acres of privately owned land, and the surrounding area is public land administered by the Bureau of Land Management.
▶ Habitats: Desert riparian, sagebrush, desert scrub.
▶ Land Use: Livestock grazing, recreational use by off-road vehicles, wildlife observation.
▶ Site Description: The site is a desert spring and oasis at the lower end of Butterbredt

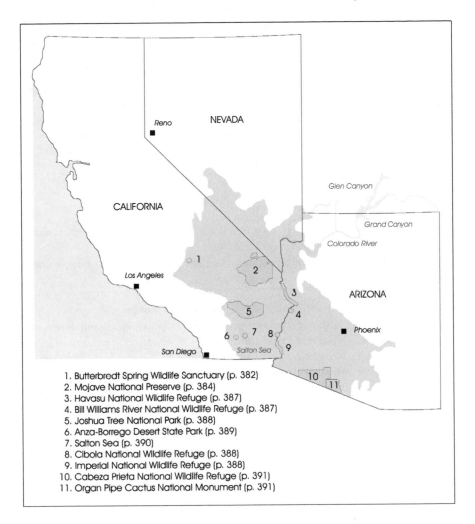

1. Butterbredt Spring Wildlife Sanctuary (p. 382)
2. Mojave National Preserve (p. 384)
3. Havasu National Wildlife Refuge (p. 387)
4. Bill Williams River National Wildlife Refuge (p. 387)
5. Joshua Tree National Park (p. 388)
6. Anza-Borrego Desert State Park (p. 389)
7. Salton Sea (p. 390)
8. Cibola National Wildlife Refuge (p. 388)
9. Imperial National Wildlife Refuge (p. 388)
10. Cabeza Prieta National Wildlife Refuge (p. 391)
11. Organ Pipe Cactus National Monument (p. 391)

Canyon; dominant vegetation there is Fremont cottonwood and red willow, with surrounding ground cover of sage, desert scrub, and Joshua tree. Because of its orientation from southeast to northwest, the canyon provides a natural passageway from the northwestern Mojave Desert into the southern Sierra Nevada.

▸ Birds: As many as 500,000 migrant landbirds, both passerine and nonpasserine, may use the site during spring migration; it is an important migrant trap and one of the top sites for birding in the Mojave Desert, especially in the spring. Brewer's and Sage Sparrows are found there seasonally, and both California and Le Conte's Thrashers breed in the area.

▸ Conservation Issues: The sanctuary owes its existence to a cooperative agreement signed between the landowner, Keith Axelson, the Santa Monica Bay Audubon Society, and the Bureau of Land Management. Mr. Alexson is the prime reason the site has the recognition that it does; he maintains fencing that prevents entry by cattle. There is off-road vehicle use in the canyon and on surrounding lands. There is always the possibility that the sale of the private land would change the existing agreement.

▶ Visitor Information: The best times to visit are fall, winter, and spring. The area is very popular with birders during spring migration. Visitors must stay on designated routes of travel and avoid damage to grasses and other plants that provide feed for livestock and wildlife. Dirt roads can become impassable after a rain. The administering office is Bureau of Land Management, Ridgecrest Field Office, 300 South Richmond Road, Ridgecrest, CA 93555, 760-384-5400. Keith Axelson can be contacted at Sageland Ranch, P.O. Box 967, Weldon, CA 93283, 760-372-6116.

Mojave National Preserve (2), California

▶ Highlight: Two high-priority species, Bendire's and Le Conte's Thrashers, breed on the preserve, as do several other significant birds.

▶ Location: Eastern San Bernadino County, beginning approximately 60 miles west of Barstow and reaching to the Nevada state line.

▶ Size: 1.6 million acres.

▶ Ownership: National Park Service, with many private inholdings.

▶ Habitats: Creosote bush flats, piñon pine and juniper woodlands, sand dunes, volcanic cinder cones, Joshua tree forests.

▶ Land Use: Recreation, cattle grazing, mining, hunting.

▶ Site Description: Mojave National Preserve incorporates lowlands and desert mountain ranges; within its borders is the largest Joshua tree forest in the world. A major feature is Cima Dome, a symmetrical granite formation approximately 75 square miles in size.

▶ Birds: Among the resident and breeding birds are the Gilded Flicker, Juniper Titmouse, and Bendire's and Le Conte's Thrashers. Other species present in the preserve are the Pinyon Jay and Black-throated Gray Warbler.

▶ Conservation Issues: The preserve was created in October 1994 when Congress passed, and President Clinton signed, the California Desert Protection Act. Cattle grazing, mining, and hunting are all allowed within the preserve boundaries, since much of the land there is privately held. Water demand from southern California threatens the aquifer that supplies part of the preserve.

▶ Visitor Information: The Mojave is a hot desert. Days with temperatures in excess of 100°F typically begin in May and can last into October. Winters, however, can bring freezing temperatures. The most pleasant temperatures and the best times to visit are in spring and fall. Contact: Mojave National Preserve Headquarters, 222 East Main Street, Suite 202, Barstow, CA 92311, 760-255-8801.

SUBSPECIES CONSERVATION

"Yuma" Clapper Rail, "Southwestern" Willow Flycatcher, "Least" Bell's Vireo, "San Clemente" Loggerhead Shrike, "California" Least Tern, "Timberline" (Brewer's) Sparrow, "Wayne's" (Black-throated Green) Warbler: the list of rare or declining subspecies is long. Should we care about their conservation, or focus instead only on full species? How different is sufficiently different to warrant the expenditure of scarce conservation resources? A large part of the answers is embedded in the practice of taxonomy and determining degrees of distinctness among taxa. Another part falls to the realm of moral and legal judgment about the job of conservation.

Those who follow scientific literature know the very definition of what constitutes a species is a subject of ongoing debate. In an unsettled taxonomy with rapidly emerging technologies for identifying relationships between taxa, and where the distinction between species is sometimes less than that between subspecies, we cannot count on current science to provide definitive answers to all conservation questions. In the legal realm, the federal listing of species and subspecies is sufficiently uneven that it cannot provide a compass for conservation action.

Scientists with Partners in Flight and American Bird Conservancy are beginning to address these questions. PIF prescribes that species recognized on the U.S. Endangered Species List, circumpolar species with a distinct North America subspecies, those with disjunct, local populations that local experts feel are a priority, and those co-occurring with other subspecies (such as the avifauna in the Southern Appalachians) receive conservation attention.

Given the scientific and legal uncertainty, the best approach for addressing subspecies conservation may be to follow the advice of Aldo Leopold, who said, "the first precaution of intelligent thinking is to save all the pieces." In other words, until we have scientific certainty regarding what it is important to conserve, it will be wisest to err on the side of caution.

Lower Colorado River IBAs, Arizona and California

Havasu National Wildlife Refuge, CA (3), Bill Williams River National Wildlife Refuge, AZ (4), Cibola National Wildlife Refuge, AZ (8), Imperial National Wildlife Refuge, AZ (9)

▶ Highlight: Important migrant corridor; wintering and migrating waterfowl; riparian and wetland breeding birds, including the "Yuma" Clapper Rail, "California" Black Rail, "Southwestern" Willow Flycatcher, "Least" Bell's Vireo. The Elf Owl, Gilded Flicker, Lucy's Warbler, and Abert's Towhee are also found here.

▶ Location: The Lower Colorado River runs through the Sonoran Desert and forms the border between Arizona and California.

▶ Size: The entire Lower Colorado River is 230,000 acres. Approximately 75,000 acres of the most significant wetland and riparian areas are protected by four key National Wildlife Refuges spread along 100 miles of the river.

▶ Ownership: Fish and Wildlife Service; elsewhere along the river, land ownership is divided among state and private interests, the Bureau of Land Management, and Indian Reservations.

▶ Habitats: Desert scrub, foothills, riparian gallery woodland, riverine, marshes, lakes, rocky cliffs.

▶ Land Use: Wildlife conservation, recreation.

Elf Owl

▶ Site Description: The four national wildlife refuge IBAs are Havasu, Bill Williams River, Cibola, and Imperial. All are generally similar in terms of bird species, composition, habitats, and vegetation. They lie along the riparian corridor of the Colorado River, which cuts through the Sonoran Desert, providing vital breeding, wintering, and migratory habitat for a range of bird species. Natural communities of gallery cottonwood and willow woodland are gradually being replaced by non-native salt cedar, introduced in the 1920s, which tolerates altered river flow conditions better than the native species. Since the 1930s, 99 percent of cottonwood-willow forests of the lower Colorado have disappeared largely due to invasion by salt cedar. The native species require periodic flooding, now severely restricted following the construction of a number of large dams upstream, beginning with Hoover Dam in 1935, which also inundated large areas of riparian habitat. Farther from the river, the galley forest gives way to mesquite, then open scrubby desert. There are also shrubby open areas, riparian washes, riverine sandbars, oxbow lakes, rocky gorges, and open desert areas dominated by cacti. The refuges also contain a number of wetlands, including areas of open water surrounded by cattail and bulrush marshes. Information applicable to all four areas is given in this introductory section, followed by a short description of features specific to each. In addition to the wildlife refuges, the corridor includes reservoirs such as Lake Mead and Lake Mojave, and broad floodplains such as the Palo Verde, Mojave, Chemihuevi, and Yuma Valleys.

▶ Birds: The river and its surrounding riparian woodland provide an important migration corridor for hundreds of thousands, perhaps millions, of neotropical migrants and large numbers of wintering and migrating waterfowl, cranes, and shorebirds. Several species of conservation concern are found within the refuges, including southwest riparian breeding specialists such as the "Western" Yellow-billed Cuckoo, "Southwestern" Willow Flycatcher, and "Least" Bell's Vireo. Other breeding birds include the "California" Black Rail, Elf Owl, Gilded Flicker, Lucy's Warbler, and Abert's Towhee. The endangered "Yuma" race of Clapper Rail is resident. Brewer's Sparrows are found during migration.

▶ Conservation Issues: Principal problems for riparian habitat are the channelization of the Colorado River, the reduction in stream flow caused by damming, and the over-utilization of water by farmers and nearby communities. Reduced stream flow has resulted in a lack of periodic flooding that is needed to maintain native willow and cottonwood gallery woodland. Native habitats have largely been replaced by introduced salt cedar. The regulation of stream flow and the control of salt cedar are the two main challenges facing conservation of riparian habitats on the Lower Colorado River, especially with increasing demand for water. All refuges have restrictions on visitor usage to limit disturbance to habitat and birds, although jet skis and off-road vehicles still cause problems in some areas. The potential for toxic pollution of the river, including from septic systems, is an ever-present threat. Destruction of native vegetation by feral donkeys is also a problem.

► Visitor Information: The best times to visit the IBAs in the Lower Colorado River corridor are during spring and fall migration. All refuges have visitor facilities, and the site accounts below provide contact information.

Havasu National Wildlife Refuge (3), California

The refuge adjoins Bill Williams River National Wildlife Refuge and occupies 37,515 acres. The refuge comprises marshy backwaters, shrubby riparian flats, steep cliffs, and arid desert. The endangered "Yuma" Clapper Rail, with a recent count of 33 birds, is found in the 4,000-acre Topock Marsh. Up to 77 "Least" Bell's Vireos have been counted on the refuge. Other resident or breeding species include the Elf Owl, Gilded Flicker, "Southwestern" Willow Flycatcher, Lucy's Warbler, and Abert's Towhee. Approximately 45 percent of the refuge is designated as wilderness. Management activities include control of salt cedar, water flow management to maintain water levels in Topock Marsh, restricted areas to protect nesting waterbirds, and the creation of the Pintail Slough Management Unit, where waterfowl feed on grain and agricultural crops planted for that purpose.

► Visitor Information: Contact: Havasu National Wildlife Refuge, P.O. Box 3009, Needles, CA 92363, 760-326-3853.

Bill Williams River National Wildlife Refuge (4), Arizona

Located near Parker and Lake Havasu City, this 6,000-acre refuge contains some of the best riparian cottonwood and willow habitat remaining in the Southwest. It encompasses the lower nine miles of the Bill Williams River, including approximately one mile of desert upland to either side of it. Habitats also include cliffs, marshes, and open water. Resident or breeding birds found here are the "Yuma" Clapper Rail, "California" Black Rail, "Southwestern" Willow Flycatcher, "Western" Yellow-billed Cuckoo, "Least" Bell's Vireo, Lucy's Warbler, and Abert's Towhee. Management activities include the control of salt cedar, tree planting and maintenance, and control of water from the Alamo Dam to return flow to natural levels. There are serious problems for the "Least" Bell's Vireo from cowbird parasitism (89.8 percent of nests were parasitized in one study). Illegal off-road vehicle traffic results in soil degradation, damage to vegetation, erosion, and alteration of stream channel. Land managers on the refuge are planting cottonwood and willow and negotiating with the Army Corps of Engineers to regulate flooding to benefit riparian communities.

► Visitor Information: The refuge can be reached by taking Arizona Highway 95 from Lake Havasu City. The refuge lies 23 miles south between mileposts 160 and 161. Contact Bill Williams River National Wildlife Refuge, 60911 Highway 95, Parker, AZ 85344, 928-857-3253.

Cibola National Wildlife Refuge (8), Arizona

Cibola lies just upriver from Imperial National Wildlife Refuge, and occupies 17,267 acres. The refuge comprises an alluvial river bottom with dense growths of salt cedar, mesquite, and arrow weed, native vegetation, open water, marshes, desert ridges and washes. There are 2,000 acres of farmland on the refuge managed for wintering waterfowl and Sandhill Cranes. The "Yuma" Clapper Rail is found in suitable marshes throughout the refuge. The Lucy's Warbler is common in spring and summer. The Abert's Towhee is also common, and breeds on the refuge. Waterfowl are abundant in winter. Management activities include control and removal of salt cedar.

▸ Visitor Information: The refuge can be reached by taking I-10 west from Blythe, three miles to Neighbors Boulevard, then driving south for 12 miles to Cibola Bridge. Contact: Cibola National Wildlife Refuge, Route 2, Box 138, Cibola, AZ 85328, 520-857-3253.

Imperial National Wildlife Refuge (9), Arizona

Imperial National Wildlife Refuge lies approximately 12 miles above Imperial Dam, north of Yuma, and occupies 25,125 acres. The refuge includes 3,000 acres of riparian habitat, with remnant stands of willow, cottonwood, and sandbars. There are also 17,000 acres of upland desert. Approximately 500 acres are actively managed for migrating and wintering waterfowl, shorebirds, and other waterbirds. The refuge boasts more than 270 species on its official bird list, and includes habitat for the "California" Black Rail and the endangered "Yuma" Clapper Rail. It is also a stopover point for migratory waterfowl and shorebirds, as well as the endangered "Southwestern" Willow Flycatcher. The range-limited Abert's Towhee is a common resident, and the "Western" Yellow-billed Cuckoo, "Least" Bell's Vireo, and Lucy's Warbler breed.

▸ Visitor Information: The refuge is reached by taking U.S. 95 north from Yuma for approximately 25 miles, then turning west onto Martinez Lake Road for 13 miles. It lies on both sides of the Colorado River. Contact: Imperial National Wildlife Refuge, P.O. Box 72217, Yuma, AZ 85365, 928-783-3371.

Joshua Tree National Park (5), California

▸ Highlight: Species breeding here include the Costa's Hummingbird, Nuttall's Woodpecker, Le Conte's and Bendire's Thrashers, and Lawrence's Goldfinch.
▸ Location: In San Bernardino and Riverside Counties, just south of Twenty-nine Palms.
▸ Size: 792,828 acres.
▸ Ownership: National Park Service.
▸ Habitats: Lower-lying arid desert (Colorado/Sonoran), and more vegetated upland desert (Mojave).
▸ Land Use: Tourism, recreation.
▸ Site Description: Joshua Tree National Park contains two principal types of desert: the more arid lowland Colorado Desert which rises to approximately 3,000 feet from

the park's eastern flank, and the upland Mojave Desert, which is found in the western portion of the park, climbing from a minimum of 2,000 feet to the park's highest point, Quail Mountain, at 5,814 feet. This part of the Mojave is characterized by Joshua trees, large granite outcrops, and boulders. The Colorado Desert comprises arid basins and rocky wilderness, scattered with creosote bushes and groups of ocotillo and cholla cactus. Annual precipitation is approximately four inches, with the higher western part of the park receiving most of this. There are six mountain ranges in total, and several oases of California fan palms.

▸ Birds: The park's avifauna includes a good range of species typical of southern Californian arid ecosystems, including the Prairie Falcon, Cactus Wren, Phainopepla, Verdin, and Bushtit. Species characteristic of the Joshua tree zone include the Ladder-backed Woodpecker and Ash-throated Flycatcher, both of which use the yuccas for nesting. Other species found there include the California, Le Conte's, and Bendire's Thrashers, Nuttall's Woodpecker, Gray Vireo, and Lawrence's Goldfinch. The Mountain Quail is resident at the higher elevations. Sage Sparrows and Lewis's Woodpeckers are occasionally seen, and migrants of conservation concern include the Lucy's Warbler, and Rufous and Allen's Hummingbirds. Cottonwood Spring is a good place to look for the Le Conte's Thrasher.

▸ Conservation Issues: The 825,340-acre Joshua Tree National Monument was created in 1936, but in 1950, 289,000 acres were removed for ore extraction. In 1994, when President Clinton signed the California Desert Protection Act, the Joshua Tree National Park was formed, with the addition of a further 243,000 acres. Eighty percent of the park is wilderness. The nonprofit Joshua Tree National Park Association assists with education and outreach activities (see www.joshuatree.org).

▸ Visitor Information: The Park's Oasis Visitor Center is located in south-central California in Twenty-nine Palms at 74485 National Park Drive. For details on visiting the park, call 760-367-7511 or 760-367-5500. Paved roads lead to lookouts, campgrounds, and nature trails.

Anza-Borrego Desert State Park (6), California

▸ Highlight: The largest state park in the lower 48 states, it is home to breeding Le Conte's Thrashers.

▸ Location: Eastern side of San Diego County, extending into Imperial and Riverside Counties.

▸ Size: 600,000 acres.

▸ Ownership: California Department of Parks and Recreation, some private inholdings.

▸ Habitats: Creosote scrub, dry lakes and washes, palm groves, riparian areas.

▸ Land Use: Recreation.

▸ Site Description: Measuring some 70 by 32 miles, this huge park incorporates the bowl of the Anza-Borrego Desert and surrounding mountains. Highest are the Santa Rosa Mountains, to the north, a wilderness area with no paved roads. The endangered desert bighorn sheep is found in the park.

▸ Birds: Among the breeding birds are California and Le Conte's Thrashers, "Southwestern" Bell's Vireos, and Lucy's Warblers, while Brewer's and Sage Sparrows are present in winter. The green areas in the park are migrant traps, and many landbirds are found there during spring and fall migration.

▶ Conservation Issues: There are 12 wilderness areas in the park. Near water, introduced salt cedar has replaced much of the native vegetation.
▶ Visitor Information: Best times to visit are fall through spring. Seasonal temperatures can be extreme. Visitors should take plenty of water in their vehicles and when hiking. Contact: Anza-Borrego Desert State Park, 200 Palm Canyon Drive, Borrego Springs, CA 92004, 760-767-5311.

Salton Sea (7), California

▶ Highlight: The site has many superlatives, including thousands of waterfowl and shorebirds seasonally present, large numbers of wintering Mountain Plovers, and the only inland breeding colonies of several species usually found only on the coast.
▶ Designation: Wetland of Hemispheric Importance in the Western Hemisphere Shorebird Reserve Network.
▶ Location: Imperial County, between Coachella and Brawley, with the north edge of the lake 12.5 miles south of Interstate 10. At the southern end of the lake lies the Sonny Bono Salton Sea National Wildlife Refuge.
▶ Size: 43,000 acres, of which the refuge is 1,800 acres.
▶ Ownership: Fish and Wildlife Service, Bureau of Land Management, California Department of Fish and Game, private.
▶ Habitats: The area includes a combination of agricultural land, riparian and lacustrine wetland, and desert scrub.
▶ Land Use: Primarily a wildlife conservation area with less than 50 percent under cultivation.
▶ Site Description: The Salton Sea is the third largest interior saline lake in North America and was formed by accidental water diversions from the Colorado River into southern California between 1905 and 1906, when a break in a canal flooded the dry alkaline basin. It is currently maintained by water imported for agricultural purposes and freshwater river flow. The area contains a mosaic of habitats from saline lake waters, through brackish and freshwater deltas, to agricultural and xerophytic habitats. The soil surrounding the sea is very alkaline; fresh water running over agricultural fields leaches out the salts and runs off into the lake, increasing its salinity each year. The area has low rainfall and summer temperatures to 120°F and higher.
▶ Birds: More than 100,000 waterfowl winter, including 8,000 Ross's Geese, 12,000 Snow Geese, 12,000 Northern Shovelers, 20,000 to 30,000 Ruddy Ducks, 10,000 Green-winged Teal, and 9,000 Northern Pintails. More than 100,000 shorebirds pass through the area on migration annually, including 10,000 Black-necked Stilts, 10,000 American Avocets, 10,000 to 15,000 Western Sandpipers, 10,000 dowitchers of both species, 5,000 to 10,000 Red-necked Phalaropes, and 1,000 Black-bellied Plovers. Long-billed Curlews, Willets, and Marbled Godwits also winter. Large numbers of colonial waterbirds nest, including 15,000 to 20,000 Cattle Egrets and 3,000 Double-crested Cormorants. The lake supports the only inland nesting colonies of the Black Skimmer (200+ nests) and Gull-billed Tern (100+ nests) in the western United States. The federally threatened western race of Snowy Plover nests; the White-faced Ibis is listed as a California species of special concern, and 16,000 winter in the Salton Sea area with small numbers breeding; the federally endangered "California" race of the Brown Peli-

can nests in small numbers (fewer than ten pairs), with a total summer population of approximately 3,500 birds; up to 25,000 American White Pelicans use the lake during fall migration; 40 percent of the world population of the "Yuma" race of Clapper Rail (approximately 400 birds) occurs around the sea. The area also supports the largest concentration of the Burrowing Owl in California, and the Abert's Towhee is resident around the lake. Close to one million Eared Grebes and approximately 400 Sandhill Cranes winter there. The sea is also a reliable location to see the Yellow-footed Gull, a Mexican species that is the most common large gull there during the summer. Surrounding burned fields may hold up to 1,000 Mountain Plovers in winter.

▶ Conservation Issues: The Salton Sea is experiencing high levels of eutrophication, salinization, and contamination, leading to large-scale mortality of birds due to botulism outbreaks, and fish die-offs due to algal blooms. A recent botulism outbreak killed more than 300 Brown Pelicans, while in the worst recorded outbreak, in 1996, more than 8,500 American White Pelicans died. Current freshwater sources are also threatened by planned diversions to coastal urban areas. In addition to its importance for birds, the lake is significant for the federally endangered desert pupfish. Other conservation issues include overapplication of pesticides, introduced non-native species, and inadequate funding for conservation.

▶ Visitor Information: Best time to visit is fall through spring. For further information contact the Sonny Bono Salton Sea National Wildlife Refuge, 906 West Sinclair Road, Calipatria, CA 92233, 760-348-5278. The refuge headquarters is located north of Calipatria at the extreme west end of Sinclair Road at its intersection with Gentry Road. The office is closed on weekends during the summer months only but open weekends during the months of October to March. A bird checklist and visitor information are available at the bulletin board.

Cabeza Prieta National Wildlife Refuge (10) and Organ Pipe Cactus National Monument (11), Arizona

▶ Highlight: Breeding Bendire's and Le Conte's Thrashers; a total of 18 Green List birds have been recorded at the site.
▶ Location: Southwestern Arizona, on the Mexican border.
▶ Size: Cabeza Prieta National Wildlife Refuge is 860,000 acres; Organ Pipe Cactus National Monument is 330,688 acres.
▶ Ownership: Fish and Wildlife Service, National Parks Service.
▶ Habitats: Sonoran Desert ecosystem, rugged mountains, valleys, desert.
▶ Land Use: Wilderness, recreation, military overflights.
▶ Site Description: Cabeza Prieta is the third largest National Wildlife Refuge in the lower 48 states. Both this and the adjoining Organ Pipe Cactus National Monument are representative of the Sonoran Desert ecosystem, with rugged mountains, arid desert, and large saguaro cacti. Cabeza Prieta is close to Ajo and has 56 miles of Mexican border running along its southern boundary; Organ Pipe Cactus National Monument, also on the border, lies east of the refuge, around six miles south of Why. Both the refuge and the monument are adjacent to the El Pinacate and Gran Desierto de Altar Biosphere Reserve in Sonora, Mexico. The area is principally arid desert with daily maximum temperatures in excess of 100°F for continuous periods between June

and October. Annual rains in Cabeza Prieta range from four to seven inches. The landscape is characterized by rugged mountains and valleys, lava flows, and arid desert, with creosote, mesquite, and bursage flats. Large cacti, including saguaro and organ pipe, are found on Organ Pipe Cactus National Monument and the eastern portions of Cabeza Prieta National Wildlife Refuge. Sand, silt, and gravel deposited by seasonal rains are found along the mountain slopes. Although the area includes some of the most inhospitable desert in North America, the lush vegetation along the washes provides important corridor habitat for migrants.

▸ Birds: The area is home to the typical avifauna of the Sonoran Desert along with many neotropical migrants in spring and fall. Resident or breeding Green List species include the Gilded Flicker, Bendire's Thrasher, Le Conte's Thrasher, Curve-billed Thrasher (most abundant of the three thrashers—the other two occur characteristically in low densities and are hard to find), Lucy's Warbler (a common breeding species), Bell's Vireo (common breeding species in riparian habitats), and seven species of owl, including the Elf Owl and the endangered "Cactus" subspecies of Ferruginous Pygmy-Owl. Migrants and winter residents include the Brewer's Sparrow, Cassin's Sparrow, Lawrence's Goldfinch, Rufous and Allen's Hummingbirds, Sprague's Pipit, Gray Vireo, and Rufous-winged, Black-chinned, and Sage Sparrows. Organ Pipe has the highest winter count of Abert's Towhees. Migration starts in late February and again in late July.

▸ Conservation Issues: Cabeza Prieta has 803,418 acres of designated wilderness. Organ Pipe Cactus National Monument was designated an International Biosphere Reserve in 1976, and 312,600 acres of the 330,688 are federally designated wilderness. Recently an invasive plant, buffel grass, has been found on the site; it is highly combustible and represents a threat to the saguaro. So far, control efforts involve simply pulling the grass up by hand. Adjacent lands in Mexico are being heavily developed.

▸ Visitor Information: The refuge center for Cabeza Prieta National Wildlife Refuge is located in Ajo, and the visitor center for Organ Pipe Cactus National Monument is approximately 23 miles south of Why, near milepost 75 on Highway 85. Cabeza Prieta has no off-road travel, and the reserve's dirt roads can be navigated only with a four-wheel drive vehicle. Visitors should carry sufficient water. Visitors must have permits that can be obtained from the reserve center. Organ Pipe Cactus National Monument can be accessed by passenger car, but no off-road driving is advised or permitted, due in part to unexploded military ordnance. A popular spot on Organ Pipe is Quitobaquito Springs, a desert oasis that attracts a variety of birds. Contact: Cabeza Prieta National Wildlife Refuge, 1611 North Second Avenue, Ajo, AZ 85321, 520-387-6483; Organ Pipe Cactus National Monument, Route 1, Box 100, Ajo, AZ 85321, 520-387-7661, ext. 7114.

This is the northern terminus of the Sierra Madre Occidental. In the United States it is made up of isolated mountain ranges in Southeast Arizona and Southwest New Mexico, as well as the more northerly forested Mogollon Rim. Of the many landbirds more typical of Mexico that extend into the United States in this region, highest conservation priorities include the Red-faced Warbler, Arizona Woodpecker, and Montezuma Quail. Riparian areas in lowlands support many in-transit migrants as well as breeding Thick-billed Kingbirds, "Western" Yellow-billed Cuckoos, and "Southwestern" Willow Flycatchers. Most uplands are publicly owned, but lower-elevation grasslands and riparian habitat are subject to development and conversion.

Buenos Aires National Wildlife Refuge (1), Arizona

▶ Highlight: In addition to several Green List species, the refuge provides the only habitat in the country for the reintroduced "Masked" Bobwhite.
▶ Location: On the Mexican border near Sasabe, west of Nogales.
▶ Size: 117,000 acres.
▶ Ownership: Fish and Wildlife Service.
▶ Habitats: Semidesert grassland, riparian.
▶ Land Use: Wildlife conservation.
▶ Site Description: The refuge is the largest ungrazed tract of grassland in Arizona.
▶ Birds: The "Masked" Bobwhite, an endangered race of the Northern Bobwhite, has been reintroduced to the site. The Rufous-winged Sparrow and Lucy's Warbler are found here, as are other rare species, such as the Montezuma Quail, Scaled Quail, Northern Beardless-Tyrannulet, Greater Pewee, Bendire's Thrasher, Bell's Vireo, Abert's Towhee, and Botteri's and Cassin's Sparrows.
▶ Conservation Issues: "Masked" Bobwhite became extirpated from the United States after the introduction of the grazing of cattle and sheep. The subspecies still existed in Mexico, and using birds captured from those flocks, research biologists with the Fish and Wildlife Service were able to build up a captive population. Finding that the bird could not survive on disturbed lands, the service purchased this former ranch and stopped the area from being grazed. Captive birds were then gradually released

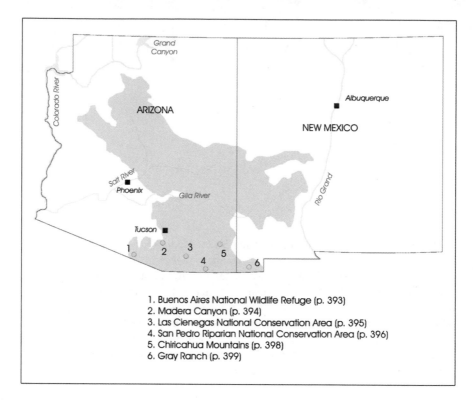

1. Buenos Aires National Wildlife Refuge (p. 393)
2. Madera Canyon (p. 394)
3. Las Cienegas National Conservation Area (p. 395)
4. San Pedro Riparian National Conservation Area (p. 396)
5. Chiricahua Mountains (p. 398)
6. Gray Ranch (p. 399)

into the recovering habitat; and some of the released birds are now breeding on their own. An African grass was introduced in the 1970s to help stop erosion due to over-grazing. Land managers are now working to piece the original ecosystem back to-gether, by restoring habitat with the native species that once grew there.

▸ Visitor Information: Best time to visit is fall through spring. Contact the refuge at P.O. Box 109, Sasabe, AZ 85633, 520-823-4251.

Madera Canyon (2), Arizona

▸ Highlight: Classic site for finding Mexican rarities; mix of habitats important to a wide range of Green List species; sky islands for neotropical migrants.

▸ Location: Midway between Tucson and Nogales.

▸ Size: 32,000 acres.

▸ Ownership: Forest Service.

▸ Habitats: Rugged mountains, desert grassland and scrub, pine-oak forest, riparian forest, canyons.

▸ Land Use: Recreation, grazing, watershed.

▸ Site Description: The Santa Rita Mountains rise from the Sonoran Desert, which borders them to the north and west, while to the east and south, they give way to exten-sive tracts of arid grassland. The range, part of a complex of 12 associated ranges, lies within the Coronado National Forest, and has some of the highest northern extension of the Sierra Madre Occidental, including Mount Wrightson at 9,453 feet. Due to the height of these mountains, which surround Madera Canyon to the east, southeast, and southwest, the area has a relatively high rainfall and a rich and diverse vegetation. Habitats include desert scrub, grassland, brushland, oak woodland, pine forest, riparian sycamore woodland, rocky mountains, steep-sided canyons, dry washes, and seasonal creeks. Typical vegetation includes ponderosa, Chihuahua, and Apache pine, Mexican piñon, Arizona cypress, evergreen silver leaf oaks, emory oak, mesquite, juniper, cacti including prickly pear, cholla, and saguaros.

▸ Birds: Madera Canyon and its environs have both the longest list of green-listed species in the United States and some of the most exciting Mexican rarities, making it among the most popular birding areas in a state that draws birders from all over the world. Resident or found seasonally include the Montezuma Quail, Band-tailed Pigeon, Arizona Woodpecker, Greater Pewee, Elf Owl, Curve-billed Thrasher, Bridled Titmouse, Rufous, Allen's, and Lucifer Hummingbirds, Bell's Vireo, Abert's Towhee, Brewer's, Black-chinned, Harris's, Cassin's, Botteri's, and Rufous-winged Sparrows, Red-faced, Virginia's, Lucy's, Grace's Hermit, and Olive Warblers, Bendire's Thrasher, Gray Vireo, Lark Bunting, and Lawrence's Goldfinch. Buff-collared Nightjars have also occurred, along with occasional vagrants such as Flame-colored Tanagers, Aztec Thrushes, and Eared Trogons.

▸ Conservation Issues: The potential for disturbance of rare breeding species by birders visiting the canyon is being addressed through a "no-taping" policy, although this is still not observed by all visitors. The entire area is subject to a cooperative agreement between the Arizona Game and Fish Department and Centro Ecológico de Sonora, leading to an international partnership that includes fieldwork, training, and financing for wildlife conservation. The Forest Service works to manage conflict between various land use activities such as timbering, watershed management, grazing, birding, sightseeing, and the protection of biodiversity. Introduced plants such as red brome are a potential problem.

▸ Visitor Information: The canyon can be reached from Tucson by taking I-19 south to East White House Canyon Road (Route 62) exit 63 east, then taking Madera Canyon Road (Route 70) south to the canyon. The popular Santa Rita Lodge is regularly booked a year ahead. For information, call 520-625-8746, e-mail lcollister@theriver.com, or see www.santaritalodge.com. Some of the roads in the area are bad, and it is advisable to check with locals before traveling far from the canyon itself. Before entering the canyon on weekends and holidays visitors must pay $2 to the Friends of Madera Canyon, a local conservation group. Information about visiting Coronado National Forest can be obtained by calling 520-670-4552. Other accommodations can be found at the Cabins at Madera Kubo 520-625-2908, and at Chuparosa Inn 520-393-7370.

Las Cienegas National Conservation Area (3), Arizona

▸ Highlight: This area, with habitats now rare in the Southwest, is an important corridor for tens of thousands of neotropical migratory birds in the spring and for several breeding and wintering Green List species.

▸ Location: Santa Cruz and Pima Counties, near Sonoita.

► Size: 45,000 acres.

► Ownership: Bureau of Land Management.

► Habitats: Grasslands, shrublands, marsh, riparian vegetation.

► Land Use: Livestock grazing, recreation, wildlife conservation.

► Site Description: The site includes nearly 20 miles of riparian cottonwood-willow, one of the most endangered habitat types in the United States. There is also natural marsh, and one of the best and largest remaining tracts of predominantly native grassland in the desert Southwest.

► Birds: Tens of thousands of neotropical migratory birds pass through the area in the spring; several pairs of "Western" Yellow-billed Cuckoos breed there, and Sprague's Pipits and Baird's and Botteri's Sparrows are found in winter.

► Conservation Issues: Overextraction of groundwater and overgrazing with the consequent spread of non-native species are critical threats to the integrity of these habitats. Recreational overuse is also a problem, as is increased residential development in the area. The Bureau of Land Management has developed a rotational grazing system and is excluding livestock from riparian areas. There are plans to restore a small section of the riparian habitat.

► Visitor Information: Best time to visit is mid-April to mid-May, during migration. For information, contact: Bureau of Land Management, Tucson Field Office, 12661 East Broadway Boulevard, Tucson, AZ 85748, 520-722-4289.

San Pedro Riparian National Conservation Area (4), Arizona

► Highlight: Best preserved riparian migrant corridor in the southwestern United States. Between three and five million passerines use the area each spring as they move from Mexico to breeding grounds to the north.

► Location: Southeastern Arizona near Sierra Vista, close to the border with Mexico.

► Size: 58,000 acres.

► Ownership: Bureau of Land Management.

► Habitats: Chihuahuan desert scrub, mesquite grassland, riparian corridor.

► Land Use: Recreation, water supply, wildlife management.

► Site Description: The San Pedro Riparian National Conservation Area is a narrow wooded corridor surrounding the San Pedro River where it flows north out of Mexico into the United States. The area stretches some 40 miles north to south, and the vegetation is comprised principally of cottonwoods, willows, and ashes, with an understorey of baccharis. Extending away from the river are groves of mesquite, surrounded by sacaton grasslands. These are among the rarest and most endangered habitats in North America. The river itself is one of the last undammed, free-flowing waterways in the Southwest, and along with its surrounding gallery woodland, appears as a thin green oasis in the midst of the vast arid Chihuahuan Desert. Average rainfall is 12 inches per year, and except during heavy rains, the river remains only five to ten feet wide, linking a series of larger pools.

► Birds: The San Pedro corridor is an important migrant conduit providing stopover and feeding habitat for between three and five million migrant passerines each spring. The majority of passage migrants are Wilson's and Yellow Warblers, and at times bird density can reach 40 birds per acre. The area also supports an important breeding population of the "Western" Yellow-billed Cuckoo (200 pairs) and is nationally important for breeding Gray Hawks and Green Kingfishers. Species occurring along the river and its environs include the Curve-billed Thrasher, Lucy's Warbler, Brewer's Sparrow, Cassin's Sparrow, Lark Bunting, Abert's Towhee (estimated at more than 1,000 pairs), Botteri's Sparrow (more than 1,000 pairs), Gilded Flicker, and "Least" Bell's Vireo (350 to 400 pairs). The San Pedro Riparian Area is also of great interest to birders because of the likelihood of southern vagrants being found during a visit there. The more recent records include the Elegant Trogon, Thick-billed Kingbird, Rufous-backed Robin, and Plain-capped Starthroat. Altogether, 355 species have been recorded within the National Conservation Area.

▶ Conservation Issues: The site was acquired by the Bureau of Land Management in 1986, and after the upper San Pedro was designated a Riparian National Conservation Area the following year, all grazing and farming were halted. The ensuing regrowth of vegetation has created one of the most important conservation areas in the southwestern United States. The possibility that grazing may at some point be re-instituted must be considered a serious threat. Another major problem is overuse of groundwater in the region due to the development of surrounding communities. There is evidence that a reduction in water flow may have already resulted from water depletion. Introduced salt cedar, the spread of toxic pollutants upriver from mines in Mexico, soil erosion, and disturbance by visitors must all be considered as potential threats, and addressed by local and cross-border management plans. A binational watershed plan was recently launched to provide funding to purchase lands and water rights along the river. Permanent protection for the river will depend on a degree of voluntary compliance from the Sierra Vista community and the Fort Huachuca Army Base. In recent years, large numbers of people have crossed the border illegally in this area; they have created trails through the vegetation and left behind piles of trash and clothing at campsites.

▶ Visitor Information: To reach San Pedro House at the center of the reserve, take Route 90 east for seven miles from Sierra Vista. The entrance road to the house is on the right. The House has an information center for visitors, and is open from 9:30 a.m. to 4:30 p.m. daily. Nearby accommodation includes the Casa de San Pedro, 520-366-1300, and the San Pedro River Inn, 520-366-5532. Additional information on visiting and conservation issues can be obtained from the Bureau of Land Management, 1763 Paseo San Luis, Sierra Vista, AZ 85635, 520-439-6400.

SOUTHWESTERN RIPARIAN WOODLAND

Among the rarest and most endangered habitats in North America is the cottonwood-willow woodland found along streams and rivers in the Southwest. Important as migratory corridors, these southwestern riparian woodlands also provide habitat for several rare and endangered subspecies limited to such habitat, such as "Southwestern" Willow Flycatchers, "Least" Bell's Vireos, and "Western" Yellow-billed Cuckoos. Not only has 90 to 95 percent of this habitat been destroyed, but the remaining fragments are often degraded. The causes for the decline of these woodlands are several. Human interruption of free-flowing water by dams, diversions, irrigation, impoundments, or channelization has been a major factor in the degrading of the natural functions of this ecological type. Without natural hydrologic systems, water tables have been lowered, resulting in the drying out of surface sediments. Cottonwoods are particularly sensitive to water stress and may decline as groundwater declines. Without periodic flooding, there is less shifting of river and stream channels and less opportunity for the establishment of cottonwood and willow seedlings, which depend on recently inundated sediments to become established. When there is no replacement within the riparian forests, they become monocultures of senescent trees that eventually die or fall victim to fire.

Overgrazing by domestic livestock has been a major factor in the alteration and degradation of these riparian areas. It destroys stabilizing vegetation, erodes banks, and favors the spread of unpalatable non-native invasive plants such as salt cedar, at the expense of the palatable native vegetation. Salt cedar has been particularly damaging; it outcompetes cottonwood and willow, and, since it is highly combustible, it increases the likelihood of periodic fires, not a feature of the native riparian woodlands. The birds suffer as well; recent studies show that up to 40 percent of riparian bird species are negatively affected by the presence of livestock and its effects.

As an endangered habitat with endangered birds, western riparian woodland is well represented by Important Bird Areas. Among those preserving riparian habitat are San Pedro Riparian National Conservation Area and Las Cienegas National Conservation Area in Arizona, Camp Pendleton, Cosumnes River Preserve, the Otay-Sweetwater Unit of the San Diego National Wildlife Refuge, the South Fork Kern River Valley in California, and the Lower Colorado River, which forms the border between the two states. In some of these areas, management to limit grazing and to restore native vegetation provides hope that this important ecological type will not decline further.

Chiricahua Mountains (5), Arizona

▶ Highlight: The "Mexican" Spotted Owl and numerous Green List species occur here, as do several species whose U.S. distribution is limited to southeastern Arizona and southwestern New Mexico.
▶ Location: Southeastern corner of Arizona, north of Douglas.
▶ Size: Approximately 600,000 acres.
▶ Ownership: Forest Service, National Park Service, private.
▶ Habitats: Desert scrub, chaparral, desert grassland, pine-oak and piñon-juniper woodlands; ponderosa pine and spruce-fir coniferous forests; riparian habitats including sycamore-dominated riparian woodland.
▶ Land Use: Recreation, grazing, some mining.
▶ Site Description: The Chiricahua Mountains offer some of the best birding in North America. Among the most famous of the birding sites is Cave Creek, where the Elegant Trogon breeds. Public lands here include the Douglas Ranger District of the Coronado National Forest (which includes 290,000 acres in the Chiricahua Mountains) and the Chiricahua National Monument (12,000 acres).
▶ Birds: The "Mexican" Spotted Owl occurs, as do the Elf Owl, Montezuma Quail, Band-tailed Pigeon, Arizona Woodpecker, Greater Pewee, Bridled Titmouse, Bell's Vireo, Bendire's Thrasher, Cassin's Sparrow, and Virginia's, Grace's Red-faced, and Olive Warblers. The Black-chinned Sparrow is an uncommon breeding resident and

Elegant Trogon

both the Buff-breasted and Sulphur-bellied Flycatchers are found. The Elegant Trogon and Mexican Chickadee are two species at the very northern limit of their range, and the Eared Trogon occurs occasionally. Many accidentals from Mexico have turned up through the years.

▶ Conservation Issues: The Chiricahua Wilderness is 87,470 acres. In the forest there are 13 Protected Activity Centers for the "Mexican" Spotted Owl, with buffer areas around each. However, not all the centers represent active breeding sites every year. Since 1993, the Forest Service has conducted four Breeding Bird Surveys in the Chiricahuas, and there is an annual survey of The Elegant Trogon conducted since 1990. There is the danger of catastrophic fire due to increasing fuel load; land managers reduce the load through managing natural fires, prescribed burning, and some removal of excess fuel, including trees killed by insect outbreaks. Increased development of private land has meant a further restriction of public access, now virtually limited to two main roads that cross the area. In the 1980s, there was a program to reintroduce Thick-billed Parrots to the mountains, but this was unsuccessful. Among the multiple uses of national forest lands are grazing and some limited mineral extraction; the forest produces no commercially harvestable timber.

▶ Visitor Information: Any time of year is worth a visit, but mid-April to June is best for breeding birds. Visitors should not make use of playback taped calls, and the South Fork Zoological-Botanical Area of Cave Creek Canyon is closed to the use of audio-recording/playback equipment from April 1 to September 1. Visitors should respect private property. The main roads in the Chiricahuas are gravel surfaced and generally in good condition. For information on the Douglas Ranger District, call 520-364-3468 and on the Chiricahua National Monument, call 520-824-3560.

Gray Ranch (6), New Mexico

▶ Highlight: Several resident, breeding, or wintering Green List species and species with restricted ranges in the United States are found there.

▶ Location: Southwestern corner of New Mexico, in Hidalgo County.

▶ Size: 321,702 acres.

▶ Ownership: Animas Foundation.

▶ Habitats: Chihuahuan Desert scrub, Chihuahuan Desert grassland, plains grassland, interior chaparral, Madrean evergreen woodland, Madrean pine-oak woodland, montane coniferous forest.

▶ Land Use: Conservation, grazing.

▶ Site Description: The Animas Peak is 8,560 feet and lies south of San Luis Pass. The uplift continues as the Sierra San Luis, approximately 4.5 miles of which are on the Gray Ranch, the balance being in Mexico at the extreme northern end of the Sierra Madre Occidental. The Animas Valley is a north-south trending rift valley, approximately 5,000 feet in elevation on the Gray Ranch. The east side of the Animas Range is a complex of old collapsed calderas and flows of tuff and welded tuff. East of the Animas Mountains, the center of the ranch is drained by a large riparian complex, Deer Creek, to the south, and by Double Adobe Creek to the north. These riparian habitats are dominated by Arizona sycamore, velvet ash, Arizona walnut, and western hackberry. Fremont cottonwood occurs in the Double Adobe Creek drainage but not in Deer Creek. The floodplain of Animas Creek north of the Animas Mountains supports a 3,000-acre stand of giant sacaton grassland, one of the most extensive examples of this community remaining.

▶ Birds: Gray Ranch is extremely significant for birds. Many species found there are on the Green List or have a limited range in the United States. The Scaled Quail is a common resident, and the Montezuma Quail is fairly common; the ranch is probably one of the strongholds of this species. The Band-tailed Pigeon is a regular but uncommon nesting species in the Animas Mountains, and the Elf Owl is fairly common in summer. There are six to eight pairs of the endangered "Mexican" Spotted Owl on the ranch. The Arizona Woodpecker is a fairly common resident, and the Greater Pewee is a fairly common nesting species. The Mexican Chickadee has been a fairly common resident in the Animas Mountains, but a recent severe drought has made it hard to find there. Gray Ranch is the only nesting site for this and for the Yellow-eyed Junco in New Mexico. The Bridled Titmouse is a fairly common resident. The Bendire's Thrasher is a probable breeding species and rare in winter. The Sprague's Pipit is uncommon but regular in winter, and the Olive Warbler is fairly common in summer, as is the Virginia's Warbler. The Lucy's Warbler and Cassin's Sparrow are common breeding species, and there is a small but significant breeding population of the Botteri's Sparrow on the ranch. The Brewer's Sparrow is abundant in some winters, while the Sage Sparrow is uncommon but regular in winter. The Black-chinned Sparrow is resident. The Lark Bunting is common during some winters, and the Baird's Sparrow is an uncommon migrant and winter resident, though it is difficult to detect.

▶ Conservation Issues: The ranch was acquired by The Nature Conservancy in 1990 and sold to the Animas Foundation in 1994 under the agreement that the land never be subdivided, that the rangelands be maintained in as good or better condition than at the time of transfer, and that the foundation set up and maintain a series of monitoring plots to ensure that the latter is honored. The mission of the foundation includes protecting biological diversity and restoring and sustaining natural habitats. A long-term research project is being conducted on the effects of grazing and fire (alone and in combination) on Chihuahuan Desert grasslands (plant composition and community structure, vertebrates, invertebrates, soil biota). Riparian restoration is underway. Rare species monitoring is conducted in conjunction with New Mexico Game and Fish Department, Endangered Species Branch. Birds monitored include the resident race of Wild Turkey, Sprague's Pipit, Mexican Chickadee, Botteri's, Baird's, and Grasshopper Sparrows, and Yellow-eyed Junco.

▶ Visitor Information: Gray Ranch is not at present open to visitors. For information about the ranch and its programs, contact: Animas Foundation/Gray Ranch, HC 65, Box 180, Animas, NM 88020, 505-548-2622.

35. Chihuahuan Desert

The Chihuahuan Desert stretches from the Madrean Mountains on the west to the Edwards Plateau in Texas, grades into the Southern Great Plains to the north, and extends over much of the central Mexican Plateau. Arid grasslands and shrublands cover broad basins, and higher elevation oak-juniper woodlands and conifers occur in numerous isolated mesas and mountains. The Scaled Quail is typical of the lowlands, with Bell's Vireo along some riparian zones, and Black-capped Vireo and Lucifer Hummingbird in the montane scrub community. The Colima Warbler is a rare inhabitant of a few of the taller mountains. The Rio Grande and adjacent wetlands provide important habitat for Sandhill Cranes, waterfowl, and other riparian and wetland-dependent birds.

Bosque Del Apache National Wildlife Refuge (1), New Mexico

▶ Highlight: A major wintering site for the Sandhill Crane and Ross's Goose, as well as a stopover site for thousands of waterfowl and shorebirds.
▶ Location: On the Rio Grande in south-central New Mexico.
▶ Size: 57,191 acres.
▶ Ownership: Fish and Wildlife Service.
▶ Habitats: Semi-desert, marshes, lakes, waterways, riparian woodland, agricultural land.
▶ Land Use: Wildlife conservation, recreation.
▶ Site Description: The refuge is located at the southern end of the 150-mile-long Middle Rio Grande Valley of New Mexico. The river corridor through this reach is dominated by an agricultural greenbelt and riparian forest. The floodplain portion of the refuge is mostly composed of a system of low-lying marshes and lakes, fed by irrigation channels and controlled by levees. Some agricultural land within the refuge is farmed through a cooperative program to provide feed for wintering wildfowl. The refuge bottomlands are surrounded by Chihuahuan semidesert, with the Chupadera Mountains lying to the west and the San Pasqual Mountains to the southeast. Cottonwoods and black willows line the waterways, as does introduced tamarisk. There are isolated cottonwood copses dotted around the landscape. The water level is generally lower during the summer.

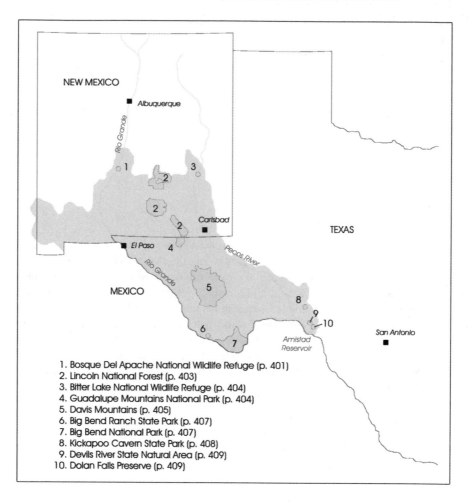

NEW MEXICO

■ Albuquerque

Rio Grande

○ 1
2
3 ○

2

2

Carlsbad ■

El Paso ■   4

Pecos River

Rio Grande

MEXICO

5

8 ○
9
─10

6 ○

7

Amistad
Reservoir

TEXAS

San Antonio ■

1. Bosque Del Apache National Wildlife Refuge (p. 401)
2. Lincoln National Forest (p. 403)
3. Bitter Lake National Wildlife Refuge (p. 404)
4. Guadalupe Mountains National Park (p. 404)
5. Davis Mountains (p. 405)
6. Big Bend Ranch State Park (p. 407)
7. Big Bend National Park (p. 407)
8. Kickapoo Cavern State Park (p. 408)
9. Devils River State Natural Area (p. 409)
10. Dolan Falls Preserve (p. 409)

▶ Birds: Up to 17,000 Sandhill Cranes of two subspecies winter on the refuge and nearby state refuges, as do up to 57,000 white geese, of which around 10 percent are Ross's. A few Greater White-fronted Geese also winter in the area. Thousands of waterfowl and shorebirds use the refuge on passage, including large numbers of American White Pelicans, a few Tundra Swans, and occasional Trumpeter Swans. Several Green List birds are found there, including the Bendire's Thrasher, Brewer's Sparrow (passage/winter), and Curve-billed Thrasher. In the past, up to six Whooping Cranes from experimental programs wintered at the refuge.

▶ Conservation Issues: The refuge was established in 1939 to protect migratory birds, especially the "Greater" Sandhill Crane, a subspecies at that time perilously close to extinction. In 1941 there were just 17 cranes on the refuge, but thanks to careful management this has increased a thousandfold to the current population. The refuge's wetlands are managed to provide sufficient habitat diversity and food resources for wintering and other migratory birds. Some lakes are completely drained each year to control botulism. Some of the refuge's roads are also closed during the winter months to prevent disturbance to roosting cranes. The refuge managers work with local farmers to manage wildfowl outside the refuge proper. Refuge management has a very active program to restore native riparian cottonwood and black willow woodlands. Salt cedar (tamarisk), an invasive non-native plant species taking over much of the riparian areas, is being removed in an effort to restore the native cottonwood-willow community that gave the refuge its name. Salt cedar forms extremely dense thickets and is of very limited use to wildlife. There are three wilderness areas, and some hunting is allowed.

▶ Visitor Information: To reach the refuge, drive south from Socorro on I-25 for nine miles to the San Antonio exit (U.S. 380). Follow 380 for one mile into San Antonio and turn right at the signal. The refuge loop road is open to visitors from one hour before dawn until one hour after sunset every day of the year. The entrance fee is $3. There are trails, observation decks, and a campsite close to the refuge entrance. The refuge can be reached at P.O. Box 1246, Socorro, NM 87801, 505-835-1828.

Lincoln National Forest (2), New Mexico

▶ Highlight: Good population of "Mexican" Spotted Owl.
▶ Location: Three units in south-central and southeastern New Mexico; forest headquarters is in Alamogorda.
▶ Size: 1.1 million acres.
▶ Ownership: Forest Service.
▶ Habitats: Mountain meadows, mixtures of pine, fir, aspen, oak, and other species; desert; subalpine vegetation.
▶ Land Use: Grazing, logging, watershed protection, and a variety of recreational activities, including hunting, fishing, wildlife observation, caving, skiing, snowmobiling, mountain biking, motorcycling.
▶ Site Description: The forest extends through several habitat zones, from Chihuahuan Desert to subalpine woodland and mountain meadows and ranges in elevation between 4,000 and 11,500 feet. The Capitan Mountains in the Smokey Bear Ranger District are among the few east-west-running mountain ranges on the continent.
▶ Birds: The endangered "Mexican" Spotted Owl is known in the Lincoln National Forest primarily from the Sacramento Ranger District, with 107 of the forest's 130 known territories found there. Only some 2,300 individuals of this subspecies are thought to be still extant in the United States.
▶ Conservation Issues: There are two designated Wilderness Areas on the forest. The Sacramento Ranger District is approximately 500,000 acres, of which 230,000 are suitable habitat for the owl. Management for the bird involves delineating an area of 600 acres around each pair, and within this, allowing no commercial logging, but permitting thinning of smaller trees (those below nine inches in diameter at chest height) for fuel reduction. All mixed conifer is considered suitable habitat, so commercial activity is restricted within that type. Some controlled burning is conducted on the forest to improve conditions for livestock and wildlife.
▶ Visitor Information: Best times to visit are spring and fall. The Sacramento Ranger

District can be reached at P.O. Box 288, Cloudcroft, NM 83317, 505-682-2551, and the Supervisor's Office at Federal Building, 1101 New York Avenue, Alamogordo, NM 88310-6992, 505-434-7200.

Bitter Lake National Wildlife Refuge (3), New Mexico

▸ Highlight: The best shorebird site in the state, this refuge also attracts many waterfowl during migration and winter.
▸ Location: On the Pecos River, about ten miles northeast of Roswell, Chaves County.
▸ Size: 24,536 acres.
▸ Ownership: Fish and Wildlife Service.
▸ Habitats: Native grassland, sand dunes, brushy bottomlands, lakes, impoundments, marshland, mudflats, riverine communities.
▸ Land Use: Recreation, wildlife conservation.
▸ Site Description: The refuge is named for a shallow playa lake fed by small springs; it often goes dry during the summer, leaving only an alkaline lake bed. The water from the springs is brackish and bitter, giving the name to the lake and the refuge.
▸ Birds: Several thousand waterfowl winter on the refuge or use it as a stopover point during migration. Between 5,000 and 15,000 "Lesser" Sandhill Cranes winter in the area, representing a major portion of its world population. It is also a major wintering site for Ross's Geese, with counts up to 8,000. It is the only nesting area in the state for the endangered "Interior" Least Tern, and up to 250 Snowy Plovers have nested there annually. Other breeding species include the American Avocet and Black-necked Stilt. The Cassin's Sparrow is present from spring to fall, and the Clay-colored Sparrow is common during migration.
▸ Conservation Issues: Two major challenges are to control non-native invasive vegetation and to restore the river channel in the reach of the Pecos River adjacent to the refuge to more closely mimic the hydrology that once prevailed at Bitter Lake. There is a threat from further groundwater loss and from possible contamination from development adjacent to the refuge.
▸ Visitor Information: Best time to visit is late summer through spring to see migrating and wintering birds. There is an eight-mile auto tour around some of the lakes, but this may sometimes be closed due to road or weather conditions. The refuge can be reached at 4065 Bitter Lake Road, Roswell, NM 88201, 505-622-6755.

Guadalupe Mountains National Park (4), Texas

▸ Highlight: Several Green List birds at the edge of their ranges breed or winter there.
▸ Location: Hudspeth and Culberson Counties, just south of the New Mexico state line.
▸ Size: 86,416 acres.
▸ Ownership: National Park Service.
▸ Habitats: Desert, canyon forest, pine forest, riparian woodland, mountains.
▸ Land Use: Recreation, wilderness.
▸ Site Description: The park incorporates a limestone massif rising abruptly from the

Chihuahuan Desert, including the highest peak in Texas, Guadalupe Peak, at 8,749 feet. Lower-lying areas have a typical Chihuahuan Desert flora with prickly pear cactus, yucca, agave, and cholla. Higher up there is a mixture of canyon forest, some riparian woodland, and pine forest. Trees include bigtooth maple, Texas walnut, Texas madrone, velvet ash, gray oak, junipers, ponderosa and southwestern white pines, aspen, and Douglas-fir.

▶ Birds: The park's bird life includes species typical both of the southwestern desert and pine forests, such as the Gray Vireo, Virginia's Warbler, and Black-chinned Sparrow. The Montezuma and Scaled Quails are resident and the Sage and Brewer's Sparrows winter. The endangered "Mexican" Spotted Owl has been recorded. Species at the edge of their range are the Juniper Titmouse (the only location for the species in Texas), Band-tailed Pigeon, Flammulated Owl, Grace's Warbler, and Cordilleran Flycatcher.

▶ Conservation Issues: 46,850 acres of the park are designated wilderness. The spread of non-native plants is being addressed by a regional team. The local Carlsbad Caverns Guadalupe Mountains Association supports conservation work in the area; it can be contacted at 505-785-2232, ext. 481. Conservation issues include management of gypsum dunes, reintroduction of extirpated species, natural habitat preservation, use of wilderness and backcountry, and fire concerns.

▶ Visitor Information: Facilities within the park are extremely limited, and visitors should bring with them everything they might need. Severe weather, including high winds, can develop rapidly. For more information, contact: Guadalupe Mountains National Park, HC 60, Box 400, Salt Flat, TX 79847, 915-828-3251.

Davis Mountains (5), Texas

▶ Highlight: The "sky islands" of the mountains support several species at the edge of their ranges, including several green-listed species.

▶ Location: The Davis Mountains lie in Jeff Davis County in southwest Texas, approximately 100 miles north-northwest of Big Bend National Park and less than 50 miles northeast of the Rio Grande and the Mexican border.

▶ Size: The Davis Mountains and its outlying plains cover some 1,500 square miles. Protected lands include The Nature Conservancy's Davis Mountain Preserve (18,000 acres) and Middle Madera Canyon Preserve (1,920 acres) plus 65,000 acres protected by the Conservancy through conservation easements. Additional public lands include the state's Davis Mountains State Park (2,700 acres), Fort Davis National Historic Site (474 acres), and McDonald Observatory (468 acres).

▶ Ownership: Private lands predominate; The Nature Conservancy and state and federal governments own the tracts mentioned above.

▶ Habitats: Plains grassland, high-altitude pine, juniper, and oak woodland, streams with riparian woodlands, marshes, stock tanks.

▶ Land Use: Ranching, recreation.

▶ Site Description: The Davis Mountains lie in the northern Chihuahuan Desert, making up the most extensive mountain range in Texas. Altitudes reach nearly 8,400 feet, and more than 800 square miles are above 5,000 feet. The area includes a range of habitats from grassland to cottonwood-willow, piñon-juniper, and pine-oak woodlands. Common trees include Mexican walnut, desert willow, Rio Grande cottonwood, Mexican piñon, southwestern white and ponderosa pine, Emory, gray, Chisos-red, silver-leaf, and Gambel's oak, rose-fruited and alligator juniper. Shrubs include acacias, scarlet bouvardia, golden lead tree, fragrant and littleleaf sumac, Apache plume, cholla, and yuccas. Annual rainfall is approximately 15 inches in the foothills and 22 inches in the mountains. In winter the temperature is regularly below freezing at night, with some snow. Summers are warm, with low humidity and cool nights. Davis Mountains State Park is at a relatively low elevation (5,000 feet) in the southeastern foothills of the range.

Painted Redstart

▶ Birds: Depending on habitat, the Montezuma and Scaled Quails, Band-tailed Pigeon, and Common Black-Hawk breed there, as do the Bell's, Hutton's, Warbling and Plumbeous Vireos, Grace's, Orange-crowned, Yellow-rumped, and Virginia's Warblers, Painted Redstart, and Black-chinned Sparrow. Several hummingbird species are known to breed there, including the Black-chinned, Broad-tailed, and Magnificent, while the White-eared, Blue-throated, and Lucifer are suspected. Rufous and Anna's are abundant in fall and usually overwinter. In winter, Williamson's Sapsuckers occur in the mountains and Chestnut-collared Longspurs are found in the basin grasslands. The Buff-breasted Flycatcher and three other *Empidonax* flycatchers breed there (Dusky, Gray, and Cordilleran Flycatchers), a high diversity site for the genus. The first state record for the breeding Greater Pewee was documented at The Nature Conservancy's Davis Mountain Preserve in 2002. A few pairs of "Mexican" Spotted Owls are known from the Davis Mountains, and there have been occurrences of territorial singing male Colima Warblers for the last three years, though there is as yet no evidence of breeding. Migrant passerines are common in spring and fall. Several unusual birds have shown up, most recently Slate-throated Redstarts and Flame-colored Tanagers.

▶ Conservation Issues: The avifauna of the Davis Mountains is among the least known in Texas, because the area has limited access and limited public lands. Basic research there is a primary necessity. As for management, The Nature Conservancy has as a goal the restoration of a natural fire regime in the "sky islands" on its preserves. At present, there is a large fuel load so that prescribed burning cannot be used until some of this load is removed. Future land use changes in the Davis Mountains could threaten habitats; thankfully, threats to the intactness of the range are few. The recent drought has meant a reduction in the size of the population of Montezuma Quail in the area.

▶ Visitor Information: Any time of year is good for a visit, but spring and early summer are usually hot and dry. Contact: Davis Mountains State Park, P.O. Box 1458, Fort Davis, TX 79734, 915-426-3337. For information on The Nature Conservancy's preserves, contact: The Nature Conservancy of Texas, Davis Mountain Preserve, P.O.

Box 2078, Fort Davis, TX 79734, 915-426-2390. Texas Parks and Wildlife Department operates a banding station two to three times per week at Davis Mountains State Park during spring and fall. Information and a bird checklist can be obtained by calling 915-426-3337. Also see the following websites: http://www.tpwd.state.tx.us/news/tpwcal/ s_0041.htm. Robert Schutsky operates birding tours in the area: 717-548-3303. Also see Texas Birder's Directory: http://www. tpwd.state.tx.us/nature/birding/birdersdirectory/ birdingclubs3.htm/1.

Big Bend Ranch State Park (6), Texas

▶ Highlight: The largest state park in Texas, it has several breeding Green List species.
▶ Location: On the Rio Grande just upstream from Big Bend National Park.
▶ Size: 280,280 acres.
▶ Ownership: Texas Parks and Wildlife.
▶ Habitats: Grassland, desert scrub, canyons, riparian woodland and thickets, streams, rivers, permanent springs.
▶ Land Use: Recreation, wildlife observation.
▶ Site Description: This relatively little-visited park encompasses some of the most remote and rugged landscape in the Southwest. With a mix of riparian and desert scrub habitats, it also contains two mountain ranges, reaching a peak elevation of 5,135 feet.
▶ Birds: Among the birds commonly found in the park are the Scaled Quail, Elf Owl, Bell's Vireo, Curve-billed Thrasher, and Cassin's Sparrow, while the Brewer's Sparrow occurs during migration and winter.
▶ Conservation Issues: Before the state acquired the land for the park in 1988, it was used for ranching operations that began in the 1850s. Sheep, goats, cattle, horses, and exotic game animals have all grazed the area at various times. The park has a herd of Texas longhorn cattle.
▶ Visitor Information: Best time to visit is fall through spring. This vast park is difficult to access due to a lack of roads and facilities. A permit is required for trips into its interior. The park may be reached at P.O. Box 2319, Presidio, TX 79845, 915-229-3416.

Big Bend National Park (7), Texas

▶ Highlight: Big Bend's Chisos Mountains are the only currently known breeding location in the United States for the rare Colima Warbler.
▶ Location: Brewster County, south of Marathon, at the Big Bend of the Rio Grande.
▶ Size: 801,163 acres.
▶ Ownership: National Park Service.
▶ Habitats: A wide variety of habitats, from river and desert in the lowlands to oak woodland and coniferous forest in the Chisos Mountains.
▶ Land Use: Wildlife conservation, recreation, tourism.
▶ Site Description: Texas is perhaps the most visited place in the world by birders, and Big Bend is one of the premier sites in this highly popular and ornithologically significant state. Despite its remoteness in a sparsely inhabited region (the nearest town, Marathon, population 800, is 70 miles away), all birders serious about their lists

come here eventually, since one breeding species, the Colima Warbler, is reliably found nowhere else in the United States. With an elevational range from 1,850 to 7,835 feet, the park incorporates a great variety of habitats, and, as a consequence not only of this but of its location on the border with Mexico, more bird species (nearly 450) have been recorded there than in any other national park.

Lucifer Hummingbird

The Colima Warbler is found in oak woodlands in Boot Canyon and other higher-elevation canyons in the Chisos Mountains, where it arrives in mid-April and departs in September. The birds are easiest to find when the males are singing, from late April to mid-June. Among other seasonally present or resident species in the park are the Elf Owl, Painted Bunting, Bell's Vireo, Lucifer Hummingbird, Gray Vireo, Black-chinned Sparrow, Cassin's Sparrow, and Band-tailed Pigeon. Brewer's and Clay-colored Sparrows, and Lark Buntings are present during winter, and the endangered Black-capped Vireo is a localized summer resident, with a population estimated at 15 to 20 birds.

▶ Conservation Issues: Big Bend was named by the National Parks Conservation Association as one of ten "Most Endangered National Parks" in 2002 because of increased air pollution that diminishes scenic visibility and the reduction in the flow of the Rio Grande which concentrates pollutants, adding a stress to wildlife. The park does not actively manipulate habitat and has recently been in an extended dry period with half the average rainfall. There has been poor reproduction for some species, including the Black-capped Vireo, for the last several years.

▶ Visitor Information: Because of the great variety of habitats and the considerable change in bird life throughout the seasons, several visits to the park are necessary to do it justice. Birding is excellent at any time but probably best during spring and fall migration. For the Colima Warbler, the best time to visit is from late April to mid-June, a time when many other species are also most easily seen.

In addition to campgrounds at several locations in the park, there is a lodge in the Chisos Mountain Basin, at 5,200 feet elevation; for reservations, call 915-477-2291. Food and gas are available at Panther Junction and Rio Grande Village during business hours. There is an entrance fee good for one week. Contact: Big Bend National Park, 1 Panther Junction, P.O. Box 129, Big Bend, TX 79834, 915-477-2251.

Kickapoo Cavern State Park (8), Texas

▶ Highlight: One of the largest populations of the endangered Black-capped Vireo.
▶ Location: 22 miles north of Brackettville on the Kinney/Edwards County line.
▶ Size: 6,368 acres.
▶ Habitats: Steep limestone hills and extensive canyons with juniper-oak woodland and small, open grassland; there are also stands of piñon pine.
▶ Land Use: Wildlife conservation.

▶ Site Description: Acquired in 1986, the park has been open to the public on a limited basis only since 1991. Of 15 known caves in the site, two are large. One of the latter, Green Cave, is famous for the spectacular flights of Brazilian freetail bats that emerge every evening from mid-March to the end of October.

▶ Birds: Kickapoo Cavern State Park has one of the largest populations of Black-capped Vireos on public lands, with 138 territorial males recorded in 1993, the last time the entire park was censused. The area also supports 15 to 20 territorial male Gray Vireos, a species first recorded at the park in the late 1980s. The Bell's Vireo and Cassin's Sparrow are common breeding species in the park. Among the other species found there are the Montezuma Quail, Long-billed Thrasher, and Painted Bunting, for which the area has the highest Breeding Bird Survey count in the country. Other species associated with the southwest or south Texas that are found in the area are the Elf Owl, Pyrrhuloxia, Varied Bunting, Black-throated Sparrow, and Scott's Oriole.

▶ Conservation Issues: Brown-headed Cowbird trapping was initiated soon after the park was established in 1986 due to high levels of nest parasitism and has met with considerable success when personnel are on hand to implement trapping early in the spring. Vegetation transects to monitor Black-capped Vireo habitat have been set up, but controlled burning has not been implemented on a large enough scale to produce results.

▶ Visitor Information: Best time for birders to visit is late March and April, when the breeding birds arrive. The park is undeveloped and open only to holders of the Texas Conservation Passport, an individual license from Texas Parks and Wildlife, costing $25 per year. The bat flight can be seen only by prearranged tour, and there is a fee to participants. There are no road signs leading to the park; best to ask precise directions when calling to arrange a visit. The park has sometimes been closed for several weeks at a time. The phone number is 830-563-2342.

Devils River State Natural Area (9) and Dolan Falls Preserve (10), Texas

▶ Highlight: Significant breeding population of the Black-capped Vireo.

▶ Location: Remote area of Val Verde County, about 45 miles north of Del Rio.

▶ Size: The protected lands in the area include Devils River State Natural Area (19,988 acres), The Nature Conservancy's Dolan Falls Preserve (about 5,000 acres), and about 13,000 acres of adjacent conservation easement land.

▶ Ownership: Texas Parks and Wildlife Department, The Nature Conservancy, private.

▶ Habitats: Riverine forest of live oak and pecans, semidesert grassland, eastern Chihuahuan Desert scrubland and Tamaulipan thornscrub habitats, springs and seeps.

▶ Land Use: Wildlife conservation, livestock ranching, recreation (hunting), subdivision.

▶ Site Description: Located at the transition where the Edwards Plateau meets the Chihuahuan Desert and Tamaulipan thornscrub, the Devils River has been called a hill country river in a Trans-Pecos setting. This spring-fed river is in a remote and little-visited section of the state, lined in places with steep limestone cliffs up to 200 feet high.

▶ Birds: In the last survey, conducted in 1991, there were 110 to 120 pairs of Black-capped Vireos breeding on the State Natural Area, one of the larger populations of this

Gray Vireo

endangered species, plus an estimated 50 pairs on the adjacent Dolan Falls Preserve. The bird is also present on the private land held under a conservation easement, and also in suitable habitat on other private lands in the area. Resident or breeding species found in the area include the Scaled and Montezuma Quails, Bell's Vireo, Cassin's Sparrow, and Painted Bunting. Neotropic Cormorants, Zone-tailed Hawks, Green and Ringed Kingfishers, Black-chinned Hummingbirds, Gray Vireos, Tropical Parulas, Groove-billed Anis, Varied Buntings, and Olive Sparrows are also found there, and many waterfowl winter on the river. Rufous-capped Warblers are also regular here and may represent a small resident population.

▶ Conservation Issues: At present, there is no management of vireo habitat, but trapping of Brown-headed Cowbirds will be implemented at the State Natural Area once new traps are in place to reduce the rate of nest parasitism. An active tagging and monitoring program for the vireo has been in place on Dolan Falls Preserve since 1995, and researchers involved in this work have lived at the preserve during the summer since 1999. Unlike the case in the bird's range farther to the east, habitat for the vireo may be created by episodic flash floods rather than periodic burning. In addition to the State Natural Area, The Nature Conservancy preserve, and the adjacent conservation easement land, there is another tract of 22,000 acres downriver to be sold by the Conservancy to a conservation buyer under easement.

▶ Visitor Information: The vireos are present from March to August. The state natural area is accessible by reservation only. Contact the park at HC 01, Box 513, Del Rio, TX 78840, 830-395-2133. Primitive campsites are available, but there is no potable water; inquire about other facilities. Best time to visit is April to May; summers are very hot. Visitation to Dolan Falls Preserve is by special arrangement or The Nature Conservancy scheduled events. Contact the Dolan Falls Preserve at HCR-1, Box 504, Del Rio, TX 78840, 915-292-4351.

36. Tamaulipan Brushlands

This plain extending into northeastern Mexico contains grassland, savannah, and thornscrub habitat, much of which has been converted to more shrubby conditions as a result of grazing. The very distinctive avifauna of this region includes the Audubon's Oriole, Buff-bellied Hummingbird, Long-billed Thrasher, and Plain Chachalaca. The Botteri's Sparrow, "Attwater's" Greater Prairie-Chicken, White-tailed Hawk, wintering Whooping Crane, and Le Conte's Sparrow are high-priority species of grassland habitats. Wetlands are habitat for most of the Black-bellied Whistling-Ducks that breed in the United States, a great variety of wading and shorebirds, as well as several wintering waterfowl species.

Lower Rio Grande Valley IBAs, Texas

Falcon State Park, Zapata County Park, and San Ygnacio (1), Bentsen-Rio Grande Valley State Park (2), Santa Ana and Lower Rio Grande Valley National Wildlife Refuges (3), Lennox Foundation Southmost Preserve (4), Sabal Palm Grove Audubon Center (5)

▸ Highlight: Many bird species, including several that are on the Green List, have a U.S. distribution exclusively or primarily in the Lower Rio Grande Valley of Texas.
▸ Location: Between Falcon Dam and the mouth of the Rio Grande.
▸ Size: At present approximately 80,000 acres are in public ownership. More are likely to be protected in the near future.
▸ Ownership: Fish and Wildlife Service, Texas Parks and Wildlife Department, Hidalgo County, The Nature Conservancy, National Audubon Society, private.
▸ Habitats: Riparian forest, brushland.
▸ Land Use: Agriculture, recreation, wildlife observation and conservation.
▸ Site Description: This area stretches from just above the Falcon Dam to the Gulf of Mexico. More than 95 percent of the vegetation of the Lower Rio Grande Valley has been destroyed and the lands converted to agriculture, which in this dry landscape requires extensive irrigation. The diverse bird life is now confined to a few wildlife sanctuaries and ranches left along the river. The situation is made worse by the fact that there has been wholesale clearing of forests in northeastern Mexico in recent

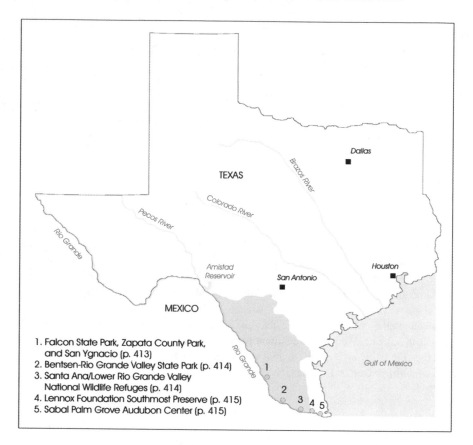

1. Falcon State Park, Zapata County Park, and San Ygnacio (p. 413)
2. Bentsen-Rio Grande Valley State Park (p. 414)
3. Santa Ana/Lower Rio Grande Valley National Wildlife Refuges (p. 414)
4. Lennox Foundation Southmost Preserve (p. 415)
5. Sabal Palm Grove Audubon Center (p. 415)

years. The Rio Grande Valley Wildlife Corridor, which extends from Falcon State Park to the Gulf, is made up of more than 100 scattered patches. Most of the remaining areas of relatively natural habitat in private ownership are in smaller holdings of less than 100 acres. The IBAs within this area are discussed individually below. These are Santa Ana/Lower Rio Grande Valley National Wildlife Refuge, Bentsen-Rio Grande Valley State Park, Falcon State Park and nearby areas, and Sabal Palm Grove Audubon Center and the nearby Lennox Foundation Southmost Preserve.

▸ Birds: Among the characteristic avifauna of natural habitats in the Lower Rio Grande Valley are the Plain Chachalaca, Red-billed Pigeon, Green and Ringed Kingfishers, Buff-bellied Hummingbird, Northern Beardless-Tyrannulet, Couch's Kingbird, Brown and Green Jays, Long-billed Thrasher, Altamira and Audubon's Orioles, and several other species at the northern end of their ranges. Many rarities from Mexico have turned up over the years.

▸ Conservation Issues: Habitat fragmentation is a threat to the native fauna of the Lower Rio Grande Valley. Studies indicate that for many songbirds, the rate of Brown-headed Cowbird parasitism and of nest predation is higher in the smaller patches of habitat. Dams, canals, and pumping stations have so changed the hydrology of the river that

Plain Chachalaca

periodic flooding no longer occurs, thus damaging the health of riparian woodland. As for protection efforts, there is a multi-agency project involving both federal and state agencies to protect a wildlife corridor and what remains of the native landscape between Falcon Dam and the mouth of the Rio Grande. This project began in 1979. At present, approximately 80,000 acres have been acquired, with a goal to protect 132,500 acres.

▸ Visitor Information: Any time of year is good for a visit. Spring and fall migrations are very rewarding; summer is very hot, but there is always the chance of a vagrant from Mexico. The first half of November is excellent, since the winter birds have arrived by then and the chances of seeing some of the rarer species is better. This is also the time when the Rio Grande Valley Birding Festival takes place in Harlingen. The remainder of the winter can also be very good. McAllen is a town chosen by many visiting birders for their trip headquarters since it is convenient to the leading Lower Rio Grande Valley sites and accommodation.

Falcon State Park, Zapata County Park, and San Ygnacio (1)

This is an important breeding area for the Red-billed Pigeon and Altamira Oriole, in addition to the Muscovy Duck and White-collared Seedeater. Located near Falcon, in Zapata County, Falcon State Park is 573 acres in size and run by the Texas Department of Parks and Wildlife, Zapata County. The area includes the riparian forest downstream from Falcon State Park to the city of Fronton, as well as upstream to include Zapata County Park and San Ygnacio, which lies approximately 30 miles upriver. The construction of Falcon Dam in the 1950s created a 60-mile-long lake. The area also includes thorn forest and Tamaulipan scrub habitat. Falcon State Park and the area immediately downriver provides critically important habitat for nesting Altamira Orioles, Red-billed Pigeons, wild Muscovy Ducks, Elf Owls, and Ferruginous Pygmy-Owls. The area above Falcon Lake to the city of San Ygnacio contains the only remaining floodplain habitat in the area and is important as the only U.S. nesting site for the White-collared Seedeater. Many migrant species are found in the area during winter, including the Sprague's Pipit. Other species found seasonally or as residents include the Plain Chachalaca, Long-billed Thrasher, Audubon's Oriole, and Cassin's, Clay-colored, and Brewer's Sparrows. The recently established Upper Rio Grande Valley Biological Station fills a gap in terms of environmental research and education since the area is not covered by any conservation group in the Lower Rio Grande Valley, and no other comparable group exists in the upper parts of the valley.

▸ Visitor Information: Best time to visit is January to April for the Texas specialties and April and May for migration. Contact: Falcon State Park, P.O. Box 2, Falcon Heights, TX 78545, 956-848-5327.

Bentsen-Rio Grande Valley State Park (2)

Near Mission, Texas, this is an important site for the South Texas specialties including the Hook-billed Kite. Much of the original subtropical vegetation has been preserved in this 587-acre park, donated to the state by the Bentsen family in 1944, and run by the Texas Department of Parks and Wildlife. It consists of resacas (former river channels whose banks support a rich forest of subtropical tree species), brushland of thorny shrubs, and small trees. The park contains many of the South Texas specialties, including the Plain Chachalaca, White-tipped Dove, Red-billed Pigeon, Northern Beardless-Tyrannulet, Green Jay, Altamira Oriole, and Olive Sparrow. Among the many wintering species are the Dickcissel, and Audubon's Oriole, and occasionally, Tropical Parula. The park is heavily visited by birdwatchers and many rarities from Mexico have been found there. The park is well protected but receives heavy use by birders and other recreationists. Nearby is Chihuahua Woods, a Nature Conservancy preserve of 243 acres. Its thornscrub vegetation supports many of the same bird species to be seen at Bentsen State Park. This site is open only during the day and can be accessed only on foot. Another area of public land along the river, located about five miles east of Bentsen-Rio Grande Valley State Park, is Anzaludas County Park, where many of the South Texas specialties may also be found.

► Visitor Information: Best time to visit is winter and early spring. Although Santa Ana is closed at night, Bentsen offers camping and is always open. Park naturalists conduct daily birding tours in the park from December to March; the tours start at 7 a.m. and last several hours. Contact: Bentsen-Rio Grande Valley State Park, P.O. Box 988, Mission, TX 78573, 956-519-6448.

Santa Ana and Lower Rio Grande Valley National Wildlife Refuges (3)

As the largest tract of public land in the Lower Rio Grande Valley, this is a critically important site for the South Texas specialties. Many vagrants from Mexico have been found through the years. Located along the river, west of Progreso, this 2,088-acre Fish and Wildlife Service refuge has the largest block of undisturbed riparian forest on the Rio Grande between Falcon Dam and Boca Chica. The refuge also has brushland and forest similar to that found in northeastern Mexico. This refuge and Laguna Atascosa (in BCR 37) protect the best remaining examples of Lower Rio Grande Valley vegetation. Virtually all of the Lower Rio Grande Valley specialties can be found at Santa Ana, and many rarities from Mexico have turned up through the years. Among the former are Plain Chachalacas, Buff-bellied Hummingbirds, Long-billed Thrashers, and Altamira and Audubon's Orioles. Migrant raptors funnel over the refuge in large numbers in spring and fall. As many as 100,000 Broad-winged Hawks have passed over the refuge on a single March day. During the twentieth century, most of the area along the Rio Grande was cleared of vegetation and converted to agriculture. Before the flow in the river was greatly reduced by damming and diversion for irrigation, the Rio Grande often flooded. The fertile soils and the geographic location of the Rio Grande's delta led to a great diversity and abundance of species unmatched elsewhere in the United States. The absence of spring flooding has changed the remnants of riparian forest; many of the tall trees have died and are being replaced by thornscrub, with a consequent decline in riparian forest birds. Land managers at the refuge are now starting to create artificial floods in the riparian forest at Santa Ana, and the results are encouraging in terms of regeneration of the vegetation.

▶ Visitor Information: Winter and spring are the best times to visit. In winter, cars are banned from the refuge, but there is a tram making a regular circuit. Contact: Santa Ana National Wildlife Refuge, Route 2, Box 202A, Alamo, TX 78516, 956-787-3079.

Lennox Foundation Southmost Preserve (4)

This 1,034-acre Nature Conservancy preserve provides habitat for several South Texas specialties, including the Buff-bellied Hummingbird. Located approximately four miles southeast of Brownsville, a mile distant from the Sabal Palm Grove Audubon Center, the preserve shares a grove of some 15 acres of sabal palm with an adjoining property recently acquired by the Fish and Wildlife Service. The preserve's sabal palm forest, resacas, and Tamaulipan thornscrub are among the largest and highest-quality examples of these native communities in the region. It is one of the most ecologically important pieces of land remaining in the valley. Much of the surrounding area is farmed. Many of the species characteristic of South Texas are found here, including the Plain Chachalaca, Buff-bellied Hummingbird, and Long-billed Thrasher. Management of this preserve, acquired by The Nature Conservancy in 1999, has so far been focused on ecological research, native brush and resaca restoration, and removal of non-native species. The site has good potential for long-term research on the compatibility of agricultural activities within a protected conservation area. Comparisons between traditional agricultural practices and environmentally friendly practices will be studied. Community-based conservation and outreach are also among the priorities of the preserve.

▶ Visitor Information: The preserve can be visited only by arrangement with The Nature Conservancy, which gives periodic tours and also sponsors volunteer workdays as well. For more information, contact the preserve at 10,000 Southmost Road, Brownsville, TX 78521, 956-546-0547.

Sabal Palm Grove Audubon Center (5)

Owned by National Audubon Society, this 527-acre preserve, located four miles southeast of Brownsville, provides habitat for several South Texas specialties, including the Buff-bellied Hummingbird. Sabal palms were once among the dominant vegetation along the Rio Grande, but now only a small fraction of the palm forests remain. This preserve has a 32-acre forest of old-growth sabal palm, the best remaining example of this type, while the nearby Southmost Preserve, only a mile or so away, shares a grove of some 15 acres with an adjoining property recently acquired by the Fish and Wildlife Service. Much of the surrounding area is comprised of agricultural fields. Many of the species characteristic of South Texas are found there, including the Plain Chachalaca, Buff-bellied Hummingbird, and Long-billed Thrasher. The area is managed as a wildlife sanctuary.

▸ Visitor Information: Trails on the sanctuary are open from 7 a.m. to 6 p.m. year-round. Contact: Sabal Palm Audubon Center and Sanctuary, Sabal Palm Road, Brownsville, TX 78523, 956-541-8034.

37. Gulf Coastal Prairie

Flat grassland and marsh hugs the coast of the Gulf of Mexico from the mouth of the Rio Grande, up into the rice country of southeast Texas and southwest Louisiana, and across the great Louisiana marshlands of the mouth of the Mississippi River. They feature one of the greatest concentrations of colonial waterbirds in the world, with breeding Reddish Egrets, Roseate Spoonbills, Brown Pelicans, and large numbers of herons, egrets, ibis, terns, and skimmers. The region provides critical in-transit habitat for migrating shorebirds, including the Buff-breasted Sandpiper and Hudsonian Godwit, and for most of the neotropical migrant forest birds of eastern North America. Mottled Ducks, Fulvous Whistling-Ducks, and Purple Gallinules also breed in wetlands, and winter numbers of waterfowl are among the highest on the continent. These include dabbling ducks (especially the Northern Pintail and Gadwall), as well as the Redhead, Lesser Scaup, and White-fronted Goose from both the Central and Mississippi Flyways. The most important waterfowl habitats of the area are coastal marsh, shallow estuarine bays and lagoons, and wetlands on agricultural lands of the rice prairies. Loss and degradation of wetland habitats due to subsidence, sea level rise, shoreline erosion, freshwater and sediment deprivation, saltwater intrusion, oil and gas canals, and navigation channels and associated maintenance dredging are the most important problems facing the area's wetland wildlife.

Laguna Atascosa National Wildlife Refuge (1), Texas

▶ Highlight: One of the top sites for shorebirds in the United States; highest winter count anywhere for Redheads; greatest number of recorded bird species of any National Wildlife Refuge.
▶ Designation: Wetland of Regional Importance in the Western Hemisphere Shorebird Reserve Network.
▶ Location: On the Gulf Coast, about 15 miles north of the mouth of the Rio Grande, across Laguna Madre from South Padre Island.
▶ Size: 45,000 acres.
▶ Ownership: Fish and Wildlife Service.
▶ Habitats: Coastal prairie and scrub, tidal wetlands and lakes, upland thorn scrubland, mesquite grassland.

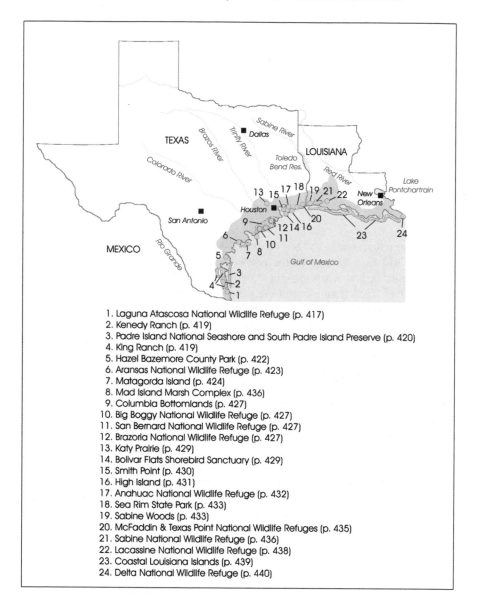

1. Laguna Atascosa National Wildlife Refuge (p. 417)
2. Kenedy Ranch (p. 419)
3. Padre Island National Seashore and South Padre Island Preserve (p. 420)
4. King Ranch (p. 419)
5. Hazel Bazemore County Park (p. 422)
6. Aransas National Wildlife Refuge (p. 423)
7. Matagorda Island (p. 424)
8. Mad Island Marsh Complex (p. 436)
9. Columbia Bottomlands (p. 427)
10. Big Boggy National Wildlife Refuge (p. 427)
11. San Bernard National Wildlife Refuge (p. 427)
12. Brazoria National Wildlife Refuge (p. 427)
13. Katy Prairie (p. 429)
14. Bolivar Flats Shorebird Sanctuary (p. 429)
15. Smith Point (p. 430)
16. High Island (p. 431)
17. Anahuac National Wildlife Refuge (p. 432)
18. Sea Rim State Park (p. 433)
19. Sabine Woods (p. 433)
20. McFaddin & Texas Point National Wildlife Refuges (p. 435)
21. Sabine National Wildlife Refuge (p. 436)
22. Lacassine National Wildlife Refuge (p. 438)
23. Coastal Louisiana Islands (p. 439)
24. Delta National Wildlife Refuge (p. 440)

▶ Land Use: Wildlife conservation, recreation.
▶ Site Description: With a great variety of habitats, the refuge is the largest protected area of natural habitat left in the Lower Rio Grande Valley. Besides its birdlife, it also harbors many mammals, including two endangered cat species—the ocelot and the jaguarundi. Coastal habitat in nearby Tamaulipas, Mexico, is part of the same system and also plays a key role in the conservation of shorebirds, waterfowl, and other birds; the designation by the Western Hemisphere Shorebird Reserve Network includes La-

guna Atascosa, nearby Tamaulipas, and part of South Padre Island, including The Nature Conservancy's South Padre Island Preserve.

Painted Bunting

▸ Birds: As one of the state's most popular destinations for birders, Laguna Atascosa holds the record for number of bird species recorded at a national wildlife refuge—currently just over 400—but it is significant for other reasons, as well. More than 700,000 wintering waterfowl have been recorded there, including up to 45,000 Redhead, the highest winter count anywhere for that species; Canvasbacks are also abundant during winter. It hosts thousands of shorebirds during migration, in addition to providing habitat for many migrating landbirds. The endangered Piping Plover winters there and at nearby South Padre Island, and the Wilson's Plover breeds. The Painted Bunting and Botteri's Sparrow are also among the breeding species, as are several South Texas specialties—Plain Chachalaca, Buff-bellied Hummingbird, and Long-billed Thrasher. Altamira Orioles, Sage Thrashers, and Le Conte's and Clay-colored Sparrows can be found in the winter. The refuge maintains an active release program to reestablish a breeding population of Aplomado Falcons in the area, using birds bred in captivity in Mexico.

▸ Conservation Issues: Water diversion upstream during times of drought is a problem to the hydrology of the refuge, as is pesticide runoff from upstream agricultural lands. Outside the refuge, conversion of brush habitat to agricultural and residential use impairs linkage of the refuge to other brush areas and impacts the ocelot population. The reintroduced Aplomado Falcon, which had been extirpated from the United States, is closely monitored. The raptor has also been reintroduced to ranches in South Texas, under the Safe Harbors program, wherein landowners voluntarily agree to take actions that would attract endangered species and in exchange are released from federal mandates affecting the use of their land.

▸ Visitor Information: Best time to visit is fall through spring. Contact: Laguna Atascosa National Wildlife Refuge, P.O. Box 450, Rio Hondo, TX 78583, 956-748-3607.

Kenedy Ranch (2) and King Ranch (4), Texas

▸ Highlight: Several of the South Texas Green List species are found on these large, privately owned ranches.

▸ Location: Entrance to King Ranch is just west of Kingsville in Kleberg County; the Kenedy Ranch is near Sarita in Kenedy County.

▸ Size: King Ranch is 825,000 acres; Kenedy Ranch is 400,000 acres.

▸ Ownership: Private; King Ranch is family-owned.

▸ Habitats: Tamaulipan brushland; Gulf Coastal Prairie.

▸ Land Use: Cattle ranching, oil and gas, agriculture, hunting, wildlife observation.

▸ Site Description: These are two large operating ranches on the border of the Tamaulipan Brushlands and the Gulf Coastal Prairie. King Ranch has more than 90 miles of undeveloped shoreline.

Long-billed Thrasher

▸ Birds: Many of the South Texas specialties may be seen on the ranches, among the species are the Mottled Duck, Buff-bellied Hummingbird, Long-billed Thrasher, Audubon's Oriole, Painted Bunting, Dickcissel and Botteri's, Cassin's and Seaside Sparrows. Other South Texas specialties are the Green Jay, Northern Beardless-Tyrannulet Tropical Parula and Ferruginous Pygmy-Owl; King Ranch has the largest populations of the latter two species in the United States. The Piping Plover and Reddish Egret can be found on both ranches.

▸ Conservation Issues: Hunting is an important source of income for both ranches. Both ranches also make money from gas and oil wells and cattle grazing, and the King Ranch also produces cotton and sorghum. The John G. and Marie Stella Kenedy Memorial Foundation owns 235,000 acres of the Kenedy Ranch. The Kenedy Foundation Ranch implements a management program designed to promote the co-existence of wildlife with grazing livestock. The ranch has been recognized by Partners in Flight for its work in bird conservation, in particular for developing tourism as a way to diversify revenue and protect bird habitat. The King Ranch has over 700,000 acres of diverse wildlife habitat and rangeland within its boundaries. This family-owned ranch has been involved in the conservation of wildlife and habitats for more than 100 years. In 1990 it began an involvement in ecotourism by allowing Victor Emanuel Nature Tours to arrange birding tours to the ranch. In 1994, King Ranch hired a full-time biologist to develop, handle, and conduct a year-round nature tour program.

▸ Visitor Information: Both ranches may be visited on organized tours. King Ranch may be contacted at P.O. Box 1090, Kingsville, TX 78364-1090, (361) 592-8055, and Kenedy Foundation Ranch at P.O. Box 70, Sarita, TX 78385, 800-757-4470.

Padre Island National Seashore and South Padre Island Preserve (3), Texas

▸ Highlight: Padre Island National Seashore and South Padre Island, along with the entire Laguna Madre system, form possibly the most important wintering site for the endangered Piping Plover. Up to 90 percent of the U.S. Redhead population winters in northern and southern Laguna Madre.

▸ Designation: The Nature Conservancy's South Padre Island Preserve is a part of a Western Hemisphere Shorebird Reserve Network site, which also includes Laguna Atascosa National Wildlife Refuge and the Rancho Rincon lands along Laguna Madre in Tamaulipas, Mexico. Padre Island National Seashore is in the process of becoming part of this designation.

▸ Location: Padre Island National Seashore and South Padre Island stretch from Corpus Christi to near the mouth of the Rio Grande. South Padre Island is also the name of the resort town at the southern end of the island system.

▸ Size: The Padre Island National Seashore is 133,000 acres, of which some 60,000 acres is owned by the state. The Nature Conservancy's South Padre Island Preserve is 24,532 acres.

▸ Ownership: National Park Service, Texas General Land Office, The Nature Conservancy, private.

▸ Habitats: Coastal dunes, grasslands, oak mottes, salt marshes, brackish lagoons, rock jetties, tidal flats, bare beach, washover channels, seagrass meadows.

▸ Land Use: Recreational use includes fishing, camping, beachcombing, and birding; there is off-road vehicle use, particularly on the flats. State lands are managed to generate oil and gas revenue for the public school system and for spoil disposal, but there are also long-term lease cabins there used by recreationists. National park and Nature Conservancy lands are also used for conservation.

▸ Site Description: Padre Island, at 113 miles, is the longest barrier island in the world. Most of Padre Island is part of the Padre Island National Seashore. On South Padre Island, the dune systems are the highest on the Texas coast, reaching 50 feet. The Nature Conservancy's South Padre Island Preserve consists of eight tracts, beginning at the northernmost end of the island, at the man-made Mansfield Channel, which divides South Padre Island from the National Seashore on Padre Island. As part of the original plans to develop South Padre, many small "beach to bay" lots were sold, many through magazine advertisements, but these were never developed. There are more than 1,000 owners involved in these tracts, but other, larger tracts are in single ownerships. The southernmost five miles of the island are highly developed, with homes, hotels, and resorts.

▸ Birds: The islands may have up to 800 Piping Plovers during the winter, a count resulting from mark/recapture studies and from the high count of surveys conducted between 1992–1994. This is a significant percent of the U.S. population and perhaps the most important wintering site for the species. Recent counts have been lower, quite likely because the international Piping Plover census takes place in midwinter, a period of low tides, when the birds are more dispersed and harder to count. There is a concentration of wintering Piping Plover, with counts of up to 400 birds, on an expansive mudflat in the northernmost part of South Padre Island on the Laguna Madre side. More than 35,000 Redhead have been censused in winter, and Least Terns and a few Snowy and Wilson Plovers are found during the breeding season. There are as many as 689 Reddish Egrets resident on the island and on offshore spoil islands, the largest concentration of this species in the United States. Long-billed Curlews winter as well as occurring as a migrant in spring migration on the shallow tidal flats, along with thousands of other shorebirds during spring and fall migration. Among the wintering birds are the Short-eared Owl, Sprague's Pipit, and Le Conte's Sparrow. There are several wooded areas on both Padre and South Padre Islands that receive tremendous migrant stopover use by passerines. A population of approximately 400 White Pelicans nests annually within Padre Island National Seashore and represents the one of two annually re-occurring saltwater populations of the species in the United States.

▸ Conservation Issues: Barge and tanker use, as well as oil and gas wells, on both sides of the park pose toxic spill threats. Recreational use is heavy; approximately

900,000 visitors use Padre Island National Seashore annually. There is a potential for hurricane damage. Some of the beach at the national seashore is open to four-wheel drive vehicles. Off-road vehicles are a problem on South Padre Island and have caused damage to sensitive ecosystems. On North Padre Island, the park does try to enforce existing regulations restricting off-road vehicle access to the flats on the bayside of the seashore. Dredge disposal is a continuing problem, less so on the island, but there remain disposal issues in the vicinity of Port Mansfield Cut. Oil and gas exploration and production continue to be activities that require constant attention to ensure they do not harm the environment. The Nature Conservancy may eventually transfer its holdings to the Fish and Wildlife Service, to be managed by Laguna Atascosa National Wildlife Refuge, which lies across Laguna Madre from South Padre Island.

▶ Visitor Information: Best time to visit is from April through the first week in May, to see the trans-gulf migrants, though fall migration and winter are also productive, especially for waterfowl and shorebirds. Padre Island National Seashore can be reached from Corpus Christi, where there are many accommodations. South Padre Island can be reached from Port Isabel, near Brownsville. At the southern end of South Padre Island is a resort area with motels, campgrounds, and restaurants. It is not possible to get to Padre Island National Seashore from South Padre Island. Contact: Padre Island National Seashore, P.O. Box 181300, Corpus Christi, TX 78480, 361-949-8173, or call the visitor center at 361-949-8068.

Hazel Bazemore County Park (5), Texas

▶ Highlight: One of the premier hawk watch sites in the country.
▶ Location: West of Corpus Christi.
▶ Size: 550 acres.
▶ Ownership: Nueces County.
▶ Habitats: Pond, riparian, Tamaulipan scrub.
▶ Site Description: The park offers a high point with a commanding view in several directions.
▶ Birds: This is perhaps the best place anywhere in the United States to watch migrating hawks, with counts of more than one million birds during fall migration. As many as 100,000, mostly Broad-winged Hawks, have been seen on a single day in mid-to-late September. The park also attracts large numbers of other landbirds and shorebirds during migration.
▶ Visitor Information: From I-37, take U.S. 77 south and turn shortly thereafter onto Farm Road 624. Within a mile turn right on County Road 69. Best time to visit is from mid-to-late September, but hawks are migrating from mid-August to mid-November. An annual four-day Celebration of Flight, sponsored by HawkWatch International, is held in late September. For more information, call Nueces County Parks at 361-888-0444.

HAWK WATCH SITES

There are some places in the United States, where, if the winds are right and it's the right time of year, one can see hundreds, even thousands, of migrating hawks in a single day. Though these places don't generally represent on-the-ground habitat important to the hawks themselves, nonetheless they serve an important function for monitoring raptor numbers and detecting population trends. Who is likely to forget the sight of thousands of hawks circling above?

Major regional concentration points for migrating hawks occur along the Pacific Coast, in the mountain ranges of the Great Basin, on the western coast of the Gulf of Mexico, along the shorelines of the Great Lakes, in the northern and central Appalachian Mountains (including the famous example of Hawk Mountain in Pennsylvania's Kittatinny Ridge), and on Atlantic Coast barrier islands and peninsulas. The numbers of hawks recorded at these sites reflect not just the numbers of birds but the numbers of humans counting them. Because of the intense interest that hawks inspire in birders, there are not only plenty of the former but plenty of the latter. The result is, according to Hawks Aloft Worldwide, that the timing and corridors of raptor migration in North America, particularly in eastern North America, are better known than those of any other region of the world.

Some of the premier U.S. sites for hawks are Braddock Bay, New York, with an average of 52,900 birds seen annually; Derby Hill, New York, with 43,700; Cape May Point, New Jersey, with 68,400; Montclair Hawk Lookout, New Jersey, with 25,800; Hawk Mountain, Pennsylvania, the oldest hawk watch of all, with 18,600; Lake Erie Metropark, Michigan, with an annual average of 109,850 but a one-day record, on September 17, 1999, of more than 501,000; Hawk Ridge Nature Reserve, Minnesota, with 60,000; Goshutes Mountains, Nevada, with 22,000; and four sites in Texas: Bentsen-Rio Grande Valley State Park, with 32,800; Smith Point, with 25,900; the Santa Ana/Lower Rio Grande Valley National Wildlife Refuges, with 30,600 and as many as 20 species recorded annually, the largest species count of any site in the United States; and the leading hawk watch of all, the Corpus Christi Hawk Watch at Hazel Bazemore Park, with an annual average of 230,467, a one-day count of up to 100,000, and a fall migration record of more than one million hawks between August and November.

Aransas National Wildlife Refuge (6), Texas

▸ Highlight: Aransas National Wildlife Refuge and environs are famous as the wintering area for the only self-sustaining natural wild population of the endangered Whooping Crane, which once wintered along the Gulf Coast from Florida to Mexico.
▸ Location: Gulf Coast in Refugio County, northeast of Rockport.
▸ Size: 115,000 acres.
▸ Ownership: Fish and Wildlife Service.
▸ Habitats: Open bay, mudflats, ponds, tidal marshes, coastal prairie, oak woodland, live oak and redbay thickets.
▸ Land Use: Wildlife protection, recreation.
▸ Site Description: Most of the refuge is located on the Blackjack Peninsula on the inland side of the Intracoastal Waterway, but part is on Matagorda Island, which lies opposite. Marshes dominated by salt grass cover much of the refuge. The interior portion is gently rolling and sandy, with oak brush, grassland, and ponds.
▸ Birds: The Aransas National Wildlife Refuge has played and continues to play a central role in the conservation of the endangered Whooping Crane. In 1941, the pop-

ulation had fallen to only 15 birds in the wild but, in a recent count, has since risen to 182 (164 adults and 18 young) wintering in and around Aransas. The cranes arrive on their Aransas wintering grounds in mid-October and leave in mid-April. Starting in March they begin their spectacular courtship behavior—bowing, leaping, and wingflapping. Most of the cranes winter on the grassy salt flats on the bayside fringe, where they feed largely on clams and crabs. Whooping Cranes also winter at nearby Matagorda Island Wildlife Management Area and State Park, administered by Aransas National Wildlife Refuge.

Among the other highlights of this vitally important refuge are wintering Black Rails and nesting Buff-bellied Hummingbirds, Swainson's Warblers, and Painted Buntings. The Seaside Sparrow is present all year. Reddish Egrets and a great variety of other herons and shorebirds feed on the mudflats and in the salt marsh. Many waterfowl, including large numbers of Redhead and Mottled Ducks, are present during the winter. Many shorebirds stop over on migration or spend the winter, including the Piping and Snowy Plovers, Long-billed Curlew, and Marbled Godwit. The refuge is also a first landfall for migrating passerines crossing the Gulf of Mexico in the spring. South Texas specialties such as the Least Grebe, White-tailed Hawk, and Couch's Kingbird are also found on the refuge.

▶ Conservation Issues: There is the constant threat of oil and chemical spills from the billions of dollars of cargoes passing through the refuge on the Intracoastal Waterway. One disastrous spill could decimate the entire wild population of Whooping Cranes. The cranes' limited habitat is also subject to damage from storms and waves from boat and barge traffic. Human disturbance through waterfowl hunting, clamming, crabbing, and planes is also a threat.

▶ Visitor's Information: Though the refuge has many species of interest throughout the year, most birders come in search of the Whooping Cranes, which are present on the refuge from late October until mid-April when they leave on their 2,500-mile journey to their nesting grounds in northern Canada's Wood Buffalo National Park. Food, motels, and campgrounds are 35 miles from the refuge, in Rockport and Port Lavaca. The interior of the refuge is closed to visitors when the cranes are present, but they can be seen in the distance from the observation tower or from the wildlife drive; by far the best way to see them, however, is to take a boat tour from Rockport Harbor or Fulton. On these tours, seeing a Whooping Crane is close to guaranteed, which is not the case from the tower on Aransas. Many other waterbirds may be seen from these tour boats. Mosquitoes and chiggers abound on the refuge. Contact: Aransas National Wildlife Refuge, P.O. Box 100, Austwell, TX 77950, 512-286-3559.

Matagorda Island (7), Texas

▶ Highlight: Several Green List species are resident or present during winter, and the Whooping Crane is occasionally seen on the tidal flats.
▶ Location: Near Port O'Conner, Calhoun County.
▶ Size: 55,393 acres.
▶ Ownership: Texas Parks and Wildlife Department, Fish and Wildlife Service,
▶ Habitats: Beach, dune communities, coastal prairie, salt cedar thickets, tidal flats.
▶ Land Use: Wildlife observation, research and environmental education.

▸ Site Description: The upper part of the island is occupied by Matagorda Island Wildlife Management Area and State Park (43,893 acres), whereas the lower part (11,500 acres) is administered by Aransas National Wildlife Refuge. Matagorda Island is one of the five major barrier islands on the Texas Gulf Coast and the only one entirely in public ownership. It is 38 miles long and from 0.75 to 4.5 miles wide. The gulf side is sandy beach while the bay side is tidal flats. Wave action, deposition of sand, and storms constantly change its contours. At the inner perimeter of the beach is a ridge of primary sand dunes from eight to 15 feet high. In conjunction with the two managing agencies, The Nature Conservancy of Texas operates the Enron Matagorda Island Environmental Education and Research Center at the southern end of the island.

▸ Birds: The Reddish Egret, Mottled Duck, Black Rail, and Seaside Sparrow are resident. In winter, Snowy and Piping Plovers are found on the beaches, while Nelson's Sharp-tailed Sparrows are seen in the marshes, and Le Conte's Sparrows in the grasslands. Whooping Cranes, part of the population wintering at Aransas, are sometimes seen on the tidal flats. There is a colony of breeding Least Terns. The island is also a staging area for shorebirds during spring and fall migration and many spend the winter there; in addition, cross-gulf migrant landbirds can be numerous in the spring. White-tailed Hawks are found there, and the island was a site for the reintroduction of the Aplomado Falcon. Six were introduced in 1996 through a partnership with The Peregrine Fund, which furnished the birds and directed the release. Falcons were also introduced in the subsequent three years. In 1999, there were two nesting attempts, and one nest fledged three birds; in 2000, there were three attempts and one bird fledged. At present, there are ten pairs of falcons and two single birds on the island.

▸ Conservation Issues: Clumps of salt cedar, an invasive non-native plant, surround some of the areas with fresh water. There is a threat of oil spills and other toxic pollution from shipping in the Intracoastal Waterway. The island was formerly the site of a military base and is not easily accessible.

▸ Visitor Information: Best time to visit is fall to spring. Visitors are limited to those with permission to dock and those taking the ferry from Port O'Connor. Inquire about schedules at the headquarters of Texas Parks and Wildlife Department. Camping is permitted, but visitors must bring all supplies, including water. The state park can be reached at P.O. Box 117, 16th Street and Maples, Port O'Connor, TX 77982, 361-983-2215. Contact: Aransas National Wildlife Refuge at P.O. Box 100, Austwell, TX 77950, 512-286-3559.

NORTH AMERICAN BIRD CONSERVATION INITIATIVE

The purpose of the North American Bird Conservation Initiative (NABCI) is to ensure the long-term health of North America's native bird populations by increasing the effectiveness of, and coordination among bird conservation initiatives, and by fostering cooperation among the continent's governments and people. NABCI aims to deliver bird conservation through culturally sensitive, regionally based, biologically driven, landscape-oriented partnerships. Culturally sensitive means conservation done in the context of local customs, people, and their needs. Regionally based partnerships involve all stakeholders across BCRs. Biologically driven conservation links population and habitat objectives with on-the-ground actions, and adapting those actions as knowledge is gained. Landscape-oriented conservation recognizes that bird populations will respond to change at multiple scales from local to BCR level.

Partners in NABCI envision collaborative habitat conservation based on the North American Waterfowl Management Plan's (NAWMP) joint venture model, covering all birds and all habitats, coast to coast, using BCRs as the ecological unit in which to achieve their goals. NABCI aims to assist and facilitate accomplishment of the goals of NAWMP, Partners in Flight, the U.S. Shorebird Conservation Plan, and the U.S. Waterbird Conservation Plan. Each of these initiatives participates in NABCI both to advance their own goals as well as contribute to and work with other initiatives to provide for more effective bird conservation.

Mad Island Marsh Complex (8), Texas

▸ Highlight: Significant areas of native coastal habitats; early winter species avian diversity is among the highest in the United States, large breeding populations of waterbirds and massive numbers of migrants pass through the area during spring and fall.

▸ Location: Southern Matagorda County at the mouth of the Colorado River below Matagorda.

▸ Size: 15-mile diameter circle.

▸ Ownership: The Nature Conservancy, Texas Parks and Wildlife Department, Lower Colorado River Authority, Texas General Land Office, other state agencies, private, commercial.

▸ Habitats: Brackish marsh, coastal prairie, coastal savannah, freshwater lake, freshwater marsh, riparian woodlands, brushlands. Also bottomland hardwood forests, riparian woodlands, live oak woodlands, Tamaulipan thornscrub brushlands, mesquite park grasslands, and coastal prairie, streams and rivers, barrier beaches and dunes.

▸ Land Use: Conservation in the form of state Wildlife Management Area, Nature Conservancy preserve, river authority property, and conservation-minded management practices and goals of private landowners. Agriculture in the form of row crops, turf farms, aquaculture facilities and ranching. Commercial wildlife and fishery management in the form of several leases of private land for hunting plus commercial fishing within the bays and river. Industry in the form of nuclear power generation and two petrochemical plants. The town of Matagorda has approximately 500 residents and one large disjunct subdivision on the river of 200 residents.

▸ Site Description: Mad Island Marsh is part of an expansive coastal wetland system that once stretched nearly unbroken along the mid- and upper-Texas Gulf Coast. The site consists of the Clive Runnells Family Mad Island Marsh Preserve (7,063 acres) and Mad Island Marsh Wildlife Management Area (7,000 acres), plus adjoining private lands. The Colorado River Delta is a very diverse complex of native habitats and agricultural land in southern Matagorda County. The river created a land bridge across Matagorda Bay during the 1940s and split Matagorda Peninsula. It empties its waters into the Gulf of Mexico and West Matagorda Bay. The peninsula contains sand dunes and grasslands grading into a brackish marsh behind the dunes. Freshwater to saline marshes occur along all drainages emptying into the bay and along bayshores. East Matagorda Bay has relatively clear water because it does not receive heavy sediments and is a preferred site for diving birds. West Matagorda Bay is very turbid because it receives most of the discharge of the river and has extensive mudflats exposed during low winter tides. It is also very valuable to shorebirds and waders. Bottomland hardwood forests grow along the narrow river floodplain, bordered by coastal prairies on both sides. Tamaulipan thornscrub communities occur along the edges of the bay and a variety of brushlands, savannahs, and riparian woods occur along the drainages emptying into the bay and draining the river. Large acreages of the coastal prairie have been converted into agriculture, producing grain crops, cotton, and lawn turf. Remaining native grasslands are grazed. Two petrochemical plants and one nuclear power plant are located along the river. Sport fishing and hunting are major recreational activities in the area.

▸ Birds: The Colorado River Delta supports in excess of 300 species. Since 1997, Mad Island Marsh has ranked first in the nation in number of species during the annual Christmas Bird Count. Wintering birds include more than 8,000 herons, including more than 30 Reddish Egrets, some 56,000 waterfowl, more than 10,000 shorebirds, and good numbers of Sandhill Cranes, Sprague's Pipits, and Le Conte's and Seaside Sparrows. Among the birds found seasonally are Roseate Spoonbills, Wood Storks, Mottled Ducks, Yellow and Black Rails, American Avocets, and Dickcissels.

▸ Conservation Issues: Tidal and freshwater wetlands bordering Matagorda Bay were damaged by saltwater intrusion and decreased freshwater inflow because of drainage and navigation. Extensive coastal prairies on Texas Parks and Wildlife Department and Nature Conservancy properties are isolated from other prairies in Texas because former prairies were converted to agriculture. Remaining native grasslands on private property are being invaded by brush because of the lack of controlled burns by private ranchers. All forests are grazed and result in degraded woodlands for wildlife.

▸ Visitor Information: Highest diversity occurs during spring and fall migration seasons. Winter months are most comfortable. Summers are hot and muggy. For information about visiting Clive Runnells Family Mad Island Marsh Preserve, contact The Nature Conservancy of Texas, P.O. Box 163, Collegeport, TX 77428, 361-972-2559. For information about Mad Island Marsh Wildlife Management Area, contact Texas Parks and Wildlife Department, County Courthouse, Room 101, Bay City, TX 77414. You may want to refer to the website for the Matagorda County Birding and Nature Center (www.mcbnc.org), which contains a map of birding locales. Also the Lower Colorado River Authority is developing a nature educational center in Matagorda. Contact: kgonzale@lcra.org.

Texas Mid-Coast National Wildlife Refuge Complex IBAs, Texas

Columbia Bottomlands (9), Big Boggy National Wildlife Refuge (10), San Bernard National Wildlife Refuge (11), Brazoria National Wildlife Refuge (12)

▸ Highlight: The refuge complex is extremely important to migrant and wintering waterfowl, shorebirds, and passerines. Brazoria lies within the Freeport Christmas Bird

Count circle, which usually ranks first or second in the entire nation in number of species seen.

▸ Location: These three refuges are along the Texas Coast, near Freeport.

▸ Size: 43,388 acres (Brazoria), 24,445 acres (San Bernard), 4,526 acres (Big Boggy).

▸ Ownership: Fish and Wildlife Service.

▸ Designation: Wetland of International Importance in the Western Hemisphere Shorebird Reserve Network.

▸ Habitats: Saline and non-saline prairie, salt and mudflats, fresh and salt marshes, saltwater lakes, woodlands, old-growth coastal live oak forests, more than 5,000 acres of native bluestem coastal prairie.

▸ Land Use: Recreation, wildlife conservation.

▸ Site Description: These three discontinuous refuges lie within 35 miles of one another in the Texas Gulf Coast Ecosystem. They support a great variety of habitats, including remnants of the native coastal prairie, more than 1.2 million acres of which have been destroyed in the last 100 years. Columbia Bottomlands, a coastal live oak forest, once covered more than 700,000 acres in the San Bernard, Brazoria, and Colorado River floodplains. Today, less than one quarter of this acreage still exists (177,000 acres). The remaining forest cover occurs as hundreds of forest patches. This forest still represents the largest contiguous forested landscape on the entire coast of the western Gulf of Mexico. Columbia Bottomlands is known to be of international significance to spring migrants after crossing the Gulf.

▸ Birds: The Texas Gulf Coast is a key wintering area for waterfowl using the Central Flyway, when thousands of geese and ducks are found there. At the three refuges combined, there are more than 200,000 waterfowl during the peak time of December through January. Among the duck species present is the Mottled Duck. All three refuges are also extremely significant as a stopover for migrating passerines and shorebirds, including the Snowy and Piping Plovers, Long-billed Curlew, Marbled Godwit, Stilt Sandpiper, and Short-billed Dowitcher. The Yellow Rail winters at the refuges, and the Black Rail is a rare resident. The Reddish Egret and Roseate Spoonbill are resident species, and Wood Storks are found in summer. Among the wintering passerines are Sprague's Pipits, Nelson's Sharp-tailed and Le Conte's Sparrows; Seaside Sparrows are residents, and the Dickcissel is a common breeding species. The area also supports high densities of breeding Prothonotary and Swainson's Warblers, in addition to huge wintering populations of passerines.

▸ Conservation Issues: Water levels are manipulated for waterfowl; controlled burns and limited grazing are also used to improve areas for waterfowl. Columbia Bottomlands (also known as Austin Woods) is at present a high priority for acquisition to add to the protected lands. The Texas Mid-Coast National Wildlife Refuge Complex has recently made several land purchases totaling more than 8,000 acres.

▸ Visitor Information: Access to Brazoria is limited during the week but open houses are held the first full weekend of each month from 8 a.m. to 4 p.m. and also on the third weekend of the month from November to April. Best times to visit are November to March for winter birds and April and May for migrants. San Bernard is open every day of the year from daylight until dark. Big Boggy is generally closed to visitors, but fishing and hunting are allowed in season. Contact: Brazoria National Wildlife Refuge, P.O. Drawer 1088, Angleton, TX 77516-1088, 979-849-6062; San Bernard National Wildlife Refuge, 1212 North Velasco, Angleton, TX 77505, 979-964-3639.

Katy Prairie (13), Texas

▸ Highlight: Important concentrations of the wintering Le Conte's Sparrow and Sprague's Pipit.
▸ Location: Just west of Houston, south of the town of Hockley.
▸ Size: 60,000 acres.
▸ Ownership: Private.
▸ Habitats: Coastal grasslands, creek corridors, depressional wetlands, agricultural wetlands (rice fields), pastureland.
▸ Land Use: Agriculture.
▸ Site Description: The area is made up of flooded rice fields, sorghum fields, and pastureland within 20 miles of Houston. Within this agricultural matrix are wetlands and brushy areas supporting much wildlife.

Buff-breasted Sandpiper

▸ Birds: In winter, the area hosts large numbers of Le Conte's Sparrows, while Sprague's Pipits, and Harris's and Henslow's Sparrows are also seen. Thousands of geese, including Ross's, and many Sandhill Cranes occur in the rice and sorghum fields in winter. Many shorebirds, including Buff-breasted Sandpipers and Hudsonian Godwits, occur in migration, as do several species of rail, including an occasional Yellow Rail, and many migrating raptors as well. In the summer, Painted Buntings and good numbers of Dickcissels breed. The "Attwater's" Greater Prairie-Chicken once occurred here.
▸ Conservation Issues: The expanding city of Houston threatens to engulf Katy Prairie, all of which is privately owned. Nonnative plants, particularly Chinese tallow, threaten open areas by crowding out native species.
▸ Visitor Information: Best time to visit is fall through spring. Since the land is private, visitors must not trespass and must confine wildlife viewing to areas visible from the roads. Bear Creek Park, just to the southeast of the prairie, has some good habitat and is open to visitors.

Bolivar Flats Shorebird Sanctuary (14), Texas

▸ Highlight: One of the most important sites for concentrations of migrating and wintering shorebirds along the Gulf Coast.
▸ Location: 25 miles down the Bolivar Peninsula from High Island.
▸ Size: 550 acres.

▸ Ownership: Owned by the State of Texas but leased for management to the Houston Audubon Society.

▸ Designation: Wetland of International Importance in the Western Hemisphere Shorebird Reserve Network.

▸ Habitats: Salt marsh, mudflats, beach, and uplands.

▸ Land Use: Wildlife observation and conservation.

▸ Site Description: This site was created (and is still being created) as the result of the activities of the Army Corps of Engineers. In 1898, the Corps built a five-mile-long jetty to protect the mouth of Galveston Bay, thus diverting the currents paralleling the coast and causing sediments to drop to the bottom. The refuge's 550 acres of salt marsh, beach, and uplands slowly came into existence through the years, as these sediments accumulated. Since sediments continue to build up, the sanctuary continues to grow. Adjacent to it are 500 to 750 acres of mudflats, whose exposed acreage fluctuates with the tides.

▸ Birds: Though shorebirds use other sites along the Bolivar Peninsula, the Bolivar Flats Shorebird Sanctuary supports the greatest concentrations of shorebirds for about ten months of the year. It is one of best wintering sites for the Piping Plover, with consistent counts of 100 birds. Both Snowy and Wilson's Plovers are also found there, and among the other shorebird species seasonally on the flats are the Red Knots and Marbled and Hudsonian Godwits. Reddish Egrets and Roseate Spoonbills can be found there; and Seaside Sparrows are resident on the sanctuary, while Nelson's Sharp-tailed Sparrows are found in winter.

▸ Conservation Issues: The site is well protected, but oil spills and pollution are potential problems.

▸ Visitor Information: A visit can be rewarding nearly any time of year, though few shorebirds are present in June. The sanctuary can be reached by driving down the Bolivar Peninsula from High Island, or, from the Galveston-Bolivar ferry, go east on highway 87 for 3.7 miles; turn south on Rettilon Road, and drive to the beach. Turn right on the beach and drive to the vehicular barrier. Contact: Houston Audubon Society, 440 Wilchester Boulevard, Houston, TX 77079, 713-932-1639.

Smith Point (15), Texas

▸ Highlight: Globally significant numbers of hawks pass over during the fall.

▸ Location: On the east side of Galveston Bay, Chambers County, about 15 miles from Anahuac National Wildlife Refuge, located in the Candy Cain Abshier Wildlife Management Area.

▸ Size: 20 acres.

▸ Ownership: Texas Parks and Wildlife.

▸ Habitats: Coastal prairie, woodland.

▸ Land Use: Recreation.

▸ Site Description: The wildlife management area offers several good vantage points from which to watch migrating birds.

▸ Birds: Counts in recent years have ranged from 26,000 to 43,000 birds, including huge flights of Broad-winged Hawks. Counts during migration are conducted by HawkWatch International and the Gulf Coast Bird Observatory. Wooded areas on

Smith Point are used heavily by cross-gulf migrant landbirds during the spring and fall.

▶ Conservation Issues: The wildlife management area is well protected.

▶ Visitor Information: Peak numbers are in the latter half of September. Contact the wildlife management area at 10 Parks and Wildlife Drive, Port Arthur, TX 77640, 409-736-2551.

COMMUNICATION TOWERS

There are approximately 80,000 communication towers in the United States, and about 5,000 new towers are being built each year. This rate will likely increase with developing cell tower and digital television networks. Nearly 50,000 of these towers are more than 200 feet tall, are in the vicinity of an airport, or are along major highways, and thus are required to be lit according to regulations established by the Federal Communications Commission.

Bird kills caused by towers, their guy wires, and related structures have been documented for over 50 years. Most birds killed by towers are neotropical migratory songbirds that migrate at night and seem to be confused by tower lights, especially in poor weather conditions. The extent of tower mortality is not well documented: the Fish and Wildlife Service estimates four to five million birds are killed each year at towers, but others estimate an annual loss of up to 40 million birds. At least 230 bird species are known to have been killed by collisions with towers. The Swainson's Warbler, Cerulean Warbler, Bachman's Sparrow, and Henslow's Sparrow, all listed as extremely high priority for conservation, have been documented as being killed at towers. In 1998, approximately 10,000 Lapland Longspurs were killed at three towers in a single night in western Kansas.

Little research has been conducted into the causes of this mortality, or into discovering ways to reduce bird kills at towers. Research protocols have been developed, and funding that research should be a priority for both government agencies and industry. Until more is learned, a number of steps can be taken to minimize bird mortality: reduce the number of towers by colocating multiple antennae on existing structures; construct towers below 200 feet to avoid the need for lights; where lighting is necessary, use minimum intensity; dismantle inactive towers as soon as possible; use visual markers in areas of raptor and waterfowl movements; down-shield security lighting for towers, and use best current knowledge in lighting towers (e.g., white strobes seem to attract fewer birds than red).

High Island (16), Texas

▶ Highlight: A famous migrant trap for birds crossing the Gulf of Mexico.

▶ Location: Upper Gulf Coast, in Chambers County.

▶ Size: The two best woodlands for migrants on High Island total 173 acres.

▶ Ownership: Houston Audubon Society, private.

▶ Habitat: Woods, fields, ponds, freshwater marshes.

▶ Land Use: Residential, tourism.

▶ Site Description: Houston Audubon Society owns and manages several tracts of woodland on the island. The most visited are Boy Scout Woods (51 acres) and Smith Oaks Bird Sanctuary (122 acres).

▶ Birds: High Island is one of the country's most famous "migrant traps." Depending on the weather, thousands of individuals of eastern woodland species crossing the gulf stop there during spring migration, and thousands can be seen again in the fall; the peaks are generally in late April and late September. The birds descend on the oak mottes (groves of live oak and hackberry surrounded by coastal prairie) to feed and rest. Such woodland "islands" in the grasslands along the coast are absolutely essential for migrants crossing the gulf. The two best places on High Island for the migrants are Boy Scout Woods and Smith Oaks Bird Sanctuary. These two small woodlands at times offer one of the greatest birding spectacles in all of North America. Many hundreds of birders a year visit High Island and the Upper Texas Coast each year, and bring considerable economic benefit to the area.

▶ Conservation Issues: A communications tower is proposed on High Island on private land. It could cause considerable mortality among migrating birds.

▶ Visitor Information: Best times to visit are late April and late September. Birding is best on a day after stormy weather. Contact: Houston Audubon at 713-932-1639.

Anahuac National Wildlife Refuge (17), Texas

▶ Highlight: An important wintering site for the green-listed Yellow Rail and a variety of waterfowl.

▶ Location: Upper Texas Coast in Chambers County, near High Island and 15 miles down the coast from McFaddin National Wildlife Refuge.

▶ Size: 34,000 acres.

▶ Ownership: Fish and Wildlife Service.

▶ Habitats: Bay, pond, freshwater and saltwater marshes, coastal prairie, the invasive non-native salt cedar, cropland.

▶ Land Use: Recreation, wildlife observation, agriculture.

▶ Site Description: Anahuac National Wildlife Refuge is one of four refuges in the Texas Chenier Plain Complex, extending from the Louisiana state line to Galveston Bay. The other refuges are McFaddin, Texas Point, and Moody National Wildlife Refuges (the latter is protected by easement and has no public use). Much of this refuge is brackish marsh and wet prairie.

▶ Birds: This is an important wintering area for waterfowl using the Central Flyway. Among the wintering species are the Yellow Rail, Black Rail, and, uncommonly, the Short-eared Owl and Sprague's Pipit, while the Mottled Duck and Saltmarsh Sharp-tailed Sparrow are common to abundant year-round. Many shorebirds, including Hudsonian and Marbled Godwits and Buff-breasted Sandpipers pass through during migration. Several species of herons, rails, and ducks nest on the refuge. During migration many passerines make use of the willows around a shallow pond on the refuge. The Roseate Spoonbill is common throughout the year. The Long-billed Curlew is common both during migration and in winter. The Dickcissel is a common breeding species.

▶ Conservation Issues: While non-native, invasive Chinese tallow is the most serious problem in the remnant coastal prairie, the problem on the coast is saltwater intrusion due, among other causes, to the Intracoastal Waterway. This has had a devastating effect on the vegetation: first the vegetation dies off, then the soil that had been stabilized by the plants is washed away, leaving open water. This means that where marshes were once a solid stand, patches of open water are developing. Coastal dune erosion resulting in saltwater breach also leads to the destruction of marshes. Fragmentation of the marshes by drainage and irrigation canals is also a serious threat to the integrity of the ecosystem. Water levels and vegetation are managed to benefit waterfowl.

▶ Visitor Information: Any time of year is good for a visit, but every spring the Friends of Anahuac Refuge host a number of walks to see Yellow Rails, which winter in the wet prairies of the Gulf Coast. At Anahuac the birds are found in the salty Spartina grass prairies close to the shore of East Bay. They prefer areas with an inch or so of water and disturbed by light cattle grazing, since disturbance of the otherwise dense carpet of Spartina creates pathways for the rails to move around. To avoid stressing and harassing the rails too much, tours are limited to 20 people. Participants should wear rubber knee-length boots. The salty prairies are burned every couple of years to keep woody plants from taking over, but the fires leave hardened stumps and sticks that can puncture less sturdy footwear. Contact Anahuac National Wildlife Refuge, 509 Washington Street, Anahuac, TX 77514, 409-267-3337.

Sea Rim State Park (18), Texas

▶ Highlight: An important site for migrant and wintering waterfowl and shorebirds and for trans-gulf migrant landbirds.
▶ Location: Jefferson County, near Sabine Woods and McFaddin and Texas Point National Wildlife Refuges.
▶ Size: 4,141 acres.
▶ Ownership: Texas Parks and Wildlife.
▶ Habitats: Beach, dunes, mudflats, marshes.
▶ Land Use: Recreation, wildlife conservation.
▶ Site Description: In addition to its marshes, the park has more than five miles of beach along the gulf.
▶ Birds: The Mottled Duck and Seaside Sparrow are resident; the Nelson's Sharptailed, Henslow's, and Le Conte's Sparrows are present in winter. Large numbers of wading birds, shorebirds, and waterfowl occur in winter and during migration, including the Reddish Egret and wintering Piping Plover. In addition, many trans-gulf migrants stop over, particularly in the spring.
▶ Visitor information: Best time to visit is fall through spring; for more information, contact the park at P.O. Box 1066, Sabine Pass, TX 77955, 409-971-2559.

Sabine Woods (19), Texas

▶ Highlight: Important fallout area for trans-gulf migrants.
▶ Location: Jefferson County, near Sea Rim State Park and McFaddin and Texas Point National Wildlife Refuges.
▶ Size: 32 acres.
▶ Ownership: Texas Ornithological Society.
▶ Habitats: Coastal woodland.

▶ Land Use: Bird conservation.

▶ Site Description: Sabine Woods is a coastal woodlot sanctuary consisting primarily of giant live oak and mulberry trees with numerous varieties of vines and shrubs.

▶ Birds: The woods are one of the most vitally important migratory stopovers on the entire continent for hundreds of thousands of birds each year. Some birders rate it above High Island as a site to see large concentrations of spring migrants.

▶ Conservation Issues: The site is owned by the Texas Ornithological Society and maintained by the Golden Triangle Audubon Society.

▶ Visitor Information: The area is best during spring migration, from late March through early May, when thousands of landbirds may alight during a fallout. Many migrants also stop over during fall migration. For information, contact: Golden Triangle Audubon Society, P.O. Box 1292, Nederland, TX 77627, 409-768-1340.

CHENIERS

Cheniers are among the most important coastal habitats used by migrants crossing the Gulf. They are found along the Gulf Coast in a 200-mile stretch between Vermilion Bay, Louisiana, and the Bolivar Peninsula and East Bay, Texas. They stretch inland from the coast from about 10 to 40 miles and cover a total of about 800 square miles, with about 95 percent on private lands. Meaning "places of oak," they are long, low forested ridges occurring in the coastal marshland; they range in elevation from a few inches to ten feet above sea level. They provide vital foraging, shelter, and resting habitat for migrating landbirds both during spring and fall migration. Cheniers are a disappearing habitat type; after decades of agricultural and residential development, no more than five percent of the natural chenier forests are left. They are typically covered by a coastal live oak and hackberry community with an understorey of palmetto, holly, and vine tangles, but on the more heavily disturbed cheniers, plant community composition usually shifts to non-native species. Studies indicate that migrant birds prefer the woodlots with greater vegetation height diversity, that is, those including larger trees and a more dense understorey.

Other woodlots along the Texas and Louisiana coasts, similar to cheniers but on salt domes, are also important to migrant birds. These woodlots are floristically similar to cheniers and are used by migratory birds for feeding and resting and as places of refuge during storms.

Use of cheniers by migrants is irregular and depends on weather conditions. During fair weather, probably 90 percent of the spring migrants overshoot the coastal areas, but in poor conditions with northerly winds or precipitation, as many as 80 percent may land there after the 600-mile journey across the Gulf of Mexico. During fall migration, many landbirds stop there as a staging area before setting out on the trans-gulf flight.

The human population along the coast is large and increasing; this means that many forest-dwelling landbird migrants must depend on degraded native woodlands and urbanized landscapes during migration. Restoration or rehabilitation of coastal woodlands such as the cheniers is important because of the abundance and species richness of migratory birds using them. Understorey structure and regeneration of these forests (important to early-arriving migrants, dead-leaf foragers, frugivores, and nectarivores) has been greatly reduced by overbrowsing by white-tailed deer and livestock grazing; essentially, all cheniers in Louisiana are grazed by cattle. A recent study indicates that most forest-dependent species are tolerant of at least some degree of degradation of chenier forest during migration.

Conditions that created the cheniers are no longer in effect, due to the construction of canals, levees, and spoil banks to control the flow of the Mississippi River, thus curtailing both input and deposition of sediments. In addition, many of the cheniers have been developed for residential, recreational, agricultural, and industrial use. Other factors include oil and gas exploration, highway construction, sea level rise, and, in particular, invasion by non-native plants such as Chinese tallow, which makes up most of the vegetation found on the levees and spoil banks. Studies indicate that this non-native species is avoided by migrants; the density of arthropods on Chinese tallow is much lower than on native species. The cumulative effect has been the disruption of the woodland which once covered these ridges. Grazing by livestock reduces the density and diversity of the understorey. The best remnants of chenier forest should be preserved and protected from grazing, to allow the understorey vegetation to recover. To regain their importance to migrants, degraded cheniers should be re-seeded with native vegetation, including live oak and hackberry. Destruction of such habitat along the coast could bring a substantial reduction of breeding bird populations in the Middle West and central Canada.

McFaddin and Texas Point National Wildlife Refuges (20), Texas

▶ Highlight: Among the features of these coastal refuges are the wintering Black and Yellow Rails and large numbers of trans-gulf migrants.

▶ Location: On the easternmost Gulf Coast of Texas in Jefferson County, bordering Louisiana. McFaddin is about 15 miles up the coast from Anahuac National Wildlife Refuge.

▶ Size: McFaddin is 54,000 acres and Texas Point is 8,952 acres.

▶ Ownership: Fish and Wildlife Service.

▶ Habitats: Fresh and brackish marsh, beach, coastal prairie, wooded uplands.

▶ Land Use: Wildlife conservation.

▶ Site Description: McFaddin and Texas Point National Wildlife Refuges contain a total combined acreage equivalent to 100 square miles of wildlife habitat. Most of McFaddin Refuge is freshwater and brackish marsh, while Texas Point Refuge is primarily saltwater and brackish marsh with some wooded uplands, including perhaps 20 acres of chenier, which receives much use by trans-gulf migrants.

▶ Birds: Both these refuges are wintering sites for Yellow and Black Rails. They also supply important feeding and resting habitat for migrating and wintering populations of waterfowl using the Central Flyway. At McFaddin, flocks of Snow Geese, which have numbered more than 70,000 birds, use feeding and resting areas in the marsh from October to March. Ducks on both the refuges can number up to 100,000, with more than two dozen species recorded. The Mottled Duck is the only species of waterfowl that nests and remains in the coastal marshes throughout the year.

▶ Conservation Issues: These two units of the National Wildlife Refuge System were acquired in 1979 and 1980, respectively, with revenues generated from the sale of duck stamps. While traditionally managed for waterfowl, today they are managed as part of the Texas Gulf Coast Ecosystem to protect and enhance habitat for the wide array of native species found on the Texas Coast. The North Unit of McFaddin, a 7,200-acre section isolated from the rest of the refuge by the Intracoastal Waterway, is not open to the public. As at nearby Anahuac National Wildlife Refuge, Chinese tallow is a serious problem, as is saltwater intrusion due to the Intracoastal Waterway. The coastal prairie at Texas Point is managed by using prescribed burns.

► Visitor Information: Best time to visit is fall through spring. Contact: McFaddin and Texas Point National Wildlife Refuges, P.O. Box 609, Sabine Pass, TX 77655, 409-971-2909.

Sabine National Wildlife Refuge (21), Louisiana

► Highlight: The largest coastal marsh refuge on the Gulf. This is one of the most important wintering refuges for waterfowl using the Mississippi Flyway.

► Designation: Wetland of Regional Importance in the Western Hemisphere Shorebird Reserve Network.

► Location: Near Hackberry in Cameron Parish.

► Size: 124,511 acres.

► Ownership: Fish and Wildlife Service.

► Habitats: Coastal marsh interspersed with canals, shallow ponds, levees, bayous, lakes, wooded islands.

► Land Use: Fishing, hunting, wildlife observation, environmental education.

► Site Description: With tidal influence from the Gulf of Mexico, the marshes on the refuge range in salinities from freshwater to almost marine concentration. Sabine is part of a larger system since it is surrounded by privately owned marshes of similar size.

Red-necked Grebe

► Birds: An important coastal waterfowl wintering site, Sabine has counts of more than 200,000 in the winter months. Among wintering ducks, the most common are Gadwall, with counts up to 130,000. Wading birds are abundant throughout the year, with large rookeries of breeding herons. Up to 100,000 shorebirds use the refuge during peak migration in the spring. Mottled Ducks are resident, with seasonal counts up to 3,000. King Rails are found there, and Black Rails have been observed on the refuge in winter, and the resident Seaside Sparrow is abundant.

► Conservation Issues: Because the mineral rights to the land are owned by an oil company, there is ongoing exploration for gas deposits and seven producing wells on the refuge. Increasing salinity brought about by the Intracoastal Waterway north of the refuge is a serious problem. The waterway has cut off freshwater drainage from the north and provides an inlet for salt water to intrude into former freshwater and brackish marshes. The refuge marshes are vulnerable to damage from natural events such as hurricanes and tidal surges. Management includes burning, grazing, and water-level and water-quality manipulation. Removal of Chinese tallow, nutria, and feral pigs is conducted to conserve and improve natural habitat.

▶ Visitor Information: The refuge is best seen by motorboat; it is open to boating from mid-spring to early fall. There is also a 1.5-mile trail with a boardwalk, open throughout the year. The refuge can be reached at 3000 Holly Beach Highway, Hackberry, LA 70645, 337-762-3816.

IS WATERFOWL MANAGEMENT GOOD FOR OTHER BIRDS?

The answer to this question is yes it can be, yes it often has been, yes it is getting more compatible as we learn more, and that it could be better and will get better under the vision of the North American Bird Conservation Initiative.

Waterfowl habitat needs are most closely aligned with those of shorebirds and other waterbirds. Most waterfowl conservation projects are good for grebes and a few rallids such as coots. Development of diverse vegetated cover in wetlands helps the Black Tern and the larger rails. The most imperiled rails (Black and Yellow) require shallower conditions than used by most ducks, and thus modifications in the slope and extent of wetlands managed for waterfowl. Many shorebirds use exposed mudflats or shallow, open water, again requiring modification of waterfowl management regimes. Shorebird migration does not, in general, coincide in time with waterfowl migration. Particularly in the fall, arctic breeding shorebirds are moving through the continent when ducks (with the exception perhaps of the Blue-winged Teal) are still on breeding or staging grounds. Waterfowl management areas were formerly either bone dry or under deep water at these key times prior to the recent upsurge of interest in integrated bird conservation. It takes special effort to create mudflats at this time, which entails expense and some decrease in the growth of food plants for ducks. Nevertheless, with some work all of the above changes are possible and are increasingly being embraced by managers across the continent.

Breeding conditions for waterfowl were badly damaged by wetland drainage and agricultural expansion throughout the 1900s. Many early waterfowl habitat conservation efforts focused strictly on wetlands. We have since learned, however, that ducks need upland cover near wetlands in order to avoid predation while nesting. Protection of uplands associated with wetlands has brought huge bonuses to a wide variety of landbirds. The creation of nesting cover using non-native plants is of some value, with protection or restoration of native vegetation bringing the greatest benefits. Where wetlands are created, care must be taken to avoid displacing habitat used by other high-priority birds. For example, wet swales used by such species as Sedge Wren and Le Conte's Sparrow should not be flooded.

Winter recommendations are similar. A diverse wetland-upland complex can support waterfowl and many other birds. Southeastern bottomland hardwoods and estuarine systems are noteworthy natural systems of importance to wintering ducks, other waterbirds, and a range of breeding passerines.

Lacassine National Wildlife Refuge (22), Louisiana

► Highlight: One of the most important coastal refuges for wintering waterfowl, with counts up to 500,000.

► Location: Near Lake Charles, Cameron Parish.

► Size: 34,760 acres.

► Ownership: Fish and Wildlife Service.

► Habitats: Freshwater impoundment, freshwater marshes, natural ridges, spoil banks, levees.

► Land Use: Wildlife observation, hunting, and in adjacent lands, grazing, rice cultivation, crawfish ponds.

► Site Description: Half the refuge is a huge freshwater impoundment, Lacassine Pool. The refuge also contains extensive freshwater marshes with emergent grasses, sedges and shrubs, a few natural ridges, and spoil banks and levees. An undisturbed 3,300-acre area on the south edge of the refuge is a Wilderness Area.

► Birds: Along with Sabine National Wildlife Refuge, Lacassine is among the most important of the coastal refuges for wintering waterfowl, with counts of more than 500,000 birds in some years; Green-winged Teal, Mallards, and Northern Pintails predominate. Nesting species include the Mottled and Wood Ducks, and Fulvous and Black-bellied Whistling-ducks. There is a heron rookery of up to 9,000 birds, including Tricolored and Little Blue Herons, Great and Cattle Egrets, and White and White-faced Ibis. Roseate Spoonbills are common in spring and summer in postbreeding dispersal, and large numbers of shorebirds are attracted each fall to the nearby rice fields and crawfish ponds in the area. American White Pelicans began nesting at the refuge over a decade ago.

► Conservation Issues: The Intracoastal Waterway and a gas pipeline canal both cut through the refuge. Agricultural pollution and conversion of surrounding lands to sugar cane production are problems, as are non-native invasive species such as the zebra mussel, Chinese tallow, and water hyacinth. There are programs to control the spread of the non-native plants. The refuge is working toward the acquisition of an additional 22,000 contiguous acres on the north side, originally prairie and marshland drained for farming and grazing but formerly a prime feeding area not only for waterfowl, but also for shorebirds and wading birds. At one time, both the "Attwater's" Greater Prairie-Chicken and Whooping Crane occurred there. If acquired, some parts of this land would be restored as natural wetlands while others would be farmed under a cooperative program with local farmers since waterfowl use farmed fields as feeding areas. The acquisitions are proposed for funding from the federally appropriated Migratory Bird Conservation Fund.

At present, 20,000 acres of private land near the refuge have been enrolled in an innovative Mini-refuges Program, effectively extending the habitat for wetland birds. Much of this land is used for rice and crawfish farming. Under the program, the owners agree to prohibit hunting and to prescribed flooding to benefit wildlife. In return, refuge personnel post these areas and provide law enforcement during the winter months when most waterfowl are present.

► Visitor Information: The best time of year to visit is in the winter, when thousands of waterfowl are found. The refuge is relatively remote, and there is no visitor center or tour road. Camping is not allowed, but hiking is permitted on about 30 miles of levees and service roads. Most human use is by fishers, who use Lacassine Pool between March 15 and October 15. To reach Lacassine Pool, travel west from Lake Arthur on Highway 14 for 15 miles or east from Hayes on Highway 14 for three miles to Parish Road 7-5, then south 4.5 miles. Waterfowl may be observed from the four miles of public roads in Lacassine Pool. For further information, contact: Lacassine National Wildlife Refuge, 209 Nature Road, Lake Arthur, LA 70549, 318-774-5923.

Coastal Louisiana Islands (23), Louisiana

▶ Highlight: Many colonial birds nest along the coast, including a sizable proportion of the U.S. populations of several species.
▶ Location: Islands along the coast, which fall into the Southeastern Coastal Plain, Gulf Coastal Prairie, and a small part of the Mississippi Alluvial Valley BCRs.
▶ Size: About 1.5 million acres.
▶ Ownership: Federal, state, and private.
▶ Habitats: Sandbars, barrier islands, marshes.
▶ Land Use: Wildlife conservation.
▶ Site Description: This covers the entire Louisiana coast, so that there is some overlap with sites described in other accounts, including the Chandeleur Islands and the coastal national wildlife refuges in the Gulf Coastal Prairie.
▶ Birds: The Louisiana coast has many seabirds that nest on sandbars, barrier islands, and marsh islands. Most are colonial nesters, feeding on small fishes within the shallow bays and near coastal waters. Since barrier islands and sandbanks appear and disappear relatively rapidly, these colonies change location frequently. A sizable proportion of the U.S. population of several species nests in such habitat on the Louisiana coast. These include 77 percent of Sandwich Tern, 44 percent of Black Skimmer, and 52 percent of Forster's Tern populations. Wading birds (herons, egrets, and ibis) are abundant all along the coast but nest in wooded areas inland from the barrier beaches, preferring freshwater and brackish marshes over salt marshes. There are large breeding colonies of Brown Pelicans. A survey from the early 1980s found 188 active colonies of colonial nesting birds in coastal Louisiana. Among the significant sites are the Grand Gosier Islands, with up to 21,000 breeding Sandwich and 11,000 breeding Royal Terns, and the Stake Islands, with up to 19,500 breeding Sandwich and 11,000 breeding Royal Terns. The Baptiste Collette Bird Islands, which is a dredge material wetland and bird island creation site, is managed by the Army Corps of Engineers and supports up to 1,500 breeding Brown Pelicans, up to 1,100 Caspian Terns, 250 Gull-billed Terns, and up to 800 Black Skimmers. Although artificially created, this site represents a typical barrier/offshore island waterbird breeding community.

Large numbers of waterfowl also winter in Coastal Louisiana and the percentages of U.S. populations of several wintering species is estimated to be very high. These include up to 63 percent of the green-listed Mottled Duck, 70 percent or more of the Gadwall and Blue-winged Teal, and close to 25 percent of the Lesser Scaup and Ring-necked Duck, plus significant percentages of several other species. Coastal Louisiana, along with coastal Texas and the Central Valley of California, is at the top of the list of areas of importance for wintering waterfowl.

► Conservation Issues: Many of the colonies are near navigational waterways where spills of chemicals and petroleum products are a threat. On some of the islands, the Army Corps of Engineers deposits dredge spoil, which sets back vegetative succession and keeps the area clear for breeding terns and other colonial birds. Among the non-native invasive species causing damage in coastal Louisiana are alligator weed, which grows in marsh ponds and at the edges of bayous, and water hyacinth, a mat-forming species obstructing navigation and interfering with drainage. Nutria, an introduced rodent that feeds on marsh vegetation, has denuded some intertidal flats and suppressed the regeneration of bald cypress. For colonial nesting birds, human disturbance can be a problem at the more accessible locations.

► Visitor Information: Most of the areas are accessible only by boat; those visiting them should take care not to disturb nesting birds at this vulnerable part of their life cycle. Best time to visit is fall through late spring.

Delta National Wildlife Refuge (24), Louisiana

► Highlight: Important wintering and stopover site for migrant waterfowl, shorebirds, and passerines.

► Location: At the mouth of the Mississippi River, in Plaquemines Parish. The refuge office is in Venice.

► Size: 48,800 acres.

► Ownership: Fish and Wildlife Service.

► Habitats: Shallow ponds, bayous, marsh, tidal mudflats.

► Land Use: Hunting, fishing, trapping, canoeing, wildlife observation.

► Site Description: There are both freshwater and brackish marshes on the refuge; freshwater marshes make up approximately 60 percent of the refuge. Tidal influences on the marshes mean that water levels fluctuate from a few inches to a foot or more. The fertile soils, composition of the vegetation, and shallow water create a highly productive habitat not only for birds but for all wildlife. The refuge is adjacent to a state-owned area, Pass A L'outre Wildlife Management Area.

► Birds: Large numbers of wading birds nest on the refuge, and thousands of shorebirds are found on the tidal mudflats both in winter and during migration. Most common are Dunlin, Western Sandpipers, and Long-billed Dowitchers, accounting for some 70 percent of the total. Piping Plovers winter there. In a peak year, more than 1.2 million waterfowl have been counted on the refuge, with Gadwall and Northern Pintails accounting for about half. In addition to nesting, thousands of ibis, egrets, and herons spend the winter on the refuge, with White Ibis and Snowy Egrets the most common.

► Conservation Issues: The majority of public recreational activity has been in the form of consumptive uses such as hunting, fishing, and trapping. Habitat is managed for waterfowl. To benefit shorebirds, land managers have cut channels in levees; the resulting sediment deposition creates splays and mudflats.

► Visitor Information: Access to the refuge is by boat only. Contact the refuge at Fish and Wildlife Service, Southeast Louisiana Refuges, 1010 Gause Boulevard, Slidell, LA 70458, 504-646-7555.

Hawaii

This chain of volcanic islands is the richest area for endemic landbirds in the United States. Because of significant disturbances from introduced species, including disease-bearing mosquitoes, and conversion of large areas to agriculture or other uses, Hawaii also has the nation's highest concentration of endangered species. Approximately 12 forest birds in the chain became extinct during the twentieth century, and many others are very close to that brink. The main island chain supports important seabird breeding populations, including the endangered Hawaiian Petrel and the Townsend's Shearwater. The Leeward Islands host immense numbers of nesting seabirds, including important colonies of the Black-footed and Laysan Albatrosses, Bonin Petrels, boobies, frigatebirds, noddies, and Gray-backed, Sooty, and White Terns. Pelagic waters provide essential foraging sites for numerous shearwaters, petrels, terns, and other seabirds.

Northwestern Hawaiian Islands (1)

▶ Highlight: Four endangered endemics and 14 million breeding seabirds of 19 species make this one of the country's most outstanding IBAs. The islands are also an important passage and wintering area for the green-listed Bristle-thighed Curlew.
▶ Location: The northwestern islands stretch some 800 miles through the central Pacific Ocean from around 160°W to 180°W, straddling the Tropic of Cancer.
▶ Ownership: Fish and Wildlife Service has two important refuges: Hawaiian Islands National Wildlife Refuge and Midway Island National Wildlife Refuge.
▶ Habitats: A series of small islands and reefs, some low and flat, others volcanic with steep cliffs. Vegetation is generally sparse; most islands with beaches, one with a central saline lake.
▶ Land Use: Mainly an uninhabited conservation area closed to the public. An Air Force base on Midway has closed.
▶ Site Description: The Hawaiian Islands National Wildlife Refuge is composed of a chain of small islands, reefs, and atolls, extending northwest from the main Hawaiian Islands. The refuge also includes 250,000 acres of marine habitat. Nihoa and Necker Islands, Gardner Pinnacles, and La Perouse Pinnacle are volcanic and fringed by steep basalt cliffs. Laysan and Lisianski Islands are low, flat, and sandy, surrounded by

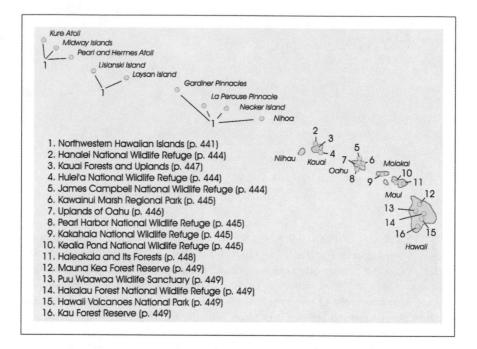

1. Northwestern Hawaiian Islands (p. 441)
2. Hanalei National Wildlife Refuge (p. 444)
3. Kauai Forests and Uplands (p. 447)
4. Huleia National Wildlife Refuge (p. 444)
5. James Campbell National Wildlife Refuge (p. 444)
6. Kawainui Marsh Regional Park (p. 445)
7. Uplands of Oahu (p. 446)
8. Pearl Harbor National Wildlife Refuge (p. 445)
9. Kakahaia National Wildlife Refuge (p. 445)
10. Kealia Pond National Wildlife Refuge (p. 445)
11. Haleakala and Its Forests (p. 448)
12. Mauna Kea Forest Reserve (p. 449)
13. Puu Waawaa Wildlife Sanctuary (p. 449)
14. Hakalau Forest National Wildlife Refuge (p. 449)
15. Hawaii Volcanoes National Park (p. 449)
16. Kau Forest Reserve (p. 449)

fringing reefs; Laysan having a central hypersaline lake that expands and contracts in size with rainfall. French Frigate Shoals, Pearl and Hermes Atoll, and Midway Atoll (a separately managed unit, the Midway Island National Wildlife Refuge) are true coral atolls comprising a few small islets surrounded by reefs.

▶ Birds: Laysan and Nihoa Islands each support two endangered endemic breeding species: the Laysan Finch (relatively common) and Laysan Duck (now, through intensive management, at approximately 600 birds, but in 1930 only one pregnant female remained, due to the decimation of vegetation by rabbits), Nihoa Finch (approximately 3,000 birds) and Millerbird (155 birds in 1996). Laysan also has a large colony of the Black-footed Albatross (14,000 to 21,000 breeding pairs). Midway Atoll supports a huge breeding colony of the Laysan Albatross that accounts for more than 50 percent of the world population (387,000 birds), and a large colony of the Black-footed Albatross (20,000 birds). The endangered Short-tailed Albatross is also a regular visitor to Midway (a few birds) and the species may eventually nest there. The Bristle-thighed Curlew occurs commonly on passage and winters throughout the reserve in small numbers. Seabird numbers and diversity are spectacular; breeding species include the Wedge-tailed Shearwater, Christmas Shearwater, Bulwer's Petrel (world's largest colony on Nihoa, at 75,000 to 100,000 pairs), Bonin Petrel (150,000 to 250,000 pairs on Lisianski), Tristram's Storm-Petrel, White-tailed Tropicbird, Red-tailed Tropicbird, Masked Booby, Brown Booby, Red-footed Booby, Great Frigatebird, Blue-gray Noddy, Brown Noddy, Black Noddy, Gray-backed Tern, Sooty Tern, and White Tern.

▶ Conservation Issues: The key conservation objectives are to prevent the introduction of non-native predators and avian diseases and to improve habitat by controlling common sandbur, an introduced grass. The Fish and Wildlife Service operates a Field Station on Tern Island in the French Frigate Shoals and is working to control sandbur on Laysan Island as well as controlling sand blowing into the lake and reducing its size. Research and monitoring are continuous, and in addition to the bird populations, activities focus on the protection of the endangered Hawaiian Monk Seal, on nesting beaches for sea turtles, and on several endemic plants. Rats have been effectively controlled on Midway, and efforts are under way to reduce infrastructure such as overhead wires, and lights that can disorient night-flying seabirds. Problems with plane collisions for albatross nesting in the vicinity of Midway Atoll's airstrip were resolved by the closure of the base in 1992. A translocation of Laysan Finches to Pearl and Hermes Atoll carried out in the 1960s was partially successful and small numbers still persist there. The Laysan Duck is a candidate for reintroduction to other islands, and the Nihoa Millerbird is a candidate for introduction to Laysan.

▶ Visitor Information: These islands are extremely remote, and most are closed to visitors. Contact Hawaiian Islands National Wildlife Refuge, P.O. Box 50167, Honolulu, HI 96850, 808-541-1201. Midway Atoll, managed as a separate National Wildlife Refuge, was recently opened to the public. Contact: Fish and Wildlife Service, Midway Atoll National Wildlife Refuge, P.O. Box 29460, Honolulu, HI 96820.

Hawaiian Wetland IBAs

Hanelai National Wildlife Refuge (2), Hulei'a National Wildlife Refuge (4), James Campbell National Wildlife Refuge (5), Kawainui Marsh Regional Park (6), Pearl Harbor National Wildlife Refuge (8), Kakahaia National Wildlife Refuge (9), Kealia Pond National Wildlife Refuge (10)

▶ Highlight: Two endangered species and two endangered subspecies are entirely confined to these areas. Important for migrating and wintering shorebirds. Seven individual sites are discussed below.

▶ Ownership: Fish and Wildlife Service, private.

▶ Habitats: Natural and man-made wetlands, taro beds, some Phragmites, open water, mudflats.

▶ Land Use: Taro farming, sugar mill settling basins, wildlife habitat.

▶ Site Description: A variety of similar wetlands found throughout the Hawaiian Islands. Man-made wetlands include taro fields and sugar mill settling basins. Most, if not all, must be managed to ensure they are not overrun by introduced plants. One (James Campbell National Wildlife Refuge) is an important natural freshwater marsh that was partially used as a settling basin for a sugarcane company, and then established as a wildlife refuge. Descriptions of individual sites follows.

▶ Birds: The endangered Hawaiian Duck was once extirpated from all islands except Kauai but has since been reintroduced on Oahu and Hawaii. Its entire world range may be confined to habitat amounting to a total of no more than 500 acres. It continues to suffer from predation by introduced species, but the population appears to be stable at approximately 2,500 individuals. The endangered Hawaiian Coot is more widespread than the duck and tolerates both fresh and saltwater habitats. Its population fluctuates from around 2,000 to 4,000 birds, and the vast majority of these are confined to Kauai,

Oahu, and Maui. The Coot also suffers from predation by introduced species, especially mongoose, except for Kauai where the mongoose is absent. The endangered
"Hawaiian" race of the Black-necked Stilt numbers approximately 1,200 individuals
and is found in small numbers throughout the wetland areas of the main islands. The
endangered "Hawaiian" race of the common Moorhen is found only on Kauai, Oahu,
and Molokai, but was formerly also present on Maui and Hawaii.
▸ Conservation Issues: Most sites require management to maintain habitat quality,
minimize disturbance from visitors, and reduce predation. Given the tiny total extent
of Hawaii's wetland reserves, additional privately owned areas could make an important contribution to bird conservation through granting of easements and adoption of
management plans to benefit these endangered wetland species.

Hanalei National Wildlife Refuge (2), Kauai County

This artificially created, 917-acre wetland in the Hanalei River Valley includes
extensive taro cultivation areas and wildlife impoundments (which are seasonally rotated). Management activities such as prescribed burning, cattle grazing,
and tilling are needed to keep exotic vegetation from overrunning waterbird
habitat. The land was acquired by the government with the understanding that
taro farmers would continue to farm and hence manage the refuge. Birds occurring here include the Hawaiian Duck, Hawaiian Coot, the "Hawaiian" race of
the Common Moorhen, and the "Hawaiian" race of the Black-necked Stilt.
▸ Visitor Information: Reached via Route 56 north from Lihue. Refuge can be
viewed from main road just north of Princeville. Hanalei National Wildlife
Refuge, 808-828-1413.

Hulei'a National Wildlife Refuge (4), Kauai

This is an abandoned taro cultivation area fed by the Hulei'a River, now managed as a wildlife reserve. The 241-acre refuge includes the Alakoko Pond,
which is a good place to see Hawaiian Ducks. Nesting islands are under construction on the refuge, and cattle grazing and vegetation clearance are used to
control invasive vegetation. Birds seen here include the Hawaiian Duck, Hawaiian Coot, and the "Hawaiian" races of the Black-necked Stilt and Common
Moorhen.
▸ Visitor Information: The refuge lies to the south of Lihue and, although
closed to visitors, can be viewed from its boundary in a number of places.
Hulei'a National Wildlife Refuge, 808-828-1413.

James Campbell National Wildlife Refuge (5), Oahu

Originally an extensive freshwater wetland close to the coast, the area was partially drained to create settling ponds for the Kahuku Sugar Mill, but when the
mill closed, a 145-acre refuge was established to inundate the settling pond to
improve waterbird habitat. The refuge was established in 1977. This and the adjacent fresh and saltwater ponds of the Amorient Aquafarm (closed to the pub-

lic) form one of the best birding sites in Hawaii for wetland endemics and migratory waterbirds. Birds occurring here include the Hawaiian Duck (reintroduced), Hawaiian Coot, the "Hawaiian" races of the Black-necked Stilt and Common Moorhen. Introduced Mallards may threaten the native duck by genetic swamping and should be controlled. The pasture area between the refuge and the beach often has Bristle-thighed Curlews during passage.

► Visitor Information: Call the refuge manager at 808-637-6330.

Kawainui Marsh Regional Park (6), Oahu

This 800-acre marsh is one of the largest freshwater wetlands in Hawaii. It was originally a fishpond used for raising mullet and degraded over the years as it became swamped with vegetation. A management plan, which has already included blasting to clear open water, is likely to improve the site for endemic waterbirds. Birds occurring here include the Hawaiian Duck (reintroduced), Hawaiian Coot, and the "Hawaiian" race of the Black-necked Stilt.

► Visitor Information: Access is currently via adjacent private properties, but a trail system is planned for the future.

Pearl Harbor National Wildlife Refuge (8), Oahu

This important wetland was artificially created in partial mitigation for the loss of natural habitat caused by runway construction at Honolulu International Airport. The 62-acre refuge consists of two separate units, located in the middle and west lochs of Pearl Harbor. The Hawaiian Duck (reintroduced), Hawaiian Coot, and the "Hawaiian" race of the Black-necked Stilt are the key wetland species.

► Visitor Information: Access is restricted and it is necessary to write ahead for permission to visit. Contact the Refuge Manager, P.O. Box 50167, Honolulu, HI 96850. Pearl Harbor National Wildlife Refuge, 808-541-1201.

Kakahaia National Wildlife Refuge (9), Molokai

This 45-acre freshwater pond close to the coast was originally used as a fishpond. The reserve was established in 1976, and in 1983 a program was initiated to improve shallow water habitat for the "Hawaiian" race of the Black-necked Stilt. The reserve is surrounded by woodland on the landward side. Birds found here are the Hawaiian Coot and "Hawaiian" Black-necked Stilt.

► Visitor Information: The refuge is closed to the public but can be viewed from Route 450 which passes right through it. Kakahaia National Wildlife Refuge 808-541-1201.

Kealia Pond National Wildlife Refuge (10), Maui

This 700-acre refuge consists of freshwater wetland and flats adjacent to the coast, surrounded by dunes and sugarcane plantations. The reserve is composed of extensive mudflats, and open water caused by sporadic flooding and siltation from the surrounding watershed. An outbreak of avian botulism in the summer and fall of 2000 killed some 100 birds. During the outbreak, the refuge was pumped as dry as possible, and by later in the year, the outbreak had subsided. Birds found here include the Hawaiian Coot and the "Hawaiian" race of Black-necked Stilt.

▶ Visitor Information: The pond lies along Route 31, between Route 30 and Route 350. Kealia Pond National Wildlife Refuge 808-875-1582.

Uplands of Oahu (7), Hawaii

▶ Highlight: The only place on Earth to find the Oahu Amakihi. The Oahu Alauahio is, however, likely extinct. The endangered "Oahu" race of Elepaio also occurs. (This may soon be split into a separate species, as may the Kauai.)

▶ Location: Higher forested elevations of the island of Oahu above approximately 1,500 feet, reaching to approximately 4,000 feet.

▶ Size: About 100,000 acres.

▶ Ownership: Private, state of Hawaii, some land owned by the Department of Defense; one 3,000-acre Nature Conservancy preserve at Honolulu.

▶ Habitats: Steep mountain slopes, ravines, peaks, and valleys, much of which is difficult to access; some native koa forest, much of the vegetation is introduced.

▶ Land Use: A major highway runs through the area. Otherwise, a combination of private landowner uses. Some hunting. The area is also an important watershed for the island.

▶ Site Description: Two isolated mountain ranges, the Waianae and the Koolau, are formed around two extinct volcanoes. The area features a steeply dissected topography with plummeting valleys and steep vegetated slopes. Parts of the mountains are still inaccessible, but the H-3 Highway, built through the southern Koolau Range, allows visitors to get unparalleled views of the area's dramatic landscape.

▶ Birds: The Oahu Amakihi occurs throughout the area in small numbers, though it is more common in the Koolau Range where it can sometimes be found as low as 150 feet, but it is rare in the north of the range. Christmas Bird Counts indicated a population decline from 1958 to 1985, but recent trends seem to be stable with birds apparently adapting to some secondary habitats. The endangered "Oahu" race of Elepaio can also be found in areas of native forest. Apapane and Iiwi also occur, although Iiwi is rare on Oahu.

▶ Conservation Issues: Previous threats included introduced species, forest clearance, and avian malaria, but some Amakihis are apparently developing resistance to this, which may explain the recent apparent increase in their numbers. The Oahu Alauahio was last reported in 1990, and is likely to be extinct. If the species does survive, it will likely be in the Halawa Valley in the Koolau Range. The construction of the H-3 Highway destroyed some habitat in the critical area for the species.

▶ Visitor Information: Contact Oahu Visitor's Bureau at: www.visit-oahu.com, or Oahu Nature Tours at www.oahunaturetours.com. Birders frequently spend only a short time in the uplands of Oahu in favor of the other large islands that now have higher species diversity among native honeyeaters. Oahu Amakihi can be seen at Round Top Drive on Mount Tantalus close to Waikiki, and the "Oahu" race of Elepaio is easily seen in Kuli'ou'ou Valley. Directions to many birding sites can be found at www.birdinghawaii.co.uk/. It is not advisable to hike alone as trail systems are often poorly marked and there are many false trails made by feral pigs. There is one National Wildlife Refuge in the forested uplands of Oahu in Koolau. For more information, contact: the Refuge Manager, Oahu National Wildlife Refuge Complex, 66-590 Kam Highway, Room 2C, Haleiwa, HI 96712, 808-637-6330, fax: 808-637-3578, e-mail: nancy_hoffman@fws.gov. Also, the Aiea trails are good birding sites in the Koolau, especially for Oahu Amakihi. Take the H-1 west from Honolulu, bear left on Route 78, then take a right onto Aiea Heights Drive to Keaiwa State Recreation Area. The Aiea Loop Trail leads to the Aiea Ridge Trail. A good map is a must, however.

Kauai Forests and Uplands (3), Hawaii

▸ Highlight: One of the most important sites for endangered birds in the United States. Five species occur nowhere else on Earth.
▸ Location: Upland areas of central-northwest Kauai.
▸ Size: 7,700 acres of protected land.
▸ Ownership: State, private; there are four protected areas.
▸ Habitats: Probably the best-preserved example of native Hawaiian forest.
▸ Land Use: Recreation, wildlife conservation, and observation.
▸ Site Description: The area is composed of rugged uplands cloaked in native rain forest and has the highest rainfall anywhere on the planet. The dominant native forest tree is koa. This IBA contains four important protected areas: the 4,345-acre Kokee State Park and Alakai Wilderness Area (State of Hawaii), the 3,150-acre Hono O Na Pali Natural Area Reserve (State of Hawaii), Waimea Canyon State Park (State of Hawaii), and the 213-acre Kaluahonu Preserve (leased to The Nature Conservancy by Grove Farm and closed to the public). Mount Waiaeale receives approximately 34 feet of rain per year, and the high plateau that lies to the northwest of the peak is known as the Alakai Swamp. This plateau is the single most important place for endemic Hawaiian birds.
▸ Birds: This is one of the most outstanding areas for native Hawaiian birds, even though several of its native species have now become extinct. The Akialoa, Kauai Oo, and Kamao are now probably extinct, and the Nukupuu may also have disappeared. The Ou has not been recorded with certainty since 1989. The endemic and endangered Puaiohi still occurs in small numbers and is benefiting from a captive-breeding and reintroduction program. The reintroduced Hawaiian Goose (Nene) occurs in the area in small numbers. Hawaiian Petrel and Townsend's Shearwaters breed (approximately 4,000 pairs in total), with the largest privately owned nesting site for the shearwater at Kaluahonu Preserve; this "Newell's" race of the species is sometimes considered a separate species. Other species of conservation concern are the Akekee, Akikiki, Kauai Amakihi, and Anianiau, all endemic to Kauai. Apapane, Iiwi, and Elepaio (the Kauai race of which may soon be considered a separate species) occur in good numbers. Waimea Canyon Overlook is a good place to look for the endemic subspecies of the Short-eared Owl.
▸ Conservation Issues: Part of the area was devastated by Hurricane Iniki in 1992. Mosquitoes carrying avian malaria were previously limited to the lowlands by temperature and altitude but have recently been found in the Alakai Wilderness. Although

Kauai is the only one of the main Hawaiian Islands free from introduced mongooses, other introduced species such as pigs are damaging the understorey. Continued intensive management of introduced species will be necessary if Kauai's endemic species are to survive. Ongoing efforts to protect the Townsend's Shearwater from collisions with urban infrastructure after being disorientated by artificial lights should be continued. Anyone finding grounded shearwaters can take them to local fire stations, which cooperate in a project to rehabilitate these birds.

▶ Visitor Information: All the protected areas except Kaluahonu Preserve are open to visitors. Terran Tours (808-335-3133) can arrange tours to the Alakai Wilderness. Some roads in the area are treacherous, especially in heavy rain. The Kokee State Park is one of the best places to see native forest birds. For information, contact: Kokee Lodge, 808-335-6061.

Haleakala and Its Forests (11), Maui

▶ Highlight: One of the most significant IBAs in the United States for endangered birds (eight species), three of which may already be extinct and another of which is down to the last few individuals. Four species found there and known to be currently extant are not known from any other site.

▶ Location: The volcano of Haleakala climbs to 10,000 feet, forming the main peak in the eastern part of the island of Maui.

▶ Size: 42,000 acres.

▶ Ownership: National Park Service, Hawaii Department of Land and Natural Resources, private.

▶ Habitats: Native forest and some grassland on the slopes, barren lava at the peak.

▶ Land Use: Watershed protection, wildlife conservation and observation.

▶ Site Description: This large and spectacular volcano is cloaked with substantial tracts of native montane rainforest, though introduced trees such as Monterey pine and species of eucalyptus are commonly found throughout. The characteristic vegetation of the windward side is wet ohia-lehua forest with a heavy growth of mosses and epiphytes, and an understorey of tree ferns. The red brushlike flowers of the native ohia trees are favored by honeycreepers. The higher slopes, and those on the leeward side of the mountain, have more koa forest. The summit and crater of the volcano are mostly barren lava with sparse alpine vegetation. There are three significant protected areas: the 28,655-acre Haleakala National Park declared in 1916, the 5,230-acre Waikamoi Preserve (managed by The Nature Conservancy and State Department of Land and Natural Resources under a permanent easement from the Haleakala Ranch Company), and the 7,500-acre Hanawi Natural Area Reserve (State of Hawaii). The adjacent Waikamoi Flume, composed of the Makawao State Forest and Koolau State Forest, is also included within this IBA.

▶ Birds: The Hawaiian Petrel breeds inside and around the crater from late February to August, where probably the world's largest and best-protected colony is located (more than 200 pairs). The Hawaiian Goose (Nene) has been reintroduced, and approximately 100 can now be found in the area of exposed lava surrounding the summit. The forests below have been the source of two major ornithological surprises in recent years. In 1973, a University of Hawaii expedition discovered a new species there: the Poo-uli. It is apparently confined to Hanawi Natural Area Reserve, which was created in 1986 to protect it. The population is likely now just three individuals which will be taken into captivity to start a breeding program as soon as possible, as their home ranges do not overlap. In 1981, a Bishop's Oo was reported from the northeastern slope of the volcano, a species that had been thought extinct after vanishing for more than 50 years (but never previously known from Maui). Despite more unconfirmed reports in the 1980s, the Oo remains an enigma. Of the other four endangered residents, the Nukupuu may now also be extinct (or at least restricted to the difficult-to-reach east Maui wilderness area and Hanawi Natural Area Reserve), but the Akohekohe persists in small numbers in and around Hanawi Natural Area Reserve, as does Maui Parrotbill. The "Maui" race of Akepa is likely extinct but has received little attention as it is generally regarded as a subspecies. The Haleakala area also supports important populations of other endemic Hawaiian species: the Maui Alauahio (endemic to Maui), Hawaii Amakihi, Apapane, and Iiwi. The "Hawaiian" race of the Short-eared Owl also occurs within this IBA.

▸ Conservation Issues: Introduced pigs and goats have severely damaged much of the understorey but are being controlled by fencing and are being removed from critical areas. Many non-native invasive trees and other plants have infested the area, as have non-native predators including rats, cats, mongooses, and a predatory snail that feeds on native snails (an important food source for Poo-uli). Avian malaria borne by introduced mosquitoes is thought to have played a large role in decimating Hawaii's bird populations. Although initially limited by temperature and altitude, there is evidence that mosquitoes are again spreading upward. Captive-breeding and reintroduction programs may assist some of the most endangered species.

▸ Visitor Information: Haleakala National Park is open to visitors (there is an entrance fee), although part of the area is a closed research reserve. To reach the area of the summit, drive east from Kahului on Route 37 and follow the signs. Visitor information is available via the park's website at: http://www.gorp.com/gorp/resource/US_National_Park/hi/hik_hal4.htm. Hanawi Reserve is difficult to reach, and the chances of seeing Poo-uli are virtually nil. Reservations are required to join hikes at Waikamoi Preserve. Call The Nature Conservancy at 808-572-7849 for more information. Intrepid birders wishing to see some of the east Maui rarities may want to volunteer for work on the National Biological Survey (write to P.O. Box 44, Hawaii National Park, HI 96718).

IBAs of the Uplands of the Island of Hawaii

Mauna Kea Forest Reserve (12), Puu Waawaa Wildlife Sanctuary (13),
Hakalau Forest National Wildlife Refuge (14), Hawaii Volcanoes
National Park (15), Kau Forest Reserve (16)

▸ Highlight: Eight endangered bird species are found here, of which six exist nowhere else on Earth (though the Ou may now be extinct and the Hawaiian Crow is close to being extinct in the wild). These uplands are the only location where the Nene, reintroduced on other islands, has remained in the wild.

▸ Designation: Hawaii Volcanoes National Park is a World Heritage site.

▸ Location: Areas on the island above 2,000 feet.

▸ Ownership: Combination of state, federal, and private, with one national park and several other protected areas, including Mauna Kea Forest Reserve, Puu Waawaa Wildlife Sanctuary, Hakalau Forest National Wildlife Refuge, and Kau Forest Reserve.

▸ Habitats: Lower slopes mostly cleared; upland streams and bogs; remaining forested areas give way to subalpine habitats above 10,000 feet.

▸ Land Use: Commercial and scientific activities, including agriculture and ranching, wood chipping, geothermal energy production, and astronomical observation.

▸ Site Description: At 4,000 square miles, the Big Island, as it is known in the state, is larger than all the other Hawaiian Islands combined and is the youngest island in the archipelago. It has five large volcanoes, three of which have been active in recent times. The island reaches an altitude of 13,796 feet at the peak of Mauna Kea, and is largely unforested above the tree line, which begins at around 10,000 feet. The native forests below 5,500 feet on the windward and leeward sides of the higher volcanoes are dominated by ohia, but above this elevation, koa becomes a major component of the forest, gaining dominance above 6,000 feet. Hakalau Forest National Wildlife Refuge, found on the east slope of Mauna Kea, was established to protect and preserve endangered forest birds and their habitat. The Kona Forest Unit is located on the western slopes of Mauna Loa and is predominantly ohia with koa found at the upper elevations. At the higher elevations on Mauna Kea, the dry forest of mamane-naio, with its open canopy and park-like grass ground cover, is critical for the endangered Palila. Ten percent of the island is covered by protected areas, including the 222,000-acre Hawaii Volcanoes National Park. There are also several Natural Area Reserves and state parks managed by the state of Hawaii.

▸ Birds: The rare Akepa, Hawaii Creeper, and Akiapolaau (all endemic to the island) are found in small numbers throughout the upland forests and occur in both the Hakalau Forest National Wildlife Refuge and Hawaii Volcanoes National Park. The endemic and endangered Palila is found only in native mamane forest on the leeward slopes of Mauna Kea above 6,500 feet (e.g., in the vicinity of the Mauna Kea Forest Reserve in the Puu Laau area). Although endangered, the species is conspicuous and the population appears stable in the low thousands. Predation by rats and feral cats limits breeding success—one study indicates that eight to 11 percent of Palila nests have been predated by cats every year since 1998—but the removal of feral goats and sheep has allowed some habitat regeneration. The distinctive pale-headed mamane-naio form of Elepaio also occurs in this area. The endangered Ou was still present (about 400 birds) in the early 1980s, but a lava flow from Mauna Loa in 1984 passed through the heart of its remaining range (Keauhou-Kilauea), and it may now be extinct. The Hawaiian Goose (Nene) occurs in the mid elevations at Hawaii Volcanoes National Park and at Hakalau Forest National Wildlife Refuge (about 350 birds), but the population's continued survival depends on the release of captive-bred stock. Hawaiian Petrels nest in the alpine zones of Mauna Loa, but little is known about the status of the species on Hawaii. The Hawaiian Hawk is endemic to the island and occurs throughout this IBA in small numbers. The endemic Omao is common in the windward forests above 3,000 feet, but has been extirpated from the leeward side of the island. Throughout the native forest, the Hawaii Amakihi, Iiwi, Apapane, and Elepaio are still relatively common. The Nukupuu may have occurred on the island (a nineteenth-century specimen and a 1971 claimed sighting), but if so, it is probably now extinct. The "Hawaiian" subspecies of the Short-eared Owl occurs within this IBA. Hawaiian Crow (Alala), found in South Kona, is on the verge of extinction in the wild, with only one remaining bird around the Kona Forest Unit of the Hakalau Forest National Wildlife Refuge. As in the case of the Hawaiian Goose, release of captive-bred birds is necessary for the species' continued survival.

▶ Conservation Issues: Land clearing by Polynesians began in the lowlands by early Polynesians long before Europeans arrived in the islands. The spread of introduced species, combined with continued habitat degradation, has wiped out much of the native flora and fauna. Most areas above 2,000 feet that still retain substantial amounts of native vegetation must be considered vital for conservation. If the island's bird species are to be preserved, several measures are necessary. Efforts to halt the spread of introduced trees and other plants should be continued, and additional conservation areas must be established. Programs to control introduced predators such as cats, rats, and mongooses must be expanded, and feral and domestic pigs, sheep, and cattle should be completely removed from forested areas. An effort to locate any remaining O'u should be mounted, and, if any birds are found, a species rescue plan should be developed and implemented immediately.

▶ Visitor Information: There are numerous opportunities to search for native birds along the Saddle Road, which has several stop-off points. The Palila can be found in the mamane-naio forest close to the Mauna Kea State Recreation Area off Saddle Road. Car rental companies require renters to avoid Saddle Road, although the pavement is generally quite good. Part of the Hakalau Forest National Wildlife Refuge is open to the public on weekends and state holidays. For information about bird watching and hiking, contact: Hakalau Forest National Wildlife Refuge, 32 Kinoole Street, Suite 101, Hilo, HI 96720, 808-933-6915. Visiting the refuge requires a 16-mile drive by four-wheel drive vehicle. Alternatively, visitors can link up with Sierra Club or Audubon volunteer groups (Sierra Club 808-538-6616, Audubon 808-528-1432). Hawaii Volcanoes National Park is open to the public (entrance fee) and there are two campgrounds. For more information, contact the park at 808-967-8226. The Big Island has 70 percent of all the public hunting areas in the state and free permits can be obtained from the Division of Forestry and Wildlife Baseyard in Hilo. Most hunting takes place on weekends, so visiting these areas is safer and quieter during the week.

STATE IBA CHECKLIST

Use this list to locate IBAs in all fifty U.S. states. Mark the IBAs you have visited in the "Date Visited" column. Photocopy your checklist and send it to American Bird Conservancy, P.O. Box 249, The Plains, VA 20198. ABC will post the checklists with the highest number of IBAs visited on its website, www.abcbirds.org. *Numbers in checklist are page references to IBA accounts in book.*

ALABAMA

IBA	Date Visited
Bon Secour National Wildlife Refuge 254	
Dauphin Island 252	
Fort Morgan Historical Park 252	
Talladega National Forest—Oakmulgee Division 256	
Wheeler National Wildlife Refuge 222	
William B. Bankhead National Forest 298	

ALASKA

IBA	Date Visited
Aleutian Islands/Alaska Maritime National Wildlife Refuge 14	
Arctic National Wildlife Refuge 24	
Copper River Delta 34	
Denali National Park and Preserve 31	
Glacier Bay National Park and Preserve 37	
Izembek National Wildlife Refuge 22	

ALASKA

IBA	Date Visited
Misty Fiords National Monument, Tongass National Forest 38	
National Petroleum Reserve 24	
North Alaska Coast 24	
Northeast Montague Island 34	
Pribilof Islands 11	
Redoubt Bay 32	
Seward Peninsula 17	
St. Lawrence Island 11	
St. Matthew and Hall Islands 11	
Yukon Delta National Wildlife Refuge 19	
Yukon Flats National Wildlife Refuge 28	

ARIZONA

IBA	Date Visited
Bill Williams River National Wildlife Refuge 387	
Buenos Aires National Wildlife Refuge 393	
Cabeza Prieta National Wildlife Refuge 391	
Chiricahua Mountains 398	
Cibola National Wildlife Refuge 388	
Havasu National Wildlife Refuge 385	
Imperial National Wildlife Refuge 388	
Las Cienegas National Conservation Area 395	
Madera Canyon 394	
Organ Pipe Cactus National Monument 391	
San Pedro Riparian National Conservation Area 396	

ARKANSAS

IBA	Date Visited
Big Lake National Wildlife Refuge 238	
Felsenthal National Wildlife Refuge 227	
Ouachita National Forest 223	
Overflow National Wildlife Refuge 227	
Ozark National Forest 208	
White River National Wildlife Refuge 239	

CALIFORNIA

IBA	Date Visited
Anza-Borrego Desert State Park 389	
Arcata Marsh 54	
Bill Williams River National Wildlife Refuge 385	
Bodega Bay 356	
Butte Sink National Wildlife Refuge 351	
Butterbredt Spring Wildlife Sanctuary 382	
Camp Pendleton (Santa Margarita River Valley) 374	
Carrizo Plain Natural Area and National Monument 368	
Cibola National Wildlife Refuge 385	
Clear Lake National Wildlife Refuge 63	
Colusa National Wildlife Refuge 351	
Cosumnes River Preserve 354	
Delevan National Wildlife Refuge 351	
Don Edwards National Wildlife Refuge 362	
East Park Reservoir 55	
Eldorado National Forest 137	
Elkhorn Slough 363	
Farallon Islands 358	
Goose Lake 65	

CALIFORNIA

IBA	Date Visited
Havasu National Wildlife Refuge 387	
Humboldt Bay National Wildlife Refuge 54	
Imperial National Wildlife Refuge 385	
Joshua Tree National Park 388	
Kings Canyon National Park 138	
Klamath National Forest 53	
Lake Abert 65	
Lake Hodges 376	
Lassen National Forest 136	
Lassen Volcanic National Park 134	
Los Banos Wildlife Management Area 365	
Los Padres National Forest 370	
Lower Klamath National Wildlife Refuge 63	
Merced National Wildlife Refuge 365	
Mojave National Preserve 384	
Mono Lake 78	
Monterey Bay National Marine Sanctuary 362	
Morro Bay 366	
Mugu Lagoon 372	
Napa-Solano Marshes 361	
North Grasslands Wildlife Management Area 365	
Plumas National Forest 137	
Point Reyes National Seashore 356	
Sacramento National Wildlife Refuge 351	
Salton Sea 390	
San Bernardino National Forest 373	
San Clemente Island 375	
San Diego National Wildlife Refuge, Otay-Sweetwater & Vernal Pools Units 377	

CALIFORNIA

IBA	Date Visited
San Diego National Wildlife Refuge, South San Diego Bay Unit 399	
San Francisco Bay 359	
San Luis National Wildlife Refuge and Great Valley Grasslands State Park 365	
Santa Cruz Island 371	
Sequoia National Forest 139	
Sequoia National Park 138	
Shasta-Trinity National Forest 57	
Sierra National Forest 138	
South Fork Kern River Valley 139	
Stanislaus National Forest 137	
Suisun Marsh 355	
Sutter National Wildlife Refuge 351	
Sweetwater Marsh National Wildlife Refuge 380	
Tahoe National Forest 137	
Tijuana River National Estuarine Research Reserve and Tijuana Slough National Wildlife Refuge 380	
Tule Lake National Wildlife Refuge 63	
Upper Klamath National Wildlife Refuge 63	
Upper Newport Bay Ecological Reserve 372	
Vandenberg Air Force Base 369	
Volta Wildlife Management Area 365	
Yosemite National Park 138	

COLORADO

IBA	Date Visited
Alamosa National Wildlife Refuge 145	
Arapaho National Forest 143	
Arapaho National Wildlife Refuge 141	

COLORADO

IBA	Date Visited
Comanche National Grassland 156	
Curecanti National Recreation Area 144	
Gunnison National Forest 144	
Monte Vista National Wildlife Refuge 145	
Pawnee National Grassland 154	
Rocky Mountain National Park 143	

CONNECTICUT

IBA	Date Visited
Stewart B. McKinney National Wildlife Refuge, Falkner Island 324	

DELAWARE

IBA	Date Visited
Bombay Hook National Wildlife Refuge 316	
Cape Henlopen State Park 316	
Delaware Bay 316	
Little Creek 316	
Prime Hook Wildlife Area and National Wildlife Refuge 316	
Ted Harvey Wildlife Area 316	
Woodland Beach 316	

FLORIDA

IBA	Date Visited
Apalachicola National Forest 258	
Archbold Biological Station and Lake Placid Scrub Preserve 341	
Arthur R. Marshall Loxahatchee National Wildlife Refuge 342	
Avon Park Air Force Range 340	
Belle Glade Area 343	

FLORIDA

IBA	Date Visited
Big Cypress National Preserve 345	
Blackwater River State Forest 255	
Canaveral National Seashore 336	
Cape Canaveral Air Force Station 336	
Cedar Key Scrub State Reserve 334	
Cedar Keys National Wildlife Refuge 334	
Corkscrew Swamp 344	
Crocodile Lake National Wildlife Refuge 348	
Cross Bar Ranch Wellfield and Al-Bar Ranch 338	
Dog Island 258	
Dry Tortugas National Park 349	
Eglin Air Force Base 255	
Everglades National Park 346	
Great White Heron National Wildlife Refuge 348	
Gulf Islands National Seashore 251	
Honeymoon Island State Recreation Area 337	
John Pennekamp Coral Reef State Park 348	
Jonathan Dickinson State Park 342	
Key Largo Hammocks State Botanical IBA 348	
Key West National Wildlife Refuge 348	
Lake Apopka Restoration Area 336	
Lower Suwannee National Wildlife Refuge 332	
Merritt Island National Wildlife Refuge 336	
National Key Deer Refuge 348	
Ocala National Forest 334	
Ochlockonee River State Park 260	
Okefenokee National Wildlife Refuge 262	
Osceola National Forest 261	

FLORIDA

IBA	Date Visited
Pinhook Swamp 261	
St. Marks National Wildlife Refuge 260	
St. Sebastian River State Buffer Preserve 339	
Three Lakes Wildlife Management Area 339	
Torchwood Hammock Preserve 348	

GEORGIA

IBA	Date Visited
Altamaha River Delta 263	
Chattahoochee National Forest 296	
Cumberland Island National Seashore 262	
Fort Benning 257	
Fort Stewart 264	
Hitchiti Experimental Forest 300	
Kennesaw Mountain National Battlefield Park 300	
Okefenokee National Wildlife Refuge 261	
Piedmont National Wildlife Refuge 300	

HAWAII

IBA	Date Visited
Hakalau Forest National Wildlife Refuge 449	
Haleakala and Its Forests 448	
Hanalei National Wildlife Refuge 444	
Hawaii Volcanoes National Park 449	
Hulei'a National Wildlife Refuge 444	
James Campbell National Wildlife Refuge 444	
Kakahaia National Wildlife Refuge 445	
Kau Forest Reserve 449	

HAWAII

IBA	Date Visited
Kauai Forests and Uplands 447	
Kawainui Marsh Regional Park 445	
Kealia Pond National Wildlife Refuge 443	
Mauna Kea Forest Reserve 449	
Northwestern Islands of Hawaii 441	
Pearl Harbor National Wildlife Refuge 443	
Puu Waawaa Wildlife Sanctuary 449	
Uplands of Oahu 446	

IDAHO

IBA	Date Visited
American Falls Reservoir/Springfield Bottoms 69	
Bear Lake National Wildlife Refuge 89	
C.J. Strike Wildlife Management Area and Reservoir 69	
Deer Flat National Wildlife Refuge 67	
Grays Lake National Wildlife Refuge 87	
Market Lake Wildlife Management Area 70	
Sand Creek Wildlife Management Area 71	
Snake River Birds of Prey National Conservation Area 68	
Yellowstone National Park 84	

ILLINOIS

IBA	Date Visited
Banner Marsh and Rice Lake State Fish and Wildlife Areas 193	
Cache River State Natural Area 211	
Carlyle Lake Wildlife Management Area 195	
Chautauqua National Wildlife Refuge 194	
Clarence Cannon National Wildlife Refuge 192	

ILLINOIS

IBA	Date Visited
Crab Orchard National Wildlife Refuge 213	
Cypress Creek National Wildlife Refuge 211	
Goose Lake Prairie State Natural Area 196	
Grassy Slough Preserve 211	
Great River National Wildlife Refuge 192	
Horseshoe Lake Conservation Area 213	
Lake Shelbyville Fish and Wildlife Management Area 196	
LaSalle Lake State Fish and Wildlife Area 196	
Limekiln Springs Preserve 211	
Mark Twain National Wildlife Refuge 192	
Marshall State Fish and Wildlife Area 195	
Middle Mississippi River National Wildlife Refuge 192	
Mississippi River State Fish and Wildlife Area 193	
Port Louisa National Wildlife Refuge 192	
Rend Lake State Fish and Wildlife Area 214	
Shawnee National Forest 209	
Trail of Tears State Forest 209	
Two Rivers National Wildlife Refuge 192	
Union County Conservation Area 210	
Upper Mississippi National Wildlife Refuge and Army Corps of Engineers Lands 201	

INDIANA

IBA	Date Visited
Big Oaks National Wildlife Refuge 220	
Brown County State Park 219	
Hoosier National Forest 219	
Jasper-Pulaski Fish and Wildlife Area 198	

INDIANA

IBA	Date Visited
Morgan-Monroe State Forest 219	
Reclaimed Coal Mine Grasslands 217	
Yellowwood State Forest 219	

IOWA

IBA	Date Visited
DeSoto National Wildlife Refuge 182	
Mark Twain National Wildlife Refuge 192	
Upper Mississippi National Wildlife Refuge and Army Corps of Engineers Lands 201	

KANSAS

IBA	Date Visited
Cheyenne Bottoms Wildlife Area and Preserve 166	
Cimarron National Grassland 168	
Flint Hills National Wildlife Refuge 188	
Flint Hills Tallgrass Prairie Preserve 188	
Fort Riley Military Reservation 188	
John Redmond Reservoir 189	
Kirwin National Wildlife Refuge 165	
Konza Prairie Research Natural Area 188	
Quivira National Wildlife Refuge 167	
Salt Plains National Wildlife Refuge 168	

KENTUCKY

IBA	Date Visited
Daniel Boone National Forest 297	
Fort Campbell 216	

LOUISIANA

IBA	Date Visited
Atchafalaya River Basin 242	
Breton National Wildlife Refuge 251	
Buckhorn Wildlife Management Area 241	
Catahoula National Wildlife Refuge and Catahoula Lake 242	
Coastal Louisiana Islands 439	
Delta National Wildlife Refuge 440	
Fort Polk 229	
Kisatchie National Forest 229	
Lacassine National Wildlife Refuge 438	
Lake Pontchartrain Causeway 244	
Sabine National Wildlife Refuge 436	
Tensas River National Wildlife Refuge 241	

MAINE

IBA	Date Visited
Acadia National Park 229	
Baxter State Park 132	
Merrymeeting Bay 128	
Northeastern Coastal Maine 130	
Upper St. John River Project 132	
Waters Around Machias Seal Island 131	
White Mountain National Forest 127	

MARYLAND

IBA	Date Visited
Assateague Island National Seashore 312	
Blackwater National Wildlife Refuge 309	
Chesapeake Bay 307	
Eastern Neck National Wildlife Refuge 311	

MARYLAND

IBA	Date Visited
Fishing Bay Wildlife Management Area (Elliott Island) 309	
Jug Bay 310	
Smith Island Archipelago (Smith Island National Wildlife Refuge) 307	

MASSACHUSETTS

IBA	Date Visited
Bird Island 327	
Cape Cod National Seashore 330	
Crane Beach 331	
Martha's Vineyard 328	
Monomoy National Wildlife Refuge 329	
Nantucket 328	
Nantucket Sound 328	
Parker River National Wildlife Refuge 331	
South Chatham Beach 329	

MICHIGAN

IBA	Date Visited
Allegan State Game Area and Kalamazoo River 204	
Hiawatha National Forest 114	
Isle Royale National Park 111	
Kirtland's Warbler Management Area 117	
Lake Erie Where the Detroit River Enters It 119	
Lake St. Clair 119	
Lake Superior State Forest 111	
Saginaw Bay 119	
Seney National Wildlife Refuge 115	
Whitefish Point 111	

MINNESOTA

IBA	Date Visited
Agassiz National Wildlife Refuge 102	
Chippewa National Forest 107	
Hawk Ridge Nature Reserve 110	
McGregor Marsh Scientific and Natural Area 109	
Rice Lake National Wildlife Refuge 109	
Superior National Forest 112	
Upper Mississippi National Wildlife Refuge and Army Corps of Engineers Lands 201	

MISSISSIPPI

IBA	Date Visited
Bienville National Forest 248	
Delta National Forest 240	
Gulf Coast Least Tern Colony 249	
Gulf Islands National Seashore 251	
Hillside National Wildlife Refuge 240	
Lower Pascagoula River 250	
Mathews Brake National Wildlife Refuge 240	
Mississippi Sandhill Crane National Wildlife Refuge 248	
Morgan Brake National Wildlife Refuge 240	
Noxubee National Wildlife Refuge 245	
Panther Swamp National Wildlife Refuge 240	
Yazoo National Wildlife Refuge 240	

MISSOURI

IBA	Date Visited
Clarence Cannon National Wildlife Refuge 192	
Great River National Wildlife Refuge 192	

MISSOURI

IBA	Date Visited
Mark Twain National Forest 191	
Mark Twain National Wildlife Refuge 192	
Middle Mississippi River National Wildlife Refuge 192	
Mingo National Wildlife Refuge 235	
Mississippi River State Fish and Wildlife Area 193	
Port Louisa National Wildlife Refuge 192	
Squaw Creek National Wildlife Refuge 186	
Swan Lake National Wildlife Refuge 190	
Trail of Tears State Forest 209	
Two Rivers National Wildlife Refuge 192	

MONTANA

IBA	Date Visited
Benton Lake National Wildlife Refuge 92	
Bowdoin National Wildlife Refuge 93	
Bureau of Land Management's 40 Complex 149	
Charles M. Russell National Wildlife Refuge 149	
Custer National Forest 84	
Freezeout Lake Wildlife Management Area 91	
Glacier National Park 81	
Medicine Lake National Wildlife Refuge Complex 94	
Red Rock Lakes National Wildlife Refuge 83	
Yellowstone National Park 84	

NEBRASKA

IBA	Date Visited
Central Platte River Valley and Rainwater Basin Area 164	
Crescent Lake National Wildlife Refuge 160	

NEBRASKA

IBA	Date Visited
DeSoto National Wildlife Refuge 182	
Fort Niobrara National Wildlife Refuge 162	
Niobrara Valley Preserve 163	
Valentine National Wildlife Refuge 162	

NEVADA

IBA	Date Visited
Carson Lake and Pasture Area 76	
Franklin Lake 75	
Great Basin National Park 78	
Ruby Lake National Wildlife Refuge 75	
Stillwater National Wildlife Refuge and Wildlife Management Area 76	

NEW HAMPSHIRE

IBA	Date Visited
White Mountain National Forest 127	

NEW JERSEY

IBA	Date Visited
Cape May Migratory Bird Refuge 319	
Cape May National Wildlife Refuge 319	
Delaware Bay 316	
Edwin B. Forsythe National Wildlife Refuge 320	
Fortescue Wildlife Management Area 316	
Sandy Hook Bay Complex 320	

NEW MEXICO

IBA	Date Visited
Bitter Lake National Wildlife Refuge 404	
Bosque Del Apache National Wildlife Refuge 401	
Gray Ranch 399	
Lincoln National Forest 403	
Mescalero Sands 159	

NEW YORK

IBA	Date Visited
Adirondack Park 124	
Derby Hill 123	
Great Gull Island 324	
Hamlin Beach State Park 122	
Long Island Piping Plover Nesting Beaches 322	
Niagara River Corridor 121	
Northern Montezuma Wetlands 122	

NORTH CAROLINA

IBA	Date Visited
Alligator River National Wildlife Refuge 279	
Cape Hatteras National Seashore 277	
Cape Lookout National Seashore 276	
Coastal Waterbird Colonies 272	
Croatan National Forest 274	
Fort Bragg 272	
Great Dismal Swamp National Wildlife Refuge 282	
Great Smoky Mountains National Park 295	
Gulf Stream/Continental Shelf Edge Marine Zone 275	
Mattamuskeet National Wildlife Refuge 280	

NORTH CAROLINA

IBA	Date Visited
Nags Head Woods Preserve 278	
Nantahala National Forest 296	
Pea Island National Wildlife Refuge 277	
Pisgah National Forest 296	
Pocosin Lakes and Pungo National Wildlife Refuge 281	
Roanoke River Floodplain and Wetland 281	
Roanoke River National Wildlife Refuge 281	
Swanquarter National Wildlife Refuge 280	

NORTH DAKOTA

IBA	Date Visited
Appam Lake Waterfowl Protection Area 95	
Chain of Lakes, McLean County 97	
Chase Lake National Wildlife Refuge 103	
Des Lacs National Wildlife Refuge 97	
Devils Lake Wetland Management District 101	
Horsehead Lake 104	
J. Clark Salyer National Wildlife Refuge 100	
Kellys Slough National Wildlife Refuge 101	
Lake Alice National Wildlife Refuge 101	
Little Missouri National Grassland 151	
Long Lake National Wildlife Refuge 103	
Lostwood National Wildlife Refuge 96	
Sheyenne National Grassland 105	
Sullys Hill National Game Preserve 101	
Upper Souris National Wildlife Refuge 98	

OHIO

IBA	Date Visited
Cedar Point National Wildlife Refuge 198	
Lakeshore Metropark 119	
Magee Marsh Wildlife Area 198	
Maumee Bay 119	
Metzger Marsh Wildlife Area 198	
Ottawa National Wildlife Refuge 198	
Sandusky Bay 199	
Wayne National Forest 291	

OKLAHOMA

IBA	Date Visited
Fort Sill Military Reservation 170	
McCurtain County Wilderness Area 226	
Ouachita National Forest 223	
Tallgrass Prairie National Preserve 190	
Washita National Wildlife Refuge 169	
Wichita Mountains National Wildlife Refuge 170	

OREGON

IBA	Date Visited
Bear Valley National Wildlife Refuge 63	
Coos Bay 49	
East Sand and Rice Islands 45	
Goose Lake 65	
Klamath Marsh National Wildlife Refuge 63	
Malheur National Wildlife Refuge, Harney Basin 65	
Medford District Bureau of Land Management 50	
Mount Hood National Forest 51	

OREGON

IBA	Date Visited
Oregon Dunes National Recreation Area 48	
Roseburg District Bureau of Land Management 50	
Siuslaw National Forest 48	
Summer Lake State Wildlife Area 63	
Tillamook Bay 47	
Umpqua National Forest 52	
Wallowa-Whitman National Forest 83	
Willamette National Forest 51	

PENNSYLVANIA

IBA	Date Visited
Allegheny National Forest 288	
Hawk Mountain and the Kittatinny Ridge 290	
Mount Zion (Piney Tract) 289	

RHODE ISLAND

IBA	Date Visited
Block Island National Wildlife Refuge 326	

SOUTH CAROLINA

IBA	Date Visited
ACE Basin 265	
Cape Romain National Wildlife Refuge 266	
Carolina Sandhills National Wildlife Refuge 270	
Congaree Swamp National Monument 270	
Francis Beidler Forest (Four Hole Swamp) 269	
Francis Marion National Forest 268	
Santee Coastal Reserve and Washo Reserve 267	

SOUTH CAROLINA

IBA	Date Visited
Sumter National Forest 296	
Tom Yawkey Wildlife Center 267	

SOUTH DAKOTA

IBA	Date Visited
Fort Pierre National Grassland 153	
Sand Lake National Wildlife Refuge 106	

TENNESSEE

IBA	Date Visited
Cherokee National Forest 295	
Fort Campbell 216	
Frozen Head State Park and Natural Area, and Royal Blue Wildlife Management Area 297	
Great Smoky Mountains National Park 295	
Reelfoot Lake 237	
Tennessee National Wildlife Refuge 214	

TEXAS

IBA	Date Visited
Anahuac National Wildlife Refuge 432	
Angelina National Forest 230	
Aransas National Wildlife Refuge 423	
Attwater Prairie Chicken National Wildlife Refuge 179	
Balcones Canyonlands National Wildlife Refuge 174	
Barton Creek Habitat Preserve 176	
Bentsen-Rio Grande Valley State Park 411	
Big Bend National Park 407	

TEXAS

IBA	Date Visited
Big Bend Ranch State Park 407	
Big Boggy National Wildlife Refuge 427	
Big Thicket National Preserve 231	
Bolivar Flats Shorebird Sanctuary 429	
Brazoria National Wildlife Refuge 427	
Caddo Lake Watershed 229	
Colorado Bend State Park 173	
Columbia Bottomlands 427	
Davis Mountains 405	
Davy Crockett National Forest 231	
Devils River State Natural Area 409	
Dolan Falls Preserve 409	
Falcon State Park, Zapata County Park, and San Ygnacio 413	
Fort Hood Military Installation 171	
Guadalupe Mountains National Park 404	
Guadalupe River State Park 177	
Hazel Bazemore County Park 422	
High Island 431	
Honey Creek State Natural Area 177	
Katy Prairie 429	
Kenedy Ranch 419	
Kerr Wildlife Management Area 176	
Kickapoo Cavern State Park 408	
King Ranch 419	
Laguna Atascosa National Wildlife Refuge 417	
Lennox Foundation Southmost Preserve 415	
Lost Maples State Natural Area 178	
Mad Island Marsh Complex 426	

TEXAS

IBA	Date Visited
Matagorda Island 424	
McFaddin and Texas Point National Wildlife Refuges 435	
Padre Island National Seashore and South Padre Island Preserve 420	
Pedernales Falls State Park 175	
Roy E. Larsen Sandyland Sanctuary 231	
Sabal Palm Grove Audubon Center 415	
Sabine Woods 433	
Sam Houston National Forest 232	
San Bernard National Wildlife Refuge 427	
Santa Ana and Lower Rio Grande Valley National Wildlife Refuges 414	
Sea Rim State Park 433	
Smith Point 430	
W.G. Jones State Forest 233	

UTAH

IBA	Date Visited
Antelope Island State Park 73	
Bear River Migratory Bird Refuge 72	
Farmington Bay Waterfowl Management Area 73	
Gillmor Audubon Sanctuary 73	
Great Salt Lake Shorelands Preserve (formerly Layton Marsh) 73	
Kennecott Inland Sea Shorebird Reserve 73	
Ogden Bay Waterfowl Management Area 73	

VERMONT

IBA	Date Visited
Green Mountain National Forest 126	
Mount Mansfield 125	

VIRGINIA

IBA	Date Visited
Assateague Island National Seashore 312	
Chesapeake Bay 307	
Chincoteague Island National Wildlife Refuge 312	
Eastern Shore of Virginia National Wildlife Refuge 303	
Fisherman Island National Wildlife Refuge 303	
George Washington National Forest 292	
Great Dismal Swamp National Wildlife Refuge 282	
Jefferson National Forest 294	
Kiptopeke State Park 303	
Piney Grove Preserve 283	
Shenandoah National Park and the Blue Ridge Parkway 294	
Virginia Coast Reserve 312	

WASHINGTON

IBA	Date Visited
Columbia National Wildlife Refuge 62	
Copalis National Wildlife Refuge 42	
Dungeness National Wildlife Refuge 39	
East Sand and Rice Islands 45	
Flattery Rocks National Wildlife Refuge 42	
Grays Harbor 42	
Olympic National Park and National Forest 40	
Padilla Bay National Estuarine Research Reserve 39	
Quillayute Needles National Wildlife Refuge 42	
Wenatchee National Forest 60	
Willapa Bay 44	

WEST VIRGINIA

IBA	Date Visited
George Washington National Forest 294	
Jefferson National Forest 292	
Monongahela National Forest 294	

WISCONSIN

IBA	Date Visited
Apostle Islands 110	
Crex Meadows Wildlife Area 113	
Horicon Marsh 203	
Nicolet National Forest 115	
Trempeleau National Wildlife Refuge 201	
Upper Mississippi National Wildlife Refuge and Army Corps of Engineers Lands 201	

WYOMING

IBA	Date Visited
Bridger-Teton National Forest 88	
Grand Teton National Park 87	
Rock Springs District Bureau of Land Management 89	
Seedskadee National Wildlife Refuge 89	
Shoshone National Forest 84	
Thunder Basin National Grassland 152	
Yellowstone National Park 85	

FURTHER IBA RESOURCES

American Bird Conservancy's IBA program aims to draw attention to the need to conserve special places for birds. In addition to publishing this book, ABC has provided public display signs to all the IBAs, and has produced a map of the sites in collaboration with National Geographic (available via American Birding Association Sales Birding Store at: *www.americanbirding.org,* while stocks last).

IMPORTANT BIRD AREA

THIS SITE HAS BEEN IDENTIFIED AS BEING SIGNIFICANT FOR WORLD BIRD CONSERVATION AND OFFICIALLY DESIGNATED A GLOBALLY IMPORTANT BIRD AREA

AMERICAN BIRD CONSERVANCY

FOR MORE INFORMATION ABOUT THE IBA PROGRAM CONTACT AMERICAN BIRD CONSERVANCY: (888) 247-3624, www.abcbirds.org

ABC's web site also includes links to the homepages of nearly every IBA, as well as photographic field guides to all the birds found in the region of each IBA in the continental United States. To access these guides, produced in collaboration with eNature, go to: *www.abcbirds.org/iba.*

BIBLIOGRAPHY

Many websites were consulted in the course of preparing this book. American Bird Conservancy's website links to virtually all the websites of Important Bird Areas and associated sites in this book. Visit abcbirds.org/iba for details of IBAs by state or www.abcbirds.org/nabci for IBAs by Bird Conservation Region.

Achenbach, J. Nature's hostile takeover? *Washington Post*. July 30, 2000.

Ainley, D. 1995. Ashy Storm-Petrel (*Oceanodroma homochroa*). In *The Birds of North America*, No. 185 (A. Poole and F. Gill, eds.). The Academy of Natural Sciences, Philadelphia, and The American Ornithologists' Union, Washington, D.C.

American Bird Conservancy. 1998. Road Threatens Alaska's Izembek NWR. *Bird Calls* 2(1):5. ABC, Washington.

American Bird Conservancy. 2000. Mute Swan population explosion threatens native species. *Bird Calls* 4 (3):6.

American Bird Conservancy. 2000. Success on horseshoe crabs, victory for shorebirds. *Bird Calls* 4(3):7.

American Bird Conservancy. 2000. Cat problems at the Cape. *Bird Calls* 4(3):9.

American Bird Conservancy. San Clemente Loggerhead Shrike increases. *Bird Calls* 6(1):15.

American Birding Association. 1994. *Birdfinding in Forty National Forests and Grasslands*. American Birding Association, Colorado Springs.

Allen, D., R. Gill, and K. Wohl. 1999. Western Hemisphere Shorebird Reserve Network Site Identification Questionnaire. Unpublished.

Andres, B. 1999. *Landbird Conservation Plan for Alaska Biogeographic Regions*, Version 1.0, Boreal Partners in Flight Working Group, Anchorage.

Armistead, H.T. 1999. Maryland's Everglades: Southern Dorchester County. *Birding* 31(2): 140–154.

Aslett, D., and A. Owsiak. 1999. Sand Creek Wildlife Management Area Management Plan.

Atwood, J.L. 1992. A closer look: California Gnatcatcher. *Birding XXIV* (4): 228–234.

Bailey, E.P. 1993. *Introduction of Foxes to Alaskan Islands—History, Effects on Avifauna, and Eradication*. U.S. Fish & Wildlife Service, Publication 193, Washington, D.C.

Bajema, R.A., T.L. DeVault, P.E. Scott, and S.L. Lima. 2001. Large reclaimed coal mine grasslands and their significance for Henslow's sparrows in the American Midwest. *Auk* 118: 422–431.

Bancroft, G.T. 1992. Rare, local, little-known, and declining breeders: a closer look: White-crowned Pigeon. *Birding XXIV* (1): 21–24.

Barrow, W.C., Jr., C.C. Chen, R.B. Hamilton, K. Ouchley, and T.J. Spengler. 2000. Disruption and restoration of en route habitat, a case study: the Chenier Plain. Pp. 71–87, in *Stopover Ecology of Nearctic-Neotropical Landbird Migrants: Habitat Relations and Conservation Implications* (F.R. Moore, ed.), *Studies in Avian Biology* No. 20: 133 pp.

Beaton, G. 1995. Kennesaw Mountain—Cerulean Warblers and Much More. *Winging It* 7(4).

Beaton, G. 2000. *Birding Georgia.* Falcon Publishing, Helena, MT.

Beedy, E.C., and W.J. Hamilton III. 1999. Tricolored Blackbird. In *The Birds of North America,* No. 423 (A. Poole and F. Gill, eds.). The Academy of Natural Sciences, Philadelphia, and The American Ornithologists' Union, Washington, D.C.

Beidleman, R.G. in cooperation with the National Park Service. No date. *Checklist of the Birds of Rocky Mountain National Park and Arapho National Recreation Area.* National Park Service. Unpaginated.

Bidwell, D. 1999. Balcones Canyonlands Conservation Plan. In *Improving Integrated Natural Resource Planning: Habitat Conservation Plans,* National Center for Environmental Decisionmaking Research. Available at http://www.ncedr.org/casestudies/hcp/balcones.htm.

Billy, C. ed. 1998. *Fodor's 99 Alaska.* Fodor's Travel Publications, Inc., New York.

Bird Observer. 1994. *A Birder's Guide to Eastern Massachusetts.* American Birding Association, Colorado Springs.

Bogan, M.A., and C.D. Allen. 1998. *Status and Trends of the Nation's Biological Resources.* Vol. 2. U.S. Department of the Interior, U.S. Geological Survey, Reston, Virginia.

Bookhout, T.A. 1995. Yellow Rail (*Coturnicops noveboracensis*). In *The Birds of North America,* No. 139 (A. Poole and F. Gill, eds.). The Academy of Natural Sciences, Philadelphia, and The American Ornithologists' Union, Washington, D.C.

Bryan, K. 1998. *Birds of Devils River State Natural Area and Vicinity, a Seasonal Checklist.* Natural Resource Program, Texas Parks and Wildlife.

Bryan, K.B. 1999. *Birds of Big Bend Ranch State Park and Vicinity: A Field Checklist.* Natural Resource Program, Texas Parks and Wildlife.

Bryan, K., P. Espy, and J. Miller. 1997. *Birds of Davis Mountains State Park and Vicinity: A Seasonal Checklist.* Natural Resource Program, Texas Parks and Wildlife.

Bryan, K.B., and J. Karges. 2001. Recent bird records in the Davis Mountains. *Texas Birds* 3(1):40–53.

Bryan, K.B., P. Espy, and J. Miller. 2001. *Birds of Davis Mountains State Park and Vicinity: A Seasonal Checklist.* Natural Resource Program, Texas Parks and Wildlife.

Buchanan, J.B., and J.R. Evenson. 1997. Abundance of shorebirds at Willapa Bay, Washington. *Western Birds* 28:158–168.

Buler, J.J., and M.S. Woodrey. 1999. The status and distribution of Swallow-tailed Kites (*Elanoides forficatus forficatus*) on the Pascagoula River, Mississippi. Unpubl. report.

Byrd, G.V., and J.C. Williams. 1993. Red-legged Kittiwake (*Rissa brevirostris*). In *The Birds of North America,* No. 60 (A. Poole and F. Gill, eds.). The Academy of Natural Sciences, Philadelphia, and The American Ornithologists' Union, Washington, D.C.

Cable, T.T., S. Seltman, and K.J. Cook. 1996. Birds of Cimarron National Grassland. General Technical Report RM-GTR-281, U.S. Department of Agriculture, Fort Collins, CO.

Canadian Nature Federation. The Niagara River Corridor—An Important Bird Area. Brochure.

Carter, R. 1993. *Finding Birds in South Carolina.* Univ. South Carolina Press, Columbia.

Clemons, C., and M. Silberstein. 2000. Elkhorn Slough: Partnerships for preservation. *Winging It* 12(7):1, 4–5.

Collar, N.J., M.J. Crosby, and A.J. Stattersfield. 1994. *Birds to Watch II.* BirdLife International, Cambridge.

Colwell, M.A. 1994. Shorebirds of Humboldt Bay, California: Abundance estimates and conservation implications. *Western Birds* 25:137–145.

Commission for Environmental Cooperation. 1999. *North American Important Bird Areas: A Directory of 150 Key Conservation Sites.* Commission for Environmental Cooperation, Montreal.

Connelly, J.W., and K.P. Reese. Greater Sage-Grouse in Idaho. Research in southern Idaho: A summary of projects and major findings, 1985–1999. Unpubl. report.

Crossley, G.J. (compiler). 1999. *A Guide to Critical Bird Habitat in Pennsylvania.* Pennsylvania Important Bird Areas Program. Pennsylvania Audubon Society, Camp Hill.

Cully, J.F., Jr., and H.L. Michaels. 2000. Henslow's Sparrow habitat associations on Kansas tallgrass prairie. *Wilson Bull.,* 112 (1): 115–123.

DeCelesta, D.J., and L. McGuinness. 1992. Impact of deer on species diversity of Allegheny hardwood stands. *Proc. of the Northeastern Weed Sci. Soc. Abstracts* 46:135.

Delaware Department of Natural Resources and Environmental Control. 1998. Delaware Bay shorebirds. Brochure.

Delorey, A. 1996. *A Birder's Guide to New Hampshire.* American Birding Association, Colorado Springs.

DeVault, T.L., P.E. Scott, R.A. Bajema, and S.L. Lima. 2002. Breeding bird communities of reclaimed coal mine grasslands in the American Midwest. *Journal of Field Ornithology,* in press.

DeVore, S. 2000. *Birding Illinois.* Falcon Publishing Co., Helena.

Dinsmore, J.G., and S.J. Dinsmore. 2001. Arctic Terns nesting in Montana. *North American Birds* 55(2):127–131.

Duncan, R.A. 1994. *Bird Migration, Weather and Fallout, Including the Migrant Traps of Alabama and Northwest Florida.* Published by the author, Gulf Breeze, FL.

Dunne, P. 1996. Cape May, New Jersey: The place that birding built. *Winging It* 8(6).

Durbin, E. 1997. Crane Creek, Ohio. *Winging It* 9(5):1, 4–7.

Eckert, K.R. 1994. *A Birder's Guide to Minnesota.* Williams Publications, Plymouth, MN.

Ellis, S., C. Kuehler, R. Lacy, K. Hughes, and U.S. Seal. 1992. Hawaiian Forest Birds Conservation and Management Plan. A publication of the Captive Breeding Specialist Group. IUCN—The World Conservation Union Species Survival Commission.

Endangered Species Habitat Conservation Program, U.S. Fish & Wildlife Service. Endangered Species Bulletin, Nov/Dec 1999, Vol. XXIV, No. 6.

Eubanks, T., P. Kerlinger, and R.H. Payne. 1993. High Island, Texas: Case study in avitourism. *Birding* 25(6):415–420.

Evanich, J.E. 1990. *Birder's Guide to Oregon.* Portland Audubon Society.

Evenson, J.R., and J.B. Buchanan. 1997. Seasonal abundance of shorebirds at Puget Sound estuaries. *Washington Birds* 6:34–62.

Evers, D. (compiler). (No date.) A guide to the birds of the Hiawatha National Forest, including directions to popular birding spots: west unit: Rapid River/Manistique and Munising Ranger Districts. A publication of Wildlife Unlimited of Delta County.

Fitzgerald, J., B. Busby, M. Howery, R. Klataska, D. Reinking, and D. Pashley. 2000. Partners in Flight Bird Conservation Plan for the Osage Plains. Unpubl.

Friebele, E. 2001. Wild rice vanishes as resident geese multiply. *Jug Bay Wetlands Sanctuary News* 16(1):1, 4–5.

Fussell, John O., III. 1994. *A Birder's Guide to Coastal North Carolina.* University of North Carolina Press, Chapel Hill.

Gossett, D.N., and S.L. Gossett. 1999. 1999 Snake River and Malad Resource Area Ferruginous Hawk and raptor monitoring. Final report.

Graves, G. 2001. Factors governing the distribution of Swainson's Warbler along a hydrological gradient in Great Dismal Swamp. *Auk* 118(3):650–664.

Gray Ranch Guide. 1996. Unpubl.

Green, J.C. 2002. Birds of the Superior National Forest: An Annotated Checklist. Boundary Waters Wilderness Foundation. 12 pp.

Groschupf, K.D., B.T. Brown, and R.R. Johnson. 1988. An annotated checklist of the birds of Organ Pipe Cactus National Monument, Arizona. Southwest Parks and Monuments Association, Tucson.

Haleakala National Park Website: http://www.gorp.com/gorp/resource/US_National_Park/hi/hik_hal4.htm.

Hamilton, W.J., III. 1998. Tricolored Blackbird itinerant breeding. *Condor* 100:218–226.

Hands, H. 1998. Kansas travelers. *Nat. Hist.* (5).

Hanowski, H.M., and G.J. Niemi. 1994. Breeding bird abundance patterns in the Chippewa and Superior National Forests from 1991 to 1993. *Loon* 66: 64–70.

Harrington, B.A., J.P. Myers, and J.S. Grear. 1989. Coastal refueling sites for global bird migrants. Proc. Symp. Coastal and Ocean Managem., 6th American Soc. Civil Engineers, New York.

Harrington, B., and E. Perry. 1995. Important shorebird staging sites meeting Western Hemisphere Shorebird Reserve Network criteria. U.S. Fish & Wildlife Service.

Harrington, B.A., J.P. Myers, and J.S. Grear. 1989. Coastal refueling sites for global bird migrants. Proc. Symp. Coastal and Ocean Managem., 6th American Soc. Civil Engineers, New York.

Harris, S.W. 1991. *Northwestern California Birds.* Humboldt State Univ. Press, Arcata.

Harrison, C. 1995. In lit.

Hawaii Natural Area Preserves Website: http://www.hawaii.gov/dlnr/dfw/nars/nars1.html.

Hawaii State Parks Website: http://www.hawaii.gov/dlnr/dsp/hawaii.html.

Hawaii Volcanoes National Park Website: http://www.hawaii.volcanoes.national-park.com/map.htm.

Hawaii's Wildlife Refuges Website: http://www.audubon.org/campaign/refuge/refuges/hawaii.html.

Heideman, R. 1996. Birds of Lost Maples State Natural Area: A field checklist. Natural Resources Program, Texas Parks and Wildlife Department.

Hilliard, G. 1996. *A Hundred Years of Horse Tracks: The Story of the Gray Ranch.* High-Lonesome Books, Silver City, NM.

Hitt, J.R., and K.T. Blackshaw (eds.). 1996. *A Birder's Guide to Georgia.* 5th ed. Occasional Publication No. 13, Georgia Ornithological Society.

Hoefler, J. 2001. Birding Crex Meadows. *Winging It* 13 (7):1–4.

Holt, H.R. 1990. *A Birder's Guide to Southern California.* American Birding Association, Colorado Springs.

Holt, H.R. 1993. *A Birder's Guide to the Texas Coast.* American Birding Association, Colorado Springs.

Holt, H.R. 1997. *A Birder's Guide to Colorado.* American Birding Association, Colorado Springs.

Hooge, P., and S. Taggart. 1998. *Status and Trends of the Nation's Biological Resources.* Vol. 2. U.S. Department of the Interior, U.S. Geological Survey, Reston, VA.

Hooper, R.G., W.E. Taylor, and J. Craig Watson. 1998. Status of the Red-cockaded Woodpecker populations in the Francis Marion National Forest based on the 1998 nesting season. Unpubl. report.

Horton, R.E., and D.H. Wolfe. 1999. Status and management of the Greater Prairie Chicken in Oklahoma. In Svedarsky, W.D., R.H. Hier, and N.J. Silvy (eds.). 1999. *The Greater Prairie-Chicken: A national look.* Misc. Publ. 99-1999, Minnesota Agricultural Experiment Station, University of Minnesota, St. Paul.

Idaho Department of Fish and Game. Birds of Sand Creek Wildlife Management Area.

———. Sand Creek Wildlife Management Area Guide.

Illinois Department of Natural Resources. 1997. Cache River area assessment. Volume 1, part II: *Living Resources*. Illinois Department of Natural Resources, Springfield.

James, F.C. 2001. A research program in ecology and ecomorphology. *Wilson Bull.* 113(2):140–163.

Johnston, D.W. 1997. *A Birder's Guide to Virginia*. American Birding Association, Colorado Springs.

Jones, I.L. 1993. Least Auklet (*Aethia pusilla*) In *The Birds of North America*, No. 69 (A. Poole and F. Gill, eds.). The Academy of Natural Sciences, Philadelphia, and The American Ornithologists' Union, Washington, D.C.

Jones, I.L. 1993. Crested Auklet (*Aethia cristatella*) In *The Birds of North America*, No. 70 (A. Poole and F. Gill, eds.). The Academy of Natural Sciences, Philadelphia, and The American Ornithologists' Union, Washington, D.C.

Karges, J., and K.B. Bryan. 2000 (revised). The Nature Conservancy of Texas' Davis Mountains Project: Bird use and conservation importance. Unpubl. report.

Keller, C.E., J.A. Spendelow, and R.D. Greer. 1984. Atlas of wading bird and seabird nesting colonies in coastal Louisiana, Mississippi, and Alabama: 1983. U.S. Fish & Wildlife Service FWS/OBS-82/13. 73 pp.

Kemper, J. 1999. *Birding Northern California*. Falcon Publishing Co., Helena.

Kerr Wildlife Management Area: A historical review of the range and wildlife management programs as related to Black-capped Vireo Management. 1954–1990. Unpubl. report.

Klein, D.R., D.F. Murray, R.H. Armstrong, and B.A. Anderson. In M.J. Mac, P.A. Opler, C.E. Puckett Haecker, and P. D. Doran. 1998. *Status and Trends of the Nation's Biological Resources*. Vol. 2. U.S. Department of the Interior, U.S. Geological Survey, Reston, VA.

Knopf, F. 1996. Mountain Plover. In *The Birds of North America*, No. 211 (A. Poole and F. Gill, eds.). The Academy of Natural Sciences, Philadelphia, and The American Ornithologists' Union, Washington, D.C.

Koch, S. WHSRN site identification form. Monomoy National Wildlife Refuge. A biological opinion on the avian diversity of the Monomoy National Wildlife Refuge. *www.provincetown.com.*

Koke'e State Park Unofficial Website: http://www.alhoa.net/~inazoo/kokee.htm.

Kress, S.W. 2000. *National Audubon Society Birder's Handbook*. Dorling Kindersley, New York.

Kutac, E.A. 1997. *Birds of Colorado Bend State Park: A Field Checklist*. Natural Resources Program, Texas Parks and Wildlife Department.

Lapp, C. 1995. Rice Lake National Wildlife Refuge holds record concentration of waterfowl. *Loon* 67:38–39.

Latta M.J., C.J. Beardmore, and T.E. Corman. 1999. *Arizona Partners in Flight Bird Conservation Plan*, Version 1.0. Nongame and Endangered Wildlife Program Technical Report 142, Arizona Game and Fish Department, Phoenix.

Laux, E.V. 2002. Sky is falling on prairie chicken, sacrifice of a rite of spring. *New York Times*, May 28, 2002.

Lee, D.S. 1995. Marine birds off the coast of North Carolina. *The Chat* 59:113–171.

Lee, D.S., and B. Browning. 1998. Conservation Concerns Related to Avian Endemism in the Southern Appalachians, draft paper.

Lethaby, N. 1994. *A Bird Finding Guide to Alaska*. Published by the author.

Lewis, J.C. 1995. Whooping Crane. In *The Birds of North America*, No. 153 (A. Poole and F. Gill, eds.). The Academy of Natural Sciences, Philadelphia, and The American Ornithologists' Union, Washington, D.C.

Lichtwardt, E. 2000. Rare, local, little-known, and declining North American breeders. *Birding* 32(5):402–408.

Lindsey, G.D., E.A. VanderWerf, H. Baker, and P.E. Baker. 1998. Amakihi spp. (*Hemignathus spp.*) In *The Birds of North America,* No. 360 (A. Poole and F. Gill, eds.). The Academy of Natural Sciences, Philadelphia, and The American Ornithologists' Union, Washington, D.C.

Lingle, G.R. 1994. *Birding Crane River: Nebraska's Platte.* Harrier Publishing, Grand Island, NE. 121 pp.

Lockwood, M.W. 1993. Kickapoo Cavern State Natural Area, Texas. *Winging It* 5(4):8–9.

Lockwood, M.W., W.B. McKinney, J.N. Paton, and B.R. Zimmer. 1999. *A Birder's Guide to the Rio Grande Valley.* American Birding Association, Colorado Springs.

Loope, L.L. In M.J. Mac, P.A. Opler, C.E. Puckett Haecker, and P.D. Doran. 1998. *Status and Trends of the Nation's Biological Resources.* Vol. 2. U.S. Department of the Interior, U.S. Geological Survey, Reston, VA.

Lukas, D. 1998. Birding Malheur National Wildlife Refuge. *Winging It* 10(6) 1, 4–6.

Lyon, B., and R. Montgomerie. 1995. Snow and McKay's Buntings (*Plectrophenax nivalis* and *Plectrophenax hyperboreus*). In *The Birds of North America,* No. 198–199 (A. Poole and F. Gill, eds.). The Academy of Natural Sciences, Philadelphia, and The American Ornithologists' Union, Washington, D.C.

Mac, M.J., P.A. Opler, C.E. Puckett Haecker, and P.D. Doran. 1998. *Status and Trends of the Nation's Biological Resources.* Vol. 1. U.S. Department of the Interior, U.S. Geological Survey, Reston, VA. 1–436 pp.

Mack, G.D. 1993. Sandhill management plan. U.S. Fish & Wildlife Service.

MacRae, D. 1995. *Birder's Guide to Washington.* Gulf Publishing Co., Houston.

Martin, G. 1998. *National Geographic's Guide to Wildlife Watching.* Round Stone Press, Washington, D.C.

McLain, P. WHSRN site nomination form: http://www.manomet.org/WHSRN/delaware.htm.

McCrae, J. 1996. Oregon developmental species: brine shrimp: Artemia sp. http://www.hmsc.orst.edu.odfw/devfish/sp/brine.html.

McEneaney, T. 1993. *The Birder's Guide to Montana.* Falcon Press, Helena.

McIvor, D.E. 1998. *Birding Utah.* Falcon Press, Helena.

McShea, W.J., H.B. Underwood, and J.H. Rappole. 1997. The science of overabundance in deer ecology and population management.

Meanley, B. 1973. The Great Dismal Swamp. Audubon Naturalist Society of the Central Atlantic States.

Meeks, W.A., and W.A. Schultze. 1997. A proposal for nominating Sand Lake National Wildlife Refuge as a Wetland of International Importance under the "RAMSAR" Convention. U.S. Fish & Wildlife Service, Region 6.

Megyesi, J.L., and D. O'Daniel. 1997. Bulwer's Petrel (*Bulweria bulwerii*). In *The Birds of North America,* No. 281 (A. Poole and F. Gill, eds.). The Academy of Natural Sciences, Philadelphia, and The American Ornithologists' Union, Washington, D.C.

Michot, T.C. 1984. Marsh loss in coastal Louisiana: Interim report on land loss and marsh creation. U.S. Fish & Wildlife Service, Ecological Services, Lafayette, La., 45 pp.

Midway Atoll National Wildlife Refuge Website: http://www.r1.fws.gov/midway/wildlife/management.html.

Mike Feighner's Hawaii Trip Report Website: http://www.xnet.com/~ugeiser/Birds/TripReports/HawaiiMF96.html.

Moulton, D.W., and A.P. Marshall. 1996. The Laysan Duck (*Anas laysanensis*). In *The Birds of North America,* No. 242 (A. Poole and F. Gill, eds.). The Academy of Natural Sciences, Philadelphia, and The American Ornithologists' Union, Washington, D.C.

Mueller, A.J. 1987. An inventory of Upper Texas Coast woodlots, valuable migratory bird habitat. *Bull. Texas Ornith. Soc.* 20(1&2):14–20.

———— and N. E. Sears. 1987. Habitat selection by spring migrants in a Texas coastal woodlot. *Bull Texas Ornith. Soc.* 20(1&2):21–26.

Natural World Heritage Website: http://www.wcmc.org.uk/protected_areas/data/wh/hawaiivo.
html.

The Nature Conservancy. 1998. Bird list of the Niobrara Valley Preserve.

The Nature Conservancy. 2000. Endangered species monitoring and management at Fort Hood,
Texas: 1999 annual report. Fort Hood Project, The Nature Conservancy of Texas. Fort
Hood, TX. 340 pp.

Newhouse, E.L. (ed.) 1997. *National Parks of the United States.* National Geographic Society,
Washington, D.C.

News from the North American Waterfowl Management Plan. 1999. *Waterfowl* 12:18.

Nisbet, I.C.T. 1992. A closer look: Roseate Tern. *Birding XXIV* (5):304–308.

Nol, E., B. Truitt, D. Allen, B. Winn, and T. Murphy. Size of the American Oystercatcher population of the United States: Results of the 1999 survey for wintering American Oystercatchers: Georgia to Virginia. Unpubl. report.

Nol, E., B. Truitt, D. Allen, B. Winn, and T. Murphy. 2000. A survey of wintering American
Oystercatchers from Georgia to Virginia, USA. *Water Study Group Bulletin* 94:46–51.

Ortego, B. Mad Island Marsh Complex birds. Texas Parks and Wildlife, Austin.

Palmer, K. (compiler). 1993. *A Guide to the Birding Areas of Missouri.* Audubon Society of
Missouri.

Pashley, D., et al. 2000. *Conservation of the Landbirds of the United States.* American Bird
Conservancy, The Plains.

Paton, P.W.C. 1999. A closer look: Snowy Plover. *Birding* 31(3):238–244.

Peregrine Fund Website: http://www.peregrinefund.org/hawaiiup.html.

Pierson, E.C., J.E. Pierson, and P.D. Vickery. 1996. *A Birder's Guide to Maine.* Down East
Books, Camden, ME.

Porter, J.F. (ed.). 2001. *A Birder's Guide to Alabama.* Univ. of Alabama Press.

Porter, J.F. and J., eds. 1999. The Alabama Coastal Birding Trail. U.S. Fish & Wildlife Service.
Available from Alabama Gulf Coast Convention and Visitors Bureau, www.gulfshores.com.

Pranty, B. 1996. *A Birder's Guide to Florida.* American Birding Association, Colorado Springs.

Pranty, B. 2000. Florida Scrub-Jay population monitoring and habitat restoration project—and
Important Bird Area surveys—for Cross Bar Ranch Wellfield and Al-Bar Ranch. Unpubl.
report. Prepared for Pinellas County Utilities Department.

Pranty, B. 2001. Florida Important Bird Areas Program website: http://www.audubon.org/bird/
iba/florida/ACCEPTED%20IBAs.htm.

Pratt, H.D. 1996. *Enjoying Birds in Hawaii.* Mutual Publishing, Honolulu.

Pratt, H.D., P.L. Bruner, and D.G. Berrett. 1989. *The Birds of Hawaii and the Tropical Pacific.*
Princeton University Press, NJ.

Pratt, T.K., C.B. Kepler, and T.L.C. Casey. 1997. Poouli (*Malamprosops phaesoma*). In *The
Birds of North America,* No. 272 (A. Poole and F. Gill, eds.). The Academy of Natural Sciences, Philadelphia, and The American Ornithologists' Union, Washington, D.C.

Raynes, B., and M. Raynes. 1996. *Birds of Jackson Hole.* Grand Teton Natural History Association. Unpaginated.

Reed, W.C., and K.J. Sage. 1975. *Merrymeeting Bay: A Guide to Conservation of a Unique Resource.* Maine Department of Conservation.

Refuge System—Detailed Unit Information Website: http://refuges.fws.gov:591/rprofiles/
record_detail.htm.

Reilly, L., and W. Riley. 1992. *Guide to the National Wildlife Refuges.* Collier Books, New York.

Ricketts, T., E. Dinerstein, D. Olson, C. Loucks, et al. 1999. *Terrestrial Ecoregions of North
America.* Island Press, Washington, D.C.

Rimmer, C.C. 1996. Rare, local, little-known, and declining North American breeders: A closer
look: Bicknell's Thrush. *Birding* 28(2):118–123.

Rimmer, C.C., K.P. McFarland, W.G. Ellison, and J.E. Goetz. 2001. Bicknell's Thrush (*Catharus bicknelli*). In *The Birds of North America,* No. 591 (A. Poole and F. Gill, eds.). The Academy of Natural Sciences, Philadelphia, and The American Ornithologists' Union, Washington, D.C.

Robert, M. 1997. A closer look: Yellow Rail. *Birding XXIX* (4):282–290.

Rockwell, D. 1998. *The Nature of North America.* Berkley Books, New York.

Rodgers, J.A., Jr., H.W. Kale, II, and H.T. Smith. 1996. *Rare and Endangered Biota of Florida: Volume V. Birds.* Univ. Press of Florida, Gainesville.

Root, T. 1988. *Atlas of Wintering North American Birds.* U. Chicago Press, Chicago.

Roth, K. Marshes vanishing at JFK Airport. Associated Press article of April 25, 2000.

Sandin, J. Horicon. 2000. Marsh's ecosystem rebounds. *Milwaukee Journal Sentinal.*

Schram, B. 1998. *A Birder's Guide to Southern California.* American Birding Association, Colorado Springs.

Scott, O.K. 1993. *A Birder's Guide to Wyoming.* American Birding Association, Colorado Springs.

Seto, N.W.H., and D. O'Daniel. 1999. Bonin Petrel (*Pterodroma hypoleuca*). In *The Birds of North America,* No. 385 (A. Poole and F. Gill, eds.). The Academy of Natural Sciences, Philadelphia, and The American Ornithologists' Union, Washington, D.C.

Shellman, D.K., Jr., and R.G. Darville. Caddo Lake. http://www.ramsar.org/lib_bio_8.htm.

Siderits, K.P. (compiler). 1978. Birds of the Superior National Forest. Eastern Region, Forest Service, United States Department of Agriculture.

Silberstein, M., and E. Cambell. 1989. *Elkhorn Slough.* Monterey Bay Aquarium Natural History Series, Monterey, CA.

Simons, T.R., G.L. Farnsworth, and S.A. Shriner. 2000. Evaluating Great Smoky Mountains National Park as a Population Source for the Wood Thrush, *Conservation Biology,* vol. 14, no. 4, pp. 1133–1144.

Simons, T.R., and C.N. Hodges. 1998. Dark-rumped Petrel (*Pterodroma phaeopygia*). In *The Birds of North America,* No. 345 (A. Poole and F. Gill, eds.). The Academy of Natural Sciences, Philadelphia, and The American Ornithologists' Union, Washington, D.C.

Simpson, M.B. 1992. Birding in Shenandoah National Park. *Winging It* 4 (5), pp. 1–6.

Simpson, M.B. 1992. *Birds of the Blue Ridge Mountains.* University of North Carolina Press, Chapel Hill.

Smith, B.A., R.J. Tyrl, and R.E. Masters. 1999. Floristic inventory of the McCurtain County Wilderness Area, Oklahoma. http://digital.library.okstate.edu/oas/oas_htm_files/v77/p99_102nf.html.

Soehren, R. 1996. *The Birdwatcher's Guide to Hawaii.* University of Hawaii Press, Honolulu.

Sommers, L.A., D.L. Rosenblatt, and M.J. DelPuerto. 2001. 1998–1999 Long Island Colonial Waterbird and Piping Plover Survey. New York Department of Environmental Conservation.

Snetsinger, T.J., M.H. Reynolds, and C.M. Herrmann. 1998. Ou (*Psittirostra psittacea*) and Lanai Hookbill (*Dysmorodrepanis munroi*). In *Birds of North America,* No. 335–336 (A. Poole and F. Gill, eds.). The Academy of Natural Sciences, Philadelphia, and The American Ornithologists' Union, Washington, D.C.

Stattersfield, A.J., M.J. Crosby, A.J. Long, and D.C. Wege. 1998. *Endemic Bird Areas of the World.* BirdLife International, Cambridge.

Steger, G.N., T.E. Munton, G.P. Eberlein, K.D. Johnson, and P.A. Shaklee. 2000. A study of Spotted Owl demographics in the Sierra National Forest and Sequoia and Kings Canyon National Parks. Annual Progress Report 2000. Pacific Southwest Research Station, Fresno.

Stern, M.A., J.F. Morawski, and G.A. Rosenberg. 1993. Rediscovery and status of a disjunct population of breeding Yellow Rails in southern Oregon. *Condor* 95:1024–1027.

Stone, W.E. 2000. Habitat relationships of breeding birds in the Bankhead National Forest. Unpubl. report, USDA Forest Service Southern Forest Research Station.

Strangis, J.M. 1996. *Birding Minnesota*. Falcon Publishing, Helena.

Svedarsky, W.D., and G. Van Amburg. 1996. Integrated management of the Greater Prairie-Chicken and Livestock on the Sheyenne National Grassland. North Dakota Game and Fish Department, Bismarck, ND.

Svedarsky, W.D., R.H. Hier, and N.J. Silvy (eds.). 1999. The Greater Prairie-Chicken: A national look. Misc. Publ. 99-1999, Minnesota Agricultural Experiment Station, University of Minnesota, St. Paul.

Svingen, D., and K. Dumroese (eds.) 1997. *A Birder's Guide to Idaho*. American Birding Association, Colorado Springs.

Svingen, D., and K. Giesen. 1999. Mountain Plover (*Charadrius montanus*) response to prescribed burns on the Comanche National Grassland. *J. Colorado Field Ornithologists* 33(4):208–212.

Sykes, P.W., Jr., and G.S. Hunter. 1978. Bird use of flooded agricultural fields during summer and early fall and some recommendations for management. *Florida Field Naturalist* 6(2):36–43.

Taylor, R.C. 1995. *A Birder's Guide to Southeastern Arizona*. American Birding Association, Colorado Springs.

Terborgh, J.W. 1980. The conservation status of neotropical migrants: present and future. In A. Keast, and E.S. Morton (eds). *Migrant Birds in the Neotropics: Ecology, Behavior, Distribution, and Conservation*. Smithsonian Institution Press, Washington, pp. 21–30.

Terborgh, J.W. 1992. Perspectives on the conservation of Neotropical migrant landbirds. In J.M. Hagan, III, and D.W. Johnston (eds). *Ecology and Conservation of Neotropical Migrant Landbirds*. Smithsonian Institution Press, Washington, pp. 7–12.

Texas Parks and Wildlife. 1994. Birds of Kickapoo Cavern State Natural Area. 12 pp.

Thomas, B. 1999. The hills have eyes. *Bird Conservation* (special Department of Defense Partners in Flight issue):6–7.

Truitt, B.R., and D.I. Schwab. 1998 Eastern Short barrier island/lagoon colonial waterbird survey. *The Raven* (in press).

Uhlman, J. 1998. Lake Mattamuskeet, North Carolina. *Winging It* 10 (12):1, 4–6.

U.S. Department of Agriculture Forest Service. 2001. Checklist of Birds of the White Mountain National Forest and Vicinity. Laconia, NH.

U.S. Department of Defense. No date. Checklist of Birds, Marine Corps Base Camp Pendleton. Department of Defense. Unpaginated.

U.S. Department of the Interior Bureau of Land Management. 2000. Roseburg District Annual Program Summary and Monitoring Report Fiscal Year 1999. Roseburg, OR. 136 pp.

U.S. Fish & Wildlife Service. No date. Birds of Buenos Aires National Wildlife Refuge. U.S. Fish & Wildlife Service. Unpaginated.

U.S. Fish & Wildlife Service. No date. Birds of Brazoria/San Bernard/Big Boggy National Wildlife Refuges. No date. U.S. Fish & Wildlife Service. Unpaginated.

U.S. Fish & Wildlife Service. No date. Birds of Malheur National Wildlife Refuge. Unpaginated.

U.S. Fish & Wildlife Service. No date. Management and Development Plan: Grays Harbor National Wildlife Refuge. Unpubl. report.

U.S. Fish & Wildlife Service. No date. Ruby Lake National Wildlife Refuge. Annual Narrative Report.

U.S. Fish & Wildlife Service. No date. Weed control on Fish & Wildlife Service Lands. Brochure.

U.S. Fish & Wildlife Service. No date. Birds of Seney National Wildlife Refuge, Seney, Michigan. U.S. Fish & Wildlife Service. Unpaginated.

U.S. Fish & Wildlife Service. No date. Merritt Island National Wildlife Refuge Checklist of Birds. U.S. Fish & Wildlife Service. Unpaginated.

U.S. Fish & Wildlife Service. 1979. Birds of Seedskadee National Wildlife Refuge. U.S. Fish & Wildlife Service. Unpaginated.

U.S. Fish & Wildlife Service. 1984. Mississippi Sandhill Crane National Wildlife Refuge. U.S. Fish & Wildlife Service. Unpaginated.

U.S. Fish & Wildlife Service. 1985. Birds of DeSoto National Wildlife Refuge. U.S. Fish & Wildlife Service. Unpaginated.

U.S. Fish & Wildlife Service. 1986. Birds of Big Lake National Wildlife Refuge. U.S. Fish & Wildlife Service. Unpaginated.

U.S. Fish & Wildlife Service. 1986. Birds of the Long Lake National Wildlife Refuge. U.S. Fish & Wildlife Service. Unpaginated.

U.S. Fish & Wildlife Service. 1989. Birds of Bitter Lake National Wildlife Refuge, New Mexico. Unpaginated.

U.S. Fish & Wildlife Service. 1990. Birds of Flint Hills National Wildlife Refuge, Kansas. U.S. Fish & Wildlife Service. Unpaginated.

U.S. Fish & Wildlife Service. 1991. Birds of Cabeza Prieta National Wildlife Refuge. U.S. Fish & Wildlife Service. Unpaginated.

U.S. Fish & Wildlife Service. 1991. Birds of Ottawa National Wildlife Refuge Complex, Ohio. U.S. Fish & Wildlife Service. Unpaginated.

U.S. Fish & Wildlife Service. 1992. Bowdoin National Wildlife Refuge Birds. U.S. Fish & Wildlife Service. Unpaginated.

U.S. Fish & Wildlife Service. 1992. A Field Checklist of Birds of Matagorda Island. U.S. Fish & Wildlife Service. Unpaginated.

U.S. Fish & Wildlife Service. 1992. Bird checklist of Ruby Lake National Wildlife Refuge. U.S. Fish & Wildlife Service. Unpaginated.

U.S. Fish & Wildlife Service. 1992. Birds of the Charles M. Russell National Wildlife Refuge, Montana. U.S. Fish & Wildlife Refuge. Unpaginated.

U.S. Fish & Wildlife Service. 1993. Birds of Benton Lake National Wildlife Refuge, Montana. U.S. Fish & Wildlife Service. Unpaginated.

U.S. Fish & Wildlife Service. 1994. Birds of Okefenokee National Wildlife Refuge. U.S. Fish & Wildlife Service. Unpaginated.

U.S. Fish & Wildlife Service. 1994. Birds of Florida Keys National Wildlife Refuge. U.S. Fish & Wildlife Service. Unpaginated.

U.S. Fish & Wildlife Service. 1994. Birds of Arthur R. Marshall Loxahatchee National Wildlife Refuge. U.S. Fish & Wildlife Service. Unpaginated.

U.S. Fish & Wildlife Service. 1995. Birds of Grays Lake National Wildlife Refuge. U.S. Fish & Wildlife Service. Unpaginated.

U.S. Fish & Wildlife Service. 1997. Willapa National Wildlife Refuge. Control of smooth cordgrass (*Spartina alterniflora*) on Willapa National Wildlife Refuge: Environmental assessment. Unpubl. report.

U.S. Fish & Wildlife Service. 1997. Birds of Wichita Mountains Wildlife Refuge. U.S. Fish & Wildlife Service. Unpubl.

U.S. Fish & Wildlife Service. 1997. Bird list of Mark Twain National Wildlife Refuge. U.S. Fish & Wildlife Service.

U.S. Fish & Wildlife Service. 1998. Bitter Lake National Wildlife Refuge annual report. Unpubl.

U.S. Fish & Wildlife Service. 1998. Birds of St. Marks National Wildlife Refuge, Florida. Unpaginated.

U.S. Fish & Wildlife Service. 1998. St. Marks National Wildlife Refuge, Annual Narrative. Unpubl. report.

U.S. Fish & Wildlife Service. 2001. Birds of Piedmont National Wildlife Refuge, Georgia. U.S. Fish & Wildlife Service. Unpaginated.

U.S. National Park Service. No date. Checklist of Birds of Big Thicket. Unpaginated.

U.S. National Park Service. No date. Cumberland Island. Official map and guide.

VanderWerf, E.A. 1998. Elepaio (*Chasiempis sandwchensis*) In *The Birds of North America,* No. 344 (A. Poole and F. Gill, eds.). The Academy of Natural Sciences, Philadelphia, and The American Ornithologists' Union, Washington, D.C.

Vaughan, R. 1994. *A Birder's Guide to Alabama and Mississippi.* Gulf Publishing Company, Houston.

Wahl, T.R., and D.R. Paulson. 1991. *A Guide to Bird Finding in Washington.* T.R. Wahl, Bellingham.

Wahlenburg, W.G. 1946. *Longleaf pine: Its Use, Ecology, Regeneration, Protection, Growth and Management.* Washington, D.C.: C.L. Pack Forestry Foundation and USDA Forest Service.

Warnock, N., S.M. Haig, and L.W. Oring. 1998. Monitoring species richness and abundance of shorebirds in the western Great Basin. *Condor* 100:589–600.

Watts, B.D., and B.R. Truitt. 2000. Abundance of shorebirds along the Virginia barrier islands during spring migration. *The Raven* 71(2):33–39.

Wauer, R.H., 1992. *The Visitor's Guide to the Birds of the Eastern National Parks.* John Muir Publications, Santa Fe.

Wauer, R.H., and M.A. Elwonger. 1998. *Birding Texas.* Falcon Publishing Co., Helena.

Wells, J.V. (compiler). 1998. *Important Bird Areas in New York State.* National Audubon Society, New York.

Westrich, L., and J. Westrick. 1991. *Birder's Guide to Northern California.* Gulf Publishing, Houston.

White, M. 1995. *A Birder's Guide to Arkansas.* American Birding Association, Colorado Springs.

White, M. 1999. National Geographic guide to birdwatching sites: Eastern U.S.

White, M. 1999. National Geographic guide to birdwatching sites: Western U.S.

Wilcove, D.S. 1999. *The Condor's Shadow.* W.H. Freeman and Co., New York.

Williams, R.B., and M. Brown. No date. Birds of Wheeler National Wildlife Refuge. U.S. Fish & Wildlife Service. Unpaginated.

Willick, D.R., and M.A. Patten. 1992. Finding the California Gnatcatcher in the U.S. *Birding* XXIV (4):234–239.

Winter, M. 1999. Relationship of fire history to territory size, breeding density, and habitat of Baird's Sparrow in North Dakota. *Studies in Avian Biology* no. 19, pp. 171–177.

Wisconsin Department of Natural Resources. Crex Meadows. Brochures.

Woolfenden, G.E., and J.W. Fitzpatrick. 1996. Florida Scrub-Jay. In *The Birds of North America,* No. 185 (A. Poole and F. Gill, eds.). The Academy of Natural Sciences, Philadelphia, and The American Ornithologists' Union, Washington, D.C.

Zack, S., H. Cooke, and G.R. Geupel. 1998. Bird abundance and diversity patterns at the East Park Reservoir site during the El Niño weather of 1998. Unpubl. report.

Zack, S., W. Richardson, G.R. Geupel, and G. Ballard. 1997. Bird abundance and diversity at East Park Reservoir and environs. Unpubl. report.

Zimmerman, J.L. 1985. Birds of Konza Prairie Research Natural Area, Kansas. *Prairie Naturalist* 17:185–192.

Zimmerman, J.L., and S.T. Pati. 1988. *Bird Finding in Kansas and Western Missouri.* Univ. Press of Kansas, Lawrence.

Zimmerman, D.A., M.A. Zimmerman, and J.N. Durrie (eds.) 1992. *New Mexico Bird Finding Guide.* The New Mexico Ornithological Society, Albuquerque.

INDEX OF PLACE NAMES

NOTE: This index includes both IBAs and other significant sites mentioned in the book. For the list of IBAs by state see page 453.

Page numbers in *italics* indicate that a site is mentioned in a side bar.

INDEX OF BIRD NAMES

NOTE: This book does not provide a comprehensive list of species found at each IBA. Species are mentioned when their occurrence at a site is of particular conservation significance. To find a field guide to the birds of each IBA, see ABC's website at www.abcbirds.org.

Page numbers in **bold** indicate bird illustrations. Those in *italics* indicate that the species is referred to in a side bar.

INDEX OF IBA MAPS BY STATE

ABOUT THE AUTHORS

American Bird Conservancy is widely recognized as the leading bird conservation organization in the United States. *The American Bird Conservancy Guide to the 500 Most Important Bird Areas in the United States* is authored by ABC staff members who are trained, experienced scientists and conservation leaders. **The Nature Conservancy,** founded in 1951, now has approximately one million members. It has protected more than 98 million acres around the world.

ROBERT M. CHIPLEY has been Director of the Important Bird Areas Program for ABC since 1998. For over twenty years he worked in various capacities with The Nature Conservancy's Science Division in building the network of Heritage Programs; his last position there was as Director of Communications. By way of scientific background, he has a Ph.D. from Cornell in biology, having done his thesis work on the wintering biology of the Blackburnian Warbler in Colombia. He retains a keen interest in neotropical ornithology and has also published on his research in the British Virgin Islands.

GEORGE H. FENWICK, ABC's President, received a Ph.D. from the Department of Pathobiology at Johns Hopkins University, studying the effects of alien species on native avifauna. He founded American Bird Conservancy in early 1994, and became President upon its merger with the U.S. and Pan American Sections of the International Council for the Preservation of Birds later that year. He worked in a variety of capacities during 15 years with The Nature Conservancy including Vice President and Director of Ecosystem Conservation, Acting Director of Science, and Chair of the Steering Committee for the Last Great Places Campaign. Prior to that, he has worked for the Chesapeake Bay Foundation, Earthsatellite Corporation, and been an instructor at the University of Virginia.

MICHAEL J. PARR, Vice President for Program Development at ABC, graduated from the University of East Anglia, U.K., in 1986. He worked at the International Council for Bird Preservation International Secretariat (now BirdLife International) as Development Officer, then he moved to the U.S.A. He joined ABC in 1996. His first book, *Parrots—A Guide to the Parrots of the World* was published by Yale University Press in April 1998. He is also co-author of the book *Wildlife Spectacles* and reviews ornithological works for both Yale and Princeton University Presses. He is a member of the Advisory Board of ProAves Colombia.

DAVID N. PASHLEY, Vice President of Conservation Programs at ABC, received a Ph.D. from the School of Forestry, Wildlife and Fisheries at Louisiana State University. His dissertation title was "A Distributional Analysis of the Warblers of the West Indies." In addition to serving six years as Director of Science and Stewardship for The Nature Conservancy of Louisiana, Dr. Pashley has had a long association with Partners in Flight. Among his responsibilities for PIF have been Chair of the Southeast Working Group and National Coordinator, a position he occupied for six years. After that, he was instrumental in the creation of the North American Bird Conservation Initiative, and served as U.S. Coordinator for that effort for four years.

ABOUT THE TYPE

This book was set in Times Roman, designed by Stanley Morison specifically for *The Times* of London. The typeface was introduced in the newspaper in 1932. Times Roman has had its greatest success in the United States as a book and commercial typeface, rather than one used in newspapers.

You can join ABC on-line at www.abcbirds.org/membership, or use the mail-in membership form below. Please photocopy the form and send it to American Bird Conservancy, P.O. Box 249, The Plains, VA 20198, with your check made payable to American Bird Conservancy.

❏ *Yes!* I want to join ABC at the introductory level and receive *Bird Conservation* magazine. I enclose payment in the amount of $18.

❏ *Yes!* I want to become a member of ABC at the level of (check one of the boxes below):

❏ $40	Vireo
❏ $100	Meadowlark
❏ $250	Tanager
❏ $500	Curlew
❏ $1,000	Falcon Club
❏ $_____	Other (please specify amount)

All members at $40 and up receive *Bird Conservation* magazine AND *Bird Calls* newsletter. In addition, while supplies last, $40 members will receive the map of Globally Important Bird Areas of the United States, produced in conjunction with the National Geographic Society.

All supporters at $100 and up receive a copy of American Bird Conservancy's field guide, *All the Birds of North America*. The fair market value of this gift is $19.95 and will reduce your tax-deductible contribution by that amount. If you do not wish to receive this gift please check here ❏. Amounts listed are in U.S. dollars. Donations are tax deductible to the extent allowable by law.

NOTES

NOTES

NOTES

NOTES

NOTES

NOTES

NOTES

NOTES